Springer Studies in the History of Economic Thought

This series offers an outlet for research in the history of economic thought. It features scholarly studies on important theoretical developments and great economic thinkers that have contributed to the evolution of the economic discipline.

Springer Studies in the History of Economic Thought (SSHET) welcomes proposals for research monographs, edited volumes and handbooks from a variety of disciplines that seek to study the history of economic thinking and help to arrive at a better understanding of modern economics. Relevant topics include, but are not limited to, various schools of thought, important pioneers and thinkers, ancient and medieval economic thought, mercantilism, cameralism and physiocracy, classical and neoclassical economics, historical, institutional and evolutionary economics, socialism and Marxism, Keynesian, Sraffian and Austrian economics, econometrics and mathematical studies as well as economic methodology and the link between economic history and history of economic thought.

More information about this series at http://www.springer.com/series/16457

Christina Anselmann

Secular Stagnation Theories

A Historical and Contemporary Analysis
with a Focus on the Distribution of Income

 Springer

Christina Anselmann
University of Hohenheim
Stuttgart, Baden-Württemberg, Germany

ISSN 2662-6098   ISSN 2662-6101   (electronic)
Springer Studies in the History of Economic Thought
ISBN 978-3-030-41089-6   ISBN 978-3-030-41087-2   (eBook)
https://doi.org/10.1007/978-3-030-41087-2

This Springer imprint is published by the registered company Springer Nature Switzerland AG
The registered company address is: Gewerbestrasse 11, 6330 Cham, Switzerland

Acknowledgements

This book could not have been written without the support of many people.

First and foremost, I thank my supervisors Prof. Dr. Harald Hagemann (University of Hohenheim) and Prof. Dr. Hagen Krämer (Karlsruhe University of Applied Sciences) for giving me the opportunity to pursue a doctorate at the University of Hohenheim. Their continuous guidance has been unparalleled, and it is hard to imagine this whole doctoral journey without their intellectual stimulus, support, and encouragement along the way.

Moreover, I am grateful to Prof. Dr. Klaus Prettner (University of Hohenheim) for chairing my thesis committee.

At the Karlsruhe University of Applied Sciences, Prof. Dr. Hagen Krämer and Prof. Dr. Johannes Schmidt (Karlsruhe University of Applied Sciences) provided me with the most fruitful research environment. Many helpful comments on my work emerged from our informal research seminars and constructive discussions, for which I am most thankful.

Moreover, I thank Prof. Dr. Heinz D. Kurz (University of Graz) for his valuable comments and suggestions, particularly regarding Chap. 8 of this book.

Of course, all remaining errors and shortcomings are my own responsibility.

I am thankful to Alois Guger (Austrian Institute of Economic Research) and the University Library of the Vienna University of Economics and Business for granting me access to several unpublished manuscripts of Josef Steindl.

Furthermore, I am grateful to the 2012–2018 dean's office of the Faculty of Management Science and Engineering at the Karlsruhe University of Applied Sciences for providing me with the best working conditions and for giving me the freedom to pursue my research.

Moreover, I thank my colleagues and friends at the University of Hohenheim, who, from day one, accepted me as one of their own. I could not have asked for a better peer group.

Last, but certainly not least, I thank my family, especially my parents, for walking beside me every step of the way.

Contents

Abbreviations

AD	Aggregate Demand
AUT	Austria
BEL	Belgium
CAN	Canada
CEO	Chief executive officer
DEU	Germany
EA	Euro area (changing composition of countries)
EA-12	Euro area 12 (fixed composition of 12 countries)
EA-16	Euro area 16 (fixed composition of 16 countries)
ESA	European System of Accounts
ESP	Spain
EU-15	European Union 15 (fixed composition of 15 countries)
EU-16	European Union 16 (fixed composition of 16 countries)
FIN	Finland
FRA	France
G20	The Group of Twenty (major world economies)
GBR	United Kingdom
GDP	Gross domestic product
GNP	Gross national product
GVA	Gross value added
ICT	Information and communications technology
IMF	International Monetary Fund
IRE	Ireland
IS	Investment-Saving
IT	Information technology
ITA	Italy
JPN	Japan
LIS	Luxembourg Income Study
LM	Liquidity preference–Money supply
LUX	Luxembourg

NED	Netherlands
OECD	Organisation for Economic Co-operation and Development
PPP	Purchasing Power Parity
PRT	Portugal
R&D	Research and development
SNA	System of National Accounts
TFP	Total factor productivity
USA	United States of America

Symbols

a_1	Dividend payout parameter
a_2	Dividend payout parameter
B	Government budget deficit
c	Value of constant capital
C_p	Consumption out of profits
D	Dividends
f	Ratio of overhead workers to variable workers at full capacity
g	Rate of capital accumulation (growth rate)
g^d	Desired rate of capital accumulation (desired growth rate)
g^s	Rate of capital accumulation (growth rate), determined from the saving side
g^*	Equilibrium rate of capital accumulation (equilibrium growth rate)
h	Rate of technological change
h_0	Autonomous rate of technological change
h_1	Effect of economic growth on the rate of technological change (Verdoorn coefficient)
H	Total hours worked
i	Interest rate
I	Investment expenditure
I_f	Private business investment
I_g	Private government investment
j	Ratio of material costs to direct labor costs
k	Capital stock internally owned by firms as a ratio of total capital (reciprocal gearing ratio)
k_0	Planned ratio of capital stock internally owned by firms as a ratio of total capital (planned reciprocal gearing ratio)
K	Capital stock
K_f	Capital stock internally owned by firms
L_f	Indirect labor (overhead labor)
L_v	Direct labor (variable labor)

m_1	Marginal profit share
m_2	Overhead labor costs as a share of capital
M	Imports
n	Constant parameter
N	Total population
p	Price level
$\hat{p}$	Inflation rate
$\hat{p}^*$	Target inflation rate
P	Section 3.2.3: Real profits (net of taxes)
	Chapter 8: Real profits (net of interest payments)
q	Constant parameter
r	Section 3.3.2: Central bank policy interest rate
	Section 4.1.4: Rate of profit
r_0	Wicksellian natural real interest rate (estimate)
R	Real profits (gross of interest payments)
s	Surplus value
s_p	Propensity to save out of profits
s_h^p	Propensity to save of the poor private households
s_h^r	Propensity to save of the rich private households
S	Private saving
S_f	Saving of firms
S_g	Government saving
S_h	Private household saving
S_h^p	Saving of the poor private households
S_h^r	Saving of the rich private households
S_w	Saving out of wages
t	Time
u	Degree of capacity utilization
u_0	Planned degree of capacity utilization
u^*	Equilibrium degree of capacity utilization
UC	Unit cost
UDC	Unit direct cost
v	Value of variable capital (sum of wages)
w	Wage share of the poor private households
w_v	Nominal wage rate of variable labor
W	Wage bill
X	Exports
$X - M$	Net foreign investment (current account balance)
y_f	Labor productivity of indirect (overhead) labor
y_v	Labor productivity of direct (variable) labor
Y	Real output (GDP)
Y_h	Private household income
Y_h^p	Income of the poor private households
Y_h^r	Income of the rich private households

Y^*	Real potential output
z	Capital income share of the poor private households
Z	Capital income of private households

Greek Letters

α_0	Effect of the animal spirits of firms on the desired rate of capital accumulation
α_1	Effect of the rate of firms' internal saving on the desired rate of capital accumulation
α_2	Effect of the rate of capacity utilization on the desired rate of capital accumulation
α_3	Effect of the rate of technological change on the desired rate of capital accumulation
β	Weight (Taylor rule)
γ	Weight (Taylor rule)
θ	Percentage mark-up on direct costs
Θ	Effect of the desired and/or actual rate of capital accumulation on the change in the rate of capital accumulation
κ	Capital–capacity ratio
π	Net profit share (share of profits (net of overhead costs) in national income)
π^d	Net profit share, determined from the demand side
π^s	Net profit share, determined from the supply side
π^*	Equilibrium net profit share
σ	Ratio of the wage of overhead labor to the wage of direct labor
φ	Time lag
ψ	Measure of personal income distribution
ψ^*	Measure of personal income distribution in long-run equilibrium
ω	Share of wages in national income

List of Figures

List of Tables

Chapter 1
Introduction

1.1 Setting the Framework

During the past decades, a slowdown in the trend rates of economic growth as well as rising income disparities have been among the economic and social challenges in several major advanced countries. While both issues have particularly moved to the forefront of the political and public debate in the aftermath of the financial crisis of 2008–2009, they are also the empirical motivation for this writing endeavor.

Although economic growth has picked up pace in most recent years, in its 2018 *Global Risk Report* the World Economic Forum (2018, p. 19) warns that "[...] this relatively upbeat picture masks numerous concerns [...]." "Productivity growth [...]," it is held, "[...] remains puzzlingly weak. Investment growth has been subdued [...]. And in many countries the social and political fabric has been badly frayed by many years of stagnating real incomes."

Especially in the lower parts of the income hierarchy, over the past decades real incomes have not grown much or have even declined, while those at the top of the distribution have seen their incomes rise considerably, most notably in the United States and other Anglo-Saxon countries. In fact, income disparities were ranked as the number one global risk in terms of likelihood in the 2012, 2013, and 2014 *Global Risk Reports* (World Economic Forum 2018, Fig. IV). Similarly, in 2018 increasing income and wealth disparities were named among the most important drivers of various global risks expected in the upcoming ten years, including social instability (World Economic Forum 2018, Fig. II and p. 9).

With the long-term slowdown in economic growth and the unequal distribution of income being the empirically motivated main themes of this book, it is useful to start off by sketching out some developments that have occurred during the past decades in major advanced countries.

© Springer Nature Switzerland AG 2020
C. Anselmann, *Secular Stagnation Theories*, Springer Studies in the History of Economic Thought, https://doi.org/10.1007/978-3-030-41087-2_1

1.1.1 From Economic Growth to Secular Stagnation?

Economic growth is a relatively recent phenomenon in history. As shown in Table 1.1 based on estimates by Maddison (2005, p. 10, 2006, pp. 640, 643), in all regions and countries considered average annual growth rates of both real gross domestic product (GDP) and real GDP per capita were almost negligible prior to the era of the first and second Industrial Revolution. While average annual real GDP growth hovered close to zero percent prior to the late eighteenth and early nineteenth century, it accelerated in the following periods, reaching values of more than four percent between 1820 and 1870 as well as almost four percent between 1870 and 1913 in several Anglo-Saxon countries (i.e., the Western offshoots). The decades following the Second World War stand out as well, with catch-up growth giving rise to average annual real GDP growth rates close to five percent in Western Europe and more than nine percent in Japan. Similar developments also hold for average real GDP per capita growth rates.

Since the early 1970s, however, economic growth has been slowing down. As compared to the post-Second World War period from 1950 to 1973, according to Table 1.1, average annual real GDP growth in Western Europe more than halved between 1973 and 2001. While the decline was even more pronounced in Japan, in the Western offshoots average annual real GDP growth fell by roughly one percentage point. In the Western world as a whole, average annual real GDP growth amounted

Table 1.1 Average annual real GDP growth rates (in %) and average annual real GDP per capita growth rates (in %), 1–2001

Period	1–1000	1000–1500	1500–1820	1820–1870	1870–1913	1913–1950	1950–1973	1973–2001
A. GDP								
Western Europe	−0.01	0.29	0.40	1.68	2.11	1.19	4.79	2.21
Western offshoots	0.05	0.07	0.78	4.31	3.92	2.83	4.03	2.95
Japan	0.10	0.18	0.31	0.41	2.44	2.21	9.29	2.71
West		0.27	0.41	1.93	2.66	1.96	4.81	2.61
World	0.01	0.15	0.32	0.93	2.11	1.82	4.90	3.05
B. GDP per capita								
Western Europe	−0.01	0.13	0.14	0.98	1.33	0.76	4.05	1.88
Western offshoots	0.00	0.00	0.34	1.41	1.81	1.56	2.45	1.84
Japan	0.01	0.03	0.09	0.19	1.48	0.88	8.06	2.14
West		0.13	0.14	1.06	1.57	1.17	3.72	1.95
World	0.00	0.05	0.05	0.54	1.30	0.88	2.92	1.41

Source Author's illustration, based on data from Maddison (2005, p. 10, 2006, pp. 640, 643). See Appendix B for detailed data sources and further notes

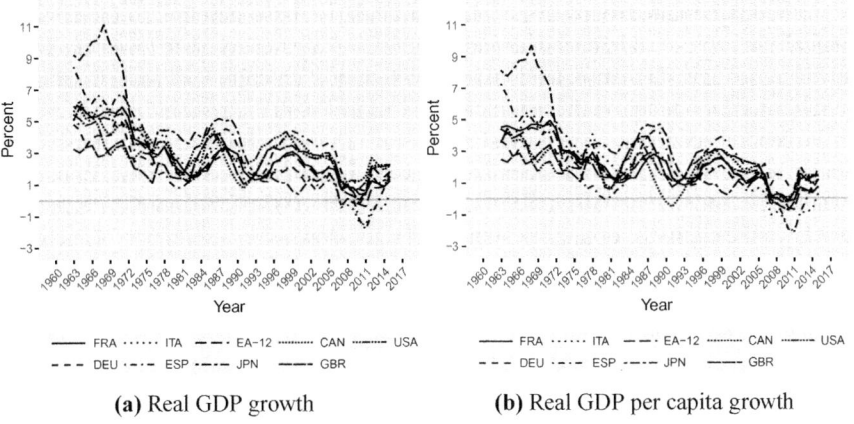

(a) Real GDP growth   **(b)** Real GDP per capita growth

Fig. 1.1 Average annual real GDP growth rates and average annual real GDP per capita growth rates (centered five-year moving averages), 1960–2017. *Source* Author's calculations and illustrations, based on data from the European Commission (2018). See Appendix A for detailed data sources and further notes

to approximately 2.6% between 1973 and 2001, while average real GDP per capita growth was down to less than two percent per year.

The growth slowdown that has been occurring during the past decades is also illustrated in Fig. 1.1, which shows centered five-year moving averages of annual real GDP and real GDP per capita growth rates from 1960 until the most recent year 2017. Apart from cyclical fluctuations, economic growth rates have gradually declined in all countries considered. In Germany, for instance, in the early 1960s five-year moving average annual real GDP growth amounted to more than four percent, while in most recent years it has been down to less than 1.8%. Similar developments also hold for five-year moving average annual real GDP per capita growth, which exceeded three percent in the first years of the 1960s, but lately has amounted to only 1.2%. As can be clearly seen in Fig. 1.1, economic growth was subdued considerably during and after the Great Recession. Although economic performances have been relatively strong in most recent years, economic growth has remained low by historical standards.

In the years following the financial crisis of 2008–2009, the slowdown in economic advance across the developed world has evoked a debate on secular stagnation, commonly understood as a long-term—secular—phase of slow economic growth. Some economists, in fact, have been afraid that secular stagnation may become a real issue in major advanced countries, most notably in the euro area, but also in the United States and Japan. While various scholars have been involved in the secular stagnation debate over the past years, it was Harvard professor Lawrence H. Summers—also a former president of Harvard University, former chief economist of the World Bank, and economic adviser in the Clinton and Obama administrations—who set the ball rolling in 2013 (Summers 2018).

Although certain groups of people—particularly those pointing to the environmental and ecological impact of economic growth—are not averse to lower economic advance, secular stagnation tendencies which may eventually lead to a cessation of long-term economic growth are typically associated with unfavorable characteristics in the general economic and political discussion. There has been a growth fetish, so to speak, as economic growth is deemed necessary in capitalist economies. Among the twentieth-century economists, Schumpeter (1939, p. 1033), for example, made clear that "[...] the capitalist organism cannot [...] settle down into a stationary stage without being vitally affected. [...] [S]tabilized capitalism is a contradiction in terms." Similarly, Alvin H. Hansen (1941, p. 173)—one of the most well-known secular stagnationists of the twentieth century—noted that "[t]o make the system of free enterprise workable, it is absolutely necessary to ensure a rising national income. [...] A static national income [...] would wreck the economic order." In more recent times, the need for economic growth in a free enterprise, profit-oriented economic system has been outlined by Galbraith (2014, pp. 241–242), for instance.

In addition to being a vital element of the capitalist system of production, economic growth is also prerequisite to sustain the welfare state and to provide public goods and services (Büchs and Koch 2017, pp. 3, 28–30). "[...] GDP growth matters [...]," Gordon (2018, pp. 2–3) notes, "[...] because slower GDP growth provides fewer resources to address the nation's problems, including faltering education, aging infrastructure, and the looming shortfall for [...] [social and medical care]." Friedman (2005, pp. 3–18), on the other hand, points to the stimulating moral and social impact of economic growth. In his own words:

> Economic growth [...] more often than not fosters greater opportunity, tolerance of diversity, social mobility, commitment to fairness, and dedication to democracy. Ever since the Enlightenment, Western thinking has regarded each of these tendencies positively, and in explicitly moral terms. (Friedman 2005, p. 4)

It may not be by chance, in fact, that the rise of populist and nationalist parties in many advanced countries over the past years has occurred at a time of overall sluggish economic performances. With a slowdown or cessation of economic growth, people are contesting over a slowly growing or non-changing national income, leading to more intense distributional struggles which may eventually become a zero-sum game. "If our growth falters [...] or if we merely continue with slower growth that benefits only a minority of our citizens [...]," Friedman (2005, p. 9) notes, "[...] the deterioration of [...] society will [...] worsen once more." While a slowdown in economic growth is unfavorable in itself, it is still worse, though, when it is accompanied by a rise in the unequal distribution of income. Yet, this is what has happened in several major advanced countries over the past decades, as the following section outlines in more detail.[1]

---

[1] While the following remarks focus on the development of income distribution, Appendix C briefly refers to the distribution of wealth in some advanced countries.

1.1.2 Income Distribution: Empirical Trends

1.1.2.1 The Functional Distribution of Income

In contrast to the personal distribution of income among private households or individuals, the functional distribution of income among the owners of the main factors of production—labor, capital, and land—has a long tradition in the history of economic thought. Following the typical three-class division of their time, the classical economists laid the foundation of the analysis of functional distribution. Already in the eighteenth century, Adam Smith ([1776] 1976) dedicated the first book of his *Wealth of Nations* to the distribution of national income between workers, capitalists, and landlords, receiving wages, profits, and rent, respectively. Eventually, with the declining economic importance of the agricultural sector in developed countries, throughout the twentieth century the traditional three-class division was mostly abandoned in favor of the nowadays common two-class distinction between workers, receiving labor income, and capitalists, receiving capital income (including profits and rent) (Glyn 2009, p. 104).

Building on the division of national income into capital income and labor compensation, Fig. 1.2a shows the long-run evolution of labor income shares—as decennial averages—in various developed countries. Although the underlying historical data should be interpreted with caution, as they are not entirely comparable over time and across nations, the general developments can be taken as a first approximation (Piketty 2014a, pp. 199–206, c, p. 39; Bengtsson and Waldenström 2018, pp. 718–720). Despite various country-specific fluctuations, in line with the empirical findings of Glyn (2009, pp. 113–122), Piketty (2014a, pp. 199–201), and Bengtsson and Waldenström (2018, pp. 722–724), at least in those nations for which there are

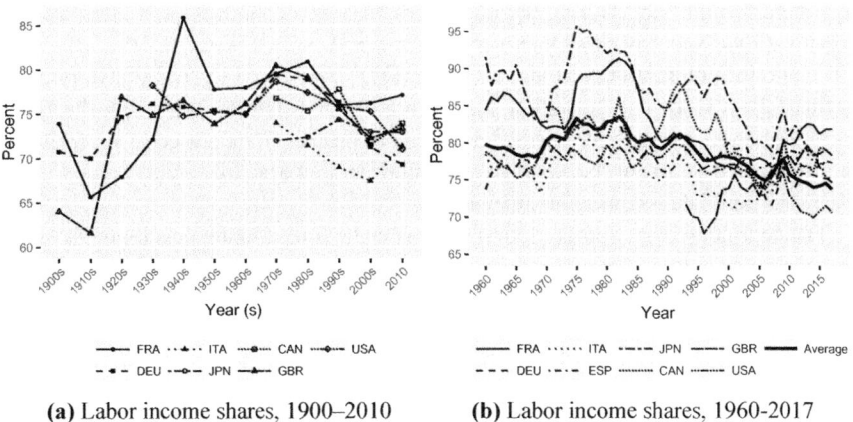

(a) Labor income shares, 1900–2010   **(b)** Labor income shares, 1960-2017

Fig. 1.2 Labor income shares. *Source* Partly author's calculations and author's illustrations, based on data from Piketty and Zucman (2014a, b) and the European Commission (2017, 2018). See Appendix A for detailed data sources and further notes

long-term data the labor share followed a slight inverted U-shaped pattern between the beginning of the twentieth and the early twenty-first century. This applies especially to Germany and the United Kingdom, but also—to a lesser extent—to France. In the early twentieth century, in Germany the labor share increased particularly during the First World War and thereafter. Although not shown in Fig. 1.2a, but as referred to by Glyn (2009, pp. 119, 121), in Italy and Japan a similar rise occurred during and after the Second World War. In Canada and the United States, on the other hand, according to Glyn (2009, pp. 118, 120–121) it was especially the Great Depression which provoked relatively strong temporary increases in the labor share. In contrast to the European countries and Japan, however, the overall developments in North America were reportedly more restrained in the early and mid-twentieth century.

In the first post-Second World War decades, labor shares remained relatively high and did not drop back to their early twentieth-century levels. Strong labor unions and favorable bargaining positions of workers have probably played a role here (Glyn 2009, pp. 115–116). In some nations, in fact, even a slight upward development continued. Starting at the end of the 1970s and the early 1980s, however, the share of labor compensation in national income generally has been declining again, reversing the overall trend of previous decades.

More detailed recent empirical developments can be seen in Fig. 1.2b, which—based on data from the European Commission (2018)—depicts the evolution of (adjusted) labor shares in net national income at factor cost since the 1960s. While differences in the underlying data and methodologies do not allow direct comparison of the labor share levels in Fig. 1.2a and b, the general developments are mostly similar. As illustrated in Fig. 1.2b, between the 1970s and at least the mid-2000s, long-term labor income shares have been declining in most countries taken into account, especially in France, Germany, Italy, Japan, and Canada. This downward trend is also visible in the weighted average of the eight national labor income shares considered (bold line). During the past years, various economists and international organizations, such as Stockhammer (2013, pp. 40–42), Piketty (2014a, pp. 199–201), and the International Monetary Fund (IMF 2017, pp. 121–122), have pointed to this fall in labor compensation shares in advanced nations. Although the labor income shares seem to have reached a plateau or have even increased to some extent in most recent years, in the majority of countries they are still low as compared to their mid- and late twentieth-century levels.[2]

The decline in labor compensation shares can be linked to the development of the personal distribution of income among private households or individuals, although—as will be outlined below—the nexus is not necessarily unambiguous from an ex-ante perspective. As mentioned by Glyn (2009, p. 122), "[t]he shift from a generally rising to a generally declining labor share over the past five decades or so represents

---

[2]It should be noted that labor and capital income shares are dependent on the business cycle. As profits fluctuate more procyclically than labor income, the share of capital income in national income typically declines during depressions and rises in years of economic prosperity. Conversely, the labor income share tends to rise during depressions and to decline in years of economic prosperity.

a parallel movement to, and has contributed to, rising personal income inequality [...]." Examining the developments in member countries of the Organisation for Economic Co-operation and Development (OECD) between the 1970s and the 1990s, Checchi and García-Peñalosa (2010), for example, find a negative nexus between labor income shares and personal income inequality as measured by the Gini coefficient. While the analysis of the functional distribution of income thus remains an important analytical tool, it is fair to say, however, that the personal distribution of income has moved to the forefront of public attention in recent decades (Atkinson and Bourguignon 2001, p.7265). Besides the availability of new and more comprehensive data sources, this also has to do with structural changes in society. While the distinction between workers, receiving labor income, and capitalists, receiving capital income, reflected the typical class division in earlier times, from today's perspective such a clear-cut allocation is not valid anymore (see also Haslinger and Stönner-Venkatarama 1998, p.24). With a rising number of people drawing on both labor and capital income, the so-called *cross-distribution* of labor and capital incomes—a term coined by Stobbe (1962, pp.35–36) but predominantly associated with the growth models of Kaldor (1955/1956) and Pasinetti (1962)—becomes increasingly important, as "[...] there is no longer any simple correspondence between classes of people and sources of income [...]" (Atkinson 2009, p.6).[3] Moreover, incomes within types of income have been diverging considerably over the past decades—a phenomenon which cannot be captured by the functional distribution of income. Labor compensation, for instance, reaches from wages barely sufficient for a decent living to the enormous salaries of top managers. Hence, while the functional distribution of income is "[...] a recognizable starting point [...]" (Atkinson 2009, p.6), the personal distribution of income—sometimes also referred to as the size distribution of income—must be considered as well.[4]

1.1.2.2 The Personal Distribution of Income

The Distribution of Pre-Tax Income

Based on tax data provided by Atkinson et al. (2017), Fig. 1.3a shows the long-term development of the shares of total gross income accruing to the top one percent of income recipients. In a number of nations, a U-shaped pattern can be observed between the early twentieth and the beginning of the twenty-first century, implying that the evolution of personal income concentration as measured by the development of top income shares contrasts with the slight inverted U-shaped trend of labor income shares. During the first years of the twentieth century, when the shares of labor compensation in national income were still comparatively low, gross income shares of the top percentile were relatively high, hovering between 15 and more than

---

[3]For further remarks on the functional distribution and cross-distribution of income, see also Kalmbach (1972, pp.154–162, 185–192) and Kurz (1977, pp.153–155).

[4]On the importance of the personal distribution of income, see also Haslinger and Stönner-Venkatarama (1998, pp.22–24).

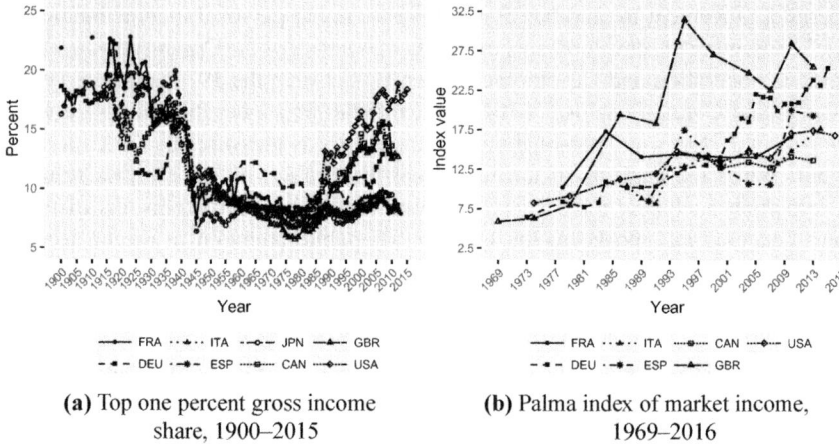

(a) Top one percent gross income
share, 1900–2015

(b) Palma index of market income,
1969–2016

Fig. 1.3 Personal pre-tax income distribution. *Source* Partly author's calculations and author's illustrations, based on data from Atkinson et al. (2017) and the Luxembourg Income Study (2018a). See Appendix A for detailed data sources and further notes

20%. In the post-Second World War era, on the other hand, high labor income shares were accompanied by low top income shares. Starting in the late 1970s and early 1980s, however, these trends have been reversed in several of the countries considered. Especially in Canada, the United Kingdom, and the United States, but also in Germany, gross income shares of top income recipients have risen considerably during the past years. Similar, though less pronounced, developments also hold for Japan and—at least until the mid-2000s—for Italy, where declining labor income shares have been accompanied by slight upward trends in top gross income shares.[5]

In line with these observations, for a panel of 15 advanced countries and Argentina, Bengtsson and Waldenström (2018, pp. 721–731) find a statistically significant positive nexus between top income and capital income shares (i.e., the counterpart to labor income shares) between the early twentieth and early twenty-first century. Despite some variations across time and within nations, this positive relation also holds for individual countries as well as for country groups (Anglo-Saxon, Continental European, and Nordic countries) in different time periods.

If it is realistically assumed that the relative importance of labor income declines as one moves from the bottom to the top of the income scale—as has been empirically shown by Piketty and Saez (2007, p. 151) for the United States as well as Dell (2007, pp. 382–383) and Bach et al. (2009, p. 318) for Germany—the overall contrasting developments of top and labor income shares are intuitively clear. Nonetheless, however, a fall (rise) in the labor income share is not necessarily accompanied by a rise (fall) in personal income inequality. For example, during the past years it has been frequently pointed out that, in contrast to the developments of the functional distribution of income, the recent increase in top income shares has been more pro-

---

[5]Similar developments also apply to the distribution of net wealth. See Appendix C.

nounced in the United States and other Anglo-Saxon countries than in Japan and most Continental European nations. In fact, while the share of labor compensation has been declining comparatively little in the USA over the past decades, the top one percent gross income share has increased considerably. As outlined by Piketty and Saez (2007, pp. 150–155), Glyn (2009, pp. 111–112), Leigh (2009, pp. 164–165), and Roine and Waldenström (2015, pp. 557–562), strong increases in managerial and Chief Executive Officer (CEO) remuneration—which are typically classified as labor income—have played a role here. Large pay increases at the top of the income hierarchy have prevented the labor income share in the United States from falling more strongly since the 1970s and 1980s, while at the same time they raised the income shares of those at the top of the distribution. As shown by Glyn (2009, pp. 112–113), subtracting the top one percent of labor income from total employee compensation reveals "[...] that the share of the 'bottom 99%' of US labor has fallen much more sharply over the past couple of decades than labor's share as a whole" (Glyn 2009, p. 112).

Looking at the development of more general measures of personal income distribution, Fig. 1.3a depicts the evolution of a modified version of the Palma index of market income in seven advanced economies since the late 1960s.[6] Based on household survey data provided by the Luxembourg Income Study (2018a), which should be interpreted with the usual caution indicated when analyzing household surveys, the Palma index in Fig. 1.3b relates the average market income of the top ten percent of the income distribution to the average market income of the combined bottom 40% of the income hierarchy. While the Palma ratio has been more or less stable in France and Canada during the past decades, it increased strongly in Germany, Italy, the United Kingdom, and the United States. In fact, as compared to the United States, the Palma index has been higher in Germany and the United Kingdom in recent years. In Germany, for example, at the beginning of the 1970s the average person in the top ten percent received about six times the market income of the average person in the bottom 40%. In 2015, on the other hand, the Palma ratio amounted to more than 25.

For Germany and the United States, more detailed developments are illustrated in Fig. 1.4, which shows the average annual growth rates in real market income in different percentiles of the income scale between the late 1970s and 2015/2016. The general pattern is quite similar in both countries, with average market incomes having declined approximately in the first 40 percentiles. At the bottom and the very top of the distribution, the developments in the United States are somewhat more abrupt

---

[6] Building on Palma's (2006, 2011) cross-country empirical finding that variations in income inequality are mainly reflected in changes in the income shares of the bottom 40% and the top ten percent of the income hierarchy, the Palma index was originally proposed by Cobham and Sumner (2013a, b) as the ratio of the income share of the top ten percent to the income share of the bottom 40% of the distribution. In contrast to the commonly used Gini coefficient, which is oversensitive to changes in the middle of the income distribution, the Palma index is better suited to capture variations at the lower and upper ends of the income scale (Cobham et al. 2016). As the bottom 40% comprise four times as many people as the top ten percent of the distribution, in Fig. 1.3b (and also in Fig. 1.6b) the Palma index as originally defined by Cobham and Sumner (2013a, b) was multiplied by a factor of four to allow for a more intuitive interpretation.

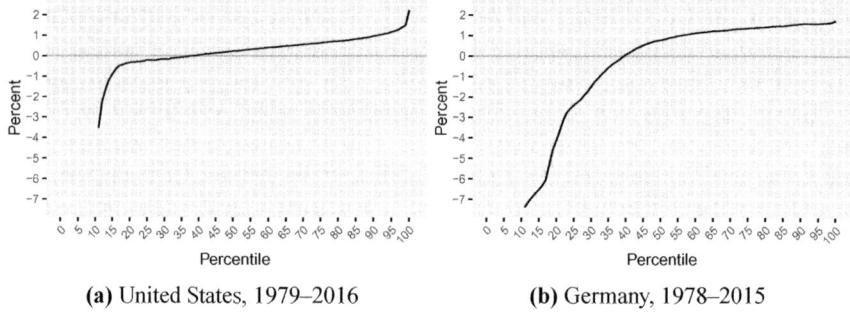

Fig. 1.4 Average annual real market income growth rates in different percentiles. *Source* Author's calculations and illustrations, based on data from the Luxembourg Income Study (2018a, b). See Appendix A for detailed data sources and further notes

than in Germany. Moreover, while the incomes at the very top rose more strongly in the United States, the decline at the bottom—between the eleventh and the 37th percentile—was more pronounced in Germany.

The Distribution of Post-Tax and Disposable Income

In contrast to the long-term development of top gross income shares shown in Fig. 1.3a, similar data on the historical evolution of post-tax income inequality are hardly available. Combined with the long-term development of top marginal income tax rates, however, the long-term development of top gross income shares may at least give an approximate idea of the historical evolution of after-tax income concentration.

As illustrated in Fig. 1.5a, in most countries considered top marginal income tax rates have roughly followed an inverted U-shaped trend over the past decades, thus standing in contrast to the evolution of top gross income shares. Although the correlation is not perfect at all times and in all nations, during the twentieth and early twenty-first century, a rise in top marginal income tax rates was generally accompanied by a decline in top gross income shares, and vice versa.[7] These developments suggest that the long-run evolution of top after-tax income shares may resemble the overall trend of top gross income shares in Fig. 1.3a. As shown in Fig. 1.5b, which

---

[7]Piketty et al. (2014) identify three channels through which high-income recipients react to changes in top tax rates, resulting in higher top gross income shares (as calculated based on tax records) when top marginal tax rates decline, and vice versa. A fall in top tax rates tends, first, to raise top income recipients' economic activity, secondly, to reduce tax avoidance, thus raising income reported to national tax authorities, and, thirdly, to increase the incentive of high-income earners "[...] to bargain more aggressively for higher pay [...]" (Piketty et al. 2014, p. 268). On the example of the United States, however, Piketty et al. (2014, p. 232) show that changes in tax avoidance and thus in income reported to tax authorities "[...] cannot account for a significant fraction of the long-run surge in top incomes [...]" since the 1960s. The evolution of top gross income shares is thus not considered a statistical artifact, but is assumed to reflect actual developments. See also Morelli et al. (2015, pp. 660–665).

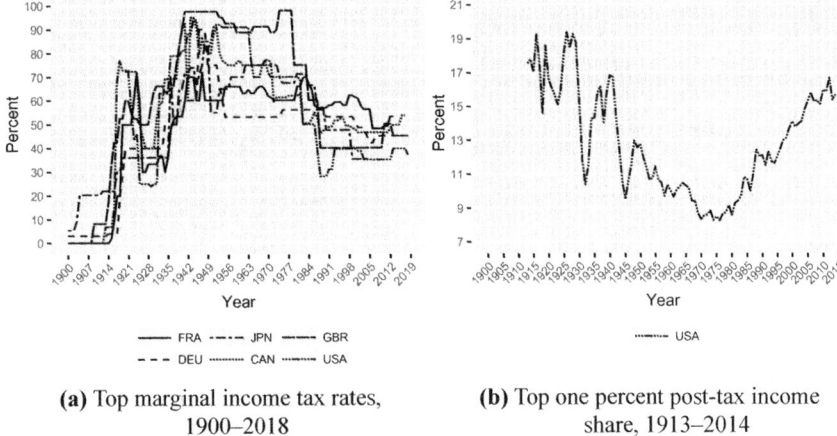

(a) Top marginal income tax rates, 1900–2018

(b) Top one percent post-tax income share, 1913–2014

Fig. 1.5 Top marginal income tax rates and the top one percent post-tax income share. *Source* Author's illustrations, based on data from Piketty (2014b), the OECD (2018), the Bundesministerium der Finanzen (2018), Gale et al. (2018, p. 2), Moriguchi and Saez (2005, pp. 65–66, 2010, pp. 162–163), Saez and Veall (2007, pp. 301–302), and Piketty et al. (2017, 2018, p. 587). See Appendix A for detailed data sources and further notes

is based on recent calculations by Piketty et al. (2017, 2018), at least for the United States this assumption can be generally confirmed.

Based on household survey data, more recent empirical developments in the distribution of disposable household income are shown in Fig. 1.6. While Fig. 1.6a depicts the evolution of the mean-to-median income ratio, Fig. 1.6b illustrates the development of the Palma ratio between the late 1960s and 2013/2016. In the United States, but also—to a lesser extent—in Canada and Germany, both inequality measures have increased during the past years. In Canada, for example, at the beginning of the 1980s average disposable household income was about 1.09 times as high as median disposable household income. In 2013, on the other hand, the mean-to-median income ratio amounted to 1.15. While no clear trend can be observed in Spain, in Italy disposable household income inequality as measured by both the mean-to-median income ratio and the Palma index has been declining since the early 1990s. In the United Kingdom, on the other hand, the Palma ratio has fallen in the most recent past, while the mean-to-median income ratio has slightly increased.

Comparing the Palma ratios of market and disposable income reveals that the ranking of countries with respect to the level of inequality is not the same in Figs. 1.3b and 1.6b. For instance, while the Palma ratio of market income has been more or less the same in Italy and the United States during the years leading up to 2014, the Palma index of disposable income has been considerably lower in Italy as compared to the USA, indicating that income redistribution through taxes and transfers is relatively more pronounced in Italy.

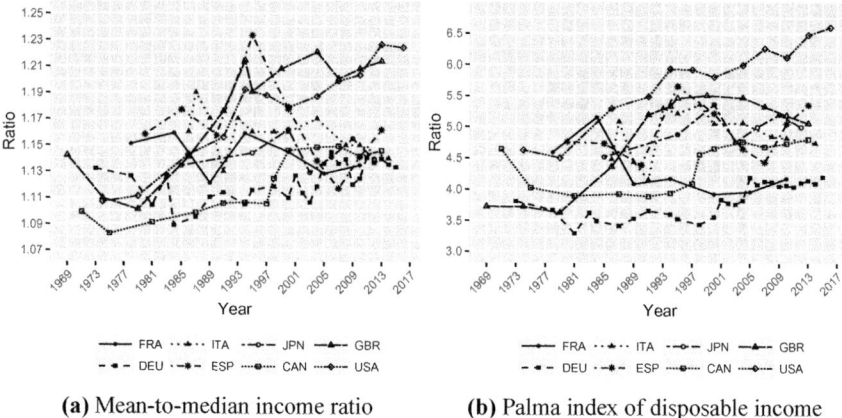

(a) Mean-to-median income ratio   **(b)** Palma index of disposable income

Fig. 1.6 Disposable household income distribution, 1969–2013/2016. *Source* Partly author's calculations and author's illustrations, based on data from the Luxembourg Income Study (2018a) and the OECD (2018). See Appendix A for detailed data sources and further notes

Similar to Fig. 1.4, for Germany and the United States Fig. 1.7 contrasts the evolution of real disposable household income in different percentiles of the distribution between the late 1970s and 2015/2016. Although in both countries the income growth rates increase as one moves from the bottom to the top of the distribution, the developments in the United States are considerably more progressive, especially at the margins of the income scale.

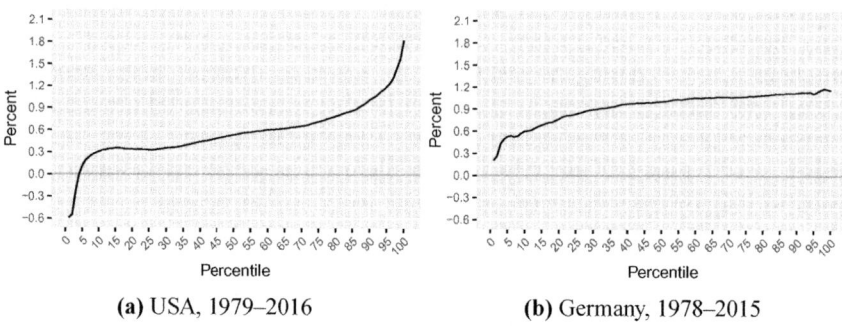

(a) USA, 1979–2016   **(b)** Germany, 1978–2015

Fig. 1.7 Average annual real disposable income growth rates in different percentiles. *Source* Author's calculations and illustrations, based on data from the Luxembourg Income Study (2018a, b). See Appendix A for detailed data sources and further notes

1.1.2.3 General Assessment and Implications

Similar to the growth slowdown over the past decades, the increase in income inequality in several advanced countries since the 1970s and 1980s has been perceived as unfavorable in the general public discussion, particularly since the aftermath of the financial crisis of 2008–2009. While it is beyond debate that some degree of inequality is necessary for the efficient functioning of capitalist economies, the question on the optimum distribution of income is a subject in its own right, with country-specific factors and social preferences playing an important role.[8] Although objective judgments about distributional issues are a difficult endeavor, in various advanced countries the rise in income inequality over the past decades has motivated discussions on so-called pay codes, intended to limit the pay differential between the highest and lowest paid employees in a company. Although these debates have been explicitly concerned with the compensation of employees, the discussed proposals may yet serve as a rough point of reference for what may be considered a decent and socially acceptable level of income inequality within individual countries.

Already in the late 1970s, in the United States Drucker (1977) argued in support of a maximum pay differential between the highest and lowest paid employees of 15:1 in small- and medium-sized firms, as well as a ratio of approximately 25:1 in large corporations. In the United Kingdom, on the other hand, in 2010 then-Prime Minister David Cameron (2010) proposed a pay differential of 20:1 in the public sector—a suggestion reportedly going back to the late nineteenth-century US-American banker J. P. Morgan (The Economist 2018). More recently, the same proposal has also been taken up again by the Labour Party (2018) in the United Kingdom, calling for a maximum pay ratio of 20:1 in both the public sector and firms "[...] bidding for public contracts [...]." In Switzerland, in turn, in a 2013 public referendum voters could decide on the introduction of a maximum pay ratio of 12:1 between the highest and lowest paid employees working for the same company. While limiting the compensation spread, with a maximum pay differential of 12:1 the monthly salary of the highest paid employee in a firm could still be as high as the annual salary of the lowest paid employee. Although the proposal was eventually rejected, almost 35% of all voters advocated the implementation of a limiting pay ratio (Schweizerischer Bundesrat 2014, p. 1775).

In light of the empirical developments outlined in the previous sections, it comes as no surprise that in major advanced countries the income differentials between the upper and lower parts of the income distribution are much higher today than all of the aforementioned proposals for maximum pay spreads. Based on household survey

---

[8]On the importance of some degree of income inequality in capitalist economies, Krelle (1962, p. 159, own translation) held, "To spur joy of work and ambition and to reward superior performances, lower [income] differences are [...] sufficient. But there is also a limit to equality, which—from an economic perspective—it is impossible to pass in a free market economy, and—if it were passed—would also be unjust and unfavorable. The slacker and the hard worker, the untalented and the talented man, he who performs simple tasks bearing little responsibility, and he whose job is characterized by high degrees of difficulty, responsibility, and perhaps risk, they also have to be differentiated in terms of their income. Dull egalitarianism is an evil."

Table 1.2 The income share of the top one percent (S99) (in %), the income share of the bottom one percent (S1) (in %), and the ratio of the two (S99/S1)

	FRA (2010)	DEU (2015)	ITA (2014)	ESP (2013)	JPN (2008)	CAN (2013)	GBR (2013)	USA (2016)
S99	4.68	4.58	4.54	4.18	4.60	4.29	5.53	5.67
S1	0.07	0.12	0.02	0.02	0.07	0.04	0.06	0.02
S99/S1	62.58	36.75	258.16	238.31	64.12	107.78	88.99	254.89

Source Author's calculations and illustration, based on data from the Luxembourg Income Study (2018a). See Appendix B for detailed data sources and further notes.

data provided by the Luxembourg Income Study (2018a), Table 1.2 reveals that in recent years the ratio of average equivalized disposable household income between the top one percent and the bottom one percent of the income hierarchy hovered between close to 37 in Germany and more than 200 in Italy, the United States, and Spain. Despite marked country-specific differences, in all nations considered the income disparities between the margins of the distribution are well above the proposed pay differentials, even more so if it is realistically assumed that household survey data tend to underestimate the income spread between the top and the bottom of the income hierarchy.

Although it is not suggested that the proposals for maximum pay differentials put forth over the past years are the absolute truth or represent an undisputed optimum range of income inequality from a social and economic perspective, following Atkinson (2015, p. 124) one may still have "[...] pragmatic concern[s] that [the] current levels of inequality are too high [...]." In several developed nations, most notably in the United States and other Anglo-Saxon countries, income disparities have been trending toward their highest levels in modern history. It is indeed questionable whether such high levels of inequality are necessary from an economic point of view, let alone from a social perspective. Considering the social and political divide that has been occurring in various countries during the past years, it is reasonable to assume that the high and partly rising levels of income inequality "[...] have reached socially unacceptable levels [...]" (Guellec and Paunov 2017, p. 34). In fact, large income disparities are worrying in their own right, because they do not seem to be compatible with the general sense of justice (Atkinson 2015, p. 12). Additionally, however, highly unequal distributions of income are also associated with various adverse social and economic effects. For example, large income disparities can inhibit social cohesion in society and may hamper economic growth through various channels. Low economic growth, on the other hand, may also boost higher income inequality, particularly if lower economic performance goes hand in hand with higher unemployment in the lower parts of the income hierarchy. This may lead to a vicious circle, in fact, provoking the socially threatening environment of low economic growth and high inequality already mentioned above. While both sluggish economic growth and a highly unequal distribution of income are problematic on their own, it is particularly the combination of the two which is potentially socially explosive.

1.2 Outline

Building on the empirical developments described in the previous Sect. 1.1, secular stagnation and the distribution of income are the main themes of this book. While the topic of secular stagnation sets the overall framework, the issue of income distribution is analyzed in the context of this stagnationist scene. The aim is, first, to provide a thorough overview of different secular stagnation theories that have been developed over the past centuries and, secondly, to assess the role of income distribution in selected stagnation theories. The motivation to address the issue from a historical perspective and to analyze the relevance of income distribution in different secular stagnation hypotheses is based on two findings:

First, the current stagnation debate that came up after the financial crisis of 2008–2009 is—in almost every sense of the word—a *contemporary* debate. Although Alvin H. Hansen is referred to by Lawrence H. Summers, other historical stagnationists are hardly mentioned in the current discussion (see also the remarks by Hein 2016, p. 4). While Hansen and Summers are the economists who typically come to mind when the topic of secular stagnation is brought up these days, the issue is not confined to the two of them. In the history of economic thought, various economists aside from Hansen and Summers have been involved in the debates on secular stagnation or have shared their opinion on stagnation-related topics. As a side issue of economic growth theory, the subject of secular stagnation is basically as old as the economic sciences, reaching back to Adam Smith and his classical contemporaries. In fact, there is not just *one* stagnation theory which has been adapted to prevailing economic circumstances over time, but there are various stagnation hypotheses, with each highlighting different aspects in terms of the causes of stagnation and the underlying mechanisms at work. To only refer to the most recent and most well-known theories would thus give an incomplete picture. Although it may indeed be assumed that the most popular theories are superior and describe economic reality most accurately, Kurz (2008, pp. 14, 15, own translation) reminds that "[e]conomics is not [...] a smoothly functioning selection process [...]. [...] [T]he selection process of ideas or theories in economics [...]," he notes, "[...] is, for various reasons, incomplete [...]." New ideas, for instance, may emerge at the wrong time, remaining largely unnoticed when they are first developed. The secular stagnation hypothesis of Josef Steindl, for example, suffered this fate. Published at the beginning of the post-Second World War economic expansion in the early 1950s, Steindl's stagnation theory received only little attention at the time. As will be outlined throughout this book, however, the general core of his theory can be a valuable addition to the contemporary stagnation debate, particularly with regard to the role of income distribution. "The history of theory is a treasury of economic ideas and theories [...]," Kurz (2008, p. 17, own translation) notes, "[...] comparable to a gene pool that can be drawn upon and from which new mutations originate."

Secondly, from an empirical perspective, most of the major secular stagnation theories that have been developed since the early and mid-twentieth century refer to time periods of high and/or rising income inequality in major advanced countries. While it may thus be assumed that the distribution of income is an important element in the respective theories, it turns out that income disparities play a heterogeneous role in different stagnation hypotheses. In most theories, however, they are not a leading characteristic. For example, despite the strong increase in the unequal distribution of income over the past decades in several developed nations, the role of income inequality is relatively minor in the contemporary stagnation debate. Although the distribution of income is not completely ignored, the empirical trends since the 1970s—with a rise in income inequality and a slowdown in economic growth—suggest that there is more room for questions of distribution. Aiming both for a stronger focus on income inequality in the stagnation debate and to bring the distribution of income to the fore, it will be shown that—in the history of economic thought—it is the twentieth-century stagnation theory of Josef Steindl which serves as the most valuable point of reference.

The remainder of this book is divided into two parts. While Part I—consisting of Chaps. 2–5—provides a critical overview of secular stagnation theories from the classical economists to the most recent stagnation debate, Part II—consisting of Chaps. 6–10—is concerned with the role of income distribution in different stagnation hypotheses. The chapters are structured as follows:

In Part I, Chap. 2 provides the basic theoretical foundations of secular stagnation. Although defining secular stagnation is a difficult endeavor, the chapter aims to give a broad definition of economic stagnation in terms of its most common symptoms. While periods of stagnation are typically characterized by weak economic growth, secular stagnation remains a multifaceted phenomenon. In fact, although sluggish economic performance is a central feature of secular stagnation, the causes of stagnation and the mechanisms at work are at least as important in the various stagnation theories. From a general perspective, it can broadly be distinguished between demand- and supply-side stagnation theories, although there are still major differences between the theories within these two groups. While demand-side stagnation is characterized by actual output (growth) falling short of potential output (growth), supply-side stagnation describes a slowdown in potential output (growth). Although this distinction is useful from an analytical point of view, the demand and the supply side of the economy are intertwined.

Over the past centuries, various economists have endorsed secular stagnation or stagnation-related issues from either a demand-side or a supply-side perspective. In this book, it is distinguished between early economists of the eighteenth to the early twentieth century, modern economists of the mid- to late twentieth century, and contemporary economists of the twenty-first century. Chapter 3 takes a look at different authors emphasizing secular stagnation as a demand-side issue, including the pre-Keynesian underconsumptionists Jean Charles Léonard Simonde de Sismondi, Thomas R. Malthus, and John A. Hobson, as well as several twentieth-century economists. The latter include John M. Keynes, whom Schumpeter (1954, p. 1172) described as the intellectual father of stagnation, and Alvin H. Hansen, also known as the *American Keynes*. Other names associated with twentieth-century demand-side stagnation are the Polish economist Michał Kalecki as well as his student and later colleague Josef Steindl. In contrast to Hansen, who advocated secular stagnation as an exogenous phenomenon, Steindl referred to stagnation as an endogenous process resulting from oligopolization tendencies and the concentration of market power among firms in the course of capitalist development. In the contemporary stagnation debate of the twenty-first century, secular stagnation with a focus on the demand side of the economy is particularly advocated by Lawrence H. Summers, who views his stagnation hypothesis as a revival of Hansen's theory.

In contrast to Chaps. 3 and 4 focuses on economists advocating secular stagnation as a supply-side issue. It includes the British classical economists Adam Smith, Thomas R. Malthus, John S. Mill, and David Ricardo, who predicted the economy to transition into a stationary state of zero economic growth. Among the early economists of the nineteenth century is also Karl Marx, who assumed the breakdown of the capitalist system of production. On the other hand, twentieth-century economists addressed in Chap. 4 include Joseph A. Schumpeter, who predicted the self-destruction and—for different reasons than Marx, though—the final breakdown of capitalism. Although they are not secular stagnationists as such, it is also referred to Robert M. Solow and Trevor W. Swan, whose standard neoclassical growth model has dominated mainstream economics since the 1970s and indirectly includes a theory of stagnation. Other twentieth-century economists who can be classified as advocates of supply-side stagnation are Jean Fourastié and William J. Baumol, referring to structural shifts in the economy toward sectors with low productivity growth as a cause of possible stagnation tendencies. Donella H. Meadows and her colleagues, on the other hand, endorsed environmental limits to economic growth. In the contemporary stagnation debate of the twenty-first century, in turn, Robert J. Gordon is the main advocate of supply-side stagnation and, as such, is usually described as the supply-side counterpart to Lawrence H. Summers.

Chapter 5 closes Part I, providing an interim conclusion and stressing that demand- and supply-side stagnation theories are not necessarily mutually exclusive. Moreover, it is emphasized that most stagnation hypotheses that emerged during the two major waves of secular stagnation theories in the mid-twentieth century and after the financial crisis of 2008–2009 refer to time periods of high and/or rising income inequality. Eventually, it is Part II which takes a closer look at the nexus between income distribution and secular stagnation, focusing especially on the impact of changes in income disparities on possible stagnation tendencies.

Part II starts with Chap. 6, which—from a more general perspective—focuses on different transmission channels through which changes in the distribution of income can impact economic growth. In this context, it is referred to demand-side, supply-side, as well as political and social mechanisms.

Chapter 7 is concerned with the role of income distribution in secular stagnation theories. While questions of distribution are generally more important in demand-side than in supply-side theories, there are still considerable differences among individual stagnation hypotheses. For example, the issue of distribution only plays a peripheral role in the twentieth-century approaches of Keynes and Hansen, and it is also not at the heart of the contemporary stagnation hypotheses of Summers and Gordon. Among the economists involved in the secular stagnation debates of the twentieth and twenty-first century, it was Steindl, one of the least recognized stagnationists in the history of economic thought, who put the issue of income distribution at the heart of his stagnation theory. With its focus on income disparities, Steindl's model of stagnation can enhance the contemporary stagnation debate by bringing the distribution of income to the fore.

In line with the classical and post-Keynesian/Kaleckian tradition, in his original demand-side stagnation theory Steindl focused on the functional distribution of income. As has already been outlined in Sect. 1.1.2, although the functional distribution of income is still important when analyzing the distribution of income, the personal distribution of income has moved to the forefront of economic research during the past decades. In Chap. 8, Steindl's twentieth-century theoretical model is therefore adjusted to include the personal distribution of income, being one of the first attempts to incorporate the personal distribution of income in a Kaleckian–Steindlian model of economic growth and stagnation. The extended model includes both the profit share and—by distinguishing between two private household groups—a measure of the personal distribution of income. Based on a comparative static analysis, it is shown that economic shocks which lead to an increase in the unequal distribution of personal income and/or a rise in the profit share *can* be accompanied by a slow-down in long-term economic growth and hence by possible stagnation tendencies. It is not a necessity, though, but depends on the specific economic shock as well as the prevailing economic circumstances. Moreover, it is shown that changes in the long-term rate of economic growth feed back on both the personal and functional distribution of income. While—in the theoretical Steindlian model—a decline (rise) in the rate of economic growth leads to a fall (rise) in the profit share, the impact on the personal distribution of income is uncertain from an ex-ante perspective. As outlined in Chap. 9, these heterogeneous findings concur with existing empirical evidence on the nexus between income distribution and economic growth.

The final chapter (Chap. 10) concludes by providing a short résumé and presenting various empirically oriented policy implications aimed at fostering both economic growth and a more equal distribution of income. In this context, it is referred to wage policy and the importance of trade unions, competition and innovation policy, public investment in infrastructure and human capital, as well as tax and transfer policy. While an adequate policy mix can foster inclusive growth, it is doubtful whether appropriate policy actions will be taken in the years ahead. Among the most important impediments to fiscal intervention are the high and partly rising public debt-to-GDP ratios in numerous advanced countries, which—particularly since the financial crisis of 2008–2009—have been pointed at to advocate public spending cuts. Collective reductions in fiscal expenditures, however, may both foster secular stagnation tendencies and have adverse long-term effects on the distribution of income.

References

Atkinson AB (2009) Factor shares: the principal problem of political economy? Oxf Rev Econ Policy 25(1):3–16

Atkinson AB (2015) Inequality: what can be done? Harvard University Press, Cambridge, MA, and London

Atkinson AB, Bourguignon F (2001) Income distribution. In: Smelser NJ, Baltes PB (eds) International encyclopedia of the social behavioral sciences. Pergamon, Oxford, pp 7265–7271

Atkinson AB, Hasell J, Morelli S, Roser M (2017) The chartbook of economic inequality (database) May 2017. Institute for New Economic Thinking (INET) at the Oxford Martin School and University of Oxford, Oxford. http://chartbookofeconomicinequality.com/wpcontent/uploads/DataForDownload/AllData_ChartbookOfEconomicInequality.xlsx. Accessed 29 Nov 2018

Bach S, Corneo G, Steiner V (2009) From bottom to top: the entire income distribution in Germany, 1992–2003. Rev Income Wealth 55(2):303–330

Bengtsson E, Waldenström D (2018) Capital shares and income inequality: evidence from the long run. J Econ Hist 78(3):712–743

Büchs M, Koch M (2017) Postgrowth and wellbeing: challenges to sustainable welfare. Palgrave Macmillan, Cham

Bundesministerium der Finanzen (2018) Lohn- und Einkommensteuerrechner. Berechnungen und Informationen zur Einkommensteuer. Berechnung der Einkommensteuer. Bundesministerium der Finanzen, Berlin. https://www.bmf-steuerrechner.de/. Accessed 20 Sept 2018

Cameron D (2010) Labour are now the reactionaries, we the radicals. The Guardian, April 08, 2010. https://www.theguardian.com/commentisfree/2010/apr/08/david-cameron-conservatives-radicals. Accessed 12 Nov 2018

Checchi D, García-Peñalosa C (2010) Labour market institutions and the personal distribution of income in the OECD. Economica 77(307):413–450

Cobham A, Sumner A (2013a) Is it all about the tails? The Palma measure of income inequality. Center for Global Development Working Paper 343. Center for Global Development, Washington, DC. https://www.cgdev.org/sites/default/files/it-all-about-tails-palma-measure-income-inequality.pdf. Accessed 02 Mar 2018

Cobham A, Sumner A (2013b) Putting the Gini back in the bottle? The Palma as a policy-relevant measure of inequality? Mimeograph. King's College London, London. https://www.kcl.ac.uk/sspp/departments/did/People/Academic-staff/Sumner/Cobham-Sumner-15March2013.pdf. Accessed 02 Mar 2018

Cobham A, Schlögl L, Sumner A (2016) Inequality and the tails: the Palma proposition and ratio. Glob Policy 7(1):25–36

Dell F (2007) Top incomes in Germany throughout the twentieth century: 1891–1998. In: Atkinson AB, Piketty T (eds) Top incomes over the twentieth century: a contrast between European and English-speaking countries. Oxford University Press, Oxford, pp 365–425

Drucker PF (1977) Is executive pay excessive? Wall Str J 20. (May 23, 1977)

European Commission (2017) Annual macro-economic database of the European Commission's Directorate General for Economic and Financial Affairs (AMECO database). European Commission, Brussels. http://ec.europa.eu/economy_finance/ameco/user/serie/SelectSerie.cfm. Data as of 11 May 2017. Accessed 19 Sept 2017

European Commission (2018) Annual macro-economic database of the European Commission's Directorate General for Economic and Financial Affairs (AMECO database). European Commission, Brussels. http://ec.europa.eu/economy_finance/ameco/user/serie/SelectSerie.cfm. Data as of 08 Nov 2018. Accessed 26 Nov 2018

Friedman BM (2005) The moral consequences of economic growth. Vintage Books, New York, NY

Galbraith JK (2014) The end of normal: the great crisis and the future of growth. Simon & Schuster, New York

Gale WG, Gelfond H, Krupkin A, Mazur MJ, Toder E (2018) Effects of the tax cuts and jobs act: a preliminary analysis. Urban-Brookings Tax Policy Center, Washington, DC. https://www.brookings.edu/wp-content/uploads/2018/06/ES_20180608_tcja_summary_paper_final.pdf. Accessed 25 Nov 2018

Glyn A (2009) Functional distribution and inequality. In: Salverda W, Nolan B, Smeeding TM (eds) The Oxford handbook of economic inequality. Oxford University Press, Oxford and New York, NY, pp 101–126

Gordon RJ (2018) Why has economic growth slowed when innovation appears to be accelerating? NBER Working Paper No. 24554. National Bureau of Economic Research, Cambridge, MA. http://www.nber.org/papers/w24554. Accessed 19 June 2018

Guellec D, Paunov C (2017) Digital innovation and the distribution of income. NBER Working Paper No. 23987. National Bureau of Economic Research, Cambridge, MA. http://www.nber. org/papers/w23987. Accessed 23 Sept 2018

Hansen AH (1941) Fiscal policy and business cycles. W. W. Norton & Company, Inc., New York, NY

Haslinger F, Stönner-Venkatarama O (1998) The theory of income distribution: a survey of some recent developments. In: Haslinger F, Stönner-Venkatarama O (eds) Aspects of the distribution of income. Metropolis-Verlag, Marburg, pp 13–71

Hein E (2016) Secular stagnation or stagnation policy? Steindl after Summers. PSL Q Rev 69(276):3–47

IMF (2017) Gaining momentum? World economic outlook September 2005. International Monetary Fund, Washington, DC. http://www.imf.org/en/Publications/WEO/Issues/2017/04/04/world-economic-outlook-april-2017. Accessed 01 Mar 2018

Kaldor N (1955/1956) Alternative theories of distribution. Rev Econ Stud 23(2):83–100

Kalmbach P (1972) Wachstum und Verteilung in neoklassischer und postkeynesianischer Sicht. Duncker & Humblot, Berlin

Krelle W (1962) Verteilungstheorie. Betriebswirtschaftlicher Verlag Dr. Th. Gabler, Wiesbaden

Kurz HD (1977) Zur neoricardianischen Theorie des Allgemeinen Gleichgewichts der Produktion und Zirkulation: Wert und Verteilung in Piero Sraffas "Production of Commodities by Means of Commodities". Duncker & Humblot, Berlin

Kurz HD (2008) Einführung. In: Kurz HD (ed) Klassiker des ökonomischen Denkens, vol I. Von Adam Smith bis Alfred Marshall. Verlag C.H.Beck, Munich, pp 9–30

Labour Party (2018) A fair deal at work: rights at work. Labour Party, London. https://labour.org. uk/manifesto/fair-deal-work/#first. Accessed 12 Nov 2018

Leigh A (2009) Top incomes. In: Salverda W, Nolan B, Smeeding TM (eds) The Oxford handbook of economic inequality. Oxford University Press, Oxford and New York, NY, pp 150–174

Luxembourg Income Study (2018a) Luxembourg Income Study (LIS) database. LIS, Luxembourg. http://www.lisdatacenter.org. Accessed 12 Nov 2018

Luxembourg Income Study (2018b) Luxembourg Income Study (LIS), PPP deflators. LIS, Luxembourg. http://www.lisdatacenter.org/data-access/web-tabulator/methods/ppp/. Data as of 04 Apr 2018. Accessed 08 Nov 2018

Maddison A (2005) Growth and interaction in the world economy: the roots of modernity. The AEI Press, Washington, DC

Maddison A (2006) The world economy vol 1 and 2. OECD Publishing, Paris

Morelli S, Smeeding T, Thompson J (2015) Post-1970 trends in within-country inequality and poverty: rich and midde-income countries. In: Atkinson AB, Bourguignon F (eds) Handbook of income distribution, vol 2A. Elsevier North-Holland, Oxford and Amsterdam, pp 593–696

Moriguchi C, Saez E (2005) The evolution of income concentration in Japan, 1885–2002: evidence from income tax statistics. Working Paper. 25 Aug 2005. https://eml.berkeley.edu//~saez/moriguchi-saez05japan.pdf. Accessed 03 Mar 2018

Moriguchi C, Saez E (2010) The evolution of income concentration in Japan, 1886–2005: evidence from income tax statistics. In: Atkinson AB, Piketty T (eds) Top incomes: a global perspective. Oxford University Press, Oxford, pp 76–170

OECD (2018) OECD. Stat OECD, Paris. http://stats.oecd.org/. Accessed 04 Dec 2018

Palma JG (2006) Globalizing inequality: Centrifugal and centripetal forces at work. DESA Working Paper No. 35. UN Department of Economic and Social Affairs, New York, NY. http://www.un. org/esa/desa/papers/2006/wp35_2006.pdf. Accessed 02 Mar 2018

Palma JG (2011) Homogeneous middles versus heterogeneous tails, and the end of the inverted-U: it's all about the share of the rich. Dev Chang 42(1):87–153

Pasinetti LL (1962) Rate of profit and income distribution in relation to the rate of economic growth. Rev Econ Stud 29(4):267–279

Piketty T (2014a) Capital in the twenty-first century. Harvard University Press, Cambridge, MA, and London

Piketty T (2014b) Capital in the twenty-first century, online appendix, March 2014. http://piketty.pse.ens.fr/en/capital21c2. Accessed 03 Dec 2018

Piketty T (2014c) Technical appendix of the book. Capital in the twenty-first century, March 2014. http://piketty.pse.ens.fr/files/capital21c/en/Piketty2014TechnicalAppendix.pdf. Accessed 03 Mar 2018

Piketty T, Saez E (2007) Income and wage inequality in the United States, 1913–2002. In: Atkinson AB, Piketty T (eds) Top incomes over the twentieth century: a contrast between European and English-speaking countries. Oxford University Press, Oxford, pp 141–225

Piketty T, Zucman G (2014a) Capital is back: wealth-income ratios in rich countries 1700–2010. Q J Econ 129(3):1255–1310

Piketty T, Zucman G (2014b) Capital is back: wealth-income ratios in rich countries 1700–2010. Online data appendix. http://gabriel-zucman.eu/capitalisback/. Accessed 06 Nov 2018

Piketty T, Saez E, Stantcheva S (2014) Optimal taxation of top labor incomes: a tale of three elasticities. Am Econ J: Econ Policy 6(1):230–271

Piketty T, Saez E, Zucman G (2017) Distributional national accounts: methods and estimates for the United States. Online data appendix. http://gabriel-zucman.eu/usdina/. Accessed 30 Nov 2018

Piketty T, Saez E, Zucman G (2018) Distributional national accounts: methods and estimates for the United States. Q J Econ 133(2):553–609

Roine J, Waldenström D (2015) Long-run trends in the distribution of income and wealth. In: Atkinson AB, Bourguignon F (eds) Handbook of income distribution, vol 2A. Elsevier North-Holland, Oxford and Amsterdam, pp 469–592

Saez E, Veall MR (2007) The evolution of high incomes in Canada 1920–2000. In: Atkinson AB, Piketty T (eds) Top incomes over the twentieth century: a contrast between European and English-speaking countries. Oxford University Press, Oxford, pp 226–308

Schumpeter JA (1939) Business cycles, vol 2. McGraw-Hill Book Company Inc, New York, NY, and London

Schumpeter JA (1954) History of economic analysis. Oxford University Press, New York, NY

Schweizerischer Bundesrat (2014) Bundesratsbeschluss über das Ergebnis der Volksabstimmung vom 24. November 2013. Schweizerischer Bundesrat, Bern. https://www.admin.ch/opc/de/federal-gazette/2014/1773.pdf. Accessed 12 Nov 2018

Smith A ([1776] 1976) An inquiry into the nature and causes of the wealth of nations. In: Campbell RH, Skinner AS (eds) The Glasgow edition of the works and correspondence of Adam Smith, vol 2. Oxford University Press, London

Stobbe A (1962) Untersuchungen zur makroökonomischen Theorie der Einkommensverteilung. Kieler Studien, 59. Tübingen: J. C. B. Mohr (Paul Siebeck)

Stockhammer E (2013) Why have wage shares fallen? An analysis of the determinants of functional income distribution. In: Lavoie M, Stockhammer E (eds) Wage-led growth: an equitable strategy for economic recovery. Palgrave Macmillan and International Labour Organization, London, pp 40–70

Summers LH (2018) Biography. http://larrysummers.com/press-contacts/biography/. Accessed 15 Nov 2018

The Economist (2018) Executive pay in America: hitting pay dirt. The Economist 427(9093):60–61. (May 26th–June 1st 2018)

World Economic Forum (2018) The global risks report 2018, 13th edn. World Economic Forum, Geneva. http://www3.weforum.org/docs/WEF_GRR18_Report.pdf. Accessed 19 Oct 2018

Part I
Secular Stagnation Theories:
Past and Present

Chapter 2
Theoretical Foundations

2.1 Defining Stagnation on Its Common Symptoms

Stagnation hypotheses have a long history in economic analysis. From classical economics until today, the idea that advanced capitalist economies might be prone to some kind of long-term—secular—stagnation which goes beyond a usual cyclical downturn has been considered in various theories of economic development (Higgins 1950, p. 255).[1] Despite its long tradition, however, as outlined by Reuter (2000, pp. 243–247) the term *stagnation* is an ambiguously defined concept and frequently misunderstood. In Eichengreen's (2014, p. 41) words, "[...] [S]tagnation [...] is an economist's Ror[s]charch [t]est. It means different things to different people." There is indeed a great variety of stagnation concepts, with each hypothesis having its own distinctive features regarding the underlying causes, mechanisms, and remedies. Defining economic stagnation in a universal, clear, and precise way is thus a difficult endeavor and—if at all—only possible with respect to the most common symptoms.

Secular stagnation is essentially an issue of economic growth theory. According to its Latin etymology (stagnum (Latin): standing water) (Riddle 1844, p. 652), stagnation is often associated with a complete cessation of economic growth. Although this notion describes the stationary state in classical economics, some of the more recent stagnation theories which evolved during the twentieth and twenty-first century are not characterized by zero output growth. In the contemporary literature of the past years, secular stagnation in a broad sense is often defined as a *prolonged period of low growth* (usually measured as long-run average annual growth in real GDP or real GDP per capita), though the terms *prolonged* and *low* are typically not further specified. While *low* may be equal to zero growth, this is not a necessity (Hamberg 1957, p. 212; Gordon 2015, p. 15). Blecker (2016, p. 203), for example, addresses stagnation as "[...] a long-term tendency toward chronically slow average

---

[1] Unless specified differently, the terms *secular stagnation*, *long-term stagnation*, and *stagnation* are used interchangeably throughout this book. They do not describe a short-term contraction or the trough of a business cycle, but refer to a long period of stagnation.

© Springer Nature Switzerland AG 2020
C. Anselmann, *Secular Stagnation Theories*, Springer Studies in the History of Economic Thought, https://doi.org/10.1007/978-3-030-41087-2_2

growth as opposed to (or in addition to) a sharp short-run downturn or slow cyclical recovery." Similarly, Backhouse and Boianovsky (2016, p. 147) speak of "[...] a long period of low growth amounting to something beyond a regular cyclical downturn." Hein (2016, p. 3) is consistent with these definitions as well and characterizes secular stagnation as "[...] low or even negative growth over a prolonged period of time." The IMF (2014, p. 83) likewise speaks of "[...] a prolonged period of very low growth [...]," and the OECD (2015, p. 2) refers to "[...] an extended period of low overall economic activity [...]."

While it is generally agreed today that slow output growth is among the typical symptoms of stagnation, it is reasonable to also consider periods in which average growth is still relatively high, but decreasing. In fact, some stagnation theorists do not refer to low economic growth as such, but are primarily concerned with a decline in the rate of growth which—if growth is not already weak—may ultimately lead to low economic growth. As a broad working definition, an economy is assumed here to be *at risk of falling into secular stagnation* if the long-term average output growth rate has not yet reached a low level, but follows a declining path. On the other hand, *secular stagnation per se* is said to prevail if the average output growth rate *is* low and perhaps declines still further for a longer period.[2]

Both situations are schematically illustrated in Fig. 2.1. While Fig. 2.1a shows long-term average annual real national output *growth rates*, Fig. 2.1b depicts the corresponding development of real national output *levels*. As long as average output growth remains fairly high, but follows a downward trend, ceteris paribus the economy is at risk of entering a period of stagnation at some point in the future. On the other hand, if average economic growth falls below a certain threshold and remains low for a prolonged period of time, the economy is experiencing secular stagnation. Although the term *secular* does not require stagnation to persist forever, low average growth must prevail for a longer period, covering at least several business cycles. Similar to the term *secular*, the expression *low* economic growth as well is a rather loose concept, with its definition being dependent on the specific time period under consideration. As a rough guide, following Streißler (1983, p. 457) low growth may broadly be defined as an average annual real output growth rate of no more than one to 1.5%. Although his assessment is from the early 1980s, Streißler (1983, p. 457) is more or less consistent with Jorgenson and Vu (2017, p. 670), who project a period of "[...] continued stagnation [...]" in several advanced countries in the upcoming years, characterized by long-term average annual economic growth rates of 1.5% and less. Similarly, on a global scale Piketty (2014, pp. 72, 101–102) expects long-term economic growth to gradually decline in the decades ahead, eventually merging

---

[2]Due to its long-term character, from an empirical point of view actual periods of secular stagnation can only be determined ex-post. From an ex-ante perspective, unless it is clear whether a low growth phase is of short- or long-term duration, one may be inclined to speak of *stagnation tendencies* rather than to refer to secular stagnation. While there may be *tendencies* toward secular stagnation, a *prolonged* period of stagnation does not necessarily have to occur, as counteracting forces may arise (Blecker 2016, pp. 211–212). This also implies that secular stagnation does *not* refer to a phenomenon which inevitably lasts forever.

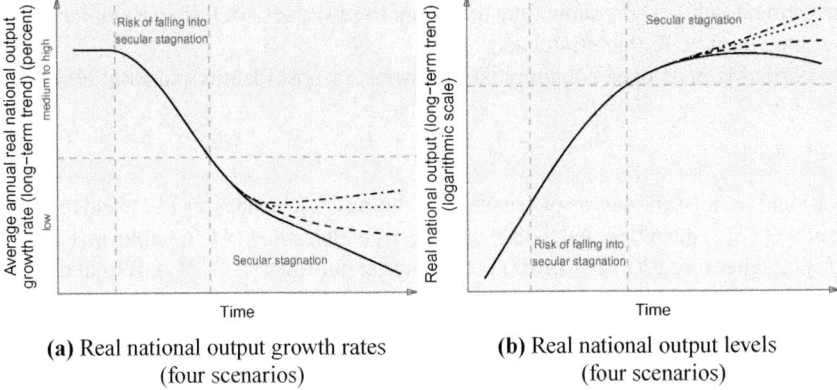

(a) Real national output growth rates
(four scenarios)

(b) Real national output levels
(four scenarios)

Fig. 2.1 Schematic illustrations of long-term trends in real national output growth and real national output levels in periods of secular stagnation. *Source* Author's illustrations

into a "[...] low-growth regime [...]," marked by average annual economic growth of no more than 1.5%.

As shown in Fig. 2.1, as long as growth remains weak, a period of stagnation as defined here may involve a constant average growth rate (dotted line) or a declining growth rate (dashed and solid lines), but may also be consistent with a rising growth rate (dot-dashed line). In contrast to the wave-like pattern of the business cycle, with each upswing leading to a downswing and vice versa, phases of secular stagnation are discrete periods which do "[...] not generate any 'forces of reversal'. If and when such forces do emerge, they originate not in the internal logic of the economy but in the larger historical context within which the economy functions" (Sweezy [1982] 1987, p. 38; see also Rosenof 1997, p. 55).

2.2   Demand- and Supply-Side Stagnation

While slow average economic growth characterizes stagnation in its most general sense, existing theories can broadly be classified into demand- and supply-side concepts. Between the individual hypotheses within these two groups, however, major differences still exist.

From a purely demand-side point of view, secular stagnation is caused by insufficient effective demand which impairs overall economic growth by holding back actual output (growth) below full-employment potential output (growth).[3] The underlying issue generally addressed is that various factors hamper the growth in planned

---

[3] Potential output is the estimated output level which can be achieved under prevailing technological conditions when labor and/or capital are fully employed, i.e., utilized at *normal* rates. It is the estimated maximum output level that can be sustained in the medium to long run without inflationary pressure.

investment, while at the same time the desire to save does not follow a similar trend, but may even be further stimulated.

Formally, in an open economy the following ex-post identity must be fulfilled:

$$S_h + S_f + S_g = I_f + I_g + (X - M). \tag{2.1}$$

National saving (i.e., saving of private households (S_h), businesses (S_f), and the government (S_g)) must be equal to the sum of private investment (I_f), public investment (I_g), and net foreign investment (i.e., net capital outflows $(X - M)$). If total desired saving exceeds total planned investment at full employment, the full-employment level of output cannot be realized. Due to a lack of effective demand, actual output settles down at a level below its full-employment potential where ex-post saving and ex-post investment are equal. If, as a result, economic growth is constrained, demand-side secular stagnation may evolve.

In fact, the expression *secular stagnation* initially characterized a demand-side phenomenon and originates with Alvin H. Hansen (1934, p. 19), a Danish-American economist who coined the term in 1934 to describe his own demand-driven stagnation thesis. Schumpeter ([1942] 2008, p. 392) later referred to him and his followers as *stagnationists*. According to Foster (1987, p. 62) and Foster and McChesney (2012, p. 59), demand-side stagnation is characterized by "[...] slow growth [...][,] rising unemployment [...][,] and idle capacity [...]." Indeed, a *growing gap* between potential output at full-employment and actual output is commonly assumed to be the main symptom of demand-driven stagnation.[4] Three examples are schematically illustrated in Fig. 2.2a. Before stagnation sets in, actual output (black lines) is assumed to be more or less equal to its full-employment potential (gray line), with both variables growing at a relatively high rate. After several periods, however, the economy enters a phase of stagnation, as actual national output (black lines) evolves more slowly and grows at comparatively weak rates. While actual output may grow at a relatively low, but constant rate (scenario I: solid black line), average economic growth may also decline further over time, but remain in positive territory (scenario II: dashed black line), or it may decline further and turn negative (scenario III: dotted black line). At the same time, however, in each scenario potential output (gray line) is not stagnating, but rises further and further above the actual output level. Although average potential output growth may slow down (not shown in Fig. 2.2a), it is assumed to remain high. Hence, if there were no lack of aggregate demand, but actual output closed up with its potential, stagnation would not prevail.

A second strand of economists advocates stagnation as a supply-side issue. These approaches, however, are not always classified as secular stagnation theories. Krugman (2014), for example, points out that the term *secular stagnation* refers to "[...] a demand-side, not a supply-side concept." Although it is true that the expression originally described Hansen's demand-side concept and continues to be mainly

---

[4]To avoid any misinterpretation, Higgins (1950, p. 166) even suggested to speak of economies "[...] with increasing under-employment and a declining rate of growth [...]" instead of using the term *stagnation*.

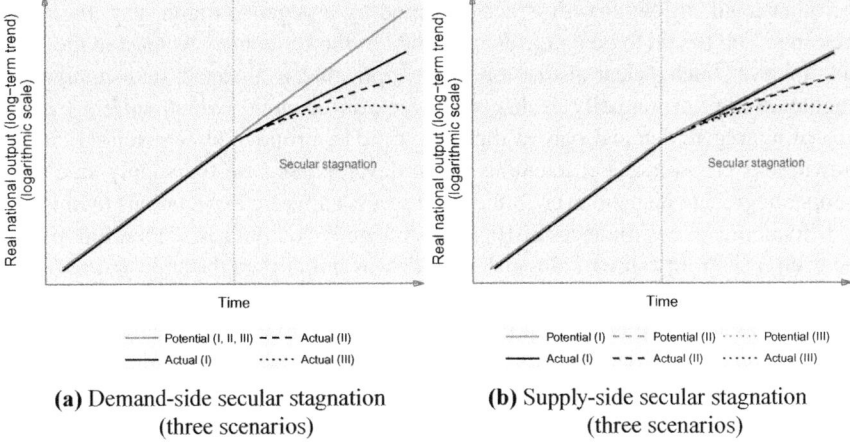

(a) Demand-side secular stagnation
(three scenarios)

(b) Supply-side secular stagnation
(three scenarios)

Fig. 2.2 Schematic illustration of demand- and supply-side secular stagnation. *Source* Author's illustrations, based on Higgins (1948, pp. 82–83, 1950, 1959, pp. 176–178), Brandt (1952, pp. 144–149), Verspohl (1971, pp. 169–171), and Meißner (1983, p. 186)

associated with Hansen, the present thesis follows today's common practice and does not confine the term to a purely demand-driven phenomenon.[5] According to supply-side stagnation theorists, the root cause of low economic growth is not that actual output (growth) is lagging behind potential output (growth). As illustrated in Fig. 2.2b on the example of three different scenarios, the main issue is rather that the development of potential output itself (gray lines) is hampered. In a period of supply-side secular stagnation, potential output may, for example, grow at a relatively low, but constant rate (scenario I: solid gray line). On the other hand, however, potential economic growth may also decline further over time, but remain in positive territory (scenario II: dashed gray line), or it may decline further and turn negative (scenario III: dotted gray line). With potential output not growing properly, economic growth remains sluggish even if—as shown in the three scenarios in Fig. 2.2b—actual output (black lines) is always at its full-employment level. The underlying causes contributing to lower potential (and hence actual) output growth differ among the various supply-side stagnation hypotheses. While several classical economists referred to the scarcity of fertile land, other scholars point to flaws in the institutional framework, a reduction in labor force growth, or sluggish potential productivity growth caused by low rates of technological progress.

Demand- and supply-side issues are commonly distinguished based on the size of the output gap, i.e., the (estimated) gap between actual and potential output. If economic growth is low and actual output is more or less equal to its potential, growth is assumed to be sluggish primarily because of supply-side constraints. On

---

[5]Gordon (2015, p. 2), for instance, refers to "[...] secular stagnation on the supply side [...]."

the other hand, if low growth is accompanied by a negative output gap, the most pressing issue is said to be on the demand side of the economy.[6] At least in the long run, however, such a clear distinction is not applicable, as demand- and supply-side stagnation are not mutually exclusive. In fact, an economy which suffers from a lack of aggregate demand may at the same time be prone to slow potential output growth and vice versa. For example, weak developments on the supply side may hamper aggregate demand even in the short run via adverse expectations (Ministère de l'Economie et des Finances 2016, p. 3). A negative output gap is therefore possible even if the root cause of sluggish growth was initially on the supply side of the economy. Similarly, a demand-side issue can well turn into a supply-side constraint. While a widening gap between potential and actual output is assumed to be among the common traits of demand-side stagnation, it is questionable whether a negative output gap can grow or persist over a prolonged period of time. In the words of Marx ([1861–1863] 1968, p. 497), "[p]ermanent crises [of overabundant capital and overproduction] do not exist." Weak demand may not just hamper the actual output path, but can also have adverse effects on the development of potential output. For instance, when low aggregate demand impairs economic activity, labor force participation rates and learning-by-doing effects may be reduced. With its multilayered character as both a demand- and supply-side component, however, it is real capital investment which plays the most crucial role. Sluggish demand can hamper the accumulation of capital due to adverse accelerator effects. While this leads to an even further slowdown in effective demand, it also harms future productive capacity. Similarly, as real investment usually incorporates a range of different technologies, lower investment demand reduces innovation, technological advance, and thus productivity growth (Setterfield 2002, pp. 4–5). These hysteresis effects are sometimes referred to as *Say's law in reverse*, indicating that a weakening of demand which inhibits the development of actual output can endogenously impair supply-side factors and thus the path of potential output (Cornwall 1970; Setterfield 2002, p. 2; Summers 2014, p. 37).[7] Hence, an existing negative output gap may not widen further over time, but is likely to close slowly until it eventually disappears. Even if a period of secular stagnation was initially caused by a lack of aggregate demand, former demand-side constraints—if left untreated—may endogenously turn into supply-side restrictions in the long run. As secular stagnation is essentially a long-term phenomenon, a stagnant economy typically tends toward a closed output gap, with overall productive capacity (growth) falling below its pre-stagnation level (Streißler 1983, p. 462).

---

[6]While the concept of the output gap is intuitive in manufacturing-driven economies, it is more contentious in service-dominated economies, with the latter having gained importance across the developed world over the past decades. Although there are exceptions—such as in the healthcare sector—capacity in the service sector tends to be more flexible than in the manufacturing sector. See also Corry et al. (2011, pp. 43–46).

[7]Hysteresis effects which do not just reduce the *level* of potential output, but which also hamper potential output *growth*, are sometimes referred to as *super-hysteresis effects* (Blanchard et al. 2015, p. 3). See also Lavoie (2018, pp. 8–9).

From a theoretical point of view, growing or persistent long-term output gaps as the ones shown in Fig. 2.2a are unlikely to evolve (Spahn 1982, p. 23). They may only exist indirectly when pre-stagnation, pre-hysteresis estimates of potential output are consulted.[8]

2.3 Stagnation Theorists: An Overview

Stagnation theories go beyond predicting prolonged periods of low economic growth triggered by a lack of effective demand and/or supply-side constraints. While the most general symptoms may be similar, careful distinctions have to be drawn between the various existing hypotheses, whose diversity mainly stems from differences in the specific, unique causes of stagnation. Although it is impossible and beyond the purpose of this book to cover all theories which are in some way related to economic stagnation, Table 2.1 attempts to give an overview of selected authors who have either influenced or even dominated the stagnation debate at different points in time. While some of these scholars, such as Solow and Swan, are not considered secular stagnationists as such, they have still contributed to the general discussion on economic growth, of which the issue of stagnation is a thematic offshoot.

Based on the general perspective which the authors take on the causes of stagnation, they are classified as either demand- or supply-side economists. While advocates of the demand side point out that actual output growth is lagging behind its potential, supply-side economists assume economic growth to be hampered by a slowdown in potential output growth. Although the demand and supply side of the economy are intertwined and not strictly separable, distinguishing between demand- and supply-side theories provides a clear structure and is useful from an analytical point of view. A second classification criterion refers to the period of time when the authors developed their respective theories. Following Backhouse and Boianovsky (2016, p. 156), recent stagnation concepts which evolved after the financial crisis of 2008–2009 are referred to as *contemporary* hypotheses. On the other hand, theories which had been established in the mid- to late twentieth century are classified as *modern* stagnation hypotheses (Schumpeter 1954, p. 1172; Verspohl 1971, p. 145). They contrast with the *early* stagnation concepts of mainly classical economists and their contemporaries.

While the following two chapters take a closer look at most of the individual theories put forth by the authors listed in Table 2.1, a brief introductory overview is indicated here.

---

[8]Higgins (1948, p. 93) also pointed to hysteresis effects when he referred to demand-side stagnation. He mentioned that "[...] the [output] gap need not go on growing forever [...] [as] the potential trend might fall [...]." Nonetheless, the Japanese experience shows that a negative output gap can persist for quite some time (Bank of Japan 2018).

Table 2.1 Economists involved in the debates on secular stagnation (and economic growth)

Chronology	Demand-side economists	Supply-side economists
Early (eighteenth to early twentieth century)	(J.C.L. Simonde de Sismondi) (Thomas R. Malthus) (John A. Hobson)	Adam Smith Thomas R. Malthus John S. Mill David Ricardo Karl Marx William S. Jevons
Modern (mid- to late twentieth century)	John M. Keynes **Alvin H. Hansen** Roy F. Harrod Michał Kalecki **Josef Steindl** Paolo Sylos-Labini Paul A. Baran Paul M. Sweezy	Joseph A. Schumpeter (Robert M. Solow) (Trevor W. Swan) Jean Fourastié William J. Baumol Donella H. Meadows
Contemporary (twenty-first century)	C. Christian von Weizsäcker Thomas I. Palley **Lawrence H. Summers** Paul Krugman	Tyler Cowen (Thomas Piketty) **Robert J. Gordon**

Source Author's illustration
Note The names of economists who are at the heart of the following discussion are written in bold letters. The names of economists who can only indirectly be referred to as "stagnationists" are put in brackets

On the demand side, Table 2.1 includes Jean Charles Léonard Simonde de Sismondi, Thomas R. Malthus, and John A. Hobson as three early representatives. While, due to conceptual flaws, these *underconsumptionists* do not classify as demand-side stagnationists as defined above, their general line of argument shares some similarities with modern and contemporary advocates of stagnation. In particular, with regard to the role of income distribution, their ideas are valuable benchmarks in the history of economic thought.

In the twentieth century, underconsumptionist concepts were endorsed by John Maynard Keynes, whom Schumpeter (1954, p. 1172) characterized as the father of modern demand-side stagnationism. While Keynes himself, however, is not always considered a stagnationist, he had a strong influence on Alvin H. Hansen, the so-called *American Keynes* who is probably the most well-known adherent of modern demand-side secular stagnation (Breit et al. 1998, p. 84). A few years after Hansen had put forward his stagnation hypothesis, the Austrian economist Josef Steindl developed a somewhat different demand-driven stagnation theory. While both Hansen (1955, p. 549) and Steindl ([1979] 1990, pp. 107–108) pointed out that Roy F. Harrod's knife-edge growth analysis incorporates the issue of secular stagnation, Steindl's ideas were particularly strongly shaped by Michał Kalecki. Several of both Steindl's and Kalecki's viewpoints were later reflected in the approach of Paul A. Baran and Paul M. Sweezy—two neo-Marxian economists who mainly contributed to the stagnation debate in the 1960s and 1970s—as well as in the work of the Italian economist Paolo Sylos-Labini.

In most recent years, after the financial crisis of 2008–2009, the issue of secular stagnation has been revived by Lawrence H. Summers. While the international contemporary debate can be traced back to him, other scholars, such as Carl Christian von Weizsäcker, Paul Krugman, and Thomas I. Palley, share some of his demand-side arguments.

Turning to stagnation on the supply side, the classical economists of the eighteenth and nineteenth century, including Karl Marx, and the neoclassical economist William S. Jevons are among the early representatives. Marx, in fact, did not just predict stagnation tendencies, but expected the capitalist system of production to ultimately break down.

Similar to Marx, although on different grounds, in the twentieth century Joseph A. Schumpeter anticipated the decline of capitalism. Writing approximately at the same time as Hansen, Schumpeter was a determined opponent of Hansen's demand-side hypothesis and offered a supply-side-oriented explanation for possible stagnation tendencies. During the post-war economic boom, however, stagnation fears eventually vanished and economic growth theory was on the rise. In the 1950s and 1960s, the debate on economic growth was dominated by the neoclassical economists Robert M. Solow and Trevor W. Swan, whose standard neoclassical growth model is still widely used and discussed today. Although Solow and Swan did not predict secular stagnation as such, von Weizsäcker (1969, p. 459) describes the neoclassical growth theory as a modern version of the classical stagnation doctrine. Other twentieth-century economists who can be related to supply-side stagnationism are Jean Fourasti and William J. Baumol, whose ideas have been somewhat revived within the contemporary stagnation debate. From an environmental point of view, in the 1970s natural limits to growth were particularly advocated by Donella H. Meadows and her colleagues.

Finally, in the contemporary debate Robert J. Gordon is the leading representative of supply-side secular stagnation, with Tyler Cowen sharing several of his viewpoints. While Gordon's theory is commonly regarded as the main counterpart to Summers's demand-side stagnation hypothesis, the French economist Thomas Piketty also offers some noteworthy growth scenarios which can be interpreted along stagnationist lines.

The following Chap. 3 takes a closer look at various demand-side stagnation theories. Chapter 4, in turn, addresses different supply-side stagnation hypotheses. Although all authors listed in Table 2.1 are mentioned in some way, shape, or form, they are not considered with equal attention to detail. While a number of theories are considered in separate subchapters, others are only peripherally mentioned. The aim is to give a critical overview of the historical development of the stagnation debate, with a focus on modern and contemporary hypotheses. As Hansen, Steindl, Summers, and Gordon are the most genuine secular stagnationists who—with the exception of Steindl—have also dominated the discussion on stagnation throughout the years, their hypotheses are at the heart of the following remarks.

References

Backhouse RE, Boianovsky M (2016) Theories of stagnation in historical perspective. Eur J Econ Econ Polic Interv 13(2):147–159

Bank of Japan (2018) Research data: output gap and potential growth rate. Bank of Japan, Tokyo. https://www.boj.or.jp/en/research/research_data/gap/index.htm/. Data as of 03 Oct 2018. Accessed 01 Dec 2018

Blanchard O, Cerutti E, Summers L (2015) Inflation and activity–two explorations and their monetary policy implications. IMF Working Paper WP/15/230. International Monetary Fund, Washington, DC. https://www.imf.org/external/pubs/ft/wp/2015/wp15230.pdf. Accessed 04 Sept 2017

Blecker RA (2016) The US economy since the crisis: slow recovery and secular stagnation. Eur J Econ Econ Polic Interv 13(2):203–214

Brandt K (1952) Struktur der Wirtschaftsdynamik. Verlag Fritz Knapp, Frankfurt am Main

Breit W, Ransom RL, Solow RM (1998) The academic scribblers. Princeton University Press, Princeton, NJ

Cornwall J (1970) The role of demand and investment in long-term growth. Q J Econ 84(1):48–69

Corry D, Valero A, Van Reenen J (2011) UK economic performance since 1997: growth, productivity and jobs. Centre for Economic Performance Special Paper No. 24, December 2011. Centre for Economic Performance, London. http://eprints.lse.ac.uk/47521/1/CEPSP24.pdf. Accessed 19 Nov 2018

Eichengreen B (2014) Secular stagnation: a review of the issues. In: Teulings C, Baldwin R (eds) Secular stagnation: facts, causes and cures. CEPR Press, London, pp 41–46

Foster JB (1987) What is stagnation? In: Cherry R, D'Onofrio C, Kurdas C, Michl TR, Moseley F, Naples MI (eds) The imperiled economy, book I: macroeconomics from a left perspective. Union for Radical Political Economics, New York, NY, pp 59–70

Foster JB, McChesney RW (2012) The endless crisis: how monopoly-finance capital produces stagnation and upheaval from the USA to China. Monthly Review Press, New York, NY

Gordon RJ (2015) Secular stagnation on the supply side: U.S. productivity growth in the short and long run. Background paper for the Philadelphia Fed policy forum, December 04, 2015. https://www.philadelphiafed.org/-/media/research-and-data/events/2015/fed-policy-forum/papers/gordon-secular_stagnation.pdf. Accessed 17 Sept 2016

Hamberg D (1957) Fiscal policy and stagnation since 1957. South Econ J 29(3):211–217

Hansen AH (1934) Capital goods and the restoration of purchasing power. Proc Acad Polit Sci 16(1):11–19

Hansen AH (1955) The stagnation thesis. In: Smithies A, Butters JK (eds) Readings in fiscal policy. George Allen and Unwin Ltd., London, pp 540–557

Hein E (2016) Secular stagnation or stagnation policy? Steindl after Summers. PSL Q Rev 69(276):3–47

Higgins B (1948) Concepts and criteria of secular stagnation. In: Metzler LA, Domar ED, Duesenberry JS, Higgins B, Goodwin RM, Samuelson PA, Wright DM, Alexander SS, Perloff HS, Musgrave RA, Lerner AP, Stettner WF, Brown EC, Bishop RL, Dunlop JT, Bourneuf A (eds) Income, employment and public policy: essays in honor of Alvin H. Hansen, W. W. Norton & Company, Inc., New York, NY, pp 82–107

Higgins B (1950) The theory of increasing under-employment. Econ J 60(238):255–274

Higgins B (1959) Economic development: principles, problems, and policies. W. W. Norton & Company, Inc., New York, NY

IMF (2014) Recovery strengthens, remains uneven. World economic outlook, April 2014. International Monetary Fund, Washington, DC. http://www.imf.org/external/pubs/ft/weo/2014/01/pdf/text.pdf. Accessed 02 Sept 2016

Jorgenson DW, Vu KM (2017) The outlook for advanced economies. J Policy Model 39(4):660–672

Krugman P (2014) What secular stagnation isn't. The New York Times. The Opinion Pages. The Conscience of a Liberal. October 27, 2014. http://krugman.blogs.nytimes.com/2014/10/27/what-secular-stagnation-isnt/?_r=0. Accessed 30 Oct 2016

Lavoie M (2018) Rethinking macroeconomic theory before the next crisis. Rev Keynes Econ 6(1):1–21

Marx K ([1861–1863] 1968) Theories of surplus-value, part II (translated from the German, edited by S. Ryazanskaya). Progress Publishers, Moscow

Meißner W (1983) Stagnation und Strukturpolitik. In: Hödl E, Schiller G (eds) Stagnation und Beschäftigung: Ursachen und Handlungsspielräume, Haag + Herchen Verlag GmbH, Frankfurt am Main, pp 186–195

Ministère de l'Economie et des Finances (2016) The debate on secular stagnation: a status report. Trésor-Economics No. 182, October 2016. Ministère de l'Economie et des Finances, Paris. https://www.tresor.economie.gouv.fr/Articles/744b6412-83b3-408f-984d-bc7e43adb22c/files/ba2cdc0f-d0eb-4b24-909c-4739cda771ce. Accessed 24 Nov 2018

OECD (2015) Escaping the stagnation trap: policy options for the euro area and Japan. OECD Publishing, Paris

Piketty T (2014) Capital in the twenty-first century. Harvard University Press, Cambridge, MA, and London

Reuter N (2000) Ökonomik der "Langen Frist": Zur Evolution der Wachstumsgrundlagen in Industriegesellschaften. Metropolis-Verlag, Marburg

Riddle JE (1844) A complete Latin-English dictionary, for the use of colleges and schools, 4th edn. Longman et al., London

Rosenof T (1997) Economics in the long run: new deal theorists and their legacies, 1933–1993. The University of North Carolina Press, Chapel Hill, NC

Schumpeter JA ([1942] 2008) Capitalism, socialism and democracy, 3rd edn. Harper Perennial Modern Thought, New York, NY

Schumpeter JA (1954) History of economic analysis. Oxford University Press, New York, NY

Setterfield M (2002) Introduction: a dissenter's view of the development of growth theory and the importance of demand-led growth. In: Setterfield M (ed) The economics of demand-led growth: challenging the supply-side vision of the long run. Edward Elgar, Cheltenham and Northhampton, MA, pp 1–16

Spahn HP (1982) Ende des Wachstums? Wirtschaftsdienst 62(1):22–27

Steindl J, ([1979] 1990) Stagnation theory and stagnation policy. In: Steindl J (ed) Economic papers 1941–88, St. Martin's Press, New York, NY, pp 107–126

Streißler E (1983) Stagnation — Analyse und Therapie. In: Bombach G, Gahlen B, Ott AE (eds) Makroökonomik Heute: Gemeinsamkeiten und Gegensätze, J. C. B, Mohr (Paul Siebeck), Tübingen, pp 457–476

Summers LH (2014) Reflections on the 'new secular stagnation hypothesis'. In: Teulings C, Baldwin R (eds) Secular stagnation: facts, causes and cures. CEPR Press, London, pp 27–38

Sweezy PM, ([1982] 1987) Why stagnation? In: Sweezy PM, Magdoff H (eds) Economic history as it happened, vol IV. Stagnation and the financial explosion. Monthly Review Press, New York, NY, pp 29–38

Verspohl E (1971) Der Stagnationsgedanke in der Nationalökonomie: Eine dogmengeschichtliche und analytische Studie. Inaugural-Dissertation zur Erlangung des Doktorgrades der Wirtschafts- und Sozialwissenschaftlichen Fakultät der Universität zu Köln. University of Cologne, Cologne

von Weizsäcker CC (1969) Forschungsinvestitionen und makroökonomische Modelle – Ein wirtschaftstheoretisches Dilemma? Kyklos: Int Rev Soc Sci 22(3):454–466

Chapter 3
Demand-Side Stagnation Theories

3.1 Pre-Keynesian Underconsumption Theories

The first attempts to explain stagnation by a lack of effective demand date back to the underconsumptionists of the nineteenth and early twentieth century. As the term indicates, underconsumption theories refer to insufficient "[...] demand for *consumption* goods [...]" as the main cause of an inherent tendency toward stagnation (Bleaney 1976, p. 11). While the general idea can partially be considered a precursor to modern demand-side stagnation concepts, early underconsumption theories suffer from major flaws. The usual line of argument is that income which is saved and thus not spent on consumption goods causes a lack of effective demand as compared to output produced. Hence, if not all (consumption) goods can be sold at their value, lower than expected profits lead to reductions in future production and hamper economic growth (Schneider 1987, p. 741; Kurz 2010, p. 378). Although underconsumptionists attempted to challenge Say's Law, they (unknowingly) adhered to it, as they failed to free themselves from the classical assumption of ex-ante saving equaling ex-ante investment (Haberler [1937] 1946, p. 124; Schneider 1987, p. 741).[1] With saving being automatically invested, however, it is impossible to ascribe stagnation to insufficient (consumption) demand, as a general glut cannot develop (Hagemann 2015, p. 165; Bleaney 1976, p. 209). The main fallacy in pre-Keynesian underconsumption theories is that investment is only associated with a more or less immediate increase in productive capacity, while its role as a source of effective demand is neglected or misconceived (Bleaney 1976, pp. 99–100, 180–181, 209).

---

[1] The classical version of Say's Law refers to the equality of ex-ante saving and ex-ante investment at full utilization of capital. Full employment of labor, however, is not assumed (Hagemann and Kurz 1997; Kurz 2010, pp. 377–378). At full employment of capital, unemployment of labor can be caused by insufficient productive capacity, a phenomenon referred to as *capacity-constrained unemployment* or *classical unemployment*. See, for example, Mitchell (2017, p. 62), Arestis et al. (1998), Spahn (1986, pp. 244–245), Burns and Mitchell (1985, p. 6), and Erber et al. (1998, p. 172).

© Springer Nature Switzerland AG 2020
C. Anselmann, *Secular Stagnation Theories*, Springer Studies in the History of Economic Thought, https://doi.org/10.1007/978-3-030-41087-2_3

Despite these flaws and the one-sided focus on consumption demand, underconsumptionism is yet a valuable reference in the history of economic thought, as it had vaguely foreshadowed several aspects which were later captured by modern demand-side stagnation theorists. While various scholars engaged in the underconsumption debate and developed their own, unique hypotheses, two types of theories which emphasize different sides of the same coin can generally be distinguished: One strand of economists referred to insufficient consumption demand due to mass poverty as the main cause of stagnation, and a second strand advocated underconsumption as an issue of over-saving (i.e., overinvestment) (Bleaney 1976, p. 14; Schumpeter 1954, p. 740). With Simonde de Sismondi and Malthus being among the first and most prominent advocates of the mass-poverty and over-saving type, respectively, Bleaney (1976, p. 211) also speaks of Sismondian and Malthusian types of underconsumption theories. As the core of each underconsumption concept can basically be assigned to one of these two groups (Bleaney 1976, pp. 14, 74), the following discussion is limited to the theories of Simonde de Sismondi and Malthus. Additionally, the rather Malthusian theory of Hobson is considered as well, as—though only peripherally—he was later referred to by several authors involved in the modern stagnation debate.

3.1.1 Simonde de Sismondi: Income Distribution and Mass Poverty

Distinguishing between a destitute working class and a rich capitalist class, with the latter including capitalists, entrepreneurs, and landlords, Simonde de Sismondi was mainly concerned about the impoverishment of workers resulting from the unequal distribution of income inherent in capitalism. As competitive capitalists pay little attention to demand developments, but are producing for an anonymous and "[...] potentially boundless market [...]," output produced is steadily rising (Dal Degan and Eyguesier 2016, p. 145; see also Simonde de Sismondi [1819] 1991, p. 278; Schneider 1987, p. 743). Consumption demand, however, is unable to keep pace. As the means of production are concentrated among the wealthy class, workers are directly dependent on the rich and exploited until wages are ultimately reduced to the subsistence level (Simonde de Sismondi [1819] 1991, pp. 82–83, 280; Luxemburg [1913] 1951, p. 182). Although the workers spend all their income on consumption goods, they are not able to buy the whole product, as the value they produce exceeds their wages. With wages diminished to the minimum and the introduction of both labor-saving machinery and mass production techniques, workers' consumption demand is falling further and further behind production. The wealthy, on the other hand, cannot compensate for this lack of demand, because their consumption capacity has a natural limit (Luxemburg [1913] 1951, p. 213). Moreover, as the rich are mainly interested in foreign luxuries, domestic consumption demand is hampered even further. Producers are therefore increasingly seeking foreign markets to sell their products and realize their surplus value, which due to the high degree of competition in the world market, however, does not prove successful (Simonde de Sismondi [1819] 1991, p. 276). While only some of the surplus value produced by the workers is thus realized by exports and the consumption of the capitalist class, still all saving is invested. Yet, although Simonde de Sismondi was aware of constant capital, such as machinery and other means of production, like most underconsumptionists of his time he had an understanding of the investment process which contrasts with modern interpretations. Similar to Smith ([1776] 1976, pp. 68–69), who omitted the accumulation of constant capital at the macroeconomic level, for Simonde de Sismondi ([1819] 1991, p. 94) accumulation meant merely that capitalists invested part of the surplus value in *variable* capital, i.e., they added to the wages fund by employing new workers who *immediately* enlarged the production of *consumption* goods and created more surplus value. In Bleaney's (1976, p. 137) words, investment was just "[...] a transfer [...] of [consumption] demand from capitalists to workers, followed by a more or less immediate increase in the production of consumption goods." Investment which adds to effective demand in one period and expands productive capacity only in the following period, however, was not considered.

Given Simonde de Sismondi's assumptions, capital investment does not realize any surplus value, i.e., it does not yield a profit. In other words, investment demand cannot absorb that part of total production which is not consumed or exported. If investment is undertaken, total output produced cannot be sold completely or cannot be sold at its value, i.e., part of the surplus value cannot be realized. While Simonde de Sismondi ([1819] 1991, pp. 104, 249) considered a *small* unrealized surplus value to be bearable by the capitalist class and was thus only concerned about *excessive* investment which would cause *great* disproportions between total production and consumption demand, Rosa Luxemburg ([1913] 1951, p. 189), on the other hand, rightly concluded that "Sismondi stands for the sheer impossibility [...] of accumulation." "[A]n expansion of production [...] must inevitably lead to slumps, crises and ever greater misery for the great masses" (Luxemburg [1913] 1951, p. 213).

Considering income inequality and the resulting impoverishment of workers as the root causes of underconsumption, Simonde de Sismondi's proposed remedies were strongly directed toward a more equal distribution of income between workers and the wealthy class.[2] To stimulate consumption expenditure, he argued in favor of government intervention, especially in terms of income redistribution from the rich to the poor (Schneider 1987, p. 743). Schumpeter (1954, p. 494) accordingly referred to Simonde de Sismondi as an important forerunner of social policy. Lutz (1999, p. 21) even called him "[t]he grandfather of social economics [...]." Given Simonde de Sismondi's interpretation of investment, however, a more equal income distribution cannot solve the problem of accumulation in a capitalist economy. In Simonde de Sismondi's world, investment does not generate any profit, implying

---

[2]The consumption-oriented, left-Keynesian position of the *Working Group Alternative Economic Policy* in Germany, also known as the *Memorandum-Group*, can be regarded a modern equivalent to Simonde de Sismondi's viewpoint. See, for example, Arbeitsgruppe Alternative Wirtschaftspolitik (1978, pp. 88–92, 1979, pp. 72–74).

that part of the capitalist surplus value cannot be realized whenever the rich save and invest.

Although Simonde de Sismondi was the first economist to explain underconsumptionism based on the distribution of income (Bleaney 1976, p. 77), his theory suffers from the erroneous interpretation of capital accumulation as investment in variable capital which immediately raises the production of consumption goods. While this notion was fairly common in his era, it does not conform to the modern interpretation of investment in constant capital which can only be deployed with a time lag. In the short run, capital investment only generates demand and realizes part of the surplus value (Bleaney 1976, p. 137). Hence, if all saving is automatically invested—as Simonde de Sismondi assumed—a lack of aggregate demand cannot occur, even if total consumption demand is insufficient to absorb output produced. Simonde de Sismondi's assertion that insufficient *consumption* demand as compared to overall production leads to inherent crises of capitalism is thus not sustainable, as—in his theory—each lack of consumption demand is compensated for by investment demand.

3.1.2   Malthus: Over-Saving by the Rich

Although Malthus is most famous for his supply-side stagnation hypothesis based on the adverse impact of population growth, he was also a representative of underconsumptionism. Only a year after Simonde de Sismondi had set forth his underconsumption theory in the *Nouveaux Principes d'Economie Politique*, in 1820 Malthus published his *Principles of Political Economy*, the last chapter of which deals with a very similar issue. Like Simonde de Sismondi ([1819] 1991), Malthus ([1820] 1836) worried about an imbalance between output produced and consumption demand. Rather than being concerned about insufficient consumption by the poor, however, he took a different perspective and identified an overabundance of saving (i.e., investment) by the rich as the main problem.

Malthus ([1820] 1836) distinguished between three social classes. While workers spend all their wage income on consumption goods, landlords consume most of their income on luxuries and save only little. Capitalists, on the other hand, save and invest a considerable part of their funds and have the lowest propensity to consume (Malthus [1820] 1836, pp. 398–400; Arnoff 2016, p. 17). Similar to Simonde de Sismondi, for Malthus ([1820] 1836, pp. 34–41), capital accumulation was equal to the employment of workers who immediately increased the production of consumption goods (Bleaney 1976, pp. 54, 99; Verspohl 1971, p. 58). As investment was not considered a separate source of effective demand which raised productive capacity only in the following period, adverse effects on profits and on the rate of capital accumulation would arise out of a deficiency of (consumption) demand (Malthus [1820] 1836, p. 327). Like Simonde de Sismondi, however, Malthus ([1820] 1836, p. 326) held that only *excessive* saving and investment were harmful for economic development. "[...] [T]he principle of saving, pushed to excess, would destroy the motive to production" (Malthus [1820] 1836, p. 7). He went on:

> Under these circumstances, it is impossible that the increased quantity of commodities, obtained by the increased number of productive labourers, should find purchasers, without such a fall of price as would probably sink their value below that of the outlay, or, at least, so reduce profits as very greatly to diminish both the power and the will to save. (Malthus [1820] 1836, p. 315)

While Malthus remained vague on this issue and did not clearly define the meaning of *excessive* capital accumulation, his line of argument cannot be maintained. As in Simonde de Sismondi's case, Malthus's interpretation of investment does not allow for any capital accumulation at all. Since no investment is able to yield a profit, *any* capital accumulation proves impossible (Bleaney 1976, p. 54).

For Malthus, an abundance of saving by the rich was the main trigger of underconsumption. The remedies he suggested were thus mainly targeted at reducing the propensity to save of the wealthy capitalists and landlords by stimulating their consumption expenditures. Workers, on the other hand, were not directly considered to be part of the solution, as they did not save by definition (Bleaney 1976, p. 74). To ensure saving and investment at a *sustainable, non-excessive* level, Malthus ([1820] 1836, pp. 372–413) suggested three alternative measures. The first approach aimed at a more equal division of landed property (Malthus [1820] 1836, pp. 375–376, 381–382). Secondly, he advocated the promotion of domestic and foreign trade, which he assumed to stimulate the consumption demand of capitalists and landlords by making available a broader range of products better suited to their wants (Malthus [1820] 1836, pp. 382–398). Finally, his third suggestion addressed the maintenance of so-called *unproductive consumers*, i.e., consumers who were not themselves involved in the production of material goods (Malthus [1820] 1836, p. 398). These mainly included landlords as well as unproductive workers engaged in the service sector, such as menial servants, judges, lawyers, and physicians predominantly demanded by the rich, but also tax-financed statesmen, soldiers, and clergy (Malthus [1820] 1836, pp. 406–410).

In fact, none of Malthus's proposed remedies is able to solve the issue of capital accumulation. Although his proposals might induce an increase in total consumption demand, still expected profits on investment cannot be realized. Landlords and unproductive workers can only consume an amount equal to the income they receive. Their income, however, does not come from nowhere, but is directly and indirectly paid for by capitalists in the form of rent, wages, and taxes (Bleaney 1976, p. 55). Part of the surplus value produced by productive workers is thus allocated to the landlords and other unproductive consumers (Luxemburg [1913] 1951, p. 220). While they spend (part of) their income on consumption goods, they are not able to realize any profit on capitalists' investment. "It remains entirely [...] [Malthus's] secret [...]," Luxemburg ([1913] 1951, p. 223) noted, "[...] how the [...] [unproductive consumers] can assist the capitalists in appropriating their profits by buying commodities [...], since they themselves obtain their purchasing power mainly from these capitalists." In other words, Malthus's considerations are subject to a fallacy of composition.

Malthus's underconsumption theory suffers from the same flaws as Simonde de Sismondi's hypothesis. The main issue is that he missed the temporal structure of the investment process. If, as Malthus ([1820] 1836, pp. 38, 314) assumed, ex-ante saving equals ex-ante investment, a lack of effective demand cannot occur. Although his underconsumption theory is thus untenable, he nonetheless anticipated that both supply and demand are necessary for economic growth (Malthus [1820] 1836, pp. 361–365). Keynes, for example, praised Malthus for considering the role of effective demand and stated, "If only Malthus, instead of Ricardo, had been the parent stem from which nineteenth-century economics proceeded, what a much wiser and richer place the world would be to-day!" (Keynes [1933b] 1972, pp. 100–101).

3.1.3 Hobson: Over-Saving and Income Distribution

One of the later pre-Keynesian underconsumptionists was Hobson, who, in conjunction with Mummery, first laid down his underconsumption hypothesis in 1889 in *The Physiology of Industry* and further advanced it in several other writings throughout the first decades of the twentieth century. While maintaining the classical assumption of ex-ante saving equaling ex-ante investment, similar to Malthus Hobson (1922, pp. 34–35, 37) traced underconsumptionism to an abundance of saving in relation to consumption spending, i.e., he approached the issue from an over-saving (i.e., overinvestment) perspective (Mummery and Hobson 1889, p. 203). According to Hobson (1922, p. 38), "[...] there must exist, at any time, an economically right proportion between [...]" total saving and consumption demand. In other words, when consumption is curtailed to save and invest in real capital, the induced increase in production must either be immediately "[...] accompanied or soon followed by a proportionately enlarged consumption." If, on the other hand, total output produced is not matched by consumption spending, prices and profits fall to such an extent that future production, capital accumulation, and economic growth come to a halt (Hobson 1922, p. 32). In fact, Hobson (1909, p. 296) assumed such an imbalance between production and consumption to be the normal state of the economy, as there was a general "[...] tendency to save a larger proportion of income than can effectively and continuously function as capital" (Hobson 1922, p. 35). Due to the introduction of modern production techniques on the one hand and rather rigid consumption habits on the other hand, productive capacity was assumed to increase much more rapidly than consumption. Additionally, a more determined rise in consumption expenditures was hampered by the unequal distribution of income (and wealth) (Hobson 1922, pp. 32–35).

The main issue for Hobson was the maldistribution of the so-called *unproductive* or *unearned* surplus. This surplus was *wasteful overpayment*, as it was not necessary to maintain production and ensure proportionate economic growth (Hobson 1911, pp. 159–161; see also Clarke 1987, p. 665). It could accrue to any scarce factor of production by virtue of "[...] the powers of combination and monopoly [...]" (Hobson 1909, p. viii), i.e., the beneficiaries were "[...] the owners of any factor strong enough to take it [...]" owing to a "[...] natural or contrived monopoly or scarcity [...]" (Hobson 1911, pp. 160–162). Unearned surplus mainly included the total rent of land received by landlords as well as abnormally high interest and profits captured by capitalists based on their superior bargaining power. While the majority of workers lived in poverty due to a general abundance of labor, some workers might occasionally enjoy unearned income in the form of excessive wages (Hobson 1909, p. viii, 1911, pp. 118–120, 161). In contrast to the mass of poor workers, however, the rich at the top of the distribution were unable to consume all their funds. By saving a large part of their unearned surplus—which was automatically invested in real capital—they reinforced the imbalance between production and consumption (Hobson 1922, pp. 35–38, 1902, p. 91).

Although both Malthus and Hobson traced underconsumptionism to excessive saving by the rich, the remedies they proposed differ considerably. While Malthus suggested to spur consumption of the well-to-do, Hobson (1922, pp. 39–41), like Simonde de Sismondi, pointed to the redistribution of income from the top to the bottom of the income hierarchy. As workers usually have a higher propensity to consume than the rich, "[...] transferring some surplus income from the 'capitalist classes' to the workers [...]" might ensure the proper proportion between saving (i.e., investment) and consumption (Hobson 1922, pp. 47–48). Establishing strong trade unions to increase workers' bargaining power might additionally contribute to higher wages for the poor and boost consumption (Hobson 1909, pp. 201–203, 1911, pp. 119, 163). Moreover, taxing the unproductive surplus of the rich would allow the state to provide a range of public services, such as national security, health care, and education, some of which mainly benefit the poor (Hobson 1911, pp. 83–85, 1922, pp. 48–50).

Similar to the earlier underconsumptionists, Hobson did not regard investment spending as an independent component of effective demand. Although—unlike Simonde de Sismondi and Malthus–Hobson (1922, p. 34) did not limit capital accumulation to investment in variable capital, but took account of constant capital as well, he maintained the assumption that any investment automatically reduced (capitalists') effective demand by adversely impacting consumption demand. At the same time, however, capital accumulation increased production immediately. Despite these flaws, Domar (1947, pp. 51–52), for example, who was a student of Alvin H. Hansen, gave kudos to Hobson and spoke highly of his underconsumption hypothesis. Although he was aware of Hobson's deficiencies, he especially acknowledged that Hobson had considered the capacity-increasing effect of investment. Similarly, Keynes ([1936] 1973, p. 366) praised Hobson for his "[...] significant and well-founded [...] intuitions." He particularly endorsed the importance which Hobson had attached to effective (consumption) demand in the investment process (Keynes [1936] 1973, p. 368). Nonetheless, Keynes ([1936] 1973, pp. 367–368) clearly stated that the root cause of all evil is not—as Hobson had claimed—excessive saving *and* investment in relation to consumption, but rather excessive ex-ante saving in relation to ex-ante investment at full employment. Hence, "[...] a relatively weak propensity to consume helps to cause unemployment by requiring and *not* receiving the accompaniment of a compensating volume of new investment [...]"

(Keynes [1936] 1973, p. 370). As Robbins (1932, p. 420) summarized, for Keynes an increase in real investment was important to spur economic development, whereas for Hobson "[...] this would simply make matters worse."

3.2 Modern Demand-Side Stagnation Theories

In contrast to the underconsumptionists of the nineteenth and early twentieth century, modern demand-side stagnation theorists did not focus solely on consumption expenditures, but included investment spending as a separate source of demand. Investment in real capital increases effective demand immediately and expands productive capacity only with a time lag. Moreover, the classical assumption of all saving being automatically invested is dismissed. In fact, the issue of ex-ante investment falling short of ex-ante saving at the full-employment level of output is at the heart of all modern (and contemporary) demand-side stagnation theories. The long-term development of output and economic growth may be hampered, so the argument runs, because specific structural changes in advanced economies retard investment and/or stimulate the desire to save.

3.2.1 Keynes: The Father of Modern Demand-Side Stagnationism?

"But this *long run* is a misleading guide to current affairs. *In the long run* we are all dead" (Keynes [1923] 1971, p. 65). This frequently quoted passage from *A Tract on Monetary Reform* has led to the common assumption that Keynes's economic analyses were only directed toward the short run. As secular stagnation is essentially a long-term phenomenon, Keynes thus does not seem to fit in the overall stagnation debate. The presumption that he ignored the long run and merely paid attention to short-run developments, however, is erroneous. In fact, while the abovementioned quote is often adduced to describe Keynes's oeuvre, it is usually taken out of context. Rather than denying the importance of the long run, Keynes ([1923] 1971, p. 65)—while referring to the quantity theory of money—merely argued in favor of economic models and analyses which take account of short-run developments.

While Keynes is best known for his theory of employment, stating that underemployment equilibria are possible whenever effective demand falls below full-employment output, he also addressed the potential future risk of developed, mature economies falling into persistent periods of economic stagnation (Verspohl 1971, pp. 50–51; Zinn 2008, p. 22). This rather "unknown long-term perspective of Keynes's theory," as Zinn (2008, p. 16, own translation) calls it, is mainly set forth in several short essays and letters, but is also addressed in some of the last chapters of *The General Theory of Employment, Interest and Money*. While Schumpeter (1946, pp. 499–501, 1954, p. 1172) traced modern stagnationism to Keynes's ([1919] 1971) *The Economic Consequences of the Peace*, it is in *The General Theory* that Keynes ([1936] 1973, p. 307) looked back with satisfaction at the special conditions prevailing during the nineteenth century, when "[...] the growth of population and of invention, the opening-up of new lands, the state of confidence and the frequency of war over the average of (say) each decade seem to have been sufficient, taken in conjunction with the propensity to consume, [...]" to generate a volume of investment high enough to ensure an adequate employment level. Keynes ([1936] 1973, pp. 308–309) doubted, however, that these economically favorable circumstances would continue, expecting investment to be hampered—ceteris paribus—by a decline in the marginal efficiency of capital. He even considered the possibility of a complete cessation of (net) investment (Keynes [1936] 1973, pp. 323–324). Moreover, because of the short-run inflexibility of long-term interest rates, which Keynes partially attributed to strong liquidity preferences, boosting investment by conventional expansionary monetary policy might prove unsuccessful to avoid longer periods of unemployment (Keynes [1936] 1973, p. 309; Leijonhufvud 1968, pp. 183, 198–200).[3] Keynes ([1936] 1973, pp. 249–250) thus concluded:

> Indeed it seems capable of remaining in a chronic condition of sub-normal activity for a considerable period without any marked tendency either towards recovery or towards complete collapse. [...] [T]he environment and the psychological propensities of the modern world must be of such a character as to produce these results.

Keynes was particularly concerned about a decrease in population. In his 1937 essay *Some Economic Consequences of a Declining Population*, he identified an increasing population as an important driver of capital investment. As a rise in population is conducive to business optimism and boosts demand—especially for houses and machinery—capital accumulation was assumed to grow pari passu with population (Keynes [1930] 1972, p. 324, [1937] 1973, pp. 125–127). Writing at the end of the 1930s, however, Keynes ([1937] 1973, pp. 125, 132) expected total population to stagnate or even decline. While this would reduce investment demand, the propensity to save might at the same time increase, such as due to smaller family sizes (Keynes [1937] 1973, pp. 128–129). Eventually, insufficient effective demand might lead to a reduction in output below its full-employment potential. According to Keynes ([1937] 1973, p. 126–127), this effect was likely to be further reinforced by capital-saving technological progress reducing the capital coefficient (and the average period of production). With both population growth and technological change unable to generate sufficient demand to ensure full employment, increases in effective demand might only be induced by a more equal distribution of income and wealth or a reduction in the rate of interest. In Keynes's ([1937] 1973, p. 131) words:

---

[3]Like Keynes, Schumpeter ([1941] 1991, p. 369) as well did not consider expansionary monetary policy an adequate remedy for economic weakness. See also Dal Pont Legrand and Hagemann (2016, p. 25, 2017, p. 250).

If follows, therefore, that to ensure equilibrium conditions of prosperity over a period of years it will be essential, *either* that we alter our institutions and the distribution of wealth in a way which causes a smaller proportion of income to be saved, *or* that we reduce the rate of interest sufficiently to [...] [call forth] a much larger use of capital in proportion to output.

As these measures, however, might not be implemented because of social and political headwinds by the upper classes, "[...] a chronic tendency towards the underemployment of resources must [...]" ultimately result (Keynes [1937] 1973, p. 132).

During the Second World War, Keynes further advanced his long-term theory. One of the most important works of this time in which he expressed a very long-run perspective is his 1943 pamphlet *The Long-Term Problem of Full Employment*. Writing about possible economic developments after the war, Keynes ([1943b] 1980) distinguished three phases which differed in terms of the balance between ex-ante investment and ex-ante saving at the full-employment level of output. In the first five post-war years or so, he expected full employment, but also inflationary pressures, as—due to the large backlog of demand—the propensity to invest was likely to exceed the propensity to save. Rationing of consumption and/or investment were thus considered suitable measures. Once excess demand had disappeared, the economy would transition into the second post-war phase. In this period, which Keynes ([1943b] 1980, p. 323) believed to last for five to ten years, full employment could be maintained, as ex-ante investment was assumed to more or less equal ex-ante saving. Possible short-term fluctuations, he held, could be mainly smoothed by countercyclical fiscal policy (Keynes [1943b] 1980, p. 322). Finally, in the third post-war phase, Keynes expected demand-side stagnation tendencies to set in, as investment demand would be saturated to such an extent that it would fall short of ex-ante saving. "[...] [S]ooner or later, we shall be faced, if not with saturation of investment, at any rate with increasing difficulties in finding satisfactory outlets for new investment" (Keynes [1943a] 1980, p. 360). To avoid secular unemployment, finding ways to increase consumption spending and reduce saving was essential, such as by redistributing income and wealth from the rich to the poor (Keynes [1943b] 1980, p. 323). "When [...] [the third phase] does come about [...]," Keynes ([1943a] 1980, p. 360) noted, "[...] we shall then have to start on very important social changes, aimed at the discouragement of saving and a redistribution of the national wealth and a tax system which encourages consumption and discourages saving." Moreover, to ensure full employment of labor despite low rates of capital accumulation, Keynes ([1943b] 1980, p. 323) was a strong advocate of a reduction in working hours.

Although he was aware of the risks of secular stagnation, it is especially because of this latter proposal that Keynes ([1943b] 1980, p. 323) spoke of the third post-war phase as a potentially *golden age*. In doing so, he embraced an earlier idea he had set forth in 1928/1930 in his essay *Economic Possibilities for Our Grandchildren*. Absent major wars and large increases in population, Keynes ([1930] 1972) predicted that in the future technological progress and increases in labor productivity would allow to satisfy the most basic material needs with much less working hours. The *economic problem*, as Keynes ([1930] 1972, p. 326) called it, "[...] may be solved, or be at least within sight of solution, within a hundred years." Instead of spending a considerable part of each day at work, people would be able to devote much more time to leisure. In fact, Keynes ([1930] 1972, p. 329) had in mind a weekly working time of 15 hours by approximately the year 2030. From today's perspective, this prediction is clearly wishful thinking. Back in 1930, Keynes, of course, could not foresee the Second World War and the strong increases in population thereafter. As Frank (2008, p. 144–146), Hagemann (2011, p. 291), and Walterskirchen (2012, p. 140–141) point out, however, he also seemed to underestimate the importance and possibilities of both luxury consumption in general and consumption springing from product innovations. Although the average number of hours worked per week has declined over the past century, this development was particularly pronounced in the decades before World War II, but has slowed down since (Gordon 2016, pp. 248, 258–261). In fact, productivity increases have not translated into a considerable reduction in working hours during the past years, but have mostly led to higher average incomes. In other words, the substitution effect of an increase in wages on hours worked has overtaken the income effect. Moreover, due to great income and wealth inequalities, many people on low pay are forced to work long hours (Freeman 2008, pp. 137–138; Hagemann 2011, pp. 287–288). It is thus doubtful whether, as Keynes ([1930] 1972, p. 331) predicted, "[...] there will be ever larger and larger classes and groups of people from whom problems of economic necessity [...] [will] practically [be] removed." A general reduction in working hours, which Keynes demanded to ensure full employment in the third post-war phase, thus does not seem to be viable.[4]

Contrary to general belief, it can be concluded that Keynes unequivocally took account of long-run economic developments and hinted at the idea of secular stagnation. Although his remarks on stagnation have a positive twist in terms of a (necessary) reduction in working hours, he clearly warned of the risks of future unfavorable conditions for economic development and employment. In fact, his long-run perspective strongly influenced Alvin H. Hansen, the most prominent modern stagnationist. It is therefore not surprising that some of Keynes's long-term views closely resemble Hansen's stagnation theory. In this regard, Schumpeter (1946, p. 501) was right in stating that the modern stagnation thesis originated with Keynes. "Keynes must be credited or debited, as the case may be, with the fatherhood of modern stagnationism" (Schumpeter 1954, p. 1172).

3.2.2 Hansen: Lack of Investment Due to Changing Exogenous Factors

3.2.2.1 Key Elements of Hansen's Stagnation Theory

Although Keynes glanced at the issue of secular stagnation, it was primarily Hansen, the so-called *American Keynes*, who further advanced the idea in the late 1930s and 1940s (Samuelson 1976, p. 25). Surprisingly, Hansen, a professor at Harvard Uni-

---

[4]For a contemporary interpretation and critical assessment of Keynes's prediction of a considerable reduction in working hours, see also the essays in Pecchi and Piga (2008).

versity from 1937 until his retirement in 1956, was initially rather cautious about Keynesian economics (Musgrave 1987, p. 591). While praising Keynes's prestige and the development of the Keynesian line of thought, in his 1936 review of *The General Theory*, for example, he mentioned, "The book [...] is not a landmark in the sense that it lays a foundation for a 'new economics.' [...] [It] is more a symptom of economic trends than a foundation stone upon which a science can be built" (Hansen 1936, p. 686). As pointed out by Rosenof (1997, pp. 49–50), however, Hansen's general attitude changed in the aftermath of the 1937/1938 recession in the United States. In the following years, he eventually developed into the most important advocate of Keynes in America (Harris in Hansen 1953, p. x). In fact, Hansen (1946a, p. 187) later acknowledged that *The General Theory* injected "[...] a new outlook [...] into economics [...]," and he admitted that earlier reviews, including his own, were partially inappropriate. Moreover, he clarified that his secular stagnation hypothesis was based "[...] fundamentally on the same foundation stones as Keynes's theory of under-employment equilibrium [...]," namely, a lack of planned investment as compared to desired saving at the full-employment level of output (Hansen 1966, p. 7).

Hansen (1934, p. 19) first mentioned the term *secular stagnation* rather incidentally in a 1934 essay and developed the underlying concept throughout subsequent years in several books and papers. As set forth in his presidential address *Economic Progress and Declining Population Growth*, which—inspired by Keynes's essay *Some Economic Consequences of a Declining Population*—he delivered at the annual meeting of the American Economic Association in December 1938, Hansen (1939, p. 3) assumed economic progress to be mainly contingent on three exogenous factors: the availability and discovery of new land and resources, the growth of population, and technological change.[5] According to Hansen, during most of the nineteenth and early twentieth century, the prosperity of these factors had provided vast opportunities for real capital investment. For example, in the United States—the country which is at the heart of Hansen's stagnation hypothesis—the expansion into the western frontier and the following urbanization had required large capital outlays (Hansen 1941, p. 43). Similarly, strong population increases had disproportionately raised the demand for housing and other capital-intensive goods (Hansen 1939, p. 7).[6] On top of that, investment had been further stimulated by profound technological advances in various areas, giving rise to major new industries, such as railroads, streetcars, telephones, electricity, and automobiles (Hansen 1941, pp. 38–41). Due to the combined impact of all these factors, most of the nineteenth and early twentieth century had been "[...] a period of rapid growth and expansion" (Hansen 1941, p. 39).

---

[5]In the form of land, labor, and technology, Hansen's three exogenous factors are also included in a typical neoclassical production function. By considering these factors merely as necessary stimuli for investment *demand*, however, Hansen took a purely demand-side point of view. See also Verspohl (1971, pp. 238–239).

[6]Hansen associated a rapidly growing population with a rising *per capita* demand for non-consumption goods, such as housing (Hansen 1939, p. 7, 1940a, p. 583; see also Cornwall 1972, pp. 261–262).

Apart from typical business cycle fluctuations, the underemployment of productive resources had not been a serious issue back then (Hansen 1939, p. 4).[7]

These favorable economic conditions could not be taken for granted, though. Writing at the end of the 1930s, Hansen was convinced that in the United States and other advanced countries deep structural changes were already under way. The nineteenth century, he assumed, had been a special and unique period characterized by flourishing exogenous factors which had provided massive opportunities for profitable investment. Starting in the 1920s, however, the overall economic environment seemed to change. Hansen was primarily concerned about both the development of population growth and the future availability of new land and resources. These two *extensive* factors, he predicted, were no longer able to spur sufficient investment to maintain full employment. While "[...] the opening of new territory and the growth of population were together responsible for a very large fraction—possibly somewhere near one-half—of the total volume of new capital formation in the nineteenth century [...]," these investment outlets were now rapidly diminishing (Hansen 1939, p. 9).

As shown in Fig. 3.1, while the absolute rate of population increase in the United States (solid line) had exhibited a slight upward trend both before and after the First World War, starting in the mid-1920s it declined considerably until the end of the 1930s.[8] According to Hansen (1939, p. 7, 1951, pp. 477–478), an ongoing downturn in population increase reduces the *widening of capital*, as less new workers have to be equipped with capital goods. While he mainly associated a slowdown in population increase with a decline in housing construction, he also pointed to potential shifts in output composition. With a stagnant population and an increasing share of older people, the demand for services requiring little investment in real capital is likely to increase (Hansen 1939, p. 7). At the same time, due to smaller families, Hansen (1940a, p. 583)—similar to Keynes ([1937] 1973, p. 128–129)—expected a rising propensity to save. As outlined by Higgins (1946, p. 140), this effect was not assumed to be compensated for by the dissaving of the elderly.[9]

---

[7]Nonetheless, according to Hansen (1938, p. 328, 1955, p. 544) secular stagnation had already occurred in the nineteenth century. He particularly pointed to the period from 1873 until 1896, the so-called *Long Depression* between the end of the railroad boom and the emergence of new industries such as electricity and automobiles.

[8]As repeatedly pointed out by Hansen (1941, p. 364, 1955, p. 546), it is the *absolute* increase in population which is relevant for stimulating investment. Ceteris paribus, a slowdown or cessation of the *absolute* increase in population reduces investment demand. See also Adler (1945).

[9] Prior to Hansen, the impact of changes in population on economic activity had been thoroughly analyzed by the German economist August Lösch, a student of Eucken, Schumpeter, and Spiethoff—with the latter two having also influenced Hansen. Described as an extraordinary economist, Lösch joined *The Kiel Institute for the World Economy* in 1940, where he was promoted to senior researcher in 1941—only four years before his sudden death (Zottmann 1949, pp. 28–29; Samuelson 1976, pp. 27–28; Christian-Albrechts-Universität zu Kiel 2017). Based on empirical developments in Germany, Lösch (1936, 1937, 1938) suggested a positive nexus between population growth and economic performance. Most important, he claimed population changes to be the driving force, with business activity following suit mainly due to the impact on capital investment. In his obituary, Wolfgang Stolper mentioned the importance of "[...] Lösch's population study [...], since the relation of population growth and business cycles has aroused new interest through the Keynes-

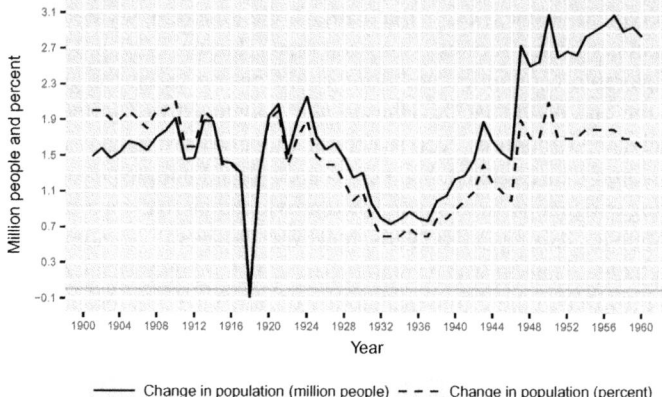

Fig. 3.1 Annual change of population in the United States, 1901–1960. *Source* Author's illustration, based on data from the Federal Reserve Bank of St. Louis (2018). See Appendix A for detailed data sources and further notes

In addition to a slower increase in population, Hansen expressed similar concerns about the disappearance of the economic frontier. Throughout the nineteenth and early twentieth century, the exploitation and development of new territory required large capital investment. Although the year 1890 marked the closing of the western frontier in the United States (Turner 1920, p. 1), its economic development continued until the First World War. "The land had to be broken, buildings had to be erected, railroads built, warehouses, commercial establishments, and houses constructed" (Hansen 1946b, p. 15). After the urbanization of the West had eventually been completed, capital exports to less developed countries opened up new investment opportunities (Hansen 1941, pp. 43–44). As compared to the nineteenth century, however, Hansen (1939, p. 9) expected future foreign investment to be much less pronounced.

With both population increase and territorial expansion diminishing, only technological progress, the *intensive* growth factor, could potentially induce sufficient investment demand. As Hansen (1939, p. 10) put it, "We are thus rapidly entering a world in which we must fall back upon a more rapid advance of technology than in the past if we are to find private investment opportunities adequate to maintain full employment."[10] Hansen was skeptical, however, whether technological change

Hansen-Terborgh discussion, through the stagnation thesis [...]" (Stolper in Lösch 1954, p. viii). Hansen (1937), on the other hand, was surprisingly critical of Lösch's (1936) work, mentioning that population changes and economic activity were likely to *mutually* influence each other.

[10]To ensure full employment of productive resources, Hansen and other economists involved in the stagnation debate frequently emphasized the need for capital investment sufficient to *absorb* full-employment saving (see, for example, Hansen 1938, pp. 313, 324, 329, 1939, p. 11, 1940b, pp. 3502, 3511, 3514, 3542; Terborgh 1945, pp. 48, 63). Investment, however, does not *absorb*, but rather *creates* an equal amount of saving by its impact on national income. If planned investment falls short of desired saving at full employment, both full-employment income and full-employment saving cannot be realized. Investment determines saving, or, as Moore (2002, p. 153) puts it, "Actual

could compensate for the decline of the two extensive growth factors. After all, it was the *combined* impact of favorable exogenous forces which had induced economic prosperity in the past (Higgins 1998, pp. 92–93). As strong population increases and the availability of new land had likely contributed to the development of new (mass) production techniques throughout the nineteenth and early twentieth century, the cessation of these factors was not assumed to be beneficial for future technological change (Hansen 1939, p. 9). Moreover, the development of new capital-intensive industries could not be taken for granted. At the end of the 1930s, Hansen did not see any major technological development which was "[...] as rich in investment opportunities as the railroad, [...] or the automobile [...]" (Hansen 1939, p. 10, 1938, pp. 288–289). Indeed, he was rather concerned about the changing character of technological progress toward capital-saving inventions and innovations reducing the capital coefficient (Hansen 1941, pp. 356–357). According to Hansen, depreciation allowances were increasingly sufficient to finance large capital investments, including improvements of existing equipment (Hansen 1940b, pp. 3538–3539).[11] Additionally, technological advances were hampered by institutional changes, most notably by the decline in competition among firms and the rise of monopolies (Hansen

---

saving is the accounting record of actual investment." It is not the flow of saving which finances investment, but the stock of money. See also Spahn (1986, pp. 93–95, 246–247) and Lindner (2012).

[11] Especially in the early 1930s, when he was still teaching at the University of Minnesota, Hansen (1931, 1932b) also addressed the issues of labor-saving technological progress and technological unemployment, arguing that it is "[...] possible that [...] [technologically] displaced labor cannot be reemployed" (Hansen 1931, p. 88). He was particularly critical of Douglas (1930), who held that technological unemployment could not be of permanent duration, as labor-saving technological progress would automatically increase the purchasing power of workers or employers, resulting in increased demand for goods and the reabsorption of the unemployed. While Haberler (1932) partially argued in favor of Douglas (1930), Hansen (1932a, p. 25, b, p. 563), similar to Mill ([1848] 1965, I, vi, pp. 96–97), stated that labor-saving technological progress as such only involves a shift, but not an additional creation, of purchasing power. "The increased purchasing power of other groups is exactly offset by the decreased purchasing power of the displaced workers" (Hansen 1932b, p. 25). Although technological unemployment is thus not automatically eliminated, Hansen (1932b) pointed to special economic conditions which could lead to the reabsorption of technologically displaced labor. He mainly referred to flexible labor and capital markets, especially advocating price and wage flexibility, as well as a rise in investment spending (Hansen 1932b, pp. 26, 29, 1941, pp. 313–326). The latter he particularly emphasized starting in the late 1930s, after he had become a Keynesian Brazelton (1993). In his secular stagnation hypothesis, however, technological unemployment plays only a minor role (Woirol 1996, p. 45). It is rather *total* unemployment, of which technological unemployment is a fraction, which was at the center of his interest. In his presidential address, Hansen (1939, p. 10) held, "There can be no greater error in the analysis of the economic trends of our times than that which finds in the advance of technology [...] a major cause of unemployment. It is true that we cannot discount the problem of technological unemployment, a problem which may be intensified by the apparently growing importance of capital-saving inventions. But, on the other side, we cannot afford to neglect that type of innovation which creates new industries and which thereby opens new outlets for real investment. The problem of our generation is, above all, the problem of inadequate private investment outlets. What we need is not a slowing down in the progress of science and technology, but rather an acceleration of that rate." For well-elaborated summaries of the technological unemployment debate in the 1930s and thereafter, see especially Woirol (1996, pp. 35–45, 69–76, 2006) and Gourvitch (1966, p. 134–142).

1939, pp. 11–12)—an issue which was later particularly emphasized by Steindl and his followers.

Although Hansen was convinced that technological progress would continue, in light of the prevailing conditions at the end of the 1930s he did not believe that technological advances were adequate to ensure full employment of productive resources (Hansen 1941, p. 41). He thus supposed the United States (and other advanced economies) to be prone to *secular stagnation* or *economic maturity*, marked by "[...] sick recoveries which die in their infancy and depressions which feed on themselves and leave a hard and seemingly immovable core of unemployment" (Hansen 1939, p. 4). Speaking of the "[...] current chronic stagnation level [...]" of income and employment, Hansen (1940b, p. 3546) at the end of the 1930s considered stagnation to be a real and immediate issue which urgently needed to be addressed.[12] Looking at the developments of gross national product (GNP) and unemployment in Fig. 3.2, it is evident that Hansen was writing at a time of great economic turmoil. Although the US economy had grown quite strongly between 1933 and 1937 during the ongoing depression, it was hit by yet another contraction in 1937 and 1938. Throughout the 1930s, actual output was consistently lacking behind its full-employment potential. The output gap, i.e., the difference between actual and potential GNP expressed as a percentage of potential GNP, reached values as low as −34% in 1933 and −19% in 1938. In the labor market, the civilian unemployment rate hovered between 14.3 and 24.9% in the years from 1931 until 1940.

While Hansen (1940b, p. 3496) declared that his conclusions might be "[...] subject to revision as new data appear [...]," he was convinced that only deliberate policy action could counteract the apparent stagnation tendencies in the United States. Although he considered a lack of private investment the main cause of general stagnation tendencies, he did not think that the stagnation issue could be solved by merely boosting private investment. Although Hansen (1941, p. 249) urged "[...] to explore to the limit every available investment opportunity [...]" and thought that policy measures such as incentive taxation could spur investment to some degree, similar to Keynes (and Schumpeter) he remained especially cautious about expansionary monetary policy (Hansen 1947, pp. 179–182, 1941, p. 82). While mentioning the importance of reducing high long-term rates of interest (Hansen 1940b, p. 3850), he concluded "[...] that the role of the rate of interest as a determinant of investment has occupied a place larger than it deserves [...]" (Hansen 1939, p. 5). Along Keynesian lines, Hansen (1941, p. 82) continued, "Cheap money can encourage investment if conditions are favorable. But it will not of itself produce an adequate volume of investment and consumption."[13]

---

[12]Speaking of income *levels*, it appears that Hansen was only concerned about the actual *level* of national income while ignoring its *growth rate*. While he certainly focused on the issue of actual output falling behind the potential output level, however, he did not neglect economic growth. For example, Hansen (1951, p. 488) mentioned, "But there is the danger that we may not achieve, on a sustained basis, our growth potential."

[13]When discussing the impact of an additional supply of (international) liquidity, Keynes ([1933a] 1972, p. 357) used the following metaphor, "We cannot [...] make the horses drink. [...] But we can provide them with water." Karl Schiller, Federal Minister of Economic Affairs in Germany from

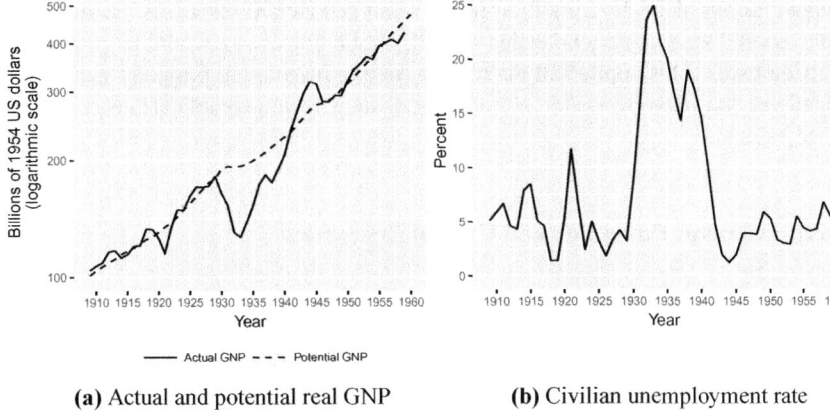

(a) Actual and potential real GNP   (b) Civilian unemployment rate

Fig. 3.2 Actual and potential real gross national product as well as civilian unemployment in the United States, 1909–1960. *Source* Author's illustrations, based on data from Knowles and Warden (1960, p. 37) and the US Bureau of the Census (1975, p. 135). See Appendix A for detailed data sources and further notes

Eventually, the major remedies which Hansen suggested were twofold. On the one hand, with reference to Hobson, he argued in favor of an increase in private consumption spending, which, however, could not be easily achieved (Hansen 1934, p. 19, 1941, pp. 247–249). Apart from short-term fluctuations over the typical business cycle, the average propensity to consume is very stable and "[...] not likely to be radically changed from one decade to another except by important modifications in fundamental institutional arrangements" (Hansen 1941, p. 248). Such institutional changes include the redistribution of income from the top to the bottom of the income hierarchy, which could be achieved by raising social benefits or by shifting the tax structure from regressive indirect taxes toward a more progressive income tax (Hansen 1941, p. 248). Due to possible adverse effects on private investment, however, he also warned of the limits of such redistribution policies (Hansen 1939, p. 12, 1947, p. 50).

As Hansen was not convinced that private investment and consumption expenditures would be sufficient to ensure full employment on a sustained basis, referring to Keynes he mainly focused on government investment spending (Hansen 1934, p. 19). Hansen (1939, p. 12) particularly stressed the importance of public investment in "[...] human and natural resources and in consumers' capital goods of a collective character designed to serve the physical, recreational and cultural needs of the community as a whole." He mainly had in mind public infrastructure investment in a variety of areas, including—but not limited to—highways, hospitals, slum clearance, schools, improved housing, and local parks (Hansen 1941, p. 440, 1947, pp. 183–184). To finance these government expenditures, Hansen was not averse to

1966 to 1972, referred to this remark in several speeches and interviews. See, for example, Schiller ([1966] 1967, p. 10, 1967, 1983, p. 28).

incurring public debt. Especially at times when productive resources are not fully employed and stagnation tendencies prevail, public borrowing would be preferable to raising taxes. This applies all the more to public investment projects, as they are typically of long-lasting character and not consumed immediately (Hansen 1940b, pp. 3853–3854).

3.2.2.2   General Perception and Critical Assessment

The issue of secular stagnation was a widely debated topic among economists in the 1930s and thereafter until the mid-twentieth century. Although some writers, such as McLaughlin and Watkins (1939), Lange (1939), and Weintraub (1939), expressed somewhat similar views as Hansen, most of the reviews were rather critical of his stagnation doctrine. Attention must be especially directed toward those authors who dismissed Hansen's theoretical concept, i.e., his explanation for secular stagnation in terms of changes in population increase, territorial expansion, and technological progress. Doubting the importance of these exogenous factors in explaining possible stagnation tendencies, Terborgh (1945), Schumpeter (1939, [1942] 2008), and also Steindl ([1952] 1976) were among Hansen's many critics.

The nexus between demographic expansion and economic performance, it was argued, might not be as clear-cut as assumed by Hansen and his followers. Steindl ([1952] 1976, p. 168), for example, rightly pointed out that population growth is likely to be both cause and effect of economic growth and capital accumulation, making it almost impossible to determine the specific impact of demographic change.[14] The main argument set forth by Hansen's critics, however, was that a slowdown in demographic expansion does not necessarily contribute to an imbalance between planned investment and desired saving at full employment. Terborgh (1945, pp. 46–47) and Sweezy (1940, pp. 66–70) did not challenge Hansen's assertion that a decline in population growth reduces the demand for housing and other capital-intensive goods while raising the demand for services. Schumpeter ([1942] 2008, p. 114) and Sweezy (1940, p. 75) even added a supply-side perspective, indicating that a stable or declining workforce might limit profitable investment opportunities due to a shortage of labor. Yet, and this is the crucial point, a slowdown in population growth might also hamper the propensity to save. Possible adverse effects on the rate of investment incident to a decline in population growth were assumed to be at least partially compensated for by similar changes in the saving rate. Terborgh (1945, pp. 56–60), for instance, held that investment and saving are not entirely independent of each other, as many private investors only save to invest in real capital goods. Moreover, a slowdown in demographic expansion must ultimately increase the share of older people in the population. As the retired elderly typically dissave, this change in the age distribution may eventually reduce the saving rate (Terborgh 1945. pp. 60–62). Sweezy (1940, p. 66), on the other hand, was aware that this effect could be

---

[14]Referring to the business cycle, Hansen (1937), in fact, also mentioned population growth to be both cause and effect of economic activity. See also footnote 9 in Sect. 3.2.2.1.

counteracted by a declining percentage of children. At least during that time of the transition period from a high to a low increase in population when the share of children has already declined and the last cohort of baby boomers has not yet retired, i.e., when the share of dependents (i.e., children and retired elderly) in the total population is relatively low, the propensity to save may increase. Schumpeter ([1942] 2008, p. 114), however, denied this effect, as he suspected "[...] the desire [of people] to expand alternative demands [...]" to be a major motive for voluntary childlessness. These alternative demands, in turn, might open new investment outlets and stimulate investment spending. After all, it is not the number of people, but effective purchasing power which is relevant (Hofmann 1959, p. 28).[15]

As to the passing of the frontier, Hofmann (1959, p. 28) criticized the issue to be a unique US-American phenomenon which was not readily applicable to other advanced countries. Terborgh (1945, pp. 64–76), on the other hand, questioned whether the availability of unsettled land in the United States had in fact required much capital investment in the nineteenth century. Moreover, he did not see any evidence of a so-called *afterglow effect* of the frontier, i.e., a positive stimulus to capital accumulation incident to the development of the Western United States after 1890. According to his line of thought, investment opportunities do not result from the existence of a physical frontier, but they arise out of technological developments, i.e., the advance of the *technological frontier* (Terborgh 1945, p. 76). A similar argument was also set forth by Schumpeter ([1942] 2008, p. 117), when he stated, "The conquest of the air may well be more important than the conquest of India was— we must not confuse geographical frontiers with economic ones." Although he did not challenge the emergence of new investment outlets, Schumpeter ([1942] 2008, p. 117) considered that these investment opportunities might be less fertile than in the past:

> [...] [A]ll we can assert is that the vanishing of investment opportunities incident to the development of new countries [...] *need* not cause a void that would necessarily affect the rate of increase in total output. We cannot assert that they actually will be replaced by at least equivalent ones.

Finally, with respect to the future of technological progress, both Terborgh (1945, p. 86) and Schumpeter (1939, p. 1034) agreed that innovation is the most important driver of investment opportunity and economic progress. Although Steindl ([1952] 1976, p. 132–134) did not share this view in the 1952 edition of his *Maturity and Stagnation in American Capitalism*, in which he criticized Hansen for exaggerating the importance of technological advance, in the introduction to the 1976 reprint he took a different stance, "In this book [of 1952] [...] I denied that innovations stimulate investment. [...] There lay my error [...]. [New] ideas [...] which are sufficiently advanced [...] are [...] in each case [...] a powerful inducement to invest"

---

[15]Lösch (1938, p. 456) also noted that consumer spending ultimately depends on purchasing power and not on the number of people. Nonetheless, he considered the number of people highly relevant for two reasons: First, the average propensity to save is likely to be smaller if a given income is spread over a larger number of people. Secondly, he assumed business confidence to be higher in economies with an increasing population.

(Steindl [1952] 1976, p. xii). Hansen's concerns about possible changes in the character of technological progress, however, were generally denied. Terborgh (1945, p. 89) doubted that only new industries similar in scope to the railway or automobile could induce sufficient real capital investment. A large number of minor technological advances, he argued, might be just as useful as a single great new industry. He also did not see any evidence of a rising share of capital-saving innovations (Terborgh 1945, p. 96). While Steindl ([1952] 1976, p. 133) took a similar attitude, Schumpeter (1939, p. 1034) at least considered the possibility of increasingly capital-saving technological advances, "[...] [C]hemical and other developments [...] *may* result in making innovation capital saving or at least less capital absorbing than, say, it has been in the railroad age." Nonetheless, technological progress is unpredictable (Terborgh 1945, p. 97). Comparing technological possibilities to an "[...] uncharted sea [...]," Schumpeter ([1942] 2008, p. 118) did not see any reason to expect a cessation of technological advance which would cause economic growth to decline. To him, it was just speculation whether past innovations "[...] were more important, more profitable, or more capital absorbing than those [...]" which were yet to come (Schumpeter 1939, p. 1034).

Although Hansen's secular stagnation hypothesis received little support, most of his critics did not challenge its logical validity in terms of the impact of the three exogenous factors on capital accumulation (Higgins 1959, p. 182). As pointed out above, they mostly shared the view that population increase, territorial expansion, and technological progress boost real capital investment. In contrast to Hansen, however, they were rather optimistic that self-regulating—though not necessarily endogenous—forces would prevent secular stagnation should these three exogenous factors fade.[16] Hansen (1946b, p. 13), in fact, accepted this view and recognized that his critics *might* be right. From a theoretical point of view, however, neither Hansen's nor his critics' position can be proved or refuted. Depending on whether counteracting forces are sufficiently powerful, secular stagnation may or may not evolve. Terborgh (1945), on the other hand, also attempted to disprove Hansen's hypothesis on empirical grounds by analyzing the impact of population increase, territorial expansion, and technological advance on economic activity during the late nineteenth and early to mid-twentieth century. His empirical critique, however, is mainly based on correlation analysis and, as rightly noted by Hansen (1946b) and Higgins (1946), partially misses the point. Even Terborgh (1945, p. 225), though, who concluded secular stagnation to be a bogey lacking any empirical relevance, did not deny the theoretical consistency of Hansen's concept. "*Persuasive as the argument may be* [...]," he held, "[...] it must yield to the evidence, which stubbornly refuses to support it" (Terborgh 1945, p. 215; emphasis added).[17]

After the Second World War, Hansen's stagnation hypothesis was almost forgotten in the wake of the post-war economic boom. It was commonly argued that the

---

[16]Fellner (1954, p. 429), for example, put it as follows: "The Keynes-Hansen pessimism [...] does not rest on a logical fallacy, but its foundations include subjective judgments which I do not happen to share."

[17]On the debate between Hansen and Terborgh, see also Dockès (2015).

strong economic performance following the war had disproved the stagnation doctrine, as Hansen had apparently confused secular with cyclical developments (Hahn 1955, p. 116). This conclusion, however, is not justified. Hansen always emphasized his prediction of secular stagnation to be only valid in the absence of counteracting forces. In the aftermath of the Second World War, however, such counteracting forces did exist. Among them were especially a large backlog of demand in the first post-war years, massive government spending (including high military expenditures during the Korean War), and the post-war baby boom. Hansen could not foresee these developments in the 1930s, and it is indeed unclear how things would have developed had there not been a major war. One can only agree with Terborgh (1945, p. 11) on that score, who mentioned that "[...] the outbreak of war deferred all possibility either of confirmation or of disproof [...]" of the stagnation thesis. Similarly, Gordon (1961, p. 449), the father of the contemporary economist Robert J. Gordon, stated, "Had the war not intervened, private investment might or might not have increased to the point where full employment would have been possible without major government intervention. We shall never know, of course." While it is thus valid to dismiss Hansen's mid-twentieth-century *prediction* of an imminent period of stagnation, his *theoretical* underpinning was not disproved by the post-Second World War period of prosperity (Clauß 1968, pp. 264–273).[18] This does not mean, however, that Hansen's hypothesis is the only reasonable stagnation concept. Based on the conviction that economic stagnation might be caused by factors other than changes in population increase, territorial expansion, and technological progress, several economists developed alternative hypotheses. Among them was Steindl ([1952] 1976, p. 134), a close follower of Kalecki, who believed his own stagnation theory to be "[...] a better basis for the understanding of long-run developments than [...] [Hansen's] exogenous theory."

3.2.3 Kalecki and Steindl: The Rise in Industrial Concentration

3.2.3.1 Kalecki's Theories of Trend and Cycle

Although it was Steindl who developed *the* other major demand-side stagnation hypothesis in the twentieth century, reference must be made to Kalecki, a contemporary of Keynes and Steindl's main inspiration. While Kalecki used to be treated as a follower of Keynes, today it is generally agreed that he discovered major aspects of *The General Theory* prior to 1936 (Laski 1987a, p. 8). The main issue was that his earlier essays were originally published in Polish and thus remained relatively unnoticed in academic circles. Among them were three of Kalecki's ([1933] 1971, [1934] 1971, [1935] 1971) papers which he later stated to contain the "[...] essentials [...]"

---

[18]As Hansen (1955, p. 549) himself mentioned, "It is amazing how many economists have been able to close their eyes and blandly announce that events since 1940 have *disproved* the stagnation thesis!"

of *The General Theory* (Kalecki 1971, p. vii). When he received a copy of Keynes's magnum opus in 1936, according to Robinson (1977, p. 8) Kalecki was shocked as "[...] it was the book that he intended to write."

Although Kalecki and Keynes developed similar theories of effective demand, their analytical frameworks differ in several respects. Like Schumpeter (1954, p. 1143–1144), in his review of *The General Theory* Kalecki ([1936] 1990, p. 231) critically reflected on Keynes's rather static analysis of essentially dynamic issues. More explicitly than Keynes, Kalecki dealt with both cyclical and long-run economic developments (Kalecki [1954] 1965, pp. 145–156; Laski 1987a, p. 9). Long- and short-run processes, he held, are heavily intertwined and cannot be separated. According to Kalecki ([1968] 1971, p. 165), "[...] the long-run trend is but a slowly changing component of a chain of short-period situations; it has no independent entity [...]." In contrast to Keynes, Kalecki ([1936] 1990, p. 223) also took account of the capacity effect of investment. While investment spending increases effective demand in the short run, in the medium to long run it raises productive capacity.

Kalecki assumed the economy to be essentially demand-constrained. Capitalists, he pointed out, usually do not fully utilize their productive capacity and—as long as capacity constraints are not binding—face constant marginal costs (Kalecki 1939, pp. 26–27, 1971, p. 169). At a given price level, an increase in output produced and sold thus raises profits, as overhead costs are spread over a larger output. Moreover, as long as there is unused capacity and real wages do not exceed labor productivity, labor demand is positively dependent on the real wage rate, i.e., the labor demand curve is upward sloping. In other words, a rise in the real wage rate increases workers' consumption spending and, ceteris paribus, output and employment (Kalecki [1935] 1971, pp. 27–28; Lavoie 2014, pp. 277–278, 291–295).

Central to Kalecki's analysis of output and employment are his theories of profits, prices, and (functional) income distribution under imperfect competition. Inspired by Marx's schemes of reproduction, he distinguished between three departments producing capitalists' investment goods, capitalists' consumption goods, and workers' consumption goods, respectively. In the most general case of an open economy with a government sector, capitalists' total real profits (net of taxes) (P) are equal to the sum of private investment (I), capitalists' consumption out of profits (C_p), the current account balance ($X - M$), and the government budget deficit (B) less workers' saving out of wages (S_w) (Kalecki [1954] 1965, pp. 48–49):

$$P = I + C_p + (X - M) + B - S_w. \qquad (3.1)$$

In the special case of a balanced government budget, balanced foreign trade, and zero workers' saving, which Kalecki ([1954] 1965, p. 50; 1971, p. 166) frequently assumed, it follows from Eq. (3.1) that total profits (P) are equal to private investment (I) and capitalists' consumption spending (C_p).[19] Profits are a passive variable here, as they are *determined* by private investment and consumption out of profits. If

---

[19]Unless otherwise stated, the assumption of a balanced government budget, balanced foreign trade, and zero workers' saving is maintained hereinafter.

capitalists as a group do not consume and/or invest, no profits are generated. Similar to Keynes's ([1930] 1971, p. 125) parable of the widow's cruse, Kaldor (1955/1956, p. 96) famously summarized Kalecki's theory of profits by stating that "[...] capitalists earn what they spend, and workers spend what they earn."[20] According to Kalecki ([1954] 1965, pp. 46, 53), in the short run capitalists' real expenditures are predetermined by decisions taken in the past (López and Assous 2010, pp. 28–29). For example, over the typical business cycle private investment decisions are stimulated by the availability of internal saving of firms (i.e., depreciation, undistributed profits, and capital increases by the issuance of new shares) and the increase in profits. On the other hand, by adversely affecting the rate of profit, a rise in the stock of fixed capital negatively impacts investment decisions (Kalecki [1954] 1965, pp. 96–99, 157).

As shown in Eq. (3.2), output (Y) and employment are determined by total profits (P), i.e., capitalists' expenditures, as well as the share of profits in national income (π), i.e., the functional distribution of income between wages and profits (López and Assous 2010, p. 67). Abstracting from overhead labor, the profit share (π) is equal to $1 - \omega$, with ω representing the share of wages in value added. The wage share (ω), in turn, is determined by the ratio of material costs to wages (j) as well as the percentage mark-up on direct costs (θ) in Kalecki's ([1954] 1965, pp. 28–29) theory (see Eq. 3.3). The latter reflects the so-called *degree of monopoly*, a key feature of Kalecki's assumption of imperfect competition among firms, with producers enjoying a mark-up of price over their unit direct costs.[21]

$$Y = \frac{P}{\pi} = \frac{P}{1 - \omega} \tag{3.2}$$

$$\omega = \frac{1}{1 + \theta\,(j + 1)}. \tag{3.3}$$

If the mark-up (θ) and/or the ratio of material costs to wages (j) rise, the wage share (ω) and—ceteris paribus—national income (Y) decline. Assuming given capitalists' real expenditures $\left(I + C_p\right)$, real profits (P) then amount to a larger proportion (π) of a lower national income (Y). The underlying mechanisms become clear if one assumes a fall in wages which, because of imperfect competition among firms, is not accompanied by a decline in prices, thus raising both θ and j. With given capitalists' profits (P) and assuming that all wages are spent on workers' consumption goods, a decrease in real wages pari passu reduces effective demand, national income, and employment. It is in this regard, in fact, that Kalecki ([1932] 1990, pp. 43–44)—similar to Keynes—opposed wage cuts in a depression.

---

[20] As Kalecki ([1954] 1965, p. 46) himself put it, "[...] [I]t is clear that capitalists may decide to consume and to invest more in a given period than in the preceding one, but they cannot decide to earn more. It is, therefore, their investment and consumption decisions which determine profits, and not vice versa."

[21] As outlined by Kalecki ([1954] 1965, pp. 28–29), in the economy as a whole both j and θ are also influenced by the industrial composition of the economy.

Kalecki (1971, p. 169) assumed the underemployment of productive resources to be the normal condition of capitalist economies. Under laissez-faire capitalism, he held, "[...] full utilisation of resources [can] only [be achieved] at the top of a boom, and frequently not even then" (Kalecki [1968] 1971, p. 169). Moreover, Kalecki ([1954] 1965, p. 161) did not believe long-term economic development to be inherent in capitalism. Being unable to generate an endogenous growth trend, the economy would be caught in a stationary state were it not for the growth-stimulating impact of several semi-exogenous development factors (Kalecki [1954] 1965, pp. 155–156; 1962, p. 134; Assous et al. 2016, p. 31). Relatively low and declining rentiers' saving (i.e., saving of capitalists outside of firms) in relation to the capital stock, for example, was considered conducive to economic growth. Moreover, Kalecki ([1954] 1965, p. 159–161) assumed robust population increases to possibly have growth-enhancing effects, although—other than Hansen—he was more skeptical. Similar to Hofmann (1959, p. 28), he pointed out that it is not the number of people, but increases in purchasing power that boost effective demand. Eventually, Kalecki ([1954] 1965, p. 158–159) stressed innovations as the most important development factor, including technological progress, the introduction of new products, as well as the opening up of new resources and raw materials. By raising expectations about future profits, a steady stream of innovations can generate a long-run upward growth trend (Kalecki [1954] 1965, pp. 151, 156, 158; Assous et al. 2016, p. 31). Long-term economic growth in advanced capitalist economies, he assumed, might at least be partially hampered by a lower intensity of innovations. Such adverse developments could be triggered by a decline in the discovery of raw materials or the changing character of technological progress—two issues which had also been emphasized by Hansen. Additionally, Kalecki ([1954] 1965, p. 30) expected monopolistic tendencies to increase in the long run. While this might be another impediment to innovation, in Kalecki's theory a rising degree of monopoly ceteris paribus also hampers real national income by its adverse impact on the wage share (Kalecki [1954] 1965, pp. 159, 161).

Kalecki ([1954] 1965, p. 161) did not see any forces which would automatically induce full utilization of productive resources in a capitalist economy. Political intervention he thus regarded to be key, and it is particularly three policy measures which he proposed to secure full employment of labor in the short and the long run (Kalecki 1944). First, output and employment could be stimulated by boosting private investment. This could be achieved by replacing a part of the income tax by a capital tax, or by introducing a modified income tax which would allow firms to deduct real capital investment spending from their taxable amount (Kalecki 1944, pp. 44–46, 54).[22] The inducement to invest could additionally be raised by lowering interest rates. To sufficiently reduce long-term interest rates might prove difficult, however, as short-term rates cannot fall considerably below zero percent. Moreover, lower interest rates do not necessarily boost private investment spending in a time of overall pessimism, as

---

[22] Keynes ([1944] 1980, pp. 381–382) supported this idea and mentioned in a letter to Kalecki, "I am very much taken with your modified income-tax." A modified income tax as proposed by Kalecki (1944, pp. 45–46, 54), however, is critical from an allocation point of view, because it favors large, established companies over new businesses.

Kalecki (1944, pp. 48, 53) noted similar to Keynes and Hansen. Taking account of the capacity effect of investment, Kalecki (1944, pp. 50–51), however, was mainly concerned about the possible self-destructing effect of investment. If private investment is pushed beyond the level at which productive capacity rises pari passu with full-employment income, idle capacity evolves, hampering future investment via a fall in the profit rate. In fact, a decline in the capital–capacity ratio reinforces the capacity-increasing effect of investment. Kalecki (1939, p. 149) concluded, "The tragedy of investment is that it causes crisis because it is useful. Doubtless many people will consider this theory paradoxical. But it is not the theory which is paradoxical, but its subject—the capitalist economy." Hence, according to Kalecki (1944, pp. 50–51, 57), private investment should be pushed to the level which increases productive capacity proportionately to full-employment output. If this level of investment is lower than the level of investment necessary to ensure full employment, private investment should not be raised further. It is the government which, secondly, should then increase its spending on public investment or—depending on social priorities—on consumption subsidies. To a certain degree, these government expenditures could also be financed by public borrowing. Moreover, and thirdly, effective demand could additionally be boosted by redistributing income from the top to the bottom of the income hierarchy, such as by changing the tax structure or by raising real wages via price controls in monopolistic markets (Kalecki 1944, pp. 39, 49–50, 53–57).

Although full employment may be achieved by government intervention, Kalecki (1943)—similar to Keynes ([1937] 1973, p. 132)—expected political opposition to full-employment policies which go beyond the typical fiscal stimulus in a cyclical downturn. Entrepreneurs and other industrial leaders, he stressed, are likely to oppose public policies designed to achieve and sustain full employment. On the one hand, he held, they reject the government to intervene in employment issues as such. Moreover, he supposed the social elite to not accept government spending on public investment and consumption subsidies. Finally, those at the top of the hierarchy tend to oppose the *maintenance* of full employment, as this would evoke several social and political changes, such as a defiant working class and lack of discipline in factories (Kalecki 1943, pp. 324, 326). Kalecki (1943, p. 330) thus expected *political business cycles*, with government spending fluctuating "[...] according to the condition of political forces" (López and Assous 2010, p. 221). In the United States, he assumed such a political business cycle to have already occurred in the recession of 1937–1938 (Kalecki 1943, p. 330). Looking back at the late 1970s, it is also reasonable to describe the developments in the United Kingdom in terms of Kalecki's political business cycle. Commonly known as the *Winter of Discontent*, in 1978/1979 conflicts between trade unions—demanding larger pay increases—and the Labour Party government—determined to tackle high inflation—eventually paved the way for the election of Margaret Thatcher, leader of the Conservative Party at the time, in the spring of 1979 (see also Hay 2009).[23]

---

[23]To counteract the threat of (cost-push) inflation due to excessive requests for wage increases by trade unions, Wallich and Weintraub (1971) proposed a so-called *tax-based incomes policy*,

Although Kalecki's (1943) hypothesis of political business cycles is one of his most tangible considerations, during his lifetime and beyond it was mainly his approach toward imperfect competition which has been continued and further advanced by numerous scholars and economists. One of his most genuine followers was Josef Steindl. As rightly outlined by Trigg (1994, p. 98), Kalecki and his work on the (functional) distribution of income under imperfect competition were the main inspiration for Steindl's secular stagnation theory.

3.2.3.2   Steindl: Maturity and Stagnation in Capitalist Economies

Key Elements of Steindl's Stagnation Theory

Competitive Versus Oligopolistic Markets

Steindl, an Austrian economist who left his home country for England after the German annexation of Austria in 1938, first met Kalecki at the University of Oxford at the beginning of the 1940s. During the Second World War, they worked together at the Oxford Institute of Statistics, where Steindl developed into one of Kalecki's closest collaborators (Laski 1987b, p. 494; Shapiro 2012, p. 167; Hagemann 2013). Steindl ([1984] 1990, p. 245–246) later described Kalecki as his *guru, inspiration*, and lifelong *reference system* and mentioned, "As an economist I am the product of England and Kalecki" (Steindl 1990, p. 98). In fact, the idea for Steindl's ([1952] 1976) magnum opus *Maturity and Stagnation in American Capitalism* grew out of Kalecki's suggestion. Steindl ([1984] 1990, p. 246) reminisced:

> On one occasion I talked with Kalecki about the crisis of capitalism. We both [...] took it for granted that capitalism was threatened by a crisis of existence, and we regarded the stagnation of the 1930s as a symptom of such a major crisis. But Kalecki [...] did not have an explanation of his own. 'I still do not know', he said, 'why there should be a crisis of capitalism.' He added: 'Could it have anything to do with monopoly?' He subsequently suggested to me and to the Institute, before he left England [in 1945], that I should work on this problem.

In the years following the Second World War, Steindl addressed the issue proposed by Kalecki and developed his own stagnation hypothesis. Inspired by developments in the United States, Steindl's analysis was mainly concerned with the micro- and macroeconomic impact of shifts in the market structure in capitalist economies from more or less free competition to oligopoly (Steindl 1987, p. 473). In the early stages of capitalism, he held, product markets are still highly competitive and characterized by the existence of a variety of different-sized firms in terms of capital endowment. Most important, the majority of industries includes a relatively large number of *small*

---

characterized by a surcharge tax on the corporate profits of those firms granting excessive wage increases.

firms, i.e., firms which can be established and operated with a little amount of capital (Steindl 1947, p. 30, [1952] 1976, p. 38).[24]

According to Steindl ([1952] 1976, p. 37), the size of a firm is negatively linked to its unit production costs at a given degree of capacity utilization. Innovations, so the argument runs, are embodied in the capital stock, implying that only the largest enterprises are able to work with the newest, most productive technologies and thus benefit from economies of scale. Larger firms within each industry therefore enjoy a cost advantage over their smaller competitors (Steindl [1966] 1984, pp. 176–177, [1952] 1976, pp. 23, 37–38). Although bigger firms may charge lower prices for their products than smaller sized enterprises, gross and—at a given degree of capacity utilization—net profit margins increase with firm size (Steindl [1952] 1976, pp. 43–44, 1947, p. 31).[25] This differential advantage allows larger enterprises to expand relative to small- and medium-sized firms. The reason is that rising profit margins which, ceteris paribus, are accompanied by rising profit rates stimulate the rate of internal accumulation of firms (i.e., corporate saving in the form of retained profits). According to Steindl ([1952] 1976, p. 112), corporate retained profits are an important inducement for firms to invest. Hence, a higher profit margin which elicits a higher profit rate provokes a higher rate of corporate saving and thus a higher rate of real capital accumulation. Assuming that firms only invest in their own industry, variations in profit margins are therefore responsible for differences in firms' rates of expansion (Steindl [1952] 1976, pp. 41, 45–46).

In contrast to the so-called *marginal producer* or *normal profit producer*, i.e., the group of the smallest firms with the highest costs and an average net profit of zero, larger firms have considerable means to invest in new technologies which reduce their production costs, raise their gross and net profit margins (at a given degree of capacity utilization), and expand their productive capacity (Steindl [1952] 1976, p. 39). These *progressive firms*, however, may expand at a rate which exceeds demand growth in the industry as a whole to such an extent that only the elimination of some competitors can prevent undesired excess capacity. In other words, a number of existing firms have to be squeezed out of the industry, i.e., *absolute concentration* takes place (Steindl [1952] 1976, p. 42). To achieve their desired degree of capacity utilization, progressive firms thus engage in fierce sales efforts: they cut prices, increase the quality of their products at the expense of higher production costs, and/or raise their

---

[24]Steindl ([1952] 1976, p. 107) assumed a closed economy without government activity. In contrast to Kalecki, he did not distinguish between capitalists and workers, but between firms and private households (Dutt 2005, p. 65).

[25]The *gross profit margin* is the share of gross profits in value added, with gross profits being defined as the excess of the value of sales over direct costs (i.e., variable costs). Similarly, the *net profit margin* is the share of net profits in value added, with net profits being defined as the excess of the value of sales over total costs (i.e., direct *and* overhead costs). For the economy as a whole, gross and net profit margins depict the share of aggregate gross and net profits, respectively, in national income. In fact, Steindl ([1952] 1976, p. 71) used the terms *profit margin* and *profit share* interchangeably. While the share of gross profits is not influenced by changes in the degree of capacity utilization, ceteris paribus the share of net profits in value added (or national income) rises with an increase in capacity utilization, as overhead costs are spread over a higher volume of output. See also Steindl ([1952] 1976, pp. 46, 71) and Lavoie (2014, p. 332).

advertising expenditures per unit of sales. As the smallest, highest cost producers are not able to withstand this intense competition and are forced out of the market, the progressive firms eventually regain their desired degree of capacity utilization.[26] Their net profit margins, however, are adversely affected by their sales effort.[27] While they probably do not completely reverse "[...] the additional differential advantage acquired by the new innovations [...]," average net profit margins in the industry as a whole, which have "[...] been temporarily raised by cost reductions of the favourably placed firms [...]," are reduced "[...] to a level which makes the rate of internal accumulation of all firms again consistent with the rate of growth of the industry" (Steindl [1952] 1976, p. 43). Abstracting from private household saving and assuming that the rate of saving out of profits, capital productivity, and the rate of real capital accumulation in the industry are given, the average net profit margin declines to its initial level if the initial degree of capacity utilization is restored. Competition among firms thus not only eliminates excess capacity, but also contains average net profit margins (at a given degree of capacity utilization).

If the process of absolute concentration continues over time, with the highest cost producers constantly being squeezed out of the market by competitive pressure, only a few large firms will eventually be left. In the later stages of capitalism, Steindl ([1952] 1976, p. 137) assumed such oligopolistic tendencies to be common in many industries, leading to a decline in the percentage of competitive sectors in the economy as a whole (Steindl [1966] 1984, p. 174). By limiting competition among enterprises, however, this structural change has important implications for economic development. In industries which are dominated by a small number of similar-sized firms, marginal producers—i.e., enterprises with the highest costs—are quite big and enjoy a profit margin which gives them a certain degree of financial strength and staying power. Driving competitors out of the market by increasing sales efforts is thus a difficult endeavor, as marginal firms have the financial means to retaliate and engage in competitive practices. Should the differential advantage of the most productive firms not be sufficiently large, "[...] the squeezing out [of] competitors and the simultaneous squeezing of the net profit margin at given levels of utilization will not happen, because it would lead to a reduction of the profit rate even for the progressive firm" (Steindl [1952] 1976, p. 53).

Secular Stagnation in Oligopoly

In oligopolistic industries, firms tend to increase their mark-ups by virtue of monopolistic practices, such as price agreements or price leadership (Steindl [1952] 1976,

---

[26]In both the short and the long run, Steindl ([1952] 1976, p. 9–11) assumed firms to intentionally hold a certain *desired* degree of excess capacity, allowing them to quickly respond to changes in demand.

[27]While price cuts and quality competition reduce both the gross profit margin and, ceteris paribus, the net profit margin (at a given degree of capacity utilization), an increase in advertising expenditures only diminishes the net profit margin (at a given degree capacity utilization) of progressive firms.

Fig. 3.3 Schematic illustration of changes in the degree of capacity utilization (u) and the share of net profits in national income (π) in oligopoly. *Source* Author's illustration, slightly modified from Lavoie (2014, p. 335)

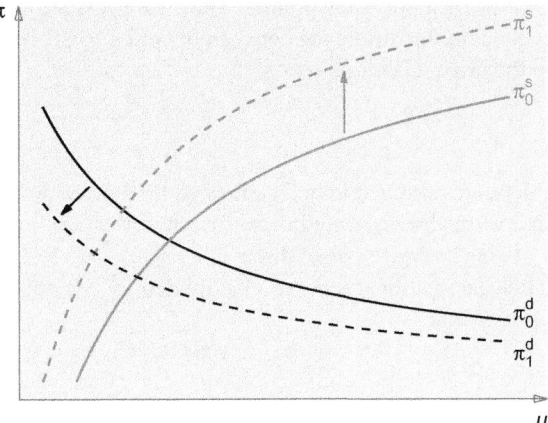

p. 137).[28] While this raises gross and—at a given degree of capacity utilization—net profit margins, ceteris paribus the redistribution of income toward profits reduces real wages and overall spending, leading to a decline in output and the degree of capacity utilization. In contrast to highly competitive markets, however, in oligopoly the initial degree of capacity utilization is not restored by price–cost adjustments. As Steindl ([1952] 1976, p. 137) put it, at a given degree of capacity utilization "[...] the profit margin becomes inelastic in the downward direction [...]," implying that equilibrium must be established by a decline in capacity utilization.

This adjustment mechanism is illustrated in Fig. 3.3, which shows the interaction between the net profit share in national income (π) and the degree of capacity utilization (u). As outlined by Marglin and Bhaduri (1990, p. 155–157), the profit share can be determined from the demand and the supply side. Following Lavoie (2014, pp. 331–335), from a demand-side perspective the profit share $\left(\pi^d\right)$ is equal to total real profits in relation to real national income. As has been shown in Sect. 3.2.3.1, in a closed economy without government and saving out of wages, real profits are determined by real private investment (I) and consumption out of profits $\left(C_p\right)$. Denoting the degree of capacity utilization Y/Y^* by u, with Y^* being the full-capacity level of output, the net share of profits in national income can be written as

$$\pi^d = \frac{P}{Y} = \frac{I + C_p}{Y} = \frac{I + C_p}{uY^*}. \tag{3.4}$$

According to Eq. (3.4), at a higher output level and thus a higher degree of capacity utilization, a given level of real profits amounts to a lower share in national income.

---

[28] With regard to the term *oligopoly*, Steindl ([1945] 1990, p. 45) mentioned, "[...] [I]n its effect on prices, oligopoly will mean much the same as monopoly."

From a supply-side point of view, the net share of profits in national income (π^s) is equal to the difference between the price level (p) and unit costs (UC) in relation to the price level, i.e.,

$$\pi^s = \frac{p - UC}{p}. \tag{3.5}$$

Prices are assumed to be determined by a mark-up (θ) on unit direct costs (UDC). In a vertically integrated economy, the latter amount to unit direct labor costs. With w_v being the wage rate of direct labor and $y_v = Y/L_v$ the labor productivity of direct labor, i.e., national income (Y) divided by the number of direct workers (L_v), the price is equal to

$$p = (1 + \theta)UDC = (1 + \theta)w_v/y_v. \tag{3.6}$$

Unit costs, on the other hand, consist of unit direct and unit overhead labor costs. With L_f being the number of overhead workers and assuming that the wage rate of overhead labor is σ times the wage rate of direct labor, unit costs can be written as

$$UC = \frac{w_v L_v + \sigma w_v L_f}{Y}, \qquad \sigma > 1. \tag{3.7}$$

With labor productivity of overhead labor being defined as $y_f = Y^*/L_f$ and the ratio of labor productivity of direct to overhead labor being equal to $f = y_v/y_f$, it follows that

$$UC = \frac{w_v}{y_v}\left(1 + \frac{\sigma f}{u}\right). \tag{3.8}$$

Finally, substituting Eqs. (3.6) and (3.8) into Eq. (3.5) yields

$$\pi^s = \frac{\theta - \sigma f/u}{1 + \theta}. \tag{3.9}$$

According to Eq. (3.9), from a supply-side perspective the net profit share in national income increases with a rise in the degree of capacity utilization, as overhead costs are spread over a higher output level. This relationship closely resembles Steindl's ([1952] 1976, p. 111, [1979] 1990, p. 111) so-called *profit function*.

If firms increase their mark-up (θ), the π^s schedule in Fig. 3.3 shifts upward, from π_0^s to π_1^s, implying that—at any given degree of capacity utilization—the net profit share is now higher than before. Ceteris paribus, however, a shift toward profits reduces output and the degree of capacity utilization, partially counteracting the rise in the net profit share. Compared to the initial equilibrium at the intersection of the π_0^s and π_0^d schedules, at the intersection of the π_1^s and π_0^d schedules the degree of capacity utilization is lower and the share of net profits in national income is higher. In highly competitive economies, this decline in the degree of capacity utilization elicits competitive pressure, i.e., price–cost adjustments push the π_1^s schedule back down toward its initial position π_0^s. In oligopoly, however, this adjustment mechanism is incapacitated. Ceteris paribus, particularly assuming that the rate of real capital accumulation I/K—with K denoting the capital stock—initially remains constant, a rise in the mark-up induces a decline in the degree of capacity utilization which is proportional to the rise in the net profit share.[29] According to Steindl ([1952] 1976, p. 124), after a time lag this decline in the degree of capacity utilization may adversely impact economic growth, i.e., the rate of real capital accumulation (I/K). If firms' investment spending is impaired by the fall in the degree of capacity utilization, the π^d schedule in Fig. 3.3 shifts downward, from π_0^d to π_1^d, leading to a further decline in output and the degree of capacity utilization (u). Although gross profit margins do not change, the net profit share declines. In fact, the net profit share in national income may even decline below its initial level. In Steindl's ([1952] 1976, p. 245) own words:

> [...] [T]he tendency for the capitalists' share in the product to increase does, after all, exist *potentially*. It is a consequence of the growth of oligopoly. The expression of this tendency can only be an *increase in the gross profit margins*. That means that the actual share of *net* incomes of capitalists need not increase at all. The increased gross profit margins may be compensated by a reduced degree of utilisation, so that there is not a shift of actual income from wages to profits, but a shift of potential income of workers to wastage in excess capacity.

While the decline in the rate of real capital accumulation (I/K) and the associated downward shift of the π^d schedule may lead to a new equilibrium at a lower degree of capacity utilization (u), Steindl ([1952] 1976, p. 137) pointed out that this is not necessarily the case. As each decline in the growth rate of real capital (I/K) further reduces the degree of capacity utilization (u), which again discourages real capital investment, the downward movement of the π^d schedule may not come to a halt.

> [A]ny reduction of the rate of capital growth will reduce the degree of utilisation, and this will further reduce the rate of growth of capital. Thus, a given reduction in capital growth will lead to a further decrease in the rate of growth. This cumulative process may again tend to a definite limit, so that the rate of growth will settle down at a new lower level, but it is not certain whether it might not continue, theoretically, without limit. (Steindl [1952] 1976, p. 138)

Steindl ([1979] 1990) himself recognized the similarities between this instability process and the knife-edge problem described by Harrod (1939). When the actual growth rate (I/K) and the natural growth rate fall short of Harrod's *warranted rate of growth*, a downward spiral continues if there is not a sufficiently pronounced downward adjustment of the desired degree of capacity utilization and/or the propensity to save (Hein 2014, pp. 38–41). "[T]he economy is unable to adjust to low growth rates [...]" Steindl ([1952] 1976, p. 107) claimed, "[...] because its savings propensity is adapted to a high one."

It should be noted, however, that a structural shift from free competition to oligopoly does not necessarily lead to a decline in the rate of growth in Steindl's

---

[29]This follows from the goods market equilibrium $\frac{I}{K} = \frac{S}{P}\frac{P}{Y}\frac{Y}{Y^*}\frac{Y^*}{K} = s_p \pi u \frac{Y^*}{K}$. Assuming that the rate of real capital accumulation (I/K), the capacity–capital ratio Y^*/K, and—for reasons of simplicity—the propensity to save out of profits (s_p) are given, a rise in the profit share (π) induces a proportional decline in the degree of capacity utilization (u).

model. Although a rise in the mark-up may reduce the rate of real capital accumulation via its adverse impact on the degree of capacity utilization, the degree of capacity utilization is not the only factor that influences real capital accumulation in Steindl's ([1952] 1976) framework. A rise in firms' internal rate of saving, for instance, may stimulate firms' rate of real capital accumulation and may thus counteract the adverse effect of a decline in the degree of capacity utilization. Depending on which of these two factors has a stronger impact on the rate of real capital accumulation, secular stagnation may or may not evolve (Steindl [1952] 1976, pp. 131, 223–225).

On the other hand, Steindl ([1952] 1976, pp. 131–132, 223–224) also offered an alternative explanation for possible stagnation tendencies in oligopoly. The π^d schedule, he held, may shift downward without a prior upward movement of the π^s schedule. As firms in oligopolistic markets are aware that competitors cannot easily be squeezed out of the market, they tend to have greater fear of undesired excess capacity and may thus increase their planned (i.e., desired) degree of capacity utilization. While each individual firm may try to avoid undesired excess capacity by cutting real investment spending, ceteris paribus a decline in the rate of real capital accumulation reduces the degree of capacity utilization in the economy as a whole. In this case, the π^d schedule moves downward without a preceding upward shift of the π^s schedule. The decline in the degree of capacity utilization, in turn, may provoke a fall in the rate of real capital accumulation in the following periods, possibly leading to economic stagnation.

General Perception and Critical Assessment

Steindl's ([1952] 1976) stagnation theory aimed at explaining the decline in the growth rate of real capital accumulation in the United States between 1890 and the beginning of the Second World War. Due to oligopolistic tendencies, he assumed private business capital accumulation to have been gradually declining since the end of the nineteenth century. While this process was partially offset by the stock market boom of the 1920s, this compensatory factor came to an abrupt end in the fall of 1929 (Steindl [1952] 1976, pp. 154–155, 166–175).

Expecting possible periods of economic stagnation to result from endogenous changes inherent in capitalism, Steindl believed his own stagnation hypothesis to be more reliable than Hansen's approach. "The doctrine of economic maturity [...]," he stressed, "[...] has been very much weakened by [...] [the] reliance on an exogenous theory of investment" (Steindl [1952] 1976, p. 132). Referring to Hansen and his followers, he went on:

> [...] [T]heir theory is 'exogenous', carrying the explanation—by and large—back to certain events like technological change which remain unexplained. This leaves us in doubt whether 'maturity' is anything more than temporary and accidental, although these authors—like Professor Hansen—do give at the same time the impression that it is something more. (Steindl [1952] 1976, p. 191)

With *Maturity and Stagnation in American Capitalism* having been finished in 1949 (Hansen 1955, p. 548) and published in the midst of the post-war economic boom in 1952, Steindl's theory suffered the same fate as Hansen's stagnation doctrine and remained largely unnoticed in academic circles. In the introduction of the 1976 reprint, Steindl ([1952] 1976, p. ix) himself mentioned that the "[...] book appeared at a time which could not have been less propitious for its success." Nonetheless, however, Steindl's magnum opus was recognized and reviewed by several economists. One of them was Hansen (1954), who pointed out that Steindl's stagnation theory might complement his own hypothesis. While continuing to emphasize the decay of exogenous factors, Hansen (1954, p. 414) acknowledged that the growth of oligopoly might have contributed to the economic turmoil of the 1920s and 1930s.[30] Similarly, Sweezy (1954) was enthusiastic about Steindl's theoretical concept, but doubted that it was sufficient to explain the actual development of capital accumulation in the United States. Empirical data, Sweezy mentioned, have to be viewed within their historical context, making it necessary to take account of such exogenous factors as the ones suggested by Hansen. Brown (1955, p. 130) pointed in a similar direction when he asked himself whether Steindl's model "[...] may not omit variables at least as important as those it includes [...]." Swanson (1953), on the other hand, who previously had criticized Hansen's stagnation doctrine in Swanson and Schmidt (1946), praised Steindl for his endogenous stagnation approach. At the same time, however, he rejected Steindl's conviction of oligopolistic tendencies being a predetermined path in capitalist economies, criticizing him for not mentioning counteracting forces which could impede such developments. Hamberg (1954), in turn, criticized Steindl for not properly considering the possibility of product innovations. According to him, new product developments can be an important inducement for firms to invest and may even give rise to new (competitive) industries.

As has already been briefly outlined in Sect. 3.2.2.2, Steindl ([1952] 1976, pp. xv–xvi) later revised his opinion on the role of technological progress and admitted its stimulating impact on investment. The petering out of a technological wave, such as the saturation of the railroad industry in the late nineteenth century, could indeed lead to a slowdown in economic growth. While acknowledging the importance of technological change, however, Steindl continued to emphasize the adverse economic effects of oligopolistic tendencies in mature capitalism. "[...] [M]ere reference to the technological development in itself [...]," Steindl ([1952] 1976, p. xvi) held, "[...] does not yield a very satisfactory explanation of the secular decline of accumulation." The general economic climate, as he called it, is important for the development of new know-how and determines whether new ideas and innovations enter the production process via real capital investment (Steindl [1989] 1990, p. 168). This mechanism, however, Steindl ([1989] 1990, p. 177–178) claimed to be severely hampered in oligopoly.

Similar to Hansen, Steindl ([1989] 1990, p. 166) did not think that his stagnation hypothesis had been disproved by the post-war economic prosperity—and rightly so. Steindl ([1979] 1990, [1989] 1990) rather referred to favorable exogenous forces which counteracted the adverse effects of oligopolistic tendencies in both the United States and Europe. Especially in the USA, economic performance improved due to

---

[30]On the coincidence of a decline in both competition and the rate of economic growth, see also Hansen (1938, p. 299).

high public (military) spending, partially financed by profit taxes. By boosting total output and sales, the increase in government expenditure raised corporate profits before taxes to such an extent that after-tax profits remained more or less unchanged. At the same time, the Cold War evoked a technological race between the West and the East, leading to high spending on education as well as on research and development (R&D). Moreover, higher capacity utilization rates, a low degree of corporate indebtedness after the war, and extensive investment opportunities encouraged private investment spending. On top of that, a strong rise in international trade enabled firms to expand their markets. In Europe, on the other hand, technological catch-up with the United States and post-war reconstruction played an important role in addition to high government spending and pent-up demand (Steindl [1989] 1990, pp. 174–175, [1979] 1990, pp. 119–121; Rothschild 1994, p. 135; see also Abramovitz 1986).

According to Steindl ([1989] 1990, p. 176), the post-war economic boom could last for more than 20 years because both foreign trade and the increased bargaining power of workers—resulting from high or even full employment—kept profit margins in check and thus secured a high level of aggregate demand. Starting in the early 1970s, however, growth slowed down and things changed. To explain these developments, Steindl ([1989] 1990, p. 166) did not directly draw on his former stagnation theory, as he "[...] did not think that these ideas were directly applicable to the new problems of the seventies." Rather than pointing to increases in mark-ups by oligopolistic firms, Steindl—in a way similar to Schumpeter ([1942] 2008, p. 139–142)—now focused on the internal transformation of companies. In oligopoly, he stressed, businesses are usually large, hierarchical, and bureaucratic and mainly concerned with their market dominance. While these structures hamper the innovation process and weaken the incentive to invest in real capital, financial investment takes on an increasingly important role. Although this process had slowly evolved over the years, in the 1970s it coincided with other unfavorable changes (Steindl [1989] 1990, pp. 177–178). For example, Steindl ([1979] 1990, p. 122–126) pointed to a rise in private households' saving as well as the petering out of the aftereffects of the Second World War, such as the technological catch-up of European countries and the tensions between the Western and Eastern powers. Additionally, environmental and energy problems created uncertainty among firms and undermined business confidence. Most important, however, Steindl ([1979] 1990, p. 124) mentioned "[...] the changed attitude of government towards full employment and growth." With governments aiming at curbing inflation and public debt, full-employment policies faded into the background. In line with Kalecki's (1943) *Political Aspects of Full Employment*, Steindl ([1979] 1990, p. 124) saw these policy changes as a response to the increased bargaining power of workers during the long period of economic prosperity after the war. He concluded, "The arguments against full employment have got the upper hand in the councils of the powers, and thus we witness stagnation not as an incomprehensible fate, as in the 1930s, but stagnation as a policy" (Steindl [1952] 1976, p. xvii).

Since the publication of *Maturity and Stagnation in American Capitalism*, Steindl's ideas have been seized on by several economists. Although he did not explicitly refer to Steindl, Sylos-Labini ([1957] 1962), for example, explained possible stagnation tendencies with a rise in industrial concentration. Like Steindl, he was critical of Hansen's secular stagnation doctrine and claimed that firms in oligopolistic markets tend to defer real capital investment especially due to a lack of demand. If investment is undertaken, however, it tends to be mainly financed out of depreciation funds and to be insufficient to ensure full employment (Sylos-Labini [1957] 1962, pp. 168, 180). Several Kaleckian and neo-Marxian economists have argued in a similar way, with the latter including the *Monthly Review* authors Baran and Sweezy (1966) as well as Sweezy and Magdoff (1972, 1973, 1977, 1987, 1988). Baran and Sweezy (1966) identified economic stagnation as a major threat to capitalism. Along Marxian lines, they argued that, while oligopolistic and monopolistic developments tend to increase the surplus value produced, due to a lack of demand it becomes increasingly difficult to realize this surplus. Absent counteracting forces, they thus believed stagnation to be the normal condition of capitalist economies (Baran and Sweezy 1966, p. 108). In more recent times, their line of thought has been taken up by Foster and McChesney (2012) and Foster (2014), who put the issue of industrial concentration in the context of today's economic reality and also elaborate on the financialization of capitalism. As current empirical studies by Autor et al. (2017) and Díez et al. (2018) have shown, industry concentration has indeed increased over the past decades, providing fertile ground for Steindl's ([1952] 1976) hypothesis.[31] Yet, although in more recent times the relevance of Steindl's ([1952] 1976) theory has been emphasized by post-Keynesian economists such as Dutt (2005) and Hein (2016), Steindl's oeuvre has been mainly ignored in the contemporary stagnation debate. As will be further outlined in Chaps. 7 and 8, however, particularly with regard to the distribution of income his theory is a valuable addition to the current discussion.

3.3   A Contemporary Demand-Side Stagnation Theory

Although the topic of secular stagnation regained some interest in the wake of the growth slowdown in the 1970s, it was only a side issue and largely forgotten during the late twentieth and early twenty-first century. In the aftermath of the financial crisis of 2008–2009, however, the subject has been revived by several economists as part of an intense discussion on the economic weakness in major advanced economies. Among the contemporary economists advocating secular stagnation as a demand-side phenomenon, Lawrence H. Summers—like Alvin H. Hansen affiliated with Harvard University—is the most well-known representative. Although other authors, such as Godley (1999), Palley (2002, 2012), and von Weizsäcker (2010), had already previously referred to related issues, it was Summers (2013) who at a conference of the International Monetary Fund (IMF) in November 2013 set the hare running and opened the public debate. In the years to come, he held, the issue of cyclical fluctu-

---

[31]On today's relevance of Steindl's ([1952] 1976) endogenous stagnation theory, see also Cowling (2005).

ations might be only of secondary importance, while the topic of secular stagnation could gain relevance in developed nations. It is commonly argued that Summers's line of thought closely resembles Hansen's exogenous stagnation doctrine. While this is true to some extent, their hypotheses also differ in several respects.

3.3.1   The Economic Environment in the Early Twenty-First Century

Summers (2015b, p. 12) assumes that stagnation tendencies in advanced countries have been around for some time, but were masked by other factors in previous years. He joins economists such as Cynamon and Fazzari (2014, p. 30) in stating that economic performances had not been excessive before the financial crisis of 2008–2009 and there had been no obvious signs of overheating (Summers 2014b, p. 38, e, p. 66). Despite a debt-fueled housing bubble, economic growth in the United States was not enormous, but most certainly unsustainable. Likewise, growth in Europe was accompanied by external imbalances between Northern and Southern countries as well as debt buildups in the European periphery that could not last forever. Japan, on the other hand, has been suffering from low economic growth and deflationary tendencies since the 1990s (Summers 2014e, pp. 66–69).

As shown in Fig. 3.4a, pre-crisis unemployment rates in Europe, Japan, and the United States did not decline to the low levels that had once prevailed in the 1960s (and before). Even with regard to the USA, where the unemployment rate around the year 2000 reached values as low as four percent, Summers (2014b, p. 38) stresses

(a) Civilian unemployment rates

(b) Employment-to-population ratios, men aged 25 to 54

Fig. 3.4 Labor market developments, 1960–2017. *Source* Author's illustrations, based on data from the European Commission (2018) and the OECD (2018). See Appendix A for detailed data sources and further notes

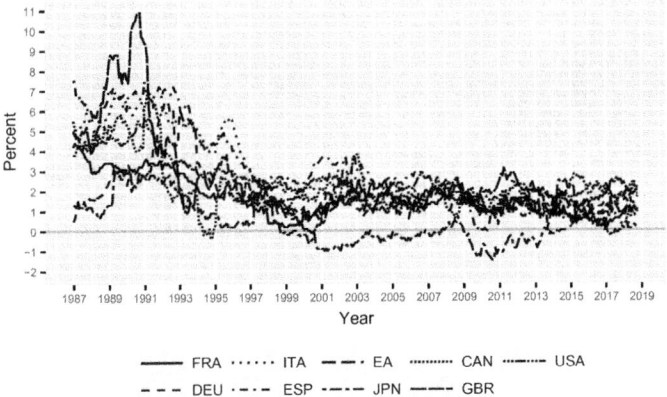

Fig. 3.5 Core inflation rates, 01/1987–10/2018. *Source* Author's illustration, based on data from the OECD (2018) and the European Central Bank (2018). See Appendix A for detailed data sources and further notes

that it did not quite approach historical lows. Additionally, Fig. 3.4b reveals that employment-to-population ratios among men aged 25–54 have been declining for several decades in the majority of countries considered. As illustrated in Fig. 3.5, similar trends also hold for core inflation rates, which were not extraordinarily high prior to the financial crisis and in most European countries and Japan have been below official target rates ever since (Summers 2015b, p. 12).[32]

As reflected by the developments of nominal three-month money market interest rates in Fig. 3.6a, at the end of the 1970s and in the early 1980s central banks in major advanced economies had pursued a rather restrictive monetary policy stance, raising their nominal policy rates to combat high inflation. In the decades thereafter, however, as inflation rates declined and settled at lower levels, key central bank interest rates were largely reduced. While policy rates were mainly lowered during recessions to stimulate economic performance, during recoveries "[...] rates were raised but by not as much [...]," leading to an overall declining trend in both nominal and real short-term market interest rates (Palley 2012, p. 42). According to Palley (2012, pp. 90–93) and others, as stagnation forces with a growing weakness of aggregate demand had already been underlying in the decades prior to 2008, monetary policy stances of relatively low interest rates were necessary to keep the economies running and to prevent stagnation from surfacing. Although in Canada, the United States, and—to a lesser extent—the United Kingdom nominal short-term market interest rates have increased slightly over the past years, in the euro area and Japan they have been

---

[32]Core inflation is the annual change of the consumer price index excluding energy and food. Summers's claim that there had been no signs of economic overheating prior to the financial crisis of 2008–2009 is not shared by all economists. Taylor (2014a, p. 62), Taylor and Wieland (2016, p. 8), and Hamilton et al. (2016, p. 16), for example, point out that in the United States inflation had amounted to more than two percent and the unemployment rate had been below its estimated natural rate in the years leading up to the financial crisis of 2008–2009.

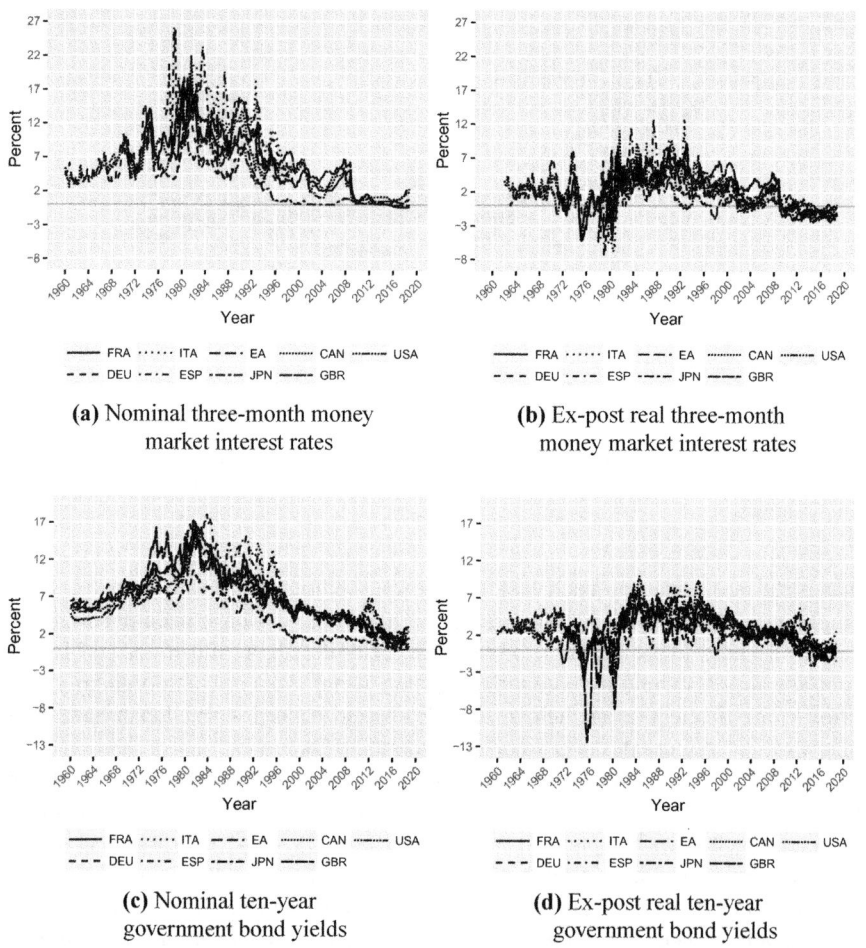

(a) Nominal three-month money
market interest rates

(b) Ex-post real three-month
money market interest rates

(c) Nominal ten-year
government bond yields

(d) Ex-post real ten-year
government bond yields

Fig. 3.6 Nominal and real short- and long-term market interest rates, 01/1960–11/2018. *Source* Partly author's calculations and author's illustrations, based on data from the OECD (2018), the European Central Bank (2018), and the Federal Reserve Bank of St. Louis (2018). See Appendix A for detailed data sources and further notes

hovering around zero percent since the financial crisis of 2008–2009. As shown in Fig. 3.6b, their inflation-adjusted counterparts have been mostly negative during the past decade.

Similar downward trends also hold for nominal and real yields on long-term government bonds shown in Fig. 3.6c and d. As compared to short-term nominal interest rates, which are mainly influenced by monetary policy, long-term nominal interest rates are determined by expectations about both inflation and future short-term interest rates (i.e., the future monetary policy stance) as well as by a term premium (European Central Bank 2015, p. 18). According to Constâncio (2016), the European Central Bank (2015, pp. 18–20), and Bernanke (2015c), all of these factors have contributed to the declining path and low levels of long-term yields in Europe and the United States over the past years. In addition to low inflation prospects and the expectation of low short-term interest rates, term premia have been declining because of a high relative demand for safe assets, which in the aftermath of the financial crisis has been exacerbated by stronger financial regulation and central banks' quantitative easing programs.[33] Today, particularly in France, Germany, and Japan nominal ten-year government bond yields are close to zero percent. With the exception of Italy and—less, though—the United States, real long-term interest rates are hovering near zero percent in all countries considered and, in fact, have even turned slightly negative in some nations.

In describing real GDP trends since the global financial crisis, Summers typically points to developments resembling those shown in Fig. 3.7. Comparing the evolutions of actual GDP (solid lines) reveals that in recent years the US economy has performed much stronger than the euro area and Japan. As an advocate of demand-side stagnation, however, Summers primarily refers to the gaps between actual real GDP (solid lines) and pre-crisis counterfactual potential real output trends (dotted lines).[34] In all three countries and regions considered, post-crisis GDP (solid lines) has not been catching up to its former (counterfactual) potential (dotted lines), but is lagging behind (Summers 2014a, 2015a, p. 60). As is apparent from Fig. 3.7, official estimates of potential output (dashed lines) have been well below their pre-crisis paths (dotted lines). In the United States, for instance, the Congressional Budget

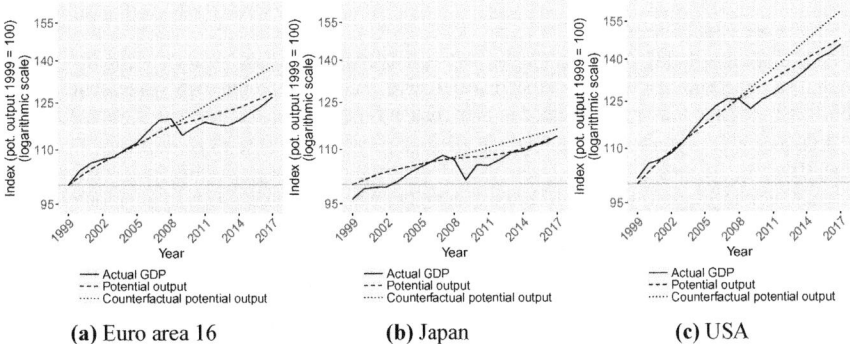

Fig. 3.7   Actual real GDP, potential real output, and counterfactual potential real output developments, 1999–2017. *Source* Author's calculations and illustrations, based on Fatás and Summers (2016, p. 3) and on data from the OECD (2018). See Appendix A for detailed data sources and further notes

---

[33] On the safe asset shortage hypothesis, see also Caballero and Farhi (2014).

[34] From 2008 onward, each dotted line extrapolates the official 1999–2007 potential real output estimate (dashed lines), assuming the average annual growth rate of potential real output between 1999 and 2007.

Office (2014) has revised potential output estimates downward several times after 2007. Due to these downward revisions, official output gaps between actual real GDP (solid lines) and potential real output (dashed lines) have been steadily declining and are currently relatively small or even closed. Although these declines in potential output estimates are, as such, not at the heart of demand-side secular stagnation hypotheses, Summers (2014c, pp. 36–37) does not neglect them and refers to possible hysteresis effects.[35] In some writings, Summers (2014a) also expands his initial demand-side argument and takes greater account of supply-side factors which might "[...] hold back the economy before constraints on the ability to create demand start to bind." Yet, although Summers (2015a, p. 63) suggests to not ignore the supply side, in light of continuously subdued inflation rates across the developed world, he is primarily supporting stagnation as a demand-side phenomenon (see also Summers 2018a, p. 246). In fact, considering the relatively low inflation rates in several major advanced countries, in recent times other economists and international economic institutions as well have suspected demand-side issues to possibly still be more relevant than suggested by official output gap estimates and labor market developments (see, for instance, Cœuré 2018; IMF 2018, p. 4).[36]

---

[35] As is evident from Fig. 3.7, all countries and regions considered have been suffering from super-hysteresis effects in the aftermath of the financial crisis of 2008–2009, although—at least in Japan—this trend seems to have been reversed in more recent times. See also footnote 7 in Sect. 2.2.

[36] Both potential output and the output gap are unobservable, but have to be estimated from real-time data and are thus subject to uncertainty. Even official output gap estimates by national and international institutions tend to differ considerably. Other indicators, such as inflation rates and labor market data, are thus typically additionally consulted to get a broad overview of the general economic climate. For example, in the United States a rather low unemployment rate and inflation close to the official target rate may be indicative of a narrow output gap. On the other hand, however, with a low and declining labor force participation rate there is still some slack in the labor market (Furman 2016, p. 8; IMF 2018, p. 4). Moreover, it is ambiguous whether the relatively high core inflation rates observed in the last years in the USA can be traced back to tight capacity constraints, as they recently have been mainly due to strong price increases in rents, motor vehicle insurances, and hospital services (U.S. Bureau of Labor Statistics 2018, p. 8). A clear negative nexus between (estimated) output gaps and inflation is indeed far from straightforward. As pointed out by Ihrig et al. (2007) and the OECD (2014, p. 16), inflation has in general become less sensitive to changes in output gaps and domestic capacity. Ihrig et al. (2007, pp. 29) suggest that this might be due to the success of monetary policy in anchoring inflation expectations. Moreover, international aspects have possibly become more important. As mentioned by Martin and Rowthorn (2012, pp. 63), the relatively high inflation rates in the United Kingdom in the immediate aftermath of the financial crisis of 2008–2009 were mainly due to rising import prices and changes in value-added taxes, and not due to the closing of the output gap.

3.3.2 Summers: A Revival of Hansen's Stagnation Theory?

3.3.2.1 Key Elements of Summers's Stagnation Theory

Secular Stagnation and the Natural Real Interest Rate

The focal point of Summers's (2015c, 2016a) stagnation hypothesis is the assumption that in major advanced economies the propensity to save has increased and the propensity to invest has declined to such an extent that the equilibrium real interest rate equating saving and investment at full employment is likely to be very low or even negative. Due to short-term nominal market interest rates close to zero percent and low inflation rates, however, this so-called *natural real interest rate* (see the following Excursus) might be unattainable (Summers 2016c). Ex-post saving and investment are thus aligned at an output level below full employment, while at the same time economic growth is likely to be relatively weak (Summers 2014b, p. 45). "[...] [I]t may be impossible [...]," Summers (2014c, p. 29) holds, "[...] for an economy to achieve full employment, satisfactory growth, and financial stability simultaneously [...]." He goes on:

> The zero lower bound on base nominal interest rates, in conjunction with low inflation, makes the achievement of sufficient demand to bring about full employment problematic. If and when ways can be found to generate sufficient demand, they will likely be associated with unsustainable financial conditions. (Summers 2014b, p. 37)

While the natural real interest rate, one of Summers's key variables, is empirically unobservable, estimates by several economists suggest that it has been trending downward for several years across major advanced countries. For instance, estimates by Laubach and Williams (2003, 2015, 2018) reveal that the natural real interest rate in the USA has been following a declining path for the past 25 years and is likely to remain low for a longer period. Decreases in natural real interest rates are also reported for the euro area and Japan (Garnier 2005; Constâncio 2016; Nakaso 2016). Comparing estimates for Canada, the euro area, the United Kingdom, and the United States, Holston and Laubach (2016) conclude that in all four economies the natural real interest rate declined slightly between 1990 and 2007, whereas a more profound downturn has probably been occurring in the aftermath of the global financial crisis of 2008–2009.[37] In trying to keep up with these (unobservable) downward trends and to push short-term market interest rates toward their natural levels, central banks have followed accommodative monetary policies and lowered their policy rates during the past decades (Gerlach and Moretti 2014; Constâncio 2016; Bernanke 2015d).

---

[37]Estimates of the natural real interest rate should be interpreted with caution, however, as results vary according to the underlying assumptions and methodologies. While most analyses point to a declining *development* of natural real interest rates, natural interest rate *levels* differ among existing estimates (Constâncio 2016; Holston and Laubach 2016; Hamilton et al. 2016; Sachverständigenrat 2015, pp. 149–152).

Excursus: The Natural Real Rate of Interest

The concept of the so-called *natural* or *normal rate of interest* goes back to the Swedish economist Wicksell ([1898] 1962, pp. 102, 120, [1935] 1978, p. 193), who defined it as the equilibrium interest rate which, first, equates households' saving decisions with firms' investment decisions at full employment and, secondly, is consistent with price stability (see also Leijonhufvud 1981, p. 154; Arestis and Sawyer 2008, pp. 282–283). Today, the Wicksellian natural rate of interest is typically understood as a short-term risk-free real interest rate which, in the medium to long run, equates saving and investment at full employment and stable inflation close to the central bank's inflation target (see, for example, Hetzel 2009; Laubach and Williams 2015; Summers 2016c; Constâncio 2016).

The (Wicksellian) natural real interest rate is a purely theoretical concept and not empirically observable. It "[...] exist[s] 'off-stage', so to speak, and assert[s] its influence behind the scenes" (Smithin 2009, p. 86). Unlike real short-term market interest rates, which are predominantly determined by monetary factors, the natural interest rate is influenced by non-monetary, real forces and serves as a benchmark for monetary policy. Determinants of the natural real interest rate include secular factors which affect desired saving and investment. Among them are the expected trend growth rate of potential output—including productivity and population growth—as well as time preferences, income inequality, and government spending (Woodford 2003, pp. 50–52; Bernanke 2015d; Rachel and Smith 2015; Weber et al. 2008, pp. 53, 61; Lansing 2016, p. 1).

To achieve full employment and stable inflation, monetary policy measures are usually designed to equate the real policy interest rate with the (unobservable) natural real interest rate in the medium to long run (Smithin 2009, pp. 86–87). Although it is not observable, economists have been eager to estimate the natural real interest rate. In fact, estimates of the natural real interest rate are part of monetary policy rules such as the Taylor (1993) rule. Referring to Taylor (1993), Smithin (2009, pp. 86–87) formally describes the link between the (estimated) natural real interest rate (r_0) and the central bank's real policy rate (r) as follows: $r = r_0 + \beta \left(\hat{p} - \hat{p}^* \right) + \gamma \left(Y - Y^* \right)$. Here, $\hat{p}$ is the actual inflation rate, $\hat{p}^*$ is the central bank's inflation target, Y is the actual real output level, Y^* is the (estimated) potential real output level, and β and γ are the weights which can take positive values between zero and one. Absent cost shocks, if inflation is below (above) its target rate and actual output is below (above) its potential level, central banks should pursue a real policy interest rate below (above) the (estimated) natural real interest rate to guide the economy to full employment and stable inflation. Once such temporary disturbances have subsided, when in the medium to long run inflation is at its target rate and actual output matches its potential, the policy rate is said to be equal to the natural interest rate. Hence, while temporary shocks may require deviations from the natural interest rate, in the medium to long run central bank policy rates trace the natural interest rate (Borio and Disyatat 2011, p. 22; Bean et al. 2015, p. 6).

The concept of the Wicksellian natural interest rate was criticized by Keynes after 1936. While he had still praised Wicksell in his *Treatise on Money* (Keynes [1930] 1971), in *The General Theory* he rejected the existence of a unique natural interest rate, mentioning that (ex-post) saving and investment can be equated at different levels of output and employment (Keynes [1936] 1973, pp. 242–243). He therefore defined a neutral (or optimum) rate of interest, which is "[...] the natural rate [...] consistent with *full* employment [...]" (Keynes [1936] 1973, p. 243).

As further outlined below, the theory of the natural real interest rate is indeed controversial, as it implicitly relies on the notion that both investment and saving depend negatively and positively, respectively, on real market interest rates. While the natural real interest rate is commonly referred to in New Keynesian approaches, it is rejected by (post-)Keynesian economists.

Causes of Secular Stagnation

Assuming that natural real interest rates in major advanced economies have fallen to such low levels that market interest rates are unable to keep up, Summers predicts a prolonged period of sluggish economic performances. Causes of this decline in natural real interest rates include several medium- to long-run factors which have hampered the propensity to invest, factors which have boosted the propensity to save, as well as open economy aspects considering changes in current accounts. Table 3.1 summarizes the main points emphasized by Summers.[38] As these factors overlap only to some extent with Hansen's three exogenous factors, Summers (2014c, p. 29) himself describes his own theory as the *new secular stagnation hypothesis*.

There is common agreement that in most recent years the supposed downward trend in natural real interest rates can be partially traced back to the aftermath of the financial crisis of 2008–2009. Debt deleveraging by the private and public sector, higher uncertainty and risk aversion, as well as higher barriers on financial intermediation have likely put upward pressure on desired saving and downward pressure on planned investment.[39] Koo (2014), in particular, is arguing along these lines. He

---

[38] See also Rachel and Smith (2015) for a comprehensive overview.
In the contemporary stagnation debate, it is often not clearly distinguished between *real* factors which influence the *natural* interest rate (by changing desired saving and/or planned investment and/or current account balances), and *monetary* factors which influence *market* interest rates (see, for instance, Blanchard et al. 2014). For example, the safe asset shortage view of Caballero and Farhi (2014) is a *financial* issue which first and foremost influences the actual *market* interest rate on safe assets. The importance of distinguishing between real and monetary/financial factors has also been outlined by Borio and Disyatat (2011) and Spahn (2016).

[39] As outlined by Yellen (2015, p. 7), the extensive and long-lasting impact of the financial crisis as well as the resulting adjustment processes go beyond a purely cyclical phenomenon. Hence, the

Table 3.1 Possible causes of stagnation tendencies and a declining natural real interest rate

Factors hampering planned investment	Factors encouraging desired saving	Other factors
Demographic changes	Demographic changes	Global imbalances
Slowdown in technological progress	Increase in inequality	
Declining relative price of capital goods	Crisis-related factors	
Shift to less capital-intensive industries		
Lower government investment		
Crisis-related factors		

Source Author's illustration, based on Summers (2015a, p. 62, 2016b, p. 103)

points out that balance sheet recessions, characterized by extensive debt repayments by private households and firms, are diminishing the propensity to invest while boosting the desire to save. Absent counteracting forces, because of a "[...] debt-related trauma that acts as a psychological block to borrowing [...] even after [...] balance sheets [...]" have been repaired, these trends may continue for a prolonged period of time (Koo 2014, p. 137). Similarly, Rogoff (2015) and Lo and Rogoff (2015) conclude that several developed nations are suffering from so-called *debt supercycles*, with high debt overhang and deleveraging by the private and government sector boosting desired saving and hampering investment.

Although crisis-related factors have probably played a role, economists advocating secular stagnation mainly refer to deeper, more structural factors which have evolved during the past decades and already had an influence prior to 2008.[40] Similar to Hansen's stagnation approach, fundamental demographic changes are among the factors stressed by Summers. During the past decades, most advanced economies have seen a slowdown in population increase, and, most important, a lower increase in the working-age population and labor force. As shown in Fig. 3.8a, the absolute change in the number of people aged 15 to 64 has been declining in several advanced economies. In Japan and a few European countries, the change has been even negative in some years. Similarly, Fig. 3.8b reveals that the share of people between 15 and 64 years of age in the population has been following a declining path in all countries considered. As has been outlined in Sect. 3.2.2, a slowdown in population increase

---

natural real interest rate (defined as a short-term real interest rate equating saving and investment at full employment in the medium to long run *once cyclical factors have dissipated*) is assumed to have declined in the aftermath of the crisis.

[40] As argued by Summers (2016b, p. 103), these underlying factors have likely contributed to the financial crisis. The crisis of 2008–2009 must therefore be considered an endogenous event which, in part, resulted from a growing imbalance between ex-ante saving and investment Summers 2016c. With reference to the Great Depression in the 1930s, Backhouse and Boianovsky (2016, p. 951) similarly mentioned, "The immediate origins of the crisis might be short-term, but its severity was the result of long-term structural factors."

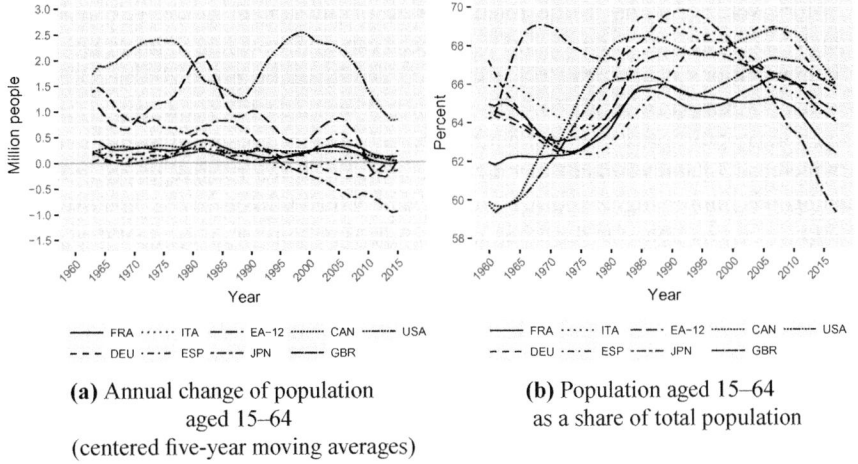

(a) Annual change of population
aged 15–64
(centered five-year moving averages)

(b) Population aged 15–64
as a share of total population

Fig. 3.8 Demographic developments, 1960–2017. *Source* Author's calculations and illustrations, based on data from the European Commission (2018). See Appendix A for detailed data sources and further notes

can impact both planned investment and desired saving through several counteracting channels. Investment may be hampered as there are potentially less new workers to equip with capital goods and because the return on investment may be reduced (Summers 2014c, p. 33; Eichengreen 2015a). The changing composition of the population, with a higher share of retirees, may at the same time exert downward pressure on the overall propensity to save. On the other hand, however, life expectancy has risen during the past decades, while the average retirement age has not increased significantly. Hence, the requirement for appropriate old-age provision has increased, boosting desired saving Summers 2016c. In Germany, this point has been especially emphasized by von Weizsäcker (2011).[41] While it is empirically ambiguous which of the described effects dominates, Carvalho et al. (2016) conclude that during the past decades demographic changes in the G7 countries have likely contributed to a decline in natural real interest rates.

Other factors which might have hampered the propensity to invest include a possible slowdown in technological progress, on which Summers (2014e, p. 69), however, does not express a clear opinion and does not comment any further.

---

[41] The German economist von Weizsäcker (2016, p. 384) describes himself as a secular stagnationist who has pointed to the underlying issues prior to Summers (see von Weizsäcker 2010). In fact, while demographic aspects are at the heart of his analysis, his general position is close to Summers's stagnation theory. Homburg (2015, p. 412), for example, in chronological order speaks of the *Hansen–Weizsäcker–Summers stagnation hypothesis*. Building on the capital theory of Eugen von Böhm-Bawerk, von Weizsäcker (2013) refers to a "provision nightmare." Aging societies, so the argument runs, postpone their time preferences into the future and increase their desired saving for old-age provision, which in turn provokes a decline in the natural interest rate. To increase demand and economic growth, the government should thus increase its debt-financed spending.

Moreover, a decline in the relative price of investment goods is considered, which—according to Moore's Law—has been especially evident in information and communications technology (ICT) (Summers 2014d; Eichengreen 2015a, pp. 67–68; see also Jorgenson 2001, 2005).[42] The impact of such a decline, however, is ambiguous. If the relative price of investment goods falls, but the volume of investment does not increase, total investment spending declines. Yet, lower relative prices of investment goods imply a higher return on investment, which is likely to trigger a rise in the volume of investment. On the other hand, a higher volume of investment diminishes the marginal product of capital, which again has an adverse impact on the return on investment (Thwaites 2015, p. 8). Which of these effects predominates depends on the elasticity of substitution between capital and labor. If it is lower than one, i.e., if capital and labor are not easily substitutable, a lower relative price of capital goods leads to a decline in investment spending and thus contributes to a fall in the natural real interest rate (Rachel and Smith 2015, pp. 42–44). While Blanchard et al. (2014, p. 105) doubt this nexus, Summers (2015a, p. 62) associates a decline in the relative price of capital goods with a decline in the natural interest rate.[43] Similarly, the IMF (2014, pp. 88–89) notes that increases in the volume of investment have not been sufficient to compensate for the decline in relative prices of investment goods in advanced economies (see also Eichengreen 2015a, pp. 67–68).

Another explanation for a lower propensity to invest addresses structural shifts toward less capital-intensive industries. Especially in the ICT sector, companies such as Google, Apple, or Facebook require relatively little real capital investment, putting downward pressure on the overall propensity to invest (Summers 2014e, p. 69; Constâncio 2016).

Additionally, Rachel and Smith (2015, pp. 44–45) refer to the declining trend in public investment, which has hampered total domestic investment demand.

Aside from the abovementioned demographic changes, other long-term factors which have possibly led to an increase in desired saving include the rise in the unequal functional and personal distribution of income that has been documented in Sect. 1.1.2. As those at the top of the income scale generally have a higher propensity to save than those at the bottom, a rise in income inequality tends to increase ex-ante saving (Summers 2014b, p. 45, c, pp. 33–34). The upward trend in corporate retained earnings during the past years has had a similar effect (Summers 2014e, p. 69).

---

[42] Moore's Law goes back to the empirical finding of Gordon E. Moore (1965) that the number of transistors on a computer chip tends to double every two years at constant costs, implying that costs (and prices) per computing power decline. In the past years, however, Moore himself and several economists have been rather skeptical as to whether this "law" is still valid. In an interview, Moore (2015) mentioned, "We won't have the rate of progress that we've had over the last few decades. I think that's inevitable with any technology; it eventually saturates out. I guess I see Moore's Law dying here in the next decade or so, but that's not surprising." See also Gordon (2016, pp. 588–589). It remains to be seen whether advances in nanotechnology and other technological innovations can perpetuate Moore's Law in the decades to come.

[43] As has been widely discussed in economic circles, Piketty (2014, pp. 220–221) in his magnum opus *Capital in the Twenty-First Century* assumes the elasticity of substitution between capital and labor to be larger than one. His assumption, however, has been criticized by various economists, including Rognlie (2014) and Semieniuk (2017).

Speaking of a rise in monopoly power, Summers (2016a) also hints at Steindl's stagnation theory in this context. Monopolistic tendencies, he says, reinforce secular stagnation as "[...] it means more income going to groups that are likely to have a high marginal propensity to save [...] and less investment demand [...]."

Finally, considering open economy aspects, changes in global imbalances as reflected by shifts in current accounts may have fostered the alleged decline in natural real interest rates in some countries. Originally described by Bernanke (2005) as a *global savings glut*, the common line of argument is that in the early and mid-2000s rising current account balances in several emerging market economies and oil-producing countries have contributed to a fall in natural real interest rates in nations with declining current account balances, most notably the United States (Bernanke 2005; Eggertsson et al. 2016). Following the regional financial crisis of 1997, most East Asian countries shifted from running current account deficits to large current account surpluses, indicating an excess of domestic saving over investment (Rachel and Smith 2015, pp. 41–42). Similarly, rising oil prices from the early to mid-2000s led to high savings and increasing current account surpluses across oil-producing countries. These mismatches between national saving and investment, however, could only be realized as other nations, such as the United States, were running equally large and rising current account deficits. Eventually, declining current account balances in the USA and other countries may have contributed to a fall in these nations' natural real interest rates.

Policy Implications

Summers addresses several policy measures which can broadly be grouped into three categories: monetary policy, structural reforms, and expansionary fiscal policy.

Although monetary policy stances have become more restrictive in most recent times, as a legacy of the highly expansionary monetary policies in the years following the financial crisis of 2008–2009, central banks in most advanced countries currently have only little room to intervene when the economic climate deteriorates again. While some economists have proposed higher inflation targets to increase the monetary scope for action, this suggestion is controversial.[44] Although Summers (2015b, p. 30, 2017a, 2018c) has argued in favor of thinking about a change in target inflation, he is more supportive of establishing a target for *nominal* GDP growth, providing a more flexible corridor for inflation (expectations). On the other hand, with short-term nominal interest rates still close to zero percent in some countries, monetary policy measures such as "[...] broader quantitative easing [...]" could be used to further reduce interest rates on longer term and riskier assets (Summers 2015b, p. 31). Trying to reduce market rates by all available means, however, bears several risks. For example, a lower interest rate environment may reduce financial stability by encouraging risk-taking and leverage. Moreover, low interest rates tend to aggravate income and wealth inequality (Summers 2014b, pp. 48–49). As argued by Williams (2016, p. 4), "[t]here are limits to what monetary policy can and, indeed,

---

[44]For example, while Ball (2014) and Krugman (2014) argue in favor of higher inflation targets, Bernanke (2010) and Mishkin (2011) are rather skeptical.

should do. The burden must also fall on fiscal and other policies to do their part [...]."
Similarly, Yellen (2011, p. 11) underlines that "[...] monetary policy is not a panacea, and it is essential for other policymakers to also do their part."

Structural reforms are typically geared toward the supply side of the economy. As pointed out by economists and international economic institutions, however, merely increasing the supply-side potential of the economy is unlikely to foster economic performance in a sustainable way (IMF 2016, pp. 101–121). Raising potential output without boosting aggregate demand could even aggravate the underlying economic problems (Summers 2015a, pp. 63–64). Yet, the supply and demand side of the economy do not operate entirely separate from one another, so certain supply-side reforms may positively affect aggregate demand (and vice versa). The IMF (2016, p. 120–128), for instance, stresses that product market reforms may lead to both higher potential output in the long run and higher aggregate demand in the short run by positively impacting investment. Similarly, Summers (2015d) underlines the importance of tax reforms and lower structural barriers to increase investment, as well as measures that foster innovation, enhance the bargaining power of trade unions, and reduce inequality (Summers 2014b, p. 50, c, p. 38, e, p. 72, 2015d, 2016c).[45]

Finally, expansionary fiscal policy is considered necessary to overcome economic weakness The Economist 2016. With both interest rates and net public investment at historical lows in advanced economies, higher public investment, partly financed by government borrowing, "[...] is potentially the key to restoring reasonable growth" (Summers 2015a, p. 64). While an increase in public spending contributes directly to aggregate demand, especially government spending on productive investment may additionally stimulate private investment—a nexus commonly associated with Aschauer (1988, 1989a, b).

General Perception and Critical Assessment

Summers's demand-side secular stagnation hypothesis has opened a lively debate and provoked various reactions among economists. While, on the one hand, his general approach shows Keynesian traits, on the other hand, the controversial concept of the Wicksellian natural real interest rate plays a crucial role in his analysis, masking the actual core of his hypothesis. In fact, Summers claims that lurking secular stagnation tendencies could be overcome if only short-term nominal market interest rates were not stuck close to zero percent, but—in the years to come—were able to decline further to trace a natural real interest rate which is estimated to remain historically low in the near future. Although he is aware of the risk of financial instability, he seems to be convinced that still lower central bank policy interest rates in times of economic hardship could be essential to boost economic growth by raising the propensity to

---

[45] As rightly outlined by Cochrane (2017), despite his plea for tax reforms that foster investment spending, Summers (2017c) has been surprisingly critical of the recent tax cuts implemented by the US government. In fact, Summers (2017c) defends his critical stance by pointing out that the tax cuts are shortsighted and do not seem to tackle any of the long-term, structural economic issues, such as the unequal distribution of income or the slow productivity growth rate. Moreover, he is afraid that the expected rise in government debt will result in (counterproductive) public spending cuts on infrastructure and social programs.

invest and hampering desired saving. In reality, however, there is not just one, but rather a whole set of different short- and long-term interest rates affecting saving and investment decisions (Hein 2016, pp. 4–5; Constâncio 2016). The response of the whole range of market interest rates to changes in short-term policy rates is therefore relevant. This also includes decisions of banks and other financial institutions on setting both credit standards and interest rates on deposits and loans (Arestis and Sawyer 2002, p. 7).

More important, though, the theory of the natural interest rate implicitly relies on the existence of an investment and a saving function which depend negatively and positively, respectively, on real market interest rates. According to Keynesian theory as well as from an empirical point of view, however, the interest rate elasticities of desired saving and planned investment are ambiguous (Arestis and Sawyer 2002, p. 6). The impact of interest rate changes on the propensity to save may be small and, in fact, can be positive or negative, depending on whether the substitution or income effect predominates (Palley 2016b, p. 29). On the other hand, along Keynesian lines investment demand is influenced by both current market interest rates and the marginal efficiency of capital, reflecting investors' future expectations and their state of confidence (Keynes [1936] 1973, pp. 135–136, 173). While desired saving, real investment, and the level of employment *may* thus change due to variations in interest rates, the precise nexus is far from clear, as there are other, potentially counteracting, factors that need to be considered.[46] From an ex-ante perspective, it is ambiguous whether lower market interest rates are actually capable of raising aggregate demand. As rightly pointed out by Palley (2016a, p. 7), "[e]conomists have forgotten Keynes' message that interest rates may not solve demand shortage." In other words, the investment-saving (IS) and aggregate demand (AD) schedules may be vertical or backward bending in such a way that, ceteris paribus, there may be no natural interest rate capable of restoring full employment (Palley 2016b, pp. 32–34). In case of a backward bending aggregate demand schedule, lower market interest rates could even aggravate the underlying demand weakness (Palley 2016a, p. 9).[47]

It is particularly with regard to the role of interest rates that the stagnation theories of Summers and his twentieth-century predecessor Hansen differ. In contrast to Summers, Hansen paid only little attention to the natural interest rate. In the relevant paragraph, he mentioned:

---

[46] Surprisingly, Summers (2015d) himself mentions that he is "[...] acutely aware of the lack of [...] simply relating the level of investment to the interest rate, and the level of savings to the interest rate."

[47] In this sense, the zero lower bound on short-term nominal interest rates may be even a *stabilizing* factor, as it may prevent aggregate demand weaknesses from deteriorating (Palley 2016b, p. 35).

During a depression the [...] [natural rate of interest] is likely to be a minus quantity. In order to bring about an increased flow of purchasing power, therefore, it would be necessary to establish a minus rate of interest in the money and capital markets. This it is not possible to do. Moreover, the Wicksellian thesis fails to recognize sufficiently the factor of uncertainty in entrepreneurial investment calculations. [...] In our view, the monetary mechanism suggested by Wicksell, directed to stabilize the flow of effective purchasing power, cannot alone accomplish the desired result. At best, monetary measures can only prepare the soil for the growth of new investment. (Hansen 1938, pp. 145–146)

In contrast to Hansen, Summers's strong focus on the natural interest rate overshadows his otherwise Keynesian line of reasoning. One may say, in fact, that his secular stagnation theory could have done without the natural interest rate, as it can be maintained on purely Keynesian grounds. Despite these flaws, however, Summers deserves credit for having brought the demand side of the economy to the fore, which was largely absent from the mainstream economic debate prior to the financial crisis of 2008–2009. In fact, several economists who have joined in the discussion on stagnation support his general line of reasoning. Krugman (2014), for example, is arguing along similar lines as Summers.[48] Eichengreen (2015a, b), though not entirely convinced by Summers's stagnation hypothesis, shares the view that hysteresis effects have caused potential output to decline and that aggregate demand is an important element in stimulating the economy. He therefore suggests governments to invest more in infrastructure, education, and training (Eichengreen 2014, pp. 44–45). Likewise, referring to the issue of balance sheet recessions, Koo (2014) expects economic weakness to remain a latent threat as long as governments fail to provide sufficient stimulus.

Although economic performances across the developed world have picked up pace more recently, a crucial question is whether secular stagnation is still relevant. Is Summers's stagnation hypothesis really plausible, or will it prove empirically invalid as it confuses temporary with secular factors? As argued by most economists, including Summers, it is uncertain whether the developed world will be characterized by weak average economic growth in the years to come.[49] Yet, absent counteracting forces and given that the factors described above tend to boost desired saving while hampering planned investment, secular stagnation tendencies could turn out to be a major problem (Blecker 2016, pp. 211–212). Some economists, though, think of

---

[48] As outlined by Palley (2016b, p. 20), though, Krugman (2014, p. 62) wrongly refers to the current zero lower bound issue as a *liquidity trap*. Hitting the zero lower bound on short-term nominal interest rates, however, does not require a conventional Keynesian liquidity trap. Following Keynes ([1936] 1973, p. 207), a liquidity trap is characterized by a perfectly elastic liquidity preference, i.e., a low demand for bonds and a horizontal liquidity preference–money supply (LM) schedule, implying that the central bank has "[...] lost effective control over the rate of interest." The current situation of very low interest rates, however, is not characterized by such a Keynesian liquidity trap (Taylor 2014b; with reference to Japan in the late twentieth century, see also Palley 2000, pp. 281–282). After all, interest rates across advanced countries have been lowered through extensive quantitative easing programs. See also Lavoie (2018, p. 14).

[49] Summers (2016d) particularly refers to the difficulty of making forecasts based on real-time data. While he admits that he might confuse temporary with long-term issues, he nonetheless assumes secular stagnation to be a plausible phenomenon (Summers 2016b, p. 104).

stagnation as a more temporary phenomenon. In contrast to Summers, who mainly reinforces his hypothesis based on a series of long-term factors, those who consider stagnation a transient phenomenon focus on temporary forces as the root causes of weak economic advance. Referring to the empirical research by Reinhart and Rogoff (2011), Rogoff (2015) and Lo and Rogoff (2015) point out that slow recoveries after severe financial crises are fairly common by historical standards. The sluggish economic performances in major advanced economies therefore fit the overall pattern of past recessions (Lo and Rogoff 2015, p. 2)—a view which, however, is not shared by economists such as Taylor (2014a, pp. 60–63) and Blecker (2016, p. 204). According to Lo and Rogoff (2015), once debt-supercycles—i.e., high debt overhangs and deleveraging—are over, advanced economies are likely to regain momentum on a sustained basis in the upcoming years.[50]

In emphasizing his global savings glut hypothesis, Bernanke (2015a, b) also paints a rather optimistic picture, especially for the United States and other countries running current account deficits. Current account surpluses of emerging market economies, he notes, have been declining for several years. While these changes have been partially offset by a positive and rising current account balance of the euro area as a whole, he assumes this trend to reverse once the economies in the European periphery grow more strongly again.

Most of the hypotheses which consider stagnation a transient phenomenon are not necessarily alternatives to Summers's approach, but they can coexist. In fact, Summers *does* consider deleveraging and other factors related to the financial crisis of 2008–2009 relevant. Moreover, he also refers to the global savings glut hypothesis and agrees with Bernanke that global imbalances with regard to emerging market economies have started to dissipate (Summers 2016b, pp. 105–106, c). Secular stagnation does not mean that temporary factors play no role at all. In reaction to the relatively good economic performances in several advanced countries during most recent years, in the spring of 2017—three and a half years after his initial speech at the IMF—Summers's (2017b) aptly noted:

> Nobody ever said that the economy was always going to be permanently in a state of deflation. If you go back to Alvin Hansen [...], he talked about weak recovery. So here we are. We've managed to get to 2% growth [in the United States], not much inflation pressure, 4% unemployment and in order to be there, we've got a fed-funds rate of eight years into a recovery of 1%. I read that as, on net, something substantial has happened relative to what anybody expected rather than nothing important happened.

It cannot be denied that various advanced countries, among them the United States, have performed comparatively well in most recent years. The Federal Reserve Bank has increased its target policy rate several times since December 2015 (Board of Governors of the Federal Reserve System 2018) and—as pointed out by Palley (2015,

---

[50]Lo and Rogoff's (2015) debt-supercycle hypothesis is similar to Koo's (2014) balance sheet recession approach. Koo's (2014) hypothesis, however, seems to be more long-run in nature, as he assumes long-term consequences for aggregate demand even after deleveraging is over. Moreover, Lo and Rogoff (2015) are much more skeptical of higher government spending, as it may result in unsustainable public debt-to-GDP ratios.

pp. 6–7), Rogoff (2015), and Summers (2015e)—deleveraging in the United States is largely over.[51] Similarly, individual European countries, such as Germany, have done reasonably well during the past years. Yet, overall growth prospects, particularly across the developed world, are characterized by high uncertainty, resting on unsound footing and remaining weak (OECD 2016; Jorgenson and Vu 2017, pp. 669–670; World Bank 2018, pp. 8–14). The main point is that aside from temporary factors a series of adverse long-term developments has been underway. These fundamental factors have not been eliminated by the financial crisis and continue to have an impact. Hence, if counteracting forces do not evolve, a general tendency toward secular stagnation may prove to be a relevant issue in the years to come. As The Economist (2018, pp. 3, 4) notes, the "[...] world is woefully unprepared [for a new recession] [...]." Particularly "[...] the rich world is ill-equipped to manage such stress [...]." Summers (2017b; 2018a, 2018b) has thus been right to hold on to his secular stagnation hypothesis in more recent times and to defend it against several critics, including Stiglitz (2018).[52] Although Summers's stagnation approach has its flaws—particularly with regard to his emphasis on the natural real interest rate—his general line of argument is reasonable.

Summers's hypothesis is all the more important, in fact, as the demand side of the economy has not only been neglected in mainstream economics prior to the financial crisis of 2008–2009, but—with output gaps assumed to currently be more or less closed in most developed countries—is at risk of fading into the background again. Yet, although he reminds of the importance of the demand side of the economy, he does not deny that there are also weaknesses on the supply side (Summers 2018a, p. 246). While Robert J. Gordon's supply-side stagnation theory is Summers's main counterpart in the current debate, supply-side stagnation approaches are not confined to Gordon, but—as the following chapter (Chap. 4) shows—have a much longer tradition in the history of economic thought.

References

Abramovitz M (1986) Catching up, forging ahead, and falling behind. J Econ History 46(2):385–406
Adler HA (1945) Absolute or relative rate of decline in population growth? Q J Econ 59(4):626–634
Arbeitsgruppe Alternative Wirtschaftspolitik (1978) Memorandum: Alternativen der Wirtschaftspolitik. Bund-Verlag, Cologne
Arbeitsgruppe Alternative Wirtschaftspolitik (1979) Memorandum: Vorrang für Vollbeschäftigung — Alternativen der Wirtschaftspolitik. Pahl-Rugenstein Verlag, Cologne
Arestis P, Sawyer M (2002) "New Consensus", New Keynesianism, and the economics of the "Third Way". Levy Economics Institute Working Paper No. 364. Levy Economics Institute of Bard

---

[51] As outlined by Palley (2015, pp. 6–7) and Gros (2014), a considerable part of private US household debt was extinguished by defaults and foreclosures. Due to more bureaucratic bankruptcy procedures, debt burdens in the euro area could not be reduced in a similar manner.

[52] As rightly pointed out by Summers (2018b), Stiglitz (2018), though criticizing his secular stagnation hypothesis, unknowingly endorses secular stagnation.

College, Annandale-on-Hudson, NY. http://www.levyinstitute.org/pubs/wp_364.pdf. Accessed 10 Sept 2016

Arestis P, Sawyer M (2008) The new consensus macroeconomics: an unreliable guide for policy. Revista Análise Econômica 26(50):275–297

Arestis P, Biefang-Frisancho Mariscal I, Hagemann H (1998) Capital shortage unemployment in Germany and the UK. Schriftenreihe des Promotionsschwerpunkts Makroökonomische Diagnosen und Therapien der Arbeitslosigkeit No. 3/1998. Evangelisches Studienwerk e. V., Universität Hohenheim, and Universität Witten/Herdecke. https://ideas.repec.org/p/zbw/hohpro/y1998i03p1-13.html. Accessed 10 May 2018

Arnoff D (2016) A theory of accumulation and secular stagnation: a Malthusian approach to understanding a contemporary malaise. Palgrave Macmillan, Basingstoke and New York, NY

Aschauer DA (1988) Is government spending stimulative? Federal Reserve Bank of Chicago Staff Memoranda SM 88-3. Federal Reserve Bank of Chicago, Chicago, IL. https://fraser.stlouisfed.org/files/docs/historical/frbchi/workingpapers/frbchi_workingpaper_1988-03.pdf. Accessed 28 Sept 2016

Aschauer DA (1989a) Does public capital crowd out private capital? J Monet Econ 24(2):171–188

Aschauer DA (1989b) Is public expenditure productive? J Monet Econ 23(2):177–200

Assous M, Dal Pont Legrand M, Hagemann H (2016) Business cycles and growth. In: Faccarello G, Kurz HD (eds) Handbook on the history of economic analysis, vol II. Developments in major fields of economics. Edward Elgar, Cheltenham, UK and Northampton, MA, USA, pp 27–39

Autor D, Dorn D, Katz LF, Patterson C, Van Reenen J (2017) Concentrating on the fall of the labor share. Am Econ Rev 107(5):180–185

Backhouse RE, Boianovsky M (2016) Secular stagnation: the history of a macroeconomic heresy. Eur J History Econ Thought 23(6):946–970

Ball L (2014) The case for a long-run inflation target of four percent. IMF Working Paper WP/14/92. International Monetary Fund, Washington, DC. https://www.imf.org/external/pubs/ft/wp/2014/wp1492.pdf. Accessed 04 Sept 2016

Baran PA, Sweezy PM (1966) Monopoly capital: an essay on the American economic and social order. Monthly Review Press, New York, NY

Bean C, Broda C, Ito T, Kroszner R (2015) Low for long? causes and consequences of persistently low interest rates. International Center for Monetary and Banking Studies (ICMB) and Centre for Economic Policy Research (CEPR), Geneva Reports on the World Economy 17, Geneva and London

Bernanke BS (2005) The global saving glut and the U.S. current account deficit. Remarks at the Sandridge Lecture. Virginia Association of Economists, Richmond, VA. http://www.federalreserve.gov/boardDocs/Speeches/2005/200503102/default.htm. Accessed 13 Sept 2016

Bernanke BS (2010) The economic outlook and monetary policy. Speech at the Federal Reserve Bank of Kansas City Economic Symposium, Jackson Hole, WY. https://www.federalreserve.gov/newsevents/speech/bernanke20100827a.htm. Accessed 04 Sept 2016

Bernanke BS (2015a) Why are interest rates so low, part 2: secular stagnation. The Brookings Institution Blog. March 31, 2015. The Brookings Institution, Washington, DC. https://www.brookings.edu/blog/ben-bernanke/2015/03/31/why-are-interest-rates-so-low-part-2-secular-stagnation/. Accessed 13 Sept 2016

Bernanke BS (2015b) Why are interest rates so low, part 3: the global savings glut. The Brookings Institution Blog. April 01, 2015. The Brookings Institution, Washington, DC. https://www.brookings.edu/blog/ben-bernanke/2015/04/01/why-are-interest-rates-so-low-part-3-the-global-savings-glut/. Accessed 13 Sept 2016

Bernanke BS (2015c) Why are interest rates so low, part 4: term premiums. The Brookings Institution Blog. April 13, 2015. The Brookings Institution, Washington, DC. https://www.brookings.edu/blog/ben-bernanke/2015/04/13/why-are-interest-rates-so-low-part-4-term-premiums/. Accessed 14 Sept 2016

Bernanke BS (2015d) Why are interest rates so low? The Brookings Institution Blog. March 30, 2015. The Brookings Institution, Washington, DC. https://www.brookings.edu/blog/ben-bernanke/2015/03/30/why-are-interest-rates-so-low/. Accessed 14 Sept 2016

Blanchard OJ, Furceri D, Pescatori A (2014) A prolonged period of low real interest rates? In: Teulings C, Baldwin R (eds) Secular stagnation: facts causes and cures. CEPR Press, London, pp 101–110

Bleaney MF (1976) Underconsumption theories. A history and critical analysis. International Publishers, New York, NY

Blecker RA (2016) The US economy since the crisis: slow recovery and secular stagnation. Eur J Econ Econ Policies Interv 13(2):203–214

Board of Governors of the Federal Reserve System (2018) Monetary policy. Policy implementations. Policy tools. Open market operations. Board of Governors of the Federal Reserve System, Washington, DC. https://www.federalreserve.gov/monetarypolicy/openmarket.htm. Accessed 21 Nov 2018

Borio C, Disyatat P (2011) Global imbalances and the financial crisis: link or no link? Bank for International Settlements Working Paper No. 346. Bank for International Settlements, Basel. http://www.bis.org/publ/work346.pdf. Accessed 09 Oct 2016

Brazelton WR (1993) Alvin Harvey Hansen: a note on his analysis of Keynes, Hayek, and Commons. J Econ Issues 27(3):940–948

Brown AJ (1955) Review of maturity and stagnation in American capitalism by J. Steindl. Int Aff 31(1):129–130

Burns ME, Mitchell WF (1985) Real wages, unemployment and economic policy in Australia. Australian Economic Papers June 1985, pp 1–23

Caballero RJ, Farhi E (2014) On the role of safe asset shortages in secular stagnation. In: Teulings C, Baldwin R (eds) Secular stagnation: facts, causes and cures. CEPR Press, London, pp 111–120

Carvalho C, Ferrero A, Nechio F (2016) Demographics and real interest rates: inspecting the mechanism. Federal Reserve Bank of San Francisco Working Paper 2016-05. Federal Reserve Bank of San Francisco, San Francisco, CA. http://www.frbsf.org/economic-research/files/wp2016-05.pdf. Accessed 14 Sept 2016

Christian-Albrechts-Universität zu Kiel (2017) August Lösch – Curriculum Vitae. August Lösch (1906–1945). Christian-Albrechts-Universität zu Kiel, Kiel. https://www.ifr.uni-kiel.de/de/alp. Accessed 14 June 2017

Clarke P (1987) Hobson, John Atkinson. In: Eatwell J, Milgate M, Newman P (eds) The New Palgrave Dictionary of Economics, vol 2. Macmillan, London, pp 664–666

Clauß FJ (1968) Konjunktur und Neoklassik: Sparen und Investieren, öffentliche Haushalte und wirtschaftliches Wachstum in der konjunkturbewegten Volkswirtschaft (USA 1929–1967). Duncker & Humblot, Berlin and Munich

Cochrane J (2017) Economists as public intellectuals. The grumpy economist: John Cochrane's blog, December 28, 2017. https://johnhcochrane.blogspot.com/2017/12/economists-as-public-intellectuals.html. Accessed 20 Nov 2018

Cœuré B (2018) Scars that never were? Potential output and slack after the crisis. In: Speech at the CEPII 40th Anniversary Conference, Paris, April 12, 2018. European Central Bank, Frankfurt am Main. https://www.ecb.europa.eu/press/key/date/2018/html/ecb.sp180412.en.html. Accessed 07 Dec 2018

Congressional Budget Office (2014) Revisions to CBO's projection of potential output since 2007. Congressional Budget Office, Washington, DC. https://www.cbo.gov/sites/default/files/113th-congress-2013-2014/reports/45150-PotentialOutput.pdf. Accessed 29 Aug 2016

Constâncio V (2016) The challenge of low real interest rates for monetary policy. Lecture at the Macroeconomics Symposium at Utrecht School of Economics, June 15, 2016. European Central Bank, Frankfurt am Main. https://www.ecb.europa.eu/press/key/date/2016/html/sp160615.en.html. Accessed 30 Aug 2016

Cornwall J (1972) Growth and stability in a mature economy. Wiley, New York, NY

Cowling K (2005) Monopoly capitalism and stagnation. In: Mott T, Shapiro N (eds) Rethinking capitalist development: essays on the economics of Josef Steindl. Routledge, New York, NY, pp 147–163

Cynamon BZ, Fazzari SM (2014) Inequality, the Great Recession, and slow recovery. June 23, 2014. http://papers.ssrn.com/sol3/papers.cfm?abstract_id=2205524. Accessed 29 Jan 2016

Dal Degan F, Eyguesier N (2016) Jean-Charles Léonard Simonde de Sismondi (1773–1842). In: Faccarello G, Kurz HD (eds) Handbook on the history of economic analysis, vol I. Great economists since Petty and Boisguilbert. Edward Elgar, Cheltenham, UK and Northhampton, MA, USA, pp 144–147

Dal Pont Legrand M, Hagemann H (2016) Business cycles, growth, and economic policy: Schumpeter and the Great Depression. J History Econ Thought 39(1):19–33

Dal Pont Legrand M, Hagemann H (2017) Retrospectives: do productive recessions show the recuperative powers of capitalism? Schumpeter's analysis of the cleansing effect. J Econ Perspect 31(1):245–256

Díez FJ, Leigh D, Tambunlertchai S (2018) Global market power and its macroeconomic implications. IMF Working Paper WP/18/137. International Monetary Fund, Washington, DC. https://www.imf.org/~/media/Files/Publications/WP/2018/wp18137. Accessed 20 Sept 2018

Dockès P (2015) Les débats sur la stagnation séculaire dans les années 1937–1950: Hansen-Terborgh et Schumpeter-Sweezy. Revue Économique 66(5):967–992

Domar ED (1947) Expansion and employment. Am Econ Rev 37(1):34–55

Douglas PH (1930) Technological unemployment. Am Fed 37(August):923–950

Dutt AK (2005) Steindl's theory of maturity and stagnation and its relevance today. In: Mott T, Shapiro N (eds) Rethinking capitalist development: essays on the economics of Josef Steindl. Routledge, New York, NY, pp 55–78

Eggertsson GB, Mehrotra NR, Singh SR, Summers LH (2016) A contagious malady? Open economy dimensions of secular stagnation. NBER Working Paper No. 22299. National Bureau of Economic Research, Cambridge, MA. http://www.nber.org/papers/w22299.pdf. Accessed 14 Sept 2016

Eichengreen B (2014) Secular stagnation: a review of the issues. In: Teulings C, Baldwin R (eds) Secular stagnation: facts, causes and cures. CEPR Press, London, pp 41–46

Eichengreen B (2015a) Secular stagnation: the long view. Am Econ Rev 105(5):66–70

Eichengreen B (2015b) Wall of worries: reflections on the secular stagnation debate. Institute for Monetary and Economic Studies of the Bank of Japan, Discussion Paper No. 2015-E-5. Bank of Japan, Tokyo. http://www.imes.boj.or.jp/research/papers/english/15-E-05.pdf. Accessed 13 Sept 2016

Erber G, Hagemann H, Seiter S (1998) Zukunftsperspektiven Deutschlands im internationalen Wettbewerb: Industriepolitische Implikationen der Neuen Wachstumstheorie. Physica-Verlag, Heidelberg

European Central Bank (2015) ECB Annual Report 2015. European Central Bank, Frankfurt am Main. https://www.ecb.europa.eu/pub/pdf/annrep/ar2015en.pdf. Accessed 08 Oct 2016

European Central Bank (2018) ECB statistical data warehouse. European Central Bank, Frankfurt am Main. http://sdw.ecb.europa.eu/. Last accessed 04 Dec 2018

European Commission (2018) Annual macro-economic database of the European Commission's Directorate General for Economic and Financial Affairs (AMECO database). European Commission, Brussels. http://ec.europa.eu/economy_finance/ameco/user/serie/SelectSerie.cfm. Accessed 26 Nov 2018. (Data as of 08 Nov 2018)

Fatás A, Summers LH (2016) The permanent effects of fiscal consolidations. NBER Working Paper No. 22374. National Bureau of Economic Research, Cambridge, MA. http://www.nber.org/papers/w22374.pdf. Accessed 29 Aug 2016

Federal Reserve Bank of St Louis (2018) FRED economic data. Federal Reserve Bank of St. Louis, St. Louis, MO. https://fred.stlouisfed.org/. Accessed 04 Dec 2018

Fellner W (1954) Full use or underutilization: appraisal of long-run factors other than defense. Am Econ Rev 44(2):423–433

Foster JB (2014) The theory of monopoly capitalism. Monthly Review Press, New York, NY

Foster JB, McChesney RW (2012) The endless crisis: how monopoly-finance capital produces stagnation and upheaval from the USA to China. Monthly Review Press, New York, NY

Frank RH (2008) Context is more important than Keynes realized. In: Pecchi L, Piga G (eds) Revisiting Keynes: economic possibilities for our grandchildren. The MIT Press, Cambridge, MA, pp 143–150

Freeman RB (2008) Why do we work more than Keynes expected? In: Pecchi L, Piga G (eds) Revisiting Keynes: economic possibilities for our grandchildren. The MIT Press, Cambridge, MA, pp 135–142

Furman J (2016) Demand and supply: learning from the United States and Japan. Council of economic advisers. In: ESRI international conference 2016, Tokyo, Japan. August 2, 2016. https://obamawhitehouse.archives.gov/sites/default/files/page/files/20160802_furman_esri_cea_0.pdf. Accessed 19 Nov 2018

Garnier J (2005) The natural real interest rate and the output gap in the euro area: A joint estimation. European Central Bank Working Paper No. 541. European Central Bank, Frankfurt am Main. https://www.ecb.europa.eu/pub/pdf/scpwps/ecbwp546.pdf?138eb74fc52db27cba6436b610546441. Accessed 14 Sept 2016

Gerlach S, Moretti L (2014) Monetary policy and TIPS yields before the crisis. BE J Macroecon 14(1):689–701

Godley W (1999) Seven unsustainable processes. Medium-term prospects and policies for the United States and the world. Special Report. The Jerome Levy Economics Institute of Bard College, New York, NY. http://www.levyinstitute.org/pubs/sevenproc.pdf. Accessed 25 Aug 2016

Gordon RA (1961) Business fluctuations, 2nd edn. Harper & Row Publishers, New York, NY, Evanston, IL, and London

Gordon RJ (2016) The rise and fall of American growth. The U.S. standard of living since the Civil War. Princeton University Press, Princeton, NJ

Gourvitch A (1966) Survey of economic theory on technological change & employment. Augustus M. Kelley, New York, NY

Gros D (2014) Why has the US recovered more quickly than Europe? World Economic Forum. https://www.weforum.org/agenda/2014/07/us-economic-recovery-faster-than-europe/. Accessed 13 Sept 2016

Haberler G (1932) Some remarks on Professor Hansen's view on technological unemployment. Q J Econ 46(3):558–562

Haberler G ([1937] 1946) Prosperity and depression: a theoretical analysis of cyclical movements. United Nations, Lake Success, NY

Hagemann H (2011) Keynes 3.0: Zu den ökonomischen Möglichkeiten unserer Enkelkinder. In: Hagemann H, Krämer H (eds) Ökonomie und Gesellschaft. Jahrbuch 23: Keynes 2.0 – Perspektiven einer modernen keynesianischen Wirtschaftstheorie und Wirtschaftspolitik. Metropolis-Verlag, Marburg, pp 281–304

Hagemann H (2013) Steindl. In: Historische Kommission bei der Bayerischen Akademie der Wissenschaften (ed) Neue Deutsche Biographie, vol 25, Duncker & Humblot, Berlin, pp 172–173

Hagemann H (2015) General glut. In: Kurz HD, Salvadori N (eds) The Elgar companion to David Ricardo. Edward Elgar, Cheltenham and Northampton, MA, pp 160–170

Hagemann H, Kurz HD (1997) Say's law. In: Glasner D (ed) Business cycles and depressions: an encyclopedia. Routledge, New York, NY, pp 599–602

Hahn LA (1955) Wirtschaftswissenschaft des gesunden Menschenverstandes. Fritz Knapp Verlag, Frankfurt am Main

Hamberg D (1954) Review of maturity and stagnation in American capitalism by J. Steindl. Am Econ Rev 44(3):414–418

Hamilton JD, Harris ES, Hatzius J, West KD (2016) The equilibrium real funds rate: past, present and future. Working Paper. February 27, 2015. Last revised May 11, 2016. University of California San Diego, San Diego, CA. http://econweb.ucsd.edu/~jhamilto/USMPF_2015.pdf. Accessed 14 Sept 2016

Hansen AH (1931) Institutional frictions and technological unemployment. Q J Econ 45(4):684–697

Hansen AH (1932a) Some remarks on Professor Hansen's view on technological unemployment: a rejoiner to Gottfried Haberler. Q J Econ 46(3):562–565

Hansen AH (1932b) The theory of technological progress and the dislocation of employment. Am Econ Rev 22(1):25–31

Hansen AH (1934) Capital goods and the restoration of purchasing power. Proc Acad Polit Sci 16(1):11–19

Hansen AH (1936) Mr. Keynes on underemployment equilibrium. J Polit Econ 44(5):667–686

Hansen AH (1937) Review of Bevölkerungswellen und Wechsellagen by August Lösch. J Am Stat Assoc 32(199):601–602

Hansen AH (1938) Full Recovery or stagnation? W. W. Norton & Company, Inc., New York, NY

Hansen AH (1939) Economic progress and declining population growth. Am Econ Rev 29(1):1–15

Hansen AH (1940a) Extensive expansion and population growth. J Polit Econ 48(4):583–585

Hansen AH (1940b) Testimony of Alvin Harvey Hansen, Professor of Political Economy, Harvard University, Cambridge, Mass. In: Temporary National Economic Committee (ed) Investigation of concentration of economic power. Hearings before the Temporary National Economic Committee Congress of the United States. Part 9: savings and investment, United States Government Printing Office, Washington, DC, pp 3495–3520, 3538–3559, 3837–3859

Hansen AH (1941) Fiscal policy and business cycles. W. W. Norton & Company, Inc., New York, NY

Hansen AH (1946a) Keynes and the general theory. Rev Econ Stat 28(4):182–187

Hansen AH (1946b) Some notes on Terborgh's "The Bogey of Economic Maturity". Rev Econ Stat 28(1):13–17

Hansen AH (1947) Economic policy and full employment. McGraw-Hill Book Company, Inc., New York, NY, and London

Hansen AH (1951) Business cycles and national income. W. W. Norton & Company, Inc., New York, NY

Hansen AH (1953) A guide to Keynes. McGraw-Hill Book Company, Inc., New York, NY

Hansen AH (1954) Growth or stagnation in the American economy. Rev Econ Stat 36(4):409–414

Hansen AH (1955) The stagnation thesis. In: Smithies A, Butters JK (eds) Readings in fiscal policy. George Allen and Unwin Ltd., London, pp 540–557

Hansen AH (1966) Stagnation and under-employment equilibrium. Rostra Economica Amstelodamensia 15 (Nov 1966), pp 7–9

Harrod RF (1939) An essay in dynamic theory. Econ J 49(139):14–33

Hay C (2009) The winter of discontent thirty years on. Polit Q 80(4):545–552

Hein E (2014) Distribution and growth after Keynes: a post-Keynesian guide. Edward Elgar, Cheltenham and Northampton, MA

Hein E (2016) Secular stagnation or stagnation policy? Steindl after Summers. PSL Q Rev 69(276):3–47

Hetzel RL (2009) Monetary policy in the 2008–2009 recession. Econ Q 95(2):201–233

Higgins B (1946) The doctrine of economic maturity. Am Econ Rev 36(1):133–141

Higgins B (1959) Economic development: principles, problems, and policies. W. W. Norton & Company, Inc., New York, NY

Higgins B (1998) Employment without inflation. Transaction Publishers, New Brunswick, NJ, and London

Hobson JA (1902) Imperialism: a study. James Pott & Company, New York, NY

Hobson JA (1909) The industrial system: an inquiry into earned and unearned income. Longmans, Green, and Co., New York, NY, Bombay, and Calcutta

Hobson JA (1911) The science of wealth. Williams & Norgate, London

Hobson JA (1922) The economics of unemployment. George Allen & Unwin Ltd., London

Hofmann W (1959) Die Lehre von der "Mature Economy": Gibt es ein tendenzielles Sinken der Zuwachsrate des Sozialproduktes? Zeitschrift für die gesamte Staatswissenschaft/J Inst Theor Econ 115(1):24–39

Holston K, Laubach T (2016) Measuring the natural rate of interest: international trends and determinants. Federal Reserve Bank of San Francisco Working Paper 2016-11. Federal Reserve Bank
of San Francisco, San Francisco, CA. http://www.frbsf.org/economic-research/files/wp2016-11.
pdf. Accessed 09 Oct 2016

Homburg S (2015) Overaccumulation, public debt and the importance of land. Ger Econ Rev
15(4):411–435

Ihrig J, Kamin SB, Lindner D, Marquez J (2007) Some simple tests of the globalization and inflation
hypothesis. International Finance Discussion Paper No. 891, April 2007. Board of Governors of
the Federal Reserve System, Washington, DC. https://www.federalreserve.gov/pubs/ifdp/2007/
891/ifdp891.pdf. Accessed 01 Nov 2016

IMF (2014) Recovery strengthens, remains uneven. World economic outlook, April 2014. International Monetary Fund, Washington, DC. http://www.imf.org/external/pubs/ft/weo/2014/01/pdf/
text.pdf. Accessed 02 Sept 2016

IMF (2016) Too slow for too long. World economic outlook, April 2016. International Monetary Fund, Washington, DC. https://www.imf.org/external/pubs/ft/weo/2016/01/pdf/text.pdf.
Accessed 04 Sept 2016

IMF (2018) Challenges to steady growth. World economic outlook, October 2018. International
Monetary Fund, Washington, DC. https://www.imf.org/en/Publications/WEO/Issues/2018/09/
24/world-economic-outlook-october-2018. Accessed 07 Dec 2018

Jorgenson DW (2001) Information technology and the U.S. economy. Am Econ Rev 91(1):1–32

Jorgenson DW (2005) Moore's law and the emergence of the new economy. In: Semiconductor
Industry Association (ed) Semiconductor Industry Association, Annual Report 2005: 2020 Is
Closer than You Think, Semiconductor Industry Association, San José, CA, pp 17–20

Jorgenson DW, Vu KM (2017) The outlook for advanced economies. J Policy Model 39(4):660–672

Kaldor N (1955/1956) Alternative theories of distribution. Rev Econ Stud 23(2):83–100

Kalecki M ([1932] 1990) Reduction of wages during crisis. In: Osiatyński J (ed) Collected works
of Michał Kalecki, vol I. Capitalism: business cycles and full employment. Clarendon Press,
Oxford, pp 41–44

Kalecki M ([1933] 1971) Outline of a theory of the business cycle. In: Kalecki M (ed) Selected
essays on the dynamics of the capitalist economy. Cambridge University Press, New York, NY,
pp 1–14

Kalecki M ([1934] 1971) On foreign trade and 'domestic exports'. In: Kalecki M (ed) Selected
essays on the dynamics of the capitalist economy. Cambridge University Press, New York, NY,
pp 15–25

Kalecki M ([1935] 1971) The mechanism of the business upswing. In: Kalecki M (ed) Selected
essays on the dynamics of the capitalist economy. Cambridge University Press, New York, NY,
pp 26–34

Kalecki M ([1936] 1990) Some remarks on Keynes's theory. In: Osiatyński J (ed) Collected works
of Michał Kalecki, vol I. Capitalism: business cycles and full employment. Clarendon Press,
Oxford, pp 223–232

Kalecki M (1939) Essays in the theory of economic fluctuations. George Allen & Unwin Ltd.,
London

Kalecki M (1943) Political aspects of full employment. Polit Q 14(4):322–331

Kalecki M (1944) Three ways to full employment. In: The Oxford University Institute of Statistics
(ed) The economics of full employment, Basil Blackwell, Oxford, pp 39–58

Kalecki M ([1954] 1965) Theory of economic dynamics. An essay on cyclical and long-run changes
in capitalist economy. Modern Reader Paperbacks, New York, NY, and London

Kalecki M (1962) Observations on the theory of growth. Econ J 72(285):134–153

Kalecki M ([1968] 1971) Trend and the business cycle. In: Kalecki M (ed) Selected essays on the
dynamics of the capitalist economy. Cambridge University Press, New York, NY, pp 165–183

Kalecki M (1971) Selected essays on the dynamics of the capitalist economy. Cambridge University
Press, New York, NY

Keynes JM ([1919] 1971) The economic consequences of the peace. In: The collected writings of John Maynard Keynes, vol II: the economic consequences of the peace. Macmillan St. Martin's Press for the Royal Economiy Society, London and Basingstoke

Keynes JM ([1923] 1971) A tract on monetary reform. In: The collected writings of John Maynard Keynes, vol IV: a tract on monetary reform. Macmillan St. Martin's Press for the Royal Economiy Society, London and Basingstoke

Keynes JM ([1930] 1971) A treatise on money. In: The collected writings of John Maynard Keynes, vol V: a treatise on money in two volumes (vol I: the pure theory of money). Macmillan and Cambridge University Press for the Royal Economic Society, London, Basingstoke, and New York, NY

Keynes JM ([1930] 1972) Economic possibilities for our grandchildren. In: The collected writings of John Maynard Keynes, vol IX: essays in persuasion. Macmillan St. Martin's Press for the Royal Economiy Society, London and Basingstoke, pp 321–332

Keynes JM ([1933a] 1972) The means to prosperity. In: The collected writings of John Maynard Keynes, vol IX: essays in persuasion. Macmillan St. Martin's Press for the Royal Economic Society, London and Basingstoke, pp 335–366

Keynes JM ([1933b] 1972) Thomas Robert Malthus. In: The collected writings of John Maynard Keynes, vol X: essays in biography. Macmillan St. Martin's Press for the Royal Economic Society, London and Basingstoke, pp 71–108

Keynes JM ([1936] 1973) The general theory of employment, interest and money. In: The collected writings of John Maynard Keynes, vol VII: the general theory of employment, interest and money. Macmillan and Cambridge University Press for the Royal Economic Society, London, Basingstoke, and New York, NY, pp xxi–384

Keynes JM ([1937] 1973) Some economic consequences of a declining population. In: Moggridge D (ed) The collected writings of John Maynard Keynes, vol XIV: the general theory and after (part II: defence and development). Macmillan St. Martin's Press for the Royal Economic Society, London and Basingstoke, pp 124–133

Keynes JM ([1943a] 1980) Letter to Sir Wilfried Eady and others (9 July 1943) In: Moggridge D (ed) The collected writings of John Maynard Keynes, vol XXVII: activities 1940–1946. Shaping the post-war world: employment and commodities, Macmillan and Cambridge University Press for the Royal Economic Society, London, Basingstoke, and New York, NY, pp 359–361

Keynes JM ([1943b] 1980) The long-term problem of full employment. In: Moggridge D (ed) The collected writings of John Maynard Keynes, vol XXVII: activities 1940–1946. Shaping the post-war world: employment and commodities. Macmillan and Cambridge University Press for the Royal Economic Society, London, Basingstoke, and New York, NY, pp 320–325

Keynes JM ([1944] 1980) Letter to M. Kalecki (30 December 1944) In: Moggridge D (ed) The collected writings of John Maynard Keynes, vol XXVII: activities 1940–1946. Shaping the post-war world: employment and commodities. Macmillan and Cambridge University Press, London, Basingstoke, and New York, NY, pp 381–383

Knowles JW, Warden CB Jr (1960) The potential economic growth in the United States. United States Government Printing Office, Washington, DC

Koo RC (2014) Balance sheet recession is the reason for secular stagnation. In: Teulings C, Baldwin R (eds) Secular stagnation: facts, causes and cures. CEPR Press, London, pp 131–142

Krugman P (2014) Four observations on secular stagnation. In: Teulings C, Baldwin R (eds) Secular stagnation: facts, causes and cures. CEPR Press, London, pp 61–68

Kurz HD (2010) On the dismal state of a dismal science? Homo Oeconomicus 27(3):369–389

Lange O (1939) Is the American economy contracting? Am Econ Rev 29(3):503–513

Lansing KJ (2016) Projecting the long-run natural rate of interest. Federal Reserve Bank of San Francisco Economic Letter 2016-25. August 29, 2016. Federal Reserve Bank of San Francisco, San Francisco, CA. http://www.frbsf.org/economic-research/files/el2016-25.pdf. Accessed 10 Oct 2016

Laski K (1987a) Kalecki, Michal. In: Eatwell J, Milgate M, Newman P (eds) The New Palgrave Dictionary of Economics, vol 3. Macmillan, London, pp 8–14

Laski K (1987b) Steindl, Josef. In: Eatwell J, Milgate M, Newman P (eds) The New Palgrave Dictionary of Economics, vol 4. Macmillan, London, p 494

Laubach T, Williams JC (2003) Measuring the natural rate of interest. Rev Econ Stat 85(4):1063–1070

Laubach T, Williams JC (2015) Measuring the natural rate of interest redux. Federal Reserve Bank of San Francisco Working Paper 2015-16. Federal Reserve Bank of San Francisco, San Francisco, CA. http://www.frbsf.org/economic-research/files/wp2015-16.pdf. Accessed 23 Aug 2016

Laubach T, Williams JC (2018) Measuring the natural rate of interest: spreadsheet of updated estimates. Federal Reserve Bank of San Francisco, San Francisco, CA. https://www.frbsf.org/economic-research/files/Laubach_Williams_updated_estimates.xlsx. Data as of 30 May 2018. Accessed 19 Nov 2018

Lavoie M (2014) Post-Keynesian economics: new foundations. Edward Elgar, Cheltenham and Northampton, MA

Lavoie M (2018) Rethinking macroeconomic theory before the next crisis. Rev Keynes Econ 6(1):1–21

Leijonhufvud A (1968) On Keynesian economics and the economics of Keynes: a study in monetary theory. Oxford University Press, New York, NY

Leijonhufvud A (1981) The Wicksell connection: variations on a theme. In: Leijonhufvud A (ed) Information and coordination: essays in macroeconomic theory. Oxford University Press, New York, NY, and Oxford, pp 131–202

Lindner F (2012) Saving does not finance investment: accounting as an indispensable guide to economic theory. IMK Working Paper No. 100-2012. Macroeconomic Policy Institute (IMK), Dusseldorf. https://www.boeckler.de/pdf/p_imk_wp_100_2012.pdf. Accessed 11 Apr 2017

Lo S, Rogoff KS (2015) Secular stagnation, debt overhang and other rationales for sluggish growth, six years on. Bank for International Settlements Working Paper No. 482. Bank for International Settlements, Basel. http://www.bis.org/publ/work482.pdf. Accessed 13 Sept 2016

López GJ, Assous M (2010) Great thinkers in economics: Michał Kalecki. Palgrave Macmillan, New York, NY

Lösch A (1936) Bevölkerungswellen und Wechsellagen im Deutschen Reich von 1871 bis 1910. Verlag von Gustav Fischer, Jena

Lösch A (1937) Population cycles as a cause of business cycles. Q J Econ 51(4):649–662

Lösch A (1938) Das Problem einer Wechselwirkung zwischen Bevölkerungs- und Wirtschaftsentwicklung. Weltwirtschaftliches Archiv 48(1938):454–469

Lösch A (1954) The economics of location (translated from the second revised edition by William H. Woglom with the assistance of Wolfang F. Stolper). Yale University Press, New Haven, CT, and London

Lutz MA (1999) Economics for the common good: two centuries of social economic thought in the humanistic tradition. Routledge, London and New York, NY

Luxemburg R ([1913] 1951) The accumulation of capital (translated from the German by Agnes Schwarzschild, with an introduction by Joan Robinson). Routledge and Kegan Paul Ltd., London

Malthus TR ([1820] 1836) Principles of political economy, 2nd edn. William Pickering, London

Marglin SA, Bhaduri A (1990) Profit squeeze and Keynesian theory. In: Marglin SA, Schor JB (eds) The golden age of capitalism: reinterpreting the postwar experience. Clarendon Press, Oxford, pp 153–186

Martin B, Rowthorn R (2012) Is the British economy supply constrained II? A renewed critique of productivity pessimism. Centre for Business Research, University of Cambridge, May 2012. UK-Innovation Research Centre, Cambridge, UK, and London. http://www.uk-irc.org/wp-content/uploads/2013/04/2012_BM_UK_economy_report.pdf. Accessed 24 Nov 2018

McLaughlin GE, Watkins RJ (1939) The problem of industrial growth in a mature economy. Am Econ Rev 29(1):1–14

Mill JS ([1848] 1965) Principles of political economy (two volumes). In: Robson JM (ed) Collected works of John Stuart Mill, vol II and III. University of Toronto Press, Toronto

Mishkin FS (2011) Monetary policy strategy: lessons from the crisis. NBER Working Paper No. 16755. National Bureau of Economic Research, Cambridge, MA. http://www.nber.org/papers/w16755.pdf. Accessed 04 Sept 2016

Mitchell W (2017) The job guarantee: a superior buffer stock option for government price stabilisation. In: Murray MJ, Forstater M (eds) The job guarantee and modern money theory: realizing Keynes's labor standard. Palgrave Macmillan, Springer Nature, Cham, pp 47–72

Moore BJ (2002) Saving and investment: the theoretical case for lower interest rates. In: Davidson P (ed) A post Keynesian perspective on twenty-first century economic problems. Edward Elgar, Cheltenham and Northhampton, MA, pp 137–157

Moore GE (1965) Cramming more components onto integrated circuits. Electronics 38(8):114–117

Moore GE (2015) Gordon Moore: the man whose name means progress. The visionary engineer reflects on 50 years of Moore's law. Interview by Rachel Courtland. IEEE Spectrum, March 30, 2015. https://spectrum.ieee.org/computing/hardware/gordon-moore-the-man-whose-name-means-progress. Accessed 11 Oct 2017

Mummery AF, Hobson JA (1889) The physiology of industry: being an exposure of certain fallacies in existing theories of economics. John Murray, London

Musgrave RA (1987) Hansen, Alvin. In: Eatwell J, Milgate M, Newman P (eds) The New Palgrave Dictionary of Economics, vol 2. Macmillan, London, pp 591–592

Nakaso H (2016) Japan's economy and monetary policy. Speech at a meeting with business leaders in Okinawa, March 03, 2016. Bank of Japan, Tokyo. https://www.boj.or.jp/en/announcements/press/koen_2016/data/ko160303a1.pdf. Accessed 30 Aug 2016

OECD (2014) OECD economic outlook no. 96, vol 2014/2, Nov 2014. OECD Publishing, Paris

OECD (2016) Stronger growth remains elusive: urgent policy response is needed. OECD Interim Economic Outlook. February 18, 2016. OECD, Paris. https://www.oecd.org/eco/outlook/OECD-Interim-Economic-Outlook-February-2016.pdf. Accessed 13 Sept 2016

OECD (2018) OECD. Stat. OECD, Paris. http://stats.oecd.org/. Accessed 04 Dec 2018

Palley TI (2000) The case for positive low inflation: some financial market considerations with special attention to the problems of Japan. Eastern Econ J 26(3):277–295

Palley TI (2002) Economic contradictions coming home to roost? Does the U.S. economy face a long-term aggregate demand generation problem? J Post Keynes Econ 25(1):9–32

Palley TI (2012) From financial crisis to stagnation: the destruction of shared prosperity and the role of economics. Cambridge University Press, New York, NY

Palley TI (2015) Inequality, the financial crisis and stagnation: competing stories and why they matter. IMK Working Paper 151, May 2015. Macroeconomic Policy Institute (IMK), Dusseldorf. http://www.boeckler.de/pdf/p_imk_wp_151_2015.pdf. Accessed 13 Sept 2016

Palley TI (2016a) Why negative interest rate policy (NIRP) is ineffective and dangerous. Real-World Economics Review, Issue No. 76, 30 Sept 2016. http://www.paecon.net/PAEReview/issue76/Palley76.pdf. Accessed 22 Oct 2016

Palley TI (2016b) Zero lower bound (ZLB) economics: the fallacy of new Keynesian explanations of stagnation. IMK Working Paper 164, February 2016. Macroeconomic Policy Institute (IMK), Dusseldorf. http://www.boeckler.de/pdf/p_imk_wp_164_2016.pdf. Accessed 22 Oct 2016

Pecchi L, Piga G (eds) (2008) Revisiting Keynes: economic possibilities for our grandchildren. The MIT Press, Cambridge, MA

Piketty T (2014) Capital in the twenty-first century. Harvard University Press, Cambridge, MA, and London

Rachel L, Smith TD (2015) Secular drivers of the global real interest rate. Bank of England Staff Working Paper No. 571. Bank of England, London. https://www.bankofengland.co.uk/working-paper/2015/secular-drivers-of-the-global-real-interest-rate. Accessed 24 Nov 2018

Reinhart CM, Rogoff KS (2011) This time is different: eight centuries of financial folly. Princeton University Press, Princeton, NJ

Robbins L (1932) Consumption and the trade cycle. Economica 38 (Nov 1932):413–430

Robinson J (1977) Michał Kalecki on the economics of capitalism. Oxford Bull Econ Stat 39(1):7–17

Rognlie M (2014) A note on Piketty and diminishing returns to capital. Working Paper, June 15, 2014. http://mattrognlie.com/piketty_diminishing_returns.pdf. Accessed 20 Nov 2018

Rogoff KS (2015) Debt supercycle, not secular stagnation. Centre for Economic Policy Research, London. http://voxeu.org/article/debt-supercycle-not-secular-stagnation. Accessed 13 Sept 2016

Rosenof T (1997) Economics in the long run: new deal theorists and their legacies, 1933–1993. The University of North Carolina Press, Chapel Hill, NC

Rothschild KW (1994) Josef Steindl: 1912–1993. Econ J 104(422):131–137

Sachverständigenrat (2015) Zukunftsfähigkeit in den Mittelpunkt. Jahresgutachten 2015/16. Statistisches Bundesamt, Wiesbaden

Samuelson PA (1976) Alvin Hansen as a creative economic theorist. Q J Econ 90(1):24–31

Schiller K ([1966] 1967) Die Talsohle liegt noch vor uns: In der Aussprache über die Regierungserklärung im Deutschen Bundestag in Bonn am 15. Dezember 1966 (Auszug). In: Bundesministerium für Wirtschaft (ed) Reden zur Wirtschaftspolitik von Professor Dr. Karl Schiller, vol 1, BMWi, Bonn, pp 7–15

Schiller K (1967) Die Pferde müssen wieder saufen! Auf der Vortragsveranstaltung der Rheinisch-Westfälischen Börse zu Düsseldorf am 25. Januar 1967. In: Bundesministerium für Wirtschaft (ed) Reden zur Wirtschaftspolitik von Professor Dr. Karl Schiller, vol 1, BMWi, Bonn, pp 23–37

Schiller K (1983) Bin ich ein Liberaler? Der Spiegel 7(1983):28–29

Schneider M (1987) Underconsumption. In: Eatwell J, Milgate M, Newman P (eds) The New Palgrave Dictionary of Economics, vol 4. Macmillan, London, pp 741–745

Schumpeter JA (1939) Business cycles, vol 2. McGraw-Hill Book Company, Inc., New York, NY, and London

Schumpeter JA ([1941] 1991) An economic interpretation of our time: the Lowell lectures. In: Swedberg R (ed) The economics and sociology of capitalism. Princeton University Press, Princeton, NJ, pp 339–400

Schumpeter JA ([1942] 2008) Capitalism, socialism and democracy, 3rd edn. Harper Perennial Modern Thought, New York, NY

Schumpeter JA (1946) John Maynard Keynes 1883–1946. Am Econ Rev 36(4):495–518

Schumpeter JA (1954) History of economic analysis. Oxford University Press, New York, NY

Semieniuk G (2017) Piketty's elasticity of substitution: a critique. Rev Polit Econ 29(1):64–79

Shapiro N (2012) Josef Steindl: an economist of his times. PSL Q Rev 65(261):167–187

Simonde de Sismondi JCL ([1819] 1991) New principles of political economy: of wealth in its relation to population (translated and annotated by Richard Hyse, with a foreword by Robert L. Heilbronner). Transaction Publishers, New Brunswick and London

Smith A ([1776] 1976) An inquiry into the nature and causes of the wealth of nations. In: Campbell RH, Skinner AS (eds) The Glasgow edition of the works and correspondence of Adam Smith, vol 2. Oxford University Press, London

Smithin J (2009) Money, enterprise and income distribution: towards a macroeconomic theory of capitalism. Routledge, New York, NY

Spahn HP (1986) Stagnation in der Geldwirtschaft: Dogmengeschichte, Theorie und Politik aus keynesianischer Sicht. Campus Verlag, Frankfurt am Main and New York, NY

Spahn P (2016) Population growth, saving, interest rates and stagnation. Discussing the Eggertsson-Mehrotra model. University of Hohenheim Discussion Paper 04-2016. University of Hohenheim, Stuttgart-Hohenheim. https://wiso.uni-hohenheim.de/fileadmin/einrichtungen/wiso/Forschungsdekan/Papers_BESS/dp_04-2016_online.pdf. Accessed 13 Sept 2016

Steindl J ([1945] 1990) Marshall and the representative firm. In: Steindl J (ed) Economic papers 1941–88, St. Martin's Press, New York, NY, pp 37–49

Steindl J (1947) Small and big business: economic problems of the size of firms. Basil Blackwell, Oxford

Steindl J ([1952] 1976) Maturity and stagnation in American capitalism (with a new introduction by the author). Monthly Review Press, New York, NY, and London

Steindl J ([1966] 1984) On maturity in capitalist economies. In: Foster JB, Szlajfer H (eds) The faltering economy: the problem of accumulation under monopoly capitalism. Monthly Review Press, New York, NY, pp 167–178

Steindl J ([1979] 1990) Stagnation theory and stagnation policy. In: Steindl J (ed) Economic papers 1941–88, St. Martin's Press, New York, NY, pp 107–126

Steindl J ([1984] 1990) Reflections on the present state of economics. In: Steindl J (ed) Economic papers 1941–88, St. Martin's Press, New York, NY, pp 241–252

Steindl J (1987) Stagnation. In: Eatwell J, Milgate M, Newman P (eds) The New Palgrave Dictionary of Economics, vol 4. Macmillan, London, pp 472–474

Steindl J ([1989] 1990) From stagnation in the 30s to slow growth in the 70s. In: Steindl J (ed) Economic papers 1941–88, St. Martin's Press, New York, NY, pp 166–179

Steindl J (1990) From stagnation in the 1930s to slow growth in the, (1970s) In: Berg M (ed) Political economy in the twentieth century, Barnes & Noble Books, Savage, MD, pp 97–115

Stiglitz JE (2018) The myth of secular stagnation. Project syndicate. 28 Aug 2018. https://www.project-syndicate.org/commentary/secular-stagnation-excuse-for-flawed-policies-by-joseph-e-stiglitz-2018-08. Accessed 16 Nov 2018

Summers LH (2013) Speech at the IMF fourteenth annual research conference in honor of Stanley Fisher, 08 Nov 2013. International Monetary Fund, Washington, DC. http://larrysummers.com/imf-fourteenth-annual-research-conference-in-honor-of-stanley-fischer/. Accessed 02 Aug 2016

Summers LH (2014a) Bold reform is the only answer to secular stagnation. Financial Times column. 14 Sept 2014. http://www.ft.com/cms/s/2/4be87390-352a-11e4-aa47-00144feabdc0.html#axzz4IkW0Licp. Accessed 29 Aug 2016

Summers LH (2014b) Low equilibrium, real rates, financial crisis, and secular stagnation. In: Baily MN, Taylor JB (eds) Across the great divide: new perspectives on the financial crisis. Hoover Institution Press, Stanford, CA, pp 37–50

Summers LH (2014c) Reflections on the 'new secular stagnation hypothesis'. In: Teulings C, Baldwin R (eds) Secular stagnation: facts, causes and cures. CEPR Press, London, pp 27–38

Summers LH (2014d) The economy hasn't grown rapidly "in a financially sustainable way" for a long time. Interview with the New Republic (by Danny Vinik), 23 July 2014. https://newrepublic.com/article/118797/larry-summers-interview-ex-im-bank-secular-stagnation-and-trade. Accessed 25 Aug 2016

Summers LH (2014e) U.S. economic prospects: secular stagnation, hysteresis, and the zero lower bound. Bus Econ 49(2):65–73

Summers LH (2015a) Demand side secular stagnation. Am Econ Rev 105(5):60–65

Summers LH (2015b) Low real rates, secular stagnation & the future of stabilization policy. Speech at the Central Bank of Chile Research Conference, 20 Nov 2015. http://larrysummers.com/wp-content/uploads/2015/12/LarrySummers-Central-Bank-of-Chile.pdf. Accessed 29 Aug 2016

Summers LH (2015c) On secular stagnation: a response to Ben Bernanke, 01 Apr 2015. http://larrysummers.com/2015/04/01/on-secular-stagnation-a-response-to-bernanke/. Accessed 25 Aug 2016

Summers LH (2015d) Reflections on secular stagnation. Keynote address at Princeton University's Julius-Rabinowitz Center for Public Policy & Finance, 19 Feb 2015. http://larrysummers.com/2015/02/25/reflections-on-secular-stagnation/. Accessed 25 Aug 2016

Summers LH (2015e) The Fed looks set to make a dangerous mistake. http://larrysummers.com/2015/08/23/the-fed-looks-set-to-make-a-dangerous-mistake/. Accessed 13 Sept 2016

Summers LH (2016a) Equitable growth in conversation: an interview with Lawrence H. Summers. Interview by Heather Boushey, 11 Feb 2016. Washington Center for Equitable Growth, Washington, DC. http://equitablegrowth.org/research-analysis/equitable-growth-in-conversation-an-interview-with-lawrence-summers/. Accessed 25 Aug 2016

Summers LH (2016b) Secular stagnation and monetary policy. Fed Reserv Bank St Louis Rev 98(2):93–110

Summers LH (2016c) The age of secular stagnation: what it is and what to do about it. For-
    eign Affairs, 15 Feb 2016. https://www.foreignaffairs.com/articles/united-states/2016-02-15/
    age-secular-stagnation. Accessed 24 Aug 2016
Summers LH (2016d) The case for secular stagnation is more convincing than ever. Financial
    Times. Larry Summers Blog, 18 Feb 2016. https://www.ft.com/content/cca662ec-d44b-3419-
    864e-ac7ccfb0d125. Accessed 20 Oct 2016
Summers LH (2017a) 5 reasons why the Fed may be making a mistake. The Washington
    Post, Wonkblog Analysis, 14 June 2017. https://wapo.st/2rxCCMh?tid=ss_mail&utm_term=.
    448ec95254ba. Accessed 20 Nov 2018
Summers LH (2017b) 'Secular stagnation' even truer today, Larry Summers says. Interview by
    David Wessel. Wall Str J, 25 May 2017. https://blogs.wsj.com/economics/2017/05/25/secular-
    stagnation-even-truer-today-larry-summers-says/. Accessed 24 Nov 2018
Summers LH (2017c) The economy is on a sugar high, and tax cuts won't help. The Washington
    Post, Opinions, 10 Dec 2017. http://wapo.st/2nMJPvh?tid=ss_mail&utm_term=.be278029dffb.
    Accessed 20 Nov 2018
Summers LH (2018a) Secular stagnation and macroeconomic policy. IMF Econ Rev 66(2):226–250
Summers LH (2018b) Setting the record straight on secular stagnation. Project Syndicate.
    03 Sept 2018. https://www.project-syndicate.org/commentary/response-to-stiglitz-attack-on-
    secular-stagnation-by-lawrence-h--summers-2018-09. Accessed 16 Nov 2018
Summers LH (2018c) Why the Fed needs a new monetary policy framework. In Hutchins Center
    on Fiscal & Monetary Policy at Brookings (ed.), Rethinking the Fed's 2 percent inflation target.
    The Brookings Institution, Washington, DC, pp 1–9. https://www.brookings.edu/wp-content/
    uploads/2018/06/ES_20180607_Hutchins-FedInflationTarget.pdf. Accessed 20 Nov 2018
Swanson EW (1953) Review of maturity and stagnation in American capitalism by J. Steindl. South
    Econ J 20(2):191–192
Swanson EW, Schmidt EP (1946) Economic stagnation or progress: a critique of recent doctrines
    on the mature economy, oversavings, and deficit spending. McGraw-Hill Book Company, Inc.,
    New York, NY, and London
Sweezy AR (1940) Population growth and investment opportunity. Q J Econ 55(1):64–79
Sweezy PM (1954) Review of maturity and stagnation in American capitalism by J. Steindl. Econo-
    metrica 22(4):531–533
Sweezy PM, Magdoff H (1972) Economic history as it happened, vol I. The dynamics of U.S.
    capitalism: corporate structure, inflation, credit, gold, and the dollar. Monthly Review Press,
    New York, NY
Sweezy PM, Magdoff H (1973) Economic history as it happened, vol II. The end of prosperity: the
    American economy in the 1970s. Monthly Review Press, New York, NY
Sweezy PM, Magdoff H (1977) Economic history as it happened, vol III. The deepening crisis of
    U.S. capitalism. Monthly Review Press, New York, NY
Sweezy PM, Magdoff H (1987) Economic history as it happened, vol IV. Stagnation and the financial
    explosion. Monthly Review Press, New York, NY
Sweezy PM, Magdoff H (1988) Economic history as it happened, vol V. The irreversible crisis.
    Monthly Review Press, New York, NY
Sylos-Labini P ([1957] 1962) Oligopoly and technical progress. Harvard University Press, Cam-
    bridge, MA
Taylor JB (1993) Discretion versus policy rules in practice. Carnegie-Rochester conference series
    on public policy 39(1993):195–214
Taylor JB (2014a) Causes of the financial crisis and the slow recovery. A ten-year perspective.
    In: Baily MN, Taylor JB (eds) Across the great divide: new perspectives on the financial crisis.
    Hoover Institution Press, Stanford, CA, pp 51–65
Taylor JB, Wieland V (2016) Finding the equilibrium real interest rate in a fog of
    policy deviations. Hoover Institution Economics Working Paper 16109. Hoover Institu-
    tion, Stanford, CA. http://www.hoover.org/research/finding-equilibrium-real-interest-rate-fog-
    policy-deviations. Accessed 05 Oct 2016

Taylor L (2014b) Paul Krugman's 'liquidity trap' and other misadventures with Keynes. Rev Keynes Econ 2(4):483–489

Terborgh G (1945) The bogey of economic maturity. Machinery and Allied Products Institute, Chicago, IL

The Economist (2016) Out of ammo? The Economist, vol 418 (8977, 20th–26th Feb 2016), p 7

The Economist (2018) Special report: The world economy. The Economist, vol 429 (9113, 3th–19th Oct 2018), pp 3–12

Thwaites G (2015) Why are real interest rates so low? Secular stagnation and the relative price of investment goods. Bank of England Staff Working Paper No. 564. Bank of England, London. https://www.bankofengland.co.uk/working-paper/2015/why-are-real-interest-rates-so-low-secular-stagnation-and-the-relative-price-of-investment-goods. Accessed 25 Nov 2018

Trigg AB (1994) On the relationship between Kalecki and the Kaleckians. J Post Keynes Econ 17(1):91–109

Turner FJ (1920) The frontier in American history. Henry Holt and Company, New York, NY

US Bureau of Labor Statistics (2018) Consumer price index–2018 Oct (USDL-18-1823). Bureau of Labor Statistics, Washington, DC. https://www.bls.gov/news.release/pdf/cpi.pdf. Accessed 22 Nov 2018

US Bureau of the Census (1975) Historical statistics of the United States, colonial times to 1970, bicentennial edition, part 2. US. Government Printing Office, Washington, DC

Verspohl E (1971) Der Stagnationsgedanke in der Nationalökonomie: Eine dogmengeschichtliche und analytische Studie. Inaugural-Dissertation zur Erlangung des Doktorgrades der Wirtschafts- und Sozialwissenschaftlichen Fakultät der Universität zu Köln. University of Cologne, Cologne

Wallich HC, Weintraub S (1971) A tax-based incomes policy. J Econ Issues 5(2):1–19

Walterskirchen E (2012) Langfristige Perspektiven von Keynes und die aktuelle Wirtschafts-entwicklung. In: Chaloupek G, Marterbauer M (eds) Wirtschaftswissenschaftliche Tagungen der Arbeiterkammer Wien, Band 17: 75 Jahre General Theory of Employment, Interest and Money, LexisNexis Verlag ARD Orac, Vienna, pp 131–147

Weber AA, Lemke W, Worms A (2008) How useful is the concept of the natural real rate of interest for monetary policy? Camb J Econ 32(1):49–63

Weintraub D (1939) Effects of current and prospective technological developments upon capital formation. Am Econ Rev 29(1):15–32

von Weizsäcker CC (2010) Das Janusgesicht der Staatsschulden. Frankfurter Allgemeine Zeitung June 4, 2010:12

von Weizsäcker CC (2011) Public debt requirements in a regime of price stability. Preprints of the Max Planck Institute for Research on Collective Goods Bonn 2011/20. Max Planck Society, Bonn. https://www.coll.mpg.de/pdf_dat/2011_20online.pdf. Accessed 05 Sept 2016

von Weizsäcker CC (2013) Der Vorsorge-Albtraum. Wirtschaftsdienst 93(13):7–15

von Weizsäcker CC (2016) Europas Mitte. Perspektiven der Wirtschaftspolitik 17(4):383–392

Wicksell K, ([1898] 1962) Interest and prices: a study of the causes regulating the value of money. Macmillan & Co., Ltd., London

Wicksell K ([1935] 1978) Lectures on political economy, vol II: Money. Augustus M. Kelley Publishers, Fairfield, NJ

Williams JC (2016) Monetary policy in a low R-star world. Federal Reserve Bank of San Francisco Economic Letter 2016-23, 15 Aug 2016. Federal Reserve Bank of San Francisco, San Francisco, CA. http://www.frbsf.org/economic-research/files/el2016-23.pdf. Accessed 04 Sept 2016

Woirol GR (1996) The technological unemployment and structural unemployment debates. Greenwood Press, Westport, CT, and London

Woirol GR (2006) New data, new issues: the origins of the technological unemployment debates. History Polit Econ 38(3):473–496

Woodford M (2003) Interest and prices. Foundations of a theory of monetary policy. Princeton University Press, Princeton, NJ

World Bank (2018) Global economic prospects: the turning of the tide? A World Bank Group flagship report, June 2018. International Bank for Reconstruction and Development and The World Bank, Washington, DC. http://www.worldbank.org/en/publication/global-economic-prospects. Accessed 16 Nov 2018

Yellen JL (2011) Aggregate demand and the global economic recovery. In: Remarks at the Asia Economic Policy Conference "Asia's Role in the Post-Crisis Global Economy" in San Francisco, California, 29 Nov 2011. Federal Reserve Bank of San Francisco, San Francisco, CA. http://www.federalreserve.gov/newsevents/speech/yellen20111129a1.pdf. Accessed 18 Oct 2016

Yellen JL (2015) Normalizing monetary policy: prospects and perspectives. In: Remarks at "The New Normal Monetary Policy" Research Conference in San Francisco, California, 27 Mar 2015. Federal Reserve Bank of San Francisco, San Francisco, CA. http://www.federalreserve.gov/newsevents/speech/yellen20150327a.pdf. Accessed 15 Oct 2016

Zinn KG (2008) Die Keynessche Alternative: Beiträge zur Keynesschen Stagnationstheorie, zur Geschichtsvergessenheit der Ökonomik und zur Frage einer linken Wirtschaftsethik. VSA-Verlag, Hamburg

Zottmann A (1949) Dr. habil. August Lösch. Gestorben am 30. Mai 1945. Weltwirtschaftliches Archiv 62(1949):28–34

Chapter 4
Supply-Side Stagnation Theories

4.1 Stagnation in Classical Economics

For the classical economists of the eighteenth and nineteenth century, stagnation was mainly associated with a complete cessation of economic (and population) growth. With most of them adhering to Say's law, they predicted economic growth to come to a halt because potential output would reach its limit. Referring to Harrod's (1948, p. 87) natural rate of growth, Verspohl (1971, p. 10) described the classical stationary state of zero output growth as *natural stagnation*.

As outlined by Schumpeter (1954, p. 563), the classical economists did not think of the stationary state as an immediate reality, but as a future condition which at the time of their writings had not yet materialized. With all of them underestimating the impact of technological progress, the British classical economists expected the rate of profit to decline in the long run, leading to a cessation of capital accumulation and thus of economic growth. While Adam Smith referred to the competition among capitalists to explain the process toward stagnation, Thomas R. Malthus, David Ricardo, and John Stuart Mill pointed to diminishing returns to labor on land. Karl Marx, on the other hand, who is included here as a classical economist, even predicted the ultimate breakdown of capitalism.

4.1.1 Smith: Saturation in the Midst of Riches

The increase in wealth, i.e., growth in per capita income, is a central element in Adam Smith's ([1776] 1976) magnum opus *The Wealth of Nations*. As outlined by Smith ([1776] 1976, p. 10), the determinants of per capita income are, first, labor productivity and, secondly, the number of productive workers in the population, with

© Springer Nature Switzerland AG 2020
C. Anselmann, *Secular Stagnation Theories*, Springer Studies in the History of Economic Thought, https://doi.org/10.1007/978-3-030-41087-2_4

both requiring real capital investment.[1] "The intention of the fixed capital [...]," Smith ([1776] 1976, II, ii, p. 287) held, "[...] is to increase the productive powers of labour, or to enable the same number of labourers to perform a much greater quantity of work." For example, a rise in labor productivity can only be achieved by making available better or more machines or by promoting the division of labor, calling for capital investment (Smith [1776] 1976, II, iii, p. 343).

Like his classical contemporaries, Smith ([1776] 1976, II, iii, pp. 337–338) believed capital investment to be determined by saving, with all saving being automatically invested. The impetus to save, in turn, he claimed to be deeply rooted in human nature, as it was the only possibility to improve one's living conditions (Smith [1776] 1976, II, iii, pp. 341–342). Although—from a theoretical point of view—workers, landlords, as well as capitalists could save (and thus invest) part of their income, Smith ([1776] 1976, II, iii, p. 333) suggested saving to mainly come from the capitalist class. While workers are usually not able to save out of their low wage incomes, landlords, on the other hand, tend to dissipate their rents on their feudal lifestyle. Hence, it is the development of capitalists' profits and, more precisely, the profit rate which is decisive for the evolution of national wealth.

With a rise in real capital in the course of economic development, Smith ([1776] 1976) expected the rate of profit to fall in the long run. He wrote:

> The increase of stock [...] tends to lower profit. When the stocks of many rich merchants are turned into the same trade, their mutual competition naturally tends to lower its profit; and when there is a like increase of stock in all the different trades carried [...] on in the same society, the same competition must produce the same effect in them all. (Smith [1776] 1976, I, ix, p. 105)

As rightly noted by Kurz and Sturn (2013, pp. 109–110) and Spahn (1986, pp. 41–42), however, Smith's conclusion is subject to a fallacy of composition, as he erroneously reasoned from the micro- to the macroeconomic level. While the influx of capital into a specific sector tends to lower the profit rate in this sector, in the economy as a whole an increase in capital raises output (and demand) and thus does not necessarily reduce the profit rate (Blaug 1968, p. 48).

By referring to the development of the real wage rate, though, Smith ([1776] 1976, II, iv, pp. 352–353) aimed to further expand his line of thought. It is not only competitive pressure among capitalists which diminishes the profit rate, so his argument went, but also a rise in the real wage rate. In Smith's ([1776] 1976, II, iv, pp. 352–353) own words:

> As capitals increase in any country, the profits which can be made by employing them necessarily diminish. It becomes gradually more and more difficult to find within the country a profitable method of employing any new capital. There arises in consequence a competition between different capitals [...]. The demand for productive labour [...] grows every day greater and greater. Labourers easily find employment, but the owners of capitals find it difficult to get labourers to employ. Their competition raises the wages of labour, and sinks the profits of

---

[1] Quotations from Smith ([1776] 1976) are given in the following form: book (uppercase Roman numbers, where applicable), chapter (lowercase Roman numbers, where applicable), page(s) (Arabic numbers).

stock. [...] [P]rofits which can be made by the use of a capital are in this manner diminished, as it were, at both ends [...].

With an increase in real capital accumulation, Smith ([1776] 1976, I, viii, pp. 86–87, 91) stressed, the real wage rate rises because of a higher demand for labor which is not immediately matched by an adequate increase in labor supply. "It is not the actual greatness of national wealth, but its continual increase, which occasions a rise in the wages of labour" (Smith [1776] 1976, I, viii, p. 87). Other than Smith ([1776] 1976, II, iv, pp.,352–353) assumed, however, a rise in the real wage rate does not necessarily diminish the profit rate, because a higher wage rate can be accompanied by an increase in labor productivity. In fact, it was Smith ([1776] 1976, I, viii, p. 99) himself who mentioned that a higher wage rate is likely to boost the productivity of workers.

Over time, changes in the wage rate influence demographic developments. If—in the wake of a strong demand for labor, triggered by high capital accumulation—the wage rate rises above the subsistence level, population increases (and vice versa). "It is in this manner [...]," Smith ([1776] 1976, I, viii, p. 98) noted, "[...] that the demand for men, like that for any other commodity, necessarily regulates the production of men; quickens it when it goes on too slowly, and stops it when it advances too fast." In other words, population was assumed to endogenously adjust to economic conditions.

Smith was convinced that the process of capital accumulation could continue for some time. A decline in the rate of profit, he stressed, might be delayed by the occurrence of new investment opportunities, such as "[t]he acquisition of new territory, or of new branches of trade [...]" (Smith [1776] 1976, I, ix, p. 110; see also Skinner 1987, p. 366). Moreover, if a falling profit rate is compensated by a rise in the share of saving out of profits, capital accumulation may continue to increase (Smith [1776] 1976, I, ix, pp. 109–110; Gehrke 1991, pp. 136–137).[2] In fact, Smith ([1776] 1976, I, viii, p. 99) looked with satisfaction at economic progress and mentioned, "[...] [I]t is in the progressive state, while the society is advancing to the further acquisition, [...] that the condition of the labouring poor, of the great body of the people, seems to be the happiest and the most comfortable."

In the long run, however, for the deficient reasons mentioned above, Smith expected capital accumulation to decline (with a fall in the profit rate) and to ultimately come to a halt. This stationary state of zero economic growth he claimed to be characterized by an intense competition among both capitalists and workers and thus low profit and wage rates.[3]

---

[2]This follows from the following identity: $\frac{I}{K} = \frac{S}{P}\frac{P}{K}$. Given Say's law, if a decline in the profit rate (P/K) is accompanied by a sufficient rise in the proportion of saving out of profits (S/P), capital accumulation (I/K) may increase. See also Kurz and Sturn (2013, pp. 78–79).

[3]With regard to the state of competition in the economy, Smith stands in contrast to Steindl. While Smith expected the stationary state to be characterized by a high degree of competition, Steindl assumed secular stagnation to grow out of a decline in competition among firms.

In a country which had acquired that full complement of riches which the nature of its soil and climate, and its situation with respect to other countries allowed it to acquire; which could, therefore, advance no further, and which was not going backwards, both the wages of labour and the profits of stock would probably be very low. In a country fully peopled in proportion to what either its territory could maintain or its stock employ, the competition for employment would necessarily be so great as to reduce the wages of labour to what was barely sufficient to keep up the number of labourers, and, the country being already fully peopled, that number could never be augmented. In a country fully stocked in proportion to all the business it had to transact, as great a quantity of stock would be employed in every particular branch as the nature and extent of the trade would admit. The competition, therefore, would everywhere be as great, and consequently the ordinary profit as low as possible. (Smith [1776] 1976, I, ix, p. 111)

At the time of writing, Smith ([1776] 1976, I, ix, p. 111) suggested that no country had yet reached this stationary state, or, as he optimistically called it, "[...] this degree of opulence [...]." Although he described the Chinese economy as stationary, he traced this condition to unfavorable institutional circumstances (Smith [1776] 1976, I, ix, pp. 111–112).

As outlined by Kurz (2018, pp. 19–21), from a stagnationist point of view reference must also be made to Smith's remarks on the so-called *natural course of things*. According to Smith ([1776] 1976, III, i, p. 380), economic growth can best unfold if real capital is first mainly directed toward the agricultural sector, then toward the manufacturing sector, and only in the later stages of economic development toward foreign trade. As "[...] nature labours along with man [...]" in agriculture, capital employed in the agricultural sector adds the greatest value to annual output (Smith [1776] 1976, II, v, p. 363). While the share of output to capital employed is lower in the manufacturing sector, capital in foreign trade has yet the lowest productivity (Smith [1776] 1976, II, v, p. 366). Hence, only if capital is allocated to the different sectors in the described sequence—i.e., according to the natural course of things—can a nation exploit its full economic potential. Especially in Europe, however, according to Smith ([1776] 1976, III, i, pp. 378–380) the order of economic development had been reversed by government intervention and other institutional interference, which had ultimately led to a slowdown in economic growth.

This order, however, being contrary to the natural course of things, is necessarily both slow and uncertain. Compare the slow progress of [...] those European countries of which the wealth depends very much upon their commerce and manufactures, with the rapid advances of our North American colonies, of which the wealth is founded altogether in agriculture. (Smith [1776] 1976, III, iv, pp. 422–423)

As rightly pointed out by Kurz and Sturn (2013, pp. 148–149) and Kurz (2018, pp. 21–22), Smith's line of thought in terms of the natural course of things is untenable. For instance, the ratios of output to capital employed are not constant in the different sectors, but change and also mutually influence each other. Moreover, Smith underestimated the rising importance of the manufacturing sector and its role as the engine of economic growth.

4.1.2 Malthus and Ricardo: Stagnation Due to Land Scarcity

Aside from his (deficient) demand-side stagnation hypothesis outlined in Sect. 3.1.2, Thomas R. Malthus had a second, supply-side-oriented explanation for stagnation, which he elaborated between 1789 and 1826 in a total of six editions of *An Essay on the Principle of Population*. Except for short-term fluctuations, he expected output per capita and real wages to remain stagnant and most people to live in misery. Referring mainly to agricultural economies, land—a scarce and more or less fixed factor of production—plays a decisive role in Malthus's (1798) reasoning, with output per capita and real wages depending positively on the availability of fertile land per capita (Malthus 1798, pp. 35, 58; Hollander 1997, p. 29).

Central to Malthus's (1798) line of thought was his conviction that population naturally tends to increase at a geometric growth rate. Especially at times when output or, more precisely, food supply per capita is plenty, he suggested population to rise rapidly (Malthus 1798, pp. 14, 58). On the other hand, however, due to the scarcity of fertile land, the means of subsistence can only grow arithmetically (Malthus 1798, p. 23). With population increasing faster than output, real wages and output per capita must eventually settle at some kind of minimum level at which "[...] the means of subsistence [...] [are] just equal to the easy support of its inhabitants" (Malthus 1798, p. 29). He wrote:

> I see no way by which man can escape from the weight of this law which pervades all animated nature. No fancied equality, no agrarian regulations in their utmost extent, could remove the pressure of it even for a single century. And it appears, therefore, to be decisive against the possible existence of society, all the members of which, should live in ease, happiness, and comparative leisure; and feel no anxiety about providing the means of subsistence for themselves and families. (Malthus 1798, pp. 16–17)

If technological progress or an increase in the availability of fertile land raise the standard of living, population growth will be encouraged until output per capita and real wages are reduced to the subsistence level (Galor and Weil 2000, p. 807; Kurz 2018, p. 38). On the other hand, if output per capita falls below its long-term minimum, population ceases to grow or even declines as a result of misery and vice, until the subsistence level is reached again (Malthus 1798, pp. 29–30, 52). The main feature of Malthus's approach, Hollander (1997, p. 43) holds, "[...] is the *secular constancy* of product per capita."

Malthus (1803, p. 509) did not believe that attempts to raise the food supply could increase the standard of living in the long run, as this "[...] would appear to be setting the tortoise [i.e., growth in food supply] to catch the hare [i.e., population growth]." To raise real wages and the proportion of food to population, he rather suggested to curb population growth by moral restraint. "If we can persuade the hare to go to sleep [...]," he wrote in the second edition of *An Essay on the Principle of Population*, "[...] the tortoise may have some chance of overtaking her" (Malthus 1803, p. 509).

David Ricardo, who was Malthus's friend, but also his intellectual opponent (Kurz 2008, p. 130), took up Malthus's population theory, claiming real wages to be at their natural (subsistence) level in the long run (Ricardo [1815] 1951, pp. 21–22, [1817] 1951, pp. 93–94). Praising Malthus (1815) for his remarks on the determinants of rent, Ricardo ([1815] 1951, [1817] 1951) in both his *Essay on the Influence of a Low Price of Corn on the Profits of Stock* and his magnum opus *The Principles of Political Economy and Taxation* was mainly concerned with the distribution of income between wages, rents, and profits accruing to workers, landlords, and capitalists, respectively. Following Ricardo ([1817] 1951, pp. 115–121), the rate of profit, which is central to capital accumulation and economic growth, is determined in the agricultural sector on the marginal, least fertile parcel of land in use (see also Eltis [1989] 2008, pp. 192–194). With a rise in the stock of capital and population over time, soil of increasingly lower fertility has to be cultivated. Due to diminishing marginal returns to labor on land, more and more workers have to be employed on the marginal land to provide a sufficient amount of food. Although Ricardo assumed real wages to be at the subsistence level in the long run, the profit rate on marginal land declines, as the number of workers and thus the aggregate of real wages increase disproportionately compared to output. "The natural tendency of profits then is to fall; for, in the progress of society and wealth, the additional quantity of food required is obtained by the sacrifice of more and more labour" (Ricardo [1817] 1951, p. 120).

While the least productive land does not yield a rent, the scarcity of fertile land allows the owners of more advantageous grades of soil to charge *differential rents* just as high to offset any differences in profit rates across the agricultural sector. Profit rates on different soils are thus equal to the profit rate on the marginal land (Ricardo [1815] 1951, pp. 12–14). As Ricardo ([1817] 1951, p. 126) put it:

> [...] [I]n all countries, and all times, profits depend on the quantity of labour requisite to provide necessaries for the labourers, on that land or with that capital which yields no rent. The effects then of accumulation will be different in different countries, and will depend chiefly on the fertility of the land. However extensive a country may be where the land is of a poor quality [...], the most moderate accumulations of capital will be attended with great reductions in the rate of profit, and a rapid rise in rent [...].

With the cultivation of more and more less fertile land, the shares of both wages and rents in output increase, while the profit share declines (de Vivo 1987, p. 190). When the output on the marginal soil is just sufficient to cover the aggregate wages necessary to cultivate this land, the total profit share (and profit rate) in the economy declines to zero.[4] Total output produced is then divided between wages and rent. With zero profits, capital accumulation and economic growth eventually come to a halt. In Ricardo's ([1817] 1951, pp. 120–121) words:

> [...] [T]here must be an end of accumulation; for no capital can then yield any profit whatever, and no additional labour can be demanded, and consequently population will have reached its highest point. Long indeed before this period, the very low rate of profits will have arrested all accumulation, and almost the whole produce of the country, after paying the labourers, will be the property of the owners of land and the receivers of tithes and taxes.

---

[4]Ricardo assumed all capital to be wage capital. Given this assumption, the profit rate is equal to the profit share divided by the wage share in output. Hence, the profit rate necessarily declines with a fall in the profit share and a corresponding rise in the wage share (de Vivo 1987, p. 190).

While the tendency of (the rate of) profit to fall is inherent, according to Ricardo ([1817] 1951, p. 120) it can be impeded—though not prevented—by technological progress, i.e., by "[...] improvements in machinery, connected with the production of necessaries, as well as by discoveries in the science of agriculture which enable us to relinquish a portion of labour before required [...]."

4.1.3 Mill: The Stationary State as a Pleasant Condition

Along Malthusian and Ricardian lines, John Stuart Mill expected economic growth to cease in the course of economic development. As outlined in his *Principles of Political Economy*, due to land scarcity and diminishing returns, a rise in capital and population raises aggregate wages and rent payments in relation to total output produced, resulting in a tendency of the rate of profit to fall and eventually a cessation of real capital accumulation (Mill [1848] 1965, IV, iii, pp. 722–723, IV, iv, p. 740).[5] Although Mill ([1848] 1965, IV, vi, p. 752) considered the stationary state inevitable, he stressed that it could be delayed by several counteracting forces, such as capital destruction, improvements in production techniques and education, capital export, and free trade (Mill [1848] 1965, I, xii, pp. 183–184; IV, iv, pp. 741–746). In fact, at the time of writing, he did not think the end of capital accumulation and economic growth to be of immediate empirical relevance (Mill [1848] 1965, IV, iv, pp. 738–739) but he optimistically compared the limits of production "[...] to a highly elastic and extensible band, which is hardly ever so violently stretched that it could not possibly be stretched any more [...]" (Mill [1848] 1965, I, xii, pp. 173–174). As outlined by Kurz (2018, pp. 41–44), although Mill predicted the stationary state, in light of his promising expectations on progress it is questionable whether economic stagnation is de facto ever reached.

While Mill's approach to economic growth is similar to that of Malthus and Ricardo, it was his explicitly well-disposed attitude toward the stationary state which sets him apart from other classical economists. Speaking of the stationary state as a future "goal" (Mill [1848] 1965, IV, vi, p. 752), he mentioned:

> I cannot [...] regard the stationary state of capital and wealth with the unaffected aversion so generally manifested towards it [...]. I am inclined to believe that it would be, on the whole, a very considerable improvement on our present condition. I confess I am not charmed with the ideal of life held out by those who think that the normal state of human beings is that of struggling to get on; that the trampling, crushing, elbowing, and treading on each other's heels [...] are the most desirable lot of human kind, or anything but the disagreeable symptoms of one of the phases of industrial progress. (Mill [1848] 1965, IV, vi, pp. 753–754)

According to Mill, the stationary state of zero output growth can be beneficial for all people in society. To ensure high-quality living conditions, however, similar to

---

[5]Quotations from Mill ([1848] 1965) are given in the following form: book (uppercase Roman numbers), chapter (lowercase Roman numbers), page(s) (Arabic numbers).

Malthus he considered preventive control of population growth essential. Mill ([1848] 1965, IV, vi, pp. 753, 756) built his hopes on the prudence of society and people's understanding that the containment of population growth is indispensable—even before the stationary state is reached—to keep real wages from declining to subsistence and all available parcels of soil from being cultivated to meet minimal nutritional requirements. On the other hand, should population growth continue unchecked, "[...] the condition of the poorest class sinks, even in a progressive state, to the lowest point which they will consent to endure" (Mill [1848] 1965, IV, vi, p. 753).

While Mill regarded preventive population controls inevitable, he was convinced that they must be supplemented by active distribution policies to ensure a good life for all people. He rejected large wealth inequalities contradicting people's sense of justice, and he did not understand "[...] why it should be matter of congratulation that persons who are already richer than any one needs to be, should have doubled their means of consuming things which give little or no pleasure except as representative of wealth [...]" (Mill [1848] 1965, IV, vi, p. 755). Accordingly, he did not think that a further increase in output was necessary in most advanced countries, but he advocated a more equal distribution of existing wealth, proposing measures such as restrictions on inheritances and a more equal distribution of landed property (Mill [1848] 1965, II, ii, pp. 224–227; IV, vi, p. 755).

If population growth could be contained and distribution policies could ensure wealth to be shared relatively equally, he predicted the future stationary state to be an overall pleasant condition, enabling a life free from compulsion. Mill ([1848] 1965, IV, vi, p. 755) wrote:

> Under this twofold influence, society would exhibit these leading features; a well-paid and affluent body of labourers; no enormous fortunes, except what were earned and accumulated during a single lifetime; but a much larger body of persons than at present, not only exempt from the coarser toils, but with sufficient leisure, both physical and mental, from mechanical details, to cultivate freely the graces of life [...]. This condition of society, so greatly preferable to the present, is not only perfectly compatible with the stationary state, but, it would seem, more naturally allied with that state than with any other.

Despite zero output growth, Mill ([1848] 1965, IV, vi, p. 756) was convinced that the stationary state would not imply stagnation of social life. He went on:

> It is scarcely necessary to remark that a stationary condition of capital and population implies no stationary state of human improvement. There would be as much scope as ever for all kinds of mental culture, and moral and social progress; as much room for improving the Act of Living, and much more likelihood of its being improved, when minds ceased to be engrossed by the art of getting on. (Mill [1848] 1965, IV, vi, p. 756)

The stationary state might even be characterized by ongoing technological progress. Instead of increasing total output, however, Mill ([1848] 1965, IV, vi, p. 756) suggested technological advances to be translated into shorter working hours.

4.1.4 Marx: Predicting the Breakdown of Capitalism

According to Karl Marx ([1894] 1909, p. 295), the generation of profit is the main purpose of capitalism. Competition for profit among capitalists is thus the main driver of capitalist production, calling for a continued accumulation of capital to make use of the most modern production techniques (Marx [1867] 1906, pp. 297, 649). "Accumulate, accumulate [...]," he held. "That is Moses and the prophets!" (Marx [1867] 1906, p. 652).

Marx distinguished between constant capital—i.e., capital invested in means of production—and variable capital—i.e., capital invested in productive labor power, paid in wages—with the latter being the only source of value (Marx [1867] 1906, p. 671; [1857–1858] 1973, p. 543). Living labor is exploited by the capitalist class, because workers do not receive as wage payments the total value they produce (Marx [1867] 1906, pp. 239–241). While average wages are just sufficient to ensure workers' reproduction, the difference between the total value produced and the sum of wages is *surplus value*, which "[...] for the capitalist [...] has all the charms of a creation out of nothing" (Marx [1867] 1906, p. 240). By selling their commodities, capitalists eventually realize all or part of the surplus value as profits (Marx [1894] 1909, pp. 49–50, 286).

> The profit of the capitalist is due to the fact that he offers something for sale for which he has not paid anything. The surplus-value, or the profit, consists precisely of the excess of the value of the commodity over its cost-price, in other words, it consists of the excess of the total amount of labor embodied in the commodity over the paid labor contained in it. (Marx [1894] 1909, p. 55)

As shown in Eq. (4.1), the rate of profit (r), which determines investment spending, is defined as the ratio of surplus value (s) to the value of total capital—i.e., the sum of constant capital (c) and variable capital (v) (Marx [1894] 1909, p. 55). Dividing both the numerator and the denominator by variable capital (v) yields that the rate of profit depends on the *rate of surplus value* (s/v) and the so-called *organic composition of capital* (c/v):

$$r = \frac{s}{c+v} = \frac{s/v}{c/v+1}.$$
(4.1)

Marx ([1894] 1909, p. 283) was aware of cyclical variations in the profit rate and considered the development of real wages a driver of the business cycle. At the top of a boom, he stressed, real wages are high because of the relative scarcity of productive labor power, leading to a fall in both the rate of surplus value (s/v) and the rate of profit ($s/(c+v)$). With a reduction in investment spending, the dismissal of workers, and a decline in wages, the resulting cyclical downturn eventually sows the seeds for the next economic upswing (Marx [1867] 1906, p. 679; [1894] 1909, pp. 295, 528).

Other than his classical predecessors, Marx ([1861–1863] 1968, pp. 507–515) did not adhere to Say's law but pointed to the general possibility of recurring crises of overproduction in monetary capitalist economies. Unlike in a barter economy, he held, in a monetary economy the acts of selling and purchasing in the metamorphosis of commodities are separated by the use of money.[6] As money is not just a medium of circulation, but also a store of value, the hoarding of money can be an attractive alternative to spending. As Marx ([1867] 1906, p. 145) put it, "Commodities are thus sold not for the purpose of buying others, but in order to replace their commodity-form by their money-form. From being the mere means of effecting the circulation of commodities, this change of form becomes the end and aim." Crises of overproduction, perhaps accompanied by credit crises, are thus always possible in monetary capitalist economies. When capitalists in a particular sector of the economy cannot sell the entire value of the commodities they produced, according to Marx—and contrary to Say's law—such a partial crisis can easily develop into a general crisis of overproduction. "For a crisis (and therefore also for over-production) to be general [...]," he held, "[...] it suffices for it to affect the principal commercial goods" (Marx [1861–1863] 1968, p. 505).

While Marx's considerations on the business cycle include a demand-side component, his long-term stagnation theory is yet to be classified as a supply-side phenomenon (Shoul 1957, p. 626). Even if demand were always equal to supply, Marx ([1894] 1909, pp. 247–271) predicted capital accumulation to fade out in the long run as an inevitable result of the so-called *law of the falling tendency of the rate of profit*, which he himself considered "[...] the most important law from the historical standpoint" (Marx [1857–1858] 1973, p. 748). Critical of Malthus's population theory and Ricardo's explanation for the profit rate to fall, Marx did not attribute a declining rate of profit to diminishing returns to labor on land, but had a different line of thought than his classical predecessors. While technological change was a possible headwind that could delay the stationary state in Ricardo's theory, Marx, in contrast, considered it the ultimate cause of a secular fall in the profit rate (Gehrke 2008, p. 233). Technological progress, he stressed, tends to be labor-saving, leading to a change in the composition of capital over time toward a relative increase in constant capital (c) as compared to variable capital (v). While this process raises the degree of capital concentration and centralization, it also increases both the organic composition of capital (c/v) and the industrial reserve army, i.e., the number of unemployed workers in the total workforce (Marx [1867] 1906, p. 681–699). As Marx ([1894] 1909, p. 290) assumed a possible increase in the rate of surplus value (s/v) to be limited, according to Eq. (4.1) an ever rising organic composition of capital (c/v) must ultimately provoke a fall in the rate of profit. Hence, while for each individual capitalist it is necessary to invest in new production techniques, capitalists as a group "[...] behave in a collectively self-destructive way [...]" by substituting constant capital for living labor, the only source of (surplus) value and profit (Elster 1986, p. 76). Although counteracting forces, such as a rise in the exploitation of labor, a decline

---

[6]The complete metamorphosis of a commodity is described by the exchange *commodity–money–commodity*, or *C–M–C*. This includes, first, the selling of a commodity in exchange for money (*C–M*). The money can then be used to purchase another commodity (*M–C*) (Marx [1867] 1906, pp. 128–129, 164–167).

in wages, and the cheapening of constant capital, can impede the long-term decline in the profit rate, they cannot prevent it (Marx [1894] 1909, pp. 272–282).[7]

Rather than predicting a mere slowdown and eventual cessation of economic growth, Marx went a step further and anticipated the ultimate breakdown of the capitalist system of production.[8] With crises getting deeper and deeper, according to Marx a proletarian revolution of the exploited working class eventually leads to the end of capitalism, paving the way for socialism (Marx and Engels [1848] 1906). Capitalism, he mentioned, is but "[...] a historical mode of production corresponding to a definite and limited epoch in the development of the material conditions of production" (Marx [1894] 1909, pp. 304–305).

Historical developments have not substantiated Marx's predictions. Critical appraisals of his law of the falling tendency of the rate of profit include the underestimation of the rate of surplus value (s/v) to rise and the overestimation of the organic composition of capital (c/v) to increase. A rise in capital productivity, in fact, can prevent a decline in the profit rate. Moreover, the value rate of profit referred to by Marx is not necessarily equal to the money rate of profit relevant for capitalists (Sweezy [1942] 1946, pp. 100–106; Higgins 1959, pp. 118–120; Steindl [1952] 1976, pp. 240–241; Steedman 1977, p. 30; Mandel 1987, p. 379).

In the twentieth century, Marx's prediction of the breakdown of capitalism was revived by Schumpeter, though based on a different line of reasoning. In contrast to Marx's objectivistic approach of capitalism, with capitalism being characterized by the objective compulsion of firms to engage in capital accumulation, Schumpeter's theory focuses on the innovator and pioneering entrepreneur, thus showing subjectivistic traits.

4.2 Modern Supply-Side Stagnation Theories

Although the stagnation debate of the twentieth century has always been mainly associated with Hansen, several economists of the time pointed to supply-side restrictions to economic growth. Aside from Schumpeter, who was a colleague of Hansen at Harvard University (Samuelson 2015), in this section it is also referred to Fourastié, Baumol, and several environmental scientists around Meadows. As representatives of neoclassical growth theory, Solow and Swan are outsiders among the economists described in the following. Yet, while they did not predict stagnation as such, their growth model can be seen from a stagnationist perspective.

---

[7]In light of the existence of counteracting factors, Marx ([1894] 1909, p. 272) explicitly referred to a falling *tendency* of the rate of profit.

[8]As Steindl (1987, p. 473) pointed out, "[...] breakdown and stagnation are not the same thing." While stagnation may lead to the decline of capitalism, it is not a necessity if adequate policy measures can be implemented. See also Riese (1965, p. 698).

4.2.1 Schumpeter: The Self-Destruction of Capitalism

It has been outlined in Sect. 3.2.2.2 that Schumpeter was a decisive critic of Hansen's demand-side stagnation hypothesis, as he was not convinced that changes in the availability of unsettled land, population growth, and technological progress contributed to the weak economic performance in the years leading up to World War II. Nonetheless, however, he cannot indeed be considered a true anti-stagnationist. In fact, Schumpeter (1954, p. 1173) thought of himself as a stagnationist of a different strand, disagreeing with Hansen's line of argument, but accepting the result of Hansen's stagnation doctrine that economic growth might slow down due to a lack of investment spending. Determined to unveil more persuasive reasons for the vanishing of investment opportunities, he developed a different kind of theory, standing in stark contrast to Hansen's thoughts (Schumpeter 1939, p. 1038). "[...] [I]t is possible to feel unconvinced by Keynes's and Hansen's arguments [...]," he held, "[...] and nevertheless to predict that capitalist evolution tends to peter out—i.e. to settle down into a condition that might be just as well described as 'stagnation' [...]" (Schumpeter 1954, p. 1173). Although Schumpeter rejected Say's law, similar to Marx his explanation for a long-term tendency toward stagnation is not primarily based on a lack of effective demand and clearly shows supply-side characteristics (Schumpeter 1939, pp. 1033, 1036, 1039–1040).

Schumpeter ([1942] 2008, p. 64) did not trace the Great Depression and its aftermath to secular economic factors which were about to reverse the general economic trend, but dismissed the economic weakness of the late 1920s and 1930s as a regular—though severe—depression which had to be expected anyway in the course of the typical cyclical development. Referring to his *three-cycle schema*, i.e., the interaction of Kondratieff long waves with classical Juglar business cycles and still shorter Kitchin cycles, he assumed the early 1930s to have been characterized by the coincidence of troughs or downgrades in all of these three cycles (Schumpeter 1935, pp. 7–8, 1931, pp. 179–180). Cyclical fluctuations, Schumpeter (1935, pp. 4–6; [1942] 2008, pp. 82–83) mentioned, are at the heart of capitalism and to a considerable extent driven by innovation clusters which do not evolve smoothly, but which come about by leaps and bounds. He did not consider cyclical downswings and depressions as futile phenomena, but rather pointed to their positive long-term influence on economic development, as they cleared "[...] the ground for revival" (Schumpeter [1934] 1989, p. 110). Schumpeter ([1942] 2008, p. 83) called this the process of *creative destruction*, which he considered "[...] the essential fact about capitalism [...]," changing "[...] the economic structure *from within*, incessantly destroying the old one, incessantly creating a new one."[9]

---

[9]Nonetheless, as thoroughly outlined by Dal Pont Legrand and Hagemann (2016; 2017), contrary to popular belief Schumpeter advocated government intervention in severe, so-called *pathological* depressions. While expansionary (deficit-financed) fiscal policy measures may be appropriate, however, the government should be committed to again balance its budget once the economy has recovered (Schumpeter [1934] 1989, p. 117).

Although Schumpeter ([1934] 1989, p. 114) neglected the influence of secular economic forces, he was aware of the severity of the Great Depression, which he primarily ascribed to certain outside, non-economic factors. Referring to the incomplete recovery after 1933 as the "disappointing Juglar," he mainly had in mind several fiscal, labor, and industrial policy measures that had been implemented between 1934 and 1935 (Schumpeter 1939, pp. 1011, 1038–1044). For example, he criticized the increase in the tax burden at the top of the income hierarchy, as this would inhibit investment spending and thus "[...] exert a serious influence on 'capital supply' [...]" (Schumpeter 1939, p. 1039). Moreover, he did not endorse labor market policies— such as the Wagner Act—which increased the bargaining power of employees, and was critical of the general hostile attitude against large-scale businesses, as this would "[...] spread paralysis in the economic organism [...]" (Schumpeter 1939, p. 1044).

Although Schumpeter ([1941] 1991, pp. 350–351; [1942] 2008, p. 70) regarded the political changes in the aftermath of the Great Depression as the first symptoms of specific secular tendencies, in contrast to Hansen he did not treat the economic turmoil of the 1930s as part of his long-term theory of capitalist development, which he mainly elaborated in his *Capitalism, Socialism and Democracy*. Speaking of the "crumbling walls" of capitalism, Schumpeter ([1942] 2008, pp. 131–142) set out three reasons for his assumption of possible long-term stagnation and the ultimate breakdown of the capitalist system of production.[10]

First, he mentioned the gradual disappearance of the entrepreneurial function. In their role as creative innovators, genuine capitalist entrepreneurs were of particular importance to Schumpeter ([1942] 2008, pp. 131–134), as they provide the main impetus to the economy by opening up new investment opportunities. With the automation and bureaucratization of technological progress, however, Schumpeter saw this social function of the entrepreneur fade away. "[...] [P]rogress is increasingly becoming the business of teams of trained specialists [...]," he stressed. "Bureau and committee work tends to replace individual action. [...] The leading man [...] is becoming just another office worker—and one who is not always difficult to replace," (Schumpeter [1942] 2008, pp. 132–133).

Secondly, Schumpeter ([1942] 2008, pp. 134–139) assumed capitalism to be threatened by the erosion of the strata protecting the capitalist bourgeoisie. In the course of economic development, he explained, feudalism as well as related institutions and organizations had been abolished. While this change had brought many advantages, Schumpeter ([1942] 2008, p. 135) wondered "[...] whether in the end such complete emancipation was good for the bourgeois and his world." In fact, he did not think so, but assumed that the end of pre-capitalist structures "[...] broke not only barriers that impeded [...] progress but also flying buttresses that prevented [...] [the] collapse [of capitalism]" (Schumpeter [1942] 2008, p. 139).

Thirdly, Schumpeter ([1942] 2008, pp. 139–142) pointed to the decay of the institutional framework of capitalism. Especially with the suppression of small- and medium-sized companies, "[...] the figure of the proprietor and with it the specifically

---

[10]Speaking of the long run, Schumpeter ([1942] 2008, p. 163) considered a century a short-run period.

proprietary interest have vanished from the picture" (Schumpeter [1942] 2008, p. 141). Managers, executives, and stockholders replaced the intrinsically motivated small-scale business owner. Schumpeter ([1942] 2008, p. 142) held, "Eventually there will be *nobody* left who really cares to stand for it—nobody within and nobody without the precincts of the big concerns."[11]

According to Schumpeter ([1942] 2008, pp. 143–163), the combined impact of these factors potentially creates a hostile, anti-capitalist atmosphere, impeding invest-ment spending and economic progress by destructive public policies and regulations which burden private companies "[...] beyond [...] [their] powers of endurance" (Schumpeter 1950, p. 450). Although he did not intend to make any predictions, he expected the natural course of things to lead to stagnation in the very long run. Moreover, as he assumed government policies themselves to be a major cause of economic decline, he did not see any effective cures. Smithies (1950, p. 640) thus described Schumpeter as "[...] the most uncompromising stagnationist of them all." Doubting the viability of a stagnant capitalist system of production, similar to Marx Schumpeter (1939, p. 1033) was convinced that capitalism must ultimately break down and give rise to socialism. For Schumpeter ([1942] 2008, p. 162), however, it was not the failure, but the very success of capitalism which would lead to its self-destruction and decay.[12] He concluded:

> Marx was wrong in his diagnosis of the manner in which capitalist society would break down; he was not wrong in the prediction that it would break down eventually. The stagnationists are wrong in their diagnosis of the reasons why the capitalist process should stagnate; they may still turn out to be right in their prognosis that it will stagnate—with sufficient help from the public sector. (Schumpeter 1950, p. 456)

Although Schumpeter (1954, pp. 1172–1173) himself primarily associated the stagnation debate with Keynes and Hansen, as outlined by Samuelson ([1970] 1972), Foster (2011; 2017, pp. 21–22), and Dockès (2015, pp. 980–988), on March 27, 1947 he engaged in a verbal debate on *The Future of Capitalism* with Paul M. Sweezy, his colleague and former student at Harvard University. Moderated by Wassily Leontief, the discussion before the Harvard Graduate Student's Economics Club was supposed to contrast their different views on the main problems of capitalism. Samuelson ([1970] 1972, p. 710) later recalled Leontief saying, "[...] The patient is capitalism. What is to be his fate? Our speakers are in fact agreed that the patient is inevitably dying. But the bases of their diagnoses could not be more different." While Schum-peter was primarily concerned about the overall business climate and the fading of the innovative entrepreneur, Sweezy, who back then mainly drew on Marx, Keynes, and Hansen (Lebowitz 2004, p. 52), believed capital accumulation as such to be the principal issue. In his notes, Sweezy ([1946/1947] 2011, pp. 12, 14) mentioned:

---

[11] Elsewhere, however, Schumpeter ([1942] 2008, pp. 87–106) did not appear reluctant to monop-olistic and oligopolistic market structures. See also Foster (2011, p. 5).

[12] Other than Marx, Schumpeter (1950, p. 447)—writing at the time of Stalin's Soviet Union—did also not endorse socialism.

There is no reason to deny the existence of Schumpeter's entrepreneurial type, but its significance is quite differently evaluated. For him the entrepreneur occupies the center of the stage; the accumulation process is derivative. For me the accumulation process is primary; the entrepreneur falls in with it and plays a part in it. [...] Generally speaking, [...] [Schumpeter's theory] denies—or at least strongly discounts—what may be called savings-and-investment troubles.

According to Foster (2011, p. 9), "[...] the Sweezy-Schumpeter debate was a disappointment to many of the economists and interested parties who crowded into the Littauer Auditorium that night [...]," mainly because Schumpeter refused to engage in an active discussion.

In general, Schumpeter certainly made some vital points, particularly with regard to the importance of (product) innovations. In fact, the invention of new products does not only foster the supply side of the economy, but can also stimulate aggregate demand. On the other hand, however, his anticipation of a breakdown of capitalism has not proved to be empirically relevant. Critics, such as Heertje (1987, p. 265) and März ([1989] 2008, p. 271), have frequently pointed to his underestimation of the dynamics and adaptability of capitalism.

4.2.2 Solow and Swan: The Vanishing of Stagnation Fears

With interest in secular stagnation waning, growth theory moved to the forefront during the post-Second World War economic boom. In the 1950s and 1960s, the issue of economic growth was dominated by Solow (1956; 1957) and (Swan 1956), who, in response to the Harrod–Domar growth model, had advanced neoclassical growth theory and developed what is commonly known as the standard neoclassical growth model (Hagemann 2009).[13] As the term suggests, it is not a *stagnation* hypothesis which explicitly predicts stagnation tendencies on theoretical or empirical grounds, but a *growth* model which first and foremost focuses on the explanation of economic growth. While Riese (1965, p. 697) concluded that neoclassical growth theory turned its back on the issue of stagnation, this is true only indirectly. With secular stagnation being a thematic offshoot of growth theory, each growth theory implicitly includes a theory of stagnation, although it is usually not at the center of interest. If there are factors which foster economic growth, the absence or interference of these factors must inhibit growth and induce stagnation tendencies (Kurz 2018, p. 9). As the Solow–Swan model is the most common neoclassical growth model, serving as a framework for many other models, its implications for stagnation are briefly outlined here, without going into detail.

The Solow–Swan growth model is based on an aggregate production function with three input factors: capital, labor, and technology. Assuming technological progress to be labor-augmenting (Harrod-neutral), output is determined by capital

---

[13] As pointed out by Rothschild (1994, p. 135), the dominance of neoclassical growth theory was one of the reasons why Steindl's ([1952] 1976) stagnation hypothesis remained largely unnoticed.

and effective labor, i.e., the quantity of labor multiplied by its efficiency. The typical neoclassical production function is characterized by, first, constant returns to scale, secondly, positive and diminishing marginal returns to labor and capital, and, thirdly, the Inada conditions, i.e., the assumption that the marginal productivity of capital (labor) approaches infinity when capital (labor) moves toward zero (and vice versa) (Barro and Sala-i Martin 2004, pp. 27, 52–54). Moreover, in contrast to the Harrod–Domar growth model, capital and labor are substitutable for each other. The economy is perfectly competitive, with all factors of production being remunerated according to their marginal productivity, ensuring full employment of labor through price and wage flexibility (Solow 1956, pp. 65–66, 68, 79; Frenkel and Hemmer 1999, p. 46).

Identifying economic growth with the rate of net capital accumulation, the model explains the long-run convergence toward a *steady state* or *balanced growth path*, an equilibrium where different variables grow at constant rates. While, ceteris paribus, a rise in the saving rate (S/Y) (and hence the investment rate (I/Y)) leads to a temporary increase in economic growth during the transition period, in the long-run steady state the saving and investment rate has no impact whatsoever on economic growth. This is due to a decline in average capital productivity, caused by the substitution of capital for labor. In fact, in long-run equilibrium output per effective labor does not change anymore. Aggregate saving and investment are just sufficient to keep output (and capital) per effective labor constant. Accordingly, the steady-state output growth rate is equal to the sum of the growth rates of labor and technology. Output per capita, in turn, changes with the rate of technological progress in the long run (Barro and Sala-i Martin 2004, pp. 33–34, 54–55).

As long-term output growth is determined by the growth rates of population and technology, it follows that secular stagnation tendencies may evolve with a decline in population growth and/or a slowdown in technological progress.[14] Although this causality resembles Hansen's stagnation doctrine, the reasoning is completely different. While Hansen was concerned with the impact of changes in population, technological progress, and the availability of land on effective demand, the neoclassical growth model is essentially a supply-side theory, with population and technology being primarily factors of production.

In the Solow–Swan model, both long-term growth factors, i.e., population growth and technological progress, are not explained in the model, but are taken as exogenously given variables. Hence, while the model identifies these factors as relevant for economic growth, it cannot explain population growth and technological progress per se. Especially technological progress is commonly stressed to fall like *manna from heaven*. Due to this exogenous character, von Weizsäcker (1966, p. 11, own translation) describes neoclassical growth theory as "[...] growth pessimistic in the sense of a lack of conviction to influence the secular economic growth rate by an increase in investment." Elsewhere, he refers to it as a "[...] modern version of the old [i.e., classical] stagnation theory [...]" (von Weizsäcker 1969, p. 459, own translation). He goes on:

---

[14]Output *per capita* growth accordingly falls with a decline in technological progress.

[...] [I]f we agree with [...] [neoclassical growth theory], we have to accept the long-term growth rate of the economy as a fate. Just as the stagnationists believed that nothing could be done to impede secular stagnation, then we are to believe that we are not able to increase the secular growth rate [...]. (von Weizsäcker 1969, pp. 459–460, own translation).[15]

To eliminate the dependence of long-term economic growth on exogenous factors, in the 1980s and thereafter the standard neoclassical growth model was advanced by various economists, such as Romer (1986) and Lucas (1986), to allow for endogenous growth in income per capita. This so-called *new* or *endogenous growth theory* abandons the long-term tendency of the marginal productivity of capital to decline with a rise in capital intensity. One strand of these models focuses on the endogenous determination of technological progress by implementing a research and development sector. In contrast, a second strand of endogenous growth models explains growth in income per capita without changes in technology, such as by assuming constant capital productivity per definition, by referring to investment in human capital, or by pointing to positive externalities of investment, including learning-by-doing effects (Frenkel and Hemmer 1999, pp. 173–180; Barro and Sala-i Martin 2004, p. 206).

4.2.3 Fourastié and Baumol: Structural Shift Toward Sectors with Low Productivity Growth

In contrast to neoclassical growth theory, in the course of the twentieth century, several economists addressed sectoral changes as possible causes of a decline in economic growth. Among them were the French economist Jean Fourastié and his US-American (neoclassical) contemporary William J. Baumol, whose theories shall serve as prominent examples here.

Based on differences in technological progress and thus labor productivity growth, Fourastié ([1949] 1969, pp. 25–28, 74–76) distinguished between three economic sectors. While he defined the primary sector as consisting of industries with medium potential for advances in labor productivity, the secondary sector includes industries with high economic progress. The tertiary sector, on the other hand, covers all types of industries eligible for only small productivity increases. In fact, one can speak of a *dynamic* sector allocation, as changes in productivity growth can lead to a rearrangement of industries among the three sectors over time. In line with the rather traditional sectoral breakdown, at the time of writing Fourastié ([1949] 1969, pp. 27–28, 74–75) assumed the primary sector to be dominated by agriculture, the secondary sector to mainly include the manufacturing industry, and the tertiary

---

[15]On the consideration of stagnation in neoclassical growth theory, see also Brandt (1988, pp. 471–472).

sector to consist of services, such as commerce, administration, liberal professions, and education.[16]

Fourastié ([1949] 1969, pp. 78–82, 89–92) referred to a structural shift in both output and employment from the primary to the secondary and finally to the tertiary sector, a process which had started with the first Industrial Revolution and which he explained by pointing to the interaction of supply- and demand-side developments. From a (hypothetical) supply-side perspective, assuming constant working hours and a given sectoral employment structure, productivity increases would lead to a rise in output in all sectors of the economy. According to the *natural productivity hierarchy* mentioned above, however, ceteris paribus in the long run, output in the secondary sector would advance the most, while output increase in the tertiary sector would be lowest. Yet, this *natural structure of growing production*, as Fourastié ([1949] 1969, p. 82) called it, stands in contrast to the *natural structure of growing consumption* on the demand side. In accordance with Gossen's (1854, pp. 4–5) First Law, Fourastié ([1949] 1969, pp. 36, 78–82) noted that human consumption of each product has a natural limit. For instance, the human body does not allow for an unlimited intake of food. Similarly, the ownership of a very large number of, say, automobiles is usually of little benefit. In other words, the marginal utility of a good diminishes with its consumption, leading to consumption saturation. In the course of economic development and with a rise in real income per capita, such consumption saturation initially occurs in the primary sector when technological progress facilitates an abundant supply of relatively cheap agricultural products (Fourastié [1949] 1969, pp. 78–84, 91–92, 132–134). As the proportion of income spent on primary products declines, consumption demand is mainly directed toward the industrial sector. After a certain level of industrialization has been reached, however, the secondary sector is also affected by saturation tendencies. Eventually, a decline in the income share spent on secondary products is accompanied by a rise in the share spent on tertiary output. Productivity and consumption developments in the tertiary sector, however, stand in contrast to those in the primary and secondary sectors, as a limited increase in productivity faces a strong desire for tertiary goods and services (Fourastié [1949] 1969, p. 112).

> [...] *[T]he structure of growing consumption does not necessarily coincide with the structure of growing production.* The consumer does not absorb all which technological progress could offer him. If we gave full scope to technological progress, it would supply the consumer with many primary products, many secondary products, and very few tertiary products. This abundance of primary products, however, is of no use to us; we rather want more secondary and, most important, more and more tertiary products and services. [...] [There is a] divergence between consumption demand and the natural supply of production in periods of technological progress. (Fourastié [1949] 1969, p. 81, own translation)

In the long run, these diverging developments need to be reconciled. According to Fourastié ([1949] 1969, pp. 101–104, 106–122), it is the demand side which takes

---

[16]As Fourastié's own classification is empirically impractical, he maintained the traditional sectoral breakdown for his empirical analysis. See Fourastié ([1949] 1969, p. 75) and Staroske (1995, p. 20).

the lead here, with the imbalances between consumption demand and the natural production pattern being offset by shifts in the labor market (see also Knottenbauer 2000, p. 92). To initially avoid overproduction in the primary sector, agricultural workers are laid off and mainly move to the expanding industrial sector. With a relative decline in the demand for secondary products, workers are finally shifting from the secondary to the tertiary sector. After a crisis-ridden transition period, characterized by intersectoral labor migration and periodical unemployment, in the final stage of *tertiary civilization* Fourastié ([1949] 1969, pp. 120–121, 187, 242) expected ten percent of the labor force to be employed in each of the primary and the secondary sectors, and 80% to work in the tertiary sector. For the United States and other Western countries, he dated the beginning of the transition period to the Industrial Revolution between 1750 and 1800, and assumed it to pass into tertiary civilization sometime after the year 2000 (Fourastié [1949] 1969, pp. 75, 120–121; 1964, p. 65).

With a shift of output and employment toward the tertiary sector, Fourastié ([1949] 1969, pp. 242–251) was aware of economic stagnation tendencies. He mentioned:

> Under current conditions, however, the living standard [measured as output per capita] is inevitably approaching an upper limit. This upper limit follows from the fact that consumption capacity will soon only be existing in the tertiary sector, in which technological progress is currently causing only minor productivity increases. [...] [T]he tertiary sector, which offers the highest resistance to technological progress, will dominate the whole economy. [...] Capitalism will be completely destroyed by technological progress; [...] investment in the primary and secondary sectors will no longer yield any significant profit [...]. (Fourastié [1949] 1969, pp. 242, 276, own translation)

Similar to Mill ([1848] 1965), however, Fourastié (1964, p. 66; [1949] 1969, p. 277) was not averse to these developments. Although he did not expect long-term real output per capita to increase infinitely, he assumed the state of tertiary civilization to be characterized by a high level of education, ethics, and culture, as well as high-quality working conditions and diverse recreational opportunities. With limited productivity growth prospects, but a high—virtually insatiable—demand for tertiary products and services, he also anticipated the tertiary sector to provide the employment opportunities which were ultimately petering out in the primary and secondary sector. In fact, Fourastié ([1949] 1969) optimistically spoke of *the great hope of the twentieth century*. The strong demand for tertiary output he ascribed to the desire for time-saving services and to consumers' requests for individualized goods. Additionally, he pointed to the rising importance of production-related services in a technologically advanced world (Fourastié [1949] 1969, pp. 244–248; see also Häußermann and Siebel 1995, pp. 32–33).

Services indeed play the dominant role in today's developed world. In the United States, 77.0% of GDP were generated in the service sector in 2016, while, in 2017, the service sector employment share amounted to 79.4%. In Germany, in 2017 the output and employment shares of the service sector were 61.9% and 71.5%, respectively (World Bank 2018; see also Krämer 2011). Nonetheless, however, Fourastié's attitude can be challenged on several grounds. As outlined by Kalmbach et al. (2005), the industrial and service sectors are heavily intertwined, leading to a rising importance of industry-related services. Moreover, while services were almost exclusively marked by low productivity prospects up until the mid-twentieth century, this has changed during the past decades (Petzina 1996, pp. 231–232). In fact, today's service sector is characterized by a high degree of heterogeneity, as it includes low-productivity activities, but also branches with high productivity growth rates. By using modern technologies, productivity growth has been especially strong in a variety of distribution and business services, such as communications, financial intermediation, and real estate activities (Breitenfellner and Hildebrandt 2006). Hence, while—in the mid-twentieth century—Fourastié (1964, pp. 27–28) correctly associated the service industry with his low-productivity tertiary sector, today a variety of services must rather be assigned to his high-productivity secondary sector. From a long-run perspective, it is thus unclear whether the economy can provide sufficient employment opportunities (Zinn 1995, p. 64). As outlined by Zinn (1993, pp. 5–7), precarious employment conditions may prevail in the tertiary sector. Moreover, even in economies with high real income per capita, effective demand for tertiary output need not be adequate to allow for full employment (Reuter 2000, pp. 202–203; Fourastié [1949] 1969, p. 127; Zinn 2004, pp. 66–67; 1994, pp. 89–90; Kalmbach 1988; Staroske 1995, pp. 96–99). The development of real wages and income inequality play an important role here, as especially those at the bottom of the income hierarchy may have only limited demand for tertiary goods. This is all the more true when the relative price of tertiary products and services increases—a point which was particularly emphasized by Baumol (1967).

In contrast to Fourastié ([1949] 1969), Baumol (1967) seemed to be more concerned about diverging sectoral productivity developments. Similar to his French contemporary, he distinguished between two economic sectors producing final consumer goods and services: a progressive sector characterized by strong increases in productivity, and a stagnant sector with no or only limited productivity growth. While the former comprises technologically advanced and innovative industries, such as manufacturing, the latter mainly consists of a range of different services, including health care, education, legal services, welfare programs, the performing arts, and police protection (Baumol and Bowen 1965, p. 499; 1966; Baumol 2012, pp. 22, 25). Based on this sectoral division, Baumol (1967, p. 417) assumed, first, all costs other than labor to be negligible, secondly, wages in the progressive and stagnant sectors to move in parallel, and, thirdly, money wages to increase in step with labor productivity in the progressive sector. While unit costs in the progressive sector thus remain constant over time, those in the stagnant sector rise continuously—a phenomenon which Baumol et al. (1985, p. 807) called the *cost disease*. With an increase in (absolute and relative) production costs and prices in the nonprogressive sector, however, demand for these products and services can be expected to fall. "In the model of unbalanced growth [...]," Baumol (1967, p. 418) mentioned, "[...] there is a tendency for the output of the 'nonprogressive' sector whose demands are not highly inelastic to decline and perhaps, ultimately, to vanish." As outlined by Robinson (1969) and later acknowledged by Baumol (2012, p. 181), however, prices rise in proportion to wages. Hence, it is not the increase in production costs as such, but rather an unfavorable distribution of income which lies at the heart of a possible lack of aggregate demand in the nonprogressive sector.

Either way, however, Baumol (1967, pp. 418–420) acknowledged that the stagnant sector can persist. For example, certain services—such as police protection—are of such social importance that governments in advanced countries are virtually required to maintain them. Moreover, demand for some services, including health care and education, is rather price inelastic. Against this background, Baumol (1967, pp. 418) assumed a constant ratio of the real outputs of the progressive sector and nonprogressive sector.[17] Due to differences in productivity developments and given the neoclassical full-employment assumption, balanced output growth rates in both sectors require an increasing share of the labor force to be employed in the stagnant sector. In case of constant productivity in the nonprogressive sector and a stable labor force, economic growth converges to zero percent (Baumol 1967, p. 419; Harvey 1998, pp. 447–449). Yet, even if productivity growth in the nonprogressive sector is positive, aggregate productivity and thus real output growth slow down over time. The reason is that aggregate productivity growth is the weighted sum of the sectoral productivity growth rates, with the sectoral shares in total nominal output serving as weights. Hence, with a shift of labor from the progressive to the stagnant sector and a rise in the nominal output share of the nonprogressive sector, aggregate productivity and output growth decline (Oulton 2001, pp. 611–613). In describing the possibility of long-term economic growth to decline in Baumol's model, Nordhaus (2008, pp. 17–18) later referred to the *growth disease*.

The cost and growth scenarios outlined by Baumol stand and fall with the underlying assumptions. For example, (unexpected) productivity increases in service industries or diverging wage developments in the progressive and stagnant sector could retard or even prevent Baumol's pessimistic prospects (Häußermann and Siebel 1995, pp. 49–50). Moreover, as outlined by Oulton (2001) and later endorsed by Baumol (2001, p. 223; 2012, pp. 120–123), if the nonprogressive sector also produces *intermediate* goods and services, a structural shift toward the stagnant sector may boost overall productivity and economic growth. From an empirical point of view, however, Nordhaus (2008) and Hartwig and Krämer (2017), for instance, largely confirm Baumol's findings. Baumol (1967, pp. 422–426) himself, on the other hand, was not so much concerned about stagnation tendencies per se, but rather worried about the government's financial burden which he expected to arise with a growth slowdown. Aiming to provide socially important, but predominantly nonprogressive, services, public authorities are particularly severely affected by the cost disease. A persistent

---

[17] As outlined by Baumol (2012, pp. 80–81, 191–192), a constant real output ratio is a simplifying assumption which is not necessarily applicable from an empirical point of view. On the example of the United States, Appelbaum and Schettkat (1999, pp. 393–397) show that the real output share of the service sector was roughly constant until the mid-1970s, but has increased thereafter. In fact, a rise in the real output share of the nonprogressive sector reinforces Baumol's predictions (see also Oulton 2001, p. 613).

cost increase in the stagnant sector can strain the government budget, leading to growing public deficits and debt, possibly calling for unpopular tax adjustments.[18]

4.2.4 Meadows et al.: Environmental Limits to Growth

In the 1970s, the classical argument of a scarcity of fertile land leading to economic stagnation was revived in a modified and extended form. Truth be told, the debate was even more reminiscent of the issues outlined by the nineteenth-century neoclassical economist William S. Jevons (1865), who, in his book *The Coal Question*, had raised the question of sustainability and natural limits to growth. Referring to the limited coal reserves in Britain, Jevons (1865) had stressed that there must ultimately be limits to economic growth imposed by nature. More than 100 years later, in the 1970s the debate on natural, ecological growth limits was particularly triggered by the pioneering work of Meadows et al. (1972), a study commissioned by the Club of Rome. While the topic is included here as a modern stagnation hypothesis of the late twentieth century, environmental issues continue to be an important part of the public and political discourse and seem to be more relevant today than ever. In fact, over the past years several studies grew out of the endeavor to continue and update the original analysis of Meadows et al. (1972), with the works of Meadows et al. (2004), Randers (2012), and Maxton and Randers (2016) being among the most prominent examples.

Environmental scientists usually take a global perspective, arguing that growth processes cannot be maintained forever in a world characterized by a finite supply of natural resources and a limited capacity to absorb pollution (Meadows et al. 1972, pp. 51, 69). While the end of output and population growth is thus considered inevitable, it is up to the global community *how* stagnation will come about. With a view to previous and actual developments, there is general concern that the world economy has been on an unsustainable growth path, that there has been an "[...] overshoot [of] the carrying capacity of this planet [...]" (Meadows et al. 1972, p. 190).[19] For several hundred years, it is argued, population and (industrial) output have been growing exponentially on a global scale. This development, in turn, has induced an exponential increase in pollution and consumption of nonrenewable resources (Meadows et al. 1972, p. 25; 2004, pp. 17, 27). Should these developments continue, the earth's physical limits in terms of the supply of natural resources and the ability to handle pollution are feared to be approached in the not too distant future, leading to an uncontrolled collapse of social welfare, accompanied by crises, conflicts, and unrest (Meadows et al. 2004, pp. x–xii).

---

[18]It must be noted, however, that fiscal adjustments are not necessarily needed. With a rise in incomes, ceteris paribus public tax revenues can be expected to increase as well, even without a rise in tax rates.

[19]Brundtland (1987, p. 40) vaguely defines sustainable development as development which "[...] seeks to meet the needs and aspirations of the present without compromising the ability to meet those of the future."

To avoid such collapse and to allow for "[...] a smooth adaptation of the human footprint to the carrying capacity of the globe [...]," proponents of the environmental narrative ask for voluntary, self-imposed limitations to growth (Meadows et al. 2004, p. xi). Rather than provoking an unmanageable breakdown of the economy and the environment, the end of population and output growth should be actively promoted as a consistent and steady process. This particularly requires the global community to forgo its growth fetish, however, and to stop pursuing growth as a means in itself (Meadows et al. 2004, p. xviii). Describing the term *equilibrium* as a state of zero population, capital, and output growth, Meadows et al. (1972, p. 193), for example, mentioned that "[...] society [must be redirected] toward goals of equilibrium rather than growth [...]." Although the transition period toward such a "[...] steady state of economic and ecological equilibrium [...]" would be characterized by painful adjustment processes, the final state of self-imposed stagnation is generally considered to be a pleasant condition (Meadows et al. 1972, p. 196). Similar to Mill ([1848] 1965), environmental scientists do not speak of a cessation of human development, but rather point to high levels of education, leisure, and social progress (Meadows et al. 1972, pp. 180, 195–196). In the words of Meadows et al. (2004, p. 255), "A sustainable society would be interested in qualitative development, not physical expansion." Similarly, Randers (2012, p. 354) speaks of "[...] a shift in focus toward human well-being rather than per capita income growth."

Referring to developments such as progress in the field of environmental technologies or the setting of climate targets, Randers (2012, pp. 84, 107, 354) acknowledges that there have been efforts to put the world economy on a sustainable growth path during the past years. Moreover, he emphasizes that economic growth in most developed countries unintentionally has been following a declining trend and is likely to remain low in the decades ahead. He traces this development to a decline in the workforce and a slowdown in productivity growth, two factors which are also at the heart of Gordon's stagnation hypothesis that will be discussed in Sect. 4.3.2. With a view to future developments, Randers (2012, p. 162) mentions:

> The lower-than-expected GDP in 2052 [...] will occur not because people and nations will want to stop growth. It will occur because there will be fewer hands (as the population ages and then declines) and, particularly, because of slower productivity growth (as the economies mature and increasing inequality and social friction take their toll). As more economies mature, they move their production into services and care, see their labor participation rates saturate, and no longer reap the emerging-economy benefits of copying methods and technology from front-runner nations. [...] The stagnation and subsequent decline of the global economy is a huge advantage from the point of view of planetary limits.

In the context of sustainability, economic stagnation tendencies are thus to be welcomed. Despite various corrective developments that have ensued in the recent past, however, it is warned that overshoot of the earth's carrying capacity remains an issue. Should human efforts not increase in the upcoming years, Randers (2012, p. 306), for example, predicts a collapse in the second half of the twenty-first century. Similarly, Maxton and Randers (2016, p. 197) are concerned that "[...] the type of collapse we fear [...] is already under way."

While the authors mentioned in this section take account of technological advances—and, in fact, regard them as essential to lead the world economy on a sustainable growth path—they do not think that technology can eliminate natural growth limits. In a finite world, so the argument runs, indefinite growth is impossible. This view stands in contrast to the neoclassical position, which implies that price changes, substitution processes, and technological progress can overcome natural resource scarcities and, in fact, may even spur growth. "[...] [T]he *effective* stocks of natural resources [...]," Blackman and Baumol (2008) explain, "[...] are continually expanded by the same technological developments that have fueled the extraordinary growth in living standards since the Industrial Revolution." While clear predictions about the long-term future are difficult to make, actual natural resource developments might lie in between these two extremes of environmental pessimism and neoclassical optimism (see also Frenkel and Hemmer 1999, pp. 321–339).

4.3 Contemporary Supply-Side Stagnation Theories

Although the issue of possible environmental limits to economic growth continues to be highly relevant today, in the contemporary stagnation debate it is particularly the stagnation hypothesis of Robert J. Gordon which has been extensively discussed over the past years. While his theory is the major supply-side counterpart to Summers's demand-side stagnation approach, it is worth to first take a brief look at Thomas Piketty's remarks on the future of economic growth.

4.3.1 Piketty: High Growth as a Historical Exception

The main contribution of Piketty's (2014) bestseller *Capital in the Twenty-First Century* is the empirical analysis and historical classification of wealth and income distribution, mainly in advanced countries. Although the development of economic growth is not at the heart of Piketty's analysis, it nonetheless plays an important role in his theoretical framework, which is partly of neoclassical nature. In a nutshell, based on his so-called *fundamental laws of capitalism*, Piketty (2014) assumes that, ceteris paribus, lower economic growth rates tend to be accompanied by a more unequal distribution of wealth and income. The reason is that with a low growth rate it is more plausible for the rate of return on capital to exceed the growth rate of the economy, implying that capital income and (inherited) wealth potentially increase more rapidly than labor income (Piketty 2014, p. 84).

While Piketty cannot be classified as a typical stagnationist, but is rather an expert on empirical developments in income and wealth distribution, the first part of his magnum opus includes a chapter on the long-term evolution of economic growth. In line with the remarks in the Introduction to this book, Piketty (2014, pp. 72–109) points out that, from a historical perspective, economic growth is a relatively new phenomenon which has only occurred since the first Industrial Revolution in the late eighteenth century. Growth, he notes, has been slow for the most part of human history and only increased in special periods or during phases of catch-up growth (Piketty 2014, p. 72). In the twentieth century, such a special period of comparatively high economic growth were the *Trente Glorieuses* in France and other European countries, i.e., the 30 years after 1945 when the war-torn nations caught up technologically with the United States.[20] In Piketty's (2014, p. 93) own words:

> [I]t is important to recall that past growth, as spectacular as it was, almost always occurred at relatively slow annual rates, generally no more than 1–1.5 percent per year. The only historical examples of noticeably more rapid growth—3–4 percent or more—occurred in countries that were experiencing accelerated catch-up with other countries. This is a process that by definition ends when catch-up is achieved and therefore can only be transitional and time limited.

While Piketty (2014, p. 95) addresses the difficulty of making predictions of long-term future developments, he presents a growth scenario for both global output and global output per capita in the twenty-first century. This median, rather optimistic scenario, reveals long-term average growth in global output per capita to steadily decline during the years ahead and to eventually amount to 1.2% in the year 2100. The underlying assumption is that output per capita in advanced countries increases at an average rate of 1.2% in the twenty-first century. On the other hand, average output per capita growth in poor and developing countries is assumed to decline from five to four percent until 2050, and then to converge to the average output per capita growth rate in developed nations (Piketty 2014, pp. 100–101).

Especially the growth scenario for developed countries Piketty (2014, pp. 95, 102) regards as highly optimistic. To maintain an average annual increase in output per capita of 1.2% until the year 2100 would require high technological progress, especially in the area of environmental technologies. "The key point is [...]," Piketty (2014, p. 93) explains, "[...] that there is no historical example of a country at the world technological frontier whose growth in per capita output exceeded 1.5 percent over a lengthy period of time."

Piketty (2014, p. 99) assumes that global population growth will decrease to close to zero percent in the second half of the twenty-first century. Based on the growth scenario for global output *per capita*, he thus expects global output growth to steadily decline to three percent between 2030 and 2050, and to eventually fall to 1.5% during the second half of the twenty-first century (Piketty 2014, p. 101). He concludes:

> [...] [T]he twenty-first century may see a return to a low-growth regime. More precisely, what we [...] find is that growth has in fact always been relatively slow except in exceptional periods or when catch-up is occurring. Furthermore, all signs are that growth—or at any rate its demographic component—will be even slower in the future. (Piketty 2014, p. 72)

According to Piketty (2014, pp. 80, 100–101), the long-term growth rates of population, output, and output per capita each exhibit a bell-shaped curve over time, with relatively low growth rates prior to the first Industrial Revolution, increasing

---

[20]The term *Trente Glorieuses* was coined by Jean Fourastié (1979) in his book *Les Trente Glorieuses: Ou la Révolution invisible de 1946 à 1975.*

growth rates from roughly the eighteenth century to the 1970s, and a decline in growth thereafter, with the latter development expected to continue until the end of the twenty-first century. In explaining these trends, Piketty (2014, pp. 94, 586–587) also refers to the stagnationist reflections of Robert J. Gordon.

4.3.2 Gordon: Sluggish Technological Progress and Four Headwinds

4.3.2.1 Key Elements of Gordon's Stagnation Theory

As a supply-side stagnationist, Gordon (2014a) assumes that actual national output growth in the United States and other advanced countries has been declining during the past years because potential output growth has been trending downward. In the long run, he stresses, the evolution of potential output can be approximated by its actual development and described by the following identity (Gordon 2015a, p. 2):

$$\hat{Y} = \widehat{Y/H} + \hat{H}. \tag{4.2}$$

Real output growth ($\hat{Y}$) equals the sum of the growth rates of real output per hour ($\widehat{Y/H}$)—i.e., labor productivity—and total hours worked ($\hat{H}$). While Gordon (2015a, p. 2) refers to secular stagnation as a decline in potential output growth (which in the long run is approximated by actual output growth ($\hat{Y}$)), he also addresses the impact of secular stagnation on the development of the average standard of living as measured by real output *per capita* growth. Similar to Eq. (4.2), real output per capita growth ($\widehat{Y/N}$) is equal to growth in labor productivity ($\widehat{Y/H}$) plus growth in hours worked per person ($\widehat{H/N}$) (Gordon 2014b, p. 186):

$$\widehat{Y/N} = \widehat{Y/H} + \widehat{H/N}. \tag{4.3}$$

In describing the developments of (potential) real output (per capita) growth ($\hat{Y}$ and $\widehat{Y/N}$) during the past years, Gordon first and foremost refers to factors which have changed labor productivity growth ($\widehat{Y/H}$). Although he predominantly focuses on the United States, he shows that similar trends also hold for other advanced nations (Gordon 2015b). As illustrated in Fig. 4.1a, labor productivity growth has been diminishing across major developed economies during the past decades. After World War II, in the 1950s and 1960s growth in real GDP per hour worked has been relatively high, most notably in continental Europe and Japan, which were both catching up technologically with the United States. Starting around the early and late 1970s, however, productivity growth has been slowing down. Although there have been temporary recoveries, especially in the USA from the mid-1990s to the mid-2000s, overall growth in real GDP per hour has been weak in recent times.[21]

Looking at the development of labor productivity, Gordon (2016) takes a broad historical perspective and distinguishes three different eras: the years between the late nineteenth century and 1920, the period from 1920 to 1970, and the years since 1970. For each period, he analyzes the evolution of the three main drivers of average labor productivity, which—according to neoclassical growth accounting—are capital deepening, labor quality, as well as total factor productivity (TFP).[22] Referring to the United States, Gordon (2016, p. 16) finds that average annual labor productivity growth amounted to 1.50% and 1.62% from 1890 to 1920 and 1970 to 2014, respectively, while it was 2.82% in the middle period between 1920 and 1970. As compared to the other two eras, higher average growth in real output per hour worked from 1920 to 1970 can be traced back almost exclusively to higher growth rates in total factor productivity, and to a much lesser extent to higher growth in educational attainment. The long-term developments shown in Fig. 4.1b reveal that—with the exception of the years between 1995 and 2005—total factor productivity growth in the United States was indeed strongest in the 50 years from 1920 to 1970. Although there are some variations in timing, which can be partially traced back to the country-specific impact of both world wars, in most developed nations considered total factor productivity growth has slowed down markedly since the early and late 1970s.[23]

Why did average total factor productivity (in the United States) grow at such high rates during the 50 years between 1920 and 1970, but was much slower in the decades before and thereafter? According to Gordon (2016, pp. 319–320), the evolution of total factor productivity growth reflects the impact of industrial revolutions. The first Industrial Revolution took place from 1770 to 1820 and gave rise to inventions such as the steam engine, railroad, steamship, and telegraph, which continued to have an effect on productivity growth throughout the nineteenth century (Gordon 2016,

---

[21] It should be noted that the productivity measures shown in Fig. 4.1 refer to *actual* developments and do not reflect the developments along full-employment potential output paths. Although it is assumed that in the long run actual and full-employment potential developments are similar, statistical data first and foremost reflect *actual* developments. In fact, productivity growth tends to fluctuate procyclically, i.e., a decline in output growth below its full-employment potential growth rate is typically accompanied by a fall in productivity growth (and vice versa). As outlined by Clauß (1968, p. 319, own translation), "Only [...] when *all* production or productivity capacities are fully employed [...] do statistical productivity data indicate the true productive force of an economy." In case of a lack of aggregate demand and a negative output gap, "[...] the term 'productivity' should only be used in quotation marks; [...] in this case changes [in statistical data] only reflect changes in demand [...] and have little or nothing to do with the true productive force of the economy."

[22] Capital deepening is a rise in the ratio of capital input to hours worked. Labor quality captures the impact of education and experience (and other factors) on the efficiency of labor hours. Total factor productivity is commonly referred to as the Solow residual and measures the efficiency of both capital and labor resulting from innovation and technological progress (Gordon 2016, pp. 15–16; Barro and Sala-i Martin 2004, pp. 436–438).

[23] It should be noted that the average annual growth rates shown in Fig. 4.1b vary according to the exact time periods chosen. Calculations based on different sub-periods, however, do not change the basic pattern.

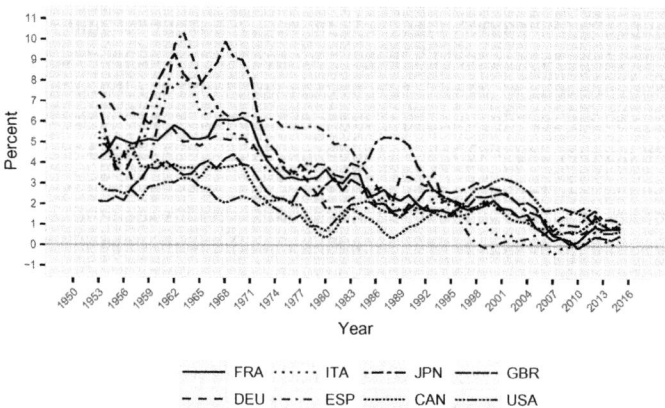

(a) Real GDP per hour growth rates (centered five-year moving averages),
1950–2017

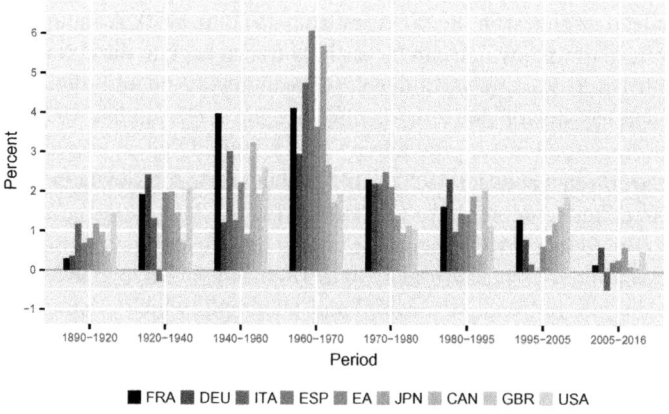

(b) Average annual total factor productivity growth rates

Fig. 4.1 Labor productivity and total factor productivity growth rates. *Source* Author's calculations
and illustrations, based on data from the The Conference Board (2018) and Bergeaud et al. (2016;
2017). See Appendix A for detailed data sources and further notes

pp. 30–31, 319). The first Industrial Revolution merged into the second Industrial
Revolution, which can be roughly dated between 1870 and 1920 and brought about
progress along many dimensions (Gordon 2016, p. 522). The invention of electricity,
electric light, the internal combustion engine, and motor vehicles, the introduction of
advanced manufacturing machinery and mass production, improvements in chem-
istry and medicine, and the networking of houses are among the numerous changes
which characterized this period (Gordon 2016, p. 285). Although the second Industrial Revolution was mainly based on inventions of the late nineteenth and early
twentieth century, their diffusion, implementation, and extension took much longer

and continued for several decades until the early 1970s. As Gordon (2016, p. 522) puts it:

> The inventions of the second industrial revolution [...] gathered momentum between 1870 and 1920 and then between 1920 and 1970 created the most rapid period of growth in labor productivity experienced in American history, bringing an utter change from 1870 in most dimensions of human life.

While the diffusion of most inventions of the second Industrial Revolution was delayed by the Great Depression and World War II, both events contributed to the progress made in the following years (Gordon 2016, pp. 18, 285). For example, it is argued that New Deal policies had a positive impact on productivity growth by reducing average working hours per week while increasing labor bargaining power and real wages. Moreover, the reorganization of manufacturing after the Great Depression as well as learning by doing and the implementation of new production techniques in the wake of the Second World War further increased efficiency. Another productivity-enhancing effect is also ascribed to the large amount of real investment by the government during the war (Gordon 2016, pp. 563–565). Against this background, Gordon (2016, p. 565) concludes that "[...] World War II saved the U.S. economy from secular stagnation, and a hypothetical scenario of economic growth after 1939 that does not include the war looks dismal at best."

According to Gordon (2016, pp. 1, 96), the era between 1870 and 1970, which was so strongly shaped by the productivity-enhancing inventions of the second Industrial Revolution, was a unique and unrepeatable period, as most of the inventions made "[...] could happen only once." That does not mean that technological change and productivity growth have come to a halt afterward. In fact, the third Industrial Revolution based on entertainment, information, and communication technologies has started around 1960 and still continues to have an impact today. The main point, however, is that the transition currently underway is quite narrow in scope as compared to the comprehensive dimension of the second Industrial Revolution (Gordon 2016, pp. 320, 578).[24] Gordon (2016, p. 575) assumes that most of the impact of the digital revolution on total factor productivity growth has already occurred during the short period between 1994 and 2004, when average annual total factor productivity growth in the United States was higher than one percent before declining again to 0.40% in the subsequent decade.[25] Although technological progress is not over, Gordon (2016, pp. 529, 589, 593) does not see any major innovation which could boost total factor productivity growth in the United States to its 1920–1970 or 1994–2004 highs in the next 25 years. While innovation and progress in fields such as medicine, robotics, and

---

[24]For example, Gordon (2016, p. 579) responds to Solow's (1987) alleged paradox that "[...] one can see the computer age everywhere but in the productivity statistics [...]" by stating that "[...] computers *are not everywhere*" (Emphasis added.) According to Gordon (2016, pp. 441–443, 578), the share of information and communication technologies in the total economy is just too small to have a similarly strong impact as the innovations of the second Industrial Revolution.

[25]As shown in Fig. 4.1, a similar temporary revival of total factor and labor productivity growth between the mid-1990s and mid-2000s has apparently not occurred in other advanced countries or—as in the case of Canada—has been less pronounced than in the United States.

big data are predicted to be steady and evolutionary (Gordon 2016, pp. 593–601), the impact on total factor productivity is assumed to be rather small (Gordon 2016, pp. 567–568, 601–604). The growing importance of the service sector, which—at least in some fields—has only comparatively little potential for large productivity gains, supports this rather gloomy forecast.

The assumption that past revivals of both total factor and labor productivity growth are unlikely to be adequate benchmarks in the years to come also shows along other dimensions. For example, business dynamism, i.e., the share of new companies among all firms, has slowed down in recent years. Similarly, growth in manufacturing capacity, net investment, and computer performance has been declining since the early 2000s and before (Gordon 2015c, p. 58; 2016, pp. 584–589). For the United States, Gordon (2016, p. 602) thus concludes that "[...] the more rapid growth of TFP during 1994–2004 represented a temporary upsurge that is unlikely to be repeated [...]" anytime soon. Forecasting the developments in the next 25 years, he predicts total factor productivity growth rates similar to those in the years from 1970 to 1994 and from 2004 to 2015 (Gordon 2016, pp. 529, 579, 589, 602, 636).

In addition to a comparatively slow pace of total factor productivity growth, there are two other forces which have hampered real output (per capita) growth during the past years and which are expected to have a continued impact over the next quarter-century. The first of these *headwinds*, as Gordon (2016, pp. 605–607) calls them, is a slowdown in the increase in educational attainment. As mentioned above, education is important for productivity growth ($\widehat{Y/H}$), because it increases labor quality and the efficiency of hours worked. Educational attainment seems to have reached a plateau, however, and has been increasing only slowly during the past decades (Gordon 2012, p. 16). While the strong rise in average years of schooling per person that took place in the twentieth century could not continue indefinitely, educational attainment has decreased along several dimensions in the recent past. For example, high school completion rates in the United States are lower today than in 1970, with secondary educational outcomes being rather unsatisfactory (Gordon 2016, p. 625). Although college completion rates in the United States are still rising, many graduates are underemployed in the sense that they cannot find adequate jobs requiring a college degree (Gordon 2016, p. 626). As pointed out by the OECD (2016, p. 16), educational progress in advanced countries is relatively diverse, with most nations, however, missing certain educational development targets.

The second headwind addresses demographic change, reducing growth in hours worked (per capita) ($\hat{H}$ and $\widehat{H/N}$), thus putting downward pressure on real output (per capita) growth rates ($\hat{Y}$ and $\widehat{Y/N}$) (Gordon 2016, pp. 627–629). While hours worked (per capita) had grown quite strongly from the 1970s to the mid-1990s as a result of women and baby boomers entering the labor force, this trend reversed in subsequent years. Slower growth in the working-age population, a decline in labor force participation rates, as well as the retirement of the first baby boomers have contributed to this development.

In addition to these two headwinds, Gordon (2016) identifies two more factors which he does not directly link to real output (per capita) growth ($\hat{Y}$ and $\widehat{Y/N}$), but which have an impact on *median* and *disposable* income growth, respectively, and are thus important to get a broader picture of the overall development of the standard of living. The first of these headwinds is rising income inequality, which has already been underway for several years in the United States and other advanced countries. While Gordon does not refer to a possible nexus between changes in income distribution and real output growth, his main point is that the fruits of economic progress are not shared equally when those at the top of the distribution enjoy a much more pronounced growth in their incomes than those at the bottom. With high and rising income inequality, so his argument runs, growth in real output per capita gives a rather distorted picture of the development of the overall standard of living (Gordon 2016, pp. 608–620). Indeed, *median* income per capita has grown considerably less than average income per capita during the past decades. Absent counteracting forces, in the years ahead the inequality headwind will likely continue to put downward pressure on real income growth in the lower parts of the income hierarchy.[26]

Finally, according to Gordon (2016, pp. 629–630) high public debt-to-GDP ratios are likely to hamper *disposable* income growth in the future. He argues that, in light of slower population growth and higher life expectancy, current developments in government debt-to-GDP ratios in the United States and other advanced countries are on the verge of becoming unsustainable. As governments sooner or later will be forced to reduce their debt by cutting transfer payments and/or by raising taxes, future growth in income after taxes and transfers—i.e., disposable income growth—will likely be slower.

Considering the impact of all four headwinds—i.e., the slowdown in educational attainment, demographic change, rising income inequality, and "[...] the strong likelihood of a fiscal correction [...]," Gordon (2016, p. 607) predicts future growth in real median disposable income to be much lower than in the past. "When combined with the implications of a smaller effect of innovation on productivity since 1970 [...]," he holds, "[...] there is little room for growth at all. [...] [T]he future growth of real median disposable income per person will be barely positive [...]" (Gordon 2016, p. 607).

4.3.2.2 Policy Implications

The policy implications proposed by Gordon (2016, pp. 643–652) mainly aim at alleviating the four headwinds. While he focuses again on the United States, the severity of each headwind differs from country to country. For instance, in Europe and Japan demographic change is more pressing, but income inequality has risen less during the past years as compared to the United States. The policy prescriptions

---

[26]Closely related to income inequality is the aforementioned issue of education, with the causal link probably holding in both directions. While differences in educational attainment are among the various causes of income inequality, by the same token a more unequal income distribution may contribute to higher educational inequalities across generations (Gordon 2016, pp. 620–624, 631). Hence, as education is an important driver of labor productivity, higher income inequality may hamper growth in real output via the educational channel.

recommended from a US-American perspective are therefore no universal remedy, but they can serve as a first point of reference, with the detailed policy designs being country-specific.

To raise the overall educational attainment, with regard to the United States Gordon (2016, pp. 647–648) advocates universal preschool education which would probably mostly benefit children and families at the bottom of the income hierarchy. Moreover, a shift from local- to state-financed public schools is assumed to reduce regional inequalities in the quality of education. On the other hand, to adequately address student indebtedness in the wake of tertiary education, a more flexible debt repayment scheme could be established.

The promotion of high-skilled immigration could mitigate the demographic headwind by boosting the share of the working-age population, while at the same time raising the average educational level (Gordon 2016, p. 650). In light of the general rise in average life expectancy, raising the retirement age is also considered (Gordon 2014b, p. 191).

The trend toward a more unequal distribution of income during the past decades could be alleviated or reversed by establishing a more progressive tax system. Raising tax rates on very high incomes, dividends, and capital gains, as well as closing loopholes in tax legislation are some of the key elements. Furthermore, inequality at the bottom of the distribution could be attenuated by raising the real minimum wage (Gordon 2016, pp. 644–645). A more far-reaching reform proposal refers to shorter prison sentences for non-violent offenders, aiming to allow for better social rehabilitation (Gordon 2016, p. 646).

In addition to the already mentioned tax reforms, a carbon tax is recommended to further increase government revenue and thus to diminish the rise in government debt (Gordon 2016, pp. 650–651). Other considerations include drug legalization, which is assumed to reduce public spending and increase tax revenue (Gordon 2016, pp. 646–647).

Although Gordon aims to address his four headwinds with this range of policy implications, he is yet aware of the limits. As especially the issues of low productivity growth—including a slowdown in the increase of educational attainment—rising income inequality, and demographic change partly rest on deep, fundamental developments, he acknowledges that the proposed policy measures may only result in small increases in median disposable income growth (Gordon 2016, p. 652).

4.3.2.3 General Perception and Critical Assessment

Gordon Versus the Techno-Optimists

While Gordon's opinion on future technological progress largely reflects the arguments put forward by Cowen (2011), his rather skeptical prospects for potential economic growth are not shared by everyone. Although there has been only little discussion on his four headwinds, his view on the future of innovation and technological progress has been highly debated and is subject to criticism. Eichengreen (2015a; 2015b), for example, has joined in the discussion on the prospects for technological advance. While he is hesitant to make any predictions, he suggests that it might just take some time for the full potential of technological progress to be reflected in total factor productivity growth. He points out that the implementation of new technologies usually requires a range of adaptations and the reorganization of economic processes (Eichengreen 2015a, pp. 69–70). While a first wave of the digital revolution showed up in official growth rates with delay between the mid-1990s and mid-2000s, a second wave of advances in information technology might well be underway. Eichengreen (2015b, pp. 9–10) thus supposes that the fact that "[...] the [...] IT revolution, as captured by TFP growth, took a decade-long pause between 2005 and 2015 may be less a portent of secular stagnation than a harbinger of better times to come."

Gordon (2016, p. 567), of course, does not share this view, stating that most applications of the third Industrial Revolution have already happened, leaving little room for technological progress to accelerate in the next 25 years. While he describes himself as a techno-pessimist, arguing that technological change in the next quarter-century is unlikely to speed up, the so-called techno-optimists, including Mokyr (2014b; 2014a) and Brynjolfsson and McAfee (2011; 2014), have high hopes for future progress. Mokyr (2014a, p. 89), for instance, criticizes the techno-pessimists around Gordon for their "[...] shortfall of imagination [...]" and for making future predictions by extrapolating only the most recent developments (Mokyr 2014b). He is convinced that science and technology will advance at high rates, and he particularly points to the interaction between the two. Powerful computers, vast databases, and nanotechnology, Mokyr (2014a, pp. 84–86) holds, are among the tools which spur science and technology today and which have great potential for promoting future progress in a variety of areas. Similar to Schumpeter ([1942] 2008, p. 118), in fact, he seems to think of technological possibilities as an "[...] uncharted sea [...]." While he expects further breakthroughs especially in information technology, genetics, biotechnology, and nanomaterials, he is convinced that advances in other fields which cannot be foreseen today will follow in the decades ahead (Mokyr 2014b; 2014a). Technology, Mokyr (2014b) predicts, "[...] will continue to develop and change human life and society at a rate that may well dwarf even the dazzling developments of the twentieth century."

Brynjolfsson and McAfee (2011; 2014, pp. 79–81) argue along similar lines, stating that Gordon is not paying enough tribute to the potential of digital technologies. According to them, the digital revolution is by no means over, but will take several decades to fully exploit its potential (Brynjolfsson and McAfee 2011, p. 76). Yet, although they are optimistic with regard to technological progress, they are worried that high unemployment could become a real problem in the future (Brynjolfsson and McAfee 2011, p. 38). In fact, they predict technological change to be so rapid that human skills and institutions are unable to adjust fast enough (Brynjolfsson and McAfee 2011, pp. 51–52). Skill-biased technological change has indeed played a role in the polarization of labor demand during the past decades. While modern technologies have mainly replaced middle-skilled workers performing routine tasks, technological progress has complemented high-skilled workers and has had little influence on low-skilled labor engaged in non-routine (service) jobs (Autor et al.

2003; Autor and Dorn 2013). Pointing to technological progress in fields such as driverless cars or electronic medical diagnostics, however, Brynjolfsson and McAfee (2014, pp. 14–15, 92; 2011, pp. 50–51) expect that even low- and high-skilled tasks are at risk of being increasingly replaced by machines in the upcoming years.

Gordon's supply-side stagnation hypothesis is only to a limited extent undermined by the arguments put forward by the techno-optimists. Most important, Mokyr, Brynjolfsson, and McAfee seem to misinterpret his assumption regarding future technological advance. As already mentioned, Gordon does not make any predictions *beyond* the next 25 years. Moreover, for the upcoming quarter-century he does not expect a *slowdown* in technological progress, but a *continuation* of the trends during the past decades. In fact, Gordon's growth pessimism mainly stems from the impact of the headwinds, not from a slowdown in technological change. While future technological progress cannot be predicted with absolute certainty, he argues that a number of past inventions—such as running water, air conditioning, and automobiles—did not come as complete surprises, but had already been discernible years before (Gordon 2016, pp. 589–591). In contrast, most of the forecasts made by the techno-optimists (still) seem like wishful thinking, making an acceleration of technological progress in the next quarter-century unlikely (Gordon 2014b, p. 188). Gordon (2016, pp. 568, 602–604) thus rejects the assumption that mass unemployment will evolve due to overly rapid technological advance. He rather supposes that technology and the labor market will change together over time, with old jobs being destroyed and new ones being created. While Gordon may be right from a long-term perspective, it is reasonable to assume, however, that—in light of downward trending employment-to-population ratios among prime-aged men (see Fig. 3.4b, p. 72)—technological change has at least played some role in the labor market over the past years. Summers (2016), for instance, has pointed this out as well.

According to the techno-optimists, high and even rising rates of technological progress are not necessarily reflected in higher total factor productivity and real output (per capita) growth rates. Their argument is that traditional measures of progress and growth tend to underestimate many dimensions of the welfare gains of technological advance. Among these unmeasured benefits are the increase in leisure, the provision of free information and services via the Internet, and the possibility to work from home (Mokyr 2014a, p. 88; 2014b; Brynjolfsson and McAfee 2011, pp. 30–31). With digital goods and services becoming more and more important, it is argued, these measurement errors are likely to increase over time (Brynjolfsson and McAfee 2011, p. 31). As rightly noted by Gordon (2014b, pp. 189–190), however, total factor productivity growth had started to slow down years before the Internet became popular. Moreover, flawed productivity growth rates are not a unique characteristic of the digital era but have always existed. Referring to the various improvements in the standard of living throughout history, according to Gordon (2016, p. 13 and p. 566; 2014b, p. 190) the unmeasured benefits of technological progress are likely to have been greatest in the nineteenth and twentieth century.

Economists rejecting Gordon's pessimistic predictions of future economic growth are generally not targeting his main concern: the four headwinds. In fact, while the issues of demographic change and government debt are not debated at all, both

Mokyr (2014a, p. 88) and Brynjolfsson and McAfee (2011, pp. 32–34, 47–50; 2014, pp. 147–162) share Gordon's concern with regard to the unequal distribution of income. Brynjolfsson and McAfee (2011, pp. 60–61) moreover agree with Gordon that educational attainment has slowed down. Hence, although the techno-optimists concur with some of Gordon's headwinds, their denial of his stagnation hypothesis is based on speculations about future technological progress. The future path of technological change, however, cannot be predicted with absolute certainty. In contrast, demographic change, high and possibly rising income inequality, a slowdown in educational attainment, as well as high government debt-to-GDP ratios have been a reality in many advanced countries for several years. While there is room for discussion on how these headwinds impact the economy, absent counteracting forces they will remain a challenge in the years to come.

Gordon Versus Summers

In the contemporary stagnation debate, Gordon's supply-side theory and Summers's demand-side hypothesis of secular stagnation are typically considered competing doctrines. Although the cores of their theories are essentially different, both approaches contain plausible arguments and are not necessarily mutually exclusive. Long-term economic growth can indeed be simultaneously restricted by factors hampering aggregate demand and by factors inhibiting the supply side of the economy. Moreover, factors such as demographic change or the unequal distribution of income are likely to have a direct impact on both demand and supply. The distinction between demand- and supply-side developments can thus become blurred. In fact, Gordon (2015a, p. 21) himself mentions that "[...] secular stagnation is not about just demand or supply, but also about the interaction between demand and supply."

As has been outlined in Sect. 2.2, output gap estimates are among the economic indicators which are typically adduced to distinguish demand- from supply-side issues. Referring to the developments since 2008–2009, it has been shown that the (estimated) negative output gaps which evolved in the wake of the financial crisis seem to have narrowed during the past years and are now more or less closed (see Fig. 3.7, p. 75). As these (estimated) developments were apparently not due to a catch-up of actual output trends to pre-crisis growth paths, but were largely based on downward revisions of potential output estimates, hysteresis effects have certainly played a role here (see also Martin 2011). For instance, speaking of the United States, Reifschneider et al. (2015, p. 71) stress that, "[...] a significant portion of the recent damage to the supply side [...] plausibly was endogenous to the weakness in aggregate demand." Moreover, Martin and Rowthorn (2012) note that labor hoarding during the crisis has been partially responsible for the slowdown in total factor productivity and overall productivity growth in several European nations.[27] In observing low growth

---

[27] As argued by Martin and Rowthorn (2012, pp. 55), due to large layoffs of labor, countries such as the United States and Spain experienced relatively stable and even rising productivity growth rates in the wake of the financial crisis of 2008–2009. In contrast, in the United Kingdom, Germany, and other European countries, productivity growth slowed down more strongly after the crisis, as labor was hoarded to some degree. On the nexus between labor productivity and labor hoarding, see also Okun (1962) and Biddle (2014).

in output per hour and total factor productivity *since the mid-2000s*, Gordon (2015a) may thus confuse cyclical and hysteresis effects with purely exogenous, long-term supply-side forces. This does not mean, however, that the secular supply-side factors mentioned by Gordon (2016) are not relevant. Demographic change, a slowdown in educational attainment, and a relatively low pace of technological progress may well hamper potential output growth over time. Yet, these factors are unlikely to have alone caused the rather sudden slowdown in potential output growth estimates after the financial crisis of 2008–2009, to which Gordon (2015a; 2018) frequently refers when describing his secular stagnation hypothesis.

From a long-run point of view, both adequate demand and supply are necessary to foster economic growth. Thus, if aggregate demand and supply are gradually hampered by the various factors mentioned by Gordon and Summers, a period of economic stagnation could become a real problem in developed countries. The question of whether major advanced countries have actually entered a *prolonged* period of stagnation cannot be answered, however, as future developments could well turn out differently than currently expected by secular stagnation advocates. Yet, the arguments put forward by Gordon and Summers are mainly based on a series of long-term factors which do not evolve or vanish overnight and are thus likely to impact economic growth during the years ahead in one way or another. As long as developments such as adverse demographic change, high and partly rising income inequalities, or a slowdown in educational attainment prevail, the possible threat of secular stagnation should be taken seriously.

References

Appelbaum E, Schettkat R (1999) Are prices unimportant? The changing structure of the industrialized economies. J Post Keynesian Econ 21(3):387–398

Autor DH, Dorn D (2013) The growth of low-skill service jobs and the polarization of the US labor market. Am Econ Rev 103(5):1553–1597

Autor DH, Levy F, Murnane RJ (2003) The skill content of recent technological change: an empirical exploration. Q J Econ 118(4):1279–1333

Barro RJ, Sala-i Martin X (2004) Economic growth, 2nd edn. The MIT Press, Cambridge, MA

Baumol WJ (1967) Macroeconomics of unbalanced growth: the anatomy of urban crisis. Am Econ Rev 57(3):415–426

Baumol WJ (2001) An interview with William J. Baumol, by Alan B. Krueger. J Econ Perspect 15(3):211–231

Baumol WJ (2012) The cost disease: why computers get cheaper and health care doesn't. Yale University Press, New Haven, CT, and London

Baumol WJ, Bowen WG (1965) On the performing arts: the anatomy of their economic problems. Am Econ Rev 55(1/2):495–502

Baumol WJ, Bowen WG (1966) Performing arts—the economic dilemma: a study of problems common to theater, opera, music and dance. The Twentieth Century Fund, New York, NY

Baumol WJ, Blackman SAB, Wolff EN (1985) Unbalanced growth revisited: asymptotic stagnancy and new evidence. Am Econ Rev 75(4):806–817

Bergeaud A, Cette G, Lecat R (2016) Productivity trends in advanced countries between 1890 and 2012. Rev Income Wealth 62(3):420–444

Bergeaud A, Cette G, Lecat R (2017) Long term productivity database. Version 2, August 2017. Available at http://www.longtermproductivity.com/. Accessed 09 Nov 2018

Biddle JE (2014) The cyclical behavior of labor productivity and the emergence of the labor hoarding concept. J Econ Perspect 28(2):197–212

Blackman SAB, Baumol WJ (2008) Natural resources. The library of economics and liberty encyclopedia. Liberty Fund, Inc., Carmel, IN. Available at http://www.econlib.org/library/Enc/NaturalResources.html. Accessed 01 Sept 2017

Blaug M (1968) Economic theory in retrospect, 2nd edn. Cambridge University Press, Cambridge, UK

Brandt K (1988) Dogmengeschichtliche Betrachtungen zur Stagnationsthese (The theory of secular stagnation: a historical view). Jahrbücher für Nationalöknomie und Statistik (Journal of Economics and Statistics) 205(6):465–479

Breitenfellner A, Hildebrandt A (2006) High employment with low productivity? The service sector as a determinant of economic development. Monet Policy Econ: Q Rev Econ Policy (Oesterreichische Nationalbank) Q1(06):110–135

Brundtland GH (ed) (1987) Our common future. The World Commission on Environment and Development. Oxford University Press, Oxford and New York, NY

Brynjolfsson E, McAfee A (2011) Race against the machine: how the digital revolution is accelerating innovation, driving productivity, and irreversibly transforming employment and the economy. Digital Frontier Press, Lexington, MA

Brynjolfsson E, McAfee A (2014) The second machine age: work, progress, and prosperity in a time of brilliant technologies. W. W. Norton & Company, New York, NY

Clauß FJ (1968) Konjunktur und Neoklassik: Sparen und Investieren, öffentliche Haushalte und wirtschaftliches Wachstum in der konjunkturbewegten Volkswirtschaft (USA 1929–1967). Duncker & Humblot, Berlin and Munich

Cowen T (2011) The great stagnation. Dutton, New York, NY

Dal Pont Legrand M, Hagemann H (2016) Business cycles, growth, and economic policy: Schumpeter and the Great Depression. J Hist Econ Thought 39(1):19–33

Dal Pont Legrand M, Hagemann H (2017) Retrospectives: do productive recessions show the recuperative powers of capitalism? Schumpeter's analysis of the cleansing effect. J Econ Perspect 31(1):245–256

de Vivo G (1987) Ricardo, David (1772–1823). In: Eatwell J, Milgate M, Newman P (eds) The New Palgrave Dictionary of Economics, vol 4. Macmillan, London, pp 183–198

Dockès P (2015) Les débats sur la stagnation séculaire dans les années 1937–1950: Hansen-Terborgh et Schumpeter-Sweezy. Revue Économique 66(5):967–992

Eichengreen B (2015a) Secular stagnation: the long view. Am Econ Rev 105(5):66–70

Eichengreen B (2015b) Wall of worries: reflections on the secular stagnation debate. Institute for Monetary and Economic Studies of the Bank of Japan, Discussion Paper No. 2015-E-5. Bank of Japan, Tokyo. Available at http://www.imes.boj.or.jp/research/papers/english/15-E-05.pdf. Accessed 13 Sept 2016

Elster J (1986) An introduction to Karl Marx. Cambridge University Press, Cambridge, UK

Eltis W ([1989] 2008) David Ricardo (1772–1823). In: Starbatty J (ed) Klassiker des ökonomischen Denkens (Gesamtausgabe), Teil 1: Von Platon bis John Stuart Mill. Nikol Verlag, Hamburg, pp 188–207

Foster JB (2011) On the laws of capitalism, 1. Insights from the Sweezy-Schumpeter debate. Month Rev 63(1):1–11, 16

Foster JB (2017) Introduction. In: Baran N, Foster JB (eds) The age of monopoly capital: selected correspondence of Paul M. Sweezy and Paul A. Baran, 1949–1964, Monthly Review Press, New York, NY, pp 13–48

Fourastié J ([1949] 1969) Die große Hoffnung des zwanzigsten Jahrhunderts. German translation of the final French edn. Bund-Verlag, Cologne

Fourastié J (1964) Die große Metamorphose des 20. Jahrhunderts. Econ-Verlag, Dusseldorf and Vienna

Fourastié J (1979) Les Trente Glorieuses: Ou la Révolution invisible de 1946 à 1975. Fayard, Paris
Frenkel M, Hemmer HR (1999) Grundlagen der Wachstumstheorie. Verlag Franz Vahlen, Munich
Galor O, Weil DN (2000) Population, technology, and growth. Am Econ Rev 90(4):806–828
Gehrke C (1991) Wachstumstheoretische Vorstellungen bei Adam Smith. In: Kurz HD (ed) Adam
    Smith (1723–1790) – Ein Werk und seine Wirkungsgeschichte. Metropolis-Verlag, Marburg, pp
    129–150
Gehrke C (2008) Karl Marx. In: Kurz HD (ed) Klassiker des ökonomischen Denkens, vol 1. Von
    Adam Smith bis Alfred Marshall. Verlag C.H.Beck, Munich, pp 217–241
Gordon RJ (2012) Is U.S. economic growth over? Faltering innovation confronts the six headwinds.
    NBER Working Paper No. 18315. National Bureau of Economic Research, Cambridge, MA.
    Available at http://www.nber.org/papers/w18315.pdf. Accessed 20 Sept 2016
Gordon RJ (2014a) The turtle's progress: secular stagnation meets the headwinds. In: Teulings C,
    Baldwin R (eds) Secular stagnation: facts, causes and cures. CEPR Press, London, pp 47–59
Gordon RJ (2014b) US economic growth is over: the short run meets the long run. In: Derviş K,
    Kharas H (eds) Think Tank 20: growth, convergence and income distribution: the road from the
    Brisbane G-20 summit. Brookings, Washington, DC, pp 185–192
Gordon RJ (2015a) Secular stagnation on the supply side: U.S. productivity growth in the
    short and long run. Background paper for the Philadelphia Fed Policy Forum, December
    04, 2015. Available at https://www.philadelphiafed.org/-/media/research-and-data/events/2015/
    fed-policy-forum/papers/gordon-secular_stagnation.pdf. Accessed 17 Sept 2016
Gordon RJ (2015b) Secular stagnation on the supply side: U.S. productivity growth in the short
    and long run. Presentation at the Bank of Canada and European Central Bank conference on the
    underwhelming global post-crisis growth performance, Ottawa, June 8, 2015. Available at http://
    www.bankofcanada.ca/wp-content/uploads/2015/08/gordon.pdf. Accessed 17 Sept 2016
Gordon RJ (2015c) The economics of secular stagnation. Secular stagnation: a supply-side view.
    Am Econ Rev 105(5):54–59
Gordon RJ (2016) The rise and fall of American growth. The U.S. standard of living since the Civil
    War. Princeton University Press, Princeton, NJ
Gordon RJ (2018) Why has economic growth slowed when innovation appears to be accelerating?
    NBER Working Paper No. 24554. National Bureau of Economic Research, Cambridge, MA.
    Available at http://www.nber.org/papers/w24554. Accessed 19 June 2018
Gossen HH (1854) Entwicklung der Gesetze des menschlichen Verkehrs, und der daraus fließenden
    Regeln für menschliches Handeln. Friedrich Vieweg und Sohn, Braunschweig
Hagemann H (2009) Solow's 1956 contribution in the context of the Harrod-Domar model. Hist
    Polit Econ 41:67–87
Harrod RF (1948) Towards a dynamic economics: some recent developments of economic theory
    and their application to policy. Macmillan & Co., Ltd., London
Hartwig J, Krämer H (2017) The growth disease at 50: Baumol after Oulton. Aggregate pro-
    ductivity growth and the service industry. Discussion Papers of the Faculty of Management
    Science and Engineering, Karlsruhe University of Applied Sciences, No. 2/2017. Karlsruhe Uni-
    versity of Applied Sciences, Karlsruhe. Available at https://www.hs-karlsruhe.de/fileadmin/hska/
    W/allgemein/Schriftenreihe_2-2017.pdf. Accessed 20 Oct 2017
Harvey MC (1998) Écarts de productivité et "maladie des coûts". Apports et limites du modèle de
    croissance déséquilibrée de William J. Baumol. Revue Économique 49(2):437–467
Häußermann H, Siebel W (1995) Dienstleistungsgesellschaften. Suhrkamp, Frankfurt am Main
Heertje A (1987) Schumpeter, Joseph Alois. In: Eatwell J, Milgate M, Newman P (eds) The New
    Palgrave Dictionary of Economics, vol 4. Macmillan, London, pp 263–267
Higgins B (1959) Economic development: principles, problems, and policies. W. W. Norton &
    Company, Inc., New York, NY
Hollander S (1997) The economics of Thomas Robert Malthus. (Studies in Classical Political
    Economy / IV). University of Toronto Press, Toronto, Buffalo, NY, and London
Jevons WS (1865) The coal question: an inquiry concerning the progress of the nation, and the
    probable exhaustion of our coal-mines. Macmillan and Co., London and Cambridge, UK

Kalmbach P (1988) Der Dienstleistungssektor: Noch immer die große Hoffnung des 20. Jahrhunderts? In: Süß W, Schroeder K (eds) Technik und Zukunft: Neue Technologien und ihre Bedeutung für die Gesellschaft. Westdeutscher Verlag, Opladen, pp 166–181

Kalmbach P, Franke R, Knottenbauer K, Krämer H (2005) Die Interdependenz von Industrie und Dienstleistungen: Zur Dynamik eines komplexen Beziehungsgeflechts. edition sigma, Berlin

Knottenbauer K (2000) Theorien des sektoralen Strukturwandels. Metropolis-Verlag, Marburg

Krämer H (2011) Dienstleistungen im Strukturwandel: Entwicklung und Perspektiven für Wachstum und Beschäftigung in Europa. Wirtschaft und Gesellschaft 37(2):269–291

Kurz HD (2008) David Ricardo (1772–1823). In: Kurz HD (ed) Klassiker des ökonomischen Denkens, vol I. Von Adam Smith bis Alfred Marshall. Verlag C.H.Beck, Munich, pp 120–139

Kurz HD (2018) Das Gespenst säkularer Stagnation. Metropolis-Verlag, Marburg

Kurz HD, Sturn R (2013) Die größten Ökonomen: Adam Smith. UVK Verlagsgesellschaft mbH, Constance and Munich

Lebowitz MA (2004) Paul M. Sweezy. Month Rev 56(5):40–68

Lucas RE (1986) On the mechanics of economic development. J Monet Econ 22(1988):3–42

Malthus TR (1798) An essay on the principles of population, 1st edn. J. Johnson, London

Malthus TR (1803) An essay on the principles of population, 2nd edn. J. Johnson, London

Malthus TR (1815) An inquiry into the nature and progress of rent. John Murray, London

Mandel E (1987) Marx, Karl Heinrich. In: Eatwell J, Milgate M, Newman P (eds) The New Palgrave Dictionary of Economics, vol 3. Macmillan, London, pp 367–383

Martin B (2011) Is the British economy supply constrained? A critique of productivity pessimism. Centre for Business Research, University of Cambridge, July 2011. UK-Innovation Research Centre, Cambridge, UK, and London. Available at http://citeseerx.ist.psu.edu/viewdoc/download? doi=10.1.1.220.9161&rep=rep1&type=pdf. Accessed 24 Nov 2018

Martin B, Rowthorn R (2012) Is the British economy supply constrained II? A renewed critique of productivity pessimism. Centre for Business Research, University of Cambridge, May 2012. UK-Innovation Research Centre, Cambridge, UK, and London. Available at http://www.uk-irc. org/wp-content/uploads/2013/04/2012_BM_UK_economy_report.pdf. Accessed 24 Nov 2018

Marx K ([1857–1858] 1973) Grundrisse: foundations of the critique of political economy (rough draft) (translated with a foreword by Martin Nicolaus). Penguin Books, Harmondsworth

Marx K ([1861–1863] 1968) Theories of surplus-value, part II (translated from the German, edited by S. Ryazanskaya). Progress Publishers, Moscow

Marx K ([1867] 1906) Capital: a critique of political economy, vol I: the process of capitalist production (edited by Frederick Engels, translated from the third German edition by Samuel Moore and Edward Aveling). Charles H. Kerr & Company, Chicago, IL

Marx K ([1894] 1909) Capital: a critique of political economy, vol III: the process of capitalist production as a whole (edited by Frederick Engels, translated from the first German edition by Ernest Untermann). Charles H. Kerr & Company, Chicago, IL

Marx K, Engels F ([1848] 1906) Manifesto of the communist party (authorized English translation: edited and annotated by Frederick Engels). Charles H. Kerr & Company, Chicago, IL

März E ([1989] 2008) Joseph Alois Schumpeter (1883–1950). In: Starbatty J (ed) Klassiker des ökonomischen Denkens (Gesamtausgabe), Teil 2: Von Karl Marx bis John Maynard Keynes. Nikol Verlag, Hamburg, pp 251–272

Maxton G, Randers J (2016) Reinventing prosperity: managing economic growth to reduce unemployment, inequality, and climate change. Greystone Books, Vancouver

Meadows DH, Meadows DL, Randers J, Behrens WW III (1972) The limits to growth. Universe Books, New York, NY

Meadows DH, Randers J, Meadows D (2004) Limits to growth: The 30-year update. Earthscan, London and Sterling, VA

Mill JS ([1848] 1965) Principles of political economy (two volumes). In: Robson JM (ed) Collected Works of John Stuart Mill, vol II and III. University of Toronto Press, Toronto

Mokyr J (2014a) Secular stagnation? Not in your life. In: Teulings C, Baldwin R (eds) Secular stagnation: facts, causes and cures, CEPR Press, London, pp 83–89

Mokyr J (2014b) The next age of invention: technology's future is brighter than pessimists allow. City J, Winter 2014. Available at http://www.city-journal.org/html/next-age-invention-13618.html. Accessed 23 Sept 2016

Nordhaus WD (2008) Baumol's diseases: a macroeconomic perspective. BE J Macroecon 8(1):Article 9

OECD (2016) Education at a glance 2016: OECD indicators. OECD Publishing, Paris

Okun AM (1962) Potential GNP: its measurement and significance. In: American Statistical Association (ed) Proceedings of the Business and Economics Statistics Section, pp 98–104

Oulton N (2001) Must the growth rate decline? Baumol's unbalanced growth revisited. Oxford Econ Papers 53(4):605–627

Petzina D (1996) Wirtschaftsstruktur und Strukturwandel: Tertiärer Bereich. In: Ambrosius G, Petzina D, Plumpe W (eds) Moderne Wirtschaftsgeschichte: Eine Einführung für Historiker und Ökonomen, R. Oldenbourg Verlag, Munich, pp 231–241

Piketty T (2014) Capital in the twenty-first century. Harvard University Press, Cambridge, MA, and London

Randers J (2012) 2052: A global forecast for the next forty years. A Report to the Club of Rome commemorating the 40th anniversary of *The Limits to Growth*. Chelsea Green Publishing, Whiter River Junction, VT

Reifschneider D, Wascher W, Wilcox D (2015) Aggregate supply in the United States: recent developments and implications for the conduct of monetary policy. IMF Econ Rev 63(1):71–109

Reuter N (2000) Ökonomik der "Langen Frist": Zur Evolution der Wachstumsgrundlagen in Industriegesellschaften. Metropolis-Verlag, Marburg

Ricardo D ([1815] 1951) An essay on the influence of a low price of corn on the profits of stock. In: Sraffa P (ed) The works and correspondence of David Ricardo, vol IV. Pamphlets and papers 1815–1823. Cambridge University Press for the Royal Economic Society, London, pp 1–41

Ricardo D ([1817] 1951) On the principles of political economy and taxation. In: Sraffa P (ed) The works and correspondence of David Ricardo, vol I: on the principles of political economy and taxation. Cambridge University Press for the Royal Economic Society, London

Riese H (1965) Ein neoklassisches Modell der säkularen Stagnation. Zeitschrift für die gesamte Staatswissenschaft 121(4):693–711

Robinson J (1969) Macroeconomics of unbalanced growth: a belated comment. Am Econ Rev 59(4):632

Romer PM (1986) Increasing returns and long-run growth. J Polit Econ 94(5):1002–1037

Rothschild KW (1994) Josef Steindl: 1912–1993. Econ J 104(422):131–137

Samuelson PA ([1970] 1972) Memories. In: Merton RC (ed) The collected scientific papers of Paul A. Samuelson, vol III, The MIT Press, Cambridge, MA, and London, pp 710–712

Samuelson PA (2015) The Harvard-circle. J Evolut Econ 25(1):31–36

Schumpeter JA (1931) The present world depression: a tentative diagnosis. Am Econ Rev 21(1):179–182

Schumpeter JA ([1934] (1989) Depressions: can we learn from past experience? In: Clemence RV (ed) Essays on entrepreneurs, innovations, business cycles, and the evolution of capitalism (with a new introduction by Richard Swedberg). Transaction Publishers, New Brunswick and London, pp 108–117

Schumpeter JA (1935) The analysis of economic change. Rev Econ Stat 17(4):2–10

Schumpeter JA (1939) Business cycles (two volumes). McGraw-Hill Book Company, Inc., New York, NY, and London

Schumpeter JA ([1941] 1991) An economic interpretation of our time: the Lowell lectures. In: Swedberg R (ed) The economics and sociology of capitalism. Princeton University Press, Princeton, NJ, pp 339–400

Schumpeter JA ([1942] 2008) Capitalism, socialism and democracy, third edn. Harper Perennial Modern Thought, New York, NY, et al

Schumpeter JA (1950) The march into socialism. Am Econ Rev 40(2):446–456

Schumpeter JA (1954) History of economic analysis. Oxford University Press, New York, NY

Shoul B (1957) Karl Marx and Say's Law. Q J Econ 71(4):611–629

Skinner AS (1987) Smith, Adam. In: Eatwell J, Milgate M, Newman P (eds) The New Palgrave Dictionary of Economics, vol 4. Macmillan, London, pp 357–375

Smith A ([1776] 1976) An inquiry into the nature and causes of the wealth of nations (two volumes). In: Campbell RH, Skinner AS (eds) The Glasgow edition of the works and correspondence of Adam Smith. Oxford University Press, London

Smithies A (1950) Memorial: Joseph Alois Schumpeter 1883–1950. Am Econ Rev 40(4):628–648

Solow RM (1956) A contribution to the theory of economic growth. Q J Econ 70(1):65–94

Solow RM (1957) Technical change and the aggregate production function. Rev Econ Stat 39(3):312–320

Solow RM (1987) We'd better watch out. New York Times Book Review. July 12, 1987, p 36

Spahn HP (1986) Stagnation in der Geldwirtschaft: Dogmengeschichte, Theorie und Politik aus keynesianischer Sicht. Campus Verlag, Frankfurt am Main and New York, NY

Staroske U (1995) Die Drei-Sektoren-Hypothese: Darstellung und kritische Würdigung. S. Roderer Verlag, Regensburg

Steedman I (1977) Marx after Sraffa. New Left Books, London

Steindl J ([1952] 1976) Maturity and stagnation in American capitalism (with a new introduction by the author). Monthly Review Press, New York, NY, and London

Steindl J (1987) Stagnation. In: Eatwell J, Milgate M, Newman P (eds) The New Palgrave Dictionary of Economics, vol 4. Macmillan, London, pp 472–474

Summers LH (2016) Will our children really not know economic growth? Prospect Magazine, February 2016. Available at http://www.prospectmagazine.co.uk/magazine/not-so-fast-economic-growth-robert-gordon. Accessed 25 Oct 2016

Swan TW (1956) Economic growth and capital accumulation. Econ Record 32(2):334–361

Sweezy PM ([1942] 1946) The theory of capitalist development: principles of Marxian political economy. Dobson Books Ltd., London

Sweezy PM ([1946/1947] 2011) On the laws of capitalism. 2. The laws of capitalism. (With a commentary by John Bellamy Foster). Month Rev 63(1):12–15

The Conference Board (2018) The conference board total economy database, March 2018. The Conference Board, New York, NY. Available at https://www.conference-board.org/data/economydatabase/. Accessed 09 Nov 2018

Verspohl E (1971) Der Stagnationsgedanke in der Nationalökonomie: Eine dogmengeschichtliche und analytische Studie. Inaugural-Dissertation zur Erlangung des Doktorgrades der Wirtschafts- und Sozialwissenschaftlichen Fakultät der Universität zu Köln. University of Cologne, Cologne

von Weizsäcker CC (1966) Zur ökonomischen Theorie des technischen Fortschritts. Vandenhoeck & Ruprecht, Göttingen

von Weizsäcker CC (1969) Forschungsinvestitionen und makroökonomische Modelle – Ein wirtschaftstheoretisches Dilemma? Kyklos: Int Rev Soc Sci 22(3):454–466

World Bank (2018) World DataBank. World Development Indicators. Variables Services, value added (% of GDP)(NV.SRV.TOTL.ZS) and Employment in services (% of total employment) (modeled ILO estimate)(SL.SRV.EMPL.ZS). World Bank, Washington, DC. Available at http://databank.worldbank.org/data/reports.aspx?source=world-development-indicators. Accessed 29 Nov 2018

Zinn KG (1993) Dienstleistungsgesellschaft oder Krise des tertiären Sektors? Zur qualitativen Analyse der Entwicklung reifer Volkswirtschaften. WSI Mitteilungen 46(1):1–10

Zinn KG (1994) Die Wirtschaftskrise: Wachstum oder Stagnation. Zum ökonomischen Grundproblem reifer Volkswirtschaften. B.I.-Taschenbuchverlag, Mannheim

Zinn KG (1995) Auf dem Weg in die tertiäre Krise? Der ungesicherte Übergang zur Dienstleistungsgesellschaft. Int Polit Soc 1995(1):59–69

Zinn KG (2004) Überkonsum und Konsumsättigung als Probleme reifer Volkswirtschaften. In: Walter R (ed) Geschichte des Konsums: Erträge der 20. Arbeitstagung der Gesellschaft für Sozial- und Wirtschaftsgeschichte, 23.–26. April 2003 in Greifswald., Franz Steiner Verlag, Wiesbaden, pp 55–74

Chapter 5
Stagnation Theories: Concluding Remarks

The historical survey of stagnation theories in the previous chapters has shown that the topic of secular stagnation has not always been en vogue, but its popularity has fluctuated with the overall economic circumstances. While stagnation hypotheses have mainly gained attention during periods of economic hardship, in times of economic prosperity they have faded into the background. Bleaney (1976, p. 218) who made a similar observation with regard to underconsumption theories, put it in a nutshell when he mentioned, "Like a desert seed which a shower of rain brings suddenly to life after years of inactivity, [...] [stagnation] theories seem to be an almost spontaneous response to a period of prolonged depression."

Considering the decades since the beginning of the twentieth century, two major eras stick out during which economic performances were so sluggish that—within a relatively short period of time—they gave rise to various secular stagnation theories: the Great Depression years of the 1930s as well as the years in the aftermath of the financial crisis of 2008–2009. While both economic downturns were the ultimate trigger for the development of several secular stagnation approaches, the respective theories that emerged during these times do not just refer to the actual economic slumps, but—with secular stagnation being a long-term phenomenon—include the years prior to the acute economic weakness.

Although most economists dealing with secular stagnation refer to empirical developments to support their hypotheses, one of the most pressing questions is whether there have been actual periods of stagnation over time. Due to secular stagnation being an inherently long-term and rather loose concept, it is indeed a difficult endeavor to empirically confirm possible phases of economic stagnation. While it is typically acknowledged that, in the mid-twentieth century, the Second World War prevented secular stagnation in the United States and other advanced countries, in the contemporary economic debate it is usually agreed that Japan has been experiencing stagnation since the 1990s. Particularly with respect to the euro area, Japan, and the United States, in fact, secular stagnation has been among the most discussed economic issues after the financial crisis of 2008–2009. In more recent times, however, with economic growth having picked up pace in most advanced countries, the

© Springer Nature Switzerland AG 2020   145
C. Anselmann, *Secular Stagnation Theories*, Springer Studies in the History
of Economic Thought, https://doi.org/10.1007/978-3-030-41087-2_5

subject has taken a back seat. There is currently a tendency to dismiss the weak economic performances in the wake of the Great Recession as just a severe cyclical phenomenon. Yet, as most of the structural weaknesses addressed in the secular stagnation debate still exist, it is rightly warned that the threat of stagnation remains. Eventually, it is the next economic downturn which is expected to be a real test for much of the developed world.

While it is still unclear whether, in the years ahead, the current risk of stagnation will develop into an actual long-term phase of sluggish average economic performance, an important question is whether the lurking stagnation tendencies are rather due to demand- or supply-side constraints. It has been argued above that a one-sided focus on either the demand or the supply side of the economy would be insufficient, as both adequate demand and supply are necessary to facilitate sustainable long-term economic growth. With demand and supply being two sides of the same coin, demand- and supply-side stagnation theories are not necessarily mutually exclusive, but they can complement each other. In the contemporary stagnation debate, for instance, the theories of Summers and Gordon both include plausible arguments. Moreover, several of the issues addressed are not only relevant from a purely demand- or supply-side perspective, but relate to both sides of the economy.

It is fair to say that in the decades leading up to the financial crisis of 2008–2009, demand-side issues were largely ignored in the mainstream economic and political debate, resulting in unsustainable debt-financed consumption spending in one part of the developed world, as well as export-driven economic growth in other advanced countries. During and after the crisis, however, when output gaps in various developed countries were estimated to be strongly negative, the demand side of the economy moved to the foreground—also triggered by Summers's demand-side stagnation hypothesis. Yet, with output gaps assumed to have closed over the past years in some nations, public attention given to demand-side economics is at risk of fading once more. The (OECD 2018, p. 10), for instance, writes that "[c]onventional estimates of economic slack, such as output gaps, suggest that spare capacity is now limited in most major advanced economies." Although country-specific variations are taken into account, it is called for "[a]mbitious supply-side policy reforms [...] to strengthen medium-term growth prospects." Similar to secular stagnation not being of major public concern when economies are performing well, so overall interest in demand-side aspects seems to vanish when estimated output gaps close in the medium to long run. It is in this regard as well that (Gordon 2014, p. 57) characterizes Summers's demand-side stagnation hypothesis as "[...] almost obsolete, because the [output] gap is steadily shrinking." While both sound supply and demand are necessary to foster economic growth, it is the demand side which is typically forgotten when it comes to long-term economic developments. Restricting demand-side issues to the short run, however, can have adverse economic effects, as—to paraphrase Kalecki ([1968] 1971, p. 165)—the long run is, after all, a succession of short-term periods. It is not claimed here that there are currently no deficiencies on the supply side, but it is unsatisfactory to base the subordinate importance of demand-side issues on such controversial concepts as the output gap. In fact, although there are topics—such as demographic change—which are equally relevant in both supply- and demand-side approaches, there are other issues which seem to be more supply- or demand-side specific. Among these topics is the distribution of income, which, as has been leaked out here and there throughout the past chapters, is somewhat more commonly addressed in demand-side approaches. Putting these issues aside in times of economic prosperity and closed output gaps seems compelling, but may backfire once economic conditions deteriorate again.

Speaking of the distribution of income and thus bringing it back to the Introduction of this book, it is striking that—from an empirical perspective—all modern and contemporary secular stagnation theories that emerged during the two major waves of stagnation hypotheses in the mid-twentieth century and after the financial crisis of 2008–2009 refer to time periods of high and/or rising income inequality. As has been shown in Sect. 1.1.2, most notably in the United States and other Anglo-Saxon countries, but also—to a lesser extent—in several European nations, three periods of income distribution can generally be distinguished: the era of a highly unequal distribution of income at the beginning of the twentieth century, the period of low inequality following World War II, as well as the years of rising inequality since the early 1970s. Most modern and contemporary stagnation theories discussed in the previous chapters can roughly be allocated to these periods, allowing for a better understanding of the distributional context in which they emerged.

It is beyond question that economists such as Keynes, Hansen, Steindl, and also Schumpeter developed their theories of stagnation and economic disruption in reaction to the economic downturn in 1929 and thereafter.[1] Nonetheless, however, although especially in Hansen's and Steindl's ([1952] 1967, p. ix) hypotheses the depression years between the late 1920s and late 1930s mark the period of acute stagnation, their theories go well beyond that specific time period. Both (Hansen 1955, pp. 540–548) and (Steindl [1952] 1967, p. 166) held that "[s]tagnation did not come over-night [...]," but was rather the result of adverse longer term developments whose effects had been masked by counteracting forces in the years prior to the Great Depression (see also (Higgins 1946; pp. 133–134) (Steindl [1989] 1990, p. 167). Referring to his own theory as well as to the hypotheses of Hansen and Schumpeter (Steindl [1952] 1967, p. 474), for example, noted that these theories "[...] were intended to explain the decline in the rate of growth of accumulation in the US which was shown [...] to have taken place between the 1880s and the beginning of World War II." Although economic growth in the early twentieth century was high by historical standards, it had already been slowly trending downward in the years prior to 1929 (see also Steindl [1952] 1967, p. 160; 1984, p. 175). Paradoxically, the (modern) stagnation theories that emerged in the 1930s and thereafter thus include the decades of strong economic performance between the late nineteenth and mid-twentieth century, which, at least with reference to the United States, are

---

[1] While the Great Depression was the ultimate trigger for the development of various secular stagnation theories in modern history, there had been some (vague) allusions and approaches before 1929. As has been outlined in Sect. 3.2.1, (Schumpeter 1954, p. 1172), for instance, traced Keynes's ([1919] 1971) stagnationist thoughts back to his book *The Economic Consequences of the Peace*, first published in 1919. Yet, Keynes clearly advanced his approach in later years, particularly in the 1930s and thereafter.

commonly known as the *Gilded Age*, the *Progressive Era*, and the *Roaring Twenties* Nugent (2002). As has been shown empirically in Sect. 1.1.2, these years were also marked by a highly unequal distribution of income.

While the subject of stagnation was not of great relevance in the economic boom and low-inequality years after World War II—reflected by the fact that stagnation theories published during that time, such as Steindl's hypothesis, were largely ignored—it regained some attention with the growth slowdown in the early 1970s. As the distribution of income, however, was still relatively equal at the beginning of the 1970s, it is not surprising that questions of distribution do not play a role in the stagnation theory of Meadows et al. (1972), for instance, which was developed toward the end of the low-inequality period.

With the continued growth weakness throughout the 1970s and thereafter, some economists drew attention to stagnation tendencies and tried to revive the stagnation debate of the 1930s. Among others, it is the collection of essays in Sweezy and Magdoff (1977, 1978, 1988) that has to be mentioned here. They especially referred to the Steindlian line of reasoning, which, as will be further pointed out below, is particularly concerned with the distribution of income.

Finally, the contemporary stagnation theories of mainly Summers and Gordon emerged a few years after the Great Recession, when most advanced countries were still struggling with the economic impact of the financial crisis of 2008–2009 and in several nations income inequality was back at its pre-World War II levels. While, similar to the modern stagnation hypotheses developed in the years following the Great Depression, the contemporary stagnation debate was triggered by the weak economic performances in the developed world after 2008–2009, both Summers and Gordon do not limit their hypotheses to the crisis years. According to both economists, adverse developments had already been underway before the Great Recession. Contemporary stagnation theories thus also include the decades of a rising unequal distribution of income before the crisis.

With both the Great Depression and the Great Recession having been preceded by years of high and/or rising income inequality, the comparatively highly unequal distribution of income is a common characteristic of the periods investigated by the stagnation hypotheses that emerged during these two major waves of stagnation theories. Yet, while all of the economists who come to mind in this context—particularly Keynes, Hansen, Schumpeter, and Steindl, as well as Summers and Gordon—refer to questions of distribution in some way, the following Part II will show that the role of income distribution in their theories is rather diverse. Surprisingly, in most secular stagnation approaches—even in those focusing on the demand side—the distribution of income is only a side issue.

References

Bleaney MF (1976) Underconsumption theories: a history and critical analysis. International Publishers, New York, NY

Gordon RJ (2014) The turtle's progress: secular stagnation meets the headwinds. In: Teulings C, Baldwin R (eds) Secular stagnation: facts, causes and cures. CEPR Press, London, pp 47–59

Hansen AH (1955) The stagnation thesis. In: Smithies A, Butters JK (eds) Readings in fiscal policy. George Allen and Unwin Ltd., London, pp 540–557

Higgins B (1946) The doctrine of economic maturity. Am Econ Rev 36(1):133–141

Kalecki M, ([1968] 1971) Trend and the business cycle. In: Kalecki M (ed) Selected essays on the dynamics of the capitalist economy. Cambridge University Press, New York, NY, pp 165–183

Keynes JM ([1919] 1971) The economic consequences of the peace. In: The collected writings of John Maynard Keynes, vol II: the economic consequences of the peace. Macmillan St. Martin's Press for the Royal Economiy Society, London and Basingstoke

Meadows DH, Meadows DL, Randers J, Behrens WW III (1972) The limits to growth. Universe Books, New York, NY

Nugent W (2002) Welcome to the journal of the Gilded Age and progressive era. J Gilded Age Progres Era 1(1):7–9

OECD (2018) High uncertainty weighing on global growth. Interim economic assessment, 20 September 2018. OECD, Paris. Available at https://www.oecd-ilibrary.org/. Accessed 23 Nov 2018

Schumpeter JA (1954) History of economic analysis. Oxford University Press, New York, NY

Steindl J ([1952] 1976) Maturity and stagnation in American capitalism (with a new introduction by the author). Monthly Review Press, New York, NY, and London

Steindl J ([1966] 1984) On maturity in capitalist economies. In: Foster JB, Szlajfer H (eds) The faltering economy: the problem of accumulation under monopoly capitalism. Monthly Review Press, New York, NY, pp 167–178

Steindl J ([1989] 1990) From stagnation in the 30s to slow growth in the 70s. In: Steindl J (ed) Economic papers 1941–88, St. Martin's Press, New York, NY, pp 166–179

Sweezy PM, Magdoff H (1977) Economic history as it happened, vol III. The deepening crisis of U.S. capitalism. Monthly Review Press, New York, NY

Sweezy PM, Magdoff H (1987) Economic history as it happened, vol IV. Stagnation and the financial explosion. Monthly Review Press, New York, NY

Sweezy PM, Magdoff H (1988) Economic history as it happened, vol V. The irreversible crisis. Monthly Review Press, New York, NY

Part II
Income Distribution and Secular Stagnation

Chapter 6
The Impact of an Unequal Distribution of Income on Economic Growth: Theoretical Considerations

6.1 Introduction

Interest in the nexus between income distribution and economic growth has a long tradition. While the distribution of income is a key element in the growth theories of Kalecki ([1954] 1965) and Kaldor (1955/1956, 1957), there are also other economists who have addressed the link between inequality and economic development. With his paper *Economic Growth and Income Inequality*, Kuznets (1955), for instance, ranks among the earliest and most well-known examples. Although he did not analyze any causal relationship, building his notion on the process of industrialization and urbanization, he assumed income inequality to initially rise and then to decline in the course of a country's economic development—a relationship which today is commonly referred to as the *Kuznets curve*. As questionable from an empirical point of view—especially considering the increases in the unequal distribution of income in a number of advanced countries during the past decades—in the recent past (Milanovic 2016, pp. 46–91) has advanced Kunets's (1955) hypothesis and is now speaking of *Kuznets waves* to describe the long-term development of inequality.

With Kuznets (1955) being one of the economists whose names typically come to mind when the link between economic development and inequality is addressed, the same is true for Okun (1975). Fostered by the publication of Okun's (1975) *Equality and Efficiency: The Big Tradeoff* in the mid-1970s, it has long been assumed that a more equal distribution of income, induced by redistribution policy, is generally harmful for economic growth. Although Okun (1975, pp. 47–48), who had been chairman of the Council of Economic Advisers under US President Lyndon Johnson from 1968 to 1969, desired both equality and efficiency, he believed that attempts to reduce inequality would frequently hamper output and growth.[1] "Any insistence

---

[1] Although Okun (1975) literally addressed the trade-off between equality and *efficiency*, with the latter being defined as "[...] getting the most out of a given input [...]" (Okun 1975, p. 2), he himself occasionally seemed to have *economic output* or *economic growth* in mind (Okun 1975, p. 48). Similarly, in the literature relating to Okun (1975), the term *efficiency* is often used synonymously with *economic growth* and/or *economic output*. See, for instance, Atkinson (2015, p. 243).

© Springer Nature Switzerland AG 2020
C. Anselmann, *Secular Stagnation Theories*, Springer Studies in the History of Economic Thought, https://doi.org/10.1007/978-3-030-41087-2_6

on carving the pie into equal slices [...]," he held, "[...] would shrink the size of the pie" (Okun 1975, p. 48). Although he acknowledged this trade-off to be a country-specific normative issue, with each nation having to decide how much efficiency it is willing to give up for more equality (Okun 1975, p. 90), he was skeptical of redistributing income from the top to the bottom of the income hierarchy, as an intact "[...] capitalist system [...] [necessarily] leaves the highest and lowest incomes far apart" (Okun 1975, p. 51). While Okun's (1975) notion is still much quoted today, the link between income distribution and economic growth is not as clear-cut as proposed by the eye-catching title of his book. In fact, by mentioning that more equality *can* go hand in hand with higher efficiency, Okun (1975, p. 4) himself was aware of the more heterogeneous nexus.

The complex nexus between income distribution and economic growth is also reflected by the role which inequality plays in secular stagnation theories. In fact, while the issue of distribution is not considered in all of the stagnation hypotheses mentioned in Part I, those theories which approach the impact of inequality do not pay equal attention to it and partly refer to different transmission channels through which inequality and growth are intertwined. While some economists consider questions of distribution essential to explaining secular stagnation tendencies—albeit for diverse reasons—others attach much less importance to inequality or do not address this issue at all.

To be able to put the stagnation debates of the twentieth and twenty-first century into a broader context of income distribution, Part I starts off with the present chapter, taking a closer look at possible transmission channels through which income inequality may impact economic growth. Drawing on various literature reviews, such as Perotti (1996), Barro (2000), Aghion et al. (1999), and Voitchovsky (2009), the following gives a short overview of the possible channels through which an unequal distribution of income can impact economic growth. It turns out that the effects are heterogeneous, making it difficult to determine a priori the precise impact of changes in the distribution of income on economic growth. While it is distinguished between demand-side, supply-side, and socio-political mechanisms, this clear-cut distinction can become blurred, especially when real capital investment is involved.

The subsequent Chap. 7, on the other hand, addresses the role of income distribution in several modern and contemporary stagnation theories. It turns out that Steindl was *the* secular stagnationist who put the distribution of income at the heart of his stagnation hypothesis. Yet, although he mentioned the personal distribution of income in some of his later writings, his focus was on the functional distribution of income. As it is the personal distribution of income which is typically at the center of public interest today, in Chap. 8 a modified Steindlian model of economic growth, stagnation, and income distribution is developed, including both the functional and personal distributions of income. Chapter 9 briefly refers to the heterogeneous results of existing empirical analyses on the nexus between income distribution and economic growth. It is followed by the final Chap. 10, which concludes with a short résumé and presents various empirically oriented policy implications aimed at fostering both economic growth and a more equal distribution of income.

It should be noted that the focus in the following is explicitly on inequality of outcome—i.e., inequality of income—not on inequality of opportunity. While it is not claimed that other dimensions of inequality are less important, they are of secondary importance in the immediate context of secular stagnation. Moreover, particularly in the present chapter and the subsequent Chap. 7, it is primarily the impact of income distribution on economic growth which is addressed, leaving aside the reverse causality from economic growth to inequality. In fact, those secular stagnation theories which refer to the distribution of income first and foremost consider inequality as a possible cause of and/or remedy for stagnation. The impact of economic growth on inequality, on the other hand, is typically not addressed.[2]

6.2   Demand-Side Mechanisms

6.2.1   The Size of Consumption Demand

From a demand-side perspective, the impact of income distribution on economic growth is typically based on the notion of non-uniform propensities to save (and consume) along the income scale. While the assumption of differences in marginal (and average) saving rates is commonly associated with the growth models of Kaldor (1955/1956) and Pasinetti (1962), in earlier years it had already been pointed out by other economists, such as Keynes ([1936b] 1937) and Kalecki (1944). In *The General Theory*, Keynes ([1936b] 1937) ([1936b] 1937, p. 97) held:

> [...] [I]t is [...] obvious that a higher absolute level of income will tend, as a rule, to widen the gap between income and consumption. For the satisfaction of the immediate primary needs of a man and his family is usually a stronger motive than the motives towards accumulation, which only acquire effective sway when a margin of comfort has been attained.

The notion that "[...] the poor have a higher propensity to consume than the rich [...]" (Kalecki 1944, p. 53), and hence a lower propensity to save, has been documented in various empirical studies. While Kuznets and Jenks (1953, pp. 186–187) provided one of the first empirical analyses endorsing a rise in the share of income saved as one moves up the income hierarchy, more recent empirical studies, coming to similar results, include Dynan et al. (2004) for the United States and Brenke and Pfannkuche (2018, pp. 187–188) for Germany.

Building on differences in the marginal (and average) propensities to save and consume, in typical demand-determined growth theories a high and rising degree of inequality is considered harmful for economic growth. The reason is that consumption demand in the economy is expected to be deficient if a considerable part of income accrues to those at the top of the distribution, who have a comparatively

---

[2]Yet, the impact of economic growth on the distribution of income is addressed in the modified Steindlian model presented in Chap. 8.

low (marginal) propensity to consume, while those at the bottom, who have a relatively high (marginal) propensity to consume, receive only a small share of total income. As rightly highlighted by Clauß (1968, p. 284), according to this underconsumptionist line of argument the lack of adequate consumption demand arises from both ends of the income scale, albeit for different reasons. While those in the lower parts of the distribution face insufficient purchasing power relative to their consumption requirements, those in the upper strata are confronted with a relative abundance of purchasing power. Along Keynesian lines, by dampening firms' expectations of future sales, inadequate consumption demand can have retarding effects on real capital investment and may thus reduce economic growth. Although Keynes ([1936b] 1937, p. 373) was well aware that some degree of income inequality is necessary in a capitalist economy to not discourage real capital investment, a highly unequal distribution of income may be likewise counterproductive. He held:

> [...] [U]p to the point where full employment prevails, the growth of capital depends not at all on a low propensity to consume but is, on the contrary, held back by it [...]. [M]easures for the redistribution of incomes in a way likely to raise the propensity to consume *may* prove positively favourable to the growth of capital. (Keynes [1936b] 1937, pp. 372–373, emphasis added)

Similarly, following Kalecki (1939, pp. 87–88; 1939 ([1954] 1965, pp. 102–103, 159) it can be argued that large savings outside of firms—which can be supposed to be higher the more unequal the distribution of income among private households or individuals—may hamper firms' profits and, ceteris paribus, the rate of profit. Assuming that the actual rate of profit affects the expected rate of profit, with the latter being an important determinant of real capital accumulation, a high degree of income inequality can inhibit economic growth.

6.2.2 The Composition of Consumption Demand

Another demand-side channel through which the distribution of income may impact economic growth has been advanced by Zweimüller (2000), Bertola et al. (2006, pp. 266–281), Foellmi and Zweimüller (2006), and Foellmi et al. (2014) in more recent years. They refer to the effects of inequality on the structure of firms' research and development expenditures, and hence on innovation and economic growth, via differences in income-specific consumption patterns.

The argument is based on the assumption that the private household sector is characterized by hierarchical consumption structures. While, due to a lack of purchasing power, those on low income consume only basic goods, the affluent also purchase luxury goods. New luxury goods are supposed to arise out of costly product innovations and initially are only affordable for rich private households. Via process innovations, however, involving the development of more productive technologies which—due to economies of scale—ultimately translate into cost and price reductions, former luxury goods can become accessible for those in the lower parts of the distribution over time. As a classic empirical example, Foellmi et al. (2014) mention the development of the automobile, which initially had been a luxury good, but became affordable to those on lower income by the introduction of the Ford Model T.

Firms' incentive to invest in product and/or process innovations, it is held, is dependent on the inequality-related consumption structure in the economy. To encourage product innovations, a sufficiently affluent class of private households is necessary. In fact, firms can charge higher prices for their newly developed products if there is a rich group of private households at the top of the distribution which has the necessary purchasing power to afford (and willingness to buy) high-priced luxury goods. While this price effect is conducive for product innovations, the initiation of process innovations, on the other hand, requires an adequate mass market. Hence, if large income differences are accompanied by small average incomes in the middle and lower parts of the income hierarchy, growth-enhancing process innovations tend to be discouraged. When those below the top of the distribution lack sufficient purchasing power, process innovations are hampered due to inadequate mass markets, which otherwise would allow for rapid market penetration.

As summarized by Voitchovsky (2009, p. 557), to foster economic growth via both product and process innovations, "[...] the optimal income distribution in these models usually consists of a small wealthy class to motivate the development of new products and a large middle class [...]" with sufficient purchasing power to encourage process innovations.

6.3 Supply-Side Mechanisms

6.3.1 Investment Indivisibility and Credit Market Imperfections

Assuming investment indivisibility, with investment projects involving large setup costs, a more unequal distribution of *wealth* may be conducive to economic growth if borrowing is constrained by insufficiently developed credit markets. A similar line of reasoning can also be applied to the impact of a more unequal distribution of *income*, which, due to saving rates being an increasing function of relative income, allows those at the top to save a comparatively large fraction of their income and hence to accumulate substantial wealth over time.

The concentration of wealth and/or income in the hands of a few, so the argument runs, may induce growth-enhancing capital investment which, given large setup costs and borrowing constraints, could not be undertaken with a more equal distribution of economic resources (Aghion et al. 1999, p. 1620; Barro 2000, pp. 5–6, 8). If indivisible investment projects have to be primarily self-financed, higher wealth and/or income inequality may thus foster economic growth and progress. As suggested by Galor and Moav (2004, pp. 1001–1002), the alleged positive impact of inequality on growth particularly occurs through investment in real capital in the early stages of industrial development, when real capital is still scarce and its accumulation is the most important driver of economic growth. Speaking of the era before World War I in Europe, Keynes ([1919] 1911, pp. 11, 13), in fact, referred to the importance of inequality for real capital accumulation and progress:[3]

> [...] [S]ociety was so framed as to throw a great part of the increased income into the control of the class least likely to consume it. [...] In fact, it was precisely the *inequality* of the distribution of wealth which made possible those vast accumulations of fixed wealth and of capital improvements which distinguished that age from all others. [...] The immense accumulations of fixed capital which, to the great benefit of mankind, were built up during the half century before the war, could never have come about in a society where wealth was divided equitably. [...] [T]he principle of accumulation based in on equality [*sic*] was a vital part of the pre-war order of society and of progress [...].[4]

According to Galor and Moav (2004, pp. 1001–1002), while a more unequal distribution of income may foster economic growth by promoting real capital accumulation at the beginning of industrial development, it may inhibit economic growth through an unfavorable allocation of human capital in more advanced countries, where real capital is abundant and human capital accumulation is one of the primary drivers of progress.

6.3.2 Human Capital Investment and Credit Market Imperfections

Given imperfect credit markets, a more unequal distribution of wealth and/or income may inhibit economic growth through an adverse allocation of human capital Galor and Zeira 1993. In contrast to those at the top of the distribution, credit-constrained poor private households can invest only little in their own and their children's education. This poverty–education nexus is typically reinforced by high fertility rates at the bottom of the distribution. As the opportunity costs of raising children are comparatively small for private households on low income, fertility rates tend to be high in the lower parts of the distribution. Eventually, assuming a positive relationship between a person's educational attainment and future income, intergenerational poverty traps may arise if uneducated poor parents with a large number of children do not have the financial means to invest adequately in the education of their children (Perotti 1996, pp. 153–154; Galor and Zang 1997; Voitchovsky 2009, pp. 554–555).

From a macroeconomic perspective, the unequal allocation of human capital may retard economic growth. As outlined by Aghion et al. (1999, p. 1630) and Galor and Moav (2004, p. 1002), human capital investment is subject to diminishing returns at the individual level. Hence, a more equal distribution of wealth and/or income,

---

[3]Hansen (1941, p. 381) later argued along similar lines.

[4]The quote from Keynes ([1919] 1911, p. 13) obviously contains a typographical error and, as in Keynes ([1919] 1920, p. 19), should read: "[...] [T]he principle of accumulation based *on inequality* was a vital part of the pre-war order [...]" (emphasis added).

allowing those at the bottom of the distribution to invest more in their own and their children's education, can increase overall productivity in the economy. In fact, the nexus between human capital investment and economic growth was also outlined by Okun (1975, pp. 80–81). Inducing a more equal allocation of human capital by providing financial aid to students on lower income, he held, may foster both economic growth and equality.[5]

6.3.3 Incentive System and Risk-Taking

As has been outlined in Sect. 1.1.2.3, there is no doubt that the efficient functioning of a capitalist economy requires some degree of inequality. If the income of an individual is positively dependent on work effort, income inequality creates financial incentives to work hard, which in turn is beneficial for productivity growth. Moreover, by providing the prospect of a monetary reward, inequality encourages risk-taking and promotes investment spending by entrepreneurs. Referring to the importance of "[...] the preservation of market incentives [...]" and arguing that "[...] opportunities for jackpot prizes should be preserved [...]," Okun (1975, p. 116), for example, was a strong advocate of this position. Similarly, Gilder (2012, p. 90) opposes high tax rates at the top of the distribution, as they would distort the incentive system in capitalist economies: "The chief threat to this system is taxation with rates so progressive [...] that the rich refuse to risk their money. Wealth is withdrawn from productive uses [...]. The rich [...] no longer contribute to the economy."[6]

While a certain degree of inequality is necessary to foster economic growth by providing performance incentives, the opposite may be true if the unequal distribution of income is too high. For instance, when excessive inequality is accompanied by low levels of social mobility, making it virtually impossible to climb up the income ladder and to move from rags to riches, especially those at the bottom of the distribution may become frustrated and discouraged. As outlined by Akerlof and Yellen (1990) based on the so-called *fair wage-effort hypothesis*, if people feel that they are underpaid, that they are not receiving what they consider a fair income, they tend to reduce their work effort, which in turn may be harmful for productivity and economic growth (see also Voitchovsky 2005, p. 276). In contrast, on the other side of the income scale, the payment of very high incomes, especially in the form of excessive executive compensation, does not appear to adequately improve overall performance

---

[5]The G.I. Bill, a US government program which, among other things, financially supported the education of veterans after World War II, serves as a suitable example of the stimulating economic impact of widespread investment in human capital. In fact, the G.I. Bill is reported to have been an important element in the strong post-war economic growth in the United States. As outlined by Humes (2006, p. 197), "[...] spending for the program was paid back many times over in the form of increased tax revenues, income, consumer spending, and productivity [...]." See also Gordon (2016, p. 606).

[6]The original edition of Gilder's *Wealth and Poverty* was published in January 1981, only a couple of days before the inauguration of US President Ronald Reagan, a proponent of supply-side economics.

(Baumol 2007, p. 547). Eventually, it is a balancing act between providing sufficient incentives to work and restraining income inequality between the top and the bottom of the income scale.

6.4 Political and Social Mechanisms

6.4.1 Redistribution Policy

According to the median voter theorem, going back to Hotelling (1929), policy measures which can only be passed with a majority vote are decided by the median voter.[7] Assuming a proportional tax on income, with tax revenues being redistributed evenly across the population, the median voter is assumed to prefer a higher degree of redistribution via the tax and transfer system if income inequality, as measured by the mean-to-median income ratio, is high (Perotti 1996, pp. 150–151). Depending on the macroeconomic impact of redistribution policy, economic growth may rise or fall.

In the models of Alesina and Rodrik (1994) and Persson and Tabellini (1994), for example, higher inequality reduces economic growth. Via the median voter mechanism, a more unequal distribution of income provokes a higher degree of redistribution, which they assume to have a distorting impact on incentives and investment spending. As rightly outlined by Voitchovsky (2009, p. 556), however, the nexus between income redistribution and economic growth depends on a variety of factors, such as the precise characteristics of the tax and transfer system and the type of redistribution policy. The impact of measures of redistribution on economic growth is thus highly country-specific.

6.4.2 Social Instability and Political Uncertainty

A high degree of inequality may reduce economic growth by disrupting social cohesion and creating uncertainty through a number of growth-retarding mechanisms (Alesina and Perotti 1994, 1996). Voitchovsky (2005, p. 276; 2009, p. 554), for example, mentions that a highly unequal distribution of income or wealth, and especially a high degree of poverty, is commonly associated with a high rate of property crime. Moreover, if those at the top of the distribution are very rich, plutocratic structures may evolve, facilitating political influence, lobbying, corruption, and rent-seeking (Voitchovsky 2009, p. 559). At the same time, if there is a sufficiently large and affluent group of private households at the top of the distribution that is not dependent on the provision of public infrastructure, such as public schools or public health care,

---

[7]On early contributions on the median voter theorem, see also Black (1948) and Downs (1957a, b).

the development of these public services may be hampered, with adverse effects for the community as a whole (Stiglitz 2012, p. 93; 2015, pp. 146–147). Finally, a highly unequal distribution of income or wealth may give rise to uncertainty and inhibit long-term growth by provoking social unrest, which may even transition into violent revolt (Voitchovsky 2009, pp. 560–561; see also Acemoglu and Robinson 2002; Hagemann and Kufenko 2016).

References

Acemoglu D, Robinson JA (2002) The political economy of the Kuznets curve. Rev Dev Econ 6(2):183–203

Aghion P, Caroli E, García-Peñalosa C (1999) Inequality and economic growth: the perspective of the new growth theories. J Econ Lit 37(4):1615–1660

Akerlof GA, Yellen JL (1990) The fair wage-effort hypothesis and unemployment. Q J Econ 105(2):255–283

Alesina A, Perotti R (1994) The political economy of growth: a critical survey of the recent literature. World Bank Econ Rev 8(3):351–371

Alesina A, Perotti R (1996) Income distribution, political instability, and investment. Eur Econ Rev 40(6):1203–1228

Alesina A, Rodrik D (1994) Distributive politics and economic growth. Q J Econ 109(2):465–490

Atkinson AB (2015) Inequality: what can be done? Harvard University Press, Cambridge, MA, and London

Barro RJ (2000) Inequality and growth in a panel of countries. J Econ Growth 5(1):5–32

Baumol WJ (2007) On income distribution and growth. J Policy Model 29(4):545–548

Bertola G, Foellmi R, Zweimüller J (eds) (2006) Income distribution in macroeconomic models. Princeton University Press, Princeton, NJ, and Oxford

Black D (1948) On the rationale of group decision-making. J Polit Econ 56(1):23–34

Brenke K, Pfannkuche J (2018) Konsum und Sparquote der privaten Haushalte hängen stark vom Erwerbsstatus, Einkommen und Alter ab. DIW Wochenbericht 10(2018):181–191

Clauß FJ (1968) Konjunktur und Neoklassik: Sparen und Investieren, öffentliche Haushalte und wirtschaftliches Wachstum in der konjunkturbewegten Volkswirtschaft (USA 1929–1967). Duncker & Humblot, Berlin and Munich

Downs A (1957a) An economic theory of democracy. Harper & Row, New York, NY

Downs A (1957b) An economic theory of political action in a democracy. J Polit Econ 65(2):135–150

Dynan KE, Skinner J, Zeldes SP (2004) Do the rich save more? J Polit Econ 112(2):397–444

Foellmi R, Zweimüller J (2006) Income distribution and demand-induced innovations. Rev Econ Stud 73(4):941–960

Foellmi R, Wuergler T, Zweimüller J (2014) The macroeonomics of model T. J Econ Theory 153(2014):617–647

Galor O, Moav O (2004) From physical to human capital accumulation: inequality and the process of development. Rev Econ Stud 71(4):1001–1026

Galor O, Zang H (1997) Fertility, income distribution, and economic growth: theory and cross-country evidence. Jpn World Econ 9(2):197–229

Galor O, Zeira J (1993) Income distribution and macroeconomics. Rev Econ Stud 60(1):35–52

Gilder G (2012) Wealth and poverty: a new edition for the twenty-first century. Regnery Publishing Inc., Washington, DC

Gordon RJ (2016) The rise and fall of American growth. The U.S. standard of living since the Civil War. Princeton University Press, Princeton, NJ

Hagemann H, Kufenko V (2016) Economic, structural and socio-psychological determinants of protests in Russia during 2011–2012: empirical analysis on a regional level. Econ Transit 24(1):3–30

Hansen AH (1941) Fiscal policy and business cycles. W. W. Norton & Company, Inc., New York, NY

Hotelling H (1929) Stability in competition. Econ J 39(153):41–57

Humes E (2006) Over here: how the G.I. bill transformed the American dream. Harcourt Inc., Orlando, FL

Kaldor N ([1955] 1956) Alternative theories of distribution. Rev Econ Stud 23(2):83–100

Kaldor N (1957) A model of economic growth. Econ J 67(268):591–624

Kalecki M (1939) Essays in the theory of economic fluctuations. George Allen & Unwin Ltd., London

Kalecki M (1944) Three ways to full employment. In: The Oxford University Institute of Statistics (ed) The economics of full employment. Basil Blackwell, Oxford, pp 39–58

Kalecki M ([1954] 1965) Theory of economic dynamics. An essay on cyclical and long-run changes in capitalist economy. Modern Reader Paperbacks, New York, NY, and London

Keynes JM ([1919] 1920) The economic consequences of the peace. Macmillan and Co., Ltd., London

Keynes JM ([1919] 1971) The economic consequences of the peace. In: The collected writings of John Maynard Keynes, vol II: the economic consequences of the peace. Macmillan St. Martin's Press for the Royal Economy Society, London and Basingstoke

Keynes JM ([1936b] 1973) The general theory of employment, interest and money. In: The collected writings of John Maynard Keynes, vol VII: the general theory of employment, interest and money. Macmillan and Cambridge University Press for the Royal Economic Society, London, Basingstoke, and New York, NY, pp xxi–384

Kuznets S (1955) Economic growth and income inequality. Am Econ Rev 45(1):1–28

Kuznets S, Jenks E (1953) Shares of upper income groups in income and savings. National Bureau of Economic Research, New York, NY

Milanovic B (2016) Global inequality: a new approach for the age of globalization. The Belknap Press of Harvard University Press, Cambridge, MA, and London

Okun AM (1975) Equality and efficiency: the big tradeoff. The Brookings Institution, Washington, DC

Pasinetti LL (1962) Rate of profit and income distribution in relation to the rate of economic growth. Rev Econ Stud 29(4):267–279

Perotti R (1996) Growth, income distribution, and democracy: what the data say. J Econ Growth 1(2):149–187

Persson T, Tabellini G (1994) Is inequality harmful for growth? Am Econ Rev 84(3):600–621

Stiglitz JE (2012) The price of inequality: how today's divided society endangers our future. W. W. Norton & Company, New York, NY, and London

Stiglitz JE (2015) Inequality and economic growth. Polit Q 86(S1):134–155

Voitchovsky S (2005) Does the profile of income inequality matter for economic growth? Distinguishing between the effects of inequality in different parts of the income distribution. J Econ Growth 10(3):273–296

Voitchovsky S (2009) Inequality and economic growth. In: Salverda W, Nolan B, Smeeding TM (eds) The Oxford handbook of economic inequality. Oxford University Press, Oxford and New York, NY, pp 549–574

Zweimüller J (2000) Schumpeterian entrepreneurs meet Engel's law: the impact of inequality on innovation-driven growth. J Econ Growth 5(2):185–206

Chapter 7
Income Distribution in Stagnation Theories

7.1 Introduction

While the theoretical literature suggests various heterogeneous transmission channels through which inequality may impact the rate of economic growth, not all of the authors referred to in Chaps. 3 and 4 consider the distribution of income relevant to explain possible stagnation tendencies. Building on Table 2.1 in Sect. 2.3, listing some of the economists who have either played a role in the secular stagnation debate or have influenced the related discussion on economic growth during specific time periods, both Tables 7.1 and 7.2 provide a first overview of the authors' general understanding of income distribution—without claiming, however, to depict the absolute truth. Although most authors refer to inequality in some way, shape or form, it is primarily in demand-side approaches that questions of distribution are considered a relevant factor in explaining weak economic performance and secular stagnation.

As shown in Table 7.1 and as has been outlined in Sect. 3.1, already the pre-Keynesian underconsumptionists regarded the unequal distribution of income between the owners of the factors of production as the main cause of economic stagnation. To spur consumption demand, Simonde de Sismondi and Hobson thus argued in favor of income redistribution from the affluent classes to the workers. Along similar lines, Malthus suggested a more equal distribution of wealth, especially of landed property.

Among the modern demand-side stagnation theories developed throughout the twentieth century, the distribution of income plays a particularly important role in (post-)Kaleckian approaches. While both Keynes and Hansen referred to questions of distribution and advocated a more equal distribution of income to spur economic activity, income distribution is a much more central element in the theories of Kalecki, Steindl, and their followers. Although it is occasionally referred to personal income inequality in their writings, the main focus is on the functional distribution of income between profits and wages. Moreover, while especially Kalecki, Steindl, as well as Baran and Sweezy doubted the implementation of adequate redistribution measures due to adverse political power relations, redistribution policy is generally considered conducive to economic growth in (post-)Kaleckian theories.

© Springer Nature Switzerland AG 2020
C. Anselmann, *Secular Stagnation Theories*, Springer Studies in the History
of Economic Thought, https://doi.org/10.1007/978-3-030-41087-2_7

Table 7.1 Income distribution as considered by economists advocating demand-side approaches of secular stagnation (and economic growth)

Chronology	Economist	Consideration of distribution			Distribution relevant to explain stagnation	Redistribution as a possible remedy for stagnation
		Addressing distribution	Main form of distribution addressed			
			Functional	Personal		
Early (eighteenth to early twentieth century)	(J.C.L. Simonde de Sismondi)	✓	✓		✓	✓
	(Thomas R. Malthus)	✓	✓		✓	✓
	(John A. Hobson)	✓	✓		✓	✓
Modern (mid- to late twentieth century)	John M. Keynes	✓	✓	?	?	✓
	Alvin H. Hansen	✓	✓	✓		✓
	Roy F. Harrod		✓			✓
	Michał Kalecki	✓	✓	?	✓	✓
	Josef Steindl	✓	✓	?	✓	✓
	Paolo Sylos-Labini	✓	✓	?	✓	✓
	Paul A. Baran	✓	✓	?	✓	✓
	Paul M. Sweezy	✓	✓	?	✓	✓
Contemporary (twenty-first century)	C. Christian von Weizsäcker	?		✓		✓
	Thomas I. Palley	✓	✓	✓	✓	✓
	Lawrence H. Summers	✓	✓	✓	✓	✓
	Paul Krugman	✓	✓	✓	?	?

Table 7.2 Income distribution as considered by economists advocating supply-side approaches of secular stagnation (and economic growth)

Chronology	Economist	Consideration of distribution				Distribution relevant to explain stagnation	Redistribution as a possible remedy for stagnation
		Addressing distribution	Main form of distribution addressed				
			Functional	Personal			
Early (eighteenth to early twentieth century)	Adam Smith	✓	✓				
	Thomas R. Malthus	✓	✓				
	John S. Mill	✓	✓			~	
	David Ricardo	✓	✓			~	
	Karl Marx	✓	✓			~	
	William S. Jevons						
Modern (mid- to late twentieth century)	Joseph A. Schumpeter	✓	✓	✓		✓	
	(Robert M. Solow)	~	✓				
	(Trevor W. Swan)	~	✓				
	Jean Fourastié						
	William J. Baumol						
	Donella H. Meadows						
Contemporary (twenty-first century)	Tyler Cowen	✓	✓	✓			
	(Thomas Piketty)	✓	✓	✓			
	Robert J. Gordon	✓	✓	✓		~	~

Source of Tables 7.1 and 7.2 Author's illustrations

Note to Tables 7.1 and 7.2 Checkmarks (✓) indicate that the respective issue is addressed. Tildes (~) indicate that the respective issue is indirectly addressed. Question marks (?) indicate that the viewpoint of the respective author is uncertain. No entry indicates that the respective issue does not play a role. In line with Table 2.1 in Sect. 2.3, the names of economists who can only indirectly be referred to as "stagnationists" are put in brackets

In the contemporary stagnation debate, the topic of income distribution is addressed by almost all authors who regard stagnation as a demand-side issue. While Palley and Summers view the highly unequal distribution of income as a cause of stagnation and hence argue in favor of income redistribution from the top to the bottom of the income hierarchy, Krugman—although concerned about rising income inequality—is more skeptical as to the impact of inequality on growth. Von Weizsäcker, on the other hand, primarily focuses on demographic change, but—at least on theoretical grounds—considers policies designed to redistribute income from the top to the bottom as a potential remedy to counteract stagnation tendencies.

Turning to supply-side theories of economic growth and stagnation in Table 7.2, the distribution of income between workers, capitalists, and landlords played an important role in classical economics. It can be argued, in fact, that the overall notion of the (inevitable) tendency toward the stationary state is at least indirectly tied to class conflicts over the distribution of national income. This applies particularly to the approaches of Ricardo and Mill, where the stationary state results from land scarcity and a corresponding increase in the share of rent and wages in national income at the expense of profits. In Marx's stagnation theory, on the other hand, the exploitation and impoverishment of the working class is an important reason for the ultimate breakdown of the capitalist system of production.

Among the economists of the twentieth century, Schumpeter occasionally referred to the functional and to the personal distribution of income. Arguing that inequality is necessary to encourage risk-taking, to foster innovation, and thus to spur economic growth, the distribution of income is of relevance in his stagnation theory. In contrast, in neoclassical growth theory, such as in the standard Solow–Swan growth model, the role of income distribution is a passive one. Given a typical Cobb–Douglas production function, the functional distribution of income is predetermined with constant factor shares.

While the distribution of income does not play a role in the theories of Fourastié, Baumol, and Meadows, in the contemporary stagnation debate the issue has been referred to by Cowen, Piketty, and Gordon. While both Cowen and Piketty are not directly considering the impact of inequality on growth, Gordon addresses the distribution of income as part of his headwinds, although not primarily with reference to overall economic growth. To spur the development of *median* household income, however, he argues in favor of income redistribution from the upper to the lower parts of the income hierarchy.

The following sections take a closer look at the role of income distribution in different stagnation theories. As inequality is mostly referred to in demand-side theories, the focus is on several modern and contemporary demand-side approaches. Although important in the history of economic thought, the early approaches of mainly the underconsumptionists and the classical economists are not considered further hereinafter. While their viewpoints on the nexus between economic growth and the distribution of income have been set forth in Sects. 3.1 and 4.1, their ideas—which are partly based on conceptual flaws—are only peripherally relevant in the modern and contemporary stagnation debates.

7.2 Distribution in Modern Stagnation Theories

Keynes, Hansen, Schumpeter, and Steindl are among the economists who engaged in the modern stagnation debate and paid attention to questions of distribution. Yet, although their hypotheses all emerged in the historical and economic context of the Great Depression years, the role which income distribution plays in their approaches is not homogeneous.

7.2.1 Keynes: Income Distribution as a Side Issue

Although Keynes ([1936b] 1973, p. 372) mentioned that "[t]he outstanding faults of the economic society in which we live are its failure to provide for full employment and its arbitrary and inequitable distribution of wealth and incomes [...]," the topic of income (and wealth) inequality does not play a leading role in his magnum opus, *The General Theory*. Steindl ([1985b] 1990, p. 288), for instance, critically noted that "[t]he book does not contain any distribution theory and distribution is rarely mentioned in it." In fact, in developing the core of his theory, Keynes mainly took as given the prevailing distribution, which he assumed to be determined, among other things, by secular, social structures (Keynes [1936b] 1973, pp. 109–110, 245). In earlier drafts of *The General Theory* and in some of his later essays, Keynes ([1934/1935] 1973, p. 452, [1939b] 1973, pp. 408–409) also pointed to existing empirical evidence on the long-run constancy of factor shares, which, for example, had been suggested by Bowley (1920) and Kalecki ([1938] 1939) at the time.

While the distribution of income (and wealth) was not Keynes's main topic, he was yet aware of the economic relevance of inequality, referring to questions of distribution in several of his writings and in various sections of *The General Theory*. For instance, he clearly considered some degree of inequality necessary for the efficient functioning of the economy, because "[t]here are valuable human activities which require the motive of money-making and the environment of private wealth-ownership for their full fruition [...]" (Keynes [1936b] 1973, p. 374). As has been indicated in Sect. 6.2.1, however, he predominantly considered inequality with reference to its impact on the aggregate propensity to consume.

Consumption, Keynes ([1936b] 1973, p. 104) held, is the ultimate goal of economic activity. In addition to being an end in itself, however, private consumption spending plays an important role in securing an adequate level of effective demand, serving both as a component of aggregate demand on its own and, by impacting the marginal efficiency of capital, as an incentive to invest (Keynes [1936b] 1973, p. 373). The total amount which, at a given national income, is spent on consumption goods, Keynes ([1936b] 1973, pp. 90–95, 107–110) assumed to be determined by a variety of factors, such as the institutional framework, cultural aspects, and social habits, but also the distribution of income in the economy.

Referring to the functional distribution of income, Keynes ([1936b] 1973, pp. 287, 290) maintained that the marginal (and average) propensities to consume vary among the main factors of production. Distinguishing between wage earners, entrepreneurs, and rentiers, he assumed the marginal propensity to consume to be highest among wage earners and lowest among rentiers, with the spending behavior of entrepreneurs lying somewhere in between. Accordingly, at a given level of national income, aggregate consumption demand tends to be higher the larger the income share of wage earners as compared to entrepreneurs, and the larger the income share of entrepreneurs as compared to rentiers.

In addition to the functional distribution of income, Keynes ([1936b] 1973, pp. 96–97) also hinted at the impact of personal income inequality on consumption demand. As outlined above, he pointed out that "[...] a higher absolute level of income will tend, as a rule, to widen the gap between income and consumption [...]," because people only start saving a part of their income after they have satisfied their most basic needs (Keynes [1936b] 1973, p. 97). Keynes himself, though, did not elaborate further on this point, remaining quite vague and failing to clearly distinguish between absolute and relative income. In fact, his assertion on consumption behavior is valid along the income hierarchy, in the sense that, at any point in time, individuals on a *relatively* high income have a lower marginal (and average) propensity to consume than those in the bottom parts of the distribution. As one moves up the income scale, the marginal and average propensities to consume tend to decline. Hence, in the static world of a given national income, the more equal the distribution of income among the individuals in society, the higher the aggregate consumption.

Keynes's ([1936b] 1973, pp. 96–97) remarks on consumption behavior do not necessarily imply that consumption as a *share* of income tends to decline when, ceteris paribus, absolute income rises in the long run. From an aggregate perspective, given that the general social and institutional framework—including the distribution of income—is not subject to major changes, the share of consumption in national income does not necessarily fall with a secular rise in national income. Indeed, Keynes ([1936b] 1973, p. 97) was first and foremost concerned with the *absolute* difference between national income and aggregate consumption, which he assumed to increase with a rise in national income in the long run. Although he pointed out that the share of consumption *might* increase from a long-run perspective, he elsewhere clarified that "[t]his is a mere statement of opinion, which requires more statistical examination than I have given it [...]" (Keynes [1939c] 1973, p. 275). In fact, existing empirical evidence, such as the early study by Kuznets (1942, p. 30, 1946, pp. 52–52), mainly suggests that the *share* of aggregate consumption in national income tends to be relatively stable over longer periods. Already at the beginning of the 1930s, Hansen (1932, pp. 373–374) had explained this empirical finding with an increase in overall minimum consumption standards along the income hierarchy, accompanying the secular rise in national income over time. In his own words:

> Higher real wages for the unskilled have not materially eased the difficulty of making both ends meet. [...] As incomes rose all around, the whole manner of living changed. It was just as difficult as ever for the unskilled class to keep up with the procession [...] Every assimilated group strives to live somewhat like other people. Each level feels the pull of the standards of

these just a step higher in the social scale. The lower the income, the more difficult it is to set aside any surplus above what is absolutely necessary in order to live according to minimum current standards. (Hansen 1932, pp. 373–374)

While Keynes ([1936b] 1973) did not refer to this line of reasoning, Hansen (1941, p. 233, 1951, pp. 164–170, 1953, pp. 76–77) repeated it in several of his later writings. In the mid-twentieth century, similar approaches were also developed by Modigliani (1949) and Duesenberry (1948, 1949), who was a former student and later colleague of Hansen (Friedman 2009, p. xiii). Mainly with respect to Duesenberry (1949), today it is commonly referred to the *relative income hypothesis*, implying that individual consumption spending is also determined by the *relative* position of a person in the income hierarchy.

It may be due to Keynes's ([1936b] 1973) vague treatment of the propensity to consume *along* the income distribution, i.e., his inadequate reference to the *relative* income position of individuals, that he was confronted with several headwinds on this matter in the years following the publication of *The General Theory*. Gilboy (1938, p. 121), for instance, claimed that Keynes ([1936b] 1973) failed to consider "[...] the present structure of income [...]"—i.e., the distribution of income among the population—as a determinant of the overall propensity to consume. On similar grounds, Staehle (1937, pp. 137–138) held that, in contrast to variations in the functional distribution of income, variations in the personal distribution of income were not adequately taken into account by Keynes ([1936b] 1973) as a factor which could change the average propensity to consume in the economy as a whole. "Among the factors capable of shifting the market curve [...]," Staehle (1937, p. 138) pointed out, "[...] he does not list changes in the size-distribution of incomes, but only mentions changes in the income-distribution as between entrepreneurs and rentiers." Keynes ([1939a] 1973, [1939c] 1973) certainly disagreed with these positions. Referring to the papers by Gilboy (1938) and Staehle (1937), in a letter to Arthur C. Pigou he expressed his displeasure and mentioned to be "[...] extremely bothered what to do about the series of articles which have been appearing [...] on the propensity to consume. [...] All of them are based on quite obvious misunderstandings of what I say" (Keynes [1938] 1973, p. 272). Determined to emphasize his viewpoint, he held:

> Since I regard the *individual* propensity to consume as being (normally) such as to leave a wider gap between income and consumption as income increases, it naturally follows that the *collective* propensity for a community as a whole may depend (*inter alia*) on the distribution of incomes within it; and I have called repeated attention to this factor in my book. (Keynes [1939c] 1973, p. 271)

Indeed, Keynes ([1936b] 1973, p. 324, [1937] 1973, p. 131) mainly expressed his notion on the distribution of income by proposing redistribution policies to increase the propensity to consume. While he acknowledged that income (and wealth) inequality had been reduced to some degree, he did not think that the large disparities that still existed in the early and mid-twentieth century could be justified from a social and economic perspective (Keynes [1936b] 1973, pp. 372–374). As investment opportunities could be expected to vanish in more advanced economies, he suspected that full employment could not be reached or maintained with the prevailing propensity to consume (Keynes [1936b] 1973, pp. 31, 325). To ensure full employment and to attenuate possible stagnation tendencies, which he assumed to set in sometime after World War II (Keynes [1943b] 1980), he thus argued in favor of "[...] a scheme of direct taxation in order to redistribute incomes in such a way as to increase the propensity to consume" (Keynes [1936a] 1973, p. 16). Along these lines, Schumpeter (1946, p. 517), in an exaggerated manner, later described Keynesianism as

> [...] a doctrine that may not actually say but can easily be made to say both that 'who tries to save destroys real capital' and that, *via* saving, 'the unequal distribution of income is the ultimate cause of unemployment.' *This* is what the Keynesian Revolution amounts to.

Although Keynes endorsed that some degree of inequality is necessary in capitalism, his general demand-side approach toward the economic impact of inequality shows clear underconsumptionist traits. While he rightly pointed to alterations in the aggregate propensity to consume as inequality changes, the dynamic backlash of such changes on real capital accumulation and investment spending is not as pronounced in his rather static analysis.

7.2.2 Hansen: Redistribution as a Remedy for Secular Stagnation

Similar to Keynes's approach to income (and wealth) distribution, the issue of inequality is also not at the heart of Hansen's secular stagnation theory. Although the early and mid-twentieth century, the time period Hansen was writing about, had been characterized by high and partly rising income inequality in the United States and other advanced countries, to him questions of distribution did not play a role in explaining a possible long-term growth slowdown. With his focus on real capital investment induced by population growth as well as on autonomous investment resulting from both technological progress and the discovery of new territory and resources (Hansen 1951, pp. 190–191, 482), Hansen did not consider the distribution of income a relevant cause of stagnation tendencies.

On the other hand, however, he regarded the reduction in income inequality as a potential remedy for stagnation, which—along Keynesian lines—could spur private consumption spending and hence effective demand in the economy. In this regard, Hansen (1941, pp. 72, 248, 291–292, 305–306, 329) repeatedly referred to the gap between the full-employment and actual level of national income, caused by a weakening of private investment. In mature economies lacking sufficient investment opportunities, he mentioned, this gap must be filled by expenditures other than private investment, most notably government spending and consumption by private households (Hansen 1941, pp. 306–309).[1]

---

[1]It must be emphasized here that Hansen was completely aware of the importance of real capital accumulation. Advocating the exploitation of all available investment opportunities (Hansen 1941, p. 249), to him real capital investment was "[...] in a sense [...] much more significant for the economy

Referring to private consumption expenditures, Hansen (1941, pp. 226, 248)—similar to Keynes ([1936b] 1973, p. 96)—pointed out that the overall propensity to consume in an economy is rather rigid, as, among other things, it is determined by institutional circumstances as well as deeply rooted habits and social structures. In advanced economies threatened by secular stagnation, however, to prevent chronic unemployment and a long-term growth slowdown, "[...] [t]he propensity to consume must somehow be increased, the consumption function must be shifted upward [...]. The problem is not to cause a cyclical fluctuation in the consumption function [...], [...] but to raise permanently the propensity to consume" (Hansen 1941, p. 298). In proposing measures designed to establish a so-called *high-consumption economy* (Hansen 1941, pp. 300, 312), i.e., to increase the share of private consumption at the full-employment level of national income, Hansen (1941, p. 299, 1945, p. 218) particularly referred to redistribution policies, advocating not only the implementation of a more progressive tax structure, but also arguing in favor of higher social and community expenditures as well as social security programs benefiting especially those in the lower parts of the income hierarchy. "These measures [...]," Hansen (1945, p. 218) noted, "[...] act like an 'irrigation system' distributing mass purchasing power throughout the economy." While emphasizing the impact of inequality on consumption spending, he also did not fail to point to its social dimension. Speaking of "[...] the socially desirable distribution [...]" (Hansen 1941, p. 444), he was aware that the extent of inequality is not only important from a demand-side perspective, but also a determinant of social cohesion.

Hansen built his argument on standard Keynesian lines, referring to declining marginal (and average) propensities to consume as one moves up the income scale. As outlined in Table 7.3, which, in a similar form, was also referred to by Hansen (1941, p. 232), in the mid-1930s those private households receiving an annual income of up to 1,000 U.S. dollars on average spent more than 100% of their income on consumption goods, i.e., they had to incur debt or draw on previously accumulated wealth to satisfy their consumption requirements. In contrast, with the share of consumption gradually declining from the bottom to the top of the income scale, those at the upper end of the distribution on average only used approximately 35% of their income to buy consumption goods.

At the same time, in the late 1930s the overall tax structure in the United States was not highly progressive. Despite strong increases in top marginal income tax rates in the mid- and late 1930s (see Fig. 1.5a, Sect. 1.1.2.2), which made the income tax schedule at the upper end more progressive, indirect (consumption) taxes, which are

---

than consumption expenditures [...]," because it increases productive capacity, allowing for a higher national income in the future (Hansen 1940, p. 3541). To boost real capital investment and discourage saving, Hansen (1941, p. 389) proposed, for instance, to partly tax firms' undistributed profits if they are not reinvested in real capital. Despite the importance of investment spending, however, based on his presumption of the fading of population growth and territorial expansion, at the time of writing Hansen (1941, pp. 298, 306) did not see sufficient investment opportunities which could secure full employment and adequate growth, especially in the US economy. It was thus considered necessary to boost other components of effective demand which could serve as a stopgap, first and foremost government spending and consumption by private households.

typically regressive, were raised as well (Hansen 1941, pp. 125–128). Taking a look at estimates on the overall tax burden by Colm and Tarasov (1940, p. 6) in Table 7.3, it can be seen that the US tax structure in 1938–1939 only started to be progressive at an annual income of 10,000 U.S. dollars and above. While the total tax schedule was more or less proportional in the middle-income brackets, it was regressive at the lower end of the income scale, with those at the very bottom paying a larger share of their income in taxes than those positioned higher in the income hierarchy. Distinguishing between federal as well as state and local taxes, Table 7.3 reveals that especially at the state and local level the tax schedule in the late 1930s was mainly flat along the income distribution and even regressive at the bottom of the income scale. As outlined by Colm and Tarasov (1940, p. 13) and Hansen (1941, p. 133), this pattern can be traced back to consumption taxes imposed by state and local authorities.

Given the overall tax structure at the end of the 1930s in the United States as well as the typical variations in the marginal (and average) propensities to consume along the income scale, Hansen (1941, pp. 398–399) argued in support of a more progressive tax scheme which would lower the tax burden at the bottom of the income hierarchy and raise it for those at the top of the distribution. While tax reductions at the lower end of the income scale are generally expected to increase consumption spending of those on low income, a higher tax burden at the upper end of the distribution is supposed to adversely impact the saving behavior of top income recipients, thus raising overall consumption spending and aggregate demand in the economy as a whole. Moreover, ceteris paribus the increase in consumption may stimulate real capital investment (Hansen 1941, pp. 278, 336, 399). Hansen (1941, pp. 398–399) himself especially favored a reduction in consumption tax rates, as they disproportionately burden those in the lower parts of the distribution. Additionally, although he was restrained as to changes in capital gains taxes, he called for a more progressive income tax structure along the total income range as well as for adequate measures to prevent tax evasion by the affluent (Hansen 1940, p. 3544, 1941, pp. 298–300, 389–391).

In the years after Hansen had outlined his secular stagnation concept, it was not just his hypothesis as such, but also the proposed countermeasures which were subject to criticism. While Abramovitz (1942, pp. 62–63), for instance, endorsed Hansen's viewpoint that a reduction in income inequality was necessary to lower the amount of saving at the full-employment level of income, Samuelson (1943, pp. 43–44), though generally supportive of some degree of income redistribution, warned to not overestimate the expected positive impact on the overall propensity to consume. Eventually, however, the debate on Hansen's proposal of a more progressive tax scheme was mainly geared toward its impact on real capital investment, bearing resemblance to Okun's (1975) later discussion on the equality–efficiency trade-off. Simons (1942, p. 177), for example, dismissed Hansen's policy implications out of hand, as they would imply "[...] taxes near the limit of taxable capacity [...]." Likewise, King (1939, pp. 618–619) did not see how aggregate demand in the economy as a whole could be increased by redistribution policies. Although he acknowledged the affluent to consume a comparatively low percentage of their income, he also assumed them to invest vast amounts in real capital. Along similar lines, Hansen was indirectly

Table 7.3 Consumption expenditures and tax payments by income group in the United States, 1935–1936 and 1938–1939

Income group (U.S. dollars)	Consumption, 1935–1936 (% of income)	Tax payments, 1938–1939 (% of income)		
		Federal	State and local	Total
Under 500	149.4	7.9	14.0	21.9
500–1,000	107.8	6.6	11.4	18.0
1,000–1,500	98.7	6.4	10.9	17.3
1,500–2,000	93.0	6.6	11.2	17.8
2,000–3,000	87.1	6.4	11.1	17.5
3,000–5,000	78.6	7.0	10.6	17.6
5,000–10,000	64.8	8.4	9.5	17.9
10,000–15,000	53.7	14.9	10.6	25.5
15,000–20,000	52.7	19.8	11.9	31.7
20,000 and over	35.4	27.2	10.6	37.8

Source Author's illustration, based on data from the National Resources Committee (1939, p. 20), Colm and Tarasov (1940, p. 6), and Hansen (1941, pp. 134, 232). See Appendix B for detailed data sources and further notes

criticized by McCord Wright (1948), one of his close associates, who was concerned about the possible adverse impact of a more progressive income tax schedule on entrepreneurial activity. Hinting at the effect of a higher tax burden at the top of the distribution on personal incentives, he wondered whether "[...] a professional hunter would bring in quite so many ducks if he knew that nine of every ten would be taken away [...]" (McCord Wright 1948, p. 170). Schumpeter (1939, pp. 1038–1039), indeed, argued on similar grounds.

Although their critics made an important point, it must be noted that Hansen and his fellows were not naive in proposing an overall more progressive tax scheme. While Hansen advocated changes in the tax structure designed to boost consumption spending by private households, he was aware that the tax system could only be adjusted with great care, so as to avoid the possible trade-off of increasing consumption at the expense of a decline in real capital accumulation (Hansen 1938, p. 30). In his *Guide to Keynes*, he later outlined that "[h]ere as so often in economics one encounters a dilemma: highly progressive taxes are favorable to a high level of consumption since such taxes promote greater equality of income, but they tend to have a deterrent effect on investment" (Hansen 1953, p. 220). By exercising caution in proposing a more progressive tax scheme, the stagnationists around Hansen actually did not make themselves vulnerable. Moreover, throughout Hansen's (1941, p. 249) works it becomes clear that, as a measure to inhibit secular stagnation tendencies, the redistribution of income via the tax and transfer system was only of secondary importance to him. In most of his writings, he put much more emphasis on (debt-financed) government investment and community expenditures.

7.2.3 *Schumpeter on the Limits of Progressive Taxation*

As an economist peripherally involved in the twentieth-century debate on secular stagnation, Schumpeter, in a way similar to Keynes and Hansen, did not lay his focus on the topic of income distribution. Nonetheless, however, he gave some insight into his perspective on inequality, also with regard to the impact on capitalist development.

Refusing to address "[...] philosophies like the one about the justice ideal [...]," Schumpeter ([1908] 2010, p. 53), unlike Hansen, did not pay attention to the social component of income distribution, but only considered the purely economic effects. For instance, critical of welfare economics such as proposed by both Arthur C. Pigou and the German economist Adolf Wagner, he opposed increases in tax progression for the sole purpose of "correcting" the distribution of income (Schumpeter 1954, pp. 945–946). Especially with respect to questions of distribution, already in his earlier writings Schumpeter ([1908] 2010, p. 225) pledged to refrain from "[...] a political attachment that strikes the essence of a science in the face. We must place so much emphasis on it [...]," he held, "[...] because the discussion of the problem of distribution [...] leads to such points time and again."

On empirical grounds, Schumpeter ([1942] 2008, pp. 65–67) adverted to the long-term constancy of income distribution with respect to nominal income and factor shares. In real terms, on the other hand, he was convinced that the capitalist system of production and the introduction of mass production techniques had elicited changes in relative income shares to the benefit of those at the lower end of the income scale. At the same time, in his 1927 essay *Social Classes in an Ethnically Homogeneous Environment*, Schumpeter ([1927] 1991, pp. 251, 273) referred to the class division in society, stating that both upward and downward social mobility are always given. Although questionable from today's perspective, with the relevant literature suggesting an overall decline in social mobility—especially in countries with a high degree of income inequality (see, for example, Krueger 2012; Corak 2013; Davis and Mazumder 2017)—he compared each social class to a hotel which is "[...] always full, but always of different people [...]" (Schumpeter [1927] 1991, p. 248). According to Schumpeter ([1927] 1991, pp. 253–254), moving up the class hierarchy is typically the result of hard work, inventive talent, and entrepreneurial initiative. In general, families tend to climb up the social hierarchy when "[...] one of their members has *done something novel*, typically the founding of a new enterprise, something that meant getting out of the conventional rut" (Schumpeter [1927] 1991, p. 253). Opportunities to go from rags to riches he thus assumed to be closely linked to entrepreneurial activity.

With entrepreneurs being the pivotal element in his theory of economic progress, along Schumpeterian lines it is essential to enable their free development and to not curtail their scope, such as by a highly progressive tax scheme. His viewpoint on taxation Schumpeter ([1918] 1991) had already outlined at the end of World War I in his essay *The Crisis of the Tax State*. Here, he described the state as "[...] an economic parasite [...]" which, via the tax system, "[...] must not demand from the people so much that they lose financial interest in production or at any rate cease to use their best energies for it" (Schumpeter [1918] 1991, p. 112). Although he referred to both indirect (consumption) and direct taxation, he placed particular emphasis on income taxes on entrepreneurial profits. If the tax burden on profits is too high, Schumpeter ([1918] 1991, pp. 113–114) noted, entrepreneurial activity and economic development will inevitably be hampered. With a highly progressive tax scheme, it can be expected that "[...] capital formation is paralyzed and may even turn into capital consumption through lack of amortization and repairs" (Schumpeter [1918] 1991, p. 115).

Disapproving of the strong and long-term increases in top marginal income tax rates in the United States in the early 1930s and thereafter (see Fig. 1.5a, Sect. 1.1.2.2), Schumpeter (1939, p. 1045) considered the tax progression at the very top of the distribution a "[...] systematic attack [...]" on real capital investment opportunities. Convinced that the rise in the highest tax rates adversely affected firms' investment threshold "[...] between 'to do and not to do [...]' [...]" (Schumpeter 1939, pp. 1038–1039), he perceived a marked degree of tax progression to be among the anti-capitalist developments which would cause stagnation and, eventually, the breakdown of the capitalist system of production (Schumpeter [1942] 2008, pp. 70, 398). Comparing Hansen's secular stagnation hypothesis with his own theory, he concluded: "[...] [E]vidently it comes to the same thing, in a profit economy, whether the objective opportunities for gainful enterprise decrease or the profits after having been made are taxed away" (Schumpeter 1954, p. 1173). Hence, although the possible trade-off between tax progression and real capital investment was not neglected by Hansen, it plays a much more important role in Schumpeter's approach and, in fact, is one of the central elements in Schumpeter's stagnation theory. Eventually, it is especially through his remarks on taxation that Schumpeter revealed himself as an economist who emphasized the incentive effect of an unequal distribution of income and thus the necessity of inequality for economic growth and development. Economic growth and progress, he stated, called for

> [...] high premia on industrial success and all the other inequalities of income that may be required in order to make the capitalist engine work [...]. *In the United States alone there need not lurk, behind modern programs of social betterment, that fundamental dilemma that everywhere else paralyzes the will of every responsible man, the dilemma between economic progress and immediate increase of the real income of the masses.* (Schumpeter [1942] 2008, p. 384)

Advocating the supply side of the economy, it is not surprising that Schumpeter's attitude toward income distribution stands in contrast to Keynes's and Hansen's demand-side perspective on inequality. Yet, with Keynes, Hansen, and Schumpeter referring approximately to the same time period in the early twentieth century, and hence to similar empirical developments in income distribution, it becomes once more clear how the underlying economic theory shapes the way in which the world is seen.

7.2.4 Kalecki and Steindl: Distribution Moves to the Forefront

While the twentieth-century economists considered thus far did not neglect the issue of distribution, Kalecki and Steindl placed much more emphasis on it, addressing the topic in a clear and precise manner. Hein (2014, p. 181), for instance, ranks Kalecki's explicit consideration of distributional issues among the differences between Keynes's and Kalecki's theoretical frameworks. Indeed, the distribution of income plays a key role in both Kalecki's and Steindl's works, not least with regard to output determination and economic growth.

7.2.4.1 Income Distribution, Output, and Economic Growth along Kaleckian Lines

As has been briefly outlined in Sect. 3.2.3.1, the functional distribution of income is essential to understanding the generation of national income in Kalecki's theory. According to Kalecki's ([1954] 1965, pp. 47, 59–61) static analysis, with a given absolute level of real investment and capitalists' consumption, and hence—in a closed economy without government activity and workers' saving—a given amount of profits, national income is higher the higher the wage share in the economy. Ceteris paribus, a decline in the wage share, such as triggered by an increase in the degree of monopoly, is thus accompanied by a fall in national income. As real wages decline with a rise in the degree of monopoly, workers' consumption, effective demand, and hence output in the economy as a whole decrease. While a given level of real profits thus represents a higher proportion of a lower national income, the wage share correspondingly declines (see also Asimakopulos 1988, p. 137).[2]

Although Kalecki predominantly referred to the functional distribution of income, especially in his essay *Three Ways to Full Employment* he also touched on the issue of personal income inequality (Kalecki 1944, p. 53). To increase output and secure full employment, here he argued in favor of income redistribution from the rich to the poor via the tax and transfer system. Just like Keynes, Kalecki (1944, p. 53) emphasized the varying (marginal) propensities to consume along the income hierarchy. By boosting the average propensity to consume in the economy as a whole, redistribution policies may be used to raise effective demand, output, and employment. Increasing national income by redistribution measures, however, requires a tax system which is both progressive, but at the same time not detrimental to private investment so as to avoid adverse dynamic effects on capital accumulation. If real capital investment were not discouraged, Kalecki (1944, p. 55) noted, a rise in income taxation aimed at redistributing income from the top to the bottom of the income scale could "[...] be

---

[2]While in the case described above aggregate demand and output fall with a reduction in real wages, the decline in national income may be mitigated or even change into an increase in an open economy with government activity and workers' saving (see, for instance, Asimakopulos 1988, p. 152; López G. and Assous 2010, pp. 134–139, 152–161).

pushed as far as practically possible [...]." In addition to endorsing adequate tax and transfer policies as a means to ensure full employment, Kalecki (1944, p. 55) also praised redistribution measures from a social perspective, as a tool that could make "[...] the distribution of incomes (after taxation) more egalitarian [...]."

While Kalecki's theory of distribution is closely connected to his idea of output, employment, and national income creation, income inequality also plays a role in his reflections on long-term economic growth. Aside from innovations, according to Kalecki ([1954] 1965, pp. 156–161) it is saving outside of firms—or *rentiers' saving*, as he called it—which, in relation to the stock of capital, impacts the long-run rate of economic growth. While innovations encourage private investment and are thus conducive to economic development, a rise in (ex-ante) non-firm saving as a share of capital hampers the rate of real capital accumulation and hence secular economic growth. Focusing on the impact of both innovations and the functional distribution of income on long-term economic growth in capitalist economies—with a rise in the profit share tending to raise the (ex-ante) amount of outside saving in relation to the capital stock—Kalecki ([1954] 1965, p. 161) summarized:

> A decline in the intensity of innovations in the later stages of capitalist development results in a retardation of the increase in capital and output. Moreover, if the effect of the increase in the degree of monopoly upon the distribution of national income is not counteracted by other factors there will be a relative shift from wages to profits and this will constitute another reason for the slowing down of the long-run rise in output.

Although not explicitly outlined by Kalecki ([1954] 1965, p. 159), the issue of non-firm saving can be linked to the personal distribution of income among private households or individuals. It can be argued, in fact, that an increase in income inequality at the private household or individual level ceteris paribus raises (ex-ante) outside saving in relation to both output and the capital stock, as those at the top of the income scale save a larger share of their income than those in the lower parts of the income hierarchy. An increase in personal income inequality, with those at the top of the income pyramid experiencing a relative rise in their income shares, may thus inhibit economic growth in the long run.

7.2.4.2 The Functional Distribution of Income: A Key Element in Steindl's Theory

Standing on the Shoulders of Kalecki: Secular Stagnation and the Profit Share
Among the "genuine" secular stagnationists of the twentieth century, it was first and foremost Josef Steindl, Kalecki's follower and contemporary, who approached the topics of output development and economic growth in the context of the functional distribution of income.

Although the tendency toward oligopoly is the dominant theme in Steindl's writings on secular stagnation, it is not industry concentration as such, but the specific characteristics involved which may reduce the long-term rate of economic growth. Along Kaleckian–Steindlian lines, in fact, the rise in oligopoly is initially accompanied by increases in gross and net profit margins and thus a rise in the profit share in national income. Ceteris paribus, this shift from wages to profits reduces effective demand and hence capacity utilization in the economy as a whole. After a time lag, the lower degree of capacity utilization, in turn, may have adverse effects on real capital accumulation, possibly leading to secular stagnation. Hence, it is the shift of income toward profits and the associated decline in effective demand that underlies Steindl's ([1952] 1976) stagnation hypothesis. Building on Kalecki's (1943) *Political Aspects of Full Employment*, Steindl (n.d.-b, p. 1, own translation) eventually traced low economic growth and the underemployment of productive resources to a lack of demand, resulting from "[...] the fact that capitalism is not inclined to provide the workers with a larger share of national income and hence to ensure the consumption of the goods produced." Capitalism, he noted, "[...] suffers from not giving the workers sufficient purchasing power" (Steindl n.d.-b, p. 2, own translation).

While Steindl's ([1952] 1976) analysis of the functional distribution of income occasionally seems to be overshadowed by his preoccupation with oligopolistic tendencies, it was Steindl (1987, p. 473) himself who repeatedly emphasized "[t]he distribution theory [...]" in his stagnation approach, noting that "[h]ere a link between distribution and the process of investment was established which so far had been missing." In an earlier unpublished version of his essay *Distribution and Growth* (Steindl, [1985a] 1990), he spoke of his "[...] own ideas on stagnation which have a lot to do with distribution [...]" (Steindl n.d.-a, p. 5). Elsewhere, Steindl (1974, p. 10) referred to his "[...] discussion of the relation of growth and distribution in Maturity & Stagnation [...]," while in his manuscript *Trend and Cycle* he concluded, "Thus distribution turns out to be a most important element in the explanation of the normal growth process" (Steindl [1988] 2005, p. 172).

Focusing on the Functional and Touching on the Personal Distribution of Income

Steindl's ([1952] 1976) focus on the nexus between income distribution, economic growth, and stagnation has also been noted by other authors. Andrews (2005, p. 79), for instance, speaks of Steindl's work as "[...] a theory of growth and development based on the interaction between the functional distribution of income, industrial structure and effective demand." In accordance with this notion, Dutt (2005, p. 73), in reflecting on Steindl's ([1952] 1976) major achievement, does not refer to the explanation of stagnation tendencies in the United States in the mid-twentieth century, but explicitly mentions Steindl's ([1952] 1976, pp. 192–228) mathematical formalization of his stagnation theory. More precisely, Dutt (2005, p. 73) acknowledges Steindl's ([1952] 1976) model as

> [...] a growth model in which it is possible for a shift in income distribution towards profits to reduce the rate of growth of the economy in the long run, thus making it possible for greater equity to go hand in hand with faster growth.

In line with the classical and Kaleckian tradition as well as most of the historical literature dealing with income distribution, Steindl's ([1952] 1976) stagnation theory and the corresponding mathematical model incorporate the *functional* distribution of income, focusing especially on the long-run economic impact of variations in the profit share. While the exclusive consideration of the functional distribution of income seems to be unsatisfactory from today's perspective, Steindl's ([1952] 1976) contribution must be interpreted within its historical context. In fact, when *Maturity and Stagnation in American Capitalism* was first published in 1952, the issue of income distribution did not play a major role in the political, economic, and public debate. As income was distributed relatively equally in the United States and other developed countries, questions of distribution were generally not of particular concern. In this regard, it was not just Steindl's ([1952] 1976) preoccupation with secular stagnation per se, but also his analysis within a theoretical framework of income distribution which did not reflect the *Zeitgeist* of the post-Second World War years. "In the second half of the [twentieth] century [...]," Atkinson and Bourguignon (2001, p. 7265) hold, "[...] there were indeed times when interest in the distribution of income was at a low ebb [...]."

At the same time, however, although the issues of both stagnation and distribution were not en vogue in the mid-twentieth century, Steindl's ([1952] 1976) focus on the *functional* distribution of income is in line with the historical development of the topic of inequality. From the classical economists to Steindl's very own teacher Kalecki, the subject of income distribution had always been primarily an issue of functional distribution in the history of economic thought. Even in the 1970s and 1980s, when the reprint of Steindl's book was published at a time of a declining labor share in national income and rising personal income inequality, it was mainly the functional distribution which due attention was paid to in the economic debate. According to Palley (2017, p. 147), this primary focus on the functional distribution of income in the 1970s and 1980s "[...] reflected the political economy concerns [...] [of that time, as] [t]his was a period of significant labor-capital conflict, marked by the rise of neoliberalism which aimed to tame labor and shift the distribution of income toward capital." In fact, although there were economists who addressed the personal distribution of income in the mid- and late twentieth century (see, for instance, the remarks in Haslinger and Stönner-Venkatarama 1998, p. 25), in more recent times this issue has clearly gained more attention. Among other things, this development can be traced back to the availability of adequate empirical data, which has largely improved since the early and mid-2000s owing to the works of Piketty (2001, 2003), Atkinson (2007, 2010), and their fellows.

Although Steindl's ([1952] 1976) focus on the profit share and thus on the functional distribution of income reflects the specific historical circumstances of his time, in some of his later writings he explicitly addressed the issue of personal income inequality, especially with reference to a rise in the saving rate of private households (Steindl 1976b, [1982b] 1990). Along Kaleckian and Steindlian lines, private household saving matters, because it constitutes outside saving which—other than firms' own saving—is not conducive to real capital investment, but is merely income which is not used for private consumption spending and hence a drag on effective demand. Absent counteracting forces, a rise in the overall propensity to save of private households or individuals, such as triggered by an increase in personal income inequality, reduces the degree of capacity utilization in the economy as a whole and may thus lead to secular stagnation (Steindl [1982b] 1990, p. 196). Steindl ([1982b] 1990, p. 183) concluded:

> In the light of these observations, the question of functional distribution (the share of profits in full employment income) ceases to be the only matter of concern, and the question of the inequality of personal incomes—which is presumably much more relevant for the personal saving ratio—moves into the foreground. Thus consideration of the trend of household saving may involve a certain shift in attitudes of economists interested in full employment.

Although Steindl was thus clearly aware of the personal distribution of income, he had never approached this topic within his model of economic growth and stagnation—an issue which will be followed up in the following Chap. 8.

To reduce the saving ratio in the economy as a whole, and thus to spur economic growth and lead the economy to its full-employment level of output, among other things Steindl ([1982b] 1990, p. 200) proposed "[...] to interfere directly with the distribution of personal incomes [...]." Referring to Kalecki (1939, pp. 148–149; 1944, pp. 46–47), who considered the potentially self-defeating capacity effect of real capital investment, Steindl (n.d.-c, p. 5) pointed to the necessity of an adequate level of private consumption to ensure both full employment of productive resources and hence—via the stimulating impact on the degree of capacity utilization—an appropriate rate of economic growth in the long run. He thus argued in favor of income redistribution toward those income groups with a relatively high (marginal) propensity to consume. "The problem of creating an adequate amount of consumption, by appropriate [*sic*] distribution of income [...]," Steindl (n.d.-c, p. 5) noted in a Keynesian and Kaleckian underconsumptionist manner, "[...] remains basic for a full employment policy." In fact, while he expected various full-employment measures—such as an excessive increase in real capital investment, public deficit spending, foreign investment, and the expansion of consumer credit—to potentially have adverse long-term economic consequences, he considered the redistribution of income toward low-saving income groups more reasonable to bring about full employment and adequate economic growth (Steindl [1990] 2012). To prevent possible adverse effects of progressive taxation on real capital investment, Steindl (1976a, p. 2) regarded Kalecki's (1944, pp. 45–46, 54) modified income tax as an appropriate solution.[3] Moreover, rather than targeting firms' profits, he suggested to tax non-investing high-income groups who only spend a comparatively low percentage of their income on consumption goods, especially the rentiers (Steindl [1990] 2012, p. 194).

Steindl ([1982b] 1990, p. 201) was aware, though, that a change in the distribution of personal income via the tax and transfer system "[...] touches a most neuralgic point [...]." Particularly with respect to managers and other occupational groups with a similarly high remuneration, already in the 1970s Steindl (1975) hinted at the irrationality of their compensation, resembling the contemporary debate on executive pay in the aftermath of the 2008–2009 financial crisis (see, for example, Bell and Van Reenen 2013; Kim et al. 2015). Assuming the highest incomes to not be determined by purely rational market forces, Steindl ([1982b] 1990, p. 201) held:

---

[3]It is surprising, however, that—as a critic of industry concentration and oligopolistic tendencies—Steindl did not reflect on the allocation issue associated with Kalecki's modified income tax. See also footnote 22 in Sect. 3.2.3.1.

The absence of a strictly rational basis for determination of higher incomes would seem to make it easier to interfere with it. In fact, the contrary is the case. The irrationality of the income structure is strong enough to resist any pressure to reform it.

Steindl's ([1982b] 1990, p. 201) doubts about the implementation of appropriate redistribution measures were similarly voiced by Sweezy ([1942] 1946, pp. 348–352) and Baran and Sweezy (1966, pp. 299–301), who particularly pointed to the rigid class hierarchy under capitalism as well as the associated unequal distribution of political power. Here, again, Kaleckian traits are clearly visible, especially with respect to Kalecki's (1943) *Political Aspects of Full Employment*. Considering the development of income distribution over the past decades, there has indeed been only little political effort to counteract the trends of rising income inequality in major advanced economies.

7.3 Distribution in Contemporary Stagnation Theories

Comparing Josef Steindl, who considered the (functional) distribution of income *the* key element in his stagnation theory, to the economists involved in the contemporary stagnation debate reveals that today's secular stagnationists tend to focus less on the issue of inequality. The more subordinate treatment of income distribution may be due to the fact that the current discussion, at least with respect to Summers and his fellows, mainly claims to be a revival of Hansen's stagnation hypothesis, whereas Steindl's inequality-focused approach has received considerably less attention.

7.3.1 The Contrasting Views of Summers and Krugman

Although Summers considers the rise in income inequality a relevant cause of a decline in the natural rate of interest and possible secular stagnation tendencies, the issue of distribution is only peripherally mentioned and not at the heart of his hypothesis. In fact, the change in the distribution of income is not a factor which stands out or to which a special role is assigned to, but it is one among the many determinants which—according to Summers—have had an impact on economic performance during the past decades. In general, Summers's strong focus on the natural rate of interest dominates the contemporary (demand-side) stagnation debate, overshadowing most of the other topics addressed.

  In those passages, however, where Summers (2015b, p. 17, 2015c, 2016b, pp. 100–103) discusses the issue of inequality, he is concerned with both the functional and personal distribution of income, referring to the rising share of profits in national income as well as to the increase in top income shares in the United States and other advanced countries. In fact, it is particularly in an interview with the *Washington Center for Equitable Growth* in which Summers (2016a) elaborates further on his position on the nexus between income inequality and secular stagnation. Endorsing the differences in the marginal propensities to save and consume along the income scale, his general line of reasoning is of Keynesian nature, implying that, ceteris paribus, income redistribution from profits to wages and/or from the top to the bottom of the income hierarchy may raise effective demand, output, and economic growth (Summers 2016a, p. 4). Without explicitly mentioning Kalecki, Steindl, or their followers, Summers (2016a, pp. 4–5) incidentally also addresses the issue of monopolistic tendencies. Although he does not approach the rise in monopolistic markets with the same importance as Steindl ([1952] 1976) did, he refers to the respective developments as yet another factor which increases the probability of a longer period of sluggish growth. Along typical Steindlian lines, Summers (2016a, p. 5) associates a rise in monopoly power with a shift in income from low to high savers as well as a decline in investment demand.

While pointing to Okun's (1975) equality–efficiency trade-off and being convinced that this trade-off is of relevance under specific circumstances, Summers (2016a, pp. 3–4) does not see any such conflict in periods of (demand-side) secular stagnation. Given secular stagnation tendencies, it is rather "[...] possible to reform policy to promote both economic efficiency and equality [...]," such as by fostering demand via adequate income redistribution (Summers 2016a, p. 4). In a similar context, referring to the empirical developments in (top) tax rates and the distribution of income in the United States and other developed nations over the past decades, Summers (2015a, p. 2) notes that "[w]ith inequality higher and [tax] progressivity lower the case for progressive reform is strong."

It is quite natural that Summers, as an advocate of demand-side secular stagnation, endorses the Keynesian consumption mechanism when linking the distribution of income to his stagnation hypothesis. Yet, even among those economists supporting his stagnation theory, different opinions on the nexus between inequality and economic growth exist. It is particularly Krugman (2014), in fact, who—although essentially agreeing with Summers's stagnation analysis—has a different view on the impact of income inequality on economic performance via the channel of private consumption spending. While he has not explicitly outlined his opinion on the inequality–growth nexus as part of the contemporary secular stagnation debate, he mainly expressed his viewpoint in reaction to Stiglitz (2013), who, along standard Keynesian lines, considers the high degree of income inequality a factor which has hampered economic recovery in the United States in the aftermath of the 2008–2009 financial crisis. In contrast to both Stiglitz and Summers, Krugman (2014) positions himself as "[...] a skeptic on the inequality-is-bad-for-performance proposition [...]." Although concerned about the high levels of inequality from a social and political perspective, Krugman (2015) warns those on the political left to "[...] not let wishful thinking drive their conclusions [...]" when relating high and rising income inequality to growth-retarding effects. "I wish I could sign on to this thesis [of a negative impact of severe inequality on economic performance] [...]," Krugman (2013a) points out, "[...] [b]ut I can't see how this works."

Krugman (2013a), who focuses on the case of the United States, mainly bases his reasoning on empirical developments, referring to a lack of evidence on the inequality-consumption–growth nexus in the relevant economic indicators. If—as

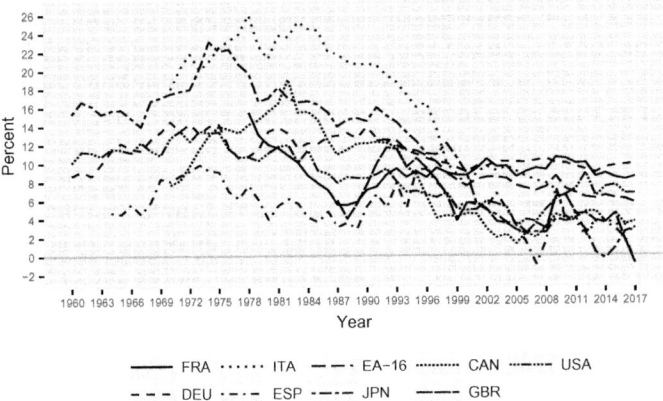

Fig. 7.1 Private household net saving rates, 1960–2017. *Source* Author's illustration, based on data from the European Commission (2018), the OECD (2011, 2018), the Deutsche Bundesbank (1976, p. 356), and the Federal Reserve Bank of St. Louis (2018). See Appendix A for detailed data sources and further notes

Summers, Stiglitz, and other economists do—differences in the (marginal) propensities to save and consume along the income scale are emphasized, so his argument runs, one would expect the aggregate private household saving rate to increase with a rise in income inequality. As shown in Fig. 7.1, however, despite an increase in income inequality in most advanced countries, private household net saving rates have generally been declining during the past decades. While the fall has been comparatively mild in France, Germany, and Spain, starting between the mid-1970s and mid-1980s, it has been particularly pronounced in Italy, Japan, Canada, and the United States. In light of these contrasting developments in income inequality and private household saving rates, Krugman (2013a) infers that consumption spending by the affluent can be sufficient to sustain an adequate percentage of private consumption demand in the economy. With the long-term rise in income inequality since the late 1970s having been accompanied by a decline in the aggregate private household saving rate in the United States and other advanced countries, according to Krugman (2013a) the standard Keynesian consumption mechanism cannot serve as an appropriate demand-side explanation for the overall decline in economic growth.

Krugman's (2013a) line of reasoning, however, is not as clear-cut. On the one hand, as has been outlined in Sect. 6.2.2, it is not only the size of consumption demand, but also its composition which matters for economic growth. A relative shift of consumption demand from mass consumption toward luxury goods may inhibit economic growth by hampering process innovations and—in line with Marshall ([1890] 2013, pp. 377–382, 450)—economies of scale. On the other hand, there is also room for discussion on Krugman's (2013a) general rejection of the Keynesian inequality-saving nexus. In fact, the assertion that an increase in income inequality tends to raise the overall propensity to save of private households is contingent on *ceteris paribus* conditions, which, however, are not fulfilled by actual (descriptive) economic data. Actual developments in saving rates, such as shown in Fig. 7.1, do not isolate the possible impact of changes in income inequality. It may thus not be contradictory to refer to the tendency of the aggregate private household saving rate to rise with an increase in income inequality, while at the same time this trend is not reflected in empirical data. Income inequality is but one of many factors which can have an impact on the aggregate private household saving rate. For instance, it is commonly agreed that the sharp decline in the private household saving rate in Japan over the past decades has been dominated by demographic effects (Koga 2006; Curtis et al. 2017), which—as has been shown in Fig. 3.8 in Sect. 3.3.2.1— have been particularly strong in Japan as compared to other advanced nations. In accordance with Modigliani's (1966) life-cycle hypothesis, the rise in the share of (dissaving) retirees in the Japanese population is a drag on the aggregate private household saving rate. This does not imply, however, that the saving rate would not have been still lower if inequality had not increased during the past decades.

Based on empirical (econometric) analyses, for the United States Dynan et al. (2004) find a positive nexus between the relative (current and permanent) income of private households and their (marginal) propensity to save. At the same time, however, they point to the "[...] difficulty in detecting a [positive] correlation between income inequality and the [aggregate private household] saving rate [...]" (Dynan et al. 2004, p. 436). Similarly, Blinder (1975, pp. 448, 467) cannot confirm a negative link between income inequality and the aggregate propensity to consume. As a possible explanation, he brings Duesenberry's (1949, pp. 44–45) relative income hypothesis into play, which, in a modified form, has also been adduced in explaining the decline in the aggregate private household saving rate in the United States prior to the 2008–2009 financial crisis (see, for instance, van Treeck and Sturn, 2012). Krugman (2013b), in fact, seems to be partially convinced by this line of reasoning. In terms of their consumption spending, so the argument runs, private households are oriented toward those households positioned slightly above themselves in the income scale. Based on a comic strip by Momand (1920), in the relevant literature this phenomenon is sometimes referred to as the *Keeping Up with the Joneses* effect (see, for instance, Perloff 1948, p. 206; Stiglitz 2012, p. 105). As a modified version of the relative income hypothesis, Frank et al. (2014, p. 57) speak of *expenditure cascades* "[...] to describe a process whereby increased expenditure by some people leads others just below them on the income scale to spend more as well, in turn leading others just below the second group to spend more, and so on [...]." With a particularly strong rise in income inequality in the United States during the past decades, the maintenance of this consumption behavior, it is argued, required those private households who saw their incomes either stagnate or increase only relatively little to lower their saving rates and to partially incur debt in the years leading up to the financial crisis of 2008–2009. While the individual propensities to save along the income hierarchy were still a positive function of private households' relative income position, they gradually declined below the top of the income scale (IMF 2012, pp. 13–16).[4] Prior to the financial crisis of 2008–2009, wealth effects have also played a role, with rising

---

[4]One can speak of a downward shift or downward rotation of an upward sloping function over time.

house prices leading to an expansion of private households' consumption spending (IMF 2012, pp. 16–18).[5] In the aggregate, these developments resulted in a fall in the overall propensity to save of private households. Despite a rise in income inequality, the private household saving rate in the US economy thus did not increase, but—to the contrary—declined. Given the impact of expenditure cascades and wealth effects, it cannot be claimed, in fact, that—along Keynesian lines—a more equal distribution of income prior to the financial crisis would have led to a lower private household saving rate and hence stronger aggregate demand and economic growth. Yet, considering the rise in private household debt, economic performance would have been more sustainable.

Eventually, given the differences in the (marginal) propensities to save along the income hierarchy, it seems empirically reasonable that a rise in income inequality *ceteris paribus* raises the aggregate private household saving rate and may thus hamper economic growth by impairing effective demand. This Keynesian effect, however, may be overcompensated by other factors. For instance, demographic change or, as in the case of the United States prior to the financial crisis of 2008–2009, behavioral adjustments by private households may lead to a decline in the aggregate private household saving rate as income inequality increases. This does not mean, however, that the typical Keynesian mechanism addressed by Summers and other economists is fundamentally without empirical relevance.

7.3.2 Gordon's Headwind of Inequality

Introducing the topic of inequality as one of his four headwinds, Gordon (2016), the supply-side advocate in the contemporary stagnation debate, shares Summers's concern about today's highly unequal distribution of income. Other than Summers, however, he builds his thoughts on different grounds and, at least in his magnum opus *The Rise and Fall of American Growth*, does not primarily address inequality because of its possible impact on overall economic growth. In fact, while Gordon (2016) bases his secular stagnation theory on his expectations regarding future innovations as well as the headwinds of education and demographic change, the headwind of inequality is first and foremost considered relevant for its own sake. It is the diverging development of material well-being at the top and the bottom of the income hierarchy, such as reflected in a relative decline in median real income as compared to average real income, which matters to him (Gordon 2016, pp. 608, 620, 628, 2018, p. 9). The comparatively low average economic growth during the past decades has not been beneficial for everyone in society, and it is this development *as such* which

---

[5]As outlined by Maki and Palumbo (2001), during the stock market boom in the 1990s, it was particularly the private households at the top of the income distribution that—due to a rise in their stock market wealth—contributed to the fall in the aggregate private household saving rate by increasing their consumption spending. In fact, saving rates at the upper end of the income hierarchy even fell into negative territory prior to the stock market downturn in the early 2000s. See also Poterba (2000) and Dynan and Maki (2001).

Gordon (2016, pp. 608–624) considers alarming. Indeed, his perception resembles Atkinson's (2015, pp. 11–14) viewpoint on inequality. A highly unequal distribution of income, Atkinson (2015, p. 12) held, is not only relevant because of its possible unfavorable economic impact, but it is also an issue in itself. He noted:

> The case for reducing inequality does not [...] depend solely on its having adverse consequences [...]. There are *intrinsic* reasons for believing that the current degree of inequality is excessive. These reasons may be framed in terms of a broader theory of justice. (Atkinson 2015, p. 12)

Although Gordon's (2016) headwind of inequality is primarily directed toward the issue of distribution as such, he occasionally addresses possible inequality-related developments that may harm economic growth in the long run. In this regard, Gordon (2016, pp. 630–632) is especially concerned about adverse social changes in the lower parts of the income hierarchy, such as a rise in the number of single-parent families or a decline in educational attainment, with the causality "[...] between stagnant incomes and social dysfunction [...]" assumed to run in both directions (Gordon 2016, p. 630). With reference to the United States, for instance, he mentions a rise in social segregation between the rich and the poor which has accompanied the surge in inequality, acting as a drag on social mobility (Gordon 2016, p. 373). Particularly via the educational channel, existing inequalities are thus increasingly perpetuated across generations, with unfavorable effects on economic growth. In a more recent paper, Gordon (2018, pp. 5–7) also emphasizes the nexus between income inequality and population growth. In the United States, long-run economic growth has been declining not least because of a fall in the growth of total hours of work, which, in turn, has been partially triggered by a decline in population growth. Among other things, this development has been caused by a reduction in life expectancy for low-educated people as well as individuals at the bottom of the income scale. An increase in the death rate due to drug abuse and suicide, which Case and Deaton (2017, p. 398) refer to as *deaths of despair*, has probably played a role here.

As has been outlined in Sect. 4.3.2.2, Gordon (2016, pp. 644–649) proposes a variety of measures aimed at reducing the high levels of income inequality in the United States and other developed nations. It is especially redistribution policy, however, which requires a political balancing act. In fact, while—in the wake of establishing a more equal distribution—those at the bottom of the income hierarchy must see their incomes grow comparatively strongly, there is "[...] no parallel desire to make those in the top 1% less productive, nor to find ways for them to contribute less to the economy and to society [...]" (Gordon 2016, p. 644). With his focus on the historical development of innovations and technological progress, it is only natural that Gordon (2016, p. 644) points to the possible adverse incentive effects of redistribution policy, which may hamper long-term economic growth through a decline in entrepreneurial activity and risk-taking. Another aspect, though, which Gordon (2016) himself does not consider, but which fits well into the discussion, refers to the possible nexus between innovation, economic development, and an efficient social safety net. As outlined by Greif and Iyigun (2013a, p. 535), social institutions positively impact economic progress, first, "[...] by directly mitigating the individual-level risk associated with discovering, adopting, and responding to new knowledge [...]," and, secondly, by promoting "[...] social order [...]," i.e., by "[...] alleviating the risk of violent social responses [...]" to innovations and economic change. Hence, as a way of risk sharing and by providing for an adequate social framework, social protection and income redistribution aimed at alleviating high inequality may be beneficial for entrepreneurial innovation and economic growth (see also Stiglitz 2015, p. 408). Focusing on England, the empirical analysis of Greif (2013a, b) shows that the longtime system of poor relief, the *Old Poor Law* (1601–1834), may have been among the factors which fostered modern economic growth and the first Industrial Revolution. Based on historical data both at the English county-level and across European countries, Greif and Iyigun (2013a, p. 538) find "[...] positive, significant, and economically meaningful correlations between innovations and the efficacy of the poor law [...]." They conclude, "Extending poor relief through some income redistribution could have fostered social peace and stability, thereby smoothing the social repercussions of the creative destruction inherent in the development process leading to and encompassing the Industrial Revolution [...]" (Greif and Iyigun 2013b, p. 25). Eventually, if an efficient social safety net is conducive to innovation, Gordon's (2016) headwind of income inequality is not only relevant from a purely distributional perspective, but it can also be linked to his analysis of technological progress.

7.4 Concluding Remarks

Although the distribution of income plays a role in all approaches considered in this chapter, in most of the theories it is not at the center of interest. While Keynes addressed the nexus between consumption demand and inequality, Hansen did not consider the unequal distribution of income in the early twentieth century a possible cause of stagnation, but nonetheless argued in favor of income redistribution to boost consumption spending and counteract secular stagnation tendencies. Schumpeter, on the contrary, emphasized the incentive effect of income inequality and was generally disapproving of income redistribution via the tax and transfer system. In the contemporary stagnation debate, Summers takes account of the topic of distribution along Keynesian lines, without, however, laying special focus on it. Gordon, on the other hand, does not primarily point to the nexus between inequality and economic growth, but first and foremost regards inequality as an issue on its own.

Among the economists involved in the modern and contemporary stagnation debates, it was clearly Steindl ([1952] 1976) who focused most strongly on the distribution of income. Emphasizing and elaborating on the nexus between income distribution, economic growth, and stagnation, his approach is a reasonable point of reference in the history of economic thought. Yet, Steindl's ([1952] 1976) theory did not only remain largely unnoticed in the years following its publication in the early 1950s, but it is also hardly mentioned in the contemporary stagnation debate. While in the recent past Hein (2016), for instance, has pointed to the importance of Steindl's contribution, Summers (2014, p. 29), the leading advocate of demand-side stagnation in the contemporary debate, rather sees his own hypothesis as a new version of Hansen's theory, with comparatively little room for questions of inequality. Given the empirical developments in income distribution in recent decades, it is surprising that the issue of inequality—and hence also Steindl's theory of stagnation—does not play a more distinct role. Steindl's inequality-focused approach, in fact, may add a different and empirically relevant perspective to the current debate.

It has been mentioned that, from today's point of view, a shortcoming of Steindl's approach is that it does not consider the role of personal income inequality, but focuses almost exclusively on the functional distribution of income. To tackle this shortcoming, in the following Chap. 8 a Steindlian model of economic growth and stagnation is developed, explicitly including the personal distribution of income.

In the recent past, a few economists have addressed the personal distribution of income in economic growth models. In addition to the functional distribution of income between profits and wages, Carvalho and Rezai (2016), for example, also analyze the unequal distribution of wages among wage earners within a neo-Kaleckian framework. Palley (2017), in turn, builds on a modified version of the Bhaduri and Marglin (1990) model to take account of personal income inequality. In his model, national income is divided between two social classes, both receiving profit and wage income. While the income of capitalist managers consists mainly of profits, the income of workers is primarily made up of wages.

Although the general approach pursued in the following chapter resembles the intention of Carvalho and Rezai (2016) and Palley (2017), the model specifications are yet different. The model presented is based on Dutt's (2005) modified version of Steindl's ([1952] 1976, pp. 192–228) original model of long-term economic growth and secular stagnation. To be able to address the personal distribution of income among private households, however, Dutt's (2005) Steindlian model is further altered.

References

Abramovitz M (1942) Savings and investment: profits vs. prosperity? Am Econ Rev 32(2):53–88

Andrews M (2005) On industry concentration and the transition to monopoly capitalism: a knife-edge model of "Steindlian" dynamics. In: Mott T, Shapiro N (eds) Rethinking capitalist development: essays on the economics of Josef Steindl. Routledge, New York, NY, pp 79–94

Asimakopulos A (1988) Post-Keynesian theories of distribution. In: Asimakopulos A (ed) Theories of income distribution. Kluwer Academic Publishers, Boston, MA, Dordrecht, and Lancaster, pp 133–157

Atkinson AB (2015) Inequality: what can be done? Harvard University Press, Cambridge, MA, and London

Atkinson AB, Bourguignon F (2001) Income Distribution. In: Smelser NJ, Baltes PB (eds) International encyclopedia of the social & behavioral sciences. Pergamon, Oxford, pp 7265–7271

Atkinson AB, Piketty T (eds) (2007) Top incomes over the twentieth century: a contrast between European and English-speaking countries. Oxford University Press, Oxford

Atkinson AB, Piketty T (eds) (2010) Top incomes: a global perspective. Oxford University Press, Oxford

Baran PA, Sweezy PM (1966) Monopoly capital: an essay on the American economic and social order. Monthly Review Press, New York, NY

Bell BD, Van Reenen J (2013) Extreme wage inequality: pay at the very top. Am Econ Rev 103(3):153–157

Bhaduri A, Marglin S (1990) Unemployment and the real wage: the economic basis for contesting political ideologies. Camb J Econ 14(4):375–393

Blinder AS (1975) Distribution effects and the aggregate consumption function. J Polit Econ 83(3):447–475

Bowley AL (1920) The change in the distribution of the national income, 1880–1913. Oxford University Press, Oxford

Carvalho L, Rezai A (2016) Personal income inequality and aggregate demand. Camb J Econ 40(2):491–505

Case A, Deaton A (2017) Mortality and morbidity in the 21st century. BrookS Pap Econ Act 2017:397–476

Colm G, Tarasov H (1940) Investigation of concentration of economic power. Temporary National Economic Committee, monograph no. 3: who pays the taxes? Allocation of federal, state, and local taxes to consumer income brackets. United States Government Printing Office, Washington, DC

Corak M (2013) Income inequality, equality of opportunity, and intergenerational mobility. J Econ Perspect 27(3):79–102

Curtis CC, Lugauer S, Mark NC (2017) Demographics and aggregate household saving in Japan, China, and India. J Macroecon 51:175–191

Davis J, Mazumder B (2017) The decline in intergenerational mobility after 1980. Federal Reserve Bank of Minneapolis Working Paper 17–21. Federal Reserve Bank of Minneapolis, Minneapolis, MN. https://www.minneapolisfed.org/institute/working-papers/17-21.pdf. Accessed 02 May 2018

Deutsche Bundesbank (1976) Deutsches Geld- und Bankwesen in Zahlen 1876–1975. Verlag Fritz Knapp, Frankfurt am Main

Duesenberry JS (1948) Income-consumption relations and their implications. In: Metzler LA, Domar ED, Duesenberry JS, Higgins B, Goodwin RM, Samuelson PA, Wright DM, Alexander SS, Perloff HS, Musgrave RA, Lerner AP, Stettner WF, Brown EC, Bishop RL, Dunlop JT, Bourneuf A (eds) Income, employment and public policy: essays in honor of Alvin H. Hansen, W. W. Norton & Company, Inc., New York, NY, pp 54–81

Duesenberry JS (1949) Income, saving and the theory of consumer behavior. Harvard University Press, Cambridge, MA

Dutt AK (2005) Steindl's theory of maturity and stagnation and its relevance today. In: Mott T, Shapiro N (eds) Rethinking capitalist development: essays on the Economics of Josef Steindl. Routledge, New York, NY, pp 55–78

Dynan KE, Maki DM (2001) Does stock market wealth matter for consumption? The Federal Reserve Board Finance and Economics Discussion Series Working Paper 2001–23. Board of Governors of the Federal Reserve System, Washington, DC. https://www.federalreserve.gov/pubs/feds/2001/200123/200123pap.pdf. Accessed 14 Nov 2018

Dynan KE, Skinner J, Zeldes SP (2004) Do the rich save more? J Polit Econ 112(2):397–444

European Commission (2018) Annual macro-economic database of the European Commission's Directorate General for Economic and Financial Affairs (AMECO database). European Commission, Brussels. http://ec.europa.eu/economy_finance/ameco/user/serie/SelectSerie.cfm. Data as of November 08, 2018. Accessed 26 Nov 2018

Federal Reserve Bank of St. Louis (2018) FRED economic data. Federal Reserve Bank of St. Louis, St. Louis, MO. https://fred.stlouisfed.org/. Accessed 04 Dec 2018

Frank RH, Levine AS, Dijk O (2014) Expenditure cascades. Rev Behav Econ 1(1–2):55–73

Friedman BM (2009) Introduction. In: Bhagwati J, Blinder AS, Friedman B (eds) Offshoring of American jobs: what response from U.S. economic policy? The Alvin Hansen symposium on public policy at Harvard University. The MIT Press, Cambridge, MA, and London, pp ix–xiv

Gilboy EW (1938) The propensity to consume. Q J Econ 53(1):120–140

Gordon RJ (2016) The rise and fall of American growth. The U.S. standard of living since the Civil War. Princeton University Press, Princeton, NJ

Gordon RJ (2018) Why has economic growth slowed when innovation appears to be accelerating? NBER Working Paper No. 24554. National Bureau of Economic Research, Cambridge, MA. http://www.nber.org/papers/w24554. Accessed 19 June 2018

Greif A, Iyigun M (2013a) Social organizations, violence, and modern growth. Am Econ Rev 103(3):534–538

Greif A, Iyigun M (2013b) What did the old poor law really accomplish? A redux. https://papers.ssrn.com/sol3/papers.cfm?abstract_id=2261497. Accessed 21 June 2018

Hansen AH (1932) Economic stabilization in an unbalanced world. Harcourt, Brace and Company, New York, NY

Hansen AH (1938) Full recovery or stagnation? W. W. Norton & Company, Inc., New York, NY

Hansen AH (1940) Testimony of Alvin Harvey Hansen, Professor of Political Economy, Harvard University, Cambridge, Mass. In: Temporary National Economic Committee (ed) Investigation of concentration of economic power. Hearings before the Temporary National Economic Committee Congress of the United States. Part 9: savings and investment, United States Government Printing Office, Washington, DC, pp 3495–3520, 3538–3559, 3837–3859

Hansen AH (1941) Fiscal policy and business cycles. W. W. Norton & Company, Inc., New York, NY

Hansen AH (1945) Stability and expansion. In: Homan PT, Machlup F (ed) Financing American prosperity. A symposium of economists. The Twentieth Century Fund, New York, NY, pp 199–265

Hansen AH (1951) Business cycles and national income. W. W. Norton & Company, Inc., New York, NY

Hansen AH (1953) A guide to Keynes. McGraw-Hill Book Company, Inc., New York, NY

Haslinger F, Stönner-Venkatarama O (1998) The theory of income distribution: a survey of some recent developments. In: Haslinger F, Stönner-Venkatarama O (eds) Aspects of the distribution of income. Metropolis-Verlag, Marburg, pp 13–71

Hein E (2014) Distribution and growth after Keynes: a post-Keynesian guide. Edward Elgar, Cheltenham and Northampton, MA

Hein E (2016) Secular stagnation or stagnation policy? Steindl after Summers. PSL Q Rev 69(276):3–47

IMF (2012) United States: selected issues. IMF country report no. 12/214. International Monetary Fund, Washington, DC. https://www.imf.org/external/pubs/ft/scr/2012/cr12214.pdf. Accessed 16 June 2018

Kalecki M ([1938] 1939) The distribution of the national income. In: Kalecki M (ed) Essays in the theory of economic fluctuations, George Allen & Unwin, Ltd., London, pp 13–41

Kalecki M (1939) Essays in the theory of economic fluctuations. George Allen & Unwin, Ltd., London

Kalecki M (1943) Political aspects of full employment. Polit Q 14(4):322–331

Kalecki M (1944) Three ways to full employment. In: The Oxford University Institute of Statistics (ed) The economics of full employment, Basil Blackwell, Oxford, pp 39–58

Kalecki M ([1954] 1965) Theory of economic dynamics. An essay on cyclical and long-run changes in capitalist economy. Modern Reader Paperbacks, New York, NY, and London

Keynes JM ([1934/1935] 1973) Appendix: variorum of drafts of the general theory. In: Moggridge D (ed) The collected writings of John Maynard Keynes, vol XIV: the general theory and after (part II: Defence and development). Macmillan St. Martin's Press for the Royal Economic Society, London and Basingstoke, pp 351–512

Keynes JM ([1936a] 1973) Letter to R. G. Hawtrey, 24, (March 1936) In: Moggridge D (ed) The collected writings of John Maynard Keynes, vol XIV: the general theory and after (part II: Defence and development). Macmillan St. Martin's Press for the Royal Economic Society, London and Basingstoke, pp 14–18

Keynes JM ([1936b] 1973) The general theory of employment, interest and money. In: The collected writings of John Maynard Keynes, vol vii: the general theory of employment, interest and money. Macmillan and Cambridge University Press for the Royal Economic Society, London, Basingstoke, and New York, NY, pp xxi–384

Keynes JM ([1937] 1973) Some economic consequences of a declining population. In: Moggridge D (ed) The collected writings of John Maynard Keynes, vol XIV: the general theory and after (part II: Defence and development). Macmillan St. Martin's Press for the Royal Economic Society, London and Basingstoke, pp 124–133

Keynes JM ([1938] 1973) Letter to A. C. Pigou, 10, (December 1938) In: Moggridge D (ed) The collected writings of John Maynard Keynes, vol xiv: the general theory and after (part II: Defence and development). Macmillan St. Martin's Press for the Royal Economic Society, London and Basingstoke, p 272

Keynes JM ([1939a] 1973) Mr Keynes on the distribution of incomes and 'propensity to consume': a reply. In: Moggridge D (ed) The collected writings of John Maynard Keynes, vol XIV: the general theory and after (part II: Defence and development). Macmillan St. Martin's Press for the Royal Economic Society, London and Basingstoke, pp 270–271

Keynes JM ([1939b] 1973) Relative movements of real wages and output. In: The collected writings of John Maynard Keynes, vol vii: the general theory of employment, interest and money. Macmillan and Cambridge University Press for the Royal Economic Society, London, Basingstoke, and New York, NY, pp 394–412

Keynes JM ([1939c] 1973) The propensity to consume: reply. In: Moggridge D (ed) The collected writings of John Maynard Keynes, vol XIV: the general theory and after (part II: Defence and development). Macmillan St. Martin's Press for the Royal Economic Society, London and Basingstoke, pp 274–277

Keynes JM ([1943b] 1980) The long-term problem of full employment. In: Moggridge D (ed) The collected writings of John Maynard Keynes, vol XXVII: activities 1940–1946. Shaping the postwar world: employment and commodities. Macmillan and Cambridge University Press for the Royal Economic Society, London, Basingstoke, and New York, NY, pp 320–325

Kim JW, Kogut B, Yang JS (2015) Executive compensation, fat cats, and best athletes. Am Sociol Rev 80(2):299–328

King WI (1939) Are we suffering from economic maturity? J Polit Econ 47(5):609–622

Koga M (2006) The decline of Japan's saving rate and demographic effects. Jpn Econ Rev 57(2):312–321

Krueger A (2012) The rise and consequences of inequality. Center for American Progress, Washington, DC. https://www.americanprogress.org/events/2012/01/12/17181/the-rise-and-consequences-of-inequality/. Accessed 02 May 2018

Krugman P (2013a) Inequality and recovery. The New York Times. The opinion pages. The conscience of a liberal, 20 Jan 2013. https://krugman.blogs.nytimes.com/2013/01/20/inequality-and-recovery/. Accessed 13 June 2018

Krugman P (2013b) Inequality as a defining challenge. The New York Times. The opinion pages. The conscience of a liberal. 14 Dec 2013. https://krugman.blogs.nytimes.com/2013/12/14/inequality-as-a-defining-challenge/. Accessed 17 June 2018

Krugman P (2014) Inequality and economic performance. The New York Times. The opinion pages. The conscience of a liberal. 02 Dec 2014. https://krugman.blogs.nytimes.com/2014/12/02/inequality-and-economic-performance/. Accessed 13 June 2018

Krugman P (2015) Musings on inequality and growth. The New York Times. The opinion pages. The conscience of a liberal. 08 June 2015. https://krugman.blogs.nytimes.com/2015/06/08/musings-on-inequality-and-growth/. Accessed 13 June 2018

Kuznets S (1942) Uses of national income in peace and war. National Bureau of Economic Research, New York, NY

Kuznets S (1946) National income: a summary of findings. National Bureau of Economic Research, New York, NY

López GJ, Assous M (2010) Great thinkers in economics: Michał Kalecki. Palgrave Macmillan, New York, NY

Maki DM, Palumbo MG (2001) Disentangling the wealth effect: a cohort analysis of household saving in the 1990s. The Federal Reserve Board Finance and Economics Discussion Series Working Paper 2001–21. Board of Governors of the Federal Reserve System, Washington, DC. https://www.federalreserve.gov/pubs/feds/2001/200121/200121pap.pdf. Accessed 14 Nov 2018

Marshall A ([1890] 2013) Principles of economics, 8th edn. Palgrave Macmillan, Basingstoke and New York, NY

McCord Wright D (1948) Income redistribution reconsidered. In: Metzler LA, Domar ED, Duesenberry JS, Higgins B, Goodwin RM, Samuelson PA, Wright DM, Alexander SS, Perloff HS, Musgrave RA, Lerner AP, Stettner WF, Brown EC, Bishop RL, Dunlop JT, Bourneuf A (eds) Income, employment and public policy: essays in honor of Alvin H. Hansen. W. W. Norton & Company, Inc., New York, NY, pp 159–176

Modigliani F (1949) Fluctuations in the saving-income ratio: a problem in economic forecasting. In: National Bureau of Economic Research (ed) Studies in income and wealth: conference on research in income and wealth. National Bureau of Economic Research, New York, NY, pp 369–444

Modigliani F (1966) The life cycle hypothesis of saving, the demand for wealth and the supply of capital. Soc Res 33(2):160–217

Momand P (1920) Keeping up with the Joneses. Cupples & Leon Co., New York, NY

National Resources Committee (1939) Consumer expenditures in the United States. Estimates for 1935–36. United States Government Printing Office, Washington, DC

OECD (2011) OECD.Stat, economic projections, OECD economic outlook no. 89 — June 2011— annual projections for OECD countries. OECD, Paris. http://stats.oecd.org/. Accessed 06 Nov 2018

OECD (2018) OECD.Stat.OECD, Paris. http://stats.oecd.org/. Accessed 04 Dec 2018

Okun AM (1975) Equality and efficiency: the big tradeoff. The Brookings Institution, Washington, DC

Palley TI (2017) Inequality and growth in neo-Kaleckian and Cambridge growth theory. Rev Keynes Econ 5(2):146–169

Perloff HS (1948) Dynamic elements in a full employment program. In: Metzler LA, Domar ED, Duesenberry JS, Higgins B, Goodwin RM, Samuelson PA, Wright DM, Alexander SS, Perloff HS, Musgrave RA, Lerner AP, Stettner WF, Brown EC, Bishop RL, Dunlop JT, Bourneuf A (eds) Income, employment and public policy: essays in honor of Alvin H. Hansen. W. W. Norton & Company, Inc., New York, NY, pp 199–217

Piketty T (2001) Les hauts revenus en France au XXe siècle: Inégalités et redistributions 1901–1998. Bernard Grasset, Paris

Piketty T (2003) Income inequality in France, 1901–1998. J Polit Econ 111(5):1004–1042

Poterba JM (2000) Stock market wealth and consumption. J Econ Perspect 14(2):99–118

Samuelson PA (1943) Full employment after the war. In: Harris SE (ed) Postwar economic problems. McGraw-Hill Book Company, Inc., New York, NY, and London, pp 27–53

Schumpeter JA ([1908] 2010) The nature and essence of economic theory (English edition and new introduction by Bruce A. McDaniel). Routledge, London and New York, NY

Schumpeter JA ([1918] 1991) The crisis of the tax state. In: Swedberg R (ed) The economics and sociology of capitalism. Princeton University Press, Princeton, NJ, pp 99–140

Schumpeter JA ([1927] 1991) Social classes in an ethnically homogeneous environment. In: Swedberg R (ed) The economics and sociology of capitalism. Princeton University Press, Princeton, NJ, pp 230–283

Schumpeter JA (1939) Business cycles (two volumes). McGraw-Hill Book Company, Inc., New York, NY, and London

Schumpeter JA ([1942] 2008) Capitalism, socialism and democracy, 3rd edn. Harper Perennial Modern Thought, New York, NY

Schumpeter JA (1946) John Maynard Keynes 1883–1946. Am Econ Rev 36(4):495–518

Schumpeter JA (1954) History of economic analysis. Oxford University Press, New York, NY

Simons HS (1942) Hansen on fiscal policy. J Polit Econ 50(2):161–196

Staehle H (1937) Short-period variations in the distribution of incomes. Rev Econ Stat 19(3):133–143

Steindl J ([1952] 1976) Maturity and stagnation in American capitalism (with a new introduction by the author). Monthly Review Press, New York, NY, and London

Steindl J (1974) Stagnation theory in the light of recent history (version 1). Unpublished manuscript. Digital collection Josef Steindl/University Library of the Vienna University of Economics and Business. Call number: S/M.45.3. https://viewer.wu-wien.ac.at/viewer/ppnresolver?id=AL00657666

Steindl J (1975) Income distribution–line of reasoning (version 1). Unpublished manuscript. Digital collection Josef Steindl/University Library of the Vienna University of Economics and Business. Call number: S/M.70.1. https://viewer.wu-wien.ac.at/viewer/ppnresolver?id=AL00659437

Steindl J (1976a) Government debts and inflation: stumbling-blocks in the way of Keynesian full employment policy. Unpublished manuscript. Digital collection Josef Steindl/University Library of the Vienna University of Economics and Business. Call number: S/M.59.5. https://viewer.wu-wien.ac.at/viewer/ppnresolver?id=AL00658474

Steindl J (1976b) Sparen und Einkommensverteilung. Empirica 3(1):55–76

Steindl J ([1982b] 1990) The role of household saving in the modern economy. In: Steindl J (ed) Economic papers 1941–88. St. Martin's Press, New York, NY, pp 183–207

Steindl J ([1985a] 1990) Distribution and growth. In: Steindl J (ed) Economic papers 1941–88. St. Martin's Press, New York, NY, pp 149–165

Steindl J ([1985b] 1990) J. M. Keynes: society and the economist. In: Steindl J (ed) Economic papers 1941–88. St. Martin's Press, New York, NY, pp 276–302

Steindl J (1987) Stagnation. In: Eatwell J, Milgate M, Newman P (eds) The New Palgrave Dictionary of Economics, vol 4. Macmillan, London, pp 472–474

Steindl J ([1988] 2005) Trend and cycle. In: Mott T, Shapiro N (eds) Rethinking capitalist development: essays on the economics of Josef Steindl. Routledge, New York, NY, pp 164–173

Steindl J ([1990] 2012) Effective demand in the short and in the long run. PSL Q Rev 65(261):189–197

Steindl J (n.d.-a) Distribution and growth. Unpublished manuscript. Digital collection Josef Steindl/University Library of the Vienna University of Economics and Business. Call number: S/M.71.4. https://viewer.wu-wien.ac.at/viewer/ppnresolver?id=AL00659620

Steindl J (n.d.-b) Kapitalismus ohne Arbeitslosigkeit. Unpublished manuscript. Digital collection Josef Steindl/University Library of the Vienna University of Economics and Business. Call number: S/M.44.5. https://viewer.wu-wien.ac.at/viewer/ppnresolver?id=AL00657581

Steindl J (n.d.-c) Policies of stimulating private investment. Unpublished manuscript. Digital collection Josef Steindl/University Library of the Vienna University of Economics and Business. Call number: S/M.45.1. https://viewer.wu-wien.ac.at/viewer/ppnresolver?id=AL00657658

Stiglitz JE (2012) The price of inequality: how today's divided society endangers our future. W. W. Norton & Company, New York, NY, and London

Stiglitz JE (2013) Inequality is holding back the recovery. New York Times. The opinion pages. Opinionator, 19 Jan 2013. https://opinionator.blogs.nytimes.com/2013/01/19/inequality-is-holding-back-the-recovery/. Accessed 13 June 2018

Stiglitz JE (2015) The great divide: unequal societies and what we can do about them. W. W. Norton & Company, New York, NY, and London

Summers LH (2014) Reflections on the 'new secular stagnation hypothesis'. In: Teulings C, Baldwin R (eds) Secular stagnation: facts, causes and cures. CEPR Press, London, pp 27–38

Summers LH (2015a) 40 Years later–the relevance of Okun's "equality and efficiency: the big tradeoff", 4 May 2005. Economic studies at Brookings. The Brookings Institution, Washington, DC. https://www.brookings.edu/wp-content/uploads/2015/05/050415-Summers-Okun-Speech.pdf. Accessed 11 June 2018

Summers LH (2015b) Low real rates, secular stagnation & the future of stabilization policy. Speech at the central bank of Chile research conference, 20 Nov 2015. http://larrysummers.com/wp-content/uploads/2015/12/LarrySummers-Central-Bank-of-Chile.pdf. Accessed 29 Aug 2016

Summers LH (2015c) Reflections on secular stagnation. Keynote address at Princeton University's Julius-Rabinowitz Center for Public Policy & Finance, 19 Feb 2015. http://larrysummers.com/2015/02/25/reflections-on-secular-stagnation/. Accessed 25 Aug 2016

Summers LH (2016a) Equitable growth in conversation: an interview with Lawrence H. Summers. Interview by Heather Boushey, 11 Feb 2016. Washington Center for Equitable Growth, Washington, DC. http://equitablegrowth.org/research-analysis/equitable-growth-in-conversation-an-interview-with-lawrence-summers/. Accessed 25 Aug 2016

Summers LH (2016b) Secular stagnation and monetary policy. Fed Reserv Bank St Louis Rev 98(2):93–110

Sweezy PM, ([1942] 1946) The theory of capitalist development: principles of Marxian political economy. Dobson Books Ltd., London

van Treeck T, Sturn S (2012) Income inequality as a cause of the Great Recession? A survey of current debates. Conditions of work and employment series no. 39. International Labour Office, Geneva. http://www.ilo.org/wcmsp5/groups/public/---ed_dialogue/---actrav/documents/meetingdocument/wcms_230194.pdf. Accessed 17 June 2018

Chapter 8
A Steindlian Model of Income Distribution, Economic Growth, and Stagnation

8.1 Introduction

In addition to the detailed verbal description of his stagnation hypothesis, Steindl ([1952] 1976, pp. 192–228) in his magnum opus also included a mathematical (growth) model of his theory. Although he was aware of the limits of both his own model and mathematical models in general, in describing economic reality (Steindl [1952] 1976, pp. xvi, 226–228, [1984] 1990, pp. 243–247), he appreciated that "[...] the mathematical formulation of the underlying theories has considerable advantages in checking the logic of the argument, and making the assumptions explicit." (Steindl [1952] 1976, p. 226).

At the heart of Steindl's ([1952] 1976, pp. 212–214) original model is the investment function

$$I_{t+\varphi} = a_1 S_{ft} + U(u_t) + G(k_t), \quad \varphi > 0, \quad \alpha_1 > 0, \tag{8.1}$$

identifying three factors which, after a time lag (φ), determine firms' investment spending (I). These factors are, first, the internal accumulation of firms (S_f), i.e., firms' internal saving in the form of retained profits, secondly, the degree of capacity utilization (u), and, thirdly, the so-called reciprocal gearing ratio (k), a measure of firms' indebtedness. While Steindl ([1952] 1976, p. 212) acknowledged that profits impact investment in addition to their indirect effect via firms' internal saving, mainly for reasons of simplicity he did not include profits as a separate (fourth) factor in his investment function.

In Eq. (8.1), Steindl ([1952] 1976, p. 212) defined $U(u_t)$ as a linear function

$$U(u_t) = K_t (nu_t - nu_0), \quad n > 0, \tag{8.2}$$

where K_t is the capital stock at time t, u_t is the degree of capacity utilization at time t, u_0 is the planned degree of capacity utilization, and n is a constant parameter. If the

© Springer Nature Switzerland AG 2020
C. Anselmann, *Secular Stagnation Theories*, Springer Studies in the History of Economic Thought, https://doi.org/10.1007/978-3-030-41087-2_8

actual degree of capacity utilization (u_t) is equal to the planned degree of capacity utilization (u_0), the impact of the degree of capacity utilization on firms' investment behavior vanishes. The degree of capacity utilization at time t Steindl ([1952] 1976, p. 212) assumed to be given by

$$u_t = \frac{\kappa Y_t}{K_t},$$ (8.3)

where Y_t is national income at time t. κ, in turn, is defined as the capital–capacity ratio

$$\kappa = \frac{K}{Y*},$$ (8.4)

with Y^* representing productive capacity, i.e., potential output.

As to the impact of the reciprocal gearing ratio on investment, Steindl ([1952] 1976, p. 213) referred to the function $G(k_t)$ as

$$G(k_t) = K_t(qk_t - qk_0), \quad q > 0,$$ (8.5)

where k_t is the actual reciprocal gearing ratio at time t, k_0 is firms' planned reciprocal gearing ratio, and q is a constant parameter. The reciprocal gearing ratio at time t is calculated as

$$k_t = \frac{K_{ft}}{K_t},$$ (8.6)

which is the ratio of firms' internally owned capital (K_f) to total capital (K) at time t. Similar to the interaction of the actual and planned degree of capacity utilization, if the actual reciprocal gearing ratio (k_t) is equal to the planned reciprocal gearing ratio (k_0), the function $G(k_t)$ becomes zero and ceases to have an impact on firms' investment spending.

Finally, substituting Eqs. (8.2), (8.3), (8.5), and (8.6) into Eq. (8.1) yields Steindl's ([1952] 1976, p. 214) investment function

$$I_{t+\varphi} = \alpha_1 S_{ft} + qK_{ft} + \kappa nY_t - K_t(nu_0 + qk_0).$$ (8.7)

By taking time lags into account, Eq. (8.7) is a so-called *delay differential equation*, formerly also commonly known as a *mixed difference-differential equation*. According to Dutt (2005, p. 56), this specific characteristic of Steindl's ([1952] 1976) investment function "[...] serves to complicate and perhaps even obfuscate the analysis."[1] He therefore reproduces Steindl's original model with a modified investment function, making two major adjustments: First, Dutt (2005, pp. 56–57) introduces a function of desired investment to which firms adjust their actual investment behavior over time. By modeling investment spending in that way, Dutt (2005) avoids to draw

---

[1] On the difficulty of solving delay differential equations, see also Andrews (2005, pp. 79–80, 92).

on a delay differential equation, but is able to model time lags with a much simpler, though not less meaningful, differential equation. Secondly, Dutt (2005, p. 56) ignores the impact of the reciprocal gearing ratio, mainly for reasons of simplicity. In fact, the reciprocal gearing ratio is not essential to Steindl's ([1952] 1976) original analysis. As pointed out by Dutt (2005, p. 56), Steindl ([1979] 1990, [1989] 1990) himself excluded the reciprocal gearing ratio in several of his later writings.

Drawing on Dutt's (2005) modified version of Steindl's ([1952] 1976, pp. 192–228) original model, in the following a Steindlian model of economic growth, stagnation, as well as functional and personal income distribution is developed. In doing so, Dutt's (2005) model, while generally maintained, is extended in two respects.

First, and most important, it is not only distinguished between a corporate sector and a private household sector, but the private household sector is further divided into two groups. In fact, by differentiating between poor and rich private households, the personal distribution of income among private households can be included in the model.

Secondly, to account for the long-run character of the model, the impact of technological change is considered. As has been outlined in Sect. 3.2.3.2, although Steindl ([1952] 1976, pp. 132–134,191–192) had explicitly excluded technological change in the 1952 release of *Maturity and Stagnation in American Capitalism*, along Kaleckian lines he later acknowledged that innovation and technological progress play a role in determining long-run economic growth (Steindl [1952] 1976, pp. xv–xvi, [1979] 1990, p. 117, [1980] 1990, [1982a] 1990). Moreover, while—following Steindl ([1952] 1976, pp. 192–228)—Dutt (2005) does not consider technological change in his model, technological progress is addressed in various post-Keynesian growth models, such as in the works of Rowthorn (1981), Kurz (1991), and Dutt (1994, 2003).

In setting the general framework, it should be noted that the model presented hereinafter certainly has its limits, as there are several factors which are not taken into account. Although it is distinguished between the short and the long run, the model is not of dynamic, but of comparative static nature. In line with the Kaleckian–Steindlian tradition, the model is also a purely demand-determined growth model and, as such, does not consider supply-side constraints. At least in the case of a stable equilibrium, it is assumed that there is always some (planned) excess capacity (see also Dutt 2005, p. 74, FN 14). Moreover, price effects as well as the financial sector remain unconsidered as well.[2]

---

[2]Dutt (2006), for instance, presents a Steindlian growth model which considers both demand- and supply-side effects. Hein (2014, pp. 375–440), on the other hand, refers to Kaleckian growth models which explicitly take account of financial markets and finance-dominated capitalism (see also Hein 2016, pp. 35–38).

8.2   Outline and Structure of the Model

8.2.1   The Corporate Sector

Considering a closed private economy which produces a single good with both labor and capital, following Dutt (1994, pp. 95, 98–100, 111, 2005, pp. 55–64) firms' desired rate of real capital accumulation is given by

$$g^d = \left(\frac{I}{K}\right)^d$$

$$= \alpha_0 + \alpha_1 \left(\frac{S_f}{K}\right) + \alpha_2 (u - u_0) + \alpha_3 h, \qquad \alpha_l > 0 \ \forall \ l = 0, 1, 2, 3.$$
(8.8)

Assuming a constant ratio of capital (K) to potential output (Y^*), the degree of capacity utilization (u) is defined as

$$u = \frac{Y}{K}, \qquad K > 0, \quad Y > 0.$$
(8.9)

In Eq. (8.8), g^d is the desired ratio of real investment (I) to capital (K), which is determined, first, by autonomous investment (α_0), driven by entrepreneurial animal spirits, secondly, by firms' internal saving as a ratio of capital (S_f/K), thirdly, by the difference between firms' actual and planned degree of capacity utilization $(u - u_0)$, as well as, fourthly, by the rate of technological change (h). The parameters α_1, α_2, and α_3 define the extent of the impact of S_f/K, $u - u_0$, and h on the desired rate of real capital accumulation, respectively.[3] As in Steindl's ([1952] 1976) original model, the term $\alpha_2 (u - u_0)$ in Eq. (8.8) vanishes if the actual degree of capacity utilization (u) is equal to its planned level (u_0).[4]

Technological change is assumed to be Harrod-neutral at heart, i.e., it is labor-saving and accompanied by a decline in the labor–output ratio, but—as in Steindl ([1989] 1990, p. 171)—does not change the ratio of capital to potential output (K/Y^*)

---

[3]On the importance of firms' internal accumulation, the degree of capacity utilization, and technological progress for firms' investment decisions, see also Guger et al. (2006, pp. 435–437).

[4]Kaleckian and Steindlian growth models treat the degree of capacity utilization (u) as an endogenous variable which, both in the short and the long run, is not necessarily equal to the planned degree of capacity utilization (u_0). This characteristic has been criticized by several authors throughout the years, such as Committeri (1986), Auerbach and Skott (1988), and Skott (2012), who argue that long-run stable equilibria cannot be attained if u is not equal to u_0 in the long run. Yet, as pointed out by Hein et al. (2011, 2012), for instance, deviations of u from u_0 can be justified. In fact, the planned degree of capacity utilization (u_0) must not be a definite, particular value, but may rather be understood as a range of values. Moreover, firms are likely to have multiple objectives, so they may accept deviations of u from u_0 to reach other targets. Along similar lines, Dutt (2005, p. 68) concludes that "[...] there is no necessary inconsistency in the Steindlian framework." See also Hein (2014, pp. 441–471) and Lavoie (2014, pp. 387–410).

(see also Dutt 1994, pp. 98–99; Rowthorn 1981, p. 22).[5] As in Dutt (1994, p. 99), the rate of technological change (h) is endogenous and, according to Kaldor's (1966) outline of *Verdoorn's Law* (Verdoorn 1949), given by

$$h = h_0 + h_1 g, \qquad h_0 > 0, \quad 0 < h_1 < 1. \tag{8.10}$$

h_0 is the autonomous rate of technological change, g is the actual rate of real capital accumulation, and h_1 is the so-called *Verdoorn coefficient*, which measures the impact of economic growth (g) on the rate of technological change (h) (see also Rowthorn 1981, p. 26). Technological change, in fact, does not only lead to economic growth, but, according to the last term in Eq. (8.10), is also the result of economic growth. As summarized by Kalmbach (2000, p. 21), it is empirically reasonable to assume positive values for both h_0 and h_1, with h_1 additionally being less than unity. While the condition $h_1 > 0$ describes learning by doing effects, $h_1 < 1$ models diminishing returns to learning (Dutt 1994, p. 99).

Firms are assumed to adjust their actual rate of real capital accumulation (g) to their desired rate of real capital accumulation (g^d) over time through

$$\frac{\mathrm{d}g}{\mathrm{d}t} = \Theta \left(g^d - g \right), \qquad \Theta > 0, \tag{8.11}$$

where t denotes time and Θ is a parameter determining the size of the impact of $g^d - g$ on $\mathrm{d}g/\mathrm{d}t$. Apart from the effect of technological change $(\alpha_3 h)$, the combined Eqs. (8.8) and (8.11) represent Steindl's ([1952] 1976, p. 214) investment function, implying that, after a time lag, the actual rate of real capital accumulation (g) is positively dependent on firms' internal saving rate (S_f/K) as well as on the gap between the actual and planned degree of capacity utilization $(u - u_0)$.

While both Eqs. (8.8) and (8.11) are Dutt's (1994, pp. 95, 99, 2005) simplified interpretation of Steindl's ([1952] 1976, p. 214) investment function, Eqs. (8.12) to (8.15) can also be found in Steindl's ([1952] 1976, p. 214) original model. Real profits gross of interest payments (R) are determined by

$$R = m_1 Y - m_2 K, \qquad m_l > 0 \ \forall \ l = 1, 2, \quad m_1 < 1, \quad R > 0. \tag{8.12}$$

With a rise in real national income (Y), real gross profits increase by $m_1 Y$, where m_1 is the marginal profit share. The latter [1952] 1976([1952] 1976, p. x) supposed

---

[5]Harrod (1948, pp. 22–23), when first defining his neutral technological progress, additionally assumed a constant interest rate. Given both a constant capital coefficient and a constant interest rate, Harrod-neutral technological progress is, in fact, characterized by a constant functional distribution of income. As will be shown further below, in the Steindlian model developed here, a change in the rate of technological progress alters the functional distribution of income. Hence, while technological progress as assumed in this Steindlian model involves key characteristics of Harrod neutrality, it does not completely conform to all of Harrod's (1948, pp. 22–23) original assumptions. On the nexus between (Harrod-neutral) technological progress and the distribution of income, see also Krämer (1996, pp. 170–178, 193–196).

to be positively influenced by the degree of monopoly and thus by Kalecki's ([1954] 1965, pp. 28–29) mark-up on direct costs (θ) mentioned in Sect. 3.2.3.1. On the other hand, gross profits depend negatively on the capital stock (K). This is due to overhead labor costs, which Steindl ([1952] 1976, pp. x, 215–216) assumed to be a fixed proportion (m_2) of the capital stock (K).

Real profits net of interest payments (P) are defined as

$$P = R - i\left(K - K_f\right), \qquad i > 0, \tag{8.13}$$

where i is the interest rate which firms have to pay on their debt. Firms' debt, in turn, is equal to the total capital stock (K) less the capital stock internally owned by firms (K_f).

Dividends (D) owed to private households are given by

$$D = a_1 K_f + a_2\left(P - a_1 K_f\right), \qquad 0 < a_l < 1 \ \forall \ l = 1, 2. \tag{8.14}$$

They consist, first, of what Steindl ([1952] 1976, p. 215) called a *basic dividend*, i.e., a proportion a_1 of firms' internally owned capital (K_f). Additionally, dividends include a proportion a_2 of the excess of net profits (P) over the basic dividend ($a_1 K_f$).

Firms' internal accumulation, i.e., firms' saving (S_f), is equivalent to the difference between profits net of interest payments (P) and dividends (D), and is thus given by

$$S_f = P - D. \tag{8.15}$$

By substituting Eqs. (8.12) to (8.14) into Eq. (8.15), firms' internal saving can be written as

$$S_f = (1 - a_2)\left[m_1 Y - m_2 K - i\left(K - K_f\right) - a_1 K_f\right]. \tag{8.16}$$

Abstracting from depreciation, changes in the capital stock are equal to real capital investment, i.e.,

$$\frac{dK}{dt} = I. \tag{8.17}$$

Similarly, changes in the capital stock internally owned by firms are equal to firms' internal saving, so that

$$\frac{dK_f}{dt} = S_f. \tag{8.18}$$

In long-run equilibrium, the growth rate of national income is equal to firms' rate of real capital accumulation (g). By disregarding depreciation and assuming that real capital is indestructible, g cannot fall below zero.

8.2.2 The Private Household Sector

Total income of private households (Y_h) is given by

$$Y_h = W + Z, \qquad (8.19)$$

where W is the wage bill and Z is private households' capital income. As national income (Y) consists of wages (W) and profits (R), wages are equal to

$$W = Y - R. \qquad (8.20)$$

By substituting Eq. (8.12) into Eq. (8.20), the wage bill can be written as

$$W = (1 - m_1) Y + m_2 K. \qquad (8.21)$$

Private households' capital income is composed of interest and dividend payments by firms, so that

$$Z = i \left(K - K_f \right) + D. \qquad (8.22)$$

Substituting Eqs. (8.12) to (8.14) into Eq. (8.22) yields

$$Z = (1 - a_2) \left[a_1 K_f + i \left(K - K_f \right) \right] + a_2 \left(m_1 Y - m_2 K \right). \qquad (8.23)$$

In contrast to the models of Steindl ([1952] 1976) and Dutt (2005), which both consider the private household sector as a collective entity, in the following it is distinguished between two private household groups of equal size. While the group of poor private households receives a total income of Y_h^p, the income of the affluent, rich private households is Y_h^r. Total private household income (Y_h) can thus be written as

$$Y_h = Y_h^p + Y_h^r, \qquad Y_h^p > 0, \quad Y_h^r > 0, \quad Y_h^p < Y_h^r, \qquad (8.24)$$

with

$$Y_h^p = wW + zZ, \qquad 0 < w < 1, \quad 0 < z < 1, \quad w > z, \qquad (8.25)$$

and

$$Y_h^r = (1 - w) W + (1 - z) Z, \qquad 0 < w < 1, \quad 0 < z < 1, \quad w > z. \qquad (8.26)$$

As can be seen from Eqs. (8.25) and (8.26), both private household groups receive wage and capital income. While w is the share of the wage bill going to the group of poor private households, $1 - w$ is the corresponding proportion of wages received by the rich private households. Likewise, z and $1 - z$ are the shares of private households' capital income accruing to the poor and the rich, respectively.

Substituting Eqs. (8.21) and (8.23) into both Eqs. (8.25) and (8.26) yields

$$Y_h^p = w\left[(1 - m_1) Y + m_2 K\right] + z\left\{(1 - a_2)\left[a_1 K_f + i\left(K - K_f\right)\right] + a_2\left(m_1 Y - m_2 K\right)\right\} \tag{8.27}$$

and

$$Y_h^r = (1 - w)\left[(1 - m_1) Y + m_2 K\right] + (1 - z)\left\{(1 - a_2)\left[a_1 K_f + i\left(K - K_f\right)\right] + a_2\left(m_1 Y - m_2 K\right)\right\}. \tag{8.28}$$

Finally, private households' saving (S_h) is given by

$$S_h = S_h^p + S_h^r = s_h^p Y_h^p + s_h^r Y_h^r, \quad 0 < s_h^p < 1, \quad 0 < s_h^r < 1, \quad s_h^p < s_h^r, \tag{8.29}$$

where S_h^p is the amount of saving of the poor, S_h^r is the amount of saving of the rich, s_h^p is the proportion of income saved by the poor, and s_h^r is the proportion of income saved by the rich.

Having defined the characteristics of the private household sector, along Kaleckian lines total profits (R) in the economy also can be determined from a demand-side (or expenditure) perspective. In line with Eq. (3.1) (see Sect. 3.2.3.1), in a closed economy without a government sector, profits (R) are equal to the sum of real capital investment (I) and consumption out of profits (C_p), less saving out of wages (S_w). While, in the Steindlian model presented here, consumption out of profits is equivalent to private households' consumption out of capital income (Z), saving out of wages corresponds to private households' saving out of the wage bill (W). From a demand-side perspective, profits (R) can thus be written as

$$R = I + Z\left[\left(1 - s_h^p\right) z + \left(1 - s_h^r\right)(1 - z)\right] - W\left[s_h^p w + s_h^r (1 - w)\right]. \tag{8.30}$$

8.2.3   Measures of Functional and Personal Income Distribution

To be able to analyze both the functional and personal distribution of income, two measures of income distribution are introduced.

The profit share

$$\pi = \frac{R}{Y} \tag{8.31}$$

is used as an index of the functional distribution of income between profits and wages. By substituting Eq. (8.12) into Eq. (8.31), the profit share (π) can be written as

$$\pi = m_1 - \frac{m_2}{u} . \tag{8.32}$$

In contrast to the profit share and similar to Palley (2017, p. 149), the ratio of the incomes of the rich to the poor private households shall serve as a measure of personal income distribution and is defined as

$$\psi = \frac{Y_h^r}{Y_h^p} , \qquad \psi > 1 . \tag{8.33}$$

Substituting Eqs. (8.27) and (8.28) into Eq. (8.33) yields

$$\psi = \frac{\begin{aligned}&(1 - w)\left[(1 - m_1)\, Y + m_2 K\right] \\ &\quad + (1 - z)\left\{(1 - a_2)\left[a_1 K_f + i\left(K - K_f\right)\right] + a_2\left(m_1 Y - m_2 K\right)\right\}\end{aligned}}{\begin{aligned}&w\left[(1 - m_1)\, Y + m_2 K\right] \\ &\quad + z\left\{(1 - a_2)\left[a_1 K_f + i\left(K - K_f\right)\right] + a_2\left(m_1 Y - m_2 K\right)\right\}\end{aligned}} . \tag{8.34}$$

By dividing both the numerator and the denominator by K and defining

$$k = \frac{K_f}{K} , \tag{8.35}$$

Eq. (8.34) can be written as

$$\psi = \frac{\begin{aligned}&(1 - w)\left[(1 - m_1)\, u + m_2\right] \\ &\quad + (1 - z)\left\{(1 - a_2)\left[a_1 k + i\left(1 - k\right)\right] + a_2\left(m_1 u - m_2\right)\right\}\end{aligned}}{\begin{aligned}&w\left[(1 - m_1)\, u + m_2\right] \\ &\quad + z\left\{(1 - a_2)\left[a_1 k + i\left(1 - k\right)\right] + a_2\left(m_1 u - m_2\right)\right\}\end{aligned}} . \tag{8.36}$$

8.3 Short- and Long-Run Effects of Economic Changes

Distinguishing between the short and the long run, the following comparative static analysis is mainly concerned with the impact of economic changes on the degree of capacity utilization (u), on both the functional and personal distribution of income (π and ψ), as well as on the rate of real capital accumulation (g). In the short run, it is assumed that the capital stock (K), firms' internally owned capital (K_f), and the rate of real capital accumulation (g) are given. As a response to different shocks to the economy, reflected in changes in the exogenous variables and parameters of the model, in the short run the goods market clears through adjustments in output and hence in capacity utilization (u). Firms' investment behavior, on the other hand, only changes in the long run. In contrast to the short run, from a long-term perspective, the capital stock (K), firms' internally owned capital (K_f), and the rate of real capital accumulation (g) are flexible and alter according to Eqs. (8.17), (8.18), and (8.11).

8.3.1 The Economy in the Short Run

8.3.1.1 Short-Run Equilibrium Conditions

From the standard investment-saving equilibrium condition $I = S$, it follows that the goods market clears when

$$I - S_f - S_h^p - S_h^r = 0. \tag{8.37}$$

Substituting Eqs. (8.16) and (8.27) to (8.29) into Eq. (8.37) yields

$$
\begin{aligned}
I &- (1 - a_2)\left[m_1 Y - m_2 K - i\left(K - K_f\right) - a_1 K_f\right] \\
&- s_h^p \left\{ w\left[(1 - m_1)\,Y + m_2 K\right] + z\left[(1 - a_2)\left(a_1 K_f + i\left(K - K_f\right)\right) \right.\right. \\
&\left.\left. + a_2\left(m_1 Y - m_2 K\right)\right]\right\} - s_h^r \left\{(1 - w)\left[(1 - m_1)\,Y + m_2 K\right] \right. \\
&\left. + (1 - z)\left[(1 - a_2)\left(a_1 K_f + i\left(K - K_f\right)\right) + a_2\left(m_1 Y - m_2 K\right)\right]\right\} \\
&= 0,
\end{aligned}
\tag{8.38}
$$

which, divided by K, results in

$$
\begin{aligned}
g &- (1 - a_2)\left[m_1 u - m_2 - i\left(1 - k\right) - a_1 k\right] \\
&- s_h^p \left\{ w\left[(1 - m_1)\,u + m_2\right] + z\left[(1 - a_2)\left(a_1 k + i\left(1 - k\right)\right) \right.\right. \\
&\left.\left. + a_2\left(m_1 u - m_2\right)\right]\right\} \\
&- s_h^r \left\{(1 - w)\left[(1 - m_1)\,u + m_2\right] + (1 - z)\left[(1 - a_2)\left(a_1 k + i\left(1 - k\right)\right) \right.\right. \\
&\left.\left. + a_2\left(m_1 u - m_2\right)\right]\right\} \\
&= 0,
\end{aligned}
\tag{8.39}
$$

with $g = I/K, k = K_f/K$, and $u = Y/K$.

Solving Eq. (8.39) for the degree of capacity utilization (u) yields

$$
u = \frac{
\begin{aligned}
g &+ (1 - a_2)(m_2 + i)\left[\left(1 - s_h^r\right) + z\left(s_h^r - s_h^p\right)\right] \\
&+ m_2\left(s_h^r - s_h^p\right)(w - z) \\
&- k\left\{(1 - a_2)(i - a_1)\left[\left(1 - s_h^r\right) - z\left(s_h^p - s_h^r\right)\right]\right\}
\end{aligned}
}{
m_1\left[(1 - a_2)\left(1 - s_h^r\right) + \left(s_h^r - s_h^p\right)(w - a_2 z)\right] + s_h^p w + s_h^r (1 - w)
}.
\tag{8.40}
$$

While Eq. (8.40) is the most general form of the equilibrium degree of capacity utilization, for reasons of simplicity in both the models of Steindl ([1952] 1976, p. 217) and Dutt (2005, pp. 59–60) it is assumed that a_1, the proportion of firms' internally owned capital which is paid out to private households as a basic dividend, is equal to the interest rate (i) which firms have to pay on their debt. The same assumption is made hereinafter. Given that $a_1 = i$, in Eq. (8.40) the impact of k on u vanishes. The degree of capacity utilization can thus be written as

$$u = \frac{g + (1 - a_2)(m_2 + i)\left[(1 - s_h^r) + z\left(s_h^r - s_h^p\right)\right] + m_2\left(s_h^r - s_h^p\right)(w - z)}{m_1\left[(1 - a_2)(1 - s_h^r) + \left(s_h^r - s_h^p\right)(w - a_2 z)\right] + s_h^p w + s_h^r(1 - w)}.$$
(8.41)

Equation (8.41) can now be substituted into both Eqs. (8.32) and (8.36), the measures of functional and personal income distribution. Keeping the assumption that $a_1 = i$, the profit share (π) in Eq. (8.32) is equal to

$$\pi = \frac{gm_1 + im_1(1 - a_2)\left[1 - s_h^r + z\left(s_h^r - s_h^p\right)\right] - m_2\left[s_h^r - w\left(s_h^r - s_h^p\right)\right]}{g + (1 - a_2)(i + m_2)\left[1 - s_h^r + z\left(s_h^r - s_h^p\right)\right] + m_2\left(s_h^r - s_h^p\right)(w - z)}.$$
(8.42)

Similarly, Eq. (8.36), which defines the ratio of the incomes of the rich to the poor private households (ψ), changes to

$$\psi = \frac{\begin{aligned}&g\left[(1 - w)(1 - m_1) + a_2 m_1(1 - z)\right] - a_2 m_2 s_h^p(w - z)\\&+ (1 - a_2)\left\{(1 - w)(i + m_2) + i(w - z)\left[s_h^p + m_1\left(1 - s_h^p\right)\right]\right\}\end{aligned}}{\begin{aligned}&g\left[a_2 m_1 z + w(1 - m_1)\right] + a_2 m_2 s_h^r(w - z)\\&+ (1 - a_2)\left\{w(i + m_2) - i(w - z)\left[s_h^r + m_1\left(1 - s_h^r\right)\right]\right\}\end{aligned}}.$$
(8.43)

8.3.1.2   Comparative Statics in the Short Run

Equations (8.41), (8.42), and (8.43) can now be used to analyze the short-run comparative static impact of changes in the model's exogenous variables and parameters on the degree of capacity utilization (u), on the functional distribution of income—measured by the profit share (π)—as well as on the personal distribution of income among private households—measured by the ratio of the incomes of the rich to the poor private households (ψ). Table 8.1 summarizes the results, with the detailed derivatives given in Appendix D.1.1.1.

Table 8.1 Comparative statics in the short run

	∂a_2	∂i	∂m_1	∂m_2	∂s_h^p	∂s_h^r	∂w	∂z
∂u	+/0/−	+	−	+	−	−	+	+
$\partial \pi$	+/0/−	+	+	−	−	−	+	+
$\partial \psi$	+/0/−	+	+	−	+/0/−	+/0/−	−	−

Source Author's illustration

While the effects of changes in the dividend payout parameter (a_2), the interest rate (i), and the saving rates (s_h^p and s_h^r) are discussed in more detail in Appendix D.1.1.2, the following remarks focus, first, on the impact of a rise in the marginal profit share (m_1) (which is equivalent to the impact of a decline in the ratio of overhead labor costs to capital (m_2)) as well as, secondly, on the impact of a rise in the wage share of the poor private households (w) (which is equivalent to the impact of a rise in the capital income share of the poor private households (z)). These variables are at the center of interest, as they most clearly relate to the distribution of income, one of the key topics in the demand-determined growth model developed here. In fact, the marginal profit share (m_1) and the ratio of overhead labor costs to capital (m_2) are directly tied to the profit share (π) and hence to the functional distribution of income. Moreover, changes in m_1 (and m_2) were of primary interest to Steindl ([1952] 1976, pp. 223–224), because they reflect variations in market power and are thus relevant to the analysis of oligopolistic tendencies. The wage and capital income shares of the poor private households (w and z), on the other hand, are most closely linked to the personal distribution of income (ψ).

Changes in the Marginal Profit Share (m_1) or the Ratio of Overhead Labor Costs to Capital (m_2)

A rise in the marginal profit share (m_1) or a decline in the ratio of overhead labor costs to capital (m_2) reduces the degree of capacity utilization (u), as it shifts income from private households to non-consuming firms. While the total income of private households (Y_h) declines, firms' profits after interest and dividend payments increase. Given firms' investment spending, this shift in income reduces aggregate demand, output (Y), and the degree of capacity utilization (u) through a decline in private households' consumption.

While the fall in output (Y) and capacity utilization (u) reduces the wage bill (W), total profits (R) increase with a rise in m_1 or a fall in m_2. The profit share (π) thus rises. Along Kaleckian lines (see Eq. 8.30), the increase in R can be traced back to a rise in dividend payments and hence to a rise in consumption out of capital income (Z). Moreover, as the wage bill (W) declines, profits (R) are additionally boosted by a reduction in the absolute amount of saving out of wages.

Personal income inequality (ψ) between the rich and the poor private households rises with an increase in the marginal profit share (m_1) or a decline in the ratio of overhead labor costs to capital (m_2). A rise in m_1 or a decline in m_2 induces a rise in private households' capital income (Z), but reduces the wage bill (W) to an even greater extent. As the wage share of the poor private households (w) is higher than their share of capital income (z), the income of the private households at the bottom of the income hierarchy (Y_h^p) declines. On the other hand, the development of the rich private households' income (Y_h^r) is ambiguous. Even if the income at the top of the distribution declines, however, this decline cannot compensate for the income reduction in the lower half of the income scale. A rise in m_1 or a decline in m_2 is thus accompanied by an increase in personal income inequality as measured by ψ.

Changes in the Income Shares of the Poor Private Households (w, z)

A rise in the wage share (w) or the capital income share (z) of the poor private households (and thus a decline in the wage share ($1 - w$) or the capital income share ($1 - z$) of the rich private households) raises private households' consumption spending and thus aggregate demand, output (Y), and the degree of capacity utilization (u).[6] The reason is that a rise in w or z redistributes income from the group of private households with a relatively high propensity to save (s_h^r) (and thus a relatively low propensity to consume ($1 - s_h^r$)) to the group of private households with a relatively low propensity to save (s_h^p) (and thus a relatively high propensity to consume ($1 - s_h^p$)).

A rise in w or z not only increases output (Y) and the degree of capacity utilization (u), but also raises the wage bill (W) and total profits (R). Along Kaleckian lines, profits (R) rise because consumption out of capital income increases. This results from the induced increase in private households' capital income (Z) and, in the case of a rise in z, from an additional increase in the average consumption rate out of capital income. Moreover, if w rises, despite an increase in total wages (W), saving out of wages declines, because the poor private households with a relatively low propensity to save (s_h^p) now have a higher share (w) of the wage bill (W). If z rises, in turn, saving out of wages rises, because total wages (W) increase while the distribution of wages does not change. With both a rise in w or z, however, total profits (R) increase. Due to the impact of overhead labor costs ($m_2 K$), profits (R) rise faster than wages (W) and output (Y), implying that the profit share (π) increases.

Finally, a rise in w or z reduces the measure of personal income inequality (ψ). Although both capital income (Z) and the wage bill (W) increase, due to the redistribution of income to the bottom of the income hierarchy the income of the poor private households (Y_h^p) rises, while the income of the households at the top of the distribution (Y_h^r) declines.

8.3.2 The Economy in the Long Run

8.3.2.1 Long-Run Equilibrium Conditions

As a response to the short-run changes in the exogenous variables and parameters outlined in Table 8.1, firms adjust their investment behavior over time. In the long run, the rate of real capital accumulation (g), the capital stock (K), and firms' internally owned capital (K_f) are thus flexible and alter according to Eqs. (8.11), (8.17), and (8.18).

---

[6]While the partial derivatives of u, π, and ψ with respect to z (see Eqs. D.8, D.16, and D.24 in Appendix D.1.1.1) seem to be uncertain, they are unambiguously defined if it is assumed that total profits (R) are positive (see Eq. 8.12). With a positive R, private households' capital income (Z) is also positive. The signs of the partial derivatives of u, π, and ψ with respect to z are given in Table 8.1.

As can be seen from Eq. (8.11), the long-run attractor of firms' actual rate of real capital accumulation (g) is their desired rate of real capital accumulation (g^d), given by Eq. (8.8). Using the definition of firms' internal saving (S_f) in Eq. (8.16) and assuming that $a_1 = i$ in Eq. (8.8), firms' internal saving as a ratio of capital (S_f/K) can be written as

$$\frac{S_f}{K} = (1 - a_2)\,(m_1 u - m_2 - i)\ . \tag{8.44}$$

In the long run, the goods market remains in equilibrium according to $I = S$, so that u is still given by Eq. (8.41). Substituting Eqs. (8.41), (8.44), and (8.10) into Eq. (8.8) yields

$$
\begin{aligned}
g^d = \alpha_0 &+ \alpha_1 \left(\frac{\begin{array}{c}(1 - a_2)\left\{ m_1 \left[g - i \left(s_h^r - s_h^p \right)(w - z) \right] \right. \\ \left. - (i + m_2)\left[s_h^p w + s_h^r (1 - w) \right] \right\}\end{array}}{\begin{array}{c} m_1 \left[(1 - a_2)\left(1 - s_h^r \right) + \left(s_h^r - s_h^p \right)(w - a_2 z) \right] \\ + s_h^p w + s_h^r (1 - w) \end{array}} \right) \\
&+ \alpha_2 \left(\frac{\begin{array}{c} g + (1 - a_2)(i + m_2)\left[\left(1 - s_h^r \right) + z \left(s_h^r - s_h^p \right) \right] \\ + m_2 \left(s_h^r - s_h^p \right)(w - z) \end{array}}{\begin{array}{c} m_1 \left[(1 - a_2)\left(1 - s_h^r \right) + \left(s_h^r - s_h^p \right)(w - a_2 z) \right] \\ + s_h^p w + s_h^r (1 - w) \end{array}} - u_0 \right) \\
&+ \alpha_3 \,(h_0 + h_1 g)\ .
\end{aligned}
\tag{8.45}
$$

Equation (8.45) can now be substituted into Eq. (8.11), which gives

$$
\begin{aligned}
\frac{dg}{dt} = \Theta \Bigg[\alpha_0 &+ \alpha_1 \left(\frac{\begin{array}{c}(1 - a_2)\left\{ m_1 \left[g - i \left(s_h^r - s_h^p \right)(w - z) \right] \right. \\ \left. - (i + m_2)\left[s_h^p w + s_h^r (1 - w) \right] \right\}\end{array}}{\begin{array}{c} m_1 \left[(1 - a_2)\left(1 - s_h^r \right) + \left(s_h^r - s_h^p \right)(w - a_2 z) \right] \\ + s_h^p w + s_h^r (1 - w) \end{array}} \right) \\
&+ \alpha_2 \left(\frac{\begin{array}{c} g + (1 - a_2)(i + m_2)\left[\left(1 - s_h^r \right) + z \left(s_h^r - s_h^p \right) \right] \\ + m_2 \left(s_h^r - s_h^p \right)(w - z) \end{array}}{\begin{array}{c} m_1 \left[(1 - a_2)\left(1 - s_h^r \right) + \left(s_h^r - s_h^p \right)(w - a_2 z) \right] \\ + s_h^p w + s_h^r (1 - w) \end{array}} - u_0 \right) \\
&+ \alpha_3 \,(h_0 + h_1 g) - g \Bigg]\ .
\end{aligned}
\tag{8.46}
$$

Long-run equilibrium is reached when $dg/dt = 0$, i.e., when firms' actual rate of real capital accumulation (g) is equal to their desired rate of real capital accumulation (g^d). The long-run equilibrium rate of real capital accumulation (g^*) can thus be calculated by equating Eq. (8.46) with zero and solving for g, yielding

$$
g^* = \left(\cfrac{1}{1 - \alpha_3 h_1 - \cfrac{\alpha_1 m_1(1-a_2)+\alpha_2}{m_1\left[(1-a_2)(1-s_h^r)+(s_h^r-s_h^p)(w-a_2z)\right]+s_h^p w+s_h^r(1-w)}} \right.
$$

$$
\cdot \quad \alpha_0 - \alpha_1(1-a_2)(i+m_2) - \alpha_2 u_0
$$

$$
\left. + \; \frac{\begin{aligned}&[\alpha_1 m_1(1-a_2)+\alpha_2]\left\{(1-a_2)(i+m_2)\right.\\ &\cdot\left[1-s_h^r+z\left(s_h^r-s_h^p\right)\right]+m_2\left(s_h^r-s_h^p\right)(w-z)\big\}\\ &\qquad + \alpha_3 h_0\left\{a_2 m_1\left[s_h^p z+s_h^r(1-z)\right]\right.\\ &\quad + (1-m_1)\left[s_h^p w+s_h^r(1-w)\right]+m_1(1-a_2)\big\}\end{aligned}}{\begin{aligned}&m_1\left[(1-a_2)\left(1-s_h^r\right)+\left(s_h^r-s_h^p\right)(w-a_2 z)\right]\\ &\qquad + s_h^p w+s_h^r(1-w)\end{aligned}} \right)
$$

$$(8.47)$$

Depending on the interaction between g and g^d, the equilibrium rate of capital accumulation (g^*) is either stable or unstable. As in Dutt (2005, pp. 60–62), the stability condition can be visualized with a phase diagram, plotting dg/dt, described by Eq. (8.46), against g.

In both Fig. 8.1a and b, the intersection of the dg/dt function with the horizontal line at $dg/dt = 0$ determines the long-run equilibrium rate of real capital accumulation (g^*). For this equilibrium to be stable, at g^* the dg/dt function must be

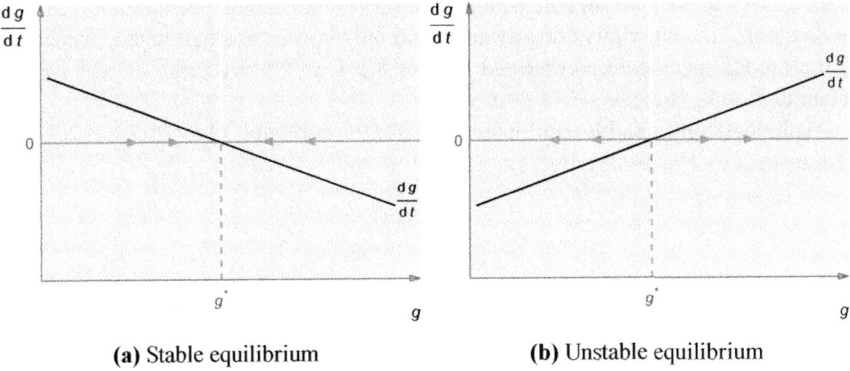

(a) Stable equilibrium   (b) Unstable equilibrium

Fig. 8.1 The long-run equilibrium rate of real capital accumulation (g^*). *Source* Author's illustrations, slightly modified from Dutt (2005, p. 61)

negatively sloped. While Fig. 8.1a depicts the case of a stable equilibrium, g^* in Fig. 8.1b is unstable.

In Fig. 8.1a, starting from the equilibrium rate of real capital accumulation (g^*), for the purpose of explanation it is assumed that firms autonomously reduce their actual rate of real capital accumulation (g), provoking a leftward movement along the dg/dt function. While the actual rate of real capital accumulation (g) thus falls below g^*, dg/dt increases from zero to a positive value. As can be seen from Eq. (8.11), with a constant desired rate of capital accumulation (g^d), a decline in g unambiguously raises dg/dt. According to Eq. (8.45), however, a change in g also impacts g^d. In fact, a decline in g has a threefold influence on the desired rate of real capital accumulation (g^d). First, a fall in g reduces the degree of capacity utilization (u) by lowering aggregate demand and output (Y). The term $\alpha_2 (u - u_0)$ in Eq. (8.8) thus declines. Secondly, the induced reduction in u provokes a fall in firms' internal saving as a ratio of capital (S_f/K) (see Eq. 8.44), leading to a fall in the term $\alpha_1 (S_f/K)$. Thirdly, through the term $\alpha_3 (h_0 + h_1 g)$, a decline in g lowers the extent of technological change. A decline in firms' actual rate of real capital accumulation (g) hence reduces the desired rate of real capital accumulation (g^d). In the case of a stable equilibrium, however, the absolute decline in g is more pronounced than the absolute fall in g^d, implying that, according to Eq. (8.11), a reduction in g is accompanied by a rise in dg/dt. From a positive dg/dt, it follows that g increases again over time, provoking a rightward movement along the dg/dt function. As the increase in g is accompanied by a lower absolute rise in g^d, dg/dt declines gradually. The interaction between g, g^d, and dg/dt eventually restores the original equilibrium, i.e., the cumulative process comes to a halt when firms' actual rate of real capital accumulation (g) is equal to g^*, and dg/dt is zero.

In contrast to Fig. 8.1a, b depicts the case of an unstable equilibrium. Starting from the equilibrium rate of real capital accumulation (g^*), an autonomous decline in g involves a stronger absolute fall in firms' desired rate of real capital accumulation (g^d). With dg/dt thus declining from zero to a negative value according to Eq. (8.11), firms reduce their actual rate of accumulation (g) still further. As this decline in g again provokes a stronger absolute fall in g^d, dg/dt as well as g continue to decline. In fact, as g keeps on falling, the equilibrium rate of real capital accumulation cannot be restored. The cumulative downward spiral only comes to a halt when, according to the model specifications outlined in Sect. 8.2.1, the desired rate of real capital accumulation (g^d) reaches its lower bound.[7]

Mathematically, a stable equilibrium requires the derivative of dg/dt (see Eq. 8.46) with respect to g to be negative, i.e.,

---

[7]In the opposite case of a cumulative upward spiral, the process comes to a halt when full capacity utilization is reached.

$$
\frac{\partial \frac{dg}{dt}}{\partial g} = \Theta \left[\frac{\alpha_1 m_1 \left(1 - a_2\right) + \alpha_2}{m_1 \left[\left(1 - a_2\right)\left(1 - s_h^r\right) + \left(s_h^r - s_h^p\right)\left(w - a_2 z\right)\right] + s_h^p w + s_h^r \left(1 - w\right)} + \alpha_3 h_1 - 1 \right] \overset{!}{<} 0, \qquad (8.48)
$$

which can be rearranged to

$$
\begin{aligned}
\alpha_1 m_1 \left(1 - a_2\right) + \alpha_2 \overset{!}{<} \; &\left(1 - \alpha_3 h_1\right) \big\{ m_1 \left[\left(1 - a_2\right)\left(1 - s_h^r\right)\right. \\
&+ \left(s_h^r - s_h^p\right)\left(w - a_2 z\right)\big] \\
&+ s_h^p w + s_h^r \left(1 - w\right) \big\}.
\end{aligned} \qquad (8.49)
$$

In fact, Eq. (8.49) represents the standard Keynesian stability condition that saving reacts more strongly to changes in the degree of capacity utilization than investment.[8]
Given Eq. (8.48), it follows that the first factor in Eq. (8.47),

$$
\frac{1}{1 - \alpha_3 h_1 - \dfrac{\alpha_1 m_1 (1 - a_2) + \alpha_2}{m_1 \left[(1 - a_2)(1 - s_h^r) + (s_h^r - s_h^p)(w - a_2 z)\right] + s_h^p w + s_h^r (1 - w)}}, \qquad (8.50)
$$

must be positive for the equilibrium rate of real capital accumulation (g^*) to be stable.

8.3.2.2   Comparative Statics of the Rate of Economic Growth

Although Steindl ([1952] 1976, pp. 225–226) himself mentioned the possibility of an unstable long-run equilibrium, in his own model he mainly paid attention to the case of a stable equilibrium. Referring to the adjustment process in the long run, he wrote, "It appears thus that, in general, this 'cumulative process' has a limit, and this limit is the new rate of growth at which the system settles down." (Steindl [1952] 1976, p. 225). In accordance with Steindl ([1952] 1976), the following remarks are confined to the case of a stable equilibrium as well.

The long-run comparative static impact of changes in the exogenous variables and parameters on the equilibrium rate of real capital accumulation (g^*) can be calculated based on either Eq. (8.47) or Eq. (8.46). If the partial derivative of g^* (see Eq. 8.47) with respect to an exogenous variable or parameter is negative (positive), the new equilibrium rate of real capital accumulation is lower (higher) than its initial value. Alternatively, the new equilibrium growth rate can be determined by deriving dg/dt (see Eq. 8.46). Requiring that the equilibrium is stable, if the partial derivative of dg/dt with respect to an exogenous variable or parameter is negative (positive), the

---

[8] See Appendix D.1.2.1 for further details. From Eq. (8.49) and given the assumption that both α_3 and h_1 are greater than zero (see Eqs. 8.8 and 8.10), it also follows that $0 < \alpha_3 h_1 < 1$.

function in Fig. 8.1a shifts downward (upward), representing a decline (rise) in $\mathrm{d}g/\mathrm{d}t$ for any given value of g^*. The new equilibrium rate of real capital accumulation is thus lower (higher) than its initial value.[9]

To relate the respective long-run changes in g^* to the short-run changes in the functional (π) and personal distribution of income (ψ) discussed in Sect. 8.3.1.2, it may be useful to refer to different growth regimes and use specific terms. If an economic shock raises (reduces) both the profit share (π) in the short run and the rate of real capital accumulation (g^*) in the long run, economic growth is referred to as *profit-led growth*. On the other hand, if the profit share (π) rises (falls) in the short run, but the rate of real capital accumulation (g^*) declines (increases) in the long run, economic growth is classified as *wage-led growth*.[10] In terms of personal income inequality, if an economic shock raises (reduces) both the measure of personal income inequality (ψ) in the short run and the rate of real capital accumulation (g^*) in the long run, economic growth is defined here as *inequality-led growth*. In contrast, if the measure of personal income inequality (ψ) rises (falls) in the short run, but the rate of real capital accumulation (g^*) declines (increases) in the long run, economic growth is referred to as *equality-led growth*.[11]

It should be noted here that, in the theoretical framework presented above, both the profit share (π) and the measure of personal income inequality (ψ) are endogenous variables. Referring to profit-, wage-, equality-, or inequality-*led* growth can thus be misleading, as the long-run rate of real capital accumulation (g^*) changes due to variations in the exogenous variables and parameters of the model. It is not the functional and/or personal distribution of income *as such* which affects the long-run rate of economic growth (g^*) (see also Palley 2017, pp. 154, 166). For instance, if an economic shock raises both the profit share (π) and the measure of personal income inequality (ψ) in the short run as well as g^* in the long run, rather than speaking of a profit-led and inequality-led growth regime it may be more appropriate to refer to short-run increases in the profit share (π) and the measure of personal income inequality (ψ) which, in the long run, *are accompanied by* a rise in economic growth

---

[9]In the case of an unstable equilibrium, if the partial derivative of $\mathrm{d}g/\mathrm{d}t$ with respect to an exogenous variable or parameter is negative (positive), the function in Fig. 8.1b shifts downward (upward) as well. A new equilibrium is not reached, however, as the actual growth rate (g) keeps on falling (rising).

[10]The terms *profit-led growth* and *wage-led growth* are used here following the discussion on *profit-led* and *wage-led economic regimes* in the existing literature, such as outlined in Bhaduri and Marglin (1990), Lavoie and Stockhammer (2013, p. 17), and Lavoie (2014, pp. 374–377). According to Lavoie (2014, p. 374), for instance, one can "[...] speak of a wage-led regime when an increase in real wages or the share of wages leads to a positive effect on the variable being considered [...]." Similarly, a profit-led regime exists "[...] when an increase in real wages or in the share of wages, that is, a decrease in the share of profits, leads to a negative effect on the variables under consideration [...]."

[11]The terms *equality-led* and *inequality-led* are also used by Dutt (2017). He writes, "[...] [A]lthough wage and profit shares are indicators of inequality in many circumstances [...], the wage share it not an adequate measure of income equality. We should be more interested in the possibility of equality-led growth than wage-led growth [...]" (Dutt 2017, p. 193).

Table 8.2 Comparative statics in the long run (I)

	∂a_2	∂i	∂m_1	∂m_2	∂s_h^p	∂s_h^r	∂w	∂z
∂g^*	+/0/−	+/0/−	+/0/−	+/0/−	−	−	+	+

Source Author's illustration

Table 8.3 Comparative statics in the long run (II)

	$\partial \alpha_0$	$\partial \alpha_1$	$\partial \alpha_2$	$\partial \alpha_3$	∂h_0	∂h_1	∂u_0
∂g^*	+	+/0/−	+/0/−	+	+	+	−

Source Author's illustration

(g^*). Hence, while the terms *profit-led*, *wage-led*, *equality-led*, and *inequality-led* are used hereinafter as a rough guidance, they should not be misinterpreted.[12]

The comparative static impact of changes in the exogenous variables and parameters on the long-run equilibrium rate of real capital accumulation (g^*) is summarized in Tables 8.2 and 8.3, with the detailed derivatives given in Appendix D.1.2.2.[13] While Table 8.2 shows the effects of changes in the variables and parameters which also have a short-run impact on u, π, and ψ, Table 8.3 outlines the effects of variations in α_0, α_1, α_2, α_3, h_0, h_1, and u_0, i.e., variables and parameters which do not have a direct impact on u, π, and ψ.

In line with the short-run analysis in Sect. 8.3.1.2, in the following the focus is again on the impact of changes in the distribution variables m_1, m_2, w, and z. Additionally, variations in the planned degree of capacity utilization (u_0) are considered as well. As has been outlined in Sect. 3.2.3.2, following Steindl ([1952] 1976, pp. 223–225) a rise in u_0 can be a symptom of oligopolistic tendencies, reflecting firms' fear of excess capacity in oligopolistic markets, which may eventually lead to economic stagnation. The effects of changes in a_2, i, s_h^p, s_h^r, α_0, α_1, α_2, α_3, h_0, and h_1 are discussed in Appendix D.1.2.3.

Changes in the Marginal Profit Share (m_1) or the Ratio of Overhead Labor Costs to Capital (m_2)

A rise in the marginal profit share (m_1) or a decline in the ratio of overhead labor costs to capital (m_2) has an ambiguous impact on the equilibrium rate of real capital accumulation (g^*). While, in the short run, an increase in m_1 or a decline in m_2 reduces the degree of capacity utilization (u), it raises firms' internal saving as a ratio of capital (S_f/K). Although the desired rate of real capital accumulation (g^d) (see Eqs. 8.8 and 8.45) is thus hampered by a fall in α_2 $(u - u_0)$, it is positively affected by a rise in α_1 (S_f/K). As can be seen from the partial derivatives of dg/dt with respect to m_1 and m_2 in Eqs. (D.35) and (D.36) (see Appendix D.1.2.2), the change in the

---

[12]See also Skott (2017) on this issue.

[13]As can be seen in Appendix D.1.2.2, the results in Tables 8.2 and 8.3 have been calculated by partially deriving Eq. (8.46) with respect to the model's exogenous variables and parameters.

equilibrium rate of capital accumulation (g^*) depends on the expression $\alpha_1 [(1 - a_2) (s_h^p w + s_h^r (1 - w))] - \alpha_2 [(s_h^r - s_h^p)(w - a_2 z) + (1 - a_2)(1 - s_h^r)]$. If it is positive (negative), a rise in the marginal profit share (m_1) or a decline in the ratio of overhead labor costs to capital (m_2) raises (reduces) the equilibrium rate of real capital accumulation (g^*), implying that economic growth is both profit-led and inequality-led (wage-led and equality-led). If it is zero, g^* is not affected by changes in m_1 or m_2. Eventually, a rise in the marginal profit share (m_1) or a decline in the ratio of overhead labor costs to capital (m_2) is more likely to raise the equilibrium rate of real capital accumulation (g^*) the higher α_1, s_h^p, and z, and the lower α_2 and w.

Changes in the Income Shares of the Poor Private Households (w, z)

In the short run, a rise in the wage share (w) or the capital income share (z) of the poor private households (and thus a decline in the wage share ($1 - w$) or the capital income share ($1 - z$) of the rich private households) increases both the degree of capacity utilization (u) and firms' internal saving as a ratio of capital (S_f/K). The desired rate of real capital accumulation (g^d) thus rises through an increase in $\alpha_2 (u - u_0)$ and a rise in $\alpha_1 (S_f/K)$. As an increase in g^d raises dg/dt (see Eq. 8.11) and hence firms' actual rate of real capital accumulation (g), the equilibrium rate of real capital accumulation (g^*) rises above its initial value.[14] As, in the short run, a rise in w or z raises the profit share (π), but reduces the measure of personal income inequality (ψ), economic growth is both profit-led and equality-led.

Changes in the Planned Degree of Capacity Utilization (u_0)

According to Eq. (8.8), a rise in the planned degree of capacity utilization (u_0) clearly reduces firms' desired rate of real capital accumulation (g^d). As a decline in g^d reduces dg/dt (see Eq. 8.11) and hence firms' actual rate of real capital accumulation (g), the equilibrium rate of real capital accumulation (g^*) declines.

8.3.2.3   Comparative Static Impact of Changes in the Rate of Economic Growth

As discussed in Sect. 8.3.1.2, the degree of capacity utilization (u), the profit share (π), and the measure of personal income inequality (ψ) vary in the short run with changes in several of the model's exogenous variables and parameters. As can be seen from Eqs. (8.41), (8.42), and (8.43), however, u, π, and ψ are also dependent on the actual rate of real capital accumulation (g), which is assumed to change only in the

---

[14]While the partial derivative of dg/dt with respect to z (see Eq. D.40 in Appendix D.1.2.2) seems to be ambiguous, it is definitely positive if it is assumed that R, and hence Z, is always positive (see Eq. 8.12). See also footnote 6 in Sect. 8.3.1.2.

Table 8.4 Comparative statics in the long run (III)

	∂g
∂u	$+$
$\partial \pi$	$+$
$\partial \psi$	$+/0/-$

Source Author's illustration

long run. Hence, when in the long run the actual rate of real capital accumulation (g) alters and settles down at a new equilibrium (g^*), the degree of capacity utilization (u), the profit share (π), and the measure of personal income inequality (ψ) change as well.

The comparative static impact of changes in the rate of real capital accumulation (g) on u, π, and ψ is summarized in Table 8.4, with the detailed derivatives given in Appendix D.1.2.2.

Impact on the Degree of Capacity Utilization (u)

As can be seen from Eq. (8.41), a rise in the rate of real capital accumulation (g), and hence an increase in firms' investment spending (I), unambiguously increases the degree of capacity utilization (u) by raising aggregate demand and thus output (Y). Equation (D.48), the partial derivative of u with respect to g, represents the Keynesian investment multiplier.

Impact on the Profit Share (π)

Via the induced increase in the degree of capacity utilization (u), an increase in the rate of real capital accumulation (g) raises the profit share (π). While a rise in firms' investment spending (I) increases both output (Y) and profits (R), profits (R) grow at a higher rate due to the impact of overhead labor costs ($m_2 K$).

From a Kaleckian perspective, profits (R) in the economy are raised directly by an increase in firms' investment spending (I). Additionally, the induced increase in output (Y) is accompanied by a rise in both private households' capital income (Z) and the wage bill (W). While private households' consumption out of capital income and their saving out of wages thus increase, the rise in saving out of wages does not compensate for the combined increase in investment and consumption out of capital income.

Impact on the Measure of Personal Income Distribution (ψ)

The impact of variations in g, and hence in firms' investment spending (I), on the measure of personal income inequality (ψ) is ambiguous. As can be seen from

Eq. (spsequ:psispsg) (see Appendix D.1.2.2), it depends on the expression $a_2 m_2 - i(1 - a_2)(1 - m_1)$. If it is positive (negative), an increase in g raises (reduces) personal income inequality as measured by ψ. If it is zero, personal income inequality (ψ) is not affected by changes in g.

It can be shown that the development of the measure of personal income inequality (ψ) depends on the impact of a change in g on both the wage bill as a ratio of capital (W/K) and private households' capital income as a ratio of capital (Z/K). By dividing both Eqs. (8.21) and (8.23) by K and assuming that $a_1 = i$, W/K and Z/K are given by

$$\frac{W}{K} = (1 - m_1)u + m_2 \tag{8.51}$$

and

$$\frac{Z}{K} = (1 - a_2)i + a_2(m_1 u - m_2) . \tag{8.52}$$

By raising the degree of capacity utilization (u), an increase in g raises both W/K and Z/K. As the poor private households benefit the most from a rise in W/K, while those at the top of the distribution are the main beneficiaries of an increase in Z/K, personal income inequality as measured by ψ increases (declines) when W/K rises less (more) than Z/K. Eventually, the higher (lower) a_2, m_1, and m_2, and the lower i, the more likely it is that, with a rise in the rate of real capital accumulation (g), W/K rises less (more) than Z/K, implying that personal income inequality as measured by ψ increases (declines).

It should be noted that if the profit share (π) were constant (i.e., if there were no overhead labor costs), a rise in the degree of capacity utilization (u) would be relatively more beneficial to the poor private households, as W/K would increase more strongly compared to Z/K.[15] An increase in u, however—triggered by a rise in the rate of real capital accumulation (g)—also raises the profit share (π), a development which is particularly beneficial to the rich private households. In general, it can be vaguely stated that, for the impact of a change in g on ψ, the impact of a change in g on u and—via u—on π plays an important role. In fact, if a rise in g raises u strongly (only slightly), while π increases only slightly (strongly), the increase in g is more likely to lower (raise) the measure of personal income inequality (ψ) from the short to the long run. Similarly, if a decline in g reduces u strongly (only slightly), while π falls only slightly (strongly), the decline in g is more likely to raise (lower) the measure of personal income inequality (ψ) from the short to the long run.

8.3.2.4 Changes to the Long-Run Equilibrium

Bringing the short and the long run together, the changes in the long-run equilibrium values of the rate of real capital accumulation (g^*), the degree of capacity

---

[15]The profit share $\pi = m_1 - m_2/u$ can be included in both Eqs. (8.51) and (8.52). While Eq. (8.51) can be written as $W/K = (1 - \pi)u$, Eq. (8.52) can be changed to $Z/K = (1 - a_2)i + a_2\pi u$.

utilization (u^*), the profit share (π^*), and the measure of personal income inequality (ψ^*) are summarized in Tables 8.5 and 8.6. More detailed descriptions are given in Appendix D.1.2.3.

Of the economic shocks in Table 8.5, changes in the dividend payout parameter (a_2), the interest rate (i), the marginal profit share (m_1), and the ratio of overhead labor costs to capital (m_2) have ambiguous effects on g^*, u^*, π^*, and ψ^*. The impact of other economic shocks, however, is more distinct. In fact, a decline in the saving rate of the poor private households (s_h^p) or the rich private households (s_h^r) as well as an increase in the wage share (w) or the capital income share (z) of the poor private households clearly raises the long-run equilibrium rate of real capital accumulation (g^*), the long-run equilibrium degree of capacity utilization (u^*), and the long-run equilibrium profit share (π^*). Although a rise in both w or z reduces the measure of personal income inequality (ψ) in the short run, the impact on ψ^* is ambiguous due to the uncertain reaction of ψ to the corresponding increase in g^*.

In Table 8.6, of the variables and parameters which have a direct effect on the rate of real capital accumulation (g), but which do only indirectly impact u, π, and ψ, a rise in both firms' animal spirits (α_0) and the technological parameters (α_3, h_0, and h_1) as well as a decline in the planned degree of capacity utilization (u_0) clearly raise g^*, u^*, and π^*. On the other hand, the impact of changes in α_1 and α_2 is ambiguous, depending on firms' internal saving as a ratio of capital (S_f/K) and the difference $u - u_0$, respectively. If S_f/K is positive, a rise in α_1 raises g^*, u^*, and π^*. Similarly, if $u - u_0$ is positive, a rise in α_2 raises g^*, u^*, and π^*. Again, the impact of changes in α_0, α_1, α_2, α_3, h_0, h_1, and u_0 on the long-run equilibrium measure of personal income inequality (ψ^*) is uncertain, as the measure of personal income inequality (ψ) may rise or fall with a change in the long-run equilibrium rate of real capital accumulation (g^*).

Table 8.5 Comparative statics of the long-run equilibrium (I)

	∂a_2	∂i	∂m_1	∂m_2	∂s_h^p	∂s_h^r	∂w	∂z
∂g^*	$+/0/-$	$+/0/-$	$+/0/-$	$+/0/-$	$-$	$-$	$+$	$+$
∂u^*	$+/0/-$	$+/0/-$	$+/0/-$	$+/0/-$	$-$	$-$	$+$	$+$
$\partial \pi^*$	$+/0/-$	$+/0/-$	$+/0/-$	$+/0/-$	$-$	$-$	$+$	$+$
$\partial \psi^*$	$+/0/-$	$+/0/-$	$+/0/-$	$+/0/-$	$+/0/-$	$+/0/-$	$+/0/-$	$+/0/-$

Source Author's illustration

Table 8.6 Comparative statics of the long-run equilibrium (II)

	$\partial \alpha_0$	$\partial \alpha_1$	$\partial \alpha_2$	$\partial \alpha_3$	∂h_0	∂h_1	∂u_0
∂g^*	$+$	$+/0/-$	$+/0/-$	$+$	$+$	$+$	$-$
∂u^*	$+$	$+/0/-$	$+/0/-$	$+$	$+$	$+$	$-$
$\partial \pi^*$	$+$	$+/0/-$	$+/0/-$	$+$	$+$	$+$	$-$
$\partial \psi^*$	$+/0/-$	$+/0/-$	$+/0/-$	$+/0/-$	$+/0/-$	$+/0/-$	$+/0/-$

Source Author's illustration

8.4 Graphical Analysis

Similar to Palley (2017), the macroeconomic relations described in Sect. 8.3 can be illustrated with a graphical analysis. Before the short- and long-run effects of changes in several of the model's exogenous variables and parameters are visualized in Sect. 8.4.2, the relevant functional relationships are described first in the following Sect. 8.4.1.

8.4.1 Functional Relationships

8.4.1.1 The Degree of Capacity Utilization (u) and the Rate of Economic Growth (g)

From the goods market equilibrium $I/K = S/K$, it follows that the rate of real capital accumulation (g), which, in the long run, is equal to the rate of economic growth, can be determined from the saving and the investment side.

From the saving side, the actual growth rate (g^s) in the economy is given by

$$g^s = \frac{S}{K} = \frac{S_f}{K} + \frac{S_h^p}{K} + \frac{S_h^r}{K}. \tag{8.53}$$

Assuming that $a_1 = i$ and substituting Eqs. (8.44) and (8.27) to (8.29) into Eq. (8.53) yields

$$\begin{aligned} g^s = \ & (1 - a_2)\,(m_1 u - m_2 - i) + s_h^p\,[(m_1 u - m_2)\,(a_2 z - w) \\ & + iz\,(1 - a_2) + uw] + s_h^r\,\{(m_1 u - m_2)\,[a_2\,(1 - z) - (1 - w)] \\ & + i\,(1 - a_2)\,(1 - z) + u\,(1 - w)\}\,. \end{aligned}$$
$$\tag{8.54}$$

In the long run, firms' rate of real capital accumulation is given by Eq. (8.8). By substituting Eqs. (8.10) and (8.44) into Eq. (8.8) and assuming that $a_1 = i$, from the investment side the growth rate (g^d) can be written as

$$g^d = \alpha_0 + \alpha_1\,[(1 - a_2)\,(m_1 u - m_2 - i)] + \alpha_2\,(u - u_0) + \alpha_3\,(h_0 + h_1 g)\,.$$
$$\tag{8.55}$$

With g being the actual rate of real capital accumulation which, at any time, must be equal to g^s from an ex-post perspective, Eq. (8.54) can be substituted into Eq. (8.55), yielding

Fig. 8.2 The degree of capacity utilization (u) and the rate of real capital accumulation (g). *Source* Author's illustration

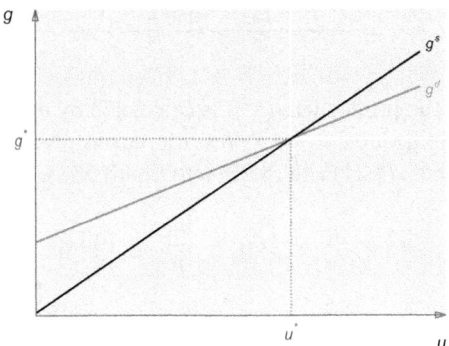

$$g^d = \alpha_0 + \alpha_1 \left[(1 - a_2)(m_1 u - m_2 - i)\right] + \alpha_2 (u - u_0)$$
$$+ \ \alpha_3 \left\{ h_0 + h_1 \left[(1 - a_2)(m_1 u - m_2 - i) + s_h^p ((m_1 u - m_2)(a_2 z - w) \right. \right.$$
$$+ \ iz (1 - a_2) + uw) + s_h^r ((m_1 u - m_2)(a_2 (1 - z) - (1 - w))$$
$$+ \ i (1 - a_2)(1 - z) + u (1 - w)) \right] \right\} .$$

$$(8.56)$$

As shown in Fig. 8.2, Eqs. (8.54) and (8.56) can be illustrated in a u-g-diagram. Both functions g^s and g^d are positively sloped, i.e., a rise in output (Y) and the degree of capacity utilization (u) increases g^s and g^d. While a rise in u raises total saving as a ratio of capital (g^s) by increasing the incomes out of which firms and private households save, it also raises the long-term growth rate (g^d) through an increase in $\alpha_1 (S_f/K)$, $\alpha_2 (u - u_0)$, and $\alpha_3 (h_0 + h_1 g)$.

The long-run equilibrium rate of real capital accumulation (g^*) and the corresponding degree of capacity utilization (u^*) are determined by the intersection of the g^s and g^d schedules. For this equilibrium to be stable, the Keynesian stability condition requires the g^s schedule to be steeper than the g^d schedule.

8.4.1.2 The Degree of Capacity Utilization (u) and the Profit Share (π)

As has been mentioned in Sect. 3.2.3.2, the profit share (π) can be determined from the supply and from the demand side. From a supply-side perspective, the profit share (π^s) is given by Eq. (8.32), i.e.,

$$\pi^s = m_1 - \frac{m_2}{u} .$$

$$(8.57)$$

From a demand-side (or expenditure) point of view, the profit share (π^d) can be deduced from Eq. (8.30). Dividing Eq. (8.30) by K gives

$$\frac{R}{K} = \frac{I + Z\left[(1 - s_h^p)z + (1 - s_h^r)(1 - z)\right] - W\left[s_h^p w + s_h^r(1 - w)\right]}{K}.$$

(8.58)

The profit share (π^d) is calculated by dividing Eq. (8.58) by the degree of capacity utilization $(u = Y/K)$. Moreover, given the assumption that $a_1 = i$, substituting Eqs. (8.21) and (8.23) into Eq. (8.58) yields

$$\pi^d = \frac{g}{u} + \left(m_1 - \frac{m_2}{u} - 1\right)\left[s_h^p w + s_h^r(1 - w)\right]$$
$$+ \left[1 - s_h^p z + s_h^r(z - 1)\right]\left[a_2\left(m_1 - \frac{m_2}{u}\right) + \frac{i}{u}(1 - a_2)\right].$$

(8.59)

According to Eq. (8.57), $m_1 - m_2/u$ is the profit share determined from the supply side (π^s). In equilibrium, π^s must be equal to the profit share determined from the demand side (π^d) as—at any point in time—there can be only one profit share in the economy. Equation (8.59) can thus be written as

$$\pi^d = \frac{g}{u} + \left(\pi^d - 1\right)\left[s_h^p w + s_h^r(1 - w)\right]$$
$$+ \left[1 - s_h^p z + s_h^r(z - 1)\right]\left[a_2\pi^d + \frac{i}{u}(1 - a_2)\right].$$

(8.60)

Finally, solving Eq. (8.60) for π^d yields

$$\pi^d = \frac{g + i(1 - a_2)\left[1 - s_h^r + z\left(s_h^r - s_h^p\right)\right] - u\left[s_h^p w + s_h^r(1 - w)\right]}{u\left[(1 - a_2)(1 - s_h^r) + \left(s_h^r - s_h^p\right)(w - a_2 z)\right]}.$$

(8.61)

Equations (8.57) and (8.61) are graphically illustrated in Fig. 8.3. Similar to Fig. 3.3 in Sect. 3.2.3.2, from a supply-side perspective, the profit share (π^s) rises with an increase in the degree of capacity utilization (u), because overhead labor costs are spread over a higher volume of output.[16] From a demand-side perspective, on the other hand, the profit share (π^d) falls with a rise in u. Although an increase in output (Y) is accompanied by a rise in consumption out of capital income, saving out of wages rises as well. With an increase in output (Y), ceteris paribus the demand-determined profit share (π^d) eventually declines, as, in any case, output (Y) rises more strongly than total profits (R).

The profit share (π) in the economy is given by the intersection of the π^s and π^d schedules. If the degree of capacity utilization (u) at this intersection is equal to its long-run equilibrium level (u^*), the profit share (π) is in long-run equilibrium (π^*) as well.

---

[16]If there were no overhead labor costs, i.e., if $m_2 K$ in Eq. (8.12) were zero, π^s would be a constant function with a value of m_1. The π^s schedule in Fig. 8.3 would thus be a horizontal line at $\pi^s = m_1$.

Fig. 8.3 The degree of capacity utilization (u) and the profit share (π). *Source* Author's illustration

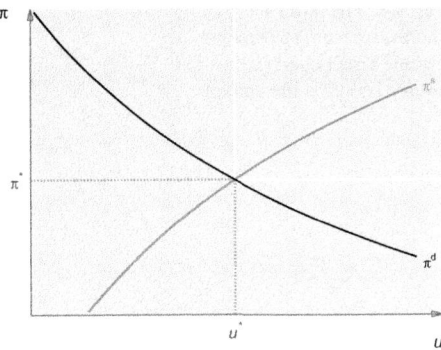

8.4.1.3 The Profit Share (π) and Personal Income Distribution (ψ)

The nexus between the profit share (π) and the measure of personal income distribution (ψ) can be deduced from Eq. (8.36). Dividing both the numerator and the denominator of Eq. (8.36) by u, assuming that $a_1 = i$, gives

$$\psi = \frac{\left(m_1 - \frac{m_2}{u}\right)[a_2(1-z)-(1-w)]+(1-w)+\frac{i}{u}(1-a_2)(1-z)}{\left(m_1 - \frac{m_2}{u}\right)(a_2 z - w) + w + \frac{i}{u}z(1-a_2)}. \tag{8.62}$$

According to Eq. (8.57), $m_1 - m_2/u$ is the supply-side determined profit share (π^s), which, in equilibrium, must be equal to the profit share determined from the demand side (π^d). As π^s and π^d jointly determine the profit share (π) realized in the economy, Eq. (8.62) can be written as

$$\psi = \frac{\pi[a_2(1-z)-(1-w)]+(1-w)+\frac{i}{u}(1-a_2)(1-z)}{\pi(a_2 z - w) + w + \frac{i}{u}z(1-a_2)}. \tag{8.63}$$

Substituting Eq. (8.41) into Eq. (8.63) eventually yields

$$\psi = \frac{\begin{array}{c}a_2\pi(1-z)+(1-\pi)(1-w)+i(1-a_2)(1-z)\\ \cdot \frac{m_1[(1-a_2)(1-s_h^r)+(s_h^r-s_h^p)(w-a_2 z)]+s_h^p w + s_h^r(1-w)}{g+(1-a_2)(m_2+i)[(1-s_h^r)+z(s_h^r-s_h^p)]+m_2(s_h^r-s_h^p)(w-z)}\end{array}}{\begin{array}{c}a_2\pi z + w(1-\pi)+iz(1-a_2)\\ \cdot \frac{m_1[(1-a_2)(1-s_h^r)+(s_h^r-s_h^p)(w-a_2 z)]+s_h^p w + s_h^r(1-w)}{g+(1-a_2)(m_2+i)[(1-s_h^r)+z(s_h^r-s_h^p)]+m_2(s_h^r-s_h^p)(w-z)}\end{array}}. \tag{8.64}$$

Equation (8.64) is graphically illustrated in Fig. 8.4, which plots the measure of personal income distribution (ψ) against the profit share (π). An increase in the profit share (π) unambiguously raises personal income inequality as measured by ψ. As the rich private households are the main receivers of private households' capital income (Z), those at the top of the distribution benefit the most from a higher share of profits (R) in national income (Y).

Fig. 8.4 The profit share (π) and the measure of personal income distribution (ψ). *Source* Author's illustration

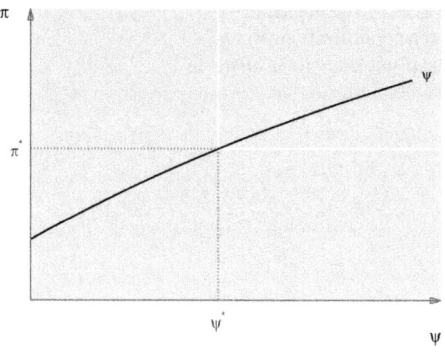

With a given set of exogenous variables and parameters, and hence a given u, g, and π, according to Eq. (8.64) the measure of personal income distribution (ψ) is uniquely defined. If the degree of capacity utilization (u), the growth rate (g), and thus the profit share (π) are at their long-run equilibrium levels (u^*, g^*, and π^*), the ratio of the incomes of the rich to the poor private households (ψ) is in long-run equilibrium (ψ^*) as well.

8.4.1.4   The Rate of Economic Growth (g) and Personal Income Distribution (ψ)

The link between the rate of real capital accumulation (g) and the measure of personal income distribution (ψ) is given by Eq. (8.43), which has been defined in Sect. 8.3.1.1 as

$$\psi = \frac{\begin{aligned}&g\left[(1-w)(1-m_1)+a_2m_1(1-z)\right]-a_2m_2s_h^p(w-z)\\&+(1-a_2)\left\{(1-w)(i+m_2)+i(w-z)\left[s_h^p+m_1\left(1-s_h^p\right)\right]\right\}\end{aligned}}{\begin{aligned}&g\left[a_2m_1z+w(1-m_1)\right]+a_2m_2s_h^r(w-z)\\&+(1-a_2)\left\{w(i+m_2)-i(w-z)\left[s_h^r+m_1\left(1-s_h^r\right)\right]\right\}\end{aligned}}.$$

As has been outlined in Sect. 8.3.2.3, the impact of changes in the rate of real capital accumulation (g) on the personal distribution of income between the rich and the poor private households (ψ) is ambiguous. In fact, an increase in g may raise, lower, or have no effect on personal income inequality (ψ). In a ψ-g-diagram, the graphical nexus between g and ψ can thus take any shape or form, i.e., the schedule can be positively sloped, negatively sloped, or be a vertical line. Figure 8.5 depicts the example of a positive relation between g and ψ, implying that a rise in the growth rate (g) increases personal income inequality (ψ).

Fig. 8.5 The rate of real
capital accumulation (g) and
the measure of personal
income distribution (ψ): The
example of a positive nexus.
Source Author's illustration

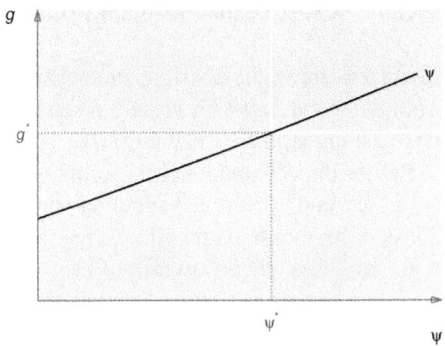

With a given set of exogenous variables and parameters, and hence a given u
and g, according to Eq. (8.43) the measure of personal income distribution (ψ) is
uniquely defined. If the degree of capacity utilization (u) and the growth rate (g) are
at their long-run equilibrium levels (u^* and g^*), ψ is in long-run equilibrium (ψ^*)
as well.

8.4.2 Graphical Illustrations of a Decline in Economic Growth

As Steindl ([1952] 1976) was concerned with economic stagnation, the following
provides a graphical analysis of several economic shocks which may cause a decline
in the long-run equilibrium rate of economic growth (g^*). In line with the previous
analyses, the focus is on a rise in the marginal profit share (m_1) (which is equivalent
to a decline in the ratio of overhead labor costs to capital (m_2)), a decline in the
wage share of the poor private households (w) (which is equivalent to a decline
in the capital income share of the poor private households (z)), as well as a rise
in the planned degree of capacity utilization (u_0) (which is equivalent to a decline
in firms' animal spirits (α_0) and a decline in the autonomous rate of technological
progress (h_0)).[17] At the center of interest is the possible short- and long-run impact
of these economic changes on the degree of capacity utilization (u), on the profit
share (π), on the measure of personal income distribution (ψ), and on the rate of
real capital accumulation (g). While the specific economic mechanisms have already
been discussed in Sect. 8.3, in the following the focus is explicitly on the graphical
analysis.[18]

---

[17] Additionally, Appendix D.2 provides a graphical analysis of a rise in the dividend payout parameter (a_2), a rise in the saving rate of the rich private households (s_h^r), and a decline in the parameter α_2.

[18] The following graphical analysis is based on computer simulations of the functional relationships that have been outlined in the previous Sect. 8.4.1.

8.4.2.1   A Rise in the Marginal Profit Share (m_1)

Figure 8.6 shows the possible short- and long-run impact of a rise in the marginal profit share (m_1), which closely resembles the impact of a decline in the ratio of overhead labor costs to capital (m_2).

Before the economic shock occurs, it is assumed that the endogenous variables (u, π, ψ, and g) are at their long-run equilibrium levels (u_0^*, π_0^*, ψ_0^*, and g_0^*). Considering the short-run effects first, in the lower right quadrant of Fig. 8.6, a rise in m_1 provokes an upward turn of the saving schedule from g_0^s to g_1^s, implying that, at u_0^*, total saving as a ratio of capital (S/K) increases. Yet, as the rate of real capital accumulation is assumed to be constant in the short run, thus remaining at g_0^*, the degree of capacity utilization declines from u_0^* to its short-run level u_{sr}. The fall in the degree of capacity utilization is also depicted in the upper right quadrant of Fig. 8.6, where the rise in m_1 leads to an upward movement of the supply-determined profit share function from π_0^s to π_1^s. In the short run, the profit share in the economy increases from π_0^* to π_{sr}. With a lower degree of capacity utilization and a higher profit share, in the short run a rise in m_1 also raises the measure of personal income distribution (ψ). As shown in the upper left quadrant of Fig. 8.6, the increase in m_1

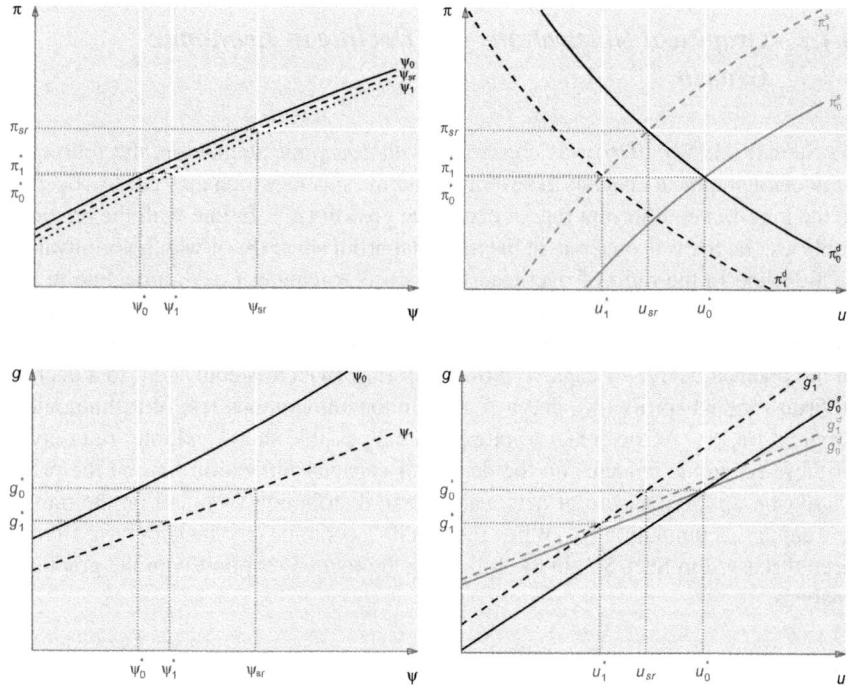

Fig. 8.6 Possible short- and long-run effects of a rise in m_1: The example of a positive nexus between g and ψ. *Source* Author's illustration

shifts the inequality schedule to the right, from ψ_0 to ψ_{sr}. In the short run, the profit share π_{sr} is accompanied by a personal income inequality measure of ψ_{sr}, which is clearly higher than its initial value ψ_0^*. Finally, the lower left quadrant of Fig. 8.6 shows the (possible) nexus between the rate of real capital accumulation (g) and the personal distribution of income (ψ). A rise in m_1 shifts the inequality function to the right, from ψ_0 to ψ_1. While the growth rate remains at g_0^*, the measure of personal income inequality increases from ψ_0^* to ψ_{sr}.

How does an increase in m_1 affect the economy in the long run? As has been outlined in Sect. 8.3.2.2, a change in m_1 has an ambiguous impact on the long-run rate of real capital accumulation (g^*). In the short run, a rise in m_1 reduces u, but increases firms' internal saving as a ratio of capital (S_f/K).[19] If the negative impact of the fall in u outweighs the positive stimulus of the increase in S_f/K, the desired rate of real capital accumulation (g^d) and hence the actual rate of real capital accumulation (g) decline in the long run. Graphically, in the lower right quadrant of Fig. 8.6, the rise in S_f/K provokes an upward turn of the g^d schedule from g_0^d to g_1^d. The more pronounced the impact of the rise in S_f/K on the desired rate of real capital accumulation (g^d) is, the stronger the function turns. In the case illustrated in Fig. 8.6, the impact of an increase in S_f/K is assumed to be relatively small. In fact, the g^d schedule moves only slightly upward, so that the g_1^s and g_1^d functions intersect at a growth rate of g_1^*, which is lower than the initial level g_0^*. In the long run, the economic growth rate thus declines from g_0^* to g_1^*. At the same time, the degree of capacity utilization falls from its short-run level u_{sr} to its new long-run equilibrium u_1^*.[20] In the upper right quadrant of Fig. 8.6, the long-term decline in the rate of real capital accumulation (g) provokes a downward movement of the demand-determined profit share function from π_0^d to π_1^d. The profit share thus declines from π_{sr} to π_1^*.[21] In the upper left quadrant, the decline in g leads to a slight rightward movement of the inequality schedule from ψ_{sr} to ψ_1. In the example illustrated in Fig. 8.6, in the long run the measure of personal income distribution declines from ψ_{sr} to ψ_1^*.[22] This decline is also depicted in the lower left quadrant, where the fall in the rate of real capital accumulation from g_0^* to g_1^* is expressed as a downward movement along the ψ_1 function, from ψ_{sr} to ψ_1^*.

As has been mentioned in Sect. 8.3.2.3, the long-run effect of a change in the rate of real capital accumulation (g) on the measure of personal income distribution (ψ)

---

[19]It should be noted that $\alpha_3 (h_0 + h_1 g)$, the term representing the impact of technological change in the g^d schedule, does not vary in the short run, as g is constant in the short run.

[20]With a rise in m_1, the g^d schedule shifts upward due to, first, the impact of m_1 on S_f/K and, secondly, the impact of m_1 on g in the term $\alpha_3 (h_0 + h_1 g)$. Yet, the impact of m_1 on technological change, i.e., on the term $\alpha_3 (h_0 + h_1 g)$ in the g^d schedule, cannot alone shift the g^d schedule to such an extent that the g_1^s and g_1^d functions intersect at a growth rate g_1^* which lies above the original growth rate g_0^*. The reason is that, according to the Keynesian stability condition, $0 < \alpha_3 h_1 < 1$. Hence, considering only the impact of m_1 on $\alpha_3 (h_0 + h_1 g)$, changes in m_1 cannot shift the g^d function to the same extent as the g^s function. Only a strong impact of m_1 on S_f/K can potentially raise the long-run equilibrium rate of real capital accumulation.

[21]While in Fig. 8.6 π_1^* is higher than π_0^*, it is also possible that π_1^* falls below π_0^*.

[22]While in Fig. 8.6 ψ_1^* is higher than ψ_0^*, it is also possible that ψ_1^* falls below ψ_0^*.

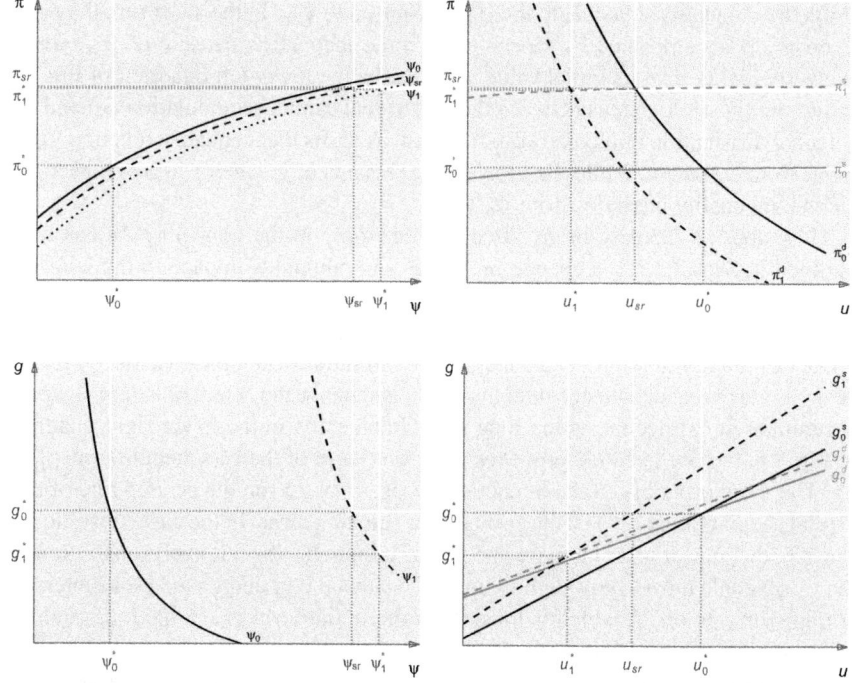

Fig. 8.7 Possible short- and long-run effects of a rise in m_1: The example of a negative nexus between g and ψ. *Source* Author's illustration

is, in fact, ambiguous. A decline in g does not necessarily reduce the measure of personal income inequality (ψ) from the short to the long run. While Fig. 8.6 depicts the example of a positive nexus, Fig. 8.7 refers to the case of a negative impact of g on ψ. In Fig. 8.7, the decline in g raises the measure of personal income distribution from ψ_{sr} to ψ_1^*. In fact, a negative nexus between the rate of real capital accumulation (g) and the personal distribution of income (ψ) requires the inequality schedule in the lower left quadrant of Fig. 8.7 to be negatively sloped. Moreover, by comparing Figs. 8.6 and 8.7, it can be seen that the π^s schedule in the upper right quadrant of Fig. 8.7 is less steep, implying that a decline in the rate of real capital accumulation (g) reduces the profit share (π) only slightly compared to the decline in the degree of capacity utilization (u). In the upper left quadrant of Fig. 8.7, a decline in g shifts the inequality schedule to the right, from ψ_{sr} to ψ_1. This rightward movement is so strongly pronounced that, despite a decline in the profit share (π), the measure of personal income distribution (ψ) rises from the short to the long run.

8.4.2.2 A Decline in the Wage Share of the Poor Private Households (w)

Figure 8.8 shows the possible short- and long-run effects of a decline in the wage share of the poor private households (w), closely resembling the impact of a decline in the capital income share of the poor private households (z).

Starting from the long-run equilibrium levels u_0^*, π_0^*, ψ_0^*, and g_0^*, in the short run a decline in w shifts the saving schedule in the lower right quadrant upward, from g_0^s to g_1^s. With a given rate of real capital accumulation (g_0^*), the degree of capacity utilization declines from u_0^* to u_{sr}. The decline in the wage share of the poor private households (w) also reduces the profit share in the economy, which, in the upper right quadrant, is depicted by a downward shift of the demand-determined profit share function from π_0^d to π_{sr}^d. Although the profit share declines from π_0^* to π_{sr}, in the short run a decline in the wage share of the poor private households (w) unambiguously raises the measure of personal income distribution (ψ). The rightward shift of the inequality schedule in the upper left quadrant from ψ_0 to ψ_{sr} is definitely accompanied by a rise in the measure of personal inequality from ψ_0^* to ψ_{sr}. The increase in ψ is also illustrated in the lower left quadrant of Fig. 8.8, where the inequality schedule shifts rightward, from ψ_0 to ψ_1.

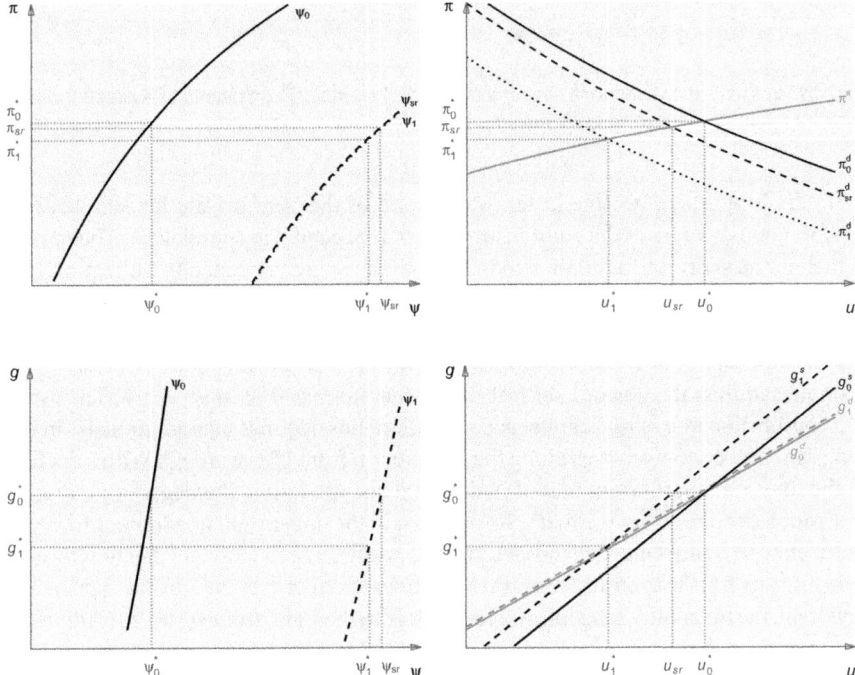

Fig. 8.8 Possible short- and long-run effects of a decline in w: The example of a positive nexus between g and ψ. *Source* Author's illustration

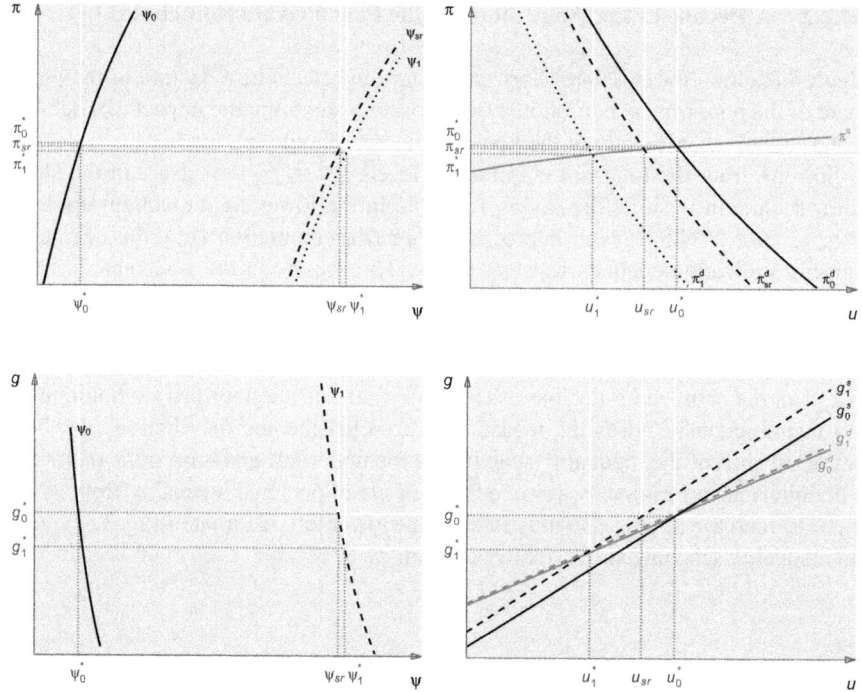

Fig. 8.9 Possible short- and long-run effects of a decline in w: The example of a negative nexus between g and ψ. *Source* Author's illustration

In the long run, a decline in the wage share of the poor private households (w) unambiguously reduces the equilibrium rate of real capital accumulation. The reason is that, in the short run, a fall in w reduces both the degree of capacity utilization (u), and—via the decline in u—also firms' internal saving as a ratio of capital (S_f/K). Although the g^d schedule in the lower right quadrant of Fig. 8.8 shifts slightly upward due to the impact of the decline in w on α_3 ($h_0 + h_1 g$), this shift is clearly less pronounced than the upward shift of the g^s function, as $0 < \alpha_3 h_1 < 1$. The long-run equilibrium rate of real capital accumulation thus declines unambiguously. In the long run, the economy moves along the g_1^s function from g_0^* toward g_1^*. With a decline in the long-run equilibrium rate of real capital accumulation, the degree of capacity utilization declines from u_{sr} to u_1^*. As depicted in the upper right quadrant of Fig. 8.8, the decline in g shifts the demand-determined profit share function further downward, from π_{sr}^d to π_1^d. The profit share thus declines from π_{sr} to π_1^*. In the upper left quadrant, the inequality schedule moves slightly to the right, from ψ_{sr} to ψ_1. Although the impact of the decline in g on the measure of personal income distribution is a priori uncertain, in the example shown in Fig. 8.8 the long-run equilibrium measure of personal income distribution declines to ψ_1^*.[23] Figure 8.9, on the other hand, shows

---

[23]While in Fig. 8.8 ψ_1^* is higher than ψ_0^*, it is also possible that ψ_1^* falls below ψ_0^*.

an example of a negative impact of g on ψ. Here, the decline in the rate of real capital accumulation from g_0^* to g_1^* raises the measure of personal income distribution from ψ_{sr} to ψ_1^*. The changes in the measure of personal income distribution are also illustrated in the lower left quadrants of Figs. 8.8 and 8.9, where the decline in the equilibrium rate of real capital accumulation from g_0^* to g_1^* leads to a downward movement along the ψ_1 schedule.

8.4.2.3 A Rise in the Planned Degree of Capacity Utilization (u_0)

Figure 8.10 depicts the possible impact of a rise in the planned degree of capacity utilization (u_0), which closely resembles the effects of a decline in the parameter reflecting firms' animal spirits (α_0) and a decline in the autonomous rate of techno-logical progress (h_0). These economic shocks do not have any short-run effects, as their impact unfolds only through changes in the g^d function.

Starting from the long-run equilibrium levels u_0^*, π_0^*, ψ_0^*, and g_0^*, a rise in u_0 provokes a downward shift of the g^d schedule in the lower right quadrant of Fig. 8.10. As the saving schedule is not affected by changes in u_0, the long-run equilibrium

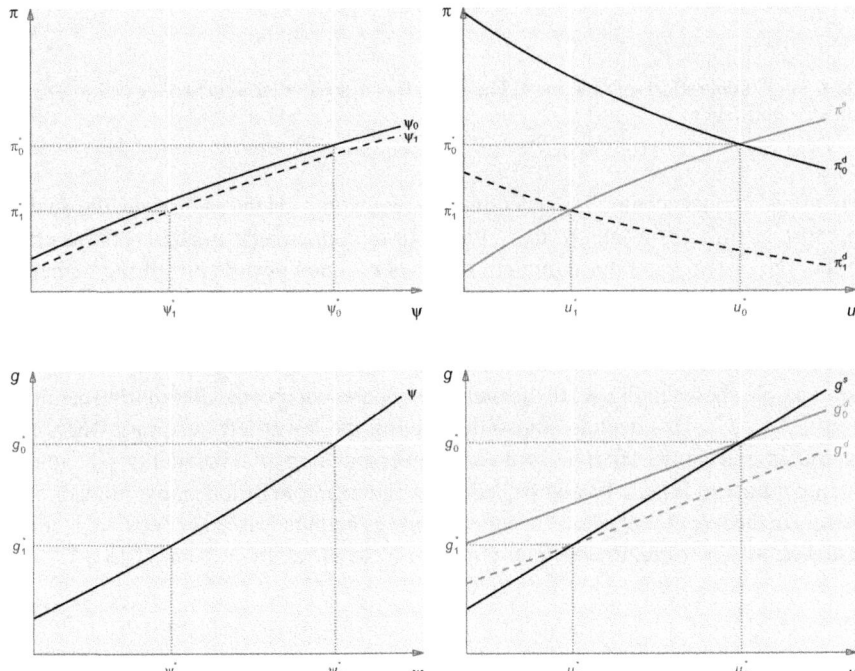

Fig. 8.10 Possible effects of a rise in u_0: The example of a positive nexus between g and ψ. *Source* Author's illustration

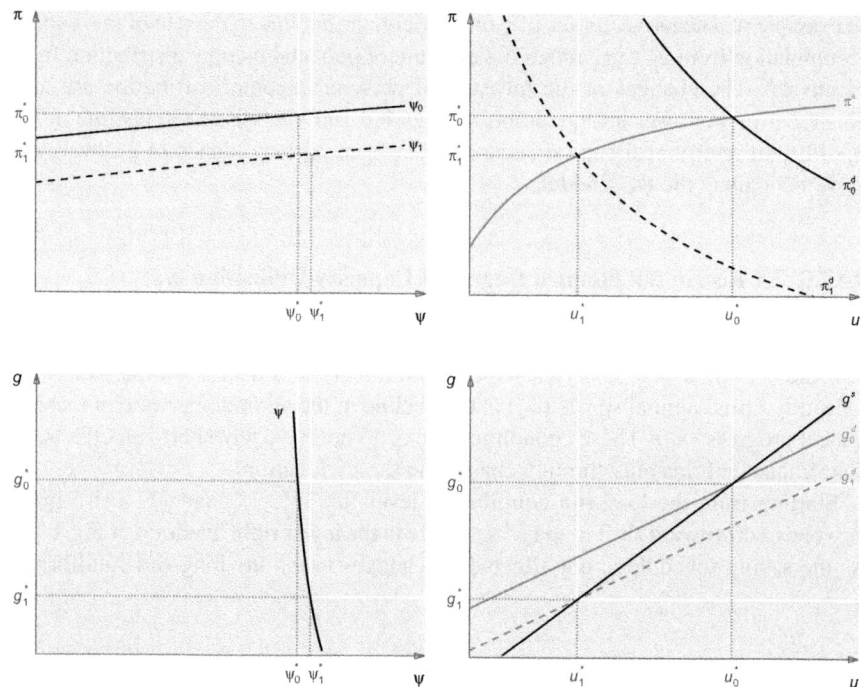

Fig. 8.11 Possible effects of a rise in u_0: The example of a negative nexus between g and ψ. *Source* Author's illustration

rate of real capital accumulation declines from g_0^* to g_1^*. At the same time, the degree of capacity utilization falls from u_0^* to u_1^*. In the upper right quadrant, the decline in the rate of real capital accumulation provokes a downward shift of the demand-determined profit share function from π_0^d to π_1^d, implying that the equilibrium profit share declines from π_0^* to π_1^*. In the upper left quadrant, the decline in the rate of real capital accumulation (g) shifts the inequality schedule to the right, from ψ_0 to ψ_1. In the example shown in Fig. 8.10, the measure of personal income distribution declines from ψ_0^* to ψ_1^*. This decline is also depicted in the lower left quadrant, where the decline in g is expressed as a downward movement along the inequality schedule.

In contrast to Figs. 8.10 and 8.11 depicts the example of a negative impact of a change in the rate of real capital accumulation (g) on the measure of personal income distribution (ψ). Here, the decline in g from g_0^* to g_1^* raises ψ from ψ_0^* to ψ_1^*.

8.5 Discussion and Final Remarks

8.5.1 Extending Steindl's Original Stagnation Theory

In *Maturity and Stagnation in American Capitalism*, Steindl ([1952] 1976) focused on the impact of monopolistic tendencies on the long-run rate of economic growth (g^*). On the one hand, according to Steindl ([1952] 1976, pp. 223–225), the rise of monopoly can be reflected in an increase in the planned degree of capacity utilization (u_0), as firms in monopolistic markets may be more averse to undesired excess capacity. As outlined in Sect. 8.3.2.2, a rise in u_0—which does not have any short-run effects in the model— unambiguously reduces the long-run equilibrium rate of real capital accumulation (g^*). On the other hand, Steindl ([1952] 1976, pp. 223–225) held, by raising firms' market power, the rise of monopoly can also manifest itself in an increase in the marginal profit share (m_1) and/or a decline in the ratio of overhead labor costs to capital (m_2). In the short run, both a rise in m_1 and a fall in m_2 clearly raise the profit share (π). In fact, it is this increase in π which puts the functional distribution of income at the heart of Steindl's ([1952] 1976, pp. 223–225) stagnation theory. Via the induced short-run decline in the degree of capacity utilization (u), the long-run rate of economic growth (g^*) *may* decrease, possibly leading to stagnation. If g^* declines with a rise in m_1 or a fall in m_2, economic growth is wage-led as defined in Sect. 8.3.2.2. With a decline in the long-run equilibrium rate of real capital accumulation (g^*), from the short to the long run the degree of capacity utilization (u) declines further, inducing a fall in the profit share (π) from its short-run level. In fact, the long-run equilibrium profit share (π^*) may even be lower than initially—a result which is in line with Steindl's ([1952] 1976, p. 245) finding that, in the long run, "[...] the tendency for the capitalists' share in the product to increase does, after all, exist *potentially* [...]" (see also Cowling 2005, p. 147).

While the model developed in this chapter is able to depict Steindl's ([1952] 1976) original stagnation hypothesis, which focuses on the functional distribution of income and long-run economic growth, the specific characteristic of the model to not only include one, but two private household groups additionally allows to analyze another dimension of income distribution, i.e., the development of personal income inequality as measured by ψ. In fact, in the short run a rise in the marginal profit share (m_1) or a decline in the ratio of overhead labor costs to capital (m_2) does not only increase the profit share (π), but also unambiguously raises the measure of personal income distribution (ψ). Hence, Steindl's original stagnation theory can be extended in the way that a rise in monopolistic tendencies, reflected in a rise in m_1 and/or a decline in m_2, raises both the profit share (π) and personal income inequality as measured by ψ in the short run. By shifting income from private households to non-consuming firms, with the income of the poor private households—who have a relatively high propensity to consume—being particularly hampered, a rise in m_1 and/or a decline in m_2 clearly reduces the degree of capacity utilization (u) in the short run. In the long run, the short-run increase in π and ψ as well as the decline in u *may* be followed by a decline in the equilibrium rate of real capital accumulation

(g^*). In fact, if g^* declines with a rise in m_1 and/or a decline in m_2, economic growth is both wage-led and equality-led.

8.5.2 Applying the Model to Other Stagnation Theories

While the model developed above extends Steindl's ([1952] 1976) original stagnation theory to include the personal distribution of income, it can also be applied to several aspects discussed in both the Keynes–Hansen and the contemporary (demand-side) stagnation debate.

Demographic change, for instance, which is part of Keynes's, Hansen's, and Summers's hypotheses, can be modeled by variations in α_0 and private households' saving rates (s_h^p, s_h^r). As outlined by Keynes ([1930] 1972, p. 324, [1937] 1973, pp. 125–126) and Lösch (1938, p. 456), a slowdown in population growth may hamper firms' business confidence. This development may be depicted by a decline in the parameter α_0, which, in the long run, clearly reduces the equilibrium rate of real capital accumulation (g^*). The decline in g^* may be reinforced by a rise in s_h^p and/or s_h^r, as smaller family sizes as well as an increased need for appropriate old-age provision may raise the desired saving of private households. In the short run, a rise in the saving rate of the poor private households (s_h^p) or the rich private households (s_h^r) clearly reduces the profit share (π), firms' internal saving as a ratio of capital (S_f/K), and the degree of capacity utilization (u), while personal income inequality as measured by ψ may rise or fall. In the long run, the equilibrium rate of real capital accumulation (g^*) unambiguously declines with a rise in s_h^p and/or s_h^r. Although economic growth is thus clearly wage-led, it may be either equality- or inequality-led.

Other drivers of secular stagnation mentioned by Hansen (1939, pp. 10–11), Summers (2014b, p. 69), and also—from a supply-side perspective—Gordon (2016, pp. 320, 578) include a (possible) slowdown of technological progress, which may be reflected in a decline in α_3, h_0, and/or h_1. While variations in these parameters and variables do not have any short-run effects in the model, a decrease in α_3, h_0, and/or h_1 clearly reduces the long-run equilibrium rate of economic growth (g^*), possibly leading to economic stagnation.

Although the model does not include the public sector, following Hein (2016, pp. 23, 28, 31) declining (autonomous and deficit-financed) government investment spending, which Summers (2016), in particular, refers to as a possible impediment to economic growth, may be depicted by a fall in the parameter α_0, reducing g^* in the long run.

Finally, it is certainly Summers's (2014a, pp. 33–34) reference to an increase in personal income inequality which can be modeled, most obviously by reductions in the wage and/or capital income share of the poor private households (w, z). A decline in w and/or z unambiguously reduces the profit share (π), firms' internal saving as a ratio of capital (S_f/K), and the degree of capacity utilization (u), while personal income inequality as measured by ψ rises in the short run. In the long run, g^* unambiguously declines, implying that economic growth is both profit-led and equality-led. This result is remarkable, as a decline in the profit share is typically associated with a decline in personal income inequality. By redistributing income toward the group of rich private households, however, in the demand-determined growth model developed in this chapter a decline in w and/or z reduces the degree of capacity utilization (u), which, due to the impact of overhead labor costs, eventually reduces the profit share (π).

8.5.3 The Impact of Changes in Economic Growth

While the effects of the described changes in α_0, α_3, h_0, h_1, s_h^p, s_h^r, u_0, w, and z on the long-run equilibrium rate of real capital accumulation (g^*) are unambiguously defined, it has been outlined in Sect. 8.3.2.3 that variations in g^* feed back on the degree of capacity utilization (u), on the profit share (π), and on the measure of personal income inequality (ψ). In fact, the impact of g^* is not always considered in economic growth models, or, as Skott (2017, p. 344) mentions in a similar context, "[...] the implications of a two-way interaction do not always seem to be fully appreciated [...]." For instance, although Steindl ([1952] 1976, p. 245) at least verbally referred to the impact of g^* on u and—via u—on π, this feedback mechanism is not at the center of his stagnation theory, as he was mainly concerned with the *causes* of secular stagnation and hence with the causal relationship from certain economic shocks to the long-run rate of real capital accumulation (g^*). In developing his modified Steindlian growth model, Dutt (2005) accordingly also does not refer to the impact of changes in the long-run equilibrium rate of real capital accumulation (g^*).[24]

Variations in g^* change both u and π in the same direction, i.e., a decline (rise) in g^* reduces (increases) u and π from the short to the long run. Hence, as has been outlined in Tables 8.5 and 8.6, an increase in s_h^p, s_h^r, and u_0 as well as a decline in α_0, α_3, h_0, h_1, w, and z clearly reduces the long-run equilibrium levels of g^*, u^*, and π^*. On the other hand, however, the impact of a change in g^* on the measure of personal income inequality (ψ) is ambiguous, implying that—for each economic shock—it is unclear how the long-run equilibrium value of personal income inequality (ψ^*) develops. Although in the political process short-term developments seem to be more important at times, particularly with regard to the distribution of income it is the long-term development which should (also) be of interest. In this regard, the results of the theoretical Steindlian model developed here are somewhat unsatisfactory, as the model does not allow for a precise prediction of the long-term development of the

---

[24]In a similar context, Dutt (2017, p. 180) writes, "Examining the effects of changes in distribution (or some determinants of it) on growth does not, of course, imply that distribution is actually exogenous, but that this relation needs to be examined prior to embedding it into an enlarged model in which distribution (or its determinants) is made endogenous in the sense that growth and other related variables are allowed to affect it."

measure of personal income inequality.[25] It has been vaguely stated, however, that the impact of a change in g^* on both u and π plays an important role in determining how variations in g^* affect ψ. If a rise in g^* raises u strongly (only slightly), while π increases only slightly (strongly), the increase in g^* is more likely to lower (raise) the measure of personal income inequality (ψ) from the short to the long run. Similarly, if a decline in g^* reduces u strongly (only slightly), while π falls only slightly (strongly), the decline in g^* is more likely to raise (lower) the measure of personal income inequality (ψ) from the short to the long run.

8.5.4   Policy Implications

Referring to policy implications which, according to the modified Steindlian model developed in this chapter, may counteract possible stagnation tendencies, from an empirical perspective it is reasonable to focus on policies which raise the long-term rate of real capital accumulation (g^*), but which, at the same time, are likely to reduce the long-term measure of personal income inequality (ψ^*). As has been outlined in the Introduction to this book, income distribution has become more unequal in major advanced countries during the past decades. Economists and international organizations have thus been eager to identify "[...] 'win-win' policies that can both reduce inequality and promote economic growth [...]" (OECD 2012, p. 182). On similar grounds, in Germany it has been suggested to expand the so-called *magic square*—a set of four potentially conflicting economic policy objectives introduced as part of the *Law to Promote Economic Stability and Growth* in 1967—by several new dimensions, such as social sustainability. For instance, while the *new magic square* as proposed by Dullien (2017) still includes the objective of "[...] continuous and adequate economic growth [...]" (Statistisches Bundesamt 2018), it also comprises the new aim to reduce the currently high levels in personal income inequality (Dullien 2017, pp. 8, 11, 15–16).

   While there are various policy measures which, according to the model outlined above, *may* potentially reduce the long-run equilibrium measure of personal income distribution (ψ^*) and raise the long-term equilibrium rate of real capital accumulation (g^*), the most straightforward policy proposed by the model is to directly redistribute income from the rich to the poor private households, i.e., to raise w and/or z. In fact, a rise in the wage share (w) and/or the capital income share (z) of the poor private households is the *only* economic change which—according to the model—unambiguously reduces personal income inequality as measured by ψ in the short run, while clearly raising the long-run equilibrium rate of real capital accumulation (g^*). Although it is unclear how this rise in g^* feeds back on ψ, as outlined in Appendix D.1.2.3, ceteris paribus it is more likely that ψ^* does not rise above its initial level the larger, for instance, the parameters α_0 and h_0. It may be suspected that especially α_0—

---

[25]The respective condition determining whether a rise (fall) in g^* raises or lowers ψ from the short to the long run has been outlined in Sect. 8.3.2.3 and Appendix D.1.2.2.

firms' animal spirits and business confidence—as well as h_0—the autonomous impact of technological change on real capital accumulation—are comparatively weak at low levels of economic growth and capacity utilization. Hence, when economic activity is low, a rise in w and/or z may be more likely to be accompanied by an *increase* in the long-run equilibrium measure of personal income inequality (ψ^*).[26] If ψ^* rises above its initial level—which is not a necessity, though—economic growth is clearly unequal, i.e., the induced increase in g^* raises personal income inequality (ψ) from the short to the long run. Moreover, this increase in ψ is so strong that the initial fall in personal income inequality is reverted.

If ψ^* *does* rise above its initial level, it may be appropriate to engage in an iterative process, i.e., to again raise w and/or z in order to lower personal income inequality (ψ) in the short run while raising g^*. In fact, it may be expected that, over time, this positive growth stimulus induces a rise in firms' business confidence (α_0) and perhaps also in the autonomous component of technological change (h_0), making it more likely that redistribution policies from the rich to the poor private households do not only reduce personal income inequality (ψ) in the short run, but also in the long run. As outlined above, the autonomous components α_0 and h_0 may also be raised proactively, such as by stimulating government investment spending or by fostering technological progress by appropriate policy measures.

Although "win-win policies," as the OECD (2012, p. 182) calls them, can be derived from the theoretical Steindlian model developed in this chapter, such theoretically based policy recommendations should be interpreted with caution. In fact, while it is the comparative static impact of individual economic shocks that has been described in the previous sections, there may be dynamic repercussions, as economic agents can be expected to react in various ways. For instance, increases in the wage and/or capital income share of the poor private households $(w$ or $z)$—i.e., redistribution policies from the top to the bottom of the income hierarchy which, in the theoretical Steindlian model, clearly raise the long-term rate of real capital accumulation (g^*)—may provoke adverse economic reactions. Assuming, for example, that it is particularly the rich private households that—due to shareholdings—own private firms, redistribution policies from the top to the bottom of the income scale may result in firms raising their mark-ups to compensate for these redistribution measures. Indeed, if a rise in w and/or z is accompanied by a rise in m_1, the equilibrium rate of real capital accumulation (g^*) may decline. This adverse impact on long-term economic growth may also be reinforced by a decline in innovation and technological progress, i.e., a fall in α_3, h_0, and/or h_1. Hence, although policies that foster both more equality and stronger economic growth are conceivable, it is key to consider possible adverse dynamic repercussions to be able to implement an effective policy mix.

---

[26]Graphically, in a typical u-π-diagram, ceteris paribus the π^s schedule is steeper the lower g and u. Hence, at low levels of economic activity, each rise in w and/or z, which shifts the π^d schedule upward, is accompanied by a relatively strong increase in the profit share (π). Ceteris paribus, a rise in the profit share (π) is more beneficial for the rich private households than for the poor private households.

8.5.5   *Concluding Remarks*

To conclude this chapter, a few words should be said about demand-driven stagnationist models in general. In the relevant literature, the well-known (post-Kaleckian) model developed by Bhaduri and Marglin (1990)—which arose from a critical assessment of the (left-)Keynesian/neo-Kaleckian stagnationist or wage-led models—is sometimes referred to as a "superior" model, as it combines different economic regimes in a single theoretical framework. For instance, while the neo-Kaleckian growth models proposed by Rowthorn (1981) and Dutt (1984) only allow for a wage-led economy, in the model of Bhaduri and Marglin (1990) a rise in the profit share may raise or lower economic activity, i.e., economic activity can be profit- or wage-led (see also Hein 2017, pp. 218–223).[27] Combining different economic regimes in a single model is possible due to the specific role assigned to the profit *share*. In fact, in Bhaduri and Marglin (1990, p. 380) and Marglin and Bhaduri (1990, p. 163), investment (and real capital accumulation) is a positive function of the profit *share* and the degree of capacity utilization.[28]

While the possibility to generate different economic regimes is a valuable feature, this characteristic is not confined to the model proposed by Bhaduri and Marglin (1990). In fact, in Steindl's ([1952] 1976) original model as well as in both Dutt's (2005) modified Steindlian model and the extended version developed above, depending on the specific economic shock a short-run rise in the profit share may be followed by either a rise or a decline in the long-term equilibrium rate of real capital accumulation (g^*). With a decline in the saving rate of private households (s_h^p, s_h^r), for instance, economic growth is clearly profit-led. Similarly, the introduction of the personal distribution of income has revealed that economic growth is unambiguously profit-led when w and z are raised. With changes in a_2, i, m_1, and m_2, on the other hand, the nexus between the short-run change in the profit share (π) and g^* is uncertain from an ex-ante perspective, allowing for either profit- or wage-led growth. In fact, different economic regimes are not only possible with respect to the functional distribution of income. As has been outlined above, depending on the specific economic shock and the prevailing economic conditions, economic activity can be either equality- or inequality-led.

---

[27]For a systematic overview of the different economic regimes, see, for instance, Blecker (2002, p. 134). It should be noted that Bhaduri and Marglin (1990, p. 384) are solely concerned with the short run. Hence, although many growth models have originated from their seminal paper, their original model cannot be characterized as a growth model. In fact, Bhaduri and Marglin (1990) do not focus on the impact of changes in the profit and wage share on economic growth, but on output and capacity utilization (see also Dutt 2017, p. 172). Marglin and Bhaduri (1990), on the other hand, also refer to the rate of real capital accumulation. They write, "One advantage of the present model is that it is normalized in terms that permit it to be applied to the determination of equilibrium over a longer period [...]" (Marglin and Bhaduri 1990, p. 155).

[28]For instance, if the degree of capacity utilization rises, but the profit rate remains constant, the profit share is necessarily lower than its initial value. Despite a higher degree of capacity utilization and a constant profit rate, real capital accumulation *may* decline if the impact of the profit *share* on real capital accumulation is relatively large. See also Lavoie (2014, pp. 370–371) and Blecker (2002, pp. 135–138).

While growth models in the Steindlian tradition thus allow for different economic regimes, the theoretical framework developed in this chapter is yet a demand-driven growth model, particularly in the sense that direct redistribution of income from the rich to the poor private households via increases in w and/or z unambiguously raises the long-term degree of capacity utilization (u^*) and economic growth (g^*). Assuming away supply-side constraints, according to the model specifications the rate of economic growth could, theoretically, be raised continuously by increasing the wage and/or capital income share of the poor private households, until the total income of the poor private households (Y_h^p) is almost as high as—and very close to—the total income of the rich private households (Y_h^r).[29] From an empirical perspective, it is clear that the redistribution of income from the top to the bottom of the income scale has its limits in capitalist economies. Although there is thus room for further development—particularly with regard to economic dynamics—the modified Steindlian model developed in this chapter is yet one of the first examples of how the personal distribution of income—which has typically been ignored in theoretical growth models—can be integrated in a theoretical framework of demand-determined economic growth.

References

Andrews M (2005) On industry concentration and the transition to monopoly capitalism: a knife-edge model of "Steindlian" dynamics. In: Mott T, Shapiro N (eds) Rethinking capitalist development: essays on the economics of Josef Steindl. Routledge, New York, NY, pp 79–94

Auerbach P, Skott P (1988) Concentration, competition and distribution—a critique of theories of monopoly capital. Int Rev Appl Econ 2(1):42–61

Bhaduri A, Marglin S (1990) Unemployment and the real wage: the economic basis for contesting political ideologies. Camb J Econ 14(4):375–393

Blecker RA (2002) Distribution, demand and growth in neo-Kaleckian macro-models. In: Setterfield M (ed) The economics of demand-led growth: challenging the supply-side vision of the long run. Edward Elgar, Cheltenham and Northhampton, MA, pp 129–152

Committeri M (1986) Some comments on recent contributions on capital accumulation, income distribution and capacity utilization. Polit Econ 2(2):161–186

Cowling K (2005) Monopoly capitalism and stagnation. In: Mott T, Shapiro N (eds) Rethinking capitalist development: essays on the economics of Josef Steindl. Routledge, New York, NY, pp 147–163

Dullien S (2017) A new, "magic square" for inclusive and sustainable economic growth: a policy framework for Germany to move beyond GDP. Friedrich-Ebert-Stiftung, Bonn

Dutt AK (1984) Stagnation, income distribution and monopoly power. Camb J Econ 8(1):25–40

Dutt AK (1994) On the long-run stability of capitalist economies: implications of a model of growth and distribution. In: Dutt AK (ed) New directions in analytical political economy. Edward Elgar Publishing, Aldershot and Brookfield, VT, pp 93–120

Dutt AK (2003) New growth theory, effective demand, and post-Keynesian dynamics. In: Salvadori N (ed) Old and new growth theories: an assessment. Edward Elgar Publishing, Cheltenham and Northampton, MA, pp 67–100

---

[29] As it has been defined that the measure of personal income inequality (ψ) is always larger than one, Y_h^p must be lower than Y_h^r, though.

Dutt AK (2005) Steindl's theory of maturity and stagnation and its relevance today. In: Mott T, Shapiro N (eds) Rethinking capitalist development: essays on the economics of Josef Steindl. Routledge, New York, NY, pp 55–78

Dutt AK (2006) Aggregate demand, aggregate supply and economic growth. Int Rev Appl Econ 20(3):319–336

Dutt AK (2017) Income inequality, the wage share, and economic growth. Rev Keynes Econ 5(2):170–195

Gordon RJ (2016) The rise and fall of American growth. The U.S. standard of living since the Civil War. Princeton University Press, Princeton, NJ

Guger A, Marterbauer M, Walterskirchen E (2006) Growth policy in the spirit of Steindl and Kalecki. Metroeconomica 57(3):428–442

Hansen AH (1939) Economic progress and declining population growth. Am Econ Rev 29(1):1–15

Harrod RF (1948) Towards a dynamic economics: some recent developments of economic theory and their application to policy. Macmillan & Co., Ltd, London

Hein E (2014) Distribution and growth after Keynes: a post-Keynesian guide. Edward Elgar, Cheltenham and Northampton, MA

Hein E (2016) Secular stagnation or stagnation policy? Steindl after Summers. PSL Quarterly Rev 69(276):3–47

Hein E (2017) The Bhaduri-Marglin post-Kaleckian model in the history of distribution and growth theories: an assessment by means of model closures. Rev Keynes Econ 5(2):218–238

Hein E, Lavoie M, van Treeck T (2011) Some instability puzzles in Kaleckian models of growth and distribution: a critical survey. Camb J Econ 35(3):587–612

Hein E, Lavoie M, van Treeck T (2012) Harrodian instability and the 'normal rate' of capacity utilization in Kaleckian models of distribution and growth—a survey. Metroeconomica 63(1):139–169

Kaldor N (1966) Causes of the slow rate of economic growth of the United Kingdom. Cambridge University Press, London

Kalecki M ([1954] 1965) Theory of economic dynamics. An essay on cyclical and long-run changes in capitalist economy. Modern Reader Paperbacks, New York, NY, and London

Kalmbach P (2000) Höhere Arbeitsmarktflexibilität oder flexiblere Wirtschaftspolitik? Zu den Ursachen der unterschiedlichen Beschäftigungsentwicklung in den USA und in Deutschland (Gutachten im Auftrag der Friedrich-Ebert-Stiftung). Wirtschafts- und Sozialpolitisches Forschungs- und Beratungszentrum der Friedrich-Ebert-Stiftung, Abteilung Wirtschaftspolitik, Bonn

Keynes JM ([1930] 1972) Economic possibilities for our grandchildren. The collected writings of John Maynard Keynes, vol IX: essays in persuasion, Macmillan St. Martin's Press for the Royal Economiy Society, London and Basingstoke, pp 321–332

Keynes JM ([1937] 1973) Some economic consequences of a declining population. In: Moggridge D (ed) The collected writings of John Maynard Keynes, vol XIV: the general theory and after (part II: Defence and development). Macmillan St Martin's Press for the Royal Economic Society, London and Basingstoke, pp 124–133

Krämer H (1996) Bowley's Law, Technischer Fortschritt und Einkommensverteilung: Eine methodische, empirische und theoretische Untersuchung der langfristigen funktionalen Einkommensverteilung. Metropolis-Verlag, Marburg

Kurz HD (1991) Technical change, growth and distribution: a steady-state approach to 'unsteady' growth on Kaldorian lines. In: Nell EJ, Semmler W (eds) Nicholas Kaldor and mainstream economics: confrontation or convergence? Macmillan, Basingstoke and London, pp 421–448

Lavoie M (2014) Post-Keynesian economics: new foundations. Edward Elgar, Cheltenham and Northampton, MA

Lavoie M, Stockhammer E (2013) Wage-led growth: concept, theories and policies. In: Lavoie M, Stockhammer E (eds) Wage-led growth: an equitable strategy for economic recovery. Palgrave Macmillan and International Labour Organization, London, pp 13–39

Lösch A (1938) Das Problem einer Wechselwirkung zwischen Bevölkerungs- und Wirtscahftsentwicklung. Weltwirtschaftliches Archiv 48(1938):454–469

Marglin SA, Bhaduri A (1990) Profit squeeze and Keynesian theory. In: Marglin SA, Schor JB (eds) The golden age of capitalism: reinterpreting the postwar experience. Clarendon Press, Oxford, pp 153–186

OECD (2012) Economic policy reforms 2012: going for growth. OECD Publishing, Paris

Palley TI (2017) Inequality and growth in neo-Kaleckian and Cambridge growth theory. Rev Keynes Econ 5(2):146–169

Rowthorn B (1981) Demand, real wages and economic growth. Thames Papers in Political Economy Autumn 1981

Skott P (2012) Theoretical and empirical shortcomings of the Kaleckian investment function. Metroeconomica 63(1):109–138

Skott P (2017) Weaknesses of 'wage-led growth'. Rev Keynes Econ 5(3):336–359

Statistisches Bundesamt (2018) Overall economic equilibrium: 50th anniversary of the magic square. Statistisches Bundesamt, Wiesbaden. https://www.destatis.de/EN/FactsFigures/NationalEconomyEnvironment/NationalAccounts/MagicSquare.html. Accessed 07 Aug 2018

Steindl J ([1952] 1976) Maturity and stagnation in American capitalism (with a new introduction by the author). Monthly Review Press, New York, NY, and London

Steindl J ([1979] 1990) Stagnation theory and stagnation policy. In: Steindl J (ed) Economic papers 1941–88. St Martin's Press, New York, NY, pp 107–126

Steindl J ([1980] 1990) Technical progress and evolution. In: Steindl J (ed) Economic papers 1941–88. St Martin's Press, New York, NY, pp 83–93

Steindl J ([1982a] 1990) Technology and the economy: the case of falling productivity growth in the 1970s. In: Steindl J (ed) Economic papers 1941–88. St Martin's Press, New York, NY, pp 94–103

Steindl J ([1984] 1990) Reflections on the present state of economics. In: Steindl J (ed) Economic papers 1941–88. St Martin's Press, New York, NY, pp 241–252

Steindl J ([1989] 1990) From stagnation in the 30s to slow growth in the 70s. In: Steindl J (ed) Economic papers 1941–88. St Martin's Press, New York, NY, pp 166–179

Summers LH (2014a) Reflections on the 'new secular stagnation hypothesis'. In: Teulings C, Baldwin R (eds) Secular stagnation: facts, causes and cures. CEPR Press, London, pp 27–38

Summers LH (2014b) US economic prospects: secular stagnation, hysteresis, and the zero lower bound. Bus Econ 49(2):65–73

Summers LH (2016) The age of secular stagnation: what it is and what to do about it. Foreign Affairs February 15, 2016. https://www.foreignaffairs.com/articles/united-states/2016-02-15/age-secular-stagnation. Accessed 24 Aug 2016

Verdoorn PJ (1949) Fattori che regolano lo sviluppo della produttività del lavoro. L'Industria 1(1949):45–53

Chapter 9
Existing Empirical Evidence on the Nexus Between Income Distribution and Economic Growth

9.1 Introduction

In the theoretical Steindlian framework developed in the Chap. 8, the nexus between both the functional and personal distribution of income and economic growth has turned out to be ambiguous. Depending on the specific economic shock and circumstances, short-run variations in the profit share (π) and the measure of personal income distribution (ψ) may be followed by any change in the long-run rate of real capital accumulation (g^*). Similarly, although a rise (fall) in the long-run equilibrium rate of real capital accumulation (g^*) clearly increases (reduces) the profit share (π), the impact on the personal distribution of income as measured by ψ is uncertain from an ex-ante perspective.

While the model presented above provides a demand-determined theoretical construct on the nexus between the functional distribution of income, the personal distribution of income, and economic growth, at the end of the day the link between the distribution of income and economic growth is also an empirical issue. During the past decades, a large body of empirical literature has emerged, particularly focusing on the impact of personal income inequality on economic growth. While comparatively few studies deal with the reverse causality from economic growth to personal income inequality, the economic effects of the functional distribution of income—i.e., the question of whether economies are rather wage- or profit-led—have also been studied extensively over the past years.

The present chapter gives a rough empirical insight on the nexus between the distribution of income and economic growth, thus providing an empirical counterpart to the theoretical model developed in the previous chapter. It is not an in-depth review of the existing empirical literature, however, as this has been provided by several authors throughout the years. For example, Onaran and Galanis (2013, pp. 85–86, 97–99) summarize the results of various analyses on the economic impact of changes in the functional distribution of income. On the other hand, recent literature reviews on the effects of personal income inequality on economic growth include Voitchovsky

C. Anselmann, *Secular Stagnation Theories*, Springer Studies in the History of Economic Thought, https://doi.org/10.1007/978-3-030-41087-2_9

(2009, pp. 561–569), Boushey and Price (2014, pp. 12–18), and Behringer et al. (2016, pp. 23–31). On the reverse impact of economic growth on personal income inequality, Bourguignon (2004, pp. 11–14) and Brueckner et al. (2015, pp. 151–152) give an overview of several empirical studies that have been conducted throughout the years. While these literature reviews provide a more profound overview of existing empirical studies, the following briefly summarizes the overall findings from a more general perspective, without going into detail.

9.2   Wage- Versus Profit-Led Economic Regimes

Empirical analyses on the economic impact of changes in the functional distribution of income are typically based on the theoretical framework of Bhaduri and Marglin (1990) and Marglin and Bhaduri (1990). In general, it is the effect of variations in the profit and wage share on aggregate demand which is analyzed. The impact on economic growth, on the other hand, has received comparatively little attention in empirical studies.

The question of whether aggregate demand is wage- or profit-led is generally addressed based on the impact of changes in the functional distribution of income on the different components of (private) aggregate demand, i.e., private consumption, private investment, and net exports. A rise in the wage share is typically found to be conducive to private consumption, as the marginal propensity to consume out of wages tends to be higher than the marginal propensity to consume out of capital income. On the other hand, ceteris paribus an increase in the wage share—and thus a decline in the profit share—is generally supposed to hamper investment. Likewise, with the wage share being closely tied to unit labor costs, ceteris paribus net exports are typically assumed to decline with a rise in the wage share (Onaran and Galanis 2013, p. 72; Bhaduri and Marglin 1990, pp. 378, 385, 387–388).

Aggregate demand is wage-led if the positive impact of a rise in the wage share on private consumption outweighs the alleged negative impact on investment and net exports. As summarized by Onaran and Galanis (2013, pp. 97–99), Hein (2014, pp. 297–307), and Lavoie (2014, pp. 375–377), for instance, most empirical studies that have been conducted over the past years for various G20 countries find that *domestic* demand—i.e., the sum of private consumption and investment—is wage-led. On the other hand, the results for total demand—i.e., the sum of private consumption, investment, and net exports—are more heterogeneous. As noted by Blecker (2016, p. 374): "[...] [A]n entire generation of empirical research has attempted to determine whether various countries have wage- or profit-led demand regimes. This now vast literature has yet to reach a consensus for many countries." To name but a few empirical analyses, Hein and Vogel (2008, p. 502), for example, find that aggregate demand in France is wage-led, while Ederer and Stockhammer (2007, p. 133) conclude that it is profit-led. Similarly, according to Onaran and Galanis (2014, p. 2509) aggregate demand in the United States is wage-led, while the empirical study of Naastepad and Storm (2006, p. 233) suggests that it may be profit-led.

Referring to groups of nations, Hartwig (2014, p. 427) finds that aggregate demand is rather wage-led in the average OECD country. For the EU-15, Onaran and Obst (2016, p. 1537) conclude that a one percentage point decline in the wage share in all of the 15 nations leads to a fall in the combined real GDP by 0.30%. Similar results pointing in the same direction are also available for a group of various G20 countries (Onaran and Galanis 2013, p. 81–85; Onaran and Galanis 2014, pp. 2509–2510).

While the empirical impact of changes in the functional distribution of income on aggregate demand and the level of output has been extensively studied over the past years, similar studies on the effect of variations in the profit and wage share on economic growth are relatively rare. As outlined by Blecker (2002, pp. 136–137; 2016, p. 374), even if aggregate demand is wage-led, long-term economic growth can be profit-led.[1] Stockhammer and Onaran (2004) and Onaran and Stockhammer (2005), in fact, are among the few empirical attempts dealing with the impact of changes in the profit and wage share on economic growth. Analyzing the growth regimes in the United States, the United Kingdom, and France, for all three countries Stockhammer and Onaran (2004, pp. 428, 433) find no significant effects of changes in the functional distribution of income on the rate of real capital accumulation. For Turkey and particularly South Korea, on the other hand, Onaran and Stockhammer (2005, p. 79) suggest economic growth to be wage-led.

9.3 Equality- Versus Inequality-Led Economic Growth

On the impact of changes in personal income inequality on economic growth, numerous empirical analyses have been conducted throughout the years, mostly in the form of cross-country regressions. As summarized by Boushey and Price (2014, pp. 12–16) and Behringer et al. (2016, pp. 24–31), the vast amount of empirical literature can be roughly divided into three groups: first, the early studies of mainly the beginning of the 1990s and mid-1990s, secondly, the analyses from the late 1990s until the financial crisis of 2008–2009, and, thirdly, the literature that has emerged in more recent years, approximately after 2010.

As noted by Boushey and Price (2014, pp. 12, 23), Behringer et al. (2016, pp. 24–25), as well as Bénabou (1996, pp. 14–15), most of the early empirical analyses suggest that higher income inequality has a negative impact on economic growth. Among the relevant studies are, for instance, the works of Alesina and Rodrik (1994), Bourguignon (1994), Persson and Tabellini (1994), and Perotti (1996), all analyzing

---

[1] The ex-post rate of real capital accumulation in goods market equilibrium is given by $g = \frac{I}{K} = s_p \pi u$. Assuming a constant ratio of total saving to profits (s_p), it is the profit share (π) and the degree of capacity utilization (u) which play the dominant role. If aggregate demand (Y) and hence the degree of capacity utilization (u) are wage-led, economic growth (g) may still decline with a rise in the wage share (i.e., a fall in the profit share) if the positive impact of a rise in the wage share on u is comparatively small. Following Marglin and Bhaduri (1990), this may happen when real capital accumulation reacts only little to a rise in u, but strongly to a decline in π.

the time period between 1960 and 1985. For different samples of various OECD and developing countries, Alesina and Rodrik (1994, pp. 478–484) find that "[...] income inequality is negatively correlated with subsequent growth [...]" in GDP per capita (Alesina and Rodrik 1994, p. 481). Similarly, based on a set of 35 developing nations, the empirical analysis of Bourguignon (1994, p. 58) suggests that "[...] income equality proves to be a significant positive determinant of growth [...]. [A] one-percentage-point increase in the total (personal) income of the bottom 40% of the distribution increases the annual rate of growth by almost 0.2 percentage points." Along similar lines, for a total of 56 democratic and non-democratic countries, Persson and Tabellini (1994, pp. 610–613) outline that a rise in the income share of the third quintile—with the third quintile representing the middle class—raises the average annual growth rate in real GDP per capita in democratic nations. Finally, for a sample of 67 democratic and non-democratic countries, Perotti (1996, pp. 154–159) concludes that a rise in the combined income shares of the third and fourth quintiles of the distribution increases real GDP per capita growth in subsequent years. From a theoretical perspective, most of these early studies suggest that the negative impact of inequality on economic growth may be due to political reasons, with supposedly distortionary tax and redistribution policies being more pronounced in more unequal societies. As outlined by Persson and Tabellini (1994, p. 615), however, "[...] the possibility remains that [...] [the empirical] findings reflect mechanisms other than the political theory [...]. After all, these regressions only estimate the reduced form of the model [...], and not the [...] specific channels identified by the theory [...]." Perotti (1996, pp. 168–173), in fact, does not find empirical support that it is distortionary tax and redistribution policies which cause economic growth to decline with a rise in income inequality.

While the availability of adequate data on income inequality had been a serious issue in earlier years, the empirical studies that were conducted after the mid-1990s could draw on more consistent databases, with the database initiated by Deininger and Squire (1996) being among the first examples. According to Deininger and Squire (1996, p. 573, 1998, p. 260), poor data quality prior to the mid-1990s casts legitimate doubt on the negative impact of income inequality on economic growth that had been suggested by the empirical literature back then. In fact, in contrast to the early empirical analyses on the impact of personal income inequality on economic growth, the results of the studies that emerged between the late 1990s and the mid-2000s are more heterogeneous. As summarized by Voitchovsky (2009, p. 561), this "[...] literature has [...] failed to reach any substantive conclusions regarding the overall influence of inequality on economic performance [...]." Aside from the empirical analysis of Deininger and Squire (1998), the studies of the mid-1990s and thereafter include the work of Li and Zou (1998), Forbes (2000), Barro (2000), Banerjee and Duflo (2003), and Voitchovsky (2005). Analyzing the time period from 1960 to 1992, for a variety of developed and developing countries Deininger and Squire (1998, pp. 266–270) find that higher income inequality as measured by the Gini coefficient reduces economic growth in subsequent years, with the results, however, not being very robust. Li and Zou (1998, pp. 321–328), on the other hand, suggest that a rise in personal income inequality stimulates real GDP per capita growth. Similarly, for a panel of 45 developed and developing countries between 1966 and 1995, Forbes (2000, pp. 873–878) concludes that an increase in personal income inequality raises the average growth rate of real GNP per capita in the following five years. Analyzing the impact of income inequality as measured by the Gini coefficient on the growth rate of real GDP per capita for a pool of 84 developed and developing countries between the 1960s and 1990s, Barro (2000, pp. 14–18), in turn, finds no significant nexus. Yet, his results suggest a rise in income inequality to hamper economic growth in poor nations, while boosting it in rich countries. Using the same data and referring to the same time period as Forbes (2000), the results of Banerjee and Duflo (2003), on the other hand, suggest that the nexus between income inequality and growth is non-linear. "[...] [C]hanges in inequality (in any direction) [...]," they hold, "[...] are associated with lower future growth rates" (Banerjee and Duflo 2003, p. 268). Finally, based on data provided by the Luxembourg Income Study, Voitchovsky (2005, pp. 286–290) finds that inequality at the top of the distribution is growth-enhancing, while inequality at the bottom end of the income hierarchy is harmful to economic growth.

As outlined by Behringer et al. (2016, p. 27), in contrast to the heterogeneous results suggested by the empirical literature of the late 1990s and thereafter, similar to the early empirical studies more recent analyses predominantly find that high income inequality is harmful to economic growth. In the years following the financial crisis of 2008–2009, it has been particularly the empirical studies of Ostry et al. (2014) and Cingano (2014) which have received wide attention in the economic and public debate. For a variety of developed and developing countries between 1960 and 2010, the results of the IMF economists Ostry et al. (2014, pp. 17, 20–24) suggest that a more unequal distribution of household disposable income reduces both the average growth rate of real GDP per capita in subsequent years as well as the "[...] duration of growth spells [...]" (Ostry et al. 2014, p. 23).[2] Additionally, the authors find that redistribution, measured as the difference between the Gini coefficients of household market and disposable income, has no statistically significant impact on growth. Except for a very large extent of redistribution, there also does not seem to be a direct negative impact of redistribution on the duration of economic growth. Rather, if income inequality is reduced via income redistribution, "[...] the resulting lower inequality seems to be associated with longer growth spells [...]" (Ostry et al. 2014, pp. 23–24).[3] Similar to Ostry et al. (2014), for 31 OECD countries in the period from 1970 to 2010, Cingano (2014, pp. 14–16, 19) concludes that higher inequality as measured by the Gini coefficient of household disposable income has a negative impact on subsequent real GDP per capita growth. Moreover, income redistribution does not seem to have a significant effect on growth. "Taken together [...]," he holds, "[...] these results suggest that inequality in disposable incomes is bad for growth, and that redistribution is, at worst, neutral to growth" (Cingano 2014, p. 19). Following

---

[2] A growth spell is defined as a period "[...] of at least five years during which growth is above 2 percent *and* significantly higher than during preceding years [...]" (Ostry et al. 2014, p. 16).

[3] In a subsequent analysis, Berg and Ostry (2017, pp. 804–808) similarly identify a more equal distribution of income as an important driver of longer growth periods.

Voitchovsky (2005), Cingano (2014, pp. 20–21) also analyzes the economic impact of disposable income inequality in different parts of the distribution. He concludes that a reduction in inequality at the bottom of the income hierarchy raises economic growth more strongly than a reduction in top income inequality. In fact, the impact of variations in top income inequality on economic growth is suggested to not be statistically significant.

9.4   The Distributional Impact of Economic Growth

In contrast to the empirical literature on the effects of income inequality on economic growth, empirical analyses on the reverse causality from economic growth to income inequality are rare. Moreover, several studies which are occasionally said to analyze the distributional impact of economic growth actually examine the existence of the Kuznets curve, i.e., an inverted U-shaped pattern of income inequality in the course of economic development. For instance, in reviewing the relevant empirical literature on the impact of economic growth on the distribution of income, Bourguignon (2004, pp. 11–14) and Brueckner et al. (2015, pp. 151–152) refer to Paukert (1973) and Ahluwalia (1976), who both focus on empirically analyzing the Kuznets curve. Yet, while Kuznets (1955, p. 1) himself wondered whether "[...] inequality in the distribution of income increase[s] or decrease[s] in the course of a country's economic growth [...]," he did not speak of a causal link, but rather referred to changes in the distribution of income which *accompany* the process of economic development.

From a more general perspective, with regard to the impact of economic growth on income inequality, Gornick and Jäntti (2013, p. 4) mention that, "[a]s any change in aggregate income must, by definition, benefit households somewhere in the distribution, economic growth is expected to shift the income distribution." Yet, the sparse empirical literature on the effects of economic growth on income inequality yields rather heterogeneous results. Among the few empirical studies assessing the distributional impact of economic growth are the analyses of Dollar and Kraay (2002), Dollar et al. (2015, 2016), Brueckner et al. (2015), and Hermansen et al. (2016). For a sample of 92 developed and developing countries between the 1960s and the early 2000s, Dollar and Kraay (2002, pp. 196, 200–201, 209) find that economic growth raises the average income of the poor—i.e., the average income of those individuals and private households in the lowest quintile of the distribution—more or less proportionately to average income in society. "[...] [E]conomic growth [...]," they hold, "[...] on average benefit[s] the poorest in society as much as anyone else [...]" (Dollar and Kraay 2002, p. 219). Aiming to update these results to include more recent years, Dollar et al. (2016) reach similar conclusions. For a set of 115 nations between 1970 and 2012, Dollar et al. (2015, pp. 338, 340) outline that changes in income inequality are not correlated with economic growth. On the other hand, for a pool of 80 countries between 1960 and 2007, the empirical analysis of Brueckner et al. (2015, pp. 154, 158) suggests that a rise in real GDP per capita reduces personal income inequality as measured by the Gini coefficient. "More specifically [...]," they mention, "[...] we find that income growth boosts the incomes of the lowest four quintiles at the expense of the top quintile, implying that the poor and the middle class benefit from it" (Brueckner et al. 2015, p. 173). Finally, for the OECD member countries between the mid-1980 and 2012, Hermansen et al. (2016, pp. 6, 35) find that "[...] growth in GDP per capita has not by itself been the driver of the well-documented rise in income inequality over the last decades [...]" (Hermansen et al. 2016, p. 35). In fact, their empirical analysis suggests that real GDP per capita growth across OECD countries has benefited all private households to a similar extent over the past years. Nonetheless, they conclude that the *source* of economic growth matters: while a rise in labor productivity seems to have been more beneficial for those in the upper parts of the income hierarchy, increases in labor utilization have disproportionately benefited those at the bottom of the distribution.

9.5 Concluding Remarks

Existing econometric analyses on the link between income distribution and economic growth yield mixed results. If any conclusion can be drawn from this, it is that the empirical nexus seems to be complex and heterogeneous. As outlined by Dollar and Kraay (2002, p. 203), Voitchovsky (2005, p. 274), and Lavoie (2014, pp. 375–376), for instance, differences in econometric techniques, the underlying data, the sample of countries, as well as the time period considered probably play an important role here. Moreover, methodological problems, such as reverse causality or endogeneity issues, are likely to affect the results as well.

Focusing on empirical studies which examine the impact of personal income inequality on economic growth, broadly speaking most econometric analyses regress the rate of economic growth on a measure of income inequality—such as the Gini coefficient—for a pool of countries at the beginning of the period under consideration. While regression analyses of this type are a well-established empirical method, they may yet obscure the underlying economic mechanisms, making it difficult to interpret the results from a more general perspective. In fact, as the theoretical Steindlian model outlined in Chap. 8 has illustrated, the nexus between the distribution of income and economic growth is likely to depend on the specific circumstances. For example, in the theoretical framework developed above, a decline in the measure of personal income distribution (ψ) from the short to the long run is clearly followed by a rise in the long-term equilibrium rate of economic growth (g^*) if the initial cause is an increase in the wage or capital income share of the poor private households (w, z). On the other hand, if the underlying economic shock is a fall in the marginal profit share (m_1) or a rise in the ratio of overhead labor costs to capital (m_2), the measure of personal income distribution (ψ) declines from the short to the long run, while the subsequent change in the long-term equilibrium rate of economic growth (g^*) is ambiguous.[4] Along these lines, Palley (2017, p. 166), in a similar context, mentions:

> [...] [T]he fact that the sign of the growth-inequality locus [...] depends on circumstance and cause of change [...], means econometric estimates of the relation require careful consideration. Single equation estimates of the growth-inequality relation are likely to be highly unreliable. Instead, it would be better to estimate separate growth and inequality equations that incorporate the deep structural factors influencing the endogenous variables, and then see how growth and inequality comove in response to changes in those factors.

Atkinson (2015, p. 260) additionally pointed to the country specificity of the nexus between economic growth and the distribution of income, making cross-country empirical analyses problematic. Moreover, even within a single country, the link between inequality and economic growth is typically not homogeneous over time. For instance, without referring to a causal relationship, Paul Krugman in a conversation with Anthony Atkinson notes that, in recent history, the United States had two periods of relatively fast economic growth: the late nineteenth century until the early twentieth century, as well as the years after World War II until the early 1970s. As has also been shown in Sect. 1.1.2, the first of these two periods was marked by high income inequality, whereas the second period was characterized by a comparatively equal distribution of income. Krugman thus concludes that "[...] both seem to be viable models [...]," i.e., depending on the specific circumstances, high levels of inequality can be accompanied by high or low rates of economic growth (and vice versa) Krugman and Atkinson 2013, min. 40:20–41:00).

While the relationship between economic growth and the distribution of income is all but clear-cut, Skott (2017) makes an important point. He holds:

> Would I advocate an increase in inequality if it could be established that a rise in inequality tends to raise the rate of economic growth? Certainly not, and I expect that many [...] would choose the same answer. It is dangerous to base policy recommendations for lower inequality on their growth-enhancing benefits. [...] Measures to increase equality and social justice need not pass a 'do they increase economic growth?' test (Skott 2017, pp. 356–357).

From both a theoretical and empirical perspective, there is no a priori trade-off between more income equality and higher economic growth. Even if the specific circumstances pose such a trade-off, however, equality-enhancing policies must not necessarily be averted. If the economy is characterized by low economic growth and a highly unequal distribution of income, the aim should indeed be to foster both economic growth and a more equal distribution of income. Yet, if both targets cannot be achieved, policy measures have to be designed based on social preferences. If income inequality is already at comparatively high levels, hampering social cohesion and the sense of justice in society, policies that promote a more equal distribution of income may be appropriate—even if they come at the cost of lower economic growth.

---

[4]On the finding that the source of economic change matters, see also Auclert and Rognlie (2017, 2018). In analyzing their theoretical framework, they find that the cause of variations in the distribution of income is important in determining their economic impact.

References

Ahluwalia MS (1976) Income distribution and development: some stylized facts. Am Econ Rev 66(2):128–135

Alesina A, Rodrik D (1994) Distributive politics and economic growth. Q J Econ 109(2):465–490

Atkinson AB (2015) Inequality: what can be done? Harvard University Press, Cambridge, MA, and London

Auclert A, Rognlie M (2017) Aggregate demand and the top 1 percent. Am Econ Rev Pap Proc 107(5):588–592

Auclert A, Rognlie M (2018) Inequality and aggregate demand. NBER Working Paper No. 24280. National Bureau of Economic Research, Cambridge, MA. https://www.nber.org/papers/w24280. Accessed 29 Nov 2018

Banerjee AV, Duflo E (2003) Inequality and growth: what can the data say? J Econ Growth 8(3):267–299

Barro RJ (2000) Inequality and growth in a panel of countries. J Econ Growth 5(1):5–32

Behringer J, Theobald T, van Treeck T (2016) Ungleichheit und makroökonomische Instabilität: Eine Bestandsaufnahme. Friedrich-Ebert-Stiftung, Bonn

Bénabou R (1996) Inequality and growth. In: Bernanke BS, Rotemberg JJ (eds) NBER macroeconomics annual 1996, vol 11. The MIT Press. Cambridge, MA, pp 11–74

Berg AG, Ostry JD (2017) Inequality and unsustainable growth: two sides of the same coin? IMF Econ Rev 65(4):792–815

Bhaduri A, Marglin S (1990) Unemployment and the real wage: the economic basis for contesting political ideologies. Camb J Econ 14(4):375–393

Blecker RA (2002) Distribution, demand and growth in neo-Kaleckian macro-models. In: Setterfield M (ed) The economics of demand-led growth: challenging the supply-side vision of the long run. Edward Elgar, Cheltenham and Northhampton, MA, pp 129–152

Blecker RA (2016) Wage-led versus profit-led demand regimes: the long and the short of it. Rev Keynes Econ 4(4):373–390

Bourguignon F (1994) Growth, distribution, and human resources. In: Ranis G (ed) En route to modern growth: essays in honor of Carlos Díaz-Alejandro. Inter-American Development Bank and The John Hopkins University Press, Washington, DC, pp 43–70

Bourguignon F (2004) The poverty-growth-inequality triangle. World Bank Working Paper 28102. The World Bank, Washington, DC. http://documents.worldbank.org/curated/en/449711468762020101/pdf/28102.pdf. Accessed 09 Mar 2018

Boushey H, Price CC (2014) How are economic inequality and growth connected? A review of recent research. Washington Center for Equitable Growth, Washington, DC. https://equitablegrowth.org/wp-content/uploads/2014/10/100914-ineq-growth.pdf. Accessed 13 Aug 2018

Brueckner M, Norris ED, Gradstein M (2015) National income and its distribution. J Econ Growth 20(2):149–175

Cingano F (2014) Trends in income inequality and its impact on economic growth. OECD Social, Employment and Migration Working Papers No. 163. OECD, Paris. https://doi.org/10.1787/5jxrjncwxv6j-en. Accessed 18 Nov 2018

Deininger K, Squire L (1996) A new data set measuring income inequality. World Bank Econ Rev 10(3):565–591

Deininger K, Squire L (1998) New ways of looking at old issues: inequality and growth. J Dev Econ 57(2):259–287

Dollar D, Kraay A (2002) Growth is good for the poor. J Econ Growth 7(3):195–225

Dollar D, Kleineberg T, Kraay A (2015) Growth, inequality and social welfare: cross-country evidence. Econ Policy 30(82):335–377

Dollar D, Kleineberg T, Kraay A (2016) Growth still is good for the poor. Eur Econ Rev 81:68–85

Ederer S, Stockhammer E (2007) Wages and aggregate demand: an empirical investigation for France. In: Hein E, Truger A (eds) Money, distribution and economic policy: alternatives to orthodox macroeconomics. Edward Elgar Publishing, Cheltenham, pp 119–138

Forbes KJ (2000) A reassessment of the relationship between inequality and growth. Am Econ Rev 90(4):869–887

Gornick JC, Jäntti M (2013) Introduction. In: Gornick JC, Jäntti M (eds) Income inequality: economic disparities and the middle class in affluent countries. Stanford University Press, Stanford, MA, pp 1–47

Hartwig J (2014) Testing the Bhaduri-Marglin model with OECD panel data. Int Rev Appl Econ 28(4):419–435

Hein E (2014) Distribution and growth after Keynes: a post-Keynesian guide. Edward Elgar, Cheltenham and Northampton, MA

Hein E, Vogel L (2008) Distribution and growth reconsidered: empirical results for six OECD countries. Camb J Econ 32(3):479–511

Hermansen M, Ruiz N, Causa O (2016) The distribution of the growth dividends. OECD Economics Department Working Papers No. 1343. OECD Publishing, Paris. https://doi.org/10.1787/7c8c6cc1-en. Accessed 19 Aug 2018

Krugman P, Atkinson AB (2013) Inequality and economic growth: Paul Krugman & Tony Atkinson in conversation. Moderated by Chrystia Freeland. May 20, 2013. Presented by the Graduate Center of the City University of New York (CUNY), the Luxembourg Income Study (LIS), and the Advanced Research Collaborative (ARC). Video available at https://www.youtube.com/watch?v=zAFCaDS4a6Q. Uploaded on 01 June 2013 by the Graduate Center of the City University of New York (CUNY). Accessed 21 Aug 2018. Duration: 1:26:54 hours

Kuznets S (1955) Economic growth and income inequality. Am Econ Rev 45(1):1–28

Lavoie M (2014) Post-Keynesian economics: new foundations. Edward Elgar, Cheltenham and Northampton, MA

Li H, Hf Zou (1998) Income inequality is not harmful for growth: theory and evidence. Rev Dev Econ 2(3):318–334

Marglin SA, Bhaduri A (1990) Profit squeeze and Keynesian theory. In: Marglin SA, Schor JB (eds) The golden age of capitalism: reinterpreting the postwar experience. Clarendon Press, Oxford, pp 153–186

Naastepad CW, Storm S (2006) OECD demand regimes (1960–2000). J Post Keynes Econ 29(2):211–246

Onaran Ö, Galanis G (2013) Is aggregate demand wage-led or profit-led? A global model. In: Lavoie M, Stockhammer E (eds) Wage-led growth: an equitable strategy for economic recovery. Palgrave Macmillan and International Labour Organization, London, pp 71–99

Onaran Ö, Galanis G (2014) Income distribution and growth: a global model. Environ Plan A 46(10):2489–2513

Onaran O, Obst T (2016) Wage-led growth in the EU15 member-states: the effects of income distribution on growth, investment, trade balance and inflation. Camb J Econ 40(6):1517–1551

Onaran Ö, Stockhammer E (2005) Two different export-oriented growth strategies: accumulation and distribution in Turkey and South Korea. Emerg Mark Financ Trade 41(1):65–89

Ostry JD, Berg A, Tsangarides CG (2014) Redistribution, inequality, and growth. IMF Staff Discussion Note 14/02. International Monetary Fund, Washington, DC. https://www.imf.org/external/pubs/ft/sdn/2014/sdn1402.pdf. Accessed 24 Nov 2018

Palley TI (2017) Inequality and growth in neo-Kaleckian and Cambridge growth theory. Rev Keynes Econ 5(2):146–169

Paukert F (1973) Income distribution at different levels of development: a survey of evidence. Int Labour Rev 108:97–125

Perotti R (1996) Growth, income distribution, and democracy: what the data say. J Econ Growth 1(2):149–187

Persson T, Tabellini G (1994) Is inequality harmful for growth? Am Econ Rev 84(3):600–621

Skott P (2017) Weaknesses of 'wage-led growth'. Rev Keynes Econ 5(3):336–359

Stockhammer E, Onaran Ö (2004) Accumulation, distribution and employment: a structural VAR approach to a Kaleckian macro model. Struct Chang Econ Dyn 15(4):421–447

Voitchovsky S (2005) Does the profile of income inequality matter for economic growth? Distinguishing between the effects of inequality in different parts of the income distribution. J Econ Growth 10(3):273–296

Voitchovsky S (2009) Inequality and economic growth. In: Salverda W, Nolan B, Smeeding TM (eds) The Oxford handbook of economic inequality. Oxford University Press, Oxford and New York, NY, pp 549–574

Chapter 10
Summary, Economic Policy Outlook, and Conclusion

10.1 Résumé

Motivated by the weak economic performances as well as the relatively high and rising income inequalities across the developed world during the past decades, secular stagnation and the distribution of income have been the defining issues of this book. With the topic of secular stagnation setting the overall framework, the aim has been, first, to provide a thorough overview of past and present stagnation debates as well as, secondly, to assess the role of income distribution in different secular stagnation hypotheses.

As a side issue of economic growth theory, secular stagnation has a long tradition in the history of economic thought, reaching from the era of classical economics to the twenty-first century. Although today stagnation is commonly referred to as an extended period of sluggish average economic growth, depending on the underlying theory there are different facets to it, particularly in terms of the causes and mechanisms at work. While it can be roughly distinguished between demand- and supply-side hypotheses, even within these two categories the theories are not homogeneous, but highlight different economic aspects.

Although most economists involved in the debates on secular stagnation refer to empirical developments to support their hypotheses, one of the most pressing questions is whether there have been actual periods of stagnation over time. In terms of empirical evidence, secular stagnation is indeed a rather difficult endeavor. First, there is no predefined trend rate of economic growth which marks the threshold between weak and adequate economic performance, implying that stagnation as such is a somewhat loose concept. Secondly, due to its long-term character, it is only after a sustained period of time, covering several business cycles, that a possible era of secular stagnation can be verified or dismissed. In the words of Terborgh (1945, p. 188), "[…] under the most favorable circumstances it would take […] years merely to confirm the existence of secular stagnation, to say nothing of identifying its causes." Hence, speaking of secular stagnation *tendencies* or the *risk* of secular stagnation is usually more appropriate than referring to secular stagnation per se.

C. Anselmann, *Secular Stagnation Theories*, Springer Studies in the History of Economic Thought, https://doi.org/10.1007/978-3-030-41087-2_10

Thirdly, policy measures or other economic shocks, such as wars, may prevent secular stagnation from actually unfolding, though the stagnation doctrine as such may still be correct. In modern history, for example, World War II possibly prevented stagnation in the United States and other advanced countries.

While economic growth has been trending downward since the 1970s, it has mainly been the weak recovery from the Great Recession that has triggered the discussion on secular stagnation in more recent times. Although it is still unclear whether a prolonged period of low economic growth is currently unfolding, secular stagnation remains a potential threat across the developed world. Despite the relatively strong economic performances in the last few years, most of the structural and long-term risk factors referred to by the economists involved in the stagnation debate still remain. Among these factors is also the unequal distribution of income, which has been rising for decades in various developed nations, but is only peripherally mentioned in most demand- and supply-side stagnation theories.

With regard to the nexus between economic growth and the distribution of income, there are usually two factions in the general public debate. While those on the political right tend to endorse Okun's (1975) trade-off between equality and efficiency, those on the political left typically support the viewpoint that a more equal distribution of income is key to prosperity and a strong economy. Both extremes, however, are only half the story. With secular stagnation having set the overall framework, this book has shown that there is no clear-cut, universal relationship between economic growth and the distribution of income, neither from a theoretical nor from an empirical perspective. The extended theoretical Steindlian model developed in Chap. 8 has illustrated that economic shocks which lower the profit share and/or reduce personal income inequality are not inevitably accompanied by a rise in the long-term rate of real capital accumulation and hence economic growth. In fact, changes in real capital accumulation in response to economic shocks do not necessarily follow a predefined direction, but depend on the type of economic shock as well as the specific economic circumstances. Similar to other demand-side stagnation hypotheses touching on the issue of income distribution, an important element in the developed model is the (Keynesian) idea of varying (marginal) propensities to consume: economic shocks which are accompanied by a redistribution of income from profits to wages and/or from the top to the bottom of the income distribution ceteris paribus raise the degree of capacity utilization in the economy, *possibly* leading to an increase in the long-term rate of real capital accumulation. While there is no a priori trade-off between a rise in both equality and economic growth, a fall in the profit share and/or a decline in personal income inequality *may* also go hand in hand with lower real capital accumulation. Recalling that it was particularly Schumpeter who, as an economist involved in the modern stagnation debate, pointed to the limits of income equality, it is in this regard that one may speak of a Schumpeterian twist in Steindlian growth models. Although being essentially a demand-determined approach, Steindl's theory allows for a more equal distribution of income to be accompanied by a rise *or* a decline in long-term economic growth. Moreover, it has been shown that changes in economic growth feed back on the distribution of income. In the extended Steindlian model developed above, ceteris paribus a rise (fall) in economic growth clearly increases (reduces) the profit share, but the impact on the personal distribution of income is ambiguous from an ex-ante perspective.

With the nexus between economic growth and the distribution of income being a priori uncertain, at times there may be a trade-off between fostering both economic growth and more equality, while at other times this trade-off may not exist. From an empirical point of view, the past decades have been characterized by a slowdown in economic performances and a rise in income inequality in numerous advanced countries. These developments suggest that there should now be sufficient room for a trend reversal in both economic advance and the distribution of income. If, for decades, a long-term slowdown in economic growth has apparently been compatible with rising income inequality, it is reasonable to assume that—in the years to come— there is potential to foster both economic growth and a more equal distribution of income. In fact, the developments since the late twentieth century may call for a reformulation of Okun's (1975) trade-off: rather than speaking of a trade-off between equality and efficiency, the empirical developments over the past decades suggest that there may currently be a *compatibility* between equality and economic growth, or—in other words—a trade-off between equality and economic stagnation.

This is not to say that a more equal distribution of income is *the* panacea for secular stagnation tendencies. As rightly noted by Mazzucato ([2013] 2014, p. 31), "[i]nequality can hurt growth but equality does not alone foster it." It is clear, for example, that attempts to boost economic performance by promoting more equality of income via the tax and transfer system have their limits, as some inequality is necessary in capitalist economies to maintain incentives to work and invest. Moreover, when thinking of the main determinants of long-term economic advance, it is not the distribution of income, but technological progress and productive investment that first come to mind. Nonetheless, however, the distribution of income is a piece in the puzzle. While it would be wrong to claim that a more equal distribution is sufficient to combat stagnation tendencies and to foster and sustain higher long-term growth, it would be equally wrong to neglect issues of distribution altogether. After having essentially been ignored by mainstream economics in the decades leading up to the financial crisis of 2008–2009, it is time to bring questions of distribution back in. While a reduction in the currently high and partly rising levels of income inequality can spur consumption demand in the economy and may thus induce higher investment spending, more equality may also stimulate economic advance by improving the sociopolitical framework. Moreover, if, for instance, triggered by well-designed spending on education which particularly benefits those at the bottom of the income hierarchy, a more equal distribution of income is also conducive to economic progress from a supply-side perspective.

With sluggish economic performances as well as high and rising income inequality having been among the economic and social challenges in major advanced countries, policy recommendations aimed at boosting economic growth and reducing income inequality have indeed been on the rise during the past years. As the nexus between economic growth and income distribution is complex and non-homogeneous, however, it is essential that policies targeted at fostering both economic growth and more equality are designed with due care.

10.2   Policy Implications and the Issue of Public Debt

10.2.1   Empirically Oriented Policy Recommendations

While some policy implications have been mentioned here and there throughout the previous chapters—particularly in the context of different secular stagnation theories and the modified Steindlian growth model—the following is a more empirically oriented compilation of policies with a focus on both economic growth and the distribution of income, including several proposals by international organizations.[1] Although policies which are expected to have a double dividend in terms of fostering economic growth and more equality are at the center of interest, from an ex-ante perspective the precise impact can be difficult to assess, as the behavioral responses of the economic actors cannot be predicted with absolute certainty. It is a balancing act, so to speak, between supporting those who are left behind and spurring incentives for firms and workers to engage in economic activity.

Of the policy options that may foster inclusive growth, in the following it is briefly referred to, first, wage policy and the role of trade unions, secondly, competition and innovation policy, thirdly, the importance of public investment in infrastructure and human capital, as well as, fourthly, tax and transfer policy reforms. While country-specific factors, such as social preferences and the institutional structure, certainly play an important role in developing appropriate policy measures, they cannot be discussed here in greater detail. The policy implications are rather to be understood as general proposals, with the actual elaboration and design varying according to country-specific circumstances.

10.2.1.1   Wage Policy and Trade Unions

In terms of the functional distribution of income, a productivity-oriented wage policy is appropriate to ensure both inclusive and sustainable long-term economic growth. Especially in the years leading up to the financial crisis of 2008–2009, in several advanced countries a decoupling of labor productivity growth from the development in labor compensation took place. As shown in Fig. 10.1 on the example of Germany, Japan, and the United States, at least between the late 1990s and the mid-2000s, labor productivity as measured by real gross value added (GVA) per working hour increased more strongly than average hourly real labor compensation, resulting in a decline in labor income shares. Although labor productivity growth has outpaced the development in labor compensation in other advanced nations as well, diverging developments across countries provoked shifts in relative international competitiveness prior to the Great Recession, especially within the euro area. In fact, the resulting

---

[1] While the proposed policy measures refer to the current economic environment in major advanced countries, they also conform to Steindl's ([1952] 1976) stagnation approach in the sense that they may foster economic growth and a more equal distribution of income along Steindlian lines. On Steindlian-oriented policy implications, see also Guger (2018, pp. 193–198).

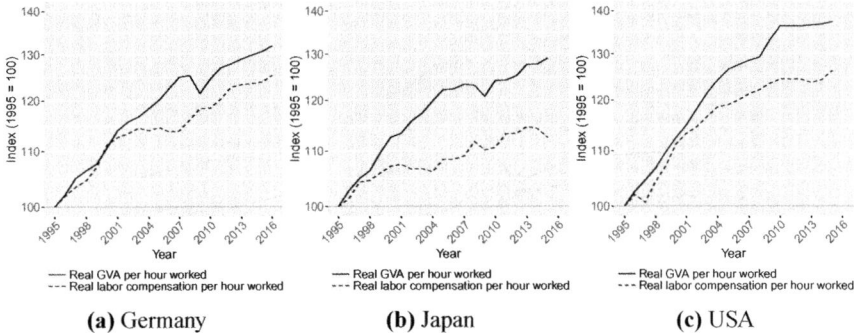

Fig. 10.1   Real gross value added (GVA) per hour worked and real average labor compensation per hour worked, 1995–2016. *Source* Author's illustrations, based on data from the OECD (2018b, pp. 85–86). See Appendix A for detailed data sources and further notes

external imbalances are among the causes of the financial and sovereign debt crisis. While there has indeed been some trend reversal in more recent years, productivity-oriented wage policy remains an important tool to ensure that labor productivity and domestic (consumption) demand can grow in parallel. With economic activity being less dependent on debt-financed domestic demand or on exports of goods and services to other countries, long-term economic growth can be more sustainable.[2]

Strengthening collective bargaining coverage can facilitate a productivity-oriented wage policy. Although there has been some stabilization in more recent years, Fig. 10.2 shows that trade union density is at relatively low levels in major advanced countries. While union density has been comparatively stable in Spain and Canada over the past decades, in all other economies considered it has declined considerably since the late 1970s and early 1980s. In Germany, for instance, roughly 35% of the workforce belonged to a trade union in 1980, whereas by 2016 this share had declined to only 17%. Similarly, in the United States trade union density fell from more than 20% in 1980 to approximately ten percent in 2017. In the context of a productivity-oriented wage policy, reversing these trends to some degree may both reduce income inequality and be beneficial to long-term economic growth.

As data by the OECD (2018c) show, particularly in Germany, Japan, the United Kingdom, and the United States, the decline in trade union density has been accompanied by a fall in collective bargaining coverage over the past decades. In Germany, the share of "[...] employees covered by collective agreements [...]" (OECD 2018c) declined from 85% in 1980 to 56% in 2016. Similarly, in the United Kingdom collective bargaining coverage amounted to roughly 69% in 1980, but by 2016 had fallen to approximately 26%. Aside from increasing trade union density, strengthening collective bargaining coverage can be an important policy tool to ensure that wage

---

[2]Correcting the existing external imbalances within the euro area would require hourly labor compensation in Germany, for instance, to temporarily rise faster than labor productivity. While such developments can be expected to be accompanied by growth distortions, future long-term economic growth would be more sustainable.

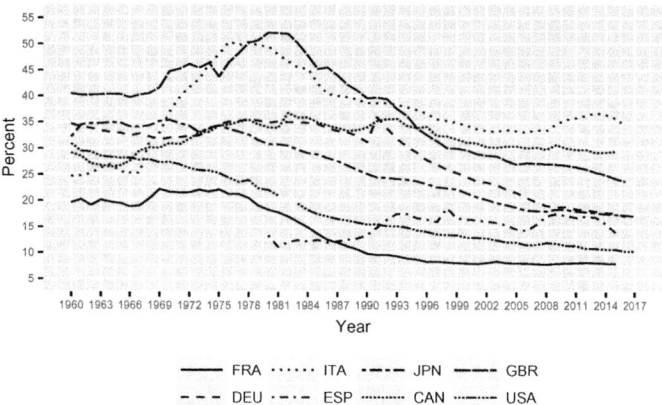

Fig. 10.2 Trade union density, 1960–2017. *Source* Author's illustration, based on data from the OECD (2018d). See Appendix A for detailed data sources and further notes

developments keep pace with labor productivity growth. This should also include a stronger representation of precarious workers, including part-time labor and employees on fixed-term contracts.

10.2.1.2   Competition and Innovation Policy

In contrast to the decline in trade union density, several empirical studies find that—on the other side of the bargaining table—industry concentration and firms' market power—two key themes in Steindl's ([1952] 1976) original secular stagnation theory—have increased over the past decades. Foster and McChesney (2012, p. 72), for instance, argue that "[...] economic concentration [in the United States] is greater today than it has ever been, and it has increased sharply over the past two decades." As measured by the share of total sales and, to a lesser extent, total employment accruing to the four and 20 largest firms in a sector, Autor et al. (2017a) similarly suggest that industry concentration in the United States has risen since the 1980s across different economic sectors. Likewise, for publicly traded firms in 33 developed countries, Díez et al. (2018) conclude that firms' market power—such as indicated by both the mark-ups of prices over marginal costs and industry concentration—has increased.

To explain this rise in industry concentration, Autor et al. (2017a, p. 184) suggest a mechanism that can be characterized as a contemporary variation of Steindl's ([1952] 1976) viewpoint on market concentration. Over the past decades, Autor et al. (2017a, pp. 180–181, 184, b, p. 2) hold, so-called *winner-take-most markets* have become increasingly important. In these markets, the most innovative and most productive firms—so-called *superstar firms*—are able to capture high market shares, also by driving smaller and less productive competitors out of the market. Over time, "[...] leading firms [thus turn] into dominating superstars [...]" Autor et al.

(2017b, pp. 25–26). Globalization as well as new information and communication technologies, it is argued, have likely contributed to the development of *winner-take-most markets*. With the rising importance of network effects, the expansion of information-intensive goods and services, as well as highly transparent product markets that allow consumers to easily compare product prices and qualities on a worldwide scale, the market dominance of the largest and most productive firms—particularly in high-tech industries—has increased over time. In fact, firms such as Amazon, Apple, Facebook, Google, and Microsoft—commonly known as *The Big Five* tech companies—are typically named among the most prominent examples (Autor et al. 2017a, pp. 180–181, 2017b, pp. 2, 23).[3] In addition to this innovation- and productivity-driven process of industry concentration, however, Autor et al. (2017a, p. 184) suggest that an increase in market entry barriers, fostered by more efficient lobbying by the largest and most dominant firms in the market, has possibly also played a role over the past decades.

In the context of Steindl's ([1952] 1976) stagnation theory, it has been outlined that a rise in market concentration can have adverse effects on the distribution of income. Indeed, Autor et al. (2017a, p. 184, b, pp. 11–15) find a negative nexus between changes in industry concentration and labor income shares. They conclude that, during the past decades, labor income shares have particularly declined in industries that have been characterized by a strong rise in concentration. Based on firm-level data, Díez et al. (2018, p. 16) similarly suggest labor income shares to be lower in firms with strong market power. To explain these results, Autor et al. (2017a, p. 180, 2017b, pp. 4–5) note that, on the one hand, large and dominating firms can enforce higher mark-ups over their marginal costs—a typical Kaleckian–Steindlian line of reasoning. Moreover, assuming that overhead labor costs are constant (or do not rise as fast as output), the share of overhead labor costs in a firm's value added declines with a rise in market dominance. While both developments hamper the labor income share in firms that grow larger and become more dominant, it is also the labor income share in the economy as a whole which is adversely affected by a rise in industry concentration. When "[...] more market share [is allocated] to superstar firms [...]," Autor et al. (2017b, p. 4) note, "[...] the aggregate labor share will fall from a reallocation effect between firms as the weight of the economy shifts to the larger, low labor share firms."[4]

---

[3] While Autor et al. (2017a, b) use the term *winner-take-most markets* to describe the dominance of a few firms in the product market, Frank and Cook ([1995] 2010) refer to *winner-take-all markets* to describe the dominance of a few individuals in the labor market. Both concepts, however, are similar. As noted by Frank and Cook ([1995] 2010), in the labor market new information and communication technologies have led to the rise of global superstars, particularly in sports and entertainment. For example, the best-performing athletes, actors, or musicians typically enjoy a global fanbase and benefit from high salaries and advertising revenues. Their close competitors, on the other hand, whose performance is only slightly inferior, are usually much less popular and receive much lower incomes.

[4] With a rise in industry concentration, both the functional and personal distribution of income also appear to be increasingly affected by pay differences among firms as well as changing employment practices. Large employers with a high degree of market dominance typically pay higher wages than smaller and less dominant firms. Yet, large and market-dominating firms are also increasingly out-

Following Steindl ([1952] 1976, [1989] 1990, pp. 168–169, 177–178), a rise in industry concentration may not only adversely affect the distribution of income, but—by hampering real capital accumulation and innovation—also the long-term rate of economic growth. For the United States, the empirical analysis of Autor et al. (2017a, p. 184, 2017b, pp. 23–25) shows that technological change, such as measured by the growth in total factor productivity or patents per worker, has been most rapid in industries that have experienced the strongest rise in concentration over the past decades. While this finding suggests that, ceteris paribus, industry concentration fosters economic advance, it is possible that these developments are only transient phenomena. In the early stages of industry concentration, firms may indeed "[...] gain high market shares by legitimately competing on the merits of their innovations or superior efficiency. Once they have gained a commanding position, however, they [may] use their market power to erect various barriers to entry to protect their position [...]" Autor et al. (2017b, p. 26). In fact, this line of reasoning complies with the inverted U relationship between competition and innovation suggested by Aghion et al. (2002, 2005). At a high degree of competition, they hold, a decline in competition is accompanied by an increase in innovation, as firms which are (technologically) lagging behind now have stronger incentives to invest in innovation. At low levels of competition, however, a further decline in competition reduces innovation, as the additional profit expected from investment in innovation is only small. The empirical analysis of Díez et al. (2018, pp. 12–14) supports this hypothesis, finding that both firms' real capital investment and expenditure on R&D are non-linearly linked to their market power. At low levels of market concentration, a rise in firms' market power is accompanied by an increase in firms' investment in real capital accumulation and innovation. At high levels of concentration, however, a further increase in market power is associated with a decline in real capital investment and R&D expenditure.

In light of the possible adverse impact of market concentration on the distribution of income, innovation, and economic growth, fostering competition among firms and boosting innovation are important policy tools to promote inclusive growth. Adequate policy measures include the enhancement of antitrust enforcement, product market reforms that reduce market entry barriers, as well as the support of start-ups and small- and medium-sized enterprises, such as by improving access to finance for these firms IMF (2018a, p. 16). At the same time, intellectual property laws should be sufficiently flexible to tackle the potential trade-off between the protection of firms' intellectual property and product market competition (see also Acemoglu and Akcigit 2012). Moreover, to counteract data monopolies among tech giants, the rules that regulate the access, use, and ownership of data should be enhanced and reformed to enable a more equal sharing of "[...] the benefits from exploiting these data and facilitating competition (while respecting other conditions such as privacy rights) [...]" Guellec and Paunov (2017, p. 35).

---

sourcing non-core (and often low-skill) tasks to lower paying firms and service providers, including temporary employment agencies. This "[...] fissuring of the workplace [...]," as Autor et al. (2017b, p. 26) call it with reference to Weil (2014), adversely impacts the labor income share and personal (labor) income inequality. See also Weil (2011).

While—in light of the suggested inverted U relationship between competition and innovation—the effect of an increase in competition among firms on innovation is uncertain from an ex-ante perspective, the government itself is one of the most important drivers of innovation and, as such, can impact the innovation process. As outlined by Mazzucato ([2013] 2014, p. 1), the state is not just an economic actor that operates in the background, intervenes during recessions, and cures market failures, but it also "[...] play[s] an *entrepreneurial* role in society [...]." Particularly with respect to innovation, the government "[...] is a key partner of the private sector [...]," she notes, "[...] and often a more daring one, willing to take the risks that business won't. [...] It *takes on* risks, shaping and creating new markets" (Mazzucato [2013] 2014, p. 5). There are numerous examples of state-funded research projects, in fact, that led to the development of new technologies and high-tech products. Apple, for instance, is among the most well-known companies that has benefited greatly from public spending on innovation, with many of its products emanating from government-funded technologies (Mazzucato [2013] 2014, pp. 87–112).[5] Product innovations, in turn, are key from an economic perspective, as they foster both supply and demand, combining the Schumpeterian and Keynesian line of reasoning.

While public investment in R&D is vital for long-term economic growth, over the past decades there have been declining trends in some advanced countries. As shown in Fig. 10.3a, public R&D expenditure as a percentage of GDP has been relatively constant in Italy, Japan, and Canada over the past years, but it has fallen in France, the United Kingdom, the United States, and—at least until the mid-2000s—Germany. In the United States, public gross domestic R&D spending as a share of GDP declined from more than one percent in 1981 to less than 0.7% in 2016. In recent years, across the eight countries and regions considered, government-financed R&D expenditure has hovered between approximately 0.5% and 0.8% of GDP. Although, as revealed by Fig. 10.3b, the sum total of public and private gross domestic spending on R&D as a percentage of GDP has generally increased during the past decades, it is the private sector which has contributed most to these rising trends. In fact, in all countries considered the percentage of R&D expenditure financed by the government has fallen. In the United States, for example, the state funded more than 47% of total R&D spending in 1981, whereas by 2016 this share had declined to roughly 25% (OECD 2018f). Particularly with regard to basic research, which is conducted in large part by public research institutes and universities, these declining trends are unfavorable (see also OECD 2014, p. 194).

While public spending on R&D is important to foster long-term economic growth, Atkinson (2015, p. 120) reminded of the possible effects on income distribution, warning that "[...] the government should explicitly consider the distributional implications [...]" of its innovation spending. Although this does not mean that growth-

---

[5]Referring to the post-Second World War period, (Steindl [1979] 1990, p. 120) also mentioned the importance of state-funded research. He held, "Although R & D expenditure (of which half to two-thirds was financed by governments in the US, Britain, and France) was to a great extent for military and space research, its indirect effects on the pace of technological progress in general, and therefore on private investment activity, were considerable. The aftermath of wartime innovation itself provided a great stimulus to industry in the post-war period."

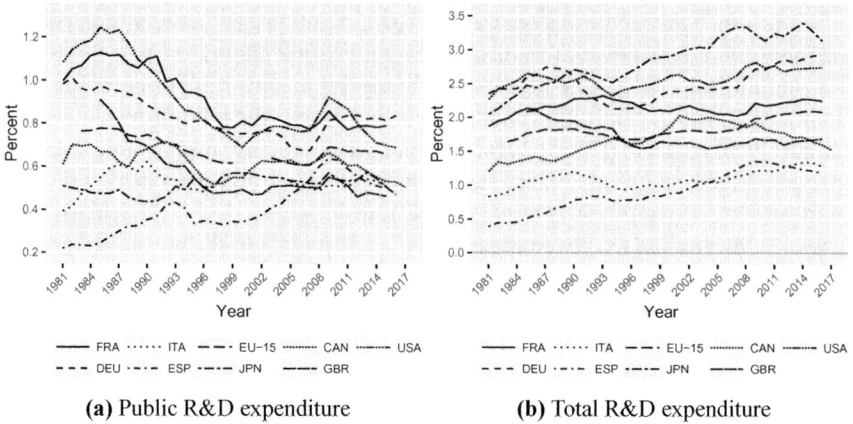

(a) Public R&D expenditure   **(b)** Total R&D expenditure

Fig. 10.3 Government-financed and total gross domestic expenditure on R&D as a share of GDP, 1981–2017. *Source* Author's illustrations, based on data from the OECD (2018d). See Appendix A for detailed data sources and further notes

enhancing innovations which may be detrimental to the distribution of income should not be initiated at all, the distributional component should be taken into account. As an example, Atkinson (2015, p. 120) mentioned government-supported research on autonomous driving in the United States. Initially aimed at providing driverless vehicles to the military, progress along these lines can be expected to also impact the private economy in the long run, such as by rendering bus and taxi drivers moot. To prevent adverse effects on employment and the distribution of income, the government must take appropriate action, for example, by investing in redeployment measures for those occupational groups most severely affected.

10.2.1.3   Public Investment in Infrastructure and Human Capital

There has not only been a decline in government-financed R&D expenditure as a share of GDP over the past decades, but relative public real capital investment as a whole has been trending downward in major advanced economies.[6] Although there are country-specific fluctuations, as shown in Fig. 10.4a in all nations and regions considered general government gross fixed capital formation as a share of GDP was lower in 2017 than at the beginning of the period investigated. Particularly in Germany, the United Kingdom, and the United States, public investment in real

---

[6]R&D expenditure, which has been referred to in the previous section, has been classified as gross fixed capital formation since the revision of national accounting standards around the years 2013/2014. In the United States, for example, the revision was implemented as part of the change in the System of National Accounts (SNA) from version SNA 1993 to version SNA 2008. In Europe, the revision was implemented as part of the change in the European System of Accounts (ESA) from version ESA 1995 to version ESA 2010. See also Dunn et al. (2014), the European Union (2014), Ravets and Mazzi (2014, p. 2–3), van de Ven (2015).

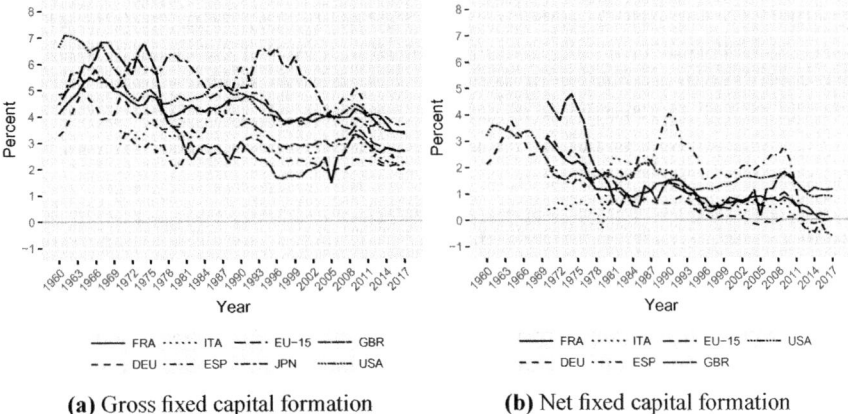

(a) Gross fixed capital formation   **(b)** Net fixed capital formation

Fig. 10.4   General government gross and net fixed capital formation as a share of GDP, 1960–2017.
Source Author's calculations and illustrations, based on data from the European Commission (2018).
See Appendix A for detailed data sources and further notes

capital as a percentage of GDP has been following a downward trend since the early
1960s. In Germany, for example, between 1960 and 2017 government gross fixed
capital formation as a share of GDP declined by one percentage point, from roughly
3.2% to 2.2%. When capital depreciation is deducted, public capital investment is
apparently even lower and, in some nations, in negative territory. In fact, Fig. 10.4b
reveals that, as a share of GDP, in 2017 public net fixed capital formation—which is
equal to public gross fixed capital formation less capital depreciation—was negative
in Italy and Spain and close to zero percent in France, Germany, and the EU-15.

While public investment is an important component of aggregate demand, it is also
key from a supply-side perspective, especially with regard to productivity growth.
For instance, government fixed capital formation includes public investment in physical and digital infrastructure, such as roads, public transportation, dwellings, and
broadband networks. As outlined by Aschauer (1989b, pp. 193–198), public investment in such "core" infrastructure is vital for the efficient functioning of an economy. Most important, he notes that "[...] public capital—particularly infrastructure
capital such as streets and highways, sewers, water systems, airports, and the like—
[...] is likely to bear a complementary relationship to private capital [...]" Aschauer
(1989a, p. 174). In other words, by raising the marginal productivity of private capital, government investment in infrastructure is able to crowd in private real capital
investment (Aschauer 1989a, pp. 171, 174; see also Aschauer 1988, 1990). Hence,
a well-developed public infrastructure system is not only beneficial in itself, but
it can also be assumed to attract private business and thus to spur private investment.[7] To foster long-term economic growth, it is therefore necessary to reverse the
downward trend in government real capital investment as a share of GDP that has

---

[7]Similar to Aschauer (1989a), Hansen (1940, p. 3546) and Steindl ([1985d] 1990, p. 238) also
referred to the stimulating impact of public investment on private investment.

occurred over the past decades (see also Hagemann et al. 2016, pp. 220–221). In fact, fiscal investment is not just important from a growth perspective, but it can also contribute to a reduction in inequality. For example, inclusive growth may be fostered by well-targeted public investment in affordable housing construction, local public transportation, or public schools, particularly in low-income neighborhoods and structurally weak regions.

While government investment in physical infrastructure is essential to a stable and productive economy, particularly with regard to human capital it is also public spending on in-kind services which is vital. With regard to education, for instance, public investment in physical infrastructure, such as school buildings, must be accompanied by well-designed educational concepts and services. As outlined by the OECD (2017a), there are still substantial gaps in educational performances among individuals from different parental backgrounds, with adults who grew up at the bottom of the socioeconomic hierarchy performing less well than their peers who were born into families of higher socioeconomic status. To boost inclusive growth and to counteract the cementation of inequality across generations, it is essential to provide more support to children and students in the lower parts of the income (and wealth) distribution. Appropriate policy measures reach from affordable early childhood education programs to lowering the financial burden of higher education, such as by granting well-targeted scholarships to students of low-income parents (Prettner 2018, p. 176). Moreover, to adequately handle the changing skill requirements coming along with technological progress, it is important to foster adult education programs and lifelong learning, allowing those who are most adversely affected by technological advance to stay in the labor market and increase their chances of employability (Geiger et al. 2018, p. 71).

In addition to public spending on education, it is also the provision of public health care services that is necessary for inclusive growth. While a healthy workforce is more productive and can thus spur economic growth, physical and mental health are also prerequisites to employment and to earning a decent income. In many advanced countries, however, there is a positive nexus between socioeconomic inequality and health inequality. For example, those with a higher level of education tend to have a higher life expectancy. Moreover, when asked for their health status, individuals at the lower end of the income distribution typically report inferior health conditions than those at the top of the income hierarchy. Differences in lifestyle habits and working conditions as well as unequal access to adequate health care services are suggested to play a role here (OECD 2017b, pp. 50–51, 62–63). Appropriate policies to tackle these issues include the expansion of health insurance coverage in countries without compulsory health insurance systems, most notably the United States, as well as the prevention of a further divergence of medical services within two-tier health care systems.

10.2.1.4 Tax and Transfer Policy

While tax and transfer policies are among the most important fiscal tools to change the distribution of income, they also rank among the most controversial political interventions, as an inadequate design can have distortive effects on the incentives to invest, innovate, and work. It is in this context, in particular, that a possible equality-efficiency trade-off—such as referred to by Okun (1975)—comes to the fore. Various tax and transfer policies which are equivalent in terms of their impact on income inequality may indeed have very different effects on economic growth—an argument in line with the theoretical Steindlian model developed in Chap. 8, which illustrated that the nexus between income distribution and economic growth depends on the specific economic shock.

Although tax and transfer policies are highly country-specific, particularly in the years leading up to the financial crisis of 2008–2009 the degree of income redistribution declined in most OECD countries, suggesting that there may be room for policy adjustments to counteract the currently high and partly rising income inequalities (Causa and Hermansen 2017, pp. 29–39; OECD 2018g, pp. 70–72). Public transfers, for instance, could be better targeted at those most in need, especially with regard to children in low-income households (IMF 2017, p. 26; Atkinson 2015, pp. 212–218). In terms of tax policy, on the other hand, Akgun et al. (2017) and the OECD (2018g), p. 74 note that changes in the tax mix may be key to foster both long-term economic growth and a more equal distribution of income. To support inclusive growth, the overall tax structure should be as little distortive as possible, but sufficiently progressive to tackle income inequality.

Taking a look at the composition of total tax revenue in selected advanced economies in Fig. 10.5a reveals that, in 2015, direct taxes—i.e., corporate and personal income taxes as well as payroll taxes—accounted for roughly 64% of tax revenue in the United States, about half of tax revenue in Germany, Japan, and Canada, and somewhat less than 50% of tax revenue in all other nations considered (OECD 2010b, p. 28). With corporate and personal income taxes being ranked as the most distortive taxes (OECD 2010b, p. 10), reductions in top marginal income tax rates over the past decades have typically been justified by their alleged positive impact on economic performance.[8] It is true that tax cuts can boost long-term economic growth by fostering incentives to work and invest, and it is in this context that the OECD (2011a, pp. 364–365) is rather skeptical of tax rate increases at the top of the distribution. "[...] [I]ncreasing marginal tax rates on high income individuals [...]," the OECD (2011a, pp. 364–365) assumes, "[...] would reduce their taxable income substantially, and so may collect little or no extra revenue which could be redistributed to people on lower incomes." Referring to Germany, von Weizsäcker (2016, p. 385)

---

[8]On the development of top marginal personal income tax rates in major advanced countries, see Fig. 1.5a (Sect. 1.1.2.2). On the development of top marginal corporate income tax rates, see OECD (2018a, e). As part of the *Tax Cuts and Jobs Act*, in recent times the US-federal government reduced the top marginal personal income tax rate from 39.6% to 37% and the top marginal corporate income tax rate from 35% to 21%. Effective as of 2018, spurring economic growth has been named among the goals of these tax policy measures (The White House 2018; Gale et al. 2018, pp. 2, 5).

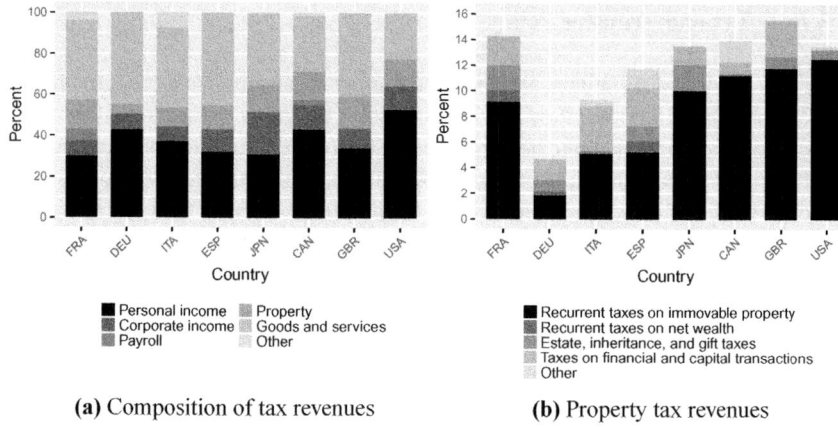

(a) Composition of tax revenues   (b) Property tax revenues

Fig. 10.5 Composition of tax revenues as a share of total tax revenue and property tax revenues as a share of total tax revenue, 2015. *Source* Author's calculations and illustrations, based on data from the OECD (2018d). See Appendix A for detailed data sources and further notes

is similarly averse to raising top tax rates, fearing unfavorable economic effects, particularly on small- and medium-sized firms, which are a key pillar of the German economy.

Although the behavioral reactions of top income recipients to tax increases cannot be assessed here, it is fair to say that the reductions in top marginal income tax rates over the past decades have not been accompanied by strong economic performances. If anything, economic growth across the developed world has proven to be unsustainable and non-inclusive. With stagnant or even declining real incomes for major parts of the population and rising real incomes at the upper end of the income hierarchy, the ability to pay has certainly become more concentrated at the top of the income pyramid. Several economists, in fact, have argued in favor of increases in top marginal income tax rates to counteract the high and rising income inequalities across developed nations. Referring to the United Kingdom, Atkinson (2015, pp. 185–188, 290), for instance, advocated a rise in the top marginal personal income tax rate up to 65% on annual taxable income exceeding 200,000 pounds sterling, supposing that similar adjustments could be made in other countries as well. For the United States, various estimates of the revenue-maximizing top tax rate include roughly 73% as suggested by Diamond and Saez (2011, pp. 171–172) and Saez et al. (2012, p. 9), as well as a range from 57% to 83% as proposed by Piketty (2014, pp. 233, 267–269) (see also Osberg, 2015, p. 10 for an overview).[9] While the optimal top marginal income tax rate depends on various (country-specific) factors, in light of the developments over the past decades it can be assumed that there is indeed "[...]

---

[9]While Piketty et al. (2014) refer to the top marginal personal income tax rate, Diamond and Saez (2011) and Saez et al. (2012) refer to the top marginal tax rate, considering "[...] the maximum federal and average state income, Medicare, and typical sales tax rates in the United States [...]" Saez et al. (2012, p. 8).

untapped revenue potential at the top of the income distribution [...]" (IMF 2013, p. 35) which could be used to redistribute income from the upper to the lower parts of the income hierarchy.

That being said, however, there are other tax policies which may additionally be considered to make the overall tax structure more progressive. To increase tax progression at the upper end of the distribution, it may be appropriate to eliminate tax expenditures that mainly benefit those at the top of the distribution, such as preferential tax rates on goods and services predominantly consumed by the affluent, or tax deductibility of certain expenses, including mortgage interest.[10] The overall tax base could additionally be broadened by aligning the tax rates on different types of income, which could also reduce tax planning activities (OECD 2011a, pp. 365–367, 2018g, pp. 74–75). In the United States, for example, the top marginal tax rate on ordinary income—i.e., all income except for long-term capital gains—amounts to 37%, being almost twice as high as the top marginal tax rate on long-term capital gains, which stands at only 20% (Internal Revenue Service 2018).[11]

To increase labor force participation rates and foster employment, the tax burden on earned income for those at the bottom of the income hierarchy should be reduced. As proposed by the OECD (2018g, pp. 107–108), for instance, after-tax earnings for low-income households could be raised by introducing or expanding earned-income tax credits and lowering social security contributions. Moreover, especially female labor force participation rates may be increased by abolishing tax practices that discriminate against second earners.

As shown in Fig. 10.5a, b, in 2015 property taxes accounted for only a relatively small share of total tax revenue in most of the eight countries considered, reaching from 4.7% in Germany to 15.6% in the United Kingdom. Reforms that increase the progressivity of particular types of property taxes may thus be appropriate to foster inclusive growth (see also IMF 2017, p. 26).[12] Among the property taxes targeted are especially recurrent taxes on immovable property as well as inheritance and gift taxes, as they are assumed to be among the least distortive taxes (OECD 2018g, p. 75, 2018h, pp. 22–23; see also Atkinson 2015, pp. 192–199). Figure 10.5b shows

---

[10]Tax expenditures are provisions that allow for tax relief. See also OECD (2010a, p. 3). As defined by the *Congressional Budget and Impoundment Act of 1974*, in the United States "[t]he term 'tax expenditures' means those revenue losses [of the government] attributable to provisions of the Federal tax laws which allow a special exclusion, exemption, or deduction from gross income or which provide a special credit, a preferential rate of tax, or a deferral of tax liability [...]" (United States Congress 1974, Sect. 3).

[11]Long-term capital gains are capital gains on assets that were held "[...] for more than one year [...]" (Internal Revenue Service 2018).

[12]Although property taxes, i.e., taxes on wealth stocks, are targeted at the distribution of wealth and not at the distribution of income, the distributions of wealth and income are intertwined. It is true that those at the top of the income hierarchy do not necessarily find themselves at the top of the wealth hierarchy. As compared to those in the lower parts of the income distribution, however, those in the upper strata of the income hierarchy typically save a larger share of their income and can thus accumulate more wealth over time. Similarly, those at the top of the wealth distribution may benefit from substantial property income, including rents, interests, and dividends. Income and wealth inequality thus reinforce each other, implying that taxes which change the distribution of wealth tend to also change the distribution of income (and vice versa) in the same direction.

that, although recurrent taxes on immovable property account for the largest share of property tax revenues in most countries considered, their share of total tax revenue is relatively small, hovering between 1.9% in Germany and 12.6% in the United States. Estate, inheritance, and gift tax revenues are almost negligible in the overall tax mix. On average, across OECD countries their share in total tax revenue has even declined over the past five decades (OECD 2018h, pp. 22–23). Eventually, a tax mix which relies more heavily on property taxes may be appropriate to foster both economic growth and a more equal distribution of income and wealth.

10.2.2   Public Debt as an Impediment to Fiscal Intervention? Lessons from the Stagnation Debates and Beyond

To spur inclusive growth, policy action is vital, and it is first and foremost the government that is in demand here. Although tax reforms and other policy measures intended to foster economic growth can generate additional government revenue, it is unrealistic to assume that reasonable fiscal endeavors could go without any deficit-financed government spending. Social support for those at the bottom of the income hierarchy and, particularly, the suggested increases in public expenditure on innovation, infrastructure, education, and health care are likely to be at least partly dependent on public deficit spending.

Despite the need for fiscal intervention, however, austerity policies have become a common characteristic in major advanced economies, especially with a view to reducing public debt-to-GDP ratios. From a long-term perspective, Fig. 10.6 reveals that government debt as a percentage of GDP has been fluctuating considerably over the past decades, increasing strongly during both world wars as well as the Great Depression. Although public debt-to-GDP ratios declined in the aftermath of the Second World War, starting in the 1970s and 1980s they have been rising again. In 2017, government debt as a share of GDP amounted to more than 130% in Italy and more than 100% in the United States. Japan's public debt even exceeded 235% of GDP and was thus higher than during World War II. Germany, on the other hand, had the lowest public debt-to-GDP ratio among the eight countries considered, amounting to roughly 64% in 2017.

Those arguing in favor of downsizing government debt do not only point to Greece and other countries that were hit by sovereign debt crises in the wake of the Great Recession and are still struggling today, but they also refer to empirical studies that emphasize the alleged burden of public debt from a more general perspective. During the past years, the debate on the adverse effects of government debt has been especially stirred up by the much-criticized analysis of Reinhart and Rogoff (2010), finding that, on average, public debt-to-GDP ratios above 90% are accompanied by lower economic growth. With reference to such "debt limits," economists and international organizations have been determined to outline consolidation scenarios that would stabilize or reduce public debt-to-GDP ratios (OECD 2011a, pp. 239, 246–247;

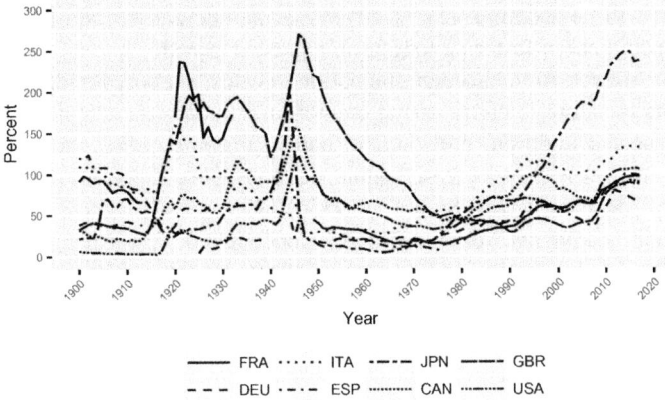

Fig. 10.6 Government debt as a percentage of GDP, 1900–2017. *Source* Author's illustration, based on data from the IMF (2018b, c). See Appendix A for detailed data sources and further notes

Merola and Sutherland 2012). After the financial crisis of 2008–2009, governments in most OECD countries have indeed planned to improve their fiscal positions. On average, two-thirds of this consolidation have been intended to come from public spending cuts, including reductions in government expenditure on welfare, health care, pensions, and infrastructure (OECD 2011b, p. 17, 22–23, 31–32, 45–49, 2012).

It is beyond question that high public debt-to-GDP ratios *can* have unfavorable effects on the economy. For example, a rise in government debt may lead to an increase in interest rates, narrowing the scope for further fiscal action. Moreover, inflationary pressures can evolve, particularly when—at full utilization of productive resources—fiscal net borrowing is accompanied by a rise in money supply. High levels of public debt as a percentage of GDP may also evoke uncertainty and lead to adverse expectations, such as with regard to future tax increases or fiscal solvency.[13] Despite these possible adverse effects, however, public net borrowing remains an important way of financing government spending. In fact, with secular stagnation tendencies lurking, the aim to simultaneously reduce government debt in various countries is likely to be counterproductive. Although it is typically aimed for growth-friendly consolidation strategies, the collective effort to bring down public debt-to-

---

[13]With regard to fiscal solvency, however, public indebtedness in foreign currency is much more problematic than government debt as such. Moreover, it is the indebtedness of a country as a whole—including both the public and the private sectors—toward the rest of the world which must be considered here. In fact, strongly negative net international investment positions can be more critical than government debt. Japan's risk of default, for example, is typically perceived to be low, as the public debt is mainly held by domestic investors and is denominated in national currency (Ministry of Finance Japan 2018a, p. 24). Additionally, Japan's net international investment position is positive, implying that the country as a whole is a net creditor toward the rest of the world (Ministry of Finance Japan 2018b).

GDP ratios will be accompanied by adverse economic and social effects, being a serious impediment to fostering long-term inclusive growth.

Bringing it back to the secular stagnation debates, support for deficit-financed government spending is particularly common in demand-side stagnation theories. In the Keynesian tradition, both Steindl and—somewhat more, though—Hansen pointed to the necessity of increased public net borrowing in periods of unemployed resources.[14] Most important, Steindl ([1985c] 1990, p. 213) rightly noted that the budget deficit is a passive variable which is dependent on government revenue and hence on the overall state of the economy. Efforts to reduce the public deficit by cutting fiscal spending thus can be counterproductive, especially in times of under-utilized productive resources. He held,

> While it is possible, in principle, to control the volume of government spending, the same is not true for the budget deficit. [...] In consequence, attempts at reducing the budget deficit by retrenchment are mostly doomed to failure. [...] On certain conditions it would seem, therefore, that the best way to combat a deficit is to increase spending (Steindl [1983] 1990, pp. 217–218).

At the same time, however, both Steindl ([1985c] 1990, p. 214) and Hansen (1943) were well aware of the potential unfavorable impact of public deficit spending. Hansen (1941, p. 117), in particular, had two major concerns about government debt and loan-financed public expenditure. First, in line with the so-called *transfer approach*, he referred to possible adverse effects of government debt on the distribution of income (and wealth). Assuming that government bonds are disproportionately held by the affluent, while taxes used to finance public interest payments are also levied on those in the middle and lower parts of the income hierarchy, public debt may be accompanied by a transfer of income toward the top of the distribution, leading to a more unequal distribution of income (and wealth). Yet, although Hansen (1938, p. 326, FN 8, 1941, p. 179) supported this line of reasoning in some of his writings, in other essays he was much more critical of this viewpoint—and rightly so (Hansen 1943, p. 265).[15] Secondly, Hansen (1939, p. 14, 1943) pointed to the threat of inflationary pressure that may result from unduly government deficit spending when the economy approaches full employment. Hence, when the output gap closes over time, as is likely to happen in the long run—either via adverse hysteresis effects

---

[14] As has been outlined in Sect. 4.2.1, Schumpeter also advocated government intervention in severe depressions.

[15] As has been particularly outlined in the relevant German-language literature of the late 1960s and 1970s, the transfer approach is indeed inadequate to capture the distributional impact of government debt. Especially Andel (1969) and Gandenberger (1970) pointed out that, although there may be a transfer of income via public interest payments and taxes used to finance these interest payments, public deficit spending also serves a purpose. For instance, if the government engages in net borrowing to raise its expenditure on education or to stimulate employment in a recession, it may be particularly those private households at the bottom of the income hierarchy that benefit from this public spending. Hence, the potentially adverse distributional impact via public interest payments and taxes may be more than offset when loan-financed government spending disproportionately benefits those in the lower parts of the distribution. For further elaboration on the transfer approach and its shortcomings, see also Lang and Koch (1980, pp. 130–136) and Anselmann and Krämer (2014).

or due to actual output catching up with potential output—public deficit spending should be undertaken with care.

While Hansen (1940, p. 3548) was averse to "[...] irresponsible public spending [...]," he made clear that the role of the government goes beyond intervening in periods of underutilized resources. Although deficit-financed public spending is particularly vital in times of underemployment, the importance of the government does not vanish once full employment has been reached. In fact, the public sector also has a developmental role to play, as Hansen (1943, pp. 262–263) called it, being necessary to foster both economic and social development. For long-term economic growth, *productive* public expenditure spurring aggregate demand and supply is particularly vital. Moreover, productive spending can in general be loan-financed, because its stimulating impact on productivity creates the economic resources necessary to pay for the public debt service. As also noted by Hansen (1940, p. 3548), productive public expenditure does not only include government investment in real capital—such as infrastructure—but also government spending on human capital, including education and health care. When fiscal expenditure of these kinds is cut back because public authorities pursue austerity policies to reduce government debt-to-GDP ratios, adverse long-run social and economic effects are to be expected.[16]

Particularly in times of historically low interest rates, deficit-financed government expenditure comes at a small cost. With real interest rates on ten-year government bonds having been negative or close to zero percent in most major advanced economies over the past years (see Fig. 3.6d, Sect. 3.3.1), it is reasonable to assume that the real rate of return on productive fiscal spending has been exceeding public borrowing costs. Moreover, as is commonly known, the development of a country's public debt-to-GDP ratio also depends on the interest-rate-growth-differential, i.e., the difference between the (average) nominal interest charge on government debt and the nominal GDP growth rate. If the interest-rate-growth-differential is negative, the government can afford a primary deficit to stabilize or even reduce the public debt-to-GDP ratio.[17] As shown in Fig. 10.7, in most countries considered the interest-

---

[16]Referring to productive expenditure, Domar (1944, p. 820), a student of Hansen at Harvard University, held, "[...] [T]he term 'investment expenditures' may be misleading, because it is too closely associated with steel and concrete. [...] If healthier people are more productive, expenditures on public health satisfy these requirements. The same holds true for expenditures on education, research, flood control, resource development and so on." Similarly, with reference to the German economist Carl Dietzel, Stettner (1948, p. 298)—another student of Hansen—outlined that productive public expenditure is a multifaceted term. Whether a particular type of government spending is productive or not also depends on the specific economic circumstances. "The most 'productive' pattern of expenditure [...]," he held, "[...] is that which contributes most toward the achievement of the economic, political, and social aims of a particular time and a particular country. This interpretation of 'productive public expenditures' has an important bearing on the question of their financing. [...] [B]oth immaterial and material capital have an equal claim on loan financing. [...] [T]he significant fact in public investment is the increase in productivity of the economy as a whole. This increase is the economic source of the interest payment on the loan." (Stettner 1948, p. 298).

[17]The primary balance is defined as public revenue (excluding public net borrowing) less public expenditure (excluding interest payments). A negative (positive) primary balance is called a primary deficit (surplus).

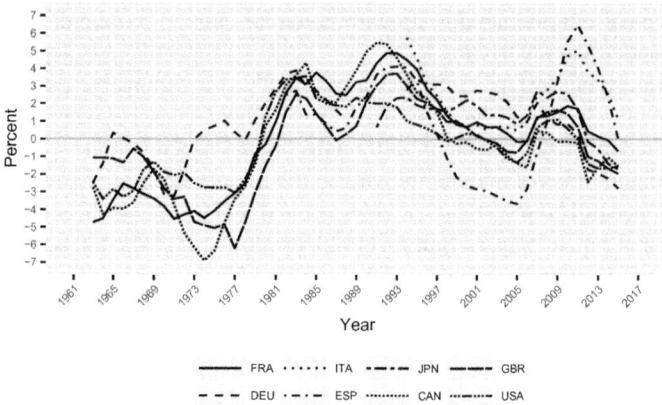

Fig. 10.7 Interest-rate-growth-differentials (centered five-year moving averages), 1961–2017. *Source* Author's calculations and illustration, based on data from the OECD (2018d) and the European Commission (2018). See Appendix A for detailed data sources and further notes

rate-growth-differential—calculated here as the difference between nominal interest rates on ten-year government bonds and nominal GDP growth—has declined for several years, reaching negative territory in the aftermath of the financial crisis of 2008–2009.[18] In Germany, for example, the average interest-rate-growth-differential has been as low as −2.7% in recent times. While the public debt-to-GDP ratio thus could have been stabilized or even reduced by running primary deficits, the German government has had primary surpluses since 2011 (European Central Bank 2018). The aim of pursuing a balanced budget ("black zero") at the federal level has fostered this trend in recent years. Moreover, the deficit limits imposed by the so-called *debt brake*, which will become fully effective in 2020, are unlikely to change this trend in the years to come.

Particularly with regard to economic stabilization in Europe, a more extensive fiscal policy stance in Germany would be advisable. In the German economic debate, von Weizsäcker (2015, pp. 154–155) has repeatedly outlined that—to boost economic activity in the euro area and prevent stagnation—the German government should engage in higher deficit-financed spending in the currently low interest rate environment. Similar proposals, though, have also been made with regard to other advanced countries. Referring to the United States, Summers (2018), for example, is concerned that necessary policy actions "[...] will not be taken because of [...] misguided concern about excessive government debt [...]." Likewise, Krugman (2018) notes that, under the current circumstances, "[...] there is [...] less reason [...] to

---

[18] As rightly outlined by Barrett (2018, p. 4), this empirical finding is not at odds with Piketty (2014, pp. 350–358), who concludes that the average rate of return on capital has been mostly exceeding the rate of economic growth throughout history. While Piketty (2014, pp. 350–358) refers to the average rate of return on capital, the calculations underlying Fig. 10.7 are based on (risk-free) ten-year government bond yields.

obsess over government debt." Although he is aware that high public debt-to-GDP ratios can be problematic, especially when interest rates are high, with a negative interest-rate-growth-differential "[...] debt is way [...] down on the list of things to worry about [...]," particularly as compared to "[...] crumbling infrastructure, which should be fixed without worrying about paying as you go." While—especially with regard to the current economic situation in the United States—both Summers and Krugman could pay somewhat more attention to the potential risk of inflationary pressure, from the perspective of long-term economic development their claim for more government investment must be endorsed.

Among the contemporary secular stagnationists, Gordon (2016, pp. 629–630) stands out with his rather averse stance toward government debt. Although he does not condemn public debt as such, he seems to be convinced that tax increases or fiscal spending cuts are inevitable to stabilize or reduce public debt-to-GDP ratios, with possible unfavorable effects on disposable incomes and the distribution of income (and wealth). This position, however, puts the cart before the horse. To stabilize or lower public debt-to-GDP ratios in a sustainable way, it is first and foremost economic growth which is key. Collective fiscal cutbacks, though, cannot be expected to be conducive to long-term economic and social development.

Fostering inclusive growth requires adequate and proactive fiscal policy, which governments across the developed world have been hesitant to implement. As has been outlined throughout this book, from both a theoretical and empirical perspective there is no a priori trade-off between a more equal distribution of income and higher long-term economic growth. There are win-win policies that can spur both economic growth and a more equal distribution of income. To what extent individual policy measures are capable of raising economic growth and lowering income inequality is a question on its own, but—as has been outlined above—there are actions that can be taken. To use similar words as Steindl ([1952] 1976, p. xvii, [1979] 1990, p. 119), the current trends of stagnation tendencies and a highly unequal distribution of income are not necessarily an inevitable fate. With governments being preoccupied with reducing public debt-to-GDP ratios by austerity policies, they are also the result of inadequate and deferred political action.

References

Acemoglu D, Akcigit U (2012) Intellectual property rights policy, competition and innovation. J Eur Econ Assoc 10(1):1–42

Aghion P, Bloom N, Blundell R, Griffith R, Howitt P (2002) Competition and innovation: an inverted U relationship. NBER Working Paper No. 9269. National Bureau of Economic Research, Cambridge, MA. http://www.nber.org/papers/w9269. Accessed 23 Sept 2018

Aghion P, Bloom N, Blundell R, Griffith R, Howitt P (2005) Competition and innovation: an inverted-U relationship. Q J Econ 120(2):701–728

Akgun O, Cournède B, Fournier J (2017) The effects of the tax mix on inequality and growth. OECD Economics Department Working Papers No. 1447. OECD Publishing, Paris. http://dx. doi.org/10.1787/c57eaa14-en. Accessed 16 Sept 2018

Andel N (1969) Zur These von den unsozialen Verteilungswirkungen öffentlicher Schulden. Pub Financ 24(1):69–79

Anselmann C, Krämer H (2014) Ungleichheit als Preis für Vollbeschäftigung? Einige Anmerkungen zu den intragenerativen Verteilungswirkungen der Staatsverschuldung. In: Dullien S, Hein E, Truger A (eds) Macroeconomics, Metropolis-Verlag, Marburg, Development and Economic Policies, pp 101–119

Aschauer DA (1988) Is government spending stimulative? Federal Reserve Bank of Chicago Staff Memoranda SM 88-3. Federal Reserve Bank of Chicago, Chicago, IL. https://fraser.stlouisfed. org/files/docs/historical/frbchi/workingpapers/frbchi_workingpaper_1988-03.pdf. Accessed 28 Sept 2016

Aschauer DA (1989a) Does public capital crowd out private capital? J Monet Econ 24(2):171–188

Aschauer DA (1989b) Is public expenditure productive? J Monet Econ 23(2):177–200

Aschauer DA (1990) Why is infrastructure important? In: Munnell AH (ed) Is there a shortfall in public capital investment? Proceedings of a conference held at Harwich Port, Massachusetts, in June 1990. Conference Series No. 34, Federal Reserve Bank of Boston, Boston, MA, pp 21–50

Atkinson AB (2015) Inequality: what can be done?. Harvard University Press, Cambridge, MA, and London

Autor D, Dorn D, Katz LF, Patterson C, Van Reenen J (2017a) Concentrating on the fall of the labor share. Am Econ Rev 107(5):180–185

Autor D, Dorn D, Katz LF, Patterson C, Van Reenen J (2017b) The fall of the labor share and the rise of superstar firms. NBER Working Paper No. 23396. National Bureau of Economic Research, Cambridge, MA. http://www.nber.org/papers/w23396. Accessed 21 Sept 2018

Barrett P (2018) Interest-growth differentials and debt limits in advanced economies. IMF Working Paper WP/18/82. International Monetary Fund, Washington, DC. https://www.imf.org/~/media/ Files/Publications/WP/2018/wp1882.pdf. Accessed 14 Oct 2018

Causa O, Hermansen M (2017) Income redistribution through taxes and transfers across OECD countries. OECD Economics Department Working Papers No. 1453. OECD Publishing, Paris. http://dx.doi.org/10.1787/bc7569c6-en. Accessed 16 Sept 2018

Diamond P, Saez E (2011) The case for a progressive tax: from basic research to policy recommendations. J Econ Perspect 25(4):165–190

Díez FJ, Leigh D, Tambunlertchai S (2018) Global market power and its macroeconomic implications. IMF Working Paper WP/18/137. International Monetary Fund, Washington, DC. https:// www.imf.org/~/media/Files/Publications/WP/2018/wp18137. Accessed 20 Sept 2018

Domar ED (1944) The "burden of the debt" and the national income. Am Econ Rev 34(4):798–827

Dunn M, Akritidis L, Biedma L (2014) The impact of ESA 2010 on key indicators of the national accounts in Europe. Eurostat Review on National Accounts and Macroeconomic Indicators special issue on the implementation of the European system of accounts (ESA 2010) 2/2014:7–27

European Central Bank (2018) ECB statistical data warehouse. Government primary deficit(-) or surplus(+) (as % of GDP), Germany. European Central Bank, Frankfurt am Main. http://sdw.ecb. europa.eu/. Data as of 24 Oct 2018. Accessed 04 Dec 2018

European Commission (2018) Annual macro-economic database of the European Commission's Directorate General for Economic and Financial Affairs (AMECO database). European Commission, Brussels. http://ec.europa.eu/economy_finance/ameco/user/serie/SelectSerie.cfm. Data as of November 08, 2018. Last accessed 26 Nov 2018

European Union (2014) Manual on measuring research and development in ESA 2010. 2014 edition. Eurostat manuals and guidelines. Publications Office of the European Union, Luxembourg. https://ec.europa.eu/eurostat/en/web/products-manuals-and-guidelines/-/ KS-GQ-14-004. Accessed 02 Oct 2018

Foster JB, McChesney RW (2012) The endless crisis: how monopoly-finance capital produces stagnation and upheaval from the USA to China. Monthly Review Press, New York, NY

Frank RH, Cook PJ, ([1995], (2010) The winner-take-all society: why the few at the top get so much more than the rest of us. Virgin Books, London

Gale WG, Gelfond H, Krupkin A, Mazur MJ, Toder E (2018) Effects of the tax cuts and jobs act: a preliminary analysis. Urban-Brookings Tax Policy Center, Washington, DC. https://www.brookings.edu/wp-content/uploads/2018/06/ES_20180608_tcja_summary_paper_final.pdf. Accessed 25 Nov 2018

Gandenberger O (1970) Öffentlicher Kredit und Einkommensverteilung. Finanzarchiv 29(1):1–16

Geiger N, Prettner K, Schwarzer JA (2018) Die Auswirkungen der Automatisierung auf Wachstum, Beschäftigung und Ungleichheit. Perspektiven der Wirtschaftspolitik 19(2):59–77

Gordon RJ (2016) The rise and fall of American growth. The U.S. standard of living since the Civil War. Princeton University Press, Princeton, NJ

Guellec D, Paunov C (2017) Digital innovation and the distribution of income. NBER Working Paper No. 23987. National Bureau of Economic Research, Cambridge, MA. http://www.nber.org/papers/w23987. Accessed 23 Sept 2018

Guger A (2018) Josef Steindl und die neue Stagnationsdiskussion: 'Kapitalismus ohne Arbeitslosigkeit'? In: Hagemann H, Kromphardt J, Marterbauer M (eds) Keynes. Metropolis-Verlag, Marburg, Geld und Finanzen, pp 173–201

Hagemann H, Erber G, Geiger N, Schwarzer J, Zwiessler O (2016) Wachstums- und Investitionsdynamik in Deutschland. Metropolis-Verlag, Marburg

Hansen AH (1938) Full recovery or stagnation? W. W, Norton, New York, NY

Hansen AH (1939) Economic progress and declining population growth. Am Econ Rev 29(1):1–15

Hansen AH (1940) Testimony of Alvin Harvey Hansen, Professor of Political Economy, Harvard University, Cambridge, MA. In: Temporary National Economic Committee (ed) Investigation of concentration of economic power. Hearings before the Temporary National Economic Committee Congress of the United States. Part 9: Savings and investment, United States Government Printing Office, Washington, DC, pp 3495–3520, 3538–3559, 3837–3859

Hansen AH (1941) Fiscal policy and business cycles. W. W, Norton, New York, NY

Hansen AH (1943) Federal debt policy. In: Proceedings of the annual conference on taxation under the auspices of the national tax association 36(November 20–22):256–268

IMF (2013) Taxing times. Fiscal monitor, October 2013. International Monetary Fund, Washington, DC. https://www.imf.org/en/Publications/FM/Issues/2016/12/31/Taxing-Times. Accessed 02 Oct 2018

IMF (2017) Fostering inclusive growth: G-20 leaders' summit, July 7–8, 2017, Hamburg, Germany. International Monetary Fund, Washington, DC. https://www.imf.org/external/np/g20/pdf/2017/062617.pdf. Accessed 17 Sept 2018

IMF (2018a) Future of work: measurement and policy challenges. Group of Twenty. International Monetary Fund, Washington, DC. https://www.imf.org/external/np/g20/pdf/2018/071818a.pdf. Accessed 26 Sept 2018

IMF (2018b) Historical public debt database. International Monetary Fund, Washington, DC. http://www.imf.org/external/datamapper/datasets/DEBT. Accessed 29 Nov 2018

IMF (2018c) World economic outlook database, October 2018. International Monetary Fund, Washington, DC. https://www.imf.org/external/pubs/ft/weo/2018/02/weodata/index.aspx. Accessed 29 Nov 2018

Internal Revenue Service (2018) Tax topics: topic no. 409 capital gains and losses. Internal Revenue Service, Washington, DC. https://www.irs.gov/taxtopics/tc409. Accessed 16 Sept 2018

Krugman P (2018) On the debt non-spiral. The New York Times. The opinion pages. The conscience of a liberal, September 11, 2018. https://www.nytimes.com/2018/09/11/opinion/on-the-debt-non-spiral.html. Accessed 14 Oct 2018

Lang E, Koch WAS (1980) Staatsverschuldung — Staatsbankrott? Physica-Verlag, Würzburg

Mazzucato M ([2013] 2014) The entrepreneurial state: debunking public vs. private sector myths. Anthem Press, London and New York, NY

Merola R, Sutherland D (2012) Fiscal consolidation: part 3. Long-run projections and fiscal gap calculations. OECD Economics Department Working Papers No. 934. OECD Publishing, Paris. http://dx.doi.org/10.1787/5k9h28p42pf1-en. Accessed 06 Oct 2018

Ministry of Finance Japan (2018a) Debt management report 2018: The government debt management and the state of public debts. Ministry of Finance Japan, Tokyo. https://www.mof.go.jp/english/jgbs/publication/debt_management_report/2018/esaimu2018.pdf. Accessed 08 Oct 2018

Ministry of Finance Japan (2018b) International investment position of Japan (end of 2017). Ministry of Finance Japan, Tokyo. https://www.mof.go.jp/english/international_policy/reference/iip/e2017.htm. Accessed 08 Oct 2018

OECD (2010a) Tax expenditures in OECD countries. OECD Publishing, Paris

OECD (2010b) Tax policy reform and economic growth. OECD Publishing, Paris

OECD (2011a) Divided we stand: why inequality keeps rising. OECD Publishing, Paris

OECD (2011b) Fiscal consolidation: targets, plans and measures. OECD J Budg 11(2):15–67

OECD (2012) Restoring public finances, 2012 update. OECD Publishing, Paris

OECD (2014) OECD science, technology and industry outlook 2014. OECD Publishing, Paris

OECD (2017a) Educational opportunity for all: overcoming inequality throughout the life course. OECD Publishing, Paris

OECD (2017b) Health at a glance 2017: OECD indicators. OECD Publishing, Paris

OECD (2018a) Corporate income tax rates: Historical table II.1 (1981–1999). OECD, Paris. http://www.oecd.org/tax/tax-policy/tax-database.htm#C_CorporateCapital. Accessed 18 Sept 2018

OECD (2018b) OECD compendium of productivity indicators 2018. OECD Publishing, Paris

OECD (2018c) OECD.Stat. Labour. Trade unions and collective bargaining. Variable collective bargaining coverage. OECD, Paris. http://stats.oecd.org/. Data as of 27 Apr 2018. Accessed 02 Dec 2018

OECD (2018d) OECD.Stat. OECD, Paris. http://stats.oecd.org/. Last accessed 04 Dec 2018

OECD (2018g) Opportunities for all: a framework for policy action on inclusive growth. OECD Publishing, Paris

OECD (2018f) OECD.Stat. Science, technology and patents. Science and technology indicators. Main science and technology indicators (MSTI Database). Variable percentage of GERD financed by government. OECD, Paris. http://stats.oecd.org/. Data as of 24 Jul 2018. Accessed 02 Dec 2018

OECD (2018h) The role and design of net wealth taxes in the OECD. OECD Publishing, Paris, OECD tax policy studies

Okun AM (1975) Equality and efficiency: the big tradeoff. The Brookings Institution, Washington, DC

Osberg L (2015) How much income tax could Canada's top 1% pay? Canadian Centre for Policy Alternatives, Ottawa. https://www.policyalternatives.ca/publications/reports/how-much-income-tax-could-canadas-top-1-pay. Accessed 20 Sept 2018

Piketty T (2014) Capital in the twenty-first century. Harvard University Press, Cambridge, MA, and London

Piketty T, Saez E, Stantcheva S (2014) Optimal taxation of top labor incomes: a tale of three elasticities. Am Econ J Econ Policy 6(1):230–271

Prettner K (2018) Verteilungsforschung: Entwicklung der Ungleichheit, sozioökonomische Konsequenzen und politische Handlungsspielräume. In: Hagemann H, Kollmer-von Oheimb-Loup G (eds) Universität Hohenheim 1818–2018: Festschrift zum 200jährigen Jubiläum. Verlag Eugen Ulmer, Stuttgart, pp 168–179

Ravets C, Mazzi GL (2014) A new European system of national and regional accounts (ESA 2010). European Commission, Luxembourg. http://www.oecd.org/sdd/na/ESA%202010.pdf. Accessed 01 Oct 2018

Reinhart CM, Rogoff KS (2010) Growth in a time of debt. Am Econ Rev 100(2):573–578

Saez E, Slemrod J, Giertz SH (2012) The elasticity of taxable income with respect to marginal tax rates: a critical review. J Econ Lit 50(1):3–50

Steindl J ([1952] (1976) Maturity and stagnation in American capitalism (with a new introduction by the author). Monthly Review Press, New York, NY, and London

Steindl J ([1979] (1990) Stagnation theory and stagnation policy. In: Steindl J (ed) Economic papers 1941–88. St. Martin's Press, New York, NY, pp 107–126

Steindl J ([1983] (1990) The control of the economy. In: Steindl J (ed) Economic Papers 1941–88. St. Martin's Press, New York, NY, pp 216–229

Steindl J ([1985c] (1990) Saving and debt. In: Steindl J (ed) Economic papers 1941–88. St. Martin's Press, New York, NY, pp 208–215

Steindl J ([1985d] (1990) Structural problems in the crisis. In: Steindl J (ed) Economic papers 1941–88. St. Martin's Press, New York, NY, pp 230–238

Steindl J ([1989] (1990) From stagnation in the 30s to slow growth in the 70s. In: Steindl J (ed) Economic papers 1941–88. St. Martin's Press, New York, NY, pp 166–179

Stettner WF (1948) Carl Dietzel, public expenditures and the public debt. In: Metzler LA, Domar ED, Duesenberry JS, Higgins B, Goodwin RM, Samuelson PA, Wright DM, Alexander SS, Perloff HS, Musgrave RA, Lerner AP, Stettner WF, Brown EC, Bishop RL, Dunlop JT, Bourneuf A (eds) Income, employment and public policy: essays in honor of Alvin H. Hansen, W. W. Norton, New York, NY, pp 276–299

Summers LH (2018) Is the world ready for the next downturn? A symposium of views. Summers responds. Int Econ Summer 2018:21

Terborgh G (1945) The bogey of economic maturity. Machinery and Allied Products Institute, Chicago, IL

The White House (2018) The tax cuts and jobs act: the most significant federal tax reform enacted in the United States in decades. The White House, Washington, DC. https://www.whitehouse.gov/wp-content/uploads/2018/02/WH_CuttingTaxesForAmericanWorkers_Feb2018.pdf. Accessed 19 Sept 2018

United States Congress (1974) Congressional budget and impoundment control act of 1974. U.S. Government Printing Office, Washington, DC

van de Ven P (2015) New standards for compiling national accounts: what's the impact on GDP and other macro-economic indicators? OECD statistics brief, February 2015, no. 20. OECD, Paris. http://www.oecd.org/sdd/na/new-standards-for-compiling-national-accounts-SNA2008-OECDSB20.pdf. Accessed 01 Oct 2018

von Weizsäcker CC (2015) How to avoid secular stagnation? In: Nowotny E, Stessl S (eds) Long-term perspectives for economic growth. In: Proceedings of the 43rd OeNB economic conference 2015. Oesterreichische Nationalbank, Vienna, pp 146–157

von Weizsäcker CC (2016) Europas Mitte. Perspektiven der Wirtschaftspolitik 17(4):383–392

Weil D (2011) Enforcing labour standards in fissured workplaces: the US experience. Econ Lab Relat Rev 22(2):33–54

Weil D (2014) The fissured workplace: why work became so bad for so many and what can be done to improve it. Harvard University Press, Cambridge, MA

Appendix A
Figure Sources and Notes in Detail

Figure 1.1a

Author's calculations and illustration. Data are from the European Commission (2018), variable *Gross domestic product at 2010 reference levels (OVGD)*. Data as of November 08, 2018. Database accessed on November 26, 2018. Real GDP growth rates shown are centered five-year moving averages from 1960 to 2017. Breaks in the data series for DEU and the EA-12 are due to German reunification. Data refer to unified Germany from 1991 onward and to West Germany prior to this year.

Figure 1.1b

Author's calculations and illustration. Data are from the European Commission (2018), variable *Gross domestic product at 2010 reference levels per head of population (RVGDP)*. Data as of November 08, 2018. Database accessed on November 26, 2018. Real GDP per capita growth rates shown are centered five-year moving averages from 1960 to 2017. Breaks in the data series for DEU and the EA-12 are due to German reunification. Data refer to unified Germany from 1991 onward and to West Germany prior to this year.

Figure 1.2a

Author's illustration. Periods considered: FRA, DEU, and GBR: 1900s–2010. ITA, JPN, and CAN: 1970s–2010. The USA: 1930s–2010. Data refer to decennial averages from 1900–1909, 1920–1929, 1930–1939, 1940–1949, 1950–1959, 1960–1969, 1970–1979, 1980–1989, 1990–1999, and 2000–2009. For FRA, DEU, and GBR, the values for the 1910s refer to 1910–1913. For all other countries, the values for the 1910s refer to 1910–1919. For DEU, the values for 2010 refer to the average of the years 2010 and 2011. For all other countries, the values for 2010 refer to 2010 only. Data are from Piketty and Zucman (2014a, b), Online Data Appendix, *Appendix Tables*, section *Structure of National Income, Table A50: Labor shares 1810–2010 (% of factor-price national income) (decennial estimates)*. Data as of June 13, 2013. Database accessed on November 06, 2018.

Figure 1.2b

Author's calculations and illustration. Periods considered: FRA, DEU, ITA, JPN, and the USA: 1960–2017. ESP: 1995–2017. CAN: 1970–2016. GBR: 1993–2017. Data for DEU refer to unified Germany from 1991 onward and to West Germany prior to this year. Data for FRA, DEU, ITA, ESP, JPN (1980–2017), CAN, GBR, and the USA are from the European Commission (2018), variables *National income at current prices (UVNN)*, *Taxes linked to imports and production minus subsidies: total economy (UTVN)*, *Compensation of employees: total economy (UWCD)*, *Employment, persons: total economy (National accounts) (NETN)*, and *Employees, persons: total economy (National accounts) (NWTN)*. Data as of November 08, 2018. Database accessed on November 26, 2018. Data for JPN (1960–1979) are from the European Commission (2017), the same variables as aforementioned. Data as of May 11, 2017. Database accessed on September 19, 2017. Figure 1.2b shows the adjusted labor share, which, following Krämer (2011, pp. 9–12), is calculated by multiplying the wage share by the ratio of employed persons (variable *NETN*) to employees (variable *NWTN*). The wage share is equal to the compensation of employees (variable *UWCD*) divided by national income at factor cost (i.e., national income at current prices (variable *UVNN*) less taxes linked to imports and production minus subsidies (variable *UTVN*)). The average labor income share (bold line) is the average of the eight national labor income shares, with the labor income share of each country weighted by net national income at factor cost based on purchasing power parity. Data for purchasing power parity are from the European Commission (2018), variable *GDP purchasing power parities, national currency units per PPS (KNP)*. Data as of November 08, 2018. Database accessed on November 26, 2018.

Figure 1.3a

Author's illustration. Periods considered: FRA: 1900–2013. DEU and JPN: 1900–2010. ITA: 1974–2009. ESP: 1981–2012. CAN: 1920–2010. GBR: 1918–2012. The USA: 1913–2015. Data for DEU refer to Prussia (including capital gains) before 1919, to the German Reich (including capital gains) from 1925 to 1938, to West Germany from 1950 to 1990, and to unified Germany thereafter. Data are from Atkinson et al. (2017b), variable *Top Income Shares, Share of top 1% in gross income*. Data as of May 2017. Database accessed on November 29, 2018. Gross income is pre-tax income "[...] before deduction of allowable outgoings" (Atkinson et al. 2017a, p. 4). Unless specified differently, data exclude capital gains. Data for FRA refer to individuals, but income is assumed to be equally split between individuals of a couple. Data for DEU and the USA refer to tax units as defined by the national tax laws at any given point in time (Alvaredo et al. 2016, p. 9). Data for ITA, JPN, and CAN refer to individuals. Data for ESP refer to tax units before 1990 and to individuals thereafter. Data for GBR refer to tax units before 1991 and to individuals thereafter.

Figure 1.3b

Author's calculations and illustration. Periods considered: FRA: 1978–2010. DEU: 1973–2015. ITA: 1987–2014. ESP: 1990–2013. CAN: 1998–2013. GBR: 1969–2013. The USA: 1974–2016. Data for DEU refer to unified Germany from 1991 onward and to West Germany prior to this year. Data are from the Luxembourg Income Study (2018a), variables *hil, hic, hitp, hpopwgt,* and *nhhmem.* Database accessed on November 08, 2018. Data refer to household equivalized market income, calculated by dividing household market income by the square root of the number of household members. Household market income is the sum of household labor income, household capital income, and household private transfers. Households where market income is missing are excluded. Data are not top- and bottom-coded. The Palma index is originally defined as the share of income received by the top ten percent of the income hierarchy divided by the share of income received by the bottom 40% of the income hierarchy. As the bottom 40% include four times as many people as the top ten percent, in Fig. 1.3b the Palma index as originally defined has been multiplied by four to allow for a more intuitive interpretation. For example, in 2013, in the United Kingdom the average household equivalized market income of the top ten percent of the income hierarchy was approximately 25.5 times as high as the average household equivalized market income of the bottom 40% of the income hierarchy.

Figure 1.4a, b
Author's calculations and illustrations. Data are from the Luxembourg Income Study (2018a), variables *hil, hic, hitp, hpopwgt,* and *nhhmem.* Database accessed on November 08, 2018. The figures show the average annual growth rates of average real household equivalized market income in different percentiles (10–11, 11–12, 12–13, ..., 97–98, 98–99, 99–100) of the income hierarchy. Household equivalized market income is calculated by dividing household market income by the square root of the number of household members. Household market income is the sum of household labor income, household capital income, and household private transfers. Households where market income is missing are excluded. Data are not top- and bottom-coded. Nominal values have been deflated by the LIS PPPs of the Luxembourg Income Study (2018b). Data as of April 04, 2018. Database accessed on November 08, 2018. Due to strong variations at the bottom of the income hierarchy, with average real household equivalized market incomes varying between strongly negative and slightly positive values, the figures do not show the income growth rates in the first ten income groups (0–1, 1–2, 2–3, ..., 7–8, 8–9, 9–10). Data for Germany refer to West Germany in 1978 and to unified Germany in 2015.

Figure 1.5a
Author's illustration. Periods considered: FRA: 1900–2013. DEU and the USA: 1900–2018. JPN: 1900–2005. CAN: 1920–2017. GBR: 1900–2017. Data for FRA, DEU (1900–2013), GBR (1900–2013), and the USA (1900–2013) are from Piketty (2014b), *The Set of Spreadsheet Files, Chapter 14 Tables Figures,* Table *TS14.1: Top Marginal Income Tax Rate in Rich Countries, 1900–2013.* Data as of March 2014. Database accessed on December 03, 2018. See also Piketty (2014a, p. 499). For FRA, "[...] [t]he top marginal income tax rate [...] includes general income tax supplements (i.e. surtaxes applying to all incomes above a certain level) and the CSG (a proportional income tax applying to all incomes), but excludes all other taxes (e.g. corporate taxes) and social contributions (except the CSG)" (Piketty 2014b,

Table TS14.1). For DEU (1900–2013) and the USA (1900–2013), "[...] [t]he top marginal income tax rate [...] includes general income tax supplements (i.e. surtaxes applying to all incomes above a certain level), but excludes all other taxes and social contributions [...]" (Piketty 2014b, Table TS14.1). Data for DEU (2014–2017), GBR (2014–2017), and the USA (2014–2017) are from the OECD (2018c), dataset *Public Sector, Taxation and Market Regulation, Taxation, Tax Database, Table I.1. Central government personal income tax rates and thresholds*, variable *Marginal rate*. Data as of April 26, 2018. Database accessed on November 06, 2018. Data for DEU (2018) are from the Bundesministerium der Finanzen (2018), variable *Grenzbelastung*. Data for the USA (2018) are from Gale et al. (2018, p. 2). Data for JPN (1900–1949) are from Moriguchi and Saez (2005, pp. 65–66), Table *2: Income Tax and Marginal Tax Rate in Japan, 1887–2002*, column *Top Marginal Tax Rate*. Data for JPN (1950–2005) are from Moriguchi and Saez (2010, pp. 162–163), Table *3C.3: Wage Income Tax and Marginal Tax Rates in Japan*, column *Top Marginal Tax Rate (%)*. The tax rate "[...] refers to the highest statutory marginal tax rate net of employment income deductions [...]" (Moriguchi and Saez 2010, p. 163). Data for CAN (1920–2000) are from Saez and Veall (2007, pp. 301–302), Table *6F.1 Marginal Income Tax Rates in Canada, 1920–2000*, column *Top*. "Marginal tax rates are calculated assuming exemptions for a married person with two dependents and average deductions by gross income level. Before 1972, only the federal income tax rates are reported as these included provincial income tax rates in most cases. Beginning in 1972, the reported income rates include then-applicable provincial income tax, assuming residence in the largest province, Ontario. All rates include applicable surtaxes and credits" (Saez and Veall 2007, p. 302). Data for CAN (2001–2017) are from the OECD (2018c), dataset *Public Sector, Taxation and Market Regulation, Taxation, Tax Database, Table I.7. Top statutory personal income tax rate and top marginal tax rates for employees*, variable *Top marginal tax rates: Personal income tax*. Data as of April 26, 2018. Database accessed on November 08, 2018.

Figure 1.5b
Author's illustration. Data are from Piketty et al. (2017), *Appendix Tables II: Distributional Series*, series *Post-Tax Income (Matching National Income), Table C1: Shares of Total Post-Tax Income*. Data as of November 09, 2017. Database accessed on November 30, 2018. See also Piketty et al. (2018, p. 587). Data refer to "[...] all U.S. residents aged 20 and above. Incomes within married couples are equally split. Pretax national income is factor income after the operation of the public and private pension systems and unemployment insurance system. Posttax national income is defined as pretax income minus all taxes plus all government transfers and spending (federal, state, and local)" (Piketty et al. 2018, p. 587).

Figure 1.6a
Author's calculations and illustration. Periods considered: FRA: 1978–2010. DEU: 1973–2015. ITA: 1986–2014. ESP: 1980–2013. JPN: 1985–2012. CAN: 1971–2013. GBR: 1969–2013. The USA: 1974–2016. Data for DEU refer to unified Germany from 1991 onward and to West Germany prior to this year. Data for FRA, DEU, ITA, ESP, CAN, GBR, and the USA are from the Luxembourg Income Study (2018a),

variables *dhi*, *hpopwgt*, and *nhhmem*. Database accessed on November 08, 2018. Data refer to household equivalized disposable income, calculated by dividing household disposable income by the square root of the number of household members. Household disposable income is the sum of household labor income, household capital income, and household transfer income less income taxes and social security contributions paid by households. Households where disposable income is missing or zero are excluded. Data are top-coded at ten times the median of household non-equivalized disposable income and bottom-coded at 1% of the mean of household equivalized disposable income. Data for JPN are from the OECD (2018c), dataset *Social Protection and Well-being, Income Distribution and Poverty*, variables *Mean disposable income (current prices)* and *Median disposable income (current prices)*. Data as of June 2018. Database accessed on November 06, 2018.

Figure 1.6b
Author's calculations and illustration. Periods considered: FRA: 1978–2010. DEU: 1973–2015. ITA: 1986–2014. ESP: 1980–2013. JPN: 1985–2012. CAN: 1971–2013. GBR: 1969–2013. The USA: 1974–2016. Data for DEU refer to unified Germany from 1991 onward and to West Germany prior to this year. Data for FRA, DEU, ITA, ESP, CAN, GBR, and the USA are from the Luxembourg Income Study (2018a), variables *dhi*, *hpopwgt*, and *nhhmem*. Database accessed on November 08, 2018. Data refer to household equivalized disposable income, calculated by dividing household disposable income by the square root of the number of household members. Household disposable income is the sum of household labor income, household capital income, and household transfer income less income taxes and social security contributions paid by households. Households where disposable income is missing or zero are excluded. Data are top-coded at ten times the median of household non-equivalized disposable income and bottom-coded at 1% of the mean of household equivalized disposable income. Data for JPN are from the OECD (2018c), dataset *Social Protection and Well-being, Income Distribution and Poverty*, variable *Palma ratio*. Data as of June 2018. Database accessed on November 06, 2018. The Palma index is originally defined as the share of income received by the top ten percent of the income hierarchy divided by the share of income received by the bottom 40% of the income hierarchy. As the bottom 40% include four times as many people as the top ten percent, in Fig. 1.6b the Palma index as originally defined has been multiplied by four to allow for a more intuitive interpretation. For example, in 2015, in Germany the average household equivalized disposable income of the top ten percent of the income hierarchy was approximately 4.2 times as high as the average household equivalized disposable income of the bottom 40% of the income hierarchy.

Figure 1.7a, b
Author's calculations and illustrations. Data are from the Luxembourg Income Study (2018a), variables *dhi*, *hpopwgt*, and *nhhmem*. Database accessed on November 08, 2018. The figures show the average annual growth rates of average real household equivalized disposable income in different percentiles (0–1, 1–2, 2–3, ..., 97–98, 98–99, 99–100) of the income hierarchy. Household equivalized disposable income is calculated by dividing household disposable income by the square root of the number

of household members. Household disposable income is the sum of household labor income, household capital income, and household transfer income less income taxes and social security contributions paid by households. Households where disposable income is missing or zero are excluded. Data are top-coded at ten times the median of household non-equivalized disposable income and bottom-coded at 1% of the mean of household equivalized disposable income. Data for Germany refer to West Germany in 1978 and to unified Germany in 2015. Nominal values have been deflated by the LIS PPPs of the Luxembourg Income Study (2018b). Data as of April 04, 2018. Database accessed on November 08, 2018.

Figure 3.1
Author's illustration. Data are from the Federal Reserve Bank of St. Louis (2018), variable *National Population (POPH)*, units *Change from Year Ago, Annual, Not Seasonally Adjusted* and *Percent Change, Annual, Not Seasonally Adjusted*. Data as of November 18, 2015. Database accessed on December 04, 2018.

Figure 3.2a
Author's illustration. Periods considered: Actual real GNP: 1909–1959. Potential real GNP: 1909–1960. Data are from Knowles and Warden Jr. (1960, p. 37), variables *Actual gross national product in 1954 dollars* and *Potential gross national product in 1954 dollars*. Data for 1959 and 1960 are preliminary estimates.

Figure 3.2b
Author's illustration. Data are from the U.S. Bureau of the Census (1975, p. 135), series *D 85–86. Unemployment: 1890 to 1970*. Data shown refer to civilian unemployment as a percentage of the civilian labor force. From 1909 to 1947, data refer to persons 14 years old and over. After 1947, data refer to persons 16 years old and over.

Figure 3.4a
Author's illustration. Data are from the European Commission (2018), variable *Unemployment, Percentage of active population (ZUTN)*. Data as of November 08, 2018. Database accessed on November 26, 2018. The unemployment rates shown refer to the share of unemployed persons in the total active population (labor force). Data for DEU (and the EA-12) refer to unified Germany from 1991 onward and to West Germany prior to this year.

Figure 3.4b
Author's illustration. Periods considered: FRA and JPN: 1968–2017. DEU and ITA: 1970–2017. ESP: 1972–2017. The EU-16: 1983–2017. CAN: 1976–2017. GBR: 1984–2017. The USA: 1960–2017. Data for DEU (and the EU-16) refer to unified Germany from 1991 onward and to West Germany prior to this year. Data are from the OECD (2018c), dataset *Labour, Labour Force Statistics, LFS by sex and age, LFS by sex and age—indicators, Employment-population ratios*, variable *Employment/population ratio, Men, Age 25 to 54*. Database accessed on November 08, 2018.

Figure 3.5
Author's illustration. Periods considered: The EA: 01/1997–10/2018. All other countries: 01/1987–10/2018. Data for DEU refer to unified Germany from 1991 onward

and to West Germany prior to this year. Data for FRA, DEU, ITA, ESP, JPN, CAN, GBR, and the USA are from the OECD (2018c), dataset *Prices and Purchasing Power Parities, Consumer and Producer Price Indices, Consumer price indices (CPIs)—Complete database*, variable *Consumer prices—Annual inflation, All items non-food non-energy*, monthly data. Data as of December 03, 2018. Database accessed on December 04, 2018. Data for the EA are from the European Central Bank (2018), dataset *ICP: Indices of Consumer prices*, variable *HICP—All-items excluding energy and food, Annual rate of change, Eurostat, Neither seasonally nor working day adjusted*. Data as of November 30, 2018. Database accessed on December 04, 2018. Core inflation rates shown are annual changes of consumer price indices excluding energy and food.

Figure 3.6a
Author's illustration. Periods considered: FRA: 01/1970–10/2018. DEU and CAN: 01/1960–10/2018. ITA: 10/1978–10/2018. ESP: 01/1977–10/2018. The EA: 01/1994–11/2018. JPN: 05/1979–11/2018. GBR: 01/1978–10/2018. The USA: 06/1964–10/2018. Data for DEU refer to unified Germany from 1991 onward and to West Germany prior to this year. Data for FRA, DEU, ITA, ESP, JPN, CAN, GBR (from 01/1986 onward), and the USA are from the OECD (2018c), dataset *Finance, Monthly Financial Statistics, Monthly Monetary and Financial Statistics (MEI), Interest rates*, variable *Short-term interest rates, Per cent per annum*, monthly data. Data as of December 03, 2018. Database accessed on December 04, 2018. Data for GBR (01/1978–12/1985) are from the OECD (2016), dataset *Finance, Monthly Financial Statistics, Monthly Monetary and Financial Statistics (MEI), Interest rates*, variable *Short-term interest rates, Per cent per annum*, monthly data. Data as of 2016. Database accessed on January 03, 2017. Data for the EA are from the European Central Bank (2018), dataset *FM: Financial market data*, variable *Euribor 3-month—Historical close, average of observations through period*. Data as of December 03, 2018. Database accessed on December 04, 2018. Data for JPN (05/1979–12/1985) are from the Federal Reserve Bank of St. Louis (2018), variable *3-Month or 90-day Rates and Yields: Certificates of Deposit for Japan (IR3TCD01JPM156N)*. Data as of November 23, 2018. Database accessed on December 04, 2018. Data for JPN (01/1986–11/2018) are from the Federal Reserve Bank of St. Louis (2018), variable *3-Month London Interbank Offered Rate (LIBOR), based on Japanese Yen (JPY3MTD156N)*. Data as of December 03, 2018. Database accessed on December 04, 2018.

Figure 3.6b
Author's calculations and illustration. Periods considered: FRA: 01/1971–10/2018. DEU: 01/1963–10/2018. ITA: 10/1978–10/2018. ESP: 01/1977–10/2018. The EA: 01/1997–10/2018. JPN: 05/1979–10/2018. CAN: 01/1962–10/2018. GBR: 01/1978–10/2018. The USA: 06/1964–10/2018. Data for DEU refer to unified Germany from 1991 onward and to West Germany prior to this year. Ex-post real short-term interest rates refer to nominal short-term interest rates less core inflation rates (i.e., inflation rates excluding energy and food) in the same year. Data sources for short-term nominal interest rates: see notes to Fig. 3.6a. Core inflation data for FRA, DEU, ITA,

ESP, JPN, CAN, GBR, and the USA are from the OECD (2018c), dataset *Prices and Purchasing Power Parities, Consumer and Producer Price Indices, Consumer price indices (CPIs)—Complete database*, variable *Consumer prices—Annual inflation, All items non-food non-energy*, monthly data. Data as of December 03, 2018. Database accessed on December 04, 2018. Core inflation data for the EA are from the European Central Bank (2018), dataset *ICP: Indices of Consumer prices*, variable *HICP—All-items excluding energy and food, Annual rate of change, Eurostat, Neither seasonally nor working day adjusted*. Data as of November 30, 2018. Database accessed on December 04, 2018.

Figure 3.6c
Author's illustration. Periods considered: FRA, CAN, GBR, and the USA: 01/1960–10/2018. DEU: 01/1960–11/2018. ITA: 03/1991–10/2018. ESP: 01/1980–10/2018. The EA: 01/1970–11/2018. JPN: 01/1989–11/2018. Data for DEU (and the EA) refer to unified Germany from 1991 onward and to West Germany prior to this year. Data for FRA, DEU, ITA, ESP, JPN, CAN, GBR, and the USA are from the OECD (2018c), dataset *Finance, Monthly Financial Statistics, Monthly Monetary and Financial Statistics (MEI), Interest rates*, variable *Long-term interest rates, Per cent per annum*, monthly data. Data as of December 03, 2018. Database accessed on December 04, 2018. Data for the EA are from the European Central Bank (2018), dataset *FM: Financial market data*, variable *Euro area 10-year Government Benchmark bond yield—Yield*. Data as of December 03, 2018. Database accessed on December 04, 2018.

Figure 3.6d
Author's calculations and illustration. Periods considered: FRA and GBR: 01/1971–10/2018. DEU: 01/1963–10/2018. ITA: 03/1991–10/2018. ESP: 01/1980–10/2018. The EA: 01/1997–10/2018. JPN: 01/1989–10/2018. CAN: 01/1962–10/2018. The USA: 01/1960–10/2018. Data for DEU refer to unified Germany from 1991 onward and to West Germany prior to this year. Ex-post real ten-year government bond yields refer to nominal ten-year government bond yields less core inflation rates (i.e., inflation rates excluding energy and food) in the same year. Data sources for nominal ten-year government bond yields: see notes to Fig. 3.6c. Core inflation data for FRA, DEU, ITA, ESP, JPN, CAN, GBR, and the USA are from the OECD (2018c), dataset *Prices and Purchasing Power Parities, Consumer and Producer Price Indices, Consumer price indices (CPIs)—Complete database*, variable *Consumer prices—Annual inflation, All items non-food non-energy*, monthly data. Data as of December 03, 2018. Database accessed on December 04, 2018. Core inflation data for the EA are from the European Central Bank (2018), dataset *ICP: Indices of Consumer prices*, variable *HICP—All items excluding energy and food, Annual rate of change, Eurostat, Neither seasonally nor working day adjusted*. Data as of November 30, 2018. Database accessed on December 04, 2018.

Figure 3.7
Author's calculations and illustrations following Fatás and Summers (2016, p. 3). Data are from the OECD (2018c), dataset *Economic Projections, OECD Economic*

Outlook, OECD Economic Outlook Latest edition, Economic Outlook No. 104—November 2018, variables *Gross domestic product, volume, market prices* and *Potential output volume*. Data as of November 21, 2018. Database accessed on November 22, 2018. The solid lines refer to actual real GDP, the dashed lines to official OECD estimates of potential real output as of November 2018. The dotted lines refer to counterfactual potential real output. The dotted lines extrapolate the 1999–2007 average annual growth rates of potential output (dashed lines) to 2017. All data are index values, with potential real output (dashed lines) in 1999 being equal to 100.

Figure 3.8a

Author's calculations and illustration. Periods considered: The EA-12: 1961–2017. All other countries: 1960–2017. The complete data series for DEU (and the EA-12) refers to unified Germany. Data are from the European Commission (2018), variable *Population: 15 to 64 years (NPAN)*. Data as of November 08, 2018. Database accessed on November 26, 2018. Absolute changes shown are centered five-year moving averages from 1960 to 2017.

Figure 3.8b

Author's calculations and illustration. Periods considered: The EA-12: 1961–2017. All other countries: 1960–2017. The complete data series for DEU (and the EA-12) refers to unified Germany. Data are from the European Commission (2018), variables *Population: 15 to 64 years (NPAN)* and *Total population (NPTN)*. Data as of November 08, 2018. Database accessed on November 26, 2018.

Figure 4.1a

Author's calculations and illustration. Data are from The Conference Board (2018), *Data, Output, Labor, and Labor Productivity, 1950–2018*, variable *Output per Hour Worked: Labor productivity per hour worked in 2017 US$ (converted to 2017 price level with updated 2011 PPPs), TCB Adjusted*. Data as of March 2018. Database accessed on November 09, 2018. Growth rates shown are centered five-year moving averages from 1950 to 2017. Data are based on real GDP levels "[...] adjusted for rapidly falling ICT prices." (The Conference Board 2018, dataset *Data, Output, Labor, and Productivity, 1950–2018*, worksheet *Contents*). See also de Vries and Erumban (2017, pp. 3–4, 9–11, 21–26).

Figure 4.1b

Author's calculations and illustration. Data are from Bergeaud et al. (2016, 2017), variable *TFP (Total Factor Productivity, $US 2010 ppp based)*. Data as of August 2017. Database accessed on November 09, 2018. Growth rates shown are average annual growth rates.

Figure 7.1

Author's illustration. Periods considered: FRA: 1978–2017. DEU, JPN, and the USA: 1960–2017. ITA and CAN: 1970–2017. ESP: 1964–2017. The EA-16: 1991–2017. GBR: 1987–2017. Data for DEU refer to unified Germany from 1991 onward and to West Germany prior to this year. Data for FRA, DEU (1980–2017), and GBR are from the European Commission (2018), variable *Saving rate, net: households and NPISH (Net saving as percentage of net disposable income) (ASNH)*. Data as of November 08, 2018. Database accessed on November 26, 2018. Data for ITA, ESP, the EA-16, JPN, and CAN (1981–2017) are from the OECD (2018c), dataset *Economic Projections, OECD Economic Outlook, OECD Economic Outlook Latest edition, Economic Outlook No. 104—November 2018*, variable *Net saving ratio of households and non-profit institutions serving households*. Data as of November 21, 2018. Database accessed on November 23, 2018. Data for DEU (1960–1969) are from the Deutsche Bundesbank (1976, p. 356), variable *Nachrichtlich: Sparquote in % (Laufende Ersparnis in % des verfügbaren Einkommens)*. Data for DEU (1970–1979) and CAN (1970–1980) are from the OECD (2011), variable *Household and non-profit institutions serving households net saving ratio*, countries *Former Federal Republic of Germany* and *Canada*. Data as of mid-June 2011. Database accessed on November 06, 2018. Data for the USA are from the Federal Reserve Bank of St. Louis (2018), variable *Personal saving as a percentage of disposable personal income (A072RC1Q156SBEA)*. Data as of November 28, 2018. Database accessed on December 04, 2018. The net saving ratio of private households is generally defined as net household saving as a share of household disposable income. Net household saving is calculated by subtracting "[...] household consumption expenditure from household disposable income, [...] [adding] the change in net equity of households in pension funds [...]" (OECD 2018b).

Figure 10.1a–c

Author's illustrations. Periods considered: EU and JPN: 1995–2016. The USA: 1995–2015. Data are from the OECD (2018a, pp. 85–86), data to *Figure 5.5. Labor productivity and average labour compensation per hour, total economy*. According to the OECD (2018a, pp. 85–86), labor productivity is measured as gross value added (GVA) per hour worked by all persons employed, deflated by the GVA deflator. Real average labor compensation per hour worked is measured as average labor compensation per hour worked by employees, deflated by the GVA deflator. All data are index values, with the data in 1995 equal to 100.

Figure 10.2

Author's illustration. Periods considered: FRA and CAN: 1960–2015. DEU, ITA, and GBR: 1960–2016. ESP: 1980–2015. JPN: 1960–2017. The USA: 1960–2017. Data for DEU refer to unified Germany from 1991 onward and to West Germany prior to this year. Data are from the OECD (2018c), dataset *Labour, Trade Unions and Collective Bargaining, Trade union density in OECD countries*, variable *Trade union density*. Data as of April 27, 2018. Database accessed on December 02, 2018. Data for the USA are survey data from 1981 onward and administrative data prior to this year. Data for all other countries are administrative data. Trade union density is defined as "[...] the ratio of union members divided by the total number of employees [...]" (OECD 2018c, dataset *Labour, Trade Unions and Collective Bargaining, Trade union density in OECD countries*).

Figure 10.3a
Author's illustration. Periods considered: FRA, ITA, ESP, the EU-15, JPN, and GBR: 1981–2015. DEU and the USA: 1981–2016. CAN: 1981–2017. Data for DEU (and the EU-15) refer to unified Germany from 1991 onward and to West Germany prior to this year. Data are from the OECD (2018c), dataset *Science, Technology and Patents, Science and Technology Indicators, Main Science and Technology Indicators (MSTI database)*, variable *Government-financed GERD as a percentage of GDP*. Data as of July 24, 2018. Database accessed on December 02, 2018. Government-financed R&D refers to "[...] all R&D performed using government funds in all sectors of the economy, such as R&D performed by businesses or universities under government contracts or grants, and within government itself [...]" (OECD 2017, p. 3).

Figure 10.3b
Author's illustration. Periods considered: CAN: 1981–2017. All other countries and the EU-15: 1981–2016. Data for DEU (and the EU-15) refer to unified Germany from 1991 onward and to West Germany prior to this year. Data are from the OECD (2018c), dataset *Science, Technology and Patents, Science and Technology Indicators, Main Science and Technology Indicators (MSTI database)*, variable *GERD as a percentage of GDP*. Data as of July 24, 2018. Database accessed on December 02, 2018.

Figure 10.4a
Author's calculations and illustration. Periods considered: ITA and ESP: 1970–2017. The EU-15: 1990–2017. All other countries: 1960–2017. Data for DEU (and the EU-15) refer to unified Germany from 1991 onward and to West Germany prior to this year. Data are from the European Commission (2018), variables *Gross fixed capital formation at current prices: general government (UIGG)* and *Gross Domestic Product at current prices (UVGD)*. Data as of November 08, 2018. Database accessed on November 26, 2018.

Figure 10.4b
Author's calculations and illustration. Periods considered: FRA, ITA, ESP, and GBR: 1970–2017. DEU and the USA: 1960–2017. The EU-15: 1990–2017. Data for DEU (and the EU-15) refer to unified Germany from 1991 onward and to West Germany prior to this year. Data are from the European Commission (2018), variables *Net fixed capital formation at current prices: general government (UING)* and *Gross Domestic Product at current prices (UVGD)*. Data as of November 08, 2018. Database accessed on November 26, 2018.

Figure 10.5a
Author's calculations and illustration. Data are from the OECD (2018c), dataset *Public Sector, Taxation and Market Regulation, Taxation, Revenue Statistics—OECD Member Countries, Revenue Statistics—OECD countries: Comparative tables, Com-*

parative tables—OECD countries, variables *1100 Taxes on income, profits and capital gains of individuals, 1200 Taxes on income, profits and capital gains of corporates, 1300 Unallocable between 1100 and 1200, 3000 Taxes on payroll and workforce, 4000 Taxes on property, 5000 Taxes on goods and services*, and *6000 Taxes other than 1000, 2000, 3000, 4000 and 5000*. Data as of November 23, 2017. Database accessed on December 02, 2018. All variables refer to total government. Data refer to tax revenues as a percentage of total tax revenue (excluding social security contributions).

Figure 10.5**b**
Author's calculations and illustration. Data are from the OECD (2018c), dataset *Public Sector, Taxation and Market Regulation, Taxation, Revenue Statistics—OECD Member Countries, Revenue Statistics—OECD countries: Comparative tables, Comparative tables—OECD countries*, variables *4100 Recurrent taxes on immovable property, 4200 Recurrent taxes on net wealth, 4300 Estate, inheritance and gift taxes, 4400 Taxes on financial and capital transactions, 4500 Non-recurrent taxes on property*, and *4600 Other recurrent taxes on property except 4100 and 4200*. Data as of November 23, 2017. Database accessed on December 02, 2018. Figure 10.5b is a close up of property taxes (orange-colored bar in Fig. 10.5a), dividing property taxes into different property tax categories. All variables refer to total government. Data refer to tax revenues as a percentage of total tax revenue (excluding social security contributions). Total taxation consists of the tax categories mentioned in the notes to Fig. 10.5a.

Figure 10.6
Author's illustration. From 1900 to 2015, data are from the IMF (2018a). Database accessed on November 29, 2018. See also Abbas et al. (2010). The data aim to report the gross debt of the general government, including central, state, and local governments. As outlined by Abbas et al. (2010, p. 6), however, particularly in earlier years, data for the general government are typically not available. In years for which there are no data at the general government level, "[...] debt data for the central government were used as an alternative [...]." From 2016 onward, data are from the IMF (2018b), variable *General government gross debt, percent of GDP*. Data as of October 2018. Database accessed on November 29, 2018. For JPN, data for 2017 are preliminary estimates by the IMF (2018b).

Figure 10.7
Author's calculations and illustration. Periods considered: FRA, DEU, CAN, GBR, and the USA: 1961–2017. ITA: 1992–2017. ESP: 1980–2017. JPN: 1989–2017. Data for DEU refer to unified Germany from 1991 onward and to West Germany prior to this year. Data on interest rates are from the OECD (2018c), dataset *Finance, Monthly Financial Statistics, Monthly Monetary and Financial Statistics (MEI), Interest rates*, variable *Long-term interest rates, Per cent per annum*, annual data. Data as of December 04, 2018. Database accessed on December 04, 2018. Data on GDP are from the European Commission (2018), variable *Gross domestic product at current prices (UVGD)*. Data as of November 08, 2018. Database accessed on November 26, 2018.

Data shown refer to the interest-rate-growth-differential, calculated by subtracting the annual nominal GDP growth rate from the nominal long-term interest rate each year. The interest-rate-growth-differentials shown are centered five-year moving averages.

Figure C.1a

Author's illustration. Periods considered: FRA: 1902–2014. GBR: 1900–2012. The USA: 1913–2014. Data are from Alvaredo et al. (2017a), dataset *Key Indicators, Wealth Inequality*, variable *Net personal wealth, Top 1% share*. Database accessed on November 29, 2018. The figure shows the share of the wealthiest 1% in total net personal wealth. As outlined by Alvaredo et al. (2017b), "[n]et personal wealth is the total value of non-financial and financial assets (housing, land, deposits, bonds, equities, etc.) held by households, minus their debts. The personal or household sector—in the national accounts sense—includes all households and private individuals (including those living in institutions), as well as unincorporated enterprises whose accounts are not separated from those of the households who own them." Data refer to adults aged 20 and over. Data for FRA and the USA refer to individuals, but wealth is assumed to be equally split between individuals of a couple. Data for GBR refer to individuals.

Figure C.1b

Author's illustration. Data are from the European Central Bank (2017, p. 58), Table *J4: Net wealth inequality indicators*, variable *Gini coefficient*. Data as of April 24, 2017. Database accessed on September 21, 2017. Data refer to net wealth, with net wealth being defined as "[...] the difference between total (gross) assets and total liabilities. Total assets consist of real assets and financial assets." (European Central Bank 2017, p. 62). Data mainly refer to the time the household interviews were conducted. Year specifications: BEL, FRA, and AUT: 2014/2015. ESP: 2011/2012. ITA: December 31, 2014. LUX, FIN, and DEU: 2014. PRT and IRE: 2013. NED: December 31, 2013. The Gini index is a summary measure of inequality which can take values between zero (complete equality) and 100 (complete inequality). In Fig. C.1b, for each country the bar chart starts at zero. For example, in 2014, in Italy the Gini index of net wealth amounted to almost 60.

References

Abbas SA, Belhocine N, ElGanainy A, Horton M (2010) A historical public debt database. IMF Working Paper WP/10/245. International Monetary Fund, Washington, DC. Available at https://www.imf.org/external/pubs/ft/wp/2010/wp10245.pdf. Accessed 08 Aug 2018

Alvaredo F, Atkinson AB, Chancel L, Piketty T, Saez E, Zucman G (2016) Distributional national accounts (DINA) guides: concepts and methods used in WID.world. WID.world Working Paper No. 2016/1, version June 9, 2017. Available at http://wid.world/document/dinaguidelines-v1/. Accessed 21 Sept 2017

Alvaredo F, Chancel L, Piketty T, Saez E, Zucman G (2017a) The world wealth and income database (WID.world). Available at http://wid.world/. Accessed 29 Nov 2018

Alvaredo F, Chancel L, Piketty T, Saez E, Zucman G (2017b) The world wealth and income database (WID.world). By country, top 1% net personal wealth share, France, United Kingdom, and USA. Sources and informations. Available at http://wid.world/. Accessed 29 Nov 2018

Atkinson AB, Hasell J, Morelli S, Roser M (2017a) The chartbook of economic inequality (book), May 2017. Institute for New Economic Thinking (INET) at the Oxford Martin School and University of Oxford, Oxford. Available at https://chartbookofeconomicinequality.com/wp-content/uploads/Chartbook_Of_Economic_Inequality_complete.pdf. Accessed 29 Nov 2018

Atkinson AB, Hasell J, Morelli S, Roser M (2017b) The chartbook of economic inequality (database), May 2017. Institute for New Economic Thinking (INET) at the Oxford Martin School and University of Oxford, Oxford. Available at https://chartbookofeconomicinequality.com/wp-content/uploads/DataForDownload/AllData_ChartbookOfEconomicInequality.xlsx. Accessed 29 Nov 2018

Bergeaud A, Cette G, Lecat R (2016) Productivity trends in advanced countries between 1890 and 2012. Review of Income and Wealth 62(3):420–444

Bergeaud A, Cette G, Lecat R (2017) Long term productivity database. Version 2, August 2017. Available at http://www.longtermproductivity.com/. Accessed 09 Nov 2018

Bundesministerium der Finanzen (2018) Lohn- und Einkommensteuerrechner. Berechnungen und Informationen zur Einkommensteuer. Berechnung der Einkommensteuer. Bundesministerium der Finanzen, Berlin. Available at https://www.bmf-steuerrechner.de/. Accessed 20 Sept 2018

Deutsche Bundesbank (1976) Deutsches Geld- und Bankwesen in Zahlen 1876–1975. Verlag Fritz Knapp, Frankfurt am Main

European Central Bank (2017) The household finance and consumption survey, wave 2, statistical tables. HFCS, April 2017. European Central Bank, Frankfurt am Main. Available at https://www.ecb.europa.eu/home/pdf/research/hfcn/HFCS_Statistical_Tables_Wave2.pdf?58cf15114aab934bcd06995c4e91505b. Accessed 21 Sept 2017

European Central Bank (2018) ECB statistical data warehouse. European Central Bank, Frankfurt am Main. Available at http://sdw.ecb.europa.eu/. Last accessed 04 Dec 2018

European Commission (2017) Annual macro-economic database of the European Commission's Directorate General for Economic and Financial Affairs (AMECO database). European Commission, Brussels. Available at http://ec.europa.eu/economy_finance/ameco/user/serie/SelectSerie.cfm. Data as of 11 May 2017. Last accessed 19 Sept 2017

European Commission (2018) Annual macro-economic database of the European Commission's Directorate General for Economic and Financial Affairs (AMECO database). European Commission, Brussels. Available at http://ec.europa.eu/economy_finance/ameco/user/serie/SelectSerie.cfm. Data as of 08 Nov 2018. Last accessed 26 Nov 2018

Fatás A, Summers LH (2016) The permanent effects of fiscal consolidations. NBER Working Paper No. 22374. National Bureau of Economic Research, Cambridge, MA. Available at http://www.nber.org/papers/w22374.pdf. Accessed 29 Aug 2016

Federal Reserve Bank of St. Louis (2018) FRED economic data. Federal Reserve Bank of St. Louis, St. Louis, MO. Available at https://fred.stlouisfed.org/. Accessed 04 Dec 2018

Gale WG, Gelfond H, Krupkin A, Mazur MJ, Toder E (2018) Effects of the tax cuts and jobs act: a preliminary analysis. Urban-Brookings Tax Policy Center, Washington, DC. Available at https://www.brookings.edu/wp-content/uploads/2018/06/ES_20180608_tcja_summary_paper_final.pdf. Accessed 25 Nov 2018

IMF (2018a) Historical public debt database. International Monetary Fund, Washington, DC. Available at http://www.imf.org/external/datamapper/datasets/DEBT. Accessed 29 Nov 2018

IMF (2018b) World economic outlook database, October 2018. International Monetary Fund, Washington, DC. Available at https://www.imf.org/external/pubs/ft/weo/2018/02/weodata/index.aspx. Accessed 29 Nov 2018

Knowles JW, Warden Jr CB (1960) The potential economic growth in the United States. United States Government Printing Office, Washington, DC

Krämer H (2011) Die Entwicklung der funktionalen Einkommensverteilung und ihrer Einflussfaktoren in ausgewählen Industrieländern 1960–2010. IMK Study 1/2011. Macroeconomic Policy Institute (IMK), Dusseldorf. Available at https://www.boeckler.de/pdf/p_imk_study_1_2011.pdf. Accessed 28 Feb 2018

Luxembourg Income Study (2018a) Luxembourg Income Study (LIS) database. LIS, Luxembourg. Available at http://www.lisdatacenter.org. Last accessed 12 Nov 2018

Luxembourg Income Study (2018b) Luxembourg Income Study (LIS), PPP deflators. LIS, Luxembourg. Available at http://www.lisdatacenter.org/data-access/web-tabulator/methods/ppp/. Data as of 04 Apr 2018. Accessed 08 Nov 2018

Moriguchi C, Saez E (2005) The evolution of income concentration in Japan, 1885–2002: Evidence from income tax statistics. Working Paper. August 25, 2005. Available at https://eml.berkeley.edu//~saez/moriguchi-saez05japan.pdf. Accessed 03 Mar 2018

Moriguchi C, Saez E (2010) The evolution of income concentration in Japan, 1886–2005: evidence from income tax statistics. In: Atkinson AB, Piketty T (eds) Top incomes: a global perspective, Oxford University Press, Oxford, pp 76–170

OECD (2011) OECD.Stat, economic projections, OECD economic outlook no. 89—June 2011—annual projections for OECD countries. OECD, Paris. Available at http://stats.oecd.org/. Accessed 06 Nov 2018

OECD (2016) OECD.Stat. Paris: OECD. Available at http://stats.oecd.org/. Data as of 2016. Accessed 03 Jan 2017

OECD (2017) Release of main science and technology indicators—latest estimates of R&D investment in OECD and major economies. OECD, Paris. Available at https://www.oecd.org/sti/inno/DataBrief_MSTI_2017.pdf. Accessed 01 Oct 2018

OECD (2018a) OECD compendium of productivity indicators 2018. OECD Publishing, Paris

OECD (2018b) OECD data: household savings. OECD, Paris. Available at https://data.oecd.org/hha/household-savings.htm. Accessed 13 June 2018

OECD (2018c) OECD.Stat.OECD, Paris. Available at http://stats.oecd.org/. Last accessed 04 Dec 2018

Piketty T (2014a) Capital in the twenty-first Century. Harvard University Press, Cambridge, MA, and London

Piketty T (2014b) Capital in the twenty-first Century, online appendix, March 2014. Available at http://piketty.pse.ens.fr/en/capital21c2. Accessed 03 Dec 2018

Piketty T, Zucman G (2014a) Capital is back: wealth-income ratios in rich countries 1700–2010. The Quarterly Journal of Economics 129(3):1255–1310

Piketty T, Zucman G (2014b) Capital is back: wealth-income ratios in rich countries 1700–2010. Online data appendix. Available at http://gabriel-zucman.eu/capitalisback/. Accessed 06 Nov 2018

Piketty T, Saez E, Zucman G (2017) Distributional national accounts: methods and estimates for the United States. Online data appendix. Available at http://gabriel-zucman.eu/usdina/. Accessed 30 Nov 2018

Piketty T, Saez E, Zucman G (2018) Distributional national accounts: methods and estimates for the United States. Q J Econ 133(2):553–609

Saez E, Veall MR (2007) The evolution of high incomes in Canada, 1920–2000. In: Atkinson AB, Piketty T (eds) Top incomes over the twentieth century: a contrast between European and English-speaking countries, Oxford University Press, Oxford, pp 226–308

The Conference Board (2018) The Conference Board total economy database, March 2018. The Conference Board, New York, NY. Available at https://www.conference-board.org/data/economydatabase/. Accessed 09 Nov 2018

US Bureau of the Census (1975) Historical statistics of the United States, colonial times to 1970, bicentennial edition, part 2. U.S. Government Printing Office, Washington, DC

de Vries K, Erumban AA (2017) Total economy database: a detailed guide to its sources and methods. Version November 2017. The Conference Board, New York, NY. Available at https://www.conference-board.org/retrievefile.cfm?filename=TED_SMDetailed_nov2017.pdf&type=subsite. Accessed 09 Nov 2018

Appendix B
Table Sources and Notes in Detail

Table 1.1

Author's illustration. Data are from Maddison (2005, p. 10; 2006, pp. 640, 643). Western Europe includes Austria, Belgium, Denmark, Finland, France, Germany, Italy, the Netherlands, Norway, Portugal, Spain, Sweden, Switzerland, the United Kingdom, as well as 14 other small Western European countries (Andorra, Cyprus, Faeroe Islands, Gibraltar, Greenland, Guernsey, Iceland, Isle of Man, Jersey, Liecht-enstein, Luxembourg, Malta, Monaco, San Marion). The Western offshoots include Australia, Canada, New Zealand, and the United States (Maddison 2010). The West includes Western Europe, the Western offshoots, and Japan. For further information on countries and regions, see Maddison (2010).

Table 1.2

Author's calculations and illustration. Data are from the Luxembourg Income Study (2018a), variables *dhi*, *hpopwgt*, and *nhhmem*. Database accessed on November 12, 2018. For each country, data refer to the latest year available. Data refer to household equivalized disposable income, calculated by dividing household disposable income by the square root of the number of household members. Household disposable income is the sum of household labor income, household capital income, and household transfer income less income taxes and social security contributions paid by households. Households where disposable income is missing or zero are excluded. Data are top-coded at ten times the median of household non-equivalized disposable income and bottom-coded at 1% of the mean of household equivalized disposable income. All data are rounded to two decimal places. Due to rounding, the S99/S1 ratios shown in Table 1.2 deviate from the S99/S1 ratios that can be obtained by dividing the income share of the top 1% (S99) shown in Table 1.2 by the income share of the bottom 1% (S1) shown in Table 1.2. It should also be noted that the data provided by the Luxembourg Income Study (2018a) are based on household surveys. Household survey data typically do not accurately capture the top and the bottom of the income distribution. It can be assumed, in fact, that the income shares of the top 1% (S99) shown in Table 1.2 underestimate the actual income shares of the top 1%, even more so because the data have been top-coded. Conversely, it can be

© Springer Nature Switzerland AG 2020
C. Anselmann, *Secular Stagnation Theories*, Springer Studies in the History of Economic Thought, https://doi.org/10.1007/978-3-030-41087-2

assumed that the income shares of the bottom 1% (S1) shown in Table 1.2 overestimate the actual income shares of the bottom 1%, even more so because the data have been bottom-coded. Accordingly, it can be assumed that the S99/S1 ratios shown in Table 1.2 underestimate the actual S99/S1 ratios. (As shown in Fig. 1.5b, for example, based on tax data the post-tax income share of the top 1% in the United States amounted to more than 15% in 2014, while, according to Table 1.2, it was below 6% in 2016. Although Fig. 1.5b and Table 1.2 refer to different income definitions, it is reasonable to assume that household survey data underestimate the income shares at the very top of the income hierarchy.)

Table 7.3

Author's illustration. Consumption, 1935–1936 (Percent of Income): Partly author's calculations. Data are from the National Resources Committee (1939, p. 20). See also Hansen (1941, p. 232). Data refer to consumer units, comprising families, single individuals, and institutional residents (National Resources Committee 1939, pp. 98–99). Tax Payments, 1938–1939 (Percent of Income): Data are from Colm and Tarasov (1940, p. 6). See also Hansen (1941, p. 134). Data refer to consumer units, comprising families and single individuals (Colm and Tarasov 1940, pp. 3, 9). Estimates on the tax burden of each income group include *all* taxes: taxes on individuals (poll taxes, income taxes, estate and gift taxes, as well as non-business personal property taxes), excise taxes on specific products, and business taxes (Colm and Tarasov 1940, pp. 3–6). Income refers to the total income "[...] received during the year by all members of the economic family, plus the value of certain items of nonmoney income." (National Resources Committee 1939, p. 99). Income is net of "[...] business operating expenses and expenses connected with income-yielding property [...]" (National Resources Committee 1938, p. 15). Moreover, income does not include capital gains and losses, inheritances which are not "[...] used for current living expenses [...]," soldiers' bonus payments, and borrowed funds (National Resources Committee 1939, p. 99).

References

Colm G, Tarasov H (1940) Investigation of concentration of economic power. Temporary National Economic Committee, monograph no. 3: who pays the taxes? Allocation of federal, state, and local taxes to consumer income brackets. United States Government Printing Office, Washington, DC

Hansen AH (1941) Fiscal policy and business cycles. W. W. Norton & Company, Inc., New York, NY

Luxembourg Income Study (2018) Luxembourg Income Study (LIS) database. LIS, Luxembourg. Available at http://www.lisdatacenter.org. Last accessed 12 Nov 2018

Maddison A (2005) Growth and interaction in the world economy: the roots of modernity. The AEI Press, Washington, DC

Maddison A (2006) The world economy (vol 1 and vol 2). OECD Publishing, Paris

Maddison A (2010) Historical statistics of the world economy: 1–2008 AD. Groningen Growth and Development Centre (GGDC), Groningen. Available at www.ggdc.net/maddison/historical_statistics/horizontal-file_02-2010.xls. Accessed 19 Oct 2018

National Resources Committee (1938) Consumer incomes in the United States: their distribution in 1935–36. United States Government Printing Office, Washington, DC

National Resources Committee (1939) Consumer expenditures in the United States. Estimates for 1935–36. United States Government Printing Office, Washington, DC

Appendix C
Wealth Distribution: Empirical Trends

Although the issue of distribution is primarily about the distribution of income in this book, a brief look shall be taken at the development of wealth distribution.

On the example of France, the United Kingdom, and the USA, Fig. C.1a shows the top percentile of the net wealth distribution owned between 35% and 75% of total net wealth in the early twentieth century. While these shares declined steadily until the early 1980s, there has been some trend reversal thereafter, especially in the United States. In 2014, the top one percent owned more than 37% of net wealth in the USA, more than 23% in France, and more than 19% in the United Kingdom. Comparing Figs. C.1a and 1.3a, it can be seen that net wealth has been more concentrated than gross income.

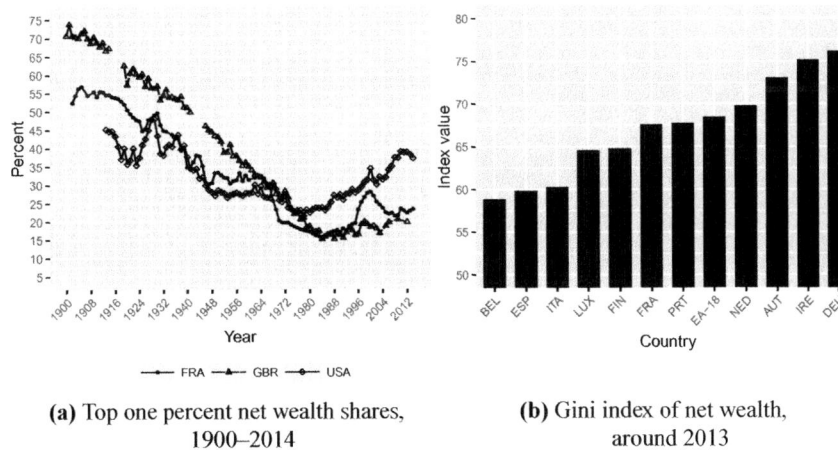

(a) Top one percent net wealth shares,
1900–2014

(b) Gini index of net wealth,
around 2013

Fig. C.1 Net wealth inequality. *Source* Author's illustrations, based on data from Alvaredo et al. (2017) and the European Central Bank (2017, p. 58). See Appendix A for detailed data sources and further notes

© Springer Nature Switzerland AG 2020   299
C. Anselmann, *Secular Stagnation Theories*, Springer Studies in the History
of Economic Thought, https://doi.org/10.1007/978-3-030-41087-2

Based on household survey data by the European Central Bank (2017), Fig. C.1b shows the extent of net wealth inequality as measured by the Gini index in several European countries around the year 2013. With a Gini index of more than 75, net wealth was particularly unequally distributed in Germany, followed by Ireland and Austria.

References

Alvaredo F, Chancel L, Piketty T, Saez E, Zucman G (2017) The world wealth and income database (WID.world). Available at http://wid.world/. Accessed 29 Nov 2018

European Central Bank (2017) The household finance and consumption survey, wave 2, statistical tables. HFCS, April 2017. European Central Bank, Frankfurt am Main. Available at https://www.ecb.europa.eu/home/pdf/research/hfcn/HFCS_Statistical_Tables_Wave2.pdf?58cf 15114aab934bcd06995c4e91505b. Accessed 21 Sept 2017

Appendix D
A Steindlian Model of Income Distribution, Economic Growth, and Stagnation: Mathematical and Graphical Appendix

D.1 Short- and Long-Run Effects of Economic Changes

D.1.1 The Economy in the Short Run

D.1.1.1 Partial Derivatives

The Degree of Capacity Utilization (u)

With a given rate of real capital accumulation (g), the short-run comparative static changes in the degree of capacity utilization (u) are calculated by partially deriving Eq. (8.41), i.e.,

$$u = \frac{g + (1 - a_2)(m_2 + i)\left[(1 - s_h^r) + z\left(s_h^r - s_h^p\right)\right] + m_2\left(s_h^r - s_h^p\right)(w - z)}{m_1\left[(1 - a_2)(1 - s_h^r) + \left(s_h^r - s_h^p\right)(w - a_2 z)\right] + s_h^p w + s_h^r (1 - w)}$$

with respect to the exogenous variables and parameters $a_2, i, m_1, m_2, s_h^p, s_h^r, w,$ and z.

The partial derivatives are given by the following Eqs. (D.1) to (D.8):

$$\frac{\partial u}{\partial a_2} = \frac{\left[1 - s_h^r + z\left(s_h^r - s_h^p\right)\right] \cdot \left\{m_1\left[g - i\left(s_h^r - s_h^p\right)(w - z)\right] - (i + m_2)\left[s_h^p w + s_h^r (1 - w)\right]\right\}}{\left\{m_1\left[(1 - a_2)(1 - s_h^r) + \left(s_h^r - s_h^p\right)(w - a_2 z)\right] + s_h^p w + s_h^r (1 - w)\right\}^2}$$
(D.1)

$$\frac{\partial u}{\partial i} = \frac{(1 - a_2)\left[1 - s_h^r + z\left(s_h^r - s_h^p\right)\right]}{m_1\left[(1 - a_2)(1 - s_h^r) + \left(s_h^r - s_h^p\right)(w - a_2 z)\right] + s_h^p w + s_h^r (1 - w)}$$
(D.2)

C. Anselmann, *Secular Stagnation Theories*, Springer Studies in the History of Economic Thought, https://doi.org/10.1007/978-3-030-41087-2

$$\frac{\partial u}{\partial m_1} = -\frac{\begin{array}{l}\left[(1 - a_2)\left(1 - s_h^r\right) + \left(s_h^r - s_h^p\right)(w - a_2 z)\right] \\ \quad\cdot\left\{g + m_2\left(s_h^r - s_h^p\right)(w - z)\right. \\ \quad + (1 - a_2)(i + m_2)\left[1 - s_h^r + z\left(s_h^r - s_h^p\right)\right]\right\}\end{array}}{\left\{m_1\left[(1 - a_2)\left(1 - s_h^r\right) + \left(s_h^r - s_h^p\right)(w - a_2 z)\right] + s_h^p w + s_h^r(1 - w)\right\}^2} \tag{D.3}$$

$$\frac{\partial u}{\partial m_2} = \frac{\left(s_h^r - s_h^p\right)(w - z) + (1 - a_2)\left[1 - s_h^r + z\left(s_h^r - s_h^p\right)\right]}{m_1\left[(1 - a_2)\left(1 - s_h^r\right) + \left(s_h^r - s_h^p\right)(w - a_2 z)\right] + s_h^p w + s_h^r(1 - w)} \tag{D.4}$$

$$\frac{\partial u}{\partial s_h^p} = \frac{\begin{array}{l}g\left[w(m_1 - 1) - a_2 m_1 z\right] + a_2 m_2 s_h^r(z - w) + m_2 w(a_2 - 1) \\ \quad + i(a_2 - 1)\left\{w(m_1 - 1)\left(s_h^r - 1\right) + z\left[m_1 + s_h^r(1 - m_1)\right]\right\}\end{array}}{\left\{m_1\left[(1 - a_2)\left(1 - s_h^r\right) + \left(s_h^r - s_h^p\right)(w - a_2 z)\right] + s_h^p w + s_h^r(1 - w)\right\}^2} \tag{D.5}$$

$$\frac{\partial u}{\partial s_h^r} = \frac{\begin{array}{l}g\left[(1 - w)(m_1 - 1) + a_2 m_1(z - 1)\right] + a_2 m_2 s_h^p(w - z) \\ \quad + (a_2 - 1)\left\{(1 - w)(i + m_2) + i(w - z)\left[m_1\left(1 - s_h^p\right) + s_h^p\right]\right\}\end{array}}{\left\{m_1\left[(1 - a_2)\left(1 - s_h^r\right) + \left(s_h^r - s_h^p\right)(w - a_2 z)\right] + s_h^p w + s_h^r(1 - w)\right\}^2} \tag{D.6}$$

$$\frac{\partial u}{\partial w} = \frac{\begin{array}{l}\left(s_h^r - s_h^p\right)\left\{g(1 - m_1) + z\left(s_h^r - s_h^p\right)\left[i(1 - a_2)(1 - m_1)\right]\right. \\ \quad + m_2\left[1 - a_2\left(1 - s_h^r + z\left(s_h^r - s_h^p\right)\right)\right] \\ \quad \left. + i(1 - a_2)(1 - m_1)\left(1 - s_h^r\right)\right\}\end{array}}{\left\{m_1\left[(1 - a_2)\left(1 - s_h^r\right) + \left(s_h^r - s_h^p\right)(w - a_2 z)\right] + s_h^p w + s_h^r(1 - w)\right\}^2} \tag{D.7}$$

$$\frac{\partial u}{\partial z} = \frac{\begin{array}{l}\left(s_h^r - s_h^p\right)\left\{a_2 g m_1 + a_2 m_2\left[w\left(s_h^r - s_h^p\right) - s_h^r\right]\right. \\ \quad \left. + i(1 - a_2)\left[m_1\left(\left(1 - s_h^r\right) + w\left(s_h^r - s_h^p\right)\right) + s_h^p w + s_h^r(1 - w)\right]\right\}\end{array}}{\left\{m_1\left[(1 - a_2)\left(1 - s_h^r\right) + \left(s_h^r - s_h^p\right)(w - a_2 z)\right] + s_h^p w + s_h^r(1 - w)\right\}^2}. \tag{D.8}$$

The Profit Share (π)

With a given rate of real capital accumulation (g), the short-run comparative static changes in the profit share (π) are calculated by partially deriving Eq. (8.42), i.e.,

$$\pi = \frac{gm_1 + im_1\left(1 - a_2\right)\left[1 - s_h^r + z\left(s_h^r - s_h^p\right)\right] - m_2\left[s_h^r - w\left(s_h^r - s_h^p\right)\right]}{g + \left(1 - a_2\right)\left(i + m_2\right)\left[1 - s_h^r + z\left(s_h^r - s_h^p\right)\right] + m_2\left(s_h^r - s_h^p\right)\left(w - z\right)}$$

with respect to the exogenous variables and parameters a_2, i, m_1, m_2, s_h^p, s_h^r, w, and z.
The partial derivatives are given by the following Eqs. (D.9) to (D.16):

$$\frac{\partial \pi}{\partial a_2} = \frac{\begin{array}{c} m_2\left[1 - s_h^r + z\left(s_h^r - s_h^p\right)\right] \\ \cdot \left\{m_1\left[g - i\left(s_h^r - s_h^p\right)\left(w - z\right)\right] - \left(i + m_2\right)\left[s_h^p w + s_h^r\left(1 - w\right)\right]\right\} \end{array}}{\begin{array}{c} \left\{g + \left(1 - a_2\right)\left(i + m_2\right)\left[1 - s_h^r + z\left(s_h^r - s_h^p\right)\right] \right. \\ \left. + m_2\left(s_h^r - s_h^p\right)\left(w - z\right)\right\}^2 \end{array}}$$

$$\text{(D.9)}$$

$$\frac{\partial \pi}{\partial i} = \frac{\begin{array}{c} \left\{m_2\left(1 - a_2\right)\left[1 - s_h^r + z\left(s_h^r - s_h^p\right)\right]\right\} \\ \cdot \left\{m_1\left[\left(1 - a_2\right)\left(1 - s_h^r\right) + \left(s_h^r - s_h^p\right)\left(w - a_2 z\right)\right] \right. \\ \left. + s_h^p w + s_h^r\left(1 - w\right)\right\} \end{array}}{\begin{array}{c} \left\{g + \left(1 - a_2\right)\left(i + m_2\right)\left[1 - s_h^r + z\left(s_h^r - s_h^p\right)\right] \right. \\ \left. + m_2\left(s_h^r - s_h^p\right)\left(w - z\right)\right\}^2 \end{array}}$$

$$\text{(D.10)}$$

$$\frac{\partial \pi}{\partial m_1} = \frac{g + i\left(1 - a_2\right)\left[1 - s_h^r + z\left(s_h^r - s_h^p\right)\right]}{g + \left(1 - a_2\right)\left(i + m_2\right)\left[1 - s_h^r + z\left(s_h^r - s_h^p\right)\right] + m_2\left(s_h^r - s_h^p\right)\left(w - z\right)}$$

$$\text{(D.11)}$$

$$\frac{\partial \pi}{\partial m_2} = \frac{\begin{array}{c} \left\{g + i\left(1 - a_2\right)\left[1 - s_h^r + z\left(s_h^r - s_h^p\right)\right]\right\} \\ \cdot \left\{-m_1\left[\left(1 - a_2\right)\left(1 - s_h^r\right) + \left(s_h^r - s_h^p\right)\left(w - a_2 z\right)\right] \right. \\ \left. - s_h^p w - s_h^r\left(1 - w\right)\right\} \end{array}}{\begin{array}{c} \left\{g + \left(1 - a_2\right)\left(i + m_2\right)\left[1 - s_h^r + z\left(s_h^r - s_h^p\right)\right] \right. \\ \left. + m_2\left(s_h^r - s_h^p\right)\left(w - z\right)\right\}^2 \end{array}}$$

$$\text{(D.12)}$$

$$\frac{\partial \pi}{\partial s_h^p} = \frac{\begin{array}{c} m_2\left\{g\left[w\left(m_1 - 1\right) - a_2 m_1 z\right] + m_2\left[w\left(a_2 - 1\right) + a_2 s_h^r\left(z - w\right)\right] \right. \\ \left. + i\left(a_2 - 1\right)\left[w\left(m_1 - 1\right)\left(s_h^r - 1\right) + z\left(m_1 + s_h^r\left(1 - m_1\right)\right)\right]\right\} \end{array}}{\begin{array}{c} \left\{g + \left(1 - a_2\right)\left(i + m_2\right)\left[1 - s_h^r + z\left(s_h^r - s_h^p\right)\right] \right. \\ \left. + m_2\left(s_h^r - s_h^p\right)\left(w - z\right)\right\}^2 \end{array}}$$

$$\text{(D.13)}$$

$$\frac{\partial \pi}{\partial s_h^r} = \frac{\begin{array}{c} m_2\left\{g\left[\left(1 - w\right)\left(m_1 - 1\right) + a_2 m_1\left(z - 1\right)\right] + a_2 m_2 s_h^p\left(w - z\right) \right. \\ \left. + \left(a_2 - 1\right)\left[\left(1 - w\right)\left(i + m_2\right) + i\left(w - z\right)\left(m_1\left(1 - s_h^p\right) + s_h^p\right)\right]\right\} \end{array}}{\begin{array}{c} \left\{g + \left(1 - a_2\right)\left(i + m_2\right)\left[1 - s_h^r + z\left(s_h^r - s_h^p\right)\right] \right. \\ \left. + m_2\left(s_h^r - s_h^p\right)\left(w - z\right)\right\}^2 \end{array}}$$

$$\text{(D.14)}$$

$$\frac{\partial \pi}{\partial w} = \frac{m_2 \left(s_h^r - s_h^p\right)\left\{g\left(1 - m_1\right) + z\left(s_h^r - s_h^p\right)\left[i\left(1 - m_1\right)\left(1 - a_2\right)\right] \atop {+ i\left(1 - a_2\right)\left(1 - m_1\right)\left(1 - s_h^r\right) \atop + m_2\left[1 - a_2\left(1 - s_h^r + z\left(s_h^r - s_h^p\right)\right)\right]\right\}}}{\left\{g + \left(1 - a_2\right)\left(i + m_2\right)\left[1 - s_h^r + z\left(s_h^r - s_h^p\right)\right] \atop + m_2\left(s_h^r - s_h^p\right)\left(w - z\right)\right\}^2}$$

(D.15)

$$\frac{\partial \pi}{\partial z} = \frac{m_2 \left(s_h^r - s_h^p\right)\left\{a_2 g m_1 + a_2 m_2\left[w\left(s_h^r - s_h^p\right) - s_h^r\right] \atop + i\left(1 - a_2\right)\left[m_1\left(\left(1 - s_h^r\right) + w\left(s_h^r - s_h^p\right)\right) + s_h^p w + s_h^r\left(1 - w\right)\right]\right\}}{\left\{g + \left(1 - a_2\right)\left(i + m_2\right)\left[1 - s_h^r + z\left(s_h^r - s_h^p\right)\right] \atop + m_2\left(s_h^r - s_h^p\right)\left(w - z\right)\right\}^2}.$$

(D.16)

The Measure of Personal Income Distribution (ψ)

With a given rate of real capital accumulation (g), the short-run comparative static changes in the ratio of rich to poor private households' income (ψ) are calculated by partially deriving Eq. (8.43), i.e.,

$$\psi = \frac{g\left[(1 - w)(1 - m_1) + a_2 m_1(1 - z)\right] - a_2 m_2 s_h^p(w - z) \atop + (1 - a_2)\left\{(1 - w)(i + m_2) + i(w - z)\left[s_h^p + m_1\left(1 - s_h^p\right)\right]\right\}}{g\left[a_2 m_1 z + w(1 - m_1)\right] + a_2 m_2 s_h^r(w - z) \atop + (1 - a_2)\left\{w(i + m_2) - i(w - z)\left[s_h^r + m_1\left(1 - s_h^r\right)\right]\right\}}$$

with respect to the exogenous variables and parameters $a_2, i, m_1, m_2, s_h^p, s_h^r, w$, and z. The partial derivatives are given by the following Eqs. (D.17)–(D.24):

$$\frac{\partial \psi}{\partial a_2} = \frac{\left[g\left(1 - m_1\right) + m_2\right]\left(w - z\right) \atop \cdot \left\{m_1\left[g - i\left(s_h^r - s_h^p\right)\left(w - z\right)\right] - \left(i + m_2\right)\left[s_h^p w + s_h^r\left(1 - w\right)\right]\right\}}{\left\{g\left[a_2 m_1 z + w(1 - m_1)\right] + a_2 m_2 s_h^r(w - z) \atop + (1 - a_2)\left[w(i + m_2) - i(w - z)\left(s_h^r + m_1\left(1 - s_h^r\right)\right)\right]\right\}^2}$$

(D.17)

$$\frac{\partial \psi}{\partial i} = \frac{\left(1 - a_2\right)\left[g\left(1 - m_1\right) + m_2\right]\left(w - z\right) \atop \cdot \left\{m_1\left[\left(1 - a_2\right)\left(1 - s_h^r\right) + \left(s_h^r - s_h^p\right)\left(w - a_2 z\right)\right] \atop + s_h^p w + s_h^r\left(1 - w\right)\right\}}{\left\{g\left[a_2 m_1 z + w(1 - m_1)\right] + a_2 m_2 s_h^r(w - z) \atop + (1 - a_2)\left[w(i + m_2) - i(w - z)\left(s_h^r + m_1\left(1 - s_h^r\right)\right)\right]\right\}^2}$$

(D.18)

$$\frac{\partial \psi}{\partial m_1} = \frac{\left[a_2 g + i\left(1 - a_2\right)\right]\left(w - z\right) \atop \cdot \left\{\left(1 - a_2\right)\left(i + m_2\right)\left[1 - s_h^r + z\left(s_h^r - s_h^p\right)\right] \atop + g + m_2\left(w - z\right)\left(s_h^r - s_h^p\right)\right\}}{\left\{g\left[a_2 m_1 z + w(1 - m_1)\right] + a_2 m_2 s_h^r(w - z) \atop + (1 - a_2)\left[w(i + m_2) - i(w - z)\left(s_h^r + m_1\left(1 - s_h^r\right)\right)\right]\right\}^2}$$

(D.19)

$$\frac{\partial \psi}{\partial m_2} = \frac{\begin{aligned}&[a_2 g + i(1-a_2)](w-z)\\ &\cdot \{-m_1[(1-a_2)(1-s_h^r) + (s_h^r - s_h^p)(w - a_2 z)]\\ &\quad - s_h^p w - s_h^r(1-w)\}\end{aligned}}{\begin{aligned}&\{g[a_2 m_1 z + w(1-m_1)] + a_2 m_2 s_h^r(w-z)\\ &\quad + (1-a_2)[w(i+m_2) - i(w-z)(s_h^r + m_1(1-s_h^r))]\}^2\end{aligned}}$$

(D.20)

$$\frac{\partial \psi}{\partial s_h^p} = \frac{(w-z)[i(1-a_2)(1-m_1) - a_2 m_2]}{\begin{aligned}&a_2 m_2 s_h^r(w-z) + g[a_2 m_1 z + w(1-m_1)] + m_2 w(1-a_2)\\ &\quad + i(1-a_2)\{w(1-m_1)(1-s_h^r) + z[m_1 + s_h^r(1-m_1)]\}\end{aligned}}$$

(D.21)

$$\frac{\partial \psi}{\partial s_h^r} = \frac{\begin{aligned}&[i(1-a_2)(1-m_1) - a_2 m_2](w-z)\\ &\cdot \{g[(1-m_1)(1-w) + a_2 m_1(1-z)] + a_2 m_2 s_h^p(z-w)\\ &\quad + (1-a_2)[(1-w)(i+m_2) + i(w-z)(m_1(1-s_h^p) + s_h^p)]\}\end{aligned}}{\begin{aligned}&\{g[a_2 m_1 z + w(1-m_1)] + a_2 m_2 s_h^r(w-z)\\ &\quad + (1-a_2)[w(i+m_2) - i(w-z)(s_h^r + m_1(1-s_h^r))]\}^2\end{aligned}}$$

(D.22)

$$\frac{\partial \psi}{\partial w} = \frac{\begin{aligned}&\{g[1 - m_1(1-a_2)] + (1-a_2)(m_2 + i)\}\\ &\cdot \{-g(1-m_1) - i(1-a_2)(1-m_1)[1 - s_h^r + z(s_h^r - s_h^p)]\\ &\quad - m_2[1 - a_2(1 - s_h^r + z(s_h^r - s_h^p))]\}\end{aligned}}{\begin{aligned}&\{g[a_2 m_1 z + w(1-m_1)] + a_2 m_2 s_h^r(w-z)\\ &\quad + (1-a_2)[w(i+m_2) - i(w-z)(s_h^r + m_1(1-s_h^r))]\}^2\end{aligned}}$$

(D.23)

$$\frac{\partial \psi}{\partial z} = \frac{\begin{aligned}&\{-g[1 - m_1(1-a_2)] - (1-a_2)(i + m_2)\}\\ &\cdot \{a_2 g m_1 + a_2 m_2[w(s_h^r - s_h^p) - s_h^r]\\ &\quad + i(1-a_2)[m_1((1-s_h^r) + w(s_h^r - s_h^p)) + s_h^p w + s_h^r(1-w)]\}\end{aligned}}{\begin{aligned}&\{g[a_2 m_1 z + w(1-m_1)] + a_2 m_2 s_h^r(w-z)\\ &\quad + (1-a_2)[w(i+m_2) - i(w-z)(s_h^r + m_1(1-s_h^r))]\}^2\end{aligned}}.$$

(D.24)

D.1.1.2 Comparative Statics in the Short Run

Changes in the Dividend Payout Parameter (a_2)

A change in a_2, the proportion of the excess of net profits (P) over the basic dividend ($a_1 K_f$) which firms pay to private households as part of their dividends, has an ambiguous impact on the degree of capacity utilization (u). It can be shown that a rise in a_2 increases u when firms' net profits (P) exceed the basic dividend ($a_1 K_f$), i.e., when $P - a_1 K_f$ in Eq. (8.14) is positive. The reason is that, with a positive $P - a_1 K_f$, a rise in a_2 redistributes income from non-consuming firms to private households who consume part of their income. As there are no adverse effects on firms' investment behavior in the short run, aggregate demand, output (Y), and hence the degree of capacity utilization (u) rise. Conversely, if firms' net profits (P) are lower than the basic dividend $(a_1 K_f)$, the degree of capacity utilization (u) declines with a rise in a_2. If $P - a_1 K_f$ is zero, u is not affected by variations in a_2.

If firms' net profits (P) exceed the basic dividend $(a_1 K_f)$, increases in output (Y) and the degree of capacity utilization (u)—induced by a rise in a_2—are accompanied by increases in both the wage bill (W) and total profits (R) in the economy. Along Kaleckian lines (see Eq. 8.30), the rise in profits (R) is due to an increase in consumption out of profits, resulting from a rise in private households' capital income (Z). Although wages (W) and hence saving out of wages rise as well, this increase does not compensate for the rise in consumption out of private households' capital income. Total profits (R) thus increase. As can be seen from Eqs. (8.12) and (8.21), due to the impact of overhead labor costs $(m_2 K)$, profits (R) eventually grow at a higher rate than wages (W) and output (Y). If firms' net profits (P) exceed the basic dividend $(a_1 K_f)$, the profit share (π) thus rises with an increase in a_2. In contrast, if $P - a_1 K_f$ is negative, the profit share (π) declines. If firms' net profits (P) are equal to the basic dividend $(a_1 K_f)$, π is not affected by changes in a_2.

Finally, if $P - a_1 K_f$ is positive, a rise in a_2 increases the measure of personal income inequality (ψ). Although both private households' capital income (Z) and the wage bill (W) increase with a rise in a_2, capital income (Z) grows at a higher rate. As the rich are the main beneficiaries of a rise in capital income (Z), ψ increases. Likewise, if firms' net profits (P) are lower than the basic dividend $(a_1 K_f)$, personal income inequality as measured by ψ declines with a rise in a_2. The ratio of the incomes of the rich to the poor private households (ψ) is not affected by a change in a_2 if $P - a_1 K_f$ is zero.

Changes in the Interest Rate (i)

As private households are the receivers of firms' interest payments, a rise in the interest rate (i) redistributes income from non-consuming firms to private households who consume part of their income. Aggregate demand, output (Y), and the degree of capacity utilization (u) thus unambiguously rise in the short run.

An increase in the interest rate (i) raises the wage bill (W) and total profits (R) in the economy. From a Kaleckian demand-side perspective (see Eq. 8.30), the total amount of profits (R) rises because an increase in the interest rate (i) raises private households' capital income (Z) and thus consumption out of profits. Although private households' saving out of wages increases as well, this rise does not compensate for the increase in consumption out of profits. Due to overhead labor costs $(m_2 K)$, profits (R) grow at a higher rate than wages (W) and output (Y). The profit share (π) thus rises with an increase in i.

Despite a rise in the wage bill (W), an increase in the interest rate (i) is most favorable for the affluent private households. With private households' capital income (Z) rising faster than total wages (W), income inequality as measured by ψ increases, as those at the top of the distribution are the main receivers of capital income (Z).

Changes in the Saving Rates of Private Households (s_h^p, s_h^r)

A rise in the saving rate of the poor private households (s_h^p) or the rich private households (s_h^r) reduces private households' consumption spending, leading to a decline in aggregate demand, output (Y), and capacity utilization (u).

The decline in output (Y) is accompanied by a fall in both the wage bill (W) and total profits (R). Along Kaleckian lines (see Eq. 8.30), the amount of profits (R) declines because private households' consumption out of capital income (Z) falls, both through the increase in the saving rate (s_h^p, s_h^r) as well as through the induced fall in private households' capital income (Z). While the development of private households' total amount of saving out of wages is ambiguous, even a decline in saving out of wages cannot compensate for the fall in consumption out of capital income. With a rise in s_h^p or s_h^r, profits (R) thus decline. Due to overhead labor costs $(m_2 K)$, profits (R) fall at a higher rate than wages (W) and output (Y), implying that the profit share (π) in the economy declines.[1]

A rise in the saving rate of private households (s_h^p, s_h^r) is accompanied by a fall in the wage bill (W) and private households' capital income (Z). While a decline in the latter mainly harms the private households at the top of the distribution, a decline in wages (W) primarily affects the private households in the lower half of the income hierarchy. From an ex-ante perspective, the magnitudes of the declines in wages (W) and capital income (Z) are ambiguous. It can be shown, however, that the development of the ratio of capital income (Z) to the wage bill (W) and the development of the measure of personal income inequality (ψ) depend on the sign of the expression $i (1 - a_2) (1 - m_1) - a_2 m_2$ (see also Eqs. D.21 and D.22 in Appendix D.1.1.1). If it is positive (negative), the wage bill (W) declines faster (less) than private households' capital income (Z), so that the measure of personal income inequality (ψ) rises (falls). If it is zero, capital income (Z) and the wage bill (W) decline at the same rate and personal income inequality (ψ) does not change at all. Eventually, $i (1 - a_2) (1 - m_1) - a_2 m_2$ is more likely to be negative the higher a_2, m_1, and m_2, and the lower i.

D.1.2   The Economy in the Long Run

D.1.2.1   The Keynesian Stability Condition

In the Steindlian model presented in Chap. 8, the Keynesian stability condition that saving reacts more strongly to changes in the degree of capacity utilization than investment is given by

$$\frac{\partial \left(\frac{I}{K}\right)^d}{\partial u} < \frac{\partial \frac{S}{K}}{\partial u}. \tag{D.25}$$

---

[1] The partial derivatives of u and π with respect to s_h^r (see Eqs. D.6 and D.14 in Appendix D.1.1.1) seem to be ambiguous. Given the assumption that total profits (R) are larger than zero (see Eq. 8.12), however, the derivatives are negative. With a positive R, the income of the rich private households (Y_h^r) is also positive. A rise in s_h^r then reduces both u and π.

Total saving as a ratio of capital is given by

$$\frac{S}{K} = \frac{S_f}{K} + \frac{S_h^p}{K} + \frac{S_h^r}{K} . \tag{D.26}$$

Assuming $a_1 = i$, substituting Eqs. (8.44) and (8.27) to (8.29) into Eq. (D.26) yields

$$\begin{aligned}\frac{S}{K} =\ & (1 - a_2)\,(m_1 u - m_2 - i)\\ & + s_h^p\,[(m_1 u - m_2)\,(a_2 z - w) + i z\,(1 - a_2) + u w]\\ & + s_h^r\,\{(m_1 u - m_2)\,[a_2\,(1 - z) - (1 - w)]\\ & + i\,(1 - a_2)\,(1 - z) + u\,(1 - w)\}\ .\end{aligned} \tag{D.27}$$

Partially deriving Eq. (D.27) with respect to u gives

$$\frac{\partial \frac{S}{K}}{\partial u} = m_1 \left[(1 - a_2)\left(1 - s_h^r\right) + \left(s_h^r - s_h^p\right)(w - a_2 z)\right] + s_h^p w + s_h^r\,(1 - w)\ . \tag{D.28}$$

The desired rate of real capital accumulation $(I/K)^d$ is the long-run attractor of firms' investment behavior and thus represents long-term investment as a ratio of capital. Substituting Eqs. (8.10) and (8.44) into Eq. (8.8) yields

$$\begin{aligned}g^d = \left(\frac{I}{K}\right)^d =\ & \alpha_0 + \alpha_1\,(1 - a_2)\,(m_1 u - m_2 - i)\\ & + \alpha_2\,(u - u_0) + \alpha_3\,(h_0 + h_1 g)\ .\end{aligned} \tag{D.29}$$

From the goods market equilibrium $g = I/K = S/K$, it follows that, at any time, the actual rate of real capital accumulation (g) is given by Eq. (D.27). Substituting Eq. (D.27) into Eq. (D.29) yields

$$\begin{aligned}g^d =\ & \alpha_0 + \alpha_1\,[(1 - a_2)\,(m_1 u - m_2 - i)] + \alpha_2\,(u - u_0)\\ & + \alpha_3 \Big\{h_0 + h_1 \Big[(1 - a_2)\,(m_1 u - m_2 - i) + s_h^p\,((m_1 u - m_2)\,(a_2 z - w)\\ & + i z\,(1 - a_2) + u w) + s_h^r\,((m_1 u - m_2)\,(a_2\,(1 - z) - (1 - w))\\ & + i\,(1 - a_2)\,(1 - z) + u\,(1 - w))\Big]\Big\}\ .\end{aligned} \tag{D.30}$$

Partially deriving Eq. (D.30) with respect to u gives

$$\begin{aligned}\frac{\partial \left(\frac{I}{K}\right)^d}{\partial u} =\ & \alpha_1 m_1\,(1 - a_2) + \alpha_2\\ & + \alpha_3 h_1 \left\{m_1 \left[(1 - a_2)\left(1 - s_h^r\right) + \left(s_h^r - s_h^p\right)(w - a_2 z)\right]\right.\\ & \left. + s_h^p w + s_h^r\,(1 - w)\right\}\ .\end{aligned} \tag{D.31}$$

By substituting Eqs. (D.28) and (D.31) into Eq. (D.25) and rearranging the terms, it follows that the Keynesian stability condition is given by

$$
\begin{aligned}
\alpha_1 m_1 (1 - a_2) + \alpha_2 < {} & (1 - \alpha_3 h_1)\{m_1 [(1 - a_2)(1 - s_h^r) \\
& + (s_h^r - s_h^p)(w - a_2 z)] + s_h^p w + s_h^r (1 - w)\},
\end{aligned}
\tag{D.32}
$$

which is equal to Eq. (8.49).

D.1.2.2   Partial Derivatives

The Rate of Real Capital Accumulation (g^*)

The long-run comparative static changes in the long-run equilibrium rate of real capital accumulation (g^*) are calculated by partially deriving Eq. (8.46), i.e.,

$$
\begin{aligned}
\frac{dg}{dt} = \Theta \Bigg[& \alpha_0 + \alpha_1 \left(\frac{\begin{array}{c} (1 - a_2)\{m_1 [g - i (s_h^r - s_h^p)(w - z)] \\ - (i + m_2) [s_h^p w + s_h^r (1 - w)]\} \end{array}}{\begin{array}{c} m_1 [(1 - a_2)(1 - s_h^r) + (s_h^r - s_h^p)(w - a_2 z)] \\ + s_h^p w + s_h^r (1 - w) \end{array}} \right) \\
& + \alpha_2 \left(\frac{\begin{array}{c} g + (1 - a_2)(i + m_2)[(1 - s_h^r) + z(s_h^r - s_h^p)] \\ + m_2 (s_h^r - s_h^p)(w - z) \end{array}}{\begin{array}{c} m_1 [(1 - a_2)(1 - s_h^r) + (s_h^r - s_h^p)(w - a_2 z)] \\ + s_h^p w + s_h^r (1 - w) \end{array}} - u_0 \right) \\
& + \alpha_3 (h_0 + h_1 g) - g \Bigg],
\end{aligned}
$$

with respect to the model's exogenous variables and parameters $a_2, i, m_1, m_2, s_h^p, s_h^r,$ $w, z, \alpha_0, \alpha_1, \alpha_2, \alpha_3, h_0, h_1,$ and u_0.

The partial derivatives are given by the following Eqs. (D.33) to (D.47):

$$
\frac{\partial \dfrac{dg}{dt}}{\partial a_2} = \frac{\begin{array}{c} \Theta \{m_1 [g - i (s_h^r - s_h^p)(w - z)] \\ - (i + m_2) [s_h^p w + s_h^r (1 - w)]\} \\ \cdot \{-\alpha_1 [s_h^r - (s_h^r - s_h^p)(w - m_1(w - z))] \\ + \alpha_2 [1 - s_h^r + z(s_h^r - s_h^p)]\} \end{array}}{\left\{ m_1 [(1 - a_2)(1 - s_h^r) + (s_h^r - s_h^p)(w - a_2 z)] + s_h^p w + s_h^r (1 - w) \right\}^2}
\tag{D.33}
$$

$$\frac{\partial \frac{dg}{dt}}{\partial i} = \frac{\Theta \left\{ -\alpha_1 (1 - a_2) \left[m_1 \left(s_h^r - s_h^p \right) (w - z) + s_h^p w + s_h^r (1 - w) \right] \right. }{ m_1 \left[(1 - a_2) \left(1 - s_h^r \right) + \left(s_h^r - s_h^p \right) (w - a_2 z) \right] + s_h^p w + s_h^r (1 - w)}$$

$$+ \alpha_2 (1 - a_2) \left[\left(1 - s_h^r \right) + z \left(s_h^r - s_h^p \right) \right] \right\}$$

(D.34)

$$\frac{\partial \frac{dg}{dt}}{\partial m_1} = \frac{\Theta \left\{ \alpha_1 \left[(1 - a_2) \left(s_h^p w + s_h^r (1 - w) \right) \right] \right. }{\left\{ m_1 \left[(1 - a_2) \left(1 - s_h^r \right) + \left(s_h^r - s_h^p \right) (w - a_2 z) \right] \right.}$$

$$- \alpha_2 \left[\left(s_h^r - s_h^p \right) (w - a_2 z) + (1 - a_2) \left(1 - s_h^r \right) \right] \right\}$$

$$\cdot \left\{ g + (1 - a_2) (i + m_2) \left[1 - s_h^r + z \left(s_h^r - s_h^p \right) \right] \right.$$

$$+ m_2 \left(s_h^r - s_h^p \right) (w - z) \right\}$$

$$\left. + s_h^p w + s_h^r (1 - w) \right\}^2$$

(D.35)

$$\frac{\partial \frac{dg}{dt}}{\partial m_2} = \frac{-\Theta \left\{ \alpha_1 \left[(1 - a_2) \left(s_h^p w + s_h^r (1 - w) \right) \right] \right. }{ m_1 \left[(1 - a_2) \left(1 - s_h^r \right) + \left(s_h^r - s_h^p \right) (w - a_2 z) \right] + s_h^p w + s_h^r (1 - w)}$$

$$- \alpha_2 \left[\left(s_h^r - s_h^p \right) (w - a_2 z) + (1 - a_2) \left(1 - s_h^r \right) \right] \right\}$$

(D.36)

$$\frac{\partial \frac{dg}{dt}}{\partial s_h^p} = \frac{-\Theta \left[\alpha_1 m_1 (1 - a_2) + \alpha_2 \right]}{\left\{ m_1 \left[(1 - a_2) \left(1 - s_h^r \right) + \left(s_h^r - s_h^p \right) (w - a_2 z) \right] \right.}$$

$$\cdot \left\{ a_2 m_2 s_h^r (w - z) + g \left[a_2 m_1 z + w (1 - m_1) \right] + m_2 w (1 - a_2) \right.$$

$$+ i (1 - a_2) \left[w (1 - m_1) \left(1 - s_h^r \right) + z \left(m_1 + s_h^r (1 - m_1) \right) \right] \right\}$$

$$\left. + s_h^p w + s_h^r (1 - w) \right\}^2$$

(D.37)

$$\frac{\partial \frac{dg}{dt}}{\partial s_h^r} = \frac{-\Theta \left[\alpha_1 m_1 (1 - a_2) + \alpha_2 \right]}{\left\{ m_1 \left[(1 - a_2) \left(1 - s_h^r \right) + \left(s_h^r - s_h^p \right) (w - a_2 z) \right] \right.}$$

$$\cdot \left\{ - a_2 m_2 s_h^p (w - z) + g \left[(1 - m_1) (1 - w) + a_2 m_1 (1 - z) \right] \right.$$

$$+ (1 - a_2) \left[(1 - w) (i + m_2) + i (w - z) \left(m_1 \left(1 - s_h^p \right) + s_h^p \right) \right] \right\}$$

$$\left. + s_h^p w + s_h^r (1 - w) \right\}^2$$

(D.38)

$$\frac{\partial \frac{dg}{dt}}{\partial w} = \frac{\Theta \left[\alpha_1 m_1 (1 - a_2) + \alpha_2 \right] \left(s_h^r - s_h^p \right)}{\left\{ m_1 \left[(1 - a_2) \left(1 - s_h^r \right) + \left(s_h^r - s_h^p \right) (w - a_2 z) \right] \right.}$$

$$\cdot \left\{ g (1 - m_1) + z \left(s_h^r - s_h^p \right) \left[i (1 - a_2) (1 - m_1) \right] \right.$$

$$+ m_2 \left[1 - a_2 \left(1 - s_h^r + z \left(s_h^r - s_h^p \right) \right) \right]$$

$$+ i (1 - a_2) (1 - m_1) \left(1 - s_h^r \right) \right\}$$

$$\left. + s_h^p w + s_h^r (1 - w) \right\}^2$$

(D.39)

$$\frac{\partial \frac{dg}{dt}}{\partial z} = \frac{\Theta \left[\alpha_1 m_1 (1 - a_2) + \alpha_2 \right] \left(s_h^r - s_h^p \right)}{\left\{ m_1 \left[(1 - a_2) \left(1 - s_h^r \right) + \left(s_h^r - s_h^p \right) (w - a_2 z) \right] \right.}$$

$$\cdot \left\{ a_2 g m_1 + a_2 m_2 \left[w \left(s_h^r - s_h^p \right) - s_h^r \right] \right.$$

$$+ i (1 - a_2) \left[m_1 \left(\left(1 - s_h^r \right) + w \left(s_h^r - s_h^p \right) \right) + s_h^p w + s_h^r (1 - w) \right] \right\}$$

$$\left. + s_h^p w + s_h^r (1 - w) \right\}^2$$

(D.40)

$$\frac{\partial \frac{\mathrm{d}g}{\mathrm{d}t}}{\partial \alpha_0} = \Theta \tag{D.41}$$

$$\frac{\partial \frac{\mathrm{d}g}{\mathrm{d}t}}{\partial \alpha_1} = \frac{\Theta (1 - a_2) \cdot \left\{ m_1 \left[g - i \left(s_h^r - s_h^p \right) (w - z) \right] - (i + m_2) \left[s_h^p w + s_h^r (1 - w) \right] \right\}}{m_1 \left[(1 - a_2)(1 - s_h^r) + \left(s_h^r - s_h^p \right) (w - a_2 z) \right] + s_h^p w + s_h^r (1 - w)} \tag{D.42}$$

$$\frac{\partial \frac{\mathrm{d}g}{\mathrm{d}t}}{\partial \alpha_2} = \frac{\Theta \left\{ g + (1 - a_2)(i + m_2) \left[\left(1 - s_h^r \right) + z \left(s_h^r - s_h^p \right) \right] + m_2 \left(s_h^r - s_h^p \right) (w - z) + u_0 \left[m_1 \left(1 - s_h^r \right) (a_2 - 1) - s_h^r + \left(s_h^r - s_h^p \right) (a_2 m_1 z + w (1 - m_1)) \right] \right\}}{m_1 \left[(1 - a_2) \left(1 - s_h^r \right) + \left(s_h^r - s_h^p \right) (w - a_2 z) \right] + s_h^p w + s_h^r (1 - w)} \tag{D.43}$$

$$\frac{\partial \frac{\mathrm{d}g}{\mathrm{d}t}}{\partial \alpha_3} = h_0 + h_1 g \tag{D.44}$$

$$\frac{\partial \frac{\mathrm{d}g}{\mathrm{d}t}}{\partial h_0} = \alpha_3 \tag{D.45}$$

$$\frac{\partial \frac{\mathrm{d}g}{\mathrm{d}t}}{\partial h_1} = \alpha_3 g \tag{D.46}$$

$$\frac{\partial \frac{\mathrm{d}g}{\mathrm{d}t}}{\partial u_0} = -\alpha_2 \Theta. \tag{D.47}$$

The Degree of Capacity Utilization (u), the Profit Share (π), and the Measure of Personal Income Distribution (ψ)

In the long run, changes in the rate of real capital accumulation (g) affect the degree of capacity utilization (u), the profit share (π), and the measure of personal income inequality (ψ).

Partially deriving Eq. (8.41), i.e.,

$$u = \frac{g + (1 - a_2)(m_2 + i) \left[\left(1 - s_h^r \right) + z \left(s_h^r - s_h^p \right) \right] + m_2 \left(s_h^r - s_h^p \right) (w - z)}{m_1 \left[(1 - a_2) \left(1 - s_h^r \right) + \left(s_h^r - s_h^p \right) (w - a_2 z) \right] + s_h^p w + s_h^r (1 - w)}$$

with respect to g yields

$$\frac{\partial u}{\partial g} = \frac{1}{m_1 \left[(1 - a_2) \left(1 - s_h^r \right) + \left(s_h^r - s_h^p \right) (w - a_2 z) \right] + s_h^p w + s_h^r (1 - w)}. \tag{D.48}$$

Partially deriving Eq. (8.42), i.e.,

$$\pi = \frac{g m_1 + i m_1 (1 - a_2) \left[1 - s_h^r + z \left(s_h^r - s_h^p \right) \right] - m_2 \left[s_h^r - w \left(s_h^r - s_h^p \right) \right]}{g + (1 - a_2) (i + m_2) \left[1 - s_h^r + z \left(s_h^r - s_h^p \right) \right] + m_2 \left(s_h^r - s_h^p \right) (w - z)}$$

with respect to g yields

$$\frac{\partial \pi}{\partial g} = \frac{\begin{array}{c} m_2 \left\{ m_1 (1 - a_2) \left(1 - s_h^r \right) + s_h^p \left[a_2 m_1 z + w (1 - m_1) \right] \right. \\ + s_h^r \left[(1 - w) + m_1 (w - a_2 z) \right] \right\} \end{array}}{\begin{array}{c} \left\{ g + (1 - a_2) (i + m_2) \left[1 - s_h^r + z \left(s_h^r - s_h^p \right) \right] \right. \\ \left. + m_2 \left(s_h^r - s_h^p \right) (w - z) \right\}^2 \end{array}}. \tag{D.49}$$

Partially deriving Eq. (8.43), i.e.,

$$\psi = \frac{\begin{array}{c} g \left[(1 - w)(1 - m_1) + a_2 m_1 (1 - z) \right] - a_2 m_2 s_h^p (w - z) \\ + (1 - a_2) \left\{ (1 - w)(i + m_2) + i (w - z) \left[s_h^p + m_1 \left(1 - s_h^p \right) \right] \right\} \end{array}}{\begin{array}{c} g \left[a_2 m_1 z + w (1 - m_1) \right] + a_2 m_2 s_h^r (w - z) \\ + (1 - a_2) \left\{ w (i + m_2) - i (w - z) \left[s_h^r + m_1 \left(1 - s_h^r \right) \right] \right\} \end{array}}$$

with respect to g yields

$$\frac{\partial \psi}{\partial g} = \frac{\begin{array}{c} (w - z) \left[a_2 m_2 - i (1 - a_2)(1 - m_1) \right] \\ \cdot \left\{ m_1 \left[(1 - a_2) \left(1 - s_h^r \right) + \left(s_h^r - s_h^p \right) (w - a_2 z) \right] \right. \\ \left. + s_h^p w + s_h^r (1 - w) \right\} \end{array}}{\begin{array}{c} \left\{ g \left[a_2 m_1 z + w (1 - m_1) \right] + a_2 m_2 s_h^r (w - z) \right. \\ \left. + (1 - a_2) \left[w (i + m_2) - i (w - z) \left(s_h^r + m_1 \left(1 - s_h^r \right) \right) \right] \right\}^2 \end{array}}. \tag{D.50}$$

D.1.2.3 Comparative Statics in the Long Run: Effects on the Long-Run Equilibrium

Changes in the Dividend Payout Parameter (a_2)

The Long-Run Equilibrium Rate of Real Capital Accumulation (g^*)

The impact of a change in the dividend payout parameter (a_2) on the long-run equilibrium rate of real capital accumulation (g^*) depends on the sign of the expression

$$- \alpha_1 \left\{ s_h^r - \left(s_h^r - s_h^p \right) \left[w - m_1 (w - z) \right] \right\} + \alpha_2 \left[1 - s_h^r + z \left(s_h^r - s_h^p \right) \right]. \tag{D.51}$$

Given a positive difference $P - a_1 K_f$, a rise in a_2 raises (reduces) g^* if expression (D.51) is positive (negative), i.e., economic growth is both profit-led and inequality-led (wage-led and equality-led). If $P - a_1 K_f$ is negative, a rise in a_2 raises (reduces) g^* if expression (D.51) is negative (positive), i.e., economic growth is both wage-led and equality-led (profit-led and inequality-led). If $P - a_1 K_f$ and/or expression (D.51) is zero, a rise in a_2 has no impact on the long-run equilibrium rate of real capital accumulation (g^*).[2]

With a positive difference $P - a_1 K_f$, in the short run a rise in a_2 reduces firms' internal saving as a ratio of capital (S_f/K), but raises the degree of capacity utilization (u). If expression (D.51) is greater than zero, the latter effect outweighs the first effect and the long-run equilibrium rate of real capital accumulation (g^*) rises. This is more likely to happen if, for instance, α_1 is relatively low compared to α_2. With a relatively low α_1, it is also likely that the long-run equilibrium degree of capacity utilization (u^*) rises. If α_2 is comparatively high, on the other hand, firms' internal saving as a ratio of capital (S_f/K) is likely to rise in the long run, although it declines in the short run.

The Long-Run Equilibrium Degree of Capacity Utilization (u^*)

The impact of a change in the dividend payout parameter (a_2) on the long-run equilibrium degree of capacity utilization (u^*) depends on the sign of the expression

$$\alpha_1 - (1 - \alpha_3 h_1) \left[1 - s_h^r + z \left(s_h^r - s_h^p\right)\right] . \tag{D.52}$$

Given a positive difference $P - a_1 K_f$, a rise in a_2 raises (reduces) u^* if expression (D.52) is negative (positive). If $P - a_1 K_f$ is negative, a rise in a_2 raises (reduces) u^* if expression (D.52) is positive (negative). If $P - a_1 K_f$ and/or expression (D.52) is zero, a change in a_2 has no impact on the long-run equilibrium degree of capacity utilization (u^*).

With a positive difference $P - a_1 K_f$, a rise in a_2 is more likely to raise u^*, for instance, the lower α_1. If $P - a_1 K_f$ is greater than zero, in the short run a rise in a_2 reduces firms' internal saving as a ratio of capital (S_f/K). This hampers firms' desired rate of real capital accumulation (g^d) and hence the long-run equilibrium rate of real capital accumulation (g^*), with the latter, in turn, being a drag on the long-run equilibrium degree of capacity utilization (u^*). If the impact of the short-run decline in S_f/K is small, however, which is more likely the lower α_1, it is more likely that both g^* and u^* rise.

The Long-Run Equilibrium Profit Share (π^*)

The impact of a change in the dividend payout parameter (a_2) on the long-run equilibrium profit share (π^*) depends on the sign of expression (D.52). Given a positive difference $P - a_1 K_f$, a rise in a_2 raises (reduces) π^* if expression (D.52) is negative

---

[2]Considering the partial derivative of dg/dt with respect to a_2 in Eq. (D.33) (see Appendix D.1.2.2), it should be noted that the expression $m_1 [g - i (s_h^r - s_h^p) (w - z)] - (i + m_2) [s_h^p w + s_h^r (1 - w)]$ is positive (negative) when firms' net profits (P) exceed (fall short of) the basic dividend $(a_1 K_f)$. It is zero when firms' net profits (P) are equal to the basic dividend $(a_1 K_f)$.

(positive). If $P - a_1 K_f$ is negative, a rise in a_2 raises (reduces) π^* if expression (D.52) is positive (negative). If $P - a_1 K_f$ and/or expression (D.52) is zero, a change in a_2 has no impact on the long-run equilibrium profit share (π^*). The impact of a change in the dividend payout parameter (a_2) on the long-run equilibrium profit share (π^*) thus depends on the same conditions as the impact of a change in a_2 on the long-run equilibrium degree of capacity utilization (u^*). If a change in a_2 raises (lowers) u^*, π^* increases (declines) as well. The reason is that, with a rise (decline) in u^* (triggered by variations in a_2), overhead labor costs are spread over a higher (lower) volume of output, implying that the long-run equilibrium profit share (π^*) rises (declines).

The Long-Run Equilibrium Measure of Personal Income Distribution (ψ^*)

The impact of a change in the dividend payout parameter (a_2) on the long-run equilibrium measure of personal income distribution (ψ^*) depends on the sign of the expression

$$(1 - m_1)(\alpha_0 - \alpha_2 u_0 + \alpha_3 h_0) + m_2 (1 - \alpha_1 - \alpha_2 - \alpha_3 h_1) . \qquad (D.53)$$

Given a positive difference $P - a_1 K_f$, a rise in a_2 raises (reduces) ψ^* if expression (D.53) is positive (negative). If $P - a_1 K_f$ is negative, a rise in a_2 raises (reduces) ψ^* if expression (D.53) is negative (positive). If $P - a_1 K_f$ and/or expression (D.53) is zero, a change in a_2 has no impact on the long-run equilibrium measure of personal income distribution (ψ^*).

   If $P - a_1 K_f$ is greater than zero, in the short run a rise in a_2 unambiguously increases personal income inequality as measured by ψ. In the long run, however, when g^* rises or falls in response to the rise in a_2, this short-run increase in personal income inequality may be reverted. In any case, ψ even falls below its initial level if expression (D.53) is negative. With a positive difference $P - a_1 K_f$, a rise in a_2 is more likely to reduce ψ^*, for instance, the larger the sum of the parameters α_1, α_2, and $\alpha_3 h_1$—the reaction coefficients of real capital accumulation—and the lower the sum of the parameters α_0, $-\alpha_2 u_0$, and $\alpha_3 h_0$—the autonomous components of real capital accumulation.[3]

Changes in the Interest Rate (i)

The conditions determining the impact of a change in the interest rate (i) on the long-run equilibrium rate of real capital accumulation (g^*), on the long-run equilibrium degree of capacity utilization (u^*), on the long-run equilibrium profit share (π^*), and on the long-run equilibrium measure of personal income distribution (ψ^*) are identical to the respective conditions determining the effects of a change in the dividend payout parameter (a_2) in case of a positive difference $P - a_1 K_f$. See the previous paragraphs for further details.

---

[3] For a stable equilibrium to hold, it should be noted that, ceteris paribus, the combined parameters α_1, α_2, and $\alpha_3 h_1$ have an upper limit.

Changes in the Marginal Profit Share (m_1)

The Long-Run Equilibrium Rate of Real Capital Accumulation (g^*)

The impact of a change in the marginal profit share (m_1) on the long-run equilibrium rate of real capital accumulation (g^*) depends on the sign of the expression

$$\alpha_1 \left\{ (1 - a_2) \left[s_h^p w + s_h^r (1 - w) \right] \right\}$$
$$- \alpha_2 \left[\left(s_h^r - s_h^p \right) (w - a_2 z) + (1 - a_2) \left(1 - s_h^r \right) \right]. \quad \text{(D.54)}$$

If it is positive (negative), a rise in m_1 raises (reduces) g^*, i.e., economic growth is both profit-led and inequality-led (wage-led and equality-led). If expression (D.54) is zero, a change in m_1 has no impact on the long-run equilibrium rate of real capital accumulation (g^*).

In the short run, a rise in m_1 raises firms' internal saving as a ratio of capital (S_f/K), but reduces the degree of capacity utilization (u). If expression (D.54) is positive, the former effect outweighs the latter effect and the long-run equilibrium rate of real capital accumulation (g^*) rises. This is more likely to happen if, for instance, α_1 is relatively large compared to α_2. With a relatively large α_1, it is also likely that the long-run equilibrium degree of capacity utilization (u^*) rises, although u declines in the short run. If α_2 is comparatively low, on the other hand, firms' internal saving as a ratio of capital (S_f/K) is likely to rise not only in the short run, but also in the long run.

The Long-Run Equilibrium Degree of Capacity Utilization (u^*)

The impact of a change in the marginal profit share (m_1) on the long-run equilibrium degree of capacity utilization (u^*) depends on the sign of the expression

$$\alpha_1 (1 - a_2) - (1 - \alpha_3 h_1) \left[(1 - a_2) \left(1 - s_h^r \right) + \left(s_h^r - s_h^p \right) (w - a_2 z) \right]. \quad \text{(D.55)}$$

If it is positive (negative), a rise in m_1 raises (reduces) u^*. If expression (D.55) is zero, a change in m_1 has no impact on the long-run equilibrium degree of capacity utilization (u^*).

A rise in m_1 is more likely to raise u^*, for instance, the larger α_1. In the short run, a rise in m_1 unambiguously raises firms' internal saving as a ratio of capital (S_f/K). This boosts firms' desired rate of real capital accumulation (g^d) and hence the long-run equilibrium rate of real capital accumulation (g^*), with the latter, in turn, being conducive to a rise in the long-run equilibrium degree of capacity utilization (u^*). Hence, if the impact of the short-run rise in S_f/K is large, which is more likely the larger α_1, it is more likely that both g^* and u^* rise.

The Long-Run Equilibrium Profit Share (π^*)

The impact of a change in the marginal profit share (m_1) on the long-run equilibrium profit share (π^*) depends on the sign of the expression

$$(\alpha_0 - \alpha_2 u_0 + \alpha_3 h_0) + i(1 - a_2)\left\{-\alpha_1 + (1 - \alpha_3 h_1)\left[1 - s_h^r + z\left(s_h^r - s_h^p\right)\right]\right\}. \quad (D.56)$$

If it is positive (negative), a rise in m_1 raises (reduces) π^*. If expression (D.56) is zero, a change in m_1 has no impact on the long-run equilibrium profit share (π^*).

In the short run, a rise in m_1 unambiguously raises the profit share (π). From the short to the long run, however, this increase in the profit share may be reverted if g^* declines sufficiently. In any case, π declines below its initial value if condition (D.56) is negative.

The Long-Run Equilibrium Measure of Personal Income Distribution (ψ^*)

The impact of a change in the marginal profit share (m_1) on the long-run equilibrium measure of personal income distribution (ψ^*) depends on the sign of the expression

$$a_2(\alpha_0 - \alpha_2 u_0 + \alpha_3 h_0) + i(1 - a_2)(1 - \alpha_1 - \alpha_2 - \alpha_3 h_1). \quad (D.57)$$

If it is positive (negative), a rise in m_1 raises (reduces) ψ^*. If expression (D.57) is zero, a change in m_1 has no impact on ψ^*.

In the short run, a rise in m_1 unambiguously increases personal income inequality as measured by ψ. In the long run, however, when g^* rises or falls in response to the rise in m_1, this short-run increase in personal income inequality may be reverted. In any case, ψ even falls below its initial level if expression (D.57) is negative. A rise in m_1 is more likely to reduce ψ^*, for instance, the larger the sum of the parameters α_1, α_2, and $\alpha_3 h_1$—the reaction coefficients of real capital accumulation—and the lower the sum of the parameters α_0, $-\alpha_2 u_0$, and $\alpha_3 h_0$—the autonomous components of real capital accumulation.

Changes in the Ratio of Overhead Labor Costs to Capital (m_2)

The conditions determining the impact of a change in the ratio of overhead labor costs to capital (m_2) on the long-run equilibrium rate of real capital accumulation (g^*), on the long-run equilibrium degree of capacity utilization (u^*), on the long-run equilibrium profit share (π^*), and on the long-run equilibrium measure of personal income distribution (ψ^*) are the exact opposite to the respective conditions determining the impact of a change in the marginal profit share (m_1). In other words:

A rise in m_2 raises (reduces) g^* if expression (D.54) is negative (positive). If expression (D.54) is zero, a change in m_2 has no impact on g^*.

A rise in m_2 raises (reduces) u^* if expression (D.55) is negative (positive). If expression (D.55) is zero, a change in m_2 has no impact on u^*.

A rise in m_2 raises (reduces) π^* if expression (D.56) is negative (positive). If expression (D.56) is zero, a change in m_2 has no impact on π^*.

A rise in m_2 raises (reduces) ψ^* if expression (D.57) is negative (positive). If expression (D.57) is zero, a change in m_2 has no impact on ψ^*.

See the previous paragraphs for further details.

Changes in the Saving Rates of Private Households (s_h^p, s_h^r)

The Long-Run Equilibrium Rate of Real Capital Accumulation (g^*)

In the short run, a rise (fall) in the saving rate of the poor private households (s_h^p) or the rich private households (s_h^r) reduces (raises) both firms' internal saving as a ratio of capital (S_f/K) as well as the degree of capacity utilization (u). The desired rate of real capital accumulation (g^d) is thus reduced (raised) by a fall (rise) in both $\alpha_1 (S_f/K)$ and $\alpha_2 (u - u_0)$. As a decline (rise) in g^d reduces (increases) dg/dt and hence firms' actual rate of real capital accumulation (g), the long-run equilibrium rate of real capital accumulation (g^*) declines (rises), implying that economic growth is clearly wage-led (profit-led).[4]

The Long-Run Equilibrium Degree of Capacity Utilization (u^*) and Profit Share (π^*)

A rise (fall) in the saving rate of the poor private households (s_h^p) or the rich private households (s_h^r) unambiguously reduces (increases) the degree of capacity utilization (u) and the profit share (π) in the short run. With a decline (rise) in the long-run equilibrium rate of real capital accumulation (g^*), from the short to the long run u and π decline (rise) still further. The long-run equilibrium degree of capacity utilization (u^*) and the long-run equilibrium profit share (π^*) are thus clearly lower (higher) than initially.

The Long-Run Equilibrium Measure of Personal Income Distribution (ψ^*)

The impact of a change in the saving rate of the poor private households (s_h^p) or the rich private households (s_h^r) on the long-run equilibrium measure of personal income distribution (ψ^*) depends on the sign of the expression

$$a_2 m_2 - i (1 - a_2) (1 - m_1) . \tag{D.58}$$

If it is positive (negative), a rise in s_h^p or s_h^r reduces (raises) ψ^*. If expression (D.58) is zero, a change in s_h^p or s_h^r has no impact on ψ^*.

In the short run, a rise in s_h^p or s_h^r has an ambiguous impact on personal income inequality as measured by ψ. It can be shown, however, that, if a rise in s_h^p or s_h^r raises (reduces) ψ in the short run, the unambiguous decline in the long-run equilibrium rate of real capital accumulation (g^*) necessarily raises (reduces) ψ further.

A rise in s_h^p or s_h^r is more likely to raise ψ^* the lower a_2, m_1, and m_2, and the higher i. See the respective remarks in Sect. 8.3.2.3 for further details.

Changes in the Income Shares of the Poor Private Households (w, z)

The Long-Run Equilibrium Rate of Real Capital Accumulation (g^*)

In the short run, a rise (fall) in the wage share (w) or the capital income share (z) of the poor private households raises (reduces) both firms' internal saving as a ratio

---

[4]While the partial derivative of dg/dt with respect to s_h^r (see Eq. D.38 in Appendix D.1.2.2) seems to be ambiguous, it is definitely negative if it is assumed that R, and hence Y_h^r, is always positive (see Eq. 8.12). See also footnote 1 in Sect. D.1.1.2.

of capital (S_f/K) as well as the degree of capacity utilization (u). The desired rate of real capital accumulation (g^d) is thus raised (reduced) by a rise (fall) in both $\alpha_1 (S_f/K)$ and $\alpha_2 (u - u_0)$. As a rise (decline) in g^d increases (reduces) dg/dt and hence firms' actual rate of real capital accumulation (g), the long-run equilibrium rate of real capital accumulation (g^*) rises (declines), implying that economic growth is both profit-led and equality-led.[5]

The Long-Run Equilibrium Degree of Capacity Utilization (u^*) and Profit Share (π^*)

A rise (fall) in the wage share (w) or the capital income share (z) of the poor private households unambiguously increases (reduces) the degree of capacity utilization (u) and the profit share (π) in the short run. With a rise (decline) in the long-run equilibrium rate of real capital accumulation (g^*), from the short to the long run u and π rise (decline) still further. The long-run equilibrium degree of capacity utilization (u^*) and the long-run equilibrium profit share (π^*) are thus clearly higher (lower) than initially.

The Long-Run Equilibrium Measure of Personal Income Distribution (ψ^*)

The impact of a change in the wage share (w) or the capital income share (z) of the poor private households on the long-run equilibrium measure of personal income distribution (ψ^*) depends on the sign of the expression

$$(\alpha_0 - \alpha_2 u_0 + \alpha_3 h_0) [1 - m_1 (1 - a_2)]$$
$$+ (1 - a_2) (i + m_2) (1 - \alpha_1 - \alpha_2 - \alpha_3 h_1) . \tag{D.59}$$

If it is positive (negative), a rise in w or z reduces (raises) ψ^*. If expression (D.59) is zero, a change in w or z has no impact on ψ^*.

In the short run, a rise in w or z unambiguously reduces personal income inequality as measured by ψ. In the long run, however, when g^* rises in response to the rise in w or z, this short-run decline in personal income inequality may be reverted. In any case, ψ even rises above its initial level if expression (D.59) is negative. A rise in w or z is more likely to raise ψ^*, for instance, the larger the sum of the parameters α_1, α_2, and $alphadh_1$—the reaction coefficients of real capital accumulation—and the lower the sum of the parameters α_0, $-\alpha_2 u_0$, and $\alpha_3 h_0$—the autonomous components of real capital accumulation.

Changes in the Parameter Reflecting Autonomous Investment (α_0), in the Parameter Reflecting the Impact of Technological Change (α_3), in the Autonomous Rate of Technological Change (h_0), and in the Verdoorn Coefficient (h_1)

The Long-Run Equilibrium Rate of Real Capital Accumulation (g^*), Degree of Capacity Utilization (u^*), and Profit Share (π^*)

---

[5] While the partial derivative of dg/dt with respect to z (see Eq. D.40 in Appendix D.1.2.2) seems to be ambiguous, it is definitely positive if it is assumed that R, and hence Z, is always positive (see Eq. 8.12). See also footnote 6 in Sect. 8.3.1.2.

According to Eqs. (8.8) and (8.10), a rise (fall) in α_0, α_3, h_0, or h_1 unambiguously raises (reduces) firms' desired rate of real capital accumulation g^d. Via a rise (fall) in dg/dt, firms' actual rate of real capital accumulation (g) and hence the equilibrium rate of real capital accumulation (g^*) increase (decline) as well. Triggered by this rise (decline) in the long-run equilibrium rate of real capital accumulation (g^*), a rise (fall) in α_0, α_3, h_0, or h_1 unambiguously raises (reduces) the long-run equilibrium degree of capacity utilization (u^*) and the long-run equilibrium profit share (π^*).

The Long-Run Equilibrium Measure of Personal Income Distribution (ψ^*)

The impact of a change in α_0, α_3, h_0, or h_1 on the long-run equilibrium measure of personal income distribution (ψ^*) depends on the sign of expression (D.58). If it is positive (negative), a rise in α_0, α_3, h_0, or h_1 raises (reduces) ψ^*. If expression (D.58) is zero, a change in α_0, α_3, h_0, or h_1 has no impact on ψ^*.

A rise in α_0, α_3, h_0, or h_1 unambiguously raises the long-run equilibrium rate of real capital accumulation (g^*). This increase in g^* is more likely to raise ψ^* the higher a_2, m_1, and m_2, and the lower i. See the respective remarks in Sect. 8.3.2.3 for further details.

Changes in the Parameter Reflecting the Impact of Firms' Internal Saving (α_1)

The Long-Run Equilibrium Rate of Real Capital Accumulation (g^*), Degree of Capacity Utilization (u^*), and Profit Share (π^*)

The impact of a change in (α_1) on the long-run equilibrium rate of real capital accumulation (g^*), on the long-run equilibrium degree of capacity utilization (u^*), and on the long-run equilibrium profit share (π^*) depends on firms' internal saving as a ratio of capital (S_f/K). If it is positive (negative), a rise in α_1 raises (reduces) g^*, u^*, and π^*. If it is zero, a change in α_1 has no impact on g^*, u^*, and π^*.[6]

The Long-Run Equilibrium Measure of Personal Income Distribution (ψ^*)

The impact of a change in (α_1) on the long-run equilibrium measure of personal income distribution (ψ^*) depends on the sign of expression (D.58).

In case of a positive ratio S_f/K, a rise in α_1 raises (reduces) ψ^* if expression (D.58) is positive (negative). In case of a negative ratio S_f/K, a rise in α_1 raises (reduces) ψ^* if expression (D.58) is negative (positive). If S_f/K and/or expression (D.58) is zero, a change in α_1 has no impact on ψ^*.

If S_f/K is positive (negative), a rise in α_1 unambiguously raises (reduces) the long-run equilibrium rate of real capital accumulation (g^*). This increase (decline) in g^* is more likely to raise ψ^* the higher (lower) a_2, m_1, and m_2, and the lower (higher) i. See the respective remarks in Sect. 8.3.2.3 for further details.

---

[6]A positive ratio S_f/K is equivalent to firms' net profits (P) exceeding the basic dividend ($a_1 K_f$).

Changes in the Parameter Reflecting the Impact of Capacity Utilization (α_2)

The Long-Run Equilibrium Rate of Real Capital Accumulation (g^*), Degree of Capacity Utilization (u^*), and Profit Share (π^*)

The impact of a change in (α_2) on the long-run equilibrium rate of real capital accumulation (g^*), on the long-run equilibrium degree of capacity utilization (u^*), and on the long-run equilibrium profit share (π^*) depends on the difference $u - u_0$. If it is positive (negative), a rise in α_2 raises (reduces) g^*, u^*, and π^*. If it is zero, a change in α_2 has no impact on g^*, u^*, and π^*.

The Long-Run Equilibrium Measure of Personal Income Distribution (ψ^*)

The impact of a change in (α_2) on the long-run equilibrium measure of personal income distribution (ψ^*) depends on the sign of expression (D.58).

In case of a positive difference $u - u_0$, a rise in α_2 raises (reduces) ψ^* if expression (D.58) is positive (negative). In case of a negative difference $u - u_0$, a rise in α_2 raises (reduces) ψ^* if expression (D.58) is negative (positive). If $u - u_0$ and/or expression (D.58) is zero, a change in α_2 has no impact on ψ^*.

If $u - u_0$ is positive (negative), a rise in α_2 unambiguously raises (reduces) the long-run equilibrium rate of real capital accumulation (g^*). This increase (decline) in g^* is more likely to raise ψ^* the higher (lower) a_2, m_1, and m_2, and the lower (higher) i. See the respective remarks in Sect. 8.3.2.3 for further details.

Changes in the Planned Degree of Capacity Utilization (u_0)

The Long-Run Equilibrium Rate of Real Capital Accumulation (g^*), Degree of Capacity Utilization (u^*), and Profit Share (π^*)

According to Eq. (8.8), a rise (fall) in u_0 unambiguously reduces (increases) firms' desired rate of real capital accumulation g^d. Via a fall (rise) in $\mathrm{d}g/\mathrm{d}t$, firms' actual rate of real capital accumulation (g) and hence the equilibrium rate of real capital accumulation (g^*) decline (increase) as well. Triggered by this decline (rise) in the long-run equilibrium rate of real capital accumulation (g^*), a rise (fall) in u_0 unambiguously reduces (raises) the long-run equilibrium degree of capacity utilization (u^*) and the long-run equilibrium profit share (π^*).

The Long-Run Equilibrium Measure of Personal Income Distribution (ψ^*)

The impact of a change in (u_0) on the long-run equilibrium measure of personal income distribution (ψ^*) depends on the sign of expression (D.58). If it is positive (negative), a rise in u_0 reduces (raises) ψ^*. If expression (D.58) is zero, a change in u_0 has no impact on ψ^*.

A fall (rise) in u_0 unambiguously raises (reduces) the long-run equilibrium rate of real capital accumulation (g^*). This increase (decline) in g^* is more likely to raise ψ^* the higher (lower) a_2, m_1, and m_2, and the lower (higher) i. See the respective remarks in Sect. 8.3.2.3 for further details.

D.2   Graphical Analysis

D.2.1   A Rise in the Dividend Payout Parameter (a_2)

Figure D.1 depicts the possible short- and long-run effects of a rise in the dividend payout parameter (a_2) in the case of a positive difference $P - a_1 K_f$. The effects closely resemble the impact of a rise in the interest rate (i).

Starting from the long-run equilibrium levels u_0^*, π_0^*, ψ_0^*, and g_0^*, in the short run a rise in a_2 provokes a downward turn of the saving schedule from g_0^s to g_1^s in the lower right quadrant of Fig. D.1, implying that at u_0^* total saving as a ratio of capital (S/K) declines. Yet, as the rate of real capital accumulation is assumed to be constant in the short run, thus remaining at g_0^*, the degree of capacity utilization rises from u_0^* to its new short-run level u_{sr}. The increase in the degree of capacity utilization is also depicted in the upper right quadrant of Fig. D.1, where the rise in a_2 leads to an upward movement of the demand-determined profit share function from π_0^d to π_{sr}^d. If P exceeds $a_1 K_f$, in the short run the profit share in the economy unambiguously increases from π_0^* to π_{sr}. Moreover, although both the wage bill (W) and private

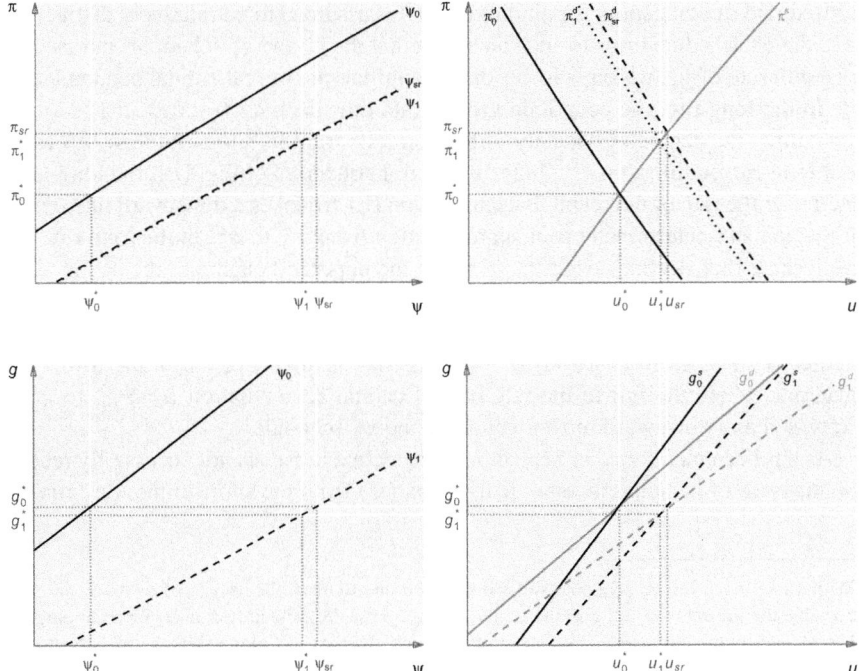

Fig. D.1 Possible short- and long-run impact of a rise in a_2: The example of a positive nexus between g and ψ. *Source* Author's illustration

households' capital income (Z) rise with an increase in a_2, the measure of personal income distribution (ψ) rises, as W increases relatively less than Z. As shown in the upper left quadrant of Fig. D.1, the increase in a_2 shifts the inequality schedule to the right, from ψ_0 to ψ_{sr}. In the short run, the profit share π_{sr} is accompanied by a personal income inequality measure of ψ_{sr}, which is unambiguously higher than ψ_0^*. Finally, the lower left quadrant of Fig. D.1 shows the (possible) nexus between the rate of real capital accumulation (g) and the personal distribution of income (ψ). A rise in a_2 shifts the inequality schedule to the right, from ψ_0 to ψ_1. While the rate of real capital accumulation remains at g_0^*, the measure of personal income distribution increases from ψ_0^* to ψ_{sr}.

As has been outlined in Sect. 8.3.2.2, a change in a_2 has an ambiguous impact on the long-run rate of real capital accumulation (g^*). If $P - a_1 K_f$ is positive, in the short run a rise in a_2 increases u, but reduces firms' internal saving as a ratio of capital (S_f/K). If the negative impact of the fall in S_f/K outweighs the positive stimulus of the increase in u, the desired rate of real capital accumulation (g^d) and hence the actual rate of real capital accumulation (g) decline in the long run. Graphically, the fall in S_f/K provokes a downward turn of the g^d function in the lower right quadrant of Fig. D.1, from g_0^d to g_1^d. The more pronounced the impact of the decline in S_f/K on the desired rate of real capital accumulation (g^d) is, the stronger the function turns. In the case illustrated in Fig. D.1, the impact of a fall in S_f/K on the desired rate of real capital accumulation (g^d) is assumed to be relatively distinct. In fact, the g^d schedule turns to such an extent that the g_1^s and g_1^d schedules intersect at a growth rate of g_1^*, which is lower than the initial rate of real capital accumulation g_0^*. In the long run, the economic growth rate thus declines from g_0^* to g_1^*. At the same time, the degree of capacity utilization falls from its short-run level u_{sr} to its new long-run equilibrium u_1^*.[7] In the upper right quadrant of Fig. D.1, the long-term decline in the rate of real capital accumulation (g) provokes a downward movement of the demand-determined profit share function from π_{sr}^d to π_1^d. In the long run, the profit share thus declines from π_{sr} to π_1^*. In the upper left quadrant, the decline in g leads to a slight rightward movement of the inequality schedule from ψ_{sr} to ψ_1. In the example illustrated in Fig. D.1, in the long run the measure of personal income inequality declines from ψ_{sr} to ψ_1^*. This decline is also depicted in the lower left quadrant, where the fall in the rate of real capital accumulation from g_0^* to g_1^* is expressed as a downward movement along the ψ_1 schedule.

As has been mentioned in Sect. 8.3.2.3, a decline in g does not necessarily reduce the measure of personal income distribution (ψ) from the short to the long run. In

---

[7]With a rise in a_2, the g^d schedule shifts downward due to, first, the impact of a_2 on S_f/K and, secondly, the impact of a_2 on g in the term $\alpha_3 (h_0 + h_1 g)$. Yet, the impact of a_2 on technological change, i.e., on the term $\alpha_3 (h_0 + h_1 g)$ in the g^d schedule, cannot alone shift the g^d schedule to such an extent that the g_1^s and g_1^d schedules intersect at a growth rate g_1^* which lies below the original growth rate g_0^*. The reason is that, according to the Keynesian stability condition, $0 < \alpha_3 h_1 < 1$. Hence, considering only the impact of a_2 on $\alpha_3 (h_0 + h_1 g)$, changes in a_2 cannot shift the g^d schedule to the same extent as the g^s function. Only a strong impact of a_2 on S_f/K can potentially reduce the long-run equilibrium rate of real capital accumulation.

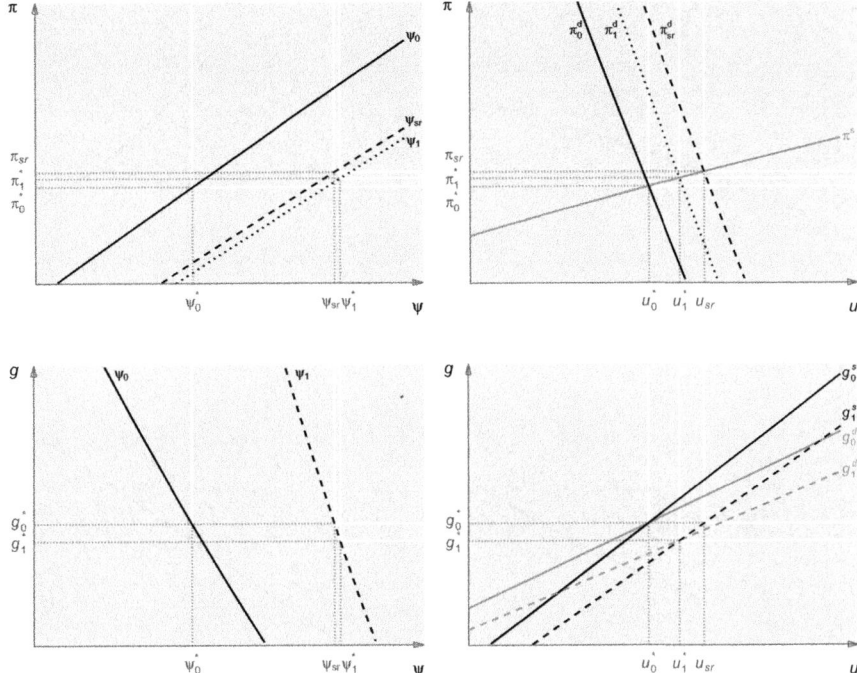

Fig. D.2 Possible short- and long-run impact of a rise in a_2: The example of a negative nexus between g and ψ. *Source* Author's illustration

contrast to Fig. D.1, which shows the example of a positive impact of g on ψ, Fig. D.2 depicts the example of a negative effect of g on ψ.

D.2.2 A Rise in the Saving Rate of the Rich Private Households (s_h^r)

Figure D.3 shows the possible short- and long-run impact of a rise in the saving rate of the rich private households (s_h^r), which closely resembles the impact of a rise in the saving rate of the poor private households (s_h^p).

Starting from the long-run equilibrium levels u_0^*, π_0^*, ψ_0^*, and g_0^*, in the short run a rise in s_h^r shifts the saving schedule in the lower right quadrant upward, from g_0^s to g_1^s. With a given rate of real capital accumulation (g_0^*), the degree of capacity utilization declines from u_0^* to u_{sr}. A rise in the saving rate of the rich private households (s_h^r) also reduces the profit share in the economy, which, in the upper right quadrant, is depicted by a downward shift of the demand-determined profit share function from π_0^d to π_{sr}^d. In the short run, a rise in s_h^r has an ambiguous impact on personal

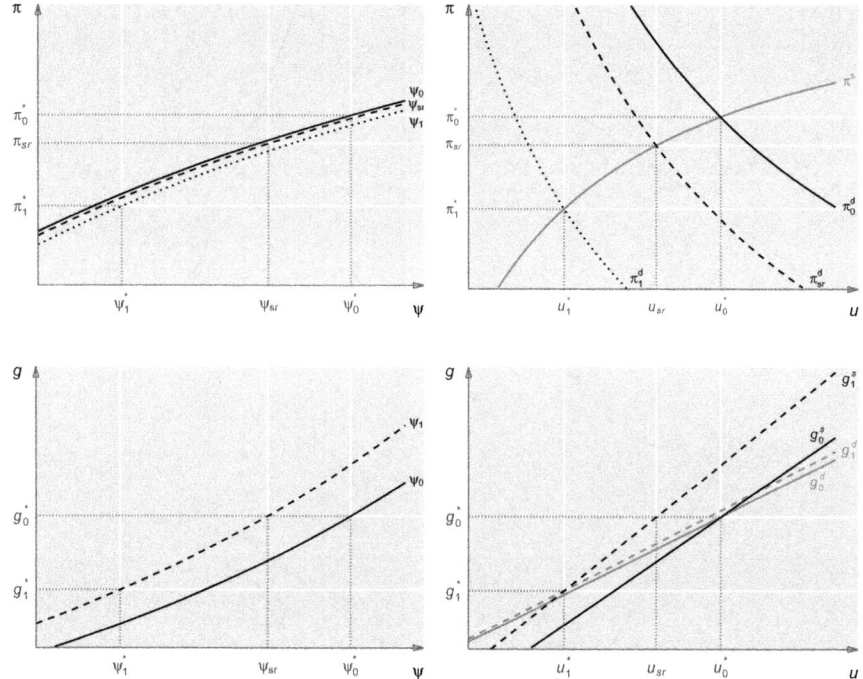

Fig. D.3 Possible short- and long-run impact of a rise in s_h^r: The example of a positive nexus between g and ψ. *Source* Author's illustration

income inequality (ψ). In the example shown in Fig. D.3, personal income inequality declines. The rightward shift of the inequality schedule in the upper left quadrant from ψ_0 to ψ_{sr} is accompanied by a decline in the measure of personal inequality from ψ_0^* to ψ_{sr}. This decline is also illustrated in the lower left quadrant of Fig. D.3, where the inequality schedule shifts leftward, from ψ_0 to ψ_1.

In the long run, a rise in the saving rate of the rich private households (s_h^r) unambiguously reduces the equilibrium rate of real capital accumulation (g). An increase in s_h^r reduces the degree of capacity utilization (u) in the short run, and, via the decline in u, also firms' internal saving as a ratio of capital (S_f/K). While the g^d schedule in the lower right quadrant of Fig. D.3 shifts slightly upward due to the impact of a rise in s_h^r on α_3 ($h_0 + h_0 g$), this shift is clearly less pronounced than the upward shift of the g^s function, as $0 < \alpha_3 h_1 < 1$. The long-run equilibrium rate of real capital accumulation thus declines unambiguously. In the long run, the economy moves along the g_1^s function from g_0^* toward the new long-run equilibrium rate of real capital accumulation g_1^*. With a decline in the long-run equilibrium rate of real capital accumulation, the degree of capacity utilization declines from u_{sr} to u_1^*. As depicted in the upper right quadrant of Fig. D.3, the decline in g shifts the demand-determined profit share function downward, from π_{sr}^d to π_1^d. The profit share thus declines from π_{sr} to π_1^*. In the upper left quadrant of Fig. D.3, the inequality schedule moves slightly to the right in the long run, from ψ_{sr} to ψ_1. As compared to the short run, the long-run equilibrium measure of personal income inequality declines from ψ_{sr} to ψ_1^*. The reduction in personal income inequality is also shown in the lower left quadrant of Fig. D.3, where the decline in the equilibrium rate of real capital accumulation from g_0^* to g_1^* involves a downward movement along the ψ_1 schedule.

As has been mentioned in Sects. 8.3.1.2 and 8.3.2.3, the impact of changes in both the saving rate of the rich private households (s_h^r) and the rate of real capital accumulation (g) on the measure of personal income inequality (ψ) is ambiguous. It can be shown, however, that, if a rise in s_h^r reduces ψ in the short run, the long-run decline in the rate of real capital accumulation (g) necessarily reduces ψ as well. On the other hand, if a rise in s_h^r increases ψ in the short run, the long-run decline in the rate of real capital accumulation (g) also must raise ψ. While Fig. D.3 depicts the former case, Fig. D.4 illustrates the latter case.

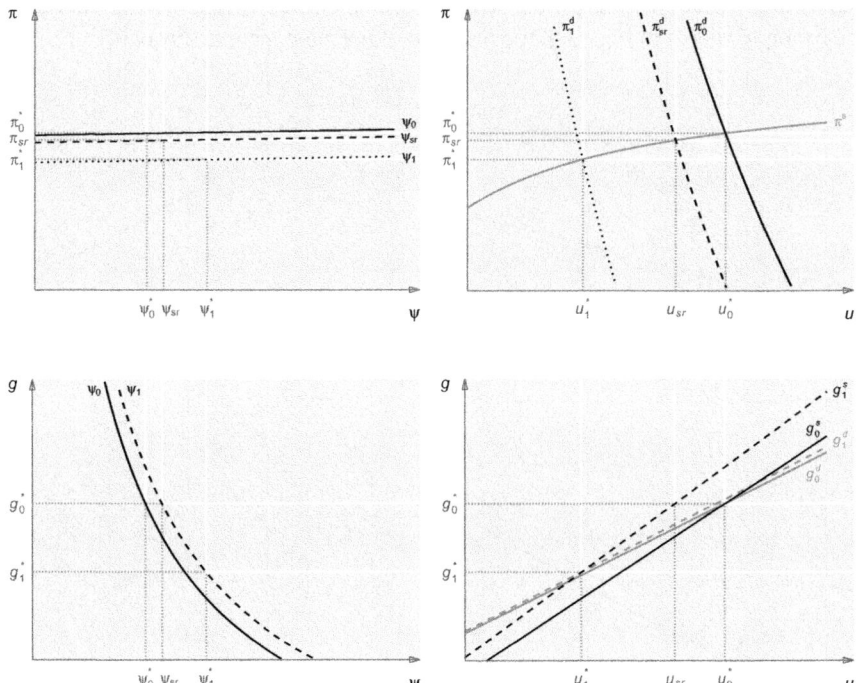

Fig. D.4 Possible short- and long-run impact of a rise in s_h^r: The example of a negative nexus between g and ψ. *Source* Author's illustration

D.2.3 A Decline in the Parameter Reflecting the Impact of the Degree of Capacity Utilization (α_2)

Figure D.5 depicts the possible impact of a decline in α_2 in the case of a positive difference $u - u_0$, which closely resembles the impact of a decline in α_1 in the case of a positive difference $P - a_1 K_f$, the impact of a decline in α_3, and the impact of a decline in h_1. These economic shocks do not have any short-run effects, as their impact unfolds only through changes in the g^d function.

Starting from the long-run equilibrium levels u_0^*, π_0^*, ψ_0^*, and g_0^*, a decline in α_2 turns the g^d schedule in the lower right quadrant of Fig. D.5 downward. As the saving schedule is not affected by changes in α_2, the long-run equilibrium rate of real capital accumulation declines from g_0^* to g_1^*. At the same time, the degree of capacity utilization falls from u_0^* to u_1^*. In the upper right quadrant, the decline in the rate of real capital accumulation (g) provokes a downward shift of the demand-determined profit share function from π_0^d to π_1^d, implying that the equilibrium profit share falls from π_0^* to π_1^*. In the upper left quadrant, the decline in the rate of real capital accumulation (g) shifts the inequality schedule to the right, from ψ_0 to ψ_1. In the example shown in Fig. D.5, the measure of personal income inequality declines

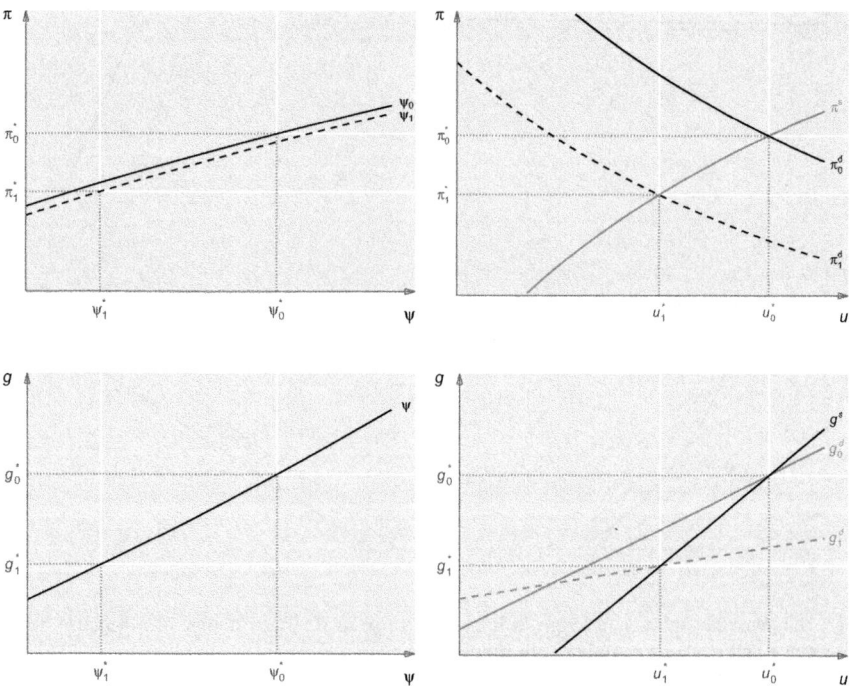

Fig. D.5 Possible impact of a decline in α_2: The example of a positive nexus between g and ψ. *Source* Author's illustration

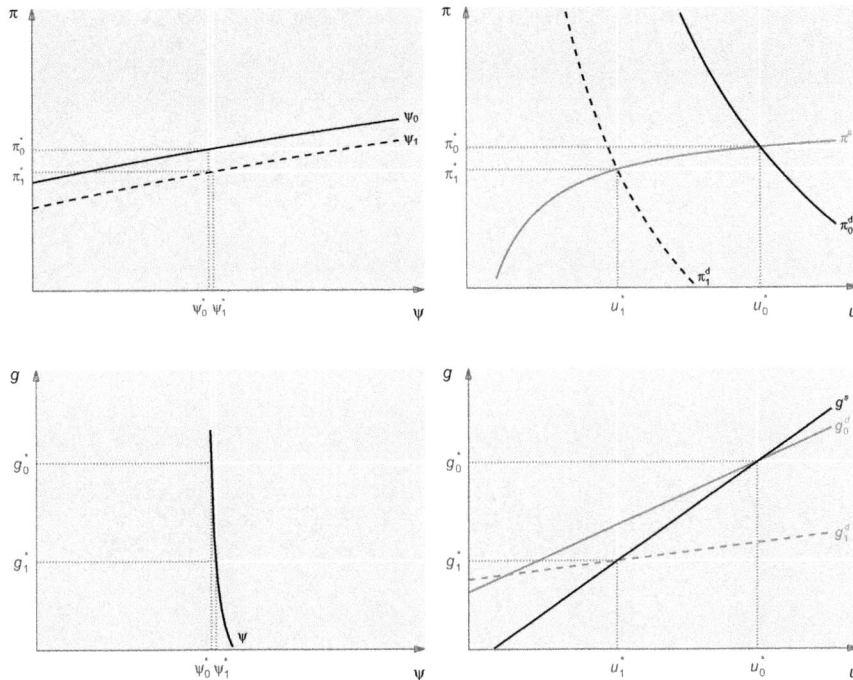

Fig. D.6 Possible impact of a decline in α_2: The example of a negative nexus between g and ψ.
Source Author's illustration

from ψ_0^* to ψ_1^*. This decline is also depicted in the lower left quadrant, where a fall in g is expressed as a downward movement along the inequality schedule.

In contrast to Figs. D.5 and D.6 depicts the example of a negative impact of a change in the rate of real capital accumulation (g) on the measure of personal income inequality (ψ). Here, the decline in g from g_0^* to g_1^* raises ψ from ψ_0^* to ψ_1^*.

Printed by Printforce, the Netherlands